CAREER ^EDITION 4
MANAGEMENT

CAREER MANAGEMENT

EDITION **4**

Jeffrey H. Greenhaus
Drexel University

Gerard A. Callanan
West Chester University

Veronica M. Godshalk
University of South Carolina, Beaufort

⑤SAGE

Los Angeles | London | New Delhi
Singapore | Washington DC

For information:

SAGE Publications, Inc.
2455 Teller Road
Thousand Oaks,
   California 91320
E-mail: order@sagepub.com

SAGE Publications Ltd.
1 Oliver's Yard
55 City Road
London EC1Y 1SP
United Kingdom

SAGE Publications India Pvt. Ltd.
B 1/I 1 Mohan Cooperative
   Industrial Area
Mathura Road, New Delhi 110 044
India

SAGE Publications Asia-Pacific Pte. Ltd.
33 Pekin Street #02-01
Far East Square
Singapore 048763

Printed in the United States of America

Library of Congress Cataloging-in-Publication Data

Greenhaus, Jeffrey H.
Career management / Jeffrey H. Greenhaus, Gerard A. Callanan, Veronica
M. Godshalk. — 4th ed.
      p. cm.
Includes bibliographical references and index.
ISBN 978-1-4129-7826-2 (pbk.: acid-free paper)
   1. Manpower planning. 2. Vocational guidance. I. Callanan, Gerard A. II. Godshalk, Veronica M.
III. Title.

HF5549.5.M3G734 2010
650.14—dc22   2009033529

This book is printed on acid-free paper.

09   10   11   12   13   10   9   8   7   6   5   4   3   2   1

Acquisitions Editor:	Lisa Cuevas Shaw
Associate Editor:	Deya Saoud
Editorial Assistant:	MaryAnn Vail
Production Editor:	Karen Wiley
Copy Editor:	Kristin Bergstad
Typesetter:	C&M Digitals (P) Ltd.
Proofreader:	Gail Fay
Indexer:	Mary Mortensen
Cover Designer:	Bryan Fishman
Marketing Manager:	Christy Guilbault

Contents

5 Applications of the Career Management Model: Goals, Strategies, and Appraisal

PART II. STAGES OF CAREER DEVELOPMENT

6 Occupational and Organizational Choice

7 The Early Career Stage: Establishment and Achievement

8 The Middle and Late Career Stages: Career Challenges for Seasoned Employees

230

PART III. CONTEMPORARY ISSUES IN CAREER MANAGEMENT

9 Job Stress and Careers   262

12 Entrepreneurial Careers

PART IV. CAREER MANAGEMENT IN WORK ORGANIZATIONS

Preface

For most individuals, work is a defining aspect of life. Indeed, our happiness and fulfillment can hinge on how well we are able to control the course of our work lives, and manage the effects of our work on our family and personal life. Yet many people enter their careers with a lack of insight and purpose, drifting to and from jobs, or lamenting unwise career choices. For others, the task of career management, because of the risks of not making personally correct decisions, is frightening and full of anxiety. We believe that individuals at any age need to approach career management with care and attention, and must have an appropriate decision-making framework in order to achieve personal success and satisfaction.

These beliefs are especially relevant in the 21st century. Realities in the world of work—economic uncertainties, mergers and acquisitions, downsizings, cost containment efforts, and the globalization of business, to mention a few—have dramatic effects on careers. We can no longer expect to spend 20 or 30 years in one company, or even in one industry. We cannot expect our employer to take responsibility for managing our career. In today's world, the relationship between employer and employee has a short-term focus, often with low levels of commitment and loyalty between the two parties. It is therefore up to the individual to take the responsibility for career management.

In the fourth edition of *Career Management* we provide a vehicle for individuals to direct their careers successfully over the life cycle. We hope this book is integral to your successful career management and all its attendant rewards.

STRUCTURE AND CONTENTS

In the fourth edition of *Career Management* we focus on four essential views of careers and career management. First, career management is a process by which individuals can guide, direct, and influence the course of their careers. The model of career management presented in this edition—an active, problem-solving approach to work and life—specifies how people can collect information, gain insight into themselves and their environment, develop appropriate goals and strategies, and obtain useful feedback regarding their efforts. The career management model is presented and examined in *Part I (Chapters 1 through 5)* of the book. Chapter 1 introduces the notion of career management as an ongoing problem-solving process.

Chapter 2 discusses traditional and contemporary views of careers and career management, including how a career develops and evolves throughout a person's life. In Chapter 3, we present the model of career management that forms the foundation for the remainder of the text. Chapters 4 and 5 apply the career management model to individual career decision making, covering such career management skills as career exploration, career goal setting, and career strategy development.

Second, it is useful to view a career in light of the different career stages. Each career stage presents unique tasks and issues, ranging from a young adult's preoccupation with choosing an initial occupation, to a middle-aged adult's concern about a devastating job loss, to an older employee's need to remain productive and to prepare for retirement. Despite these differences, the role of career management is fundamentally the same at each stage of career development: to make sound decisions based on insight and to implement the decisions effectively. *Part II (Chapters 6 through 8)* of *Career Management* discusses the different stages of career development and emphasizes the role of active career management at each stage. Chapter 6 traces the processes by which people choose occupations and enter organizations. Chapter 7 deals with the tasks facing employees in their early career, and Chapter 8 concentrates on issues relevant to seasoned employees who are in the middle and later phases of their careers.

Third, career management efforts must take into account a number of additional demands, including dealing with job stress, the intertwining of work and personal lives, facing the challenges of a culturally diverse workforce, and the potential for embarking on an entrepreneurial career. *Part III (Chapters 9 through 12)* of *Career Management* is devoted to these issues. In Chapter 9, we examine the effect of work stress on the individual's quality of life. Chapter 10 considers the relationship between work and family, focusing on the two-career relationship as a dominant lifestyle. Chapter 11 discusses career management in the context of cultural diversity, with material on the careers of women and men in contemporary organizations, the careers of minority employees, and the career challenges faced by employees and employers in culturally diverse settings. In Chapter 12, which discusses the choice of an entrepreneurial career, we profile the entrepreneur; review different forms of social, educational, and emotional support; address issues facing female and minority entrepreneurs; and describe the unique demands of entrepreneurial career management. We hope this chapter will help individuals decide whether an entrepreneurial career and lifestyle are right for them.

Fourth, individual career management can be assisted through a number of organizationally sponsored programs. In *Part IV (Chapters 13 and 14)*, we discuss a variety of career management practices available to organizations, and we offer specific examples of these practices as used by real companies. Chapter 13 offers an overview of the broader spectrum of human resource activities, with special emphasis on how human resource systems can support employee career management. We illustrate how human resource and career management systems must be integrated to maximize individual and organizational well-being, and we encourage the development of career-oriented human resource support systems. Throughout this chapter we describe and illustrate career management practices in organizations. This information should be useful to human resource specialists in organizations as well as students and employees assessing employers' or prospective employers' support of career management. Moreover, an understanding of the organization's role in career management can help individuals become more effective managers of people over the course of their careers. Chapter 14 provides our closing thoughts on career management and reinforces our belief that individuals can—and must—take the initiative to manage their own careers.

Career Management is intended for several different audiences. First, it is ideal for all individuals who wish to learn more about career dynamics and how to manage their careers, whether they are students, working adults, or simply intellectually curious. *Career Management* was written to provide an understanding of career development and a framework in which career management can be pursued. Indeed, the fourth edition contains updated and comprehensive information on different forms of self-assessment—the ways in which individuals can learn more about themselves, their values, interests, talents, personality, and lifestyle preferences. *Career Management* can be used as a primary or supplementary text for undergraduate and graduate courses in careers, human resource management, organizational behavior, psychology, and education. And it can also be utilized in organizations as a resource for employees seeking guidance in the management of their careers.

Our second audience, human resource professionals, can certainly profit from the material in the fourth edition. It is impossible to develop effective career management programs in organizations without a full appreciation of the kinds of decisions and dilemmas individuals face in their careers. The material on the career management process, the emerging contexts of career management and development, job stress, work–family integration, and the management of diversity sets the stage for Chapter 13, which deals explicitly with strategic human resource and career management initiatives.

Finally, this edition of the book was written for our peers, researchers in career management and decision making. As with the prior editions, we hope the fourth edition of *Career Management* helps pull together the most recent research and theory on careers and stimulates additional research in this area.

LEARNING-ORIENTED FEATURES

To meet the needs of these audiences, the fourth edition contains the following learning-oriented features:

A Balance of Theory and Application. The material in *Career Management* is theory- and research-based because individuals, whether they are students or working adults, must appreciate the concepts that underlie career management principles and techniques. In addition, every chapter offers pragmatic applications of the concepts. It is hoped that readers of this text will emerge with a framework and a set of guidelines that can serve as a career management "map" throughout their work lives.

Mixture of Individual and Organizational Actions. Although career management is viewed as an individual problem-solving and decision-making process, work organizations can play an integral part in stimulating and fostering effective career management. Therefore, most chapters include examples of actions or programs that organizations can provide to promote employee career management, and Chapter 13 provides a number of examples of organizational career management programs that are tied into the overall process of human resource management and development.

Learning Exercises to Help Readers Practice Career Management Skills. The exercises offer an opportunity for the reader to engage in career exploration, career goal setting, and career strategy development, key ingredients in the career management process. Although the conceptual material can be grasped independently of the learning exercises, the experiential learning derived from the exercises can provide extremely valuable insight into one's career. There are three issues to consider regarding the use of the learning exercises. First is the question of timing. Learning Exercises 1 through 4 appear at the end of Chapter 4. It is suggested that individuals read Chapter 4 fully before beginning these exercises. Learning Exercises 5 and 6 are provided at the end of Chapter 5, and Learning Exercises 7 and 8 at the end of Chapter 6. Again, it is suggested that the relevant chapters be read before the exercises are begun.

Second is the issue of where readers should enter their responses to the learning exercises. We recommend that you create a separate notebook or computer file in which to write your responses to these exercises. A separate career management notebook or file provides the flexibility to add more information to an exercise at a later point.

Third, the learning exercises can be—at an instructor's discretion—converted into group or team assignments. Although the learning exercises should initially be completed by individuals working alone, some instructors have found it helpful for groups of students to share their responses to the learning exercises so that they can provide feedback and guidance to each other in a supportive environment.

Cases to Examine Individual and Organizational Career Management. The fourth edition includes a case at the end of each chapter that serves to highlight the career management issues that are covered in that chapter. The cases are a great learning tool since they offer competing perspectives on various career management issues and contain real-life complexities that individuals face in making career decisions. Each case is accompanied by questions that facilitate analysis and group discussions. In addition to the end-of-chapter cases, there are many short vignettes interspersed throughout the book as a means to give real-life examples and meaning to particular career management topics. We believe that a major strength of the fourth edition is that it allows students to relate sometimes abstract concepts to the everyday realities and demands of work life and career management.

Summaries. Each chapter concludes with a summary of the material and key issues contained in the chapter. The summaries reiterate main themes and give a useful synopsis of important concepts.

Assignments and Discussion Questions. At the end of each chapter the reader is asked to complete an assignment that links the material in the chapter with real-life experience. Further, nearly every chapter is supplemented with a series of relevant questions that are useful in guiding discussion of the important material presented in the chapter.

ANCILLARIES

Instructor Resources. Instructors can access password-protected resources at www.sagepub .com/greenhaus4e. These include guidelines for all in-text discussion questions and assignments, PowerPoint slides for each chapter, and a test bank containing multiple-choice, true/false, and essay questions. Qualified instructors can contact Customer Care to receive access to the site.

Student Resources. An open-access Student Study Site includes electronic versions of the in-text exercises, relevant Web sites (including links to career resources, assessments, and questionnaires), links to SAGE Journal Articles, and more. Go to www.sagepub.com/ greenhaus4e to access the site.

ACKNOWLEDGMENTS

A number of people have provided stimulation, advice, and support and have directly or indirectly contributed to this edition of the book. First, we are indebted to the many other scholars whose research has influenced our thinking about careers and whose works are cited extensively in this book. We hope our interpretation of others' research does justice to their contributions.

We also thank our students for their enthusiasm in discussing their views of career management and their willingness to share many personal career experiences. We appreciate the many contributions of the late Professor Saroj Parasuraman of Drexel University's Department of Management, who provided critical and constructive reviews of selected chapters in the original and revised editions of the book. We are also grateful to the administrators and faculty colleagues at our respective universities—their help and support have made the process of creating the fourth edition much easier.

We are also very grateful to Tammy Allen of The University of South Florida, William S. Brown of Marist College, Laura Byars of Arvin Meritor, Cristina Giannantonio of Chapman University, Wyat P. Gregory III of Webster University, Gerald Klein of Rider University, Barbara Ribbens of Western Illinois University, and Belle Rose Ragins of University of Wisconsin–Milwaukee for their critical assessments of the third edition of *Career Management,* all of which were helpful in preparing the fourth edition. We also gratefully acknowledge the thorough reviews of the draft manuscript of the fourth edition provided by Lillian T. Eby of the University of Georgia; Cristina Giannantonio of Chapman University; David M. Leuser of Plymouth State University; Lisa A. Mainiero of Fairfield University; Sam Rabinowitz of Rutgers State University of New Jersey; Camden; and Barbara Ribbens of Western Illinois University. Their insightful comments helped us to refine the final version of the fourth edition.

We especially thank the editorial team at SAGE—Al Bruckner, former Senior Editor; Deya Saoud, Senior Associate Editor; and Lisa Cuevas Shaw, Executive Editor—for their assistance and support throughout the process of taking the fourth edition from conception to publication. We are also grateful for the expertise, dedication, and care provided by MaryAnn Vail, Editorial Assistant, and Kristin Bergstad, our copy editor. Our deep appreciation goes to Karen Wiley, Production Editor at SAGE. We also appreciate the efforts of the SAGE production and design staff.

On a more personal level, we are forever grateful for the love, guidance, and support of our parents—Marjorie and Sam Greenhaus, Loretta and Augustine Callanan, and Catherine and Lawrence Brooks—whose influence extends far beyond this book. Our nuclear families deserve our deepest heartfelt thanks: Adele Greenhaus, Joanne, Tim, Riley, and Hunter Noble, and Michele, Jeff, Hallie, Carly, and Mackenzie Levine; Laura, Michael, Timothy, and Ryan Callanan; and Robert, Timothy, and Lauren Godshalk. Their love and support made this edition of the book possible. We are forever grateful for the love you have given and the sacrifices you have made.

Jeffrey H. Greenhaus
Gerard A. Callanan
Veronica M. Godshalk

The Career Management Process

Theory and Application

Introduction to the Study of Careers

We begin Chapter 1 by recognizing a fundamental quality about career management: career decisions have their roots not only in past experiences but also in a vision of the future. Encounters with the world can teach people about themselves—what they enjoy doing, what they're good at, and what really matters in work and in life. In most cases, career decisions are based on the belief that the future in a particular occupation, job, or organization can provide experiences, opportunities, and rewards that are meaningful and satisfying. But careers can be highly unpredictable—especially in today's world. It is often difficult and sometimes impossible to foresee the roadblocks and detours that can arise as we progress through our work lives. How we cope with the twists and turns in our careers is what distinguishes effective from ineffective career management.

The aim of this book is to help the reader understand the principles of effective career management and to provide opportunities to develop and practice skills in career management. The book devotes a great deal of attention to the issues faced by people at different times in their careers, so that individuals can manage their careers effectively throughout their lives. This book is also designed to help managers and future managers respond constructively to their subordinates' career needs, and to help human resource specialists develop effective career management systems within their organizations.

A major premise of *Career Management* is that individuals can exert considerable—although not total—control over their careers. Effective career management requires not only keen insight into oneself and the world of work but also sound decision-making skills that can be developed and improved. As we will discuss in Chapter 3, career management is essentially a problem-solving process in which information is gathered, insight is acquired, goals are set, and strategies are developed to attain those goals.

The study of careers is a popular area of interest and inquiry. There are a number of career planning and other self-help books in local bookstores, and the Internet provides many avenues for self-discovery and also serves to facilitate the career exploration process.

In addition, there are a number of career planning activities provided by corporations, libraries, social or professional organizations, and adult education programs. Research on careers also has a prominent place in the fields of human resource management and organizational behavior. The Academy of Management, one of the most prestigious professional organizations for management scholars,[1] has a division devoted to the study of the career, and professional journals have published a wide range of articles on career-related issues.

The primary reason for this popularity lies in the belief that the concept of career, like no other, can help one to understand the fundamental relationship between people and work, a relationship that has intrigued scholars, mystified organizations, and frustrated people in all sorts of occupations. Consider the following situations:

- An engineer, 20 years out of college, has recently been laid off in a corporate downsizing move. She is beginning to question her competence and drive to succeed.

- A young physician realizes that he chose a career in medicine to please his parents and dreads spending the next 40 years pursuing someone else's dream.

- A regional sales manager in Denver, Colorado, refuses a promotion to corporate headquarters in New York. He enjoys the outdoor life, and his wife is committed to her successful career. He wonders about his future in the company.

- A 35-year-old financial analyst whose employer has just been acquired by an international conglomerate watches nervously as her colleagues are terminated one after another. Will she be next?

- A recent college graduate has been unable to find employment in his chosen field, and has no idea about what career options to pursue.

- A harried mother in a dual-career relationship is frustrated in her career because she receives little support from her husband, children, or company.

- A 39-year-old manager feels unfulfilled by a stalled career with no promotions in sight.

Each one of these situations requires the individual to actively manage his or her career. They provide an opportunity for the person to make an effective career decision or, by default, to allow someone else to make the decision. This book provides a framework for individuals to manage their careers more effectively, and for organizations to develop policies and practices to help their employees with the task of career management.

Before we provide a more formal definition of a career, we need to set the stage by describing changes in the world of work that have occurred over the past several decades. After all, it is in this new economic reality—amidst a great deal of uncertainty and turbulence—that our careers will unfold and our efforts to manage our careers will take place.

THE CHANGING LANDSCAPE OF WORK AND CAREERS

The world is changing constantly, and these changes—economic, political, technological, and cultural—have profound effects on the world of work. Accompanying these changes is a level of uncertainty that can play havoc with people's careers and lives. Intense competition in all industries has been fueled by increased global business and an uncertain world economy. This fierce competition has produced numerous acquisitions, internal reorganizations, a restructuring of jobs and outsourcing as a means to contain costs, and a related change in the psychological bond between employers and employees. The following sections discuss these various changes in the landscape of work and careers.

Organizational Cost Cutting and the Loss of Job Security

The number of incidents and the magnitude of mass layoffs and downsizings that occurred in the United States over the 1980s and 1990s are well documented. During the period from 1979 through 1995, it is estimated that 43 million jobs were lost in the United States alone, or an average of roughly 2.5 million jobs lost per year.[2] In addition, since 1995 the United States Bureau of Labor Statistics (BLS) has tracked the total number of individuals in the United States who experienced a mass layoff.[3] During the 10 years from 1996 to 2005, more than 18 million workers went through a mass layoff incident, or approximately 1.8 million per year. Discounting the recession years of 2000 and 2001, the incidents and number of individuals in a mass layoff remained fairly constant over that 10-year period. In addition, the worldwide economic recession that became manifest in 2008 and 2009 led to a further acceleration in mass layoffs of workers around the globe. Indeed, while mass layoffs were originally concentrated in the United States, more recently they have been experienced by workers in Europe and Asia as major corporations in these regions find it necessary to contain labor costs to stay competitive and also respond to economic downturns.[4] Downsizings in these geographic sectors can be particularly traumatic given the cultural mores and laws that traditionally restricted the degree of job loss experienced by these workers.[5]

Uncertainties in the job market are not limited to the private sector, as local, state, and federal governments are also under severe financial strains. In addition, these streamlining activities are hitting many of us closer to home, as white-collar, professional, and managerial employees are becoming increasingly vulnerable to reductions in force and the outsourcing of jobs to other parts of the world. Clearly, the prospect of a continuous, lifetime career with one employer (or even within one industry) has faded. As a consequence, job security, defined as the stability and continuance of one's employment,[6] has declined significantly over the last three decades. Individuals who are just beginning their careers can expect to work for anywhere from 7 to 12 different employers during their lifetimes.[7] The decline in job security has major implications for career management as individuals must be on constant alert for abrupt changes in their jobs and career direction.

The Changing Structure of Organizations

To meet the challenges of a highly competitive, global marketplace, many organizations have made significant changes in their internal structure. Organizations have become "flatter" and more decentralized than the bureaucratic forms of organizational design that existed through the second half of the 20th century.[8] Customer-driven "horizontal" organizational structures contain fewer levels of management and use cross-functional autonomous work teams to manage virtually every process from manufacturing to marketing.[9] Consequently, modern organizations employ a relatively small number of employees to handle core business functions, but use outsourcing and a large cadre of temporary or contingent workers to deal with secondary and back office activities.

In addition, contemporary organizations use network structures to form partnerships or networks with other organizations and individuals outside their formal boundaries. Not unlike a computer network, network organizations link a variety of firms together to provide the expertise and resources necessary to complete particular projects or manufacture specific products.[10] Some scholars have used the term *boundaryless* to describe the characteristics of these organizations because the organization typically accomplishes its goals through collaboration with many resource providers that lie outside its boundaries.[11]

In sum, although bureaucratic organizations, with their emphasis on stability and predictability, will undoubtedly continue into the future, most organizations have opted for greater flexibility by utilizing a small permanent workforce with an extensive reliance on contingent, part-time, and contract workers and by creating a flatter hierarchy with fewer levels of management.

The Changing Nature of Work

Another significant philosophical shift in organizational management over the past two decades is the widespread adoption of team-based structures as a mechanism for task accomplishment, decision making, and problem solving.[12] The move to collaborative teams as a preferred means of organization has happened at all levels within corporate hierarchies, from the executive suite to the shop floor. Team-based structures involve the "structural empowerment" of workers, meaning that employees and teams of employees are given decision-making responsibility for an entire job or project and for knowing how that job or project fits within the organizational purpose and mission.[13] The move to team-based collaborative structures and the use of empowerment have significant implications for the type of work performed by managers and professionals. Managers and nonmanagers must be effective members and leaders of cross-functional and cross-organizational teams, and attain power and influence as they gain greater information and visibility through their participation in these groups. In addition, it is more difficult for managers in flatter, team-based organizations to supervise their people in a traditional manner and to monitor their performance closely.[14] Indeed, there are fewer managers in the organization to supervise anyone. And the managers who do remain derive their power from their expertise and the respect they have earned rather than from their position in the organizational hierarchy.

Further, in order to advance, employees must be skilled in self-management as the locus of responsibility shifts downward in the organization. These critical requirements include the flexibility to move skillfully from one project to another, the ability to interact with people from a variety of different functional areas, and the utilization of a more collaborative and participative interpersonal style.[15]

Change in the Psychological Contract

The changes in organizational structure and the nature of work have been accompanied by a revision in the basic "psychological contract" between employer and employee. When applied in the context of an employment relationship, a psychological contract is an implicit, unwritten understanding that specifies the contributions an employee is expected to make to the organization and the rewards the employee believes the organization will provide in exchange for his or her contributions.[16] Up until the 1980s, a traditional or "relational" contract was prevalent whereby the employee received job security in exchange for satisfactory performance and loyalty to the organization.[17] A relational contract is normally longer term and involves a high degree of commitment to the relationship on the part of the employee and the employer.[18]

However, because of their need for flexibility in a highly competitive environment, most organizations have adopted a more "transactional" psychological contract in their relationship with their employees. A transactional contract is usually shorter term and involves performance-based pay, lower levels of commitment by both parties, and an allowance for easy exit from the implicit agreement.[19] Instead of exchanging performance and loyalty for job security, employees are expected to be flexible in accepting new work assignments and be willing to develop new skills in response to the organization's needs. In return, the organization does not offer promises of future employment but rather "employability" (with the current employer or some other organization) by providing opportunities for continued professional growth and development. As we will discuss in Chapter 2, this shift in the psychological contract from relational to transactional—from employment to employability—has major implications for employees' careers.

International Competition

The evolving global economy reflects another major change in the world of work. The emergence of new world markets, foreign competition, and political realignments has forced both large and small organizations to adopt more global business strategies as a means to optimize competitiveness. The presence of a global perspective has radically changed the face of business and, as a result, how careers develop within these multinational organizations. As of

2005, international trade of merchandise and commercial services throughout the world totaled $12.5 trillion.[20] In the year 2006 alone, the total dollar value of exports and imports in the United States was $3.6 trillion, an increase of 44 percent since the year 2000 and more than three times greater than the level in 1990.[21]

The emergence of the multinational corporation, with extensive sales revenues coming from operations outside the company's home country, has transformed managerial careers immensely.[22] In many such firms, the route to the top now includes significant exposure to the management of international operations. These international experiences can include expatriation, wherein the employee who is a citizen of the country in which the parent company is located works in a foreign country at a branch or a subsidiary of the parent company.[23] In a reverse of this process, international careers can include repatriation where the expatriate is brought back to work in the home country. Both expatriation and repatriation hold career management challenges for individuals as they navigate differences between the home and host countries in terms of language, culture, business practices, and local customs.

In general, all managers, whether or not they are executive-bound, must learn to understand foreign markets, consumer preferences, and new management styles if they are to be effective in today's multinational corporation. The fall of communism in the early 1990s and the worldwide shift to more free market economies has led many multinational corporations to relocate significant facilities to areas of greater opportunity and lower cost. Job assignments and career paths in these corporations will never be the same, and it is incumbent on individuals to manage their careers to take advantage of these experiences.

Technology and the Churning of Jobs

Technological advances have affected every phase of business from operations to sales to financial management. Computer technology has upgraded the skill requirements of many jobs and eliminated the existence of others.[24] Rapidly changing technologies have created new career paths for employees with the proper mix of skills, while their less adaptable colleagues have often found themselves out of tune with their employers' future plans. In addition, technology, in combination with shifting demands for products and services, will continue to create new occupations. The creation of new and more technologically advanced jobs combined with the elimination of old "lower-tech" jobs has been referred to as the churning of jobs.[25] As a technology-driven process, the churning of jobs produces new—but unpredictable—options, thereby making career management even more crucial in the years ahead. What is required, as we will see, is a career management style that is flexible and attuned to the many technological changes that lie ahead in the world of work.

Changes in Workforce Diversity and Demographics

A more culturally diverse workforce has produced changes in the way organizations function. These changes are as significant as the changes arising from economic competition and technological change. The labor force has and will become older, more female, and more diverse.[26] The increasing proportion of women, racial minorities, and immigrants in the workforce has put pressure on organizations to manage this sexual, racial, and ethnic diversity effectively. But it has also challenged employees to understand different cultures, and to work cooperatively with others who might hold different values and perspectives. Career success in many organizations can often depend on an employee's ability to thrive in a multicultural environment.

Of particular note, the aging and ultimate retirement of the baby boom generation represents a major demographic and sociological phenomenon that has far-reaching implications for individual career management and for organizational human resource management systems.[27] The baby boom generation consists of the roughly 78 million people born in the United States during the 20-year period after World War II. For individuals who are part of this generation, career management is fraught with concerns and challenges, including dealing with the possibility of a plateaued career, maintaining a skill set that is desired by employers, and ultimately deciding on the timing of, and the financial planning for, retirement. For individuals who were born after the baby boom, the potential exists that advancement will be blocked or stalled by the presence of a mass cohort of employees who might be reluctant or financially unable to leave the workforce to make room for younger, upwardly mobile employees.

For organizations, the baby boom workforce is a paradox, simultaneously representing both a critical success factor as well as a potential drag on corporate performance and financial resources. At present, the baby boom generation can be seen as a pool of talented, experienced, and highly educated workers who occupy critical leadership and senior management positions and who, accordingly, are an important resource that must be nurtured and maintained in order to achieve continued success. In the future, baby boom workers will be an ever more valuable resource as a forecasted shortage of skilled and unskilled labor in the industrialized world will dictate that employers find ways to keep these workers engaged past standard retirement ages and continue to develop them to optimize present and future contributions to the firm.[28] From an opposite perspective, the baby boom can be seen as a crippling force within organizations, not only in the sense that it will overwhelm pension and retirement systems,[29] but also that plateaued boomers can become organizational "deadwood" and block the advancement of younger and presumably more creative employees.

Work and Family Life

The management of work and family lives has posed a substantial challenge to employee and employer alike. The neat separation of work and family, where neither role interferes with the other, now seems like a distant memory. In 2007, 69 percent of married women in the United States with children under the age of 18 were participating in the workforce, compared to just 45 percent in 1975 and 30 percent in 1960.[30] In addition, 63 percent of married women with children younger than age six were in the workforce in 2007, compared to only 37 percent in 1975 and only 19 percent in 1960.[31] The employment participation rate for married women with children ages 6–17 was 77 percent in 2007, almost 50 percent higher than the rate in 1975 (52 percent) and nearly double the rate (39 percent) of 1960.[32]

The burgeoning employment of women has created new challenges of juggling work and family commitments. Moreover, the divorce rate and a higher degree of out-of-wedlock births have substantially increased the number of single-parent households—the vast majority headed by women—with particularly intense work and family pressures.[33] Data from the U.S. Census Bureau indicate that as of 2006 roughly 28 percent of all households in the United States with children under the age of 18 were single-parent households, and of these, the vast majority (82 percent) were headed by the mother.[34] Dual-career couples and single parents must learn to balance their careers with extensive family responsibilities, often including the care of elderly parents or in-laws. The 21st century is providing even more challenges to women and men pursuing demanding careers and active family and personal lives.

Work and family roles have also been altered by technological advances, which have blurred the demarcation between these two spheres of life. Widespread advances in communications technology have moved work activities from the office to the dining room or study, and even the most remote location can function as an office. These changes provide opportunities for achieving work–family balance but also require considerable support from spouses, children, and employers.

DEFINITIONS OF CAREER CONCEPTS

Now that we have painted the changing landscape of the world of work, we will discuss what constitutes a career, first presenting its historical meaning and then presenting a definition of a career that more closely fits today's world. We will also introduce the career management process and examine the concept of career development.

What Is a Career?

In Chapter 2 we will discuss in detail a number of different perspectives on careers and career management. In broad terms, however, there are two primary ways to view a career. One approach sees a career as a structural property of an *occupation* or an *organization*.[35] For example, one could think of a career in law as a sequence of positions held by a typical or "ideal" practitioner of the occupation: law student, law clerk, junior member of a law firm, senior member of a law firm, judge, and ultimately retirement. A career could also be seen as a mobility path within a single organization or multiple employers,[36] as the following functional path in marketing illustrates: sales representative, product manager, district marketing manager, regional marketing manager, and divisional vice president of marketing, with several staff assignments interspersed among these positions.

The other primary approach views a career as a property of an *individual* rather than an occupation or an organization. Since almost everyone accumulates a unique series of jobs, positions, and experiences, this view acknowledges that each person, in effect, pursues a unique career. Even within this individual perspective, however, a number of different definitions of career have appeared over the years, each reflecting a certain theme embodied in the meaning of a career.[37]

In *Career Management,* we define a career as

the pattern of work-related experiences that span the course of a person's life.

In our definition, work-related experiences are broadly construed to include (a) objective events or situations such as job positions, job duties or activities, and work-related decisions and (b) subjective interpretations of work-related events such as work aspirations, expectations, values, needs, and feelings about particular work experiences. Exhibit 1.1 portrays some significant elements of a person's hypothetical career. Notice that an examination of the objective events by themselves would not provide a full, rich understanding of a person's career. Similarly, an exclusive focus on subjective feelings or values would not do justice to the complexity of a career. Both objective and subjective components are necessary. As we will see in subsequent chapters, one can manage a career by changing the objective environment (e.g., switching jobs) or by modifying one's subjective perception of a situation (e.g., changing expectations). Similarly, the unfolding or development of a career frequently involves systematic changes in objective events (as when a person's opportunity for future promotions becomes limited) as well as changes in subjective reactions to events (such as changes in values or goals).

Our definition of a career does not require that a person's work roles be professional in nature, be stable within a single occupation or organization, or be characterized by upward mobility. Indeed, anyone engaging in work-related activities is, in effect, pursuing a career. This broad definition fits nicely with the changes in the work world discussed earlier in the chapter. For example, the definition's omission of advancement in the corporate hierarchy as a defining characteristic of a career meshes well with the limited vertical mobility opportunities within today's flat organizations. Similarly, to require that a career provide stability within one organization—or even one career path—is unrealistic in today's world of downsizing, contingent employment, and constantly changing jobs. As we will see throughout this book, individuals need to take responsibility for understanding the type of career they wish to pursue and making career decisions that are consistent with these preferences.

EXHIBIT 1.1 Objective and Subjective Elements of a Hypothetical Career

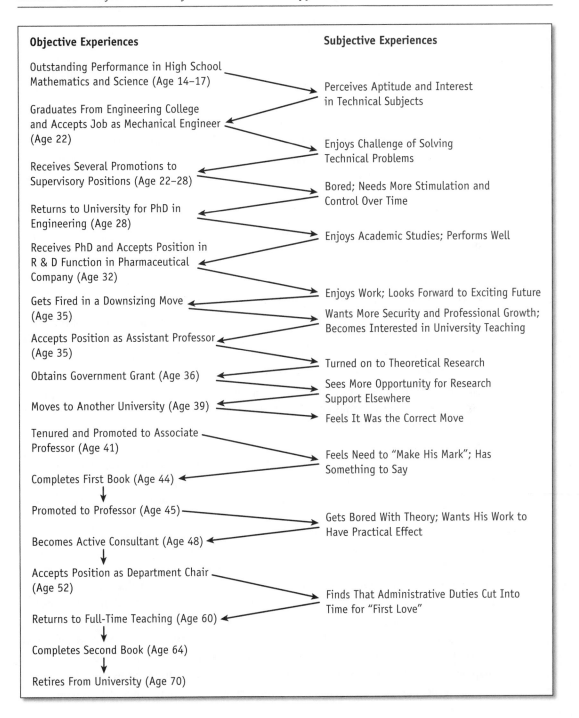

Career Management

Like the concept of the career itself, career management has been defined in a number of ways. We view career management as

> a process by which individuals develop, implement, and monitor career goals and strategies.[38]

Since the process of career management is central to this book, Chapters 3, 4, and 5 are devoted to the explanation and application of our model of career management. For the time being, career management can be briefly described as an ongoing process in which an individual

- Gathers relevant information about himself or herself and the world of work
- Develops an accurate picture of his or her talents, interest, values, and preferred lifestyle as well as alternative occupations, jobs, and organizations
- Develops realistic career goals based on this information
- Develops and implements a strategy designed to achieve the goals
- Obtains feedback on the effectiveness of the strategy and the relevance of the goals

Notice that career management is an individual—not an organizational—activity. Indeed, as we will show in Chapter 3, it is the individual's responsibility to manage his or her career. More and more organizations are relinquishing an activist role in their employees' careers and are laying the responsibility for career management squarely on the shoulders of the individual.[39]

Moreover, individuals will need to develop a set of career competencies that enable them to develop insight into themselves and their environment so they can navigate their increasingly unpredictable and "chaotic" careers. The specific steps in the career management process—and the qualities necessary to carry them out—will be discussed extensively in Chapters 3, 4, and 5.

Career Development

As we will discuss in Chapter 2, people face a number of developmental tasks and challenges as they progress through their careers. The traditional view of career development holds that individuals go through relatively predictable phases or stages in their careers, with each career stage being characterized by a somewhat distinctive set of themes or tasks that need to be confronted.[40] Although the economic and career uncertainty discussed earlier in this chapter can certainly disrupt one's progress through a career and the career stages, it is still true that as people age they will likely confront a changing set of requirements and demands.

For example, a 23-year-old trainee is likely to be preoccupied with gaining competence, acceptance, and credibility in his or her early career. The same person at midcareer (age 45, for example) might be wrestling with gnawing self-doubts about the sacrifices his or her career has required. At age 55 or 60, that person might be faced with the task of remaining productive in later career years, or even switching career fields entirely.

We define career development as follows:

> an ongoing process by which individuals progress through a series of stages, each of which is characterized by a relatively unique set of issues, themes, and tasks

One primary goal of this book is to demonstrate the interplay between career management and career development. If individuals understand the developmental tasks as they progress through their careers, they can formulate goals and strategies that are most appropriate for that particular time in their career and life. Moreover, organizations attuned to the unfolding of careers can design developmental programs most relevant to an employee's career stage.

THE NEED TO UNDERSTAND CAREER MANAGEMENT

An understanding of career management is important in two respects. First, it can help individuals manage their careers more effectively. Second, organizations can profit from understanding the career decisions and dilemmas that confront their employees. In this section, we will consider the importance of career management both from an individual employee's perspective and from an organization's viewpoint.

The Individual Perspective

From an individual's point of view, effective career management is particularly important in light of the turbulent economic, technological, and cultural environments discussed earlier in the chapter. In rapidly changing and uncertain times, career success and satisfaction will most likely be achieved by individuals who understand themselves, know how to detect changes in the environment, create opportunities for themselves, and learn from their mistakes—all elements of effective career management. In an era of downsizing, outsourcing, and changing corporate structures, individuals who have insights into themselves and their options should be more able to overcome obstacles to their career growth.

Moreover, careers have become less structured, less automatic, and more unpredictable. Established career paths are being replaced by more innovative and idiosyncratic routes to success. As organizations become more responsive to rapidly changing business priorities, greater flexibility will be required on the part of the employee. Flexibility and adaptability are hallmarks of effective career management.

Another pressure for effective career management is the very nature of contemporary employees—active and assertive—who demand a high degree of control over their careers and their lives. Behavioral scientists have observed the following significant changes in the workforce in recent years:

High Expectations. The desire for interesting and meaningful work has been matched by the belief that the attainment of these outcomes is likely. To want something from life is one thing; to expect it is another matter. New employees often hold inflated, unrealistic expectations about work. High expectations can produce anger, disappointment, and dissatisfaction if work experiences do not live up to values and expectations. Effective career management can play a particularly significant role in the attempt to secure a match between expectations and experiences.

Autonomy. One of the most significant values held by the contemporary employee is the achievement of freedom, autonomy, and discretion in the workplace.[41] Having substantial freedom to select work projects, to decide how a job is accomplished, and to set work schedules is crucial to a large number of employees in today's world. Indeed, for many employees, attaining high-quality job performance on challenging, autonomous projects can be more important than receiving a promotion.

Weakening of Sex-Role Boundaries. The arbitrary divisions of labor between men's and women's participation in work roles have become progressively less rigid during the past three decades. As occupational sex-typing continues to weaken, women and men will perceive a much wider range of career options and will need to choose from these options wisely, therefore increasing the need for effective career management.

A Concern for Total Lifestyle. The quest for meaningful and challenging work has been accompanied by an intense concern for a satisfying personal life. The unwavering pursuit of promotions and a higher salary has potential costs—less time or energy for family, recreation, and self-development—and might even lead to a compromising of one's ethical and moral beliefs.[42] From an opposite perspective, refused promotions or relocations and an unwillingness to work 14-hour days reflect a belief among many employees that the trade-offs associated with the pursuit of the tangible outcomes of career success can be excessive.

A desire for a more balanced lifestyle can produce ambivalent feelings in many employees. On one hand, money, advancement, challenge, responsibility, and interesting work are sought and valued. On the other hand, leisure, family, and self-development are also seen as legitimate and important activities that, at times, take precedence over work. In a sense, then, many employees seem to be seeking a bounded involvement with work. That is, they are placing boundaries around their work involvement so that work does not incessantly intrude into other parts of their lives. As we will see in later chapters, career decisions must take into account the satisfaction of work, family, and personal needs. Whether the blurring of work and family lives has positive or negative consequences (and it probably has elements of both), career management as we move forward in the 21st century requires new insights and strategies to manage not only one's career but one's overall life as well.

Moreover, the increasing prevalence of single-parent households and dual-career couples puts immense pressures on women and men to balance their own work, family, and personal responsibilities. The interaction between work and family will be considered in detail in Chapter 10. At this point, however, one must note that the added complexity of a nontraditional family structure requires effective career management on the part of women and men.

Diversity of Career Orientations. Our discussion of the contemporary workforce does not imply that all employees hold the same values and pursue the same type of careers. In fact, there is considerable diversity among employees' career orientations and work values.[43] While some of us value advancement or freedom above all else, others primarily value the intrinsic excitement of work, and still others place the most significance on security and balance in their lives.[44] Although we will examine career orientations more extensively in later chapters of the book, we should realize at this point that active career management is essential if we are to satisfy our unique career values, whatever they might be.

The Organizational Perspective

As indicated in the preceding section, individuals who define career success in broad terms and who feel the need to combine different parts of their lives into a satisfying lifestyle have a real need to understand the nature of careers and to manage their careers actively. Organizations also have incentives for understanding careers. In fact, an organization's ability to manage its human resources effectively depends on how well it understands its employees' career needs and helps them engage in effective career management.[45]

Selection of Human Resources. Successful human resource management begins with the effective recruitment, selection, and socialization of new employees.[46] An organization needs to be concerned with identifying a pool of talented applicants, selecting those applicants with the greatest likelihood of success, and bringing the new recruits on board in a way that increases their contribution to the organization. In order to accomplish these tasks, an organization must understand the type of careers it provides and the career values that it believes are most conducive to success and satisfaction in the organization.

Moreover, an organization must understand the way applicants approach the job search process so it can present itself to these applicants in the most favorable way. Yet an organization must also avoid overselling itself to the point where new recruits hold unrealistic and unattainable expectations.[47] Finally, an organization must orient new employees to their work roles and positions by helping them understand their jobs, appreciate the organization's culture, and learn required tasks.[48] An organization is more likely to succeed in these activities if it understands the career needs experienced by job applicants and new employees, a topic we will treat in depth in Chapter 6.

Development and Utilization of Human Resources. Many organizations contend that their employees are their most valued assets. However, employees who are placed in inappropriate jobs and who are frustrated with their opportunities for growth and development can ultimately turn into liabilities, either through poor performance or through voluntary termination. Therefore, it is in the best interest of the organization to help its employees plan and manage their careers. Career planning workshops, job posting, supportive performance appraisal systems, career counseling, and job redesign are but a few of the career-related programs that organizations have used to facilitate effective career management.

Further, to enhance the performance and development of its employees, an organization should understand the critical tasks faced by people at different times in their careers. Programs designed to help employees in their early careers, such as a challenging initial job assignment, are likely to be different to some extent from developmental activities most relevant to someone in midcareer (e.g., learning to become a mentor) or in late career (preretirement counseling).

Moreover, to ensure a steady movement of human resources to key positions, an organization needs to understand the basis upon which employees make their career decisions. It is no longer practical for an organization to assume that employees will automatically accept promotions or other job assignments offered to them. Personal career interests, family considerations, and lifestyle choices often upset a company's best laid plans. Therefore, the organization needs to understand the dynamics of career decision making and be aware of its employees' career concerns to avoid miscalculation of its human resource needs.

Management of the Career Plateau. There is an additional problem experienced by companies that are either not expanding rapidly or are contracting in size. In these firms, there are fewer advancement opportunities for managers and other employees since the number of employees ready for a position may greatly exceed the number of openings. This problem is exacerbated by the aging baby boom generation that is now in middle age or older, where advancement of younger workers is blocked by a massive pool of employees who are not ready or are unable to fully retire.[49] Employees can become plateaued relatively early in their careers, stuck in jobs with little likelihood of promotion or with few opportunities for increased responsibility.[50] Many of these employees may experience a diminished level of work motivation or, as seen in Chapter 12, may leave their employers to establish an entrepreneurial career. Organizations need to keep plateaued employees performing effectively. To a considerable extent, success in meeting this challenge depends on an understanding of the principles of career management.

The Management of Cultural Diversity. The movement toward equal employment opportunity—fueled by the passage of the Civil Rights Act of 1964 and reinforced by judicial decisions and the Civil Rights Act of 1991—has had a profound effect on organizations' management of their human resources.[51] The focus on equitable career opportunities within organizations requires companies to develop fair assessment techniques so candidates for promotions or other job assignments will be judged on their competence, not on their sex, race, ethnicity, or age. Beyond that, however, employers need to leverage the perspectives of different cultural groups to create a more effective workforce.[52] As Chapter 11 will demonstrate, an understanding of career management is essential to accomplish this goal.

Family Responsiveness. Organizations recognize that they stand to lose the services of valuable human resources—women and men—if they fail to help their employees resolve difficulties in achieving balance between work and family responsibilities. Family-responsive organizations increasingly provide more flexible work schedules, part-time employment, opportunities for job sharing, telecommuting, and child care arrangements in an attempt to retain employees who are experiencing extensive work–family conflicts.[53] Moreover, employers may well need to reconsider the level of commitment and involvement they can reasonably expect from employees who are juggling work and family pressures. As we will see in Chapter 10, an understanding of the work and family demands facing employees at different stages of their career development will be required to attract, motivate, and retain an effective workforce.

Summary of the Contemporary Workplace

Modern organizations are staffed by an increasingly diverse group of employees. In general, employees want to derive more meaning from work than simply money and security, and are paying considerable attention to balancing their work, family, and personal lives. As part of a more general trend, employees are more assertive and vocal about their needs and are willing to leave organizations that fail to provide opportunities to meet these needs.

In addition, work organizations will face pressures from other sources. International competition, technological advances, and the constant focus on efficiency and productivity present a variety of human resource problems. "Lean and mean" may be a corporate rallying cry, but it can violate employees' expectations for rapid advancement and thereby frustrate the attainment of previously reasonable goals. Changing technologies can eliminate jobs and career paths in favor of other career routes. Work and family lives are increasingly intertwined as individuals and families attempt to achieve balance in their lives. The adoption of a global perspective and increasing prevalence of a multicultural work environment require new insights into the cultural underpinnings of behavior.

This turbulence exists in an era of employee rights and insistence on social justice on one hand, and the need for greater organizational efficiency on the other. Although an understanding of careers will not by itself solve these problems, a failure to understand and apply principles of career management could have unfortunate consequences for employees and their employers.

SUMMARY

A career is defined as the pattern of work-related experiences that span the course of a person's life. All careers have objective and subjective elements that together form the basis of an individual's career.

Career management is seen as an ongoing problem-solving process in which information is gathered, awareness of oneself and the environment is increased, career goals and strategies are developed, and feedback is obtained. This process can help individuals deal with the tasks and issues they face in various stages of their careers.

It is essential that employees and organizations develop an understanding of career management in today's turbulent world. Contemporary employees tend to be assertive and vocal about their needs, and they desire control over their professional and private lives. Organizations concerned with the productive utilization of their human resources can also benefit from understanding the many dilemmas and challenges faced by employees, as they attempt to help them plan and manage their careers.

ASSIGNMENT

Interview a friend, family member, or coworker to review the key events in his or her career. Remember to examine objective and subjective factors. Sketch a diagram of the person's career as in Exhibit 1.1.

DISCUSSION QUESTIONS

1. What is the impact of recent changes in the business environment on individuals' careers? Consider the consequences of intense competition, changes in organizational structure and the nature of work, internationalization, technology, work–family issues, and cultural diversity on career management.

2. Does the characterization of the contemporary workforce described in this chapter (high expectations, autonomy, weakening sex-role stereotypes, and concern for total lifestyle) fit your picture of yourself, your friends, or your family members? Could there be age, social class, cultural, or gender differences in how people view work and life?

3. Why should people be concerned about managing their careers? What can happen if people do not actively plan and manage their careers?

4. What is the incentive for an organization to help its employees manage their careers? How can the organization stand to gain from this venture? Are there any risks?

CHAPTER 1 CASE

Richard the Information Systems Executive

Why was Richard's decision to leave his employer of 14 years such a shock? Maybe it was the outstanding reputation of the company he had decided to leave—a company known for innovative computer technology and progressive human resource practices. Perhaps it was his steady advancement in title, responsibilities, and salary, or his obvious enthusiasm for his work and for the company that had treated him so well. Or possibly it was the fact that Richard had started with this paternalistic company right out of college and it was rare for any employee to leave when he or she had such high job security.

Richard had made a significant career decision that, in retrospect, should not have been so surprising. At 38 years of age he yearned for more—more money and a more prestigious title—but, most significantly, he wanted more responsibility and an opportunity to make a meaningful contribution to the destiny of his employer. This opportunity may have come eventually with his current company, but it would have taken a while, and Richard was growing impatient. Richard was in the phase of his career where he needed to have a greater degree of authority and independence, to be listened to seriously, and to make a name for himself. With a stay-at-home spouse and a young daughter, Richard was also concerned about increasing his compensation to provide a nice lifestyle for himself and his family, now and in the future. Aware of his needs and the opportunities at his current company, Richard, with the support of his spouse, decided to risk security in a safe, known environment and pursue his goals. This decision shaped the course of his career and life in profound ways.

Richard left his former employer with goodwill and enormous optimism. He accepted a position as Director of Customer Support with a rapidly growing computer firm. In this new position, he and his staff were in charge of providing technical support for all of the company's private and corporate clients. Richard approached his new job with the enthusiasm and energy that had produced success in earlier years. He upgraded his employer's back office information system, and built a management structure within his division that was sorely needed. His accomplishments were substantial and were recognized by his superiors, peers, and subordinates alike. It looked like his decision had paid off!

Unfortunately, Richard did not count on, nor did he anticipate, the corporate changes in strategy that were about to take place. Not that he was particularly naive, but how could he have known that the senior management of the company was planning on "offshoring" all of its customer support to Asia. Facing intense competition and resultant pressures to cut costs, the company's senior management team, with the blessing of the Board of Directors, decided to reduce labor costs by 40 percent by outsourcing Richard's entire department. After just a few months in what he thought was going to be his dream job, Richard was facing a great deal of uncertainty about his future. It's one thing to know intellectually that a change in corporate strategy can outweigh job performance in the real world; it's

(Continued)

(Continued)

quite another to be the victim of a major corporate cost-cutting move. Richard was worried; he had a family to support, a child to eventually put through college, and a heavy mortgage to pay each month.

At the age of 40, Richard found himself unemployed for the first time since high school. Finding a new position became a full-time job, and he approached this task with alacrity and extensive planning. After what seemed like an eternity, he found a position with a brokerage firm, heading up its information systems group. Burned once, he comforted himself that this new company was less likely than his previous employer to make a major change in strategy. But after two years of outstanding contributions, this firm is now undergoing a major reorganization and a reshuffling of personnel. Richard's future? Although he was recently promoted to Vice President, he's not so sure of himself anymore. When a friend asked whether he had any regrets about his decision to leave his initial employer, Richard gave an emphatic "maybe."

Case Analysis Questions

1. What do Richard's experiences indicate about the process of career management?

2. What environmental factors have affected Richard's career?

3. When Richard decided to leave his initial employer, what career trade-offs, either consciously or subconsciously, did he make? Do you believe that Richard has done a good job of managing his career? Why or why not?

4. If Richard sought your help, what advice would give him in terms of the future management of his career?

Career Contexts and Stages

In Chapter 1 we defined a career as the pattern of work-related experiences that span the course of a person's life. While this definition is straightforward, there are many different perspectives and themes from which a career can be seen and analyzed. As we move through the early part of the 21st century, the concept of a career continues to evolve. In this chapter we present a number of ways in which a career and career-related topics can be viewed. We start by looking at the more traditional perspectives on careers, namely, the *advancement/stability* theme, the *professional* view of careers, and the career as a *calling* concept. We then provide a discussion of more contemporary perspectives, including the *boundaryless* and *protean* themes, the effects of *social influences* on careers, and the differing meanings of *career success.* We conclude this chapter by discussing the *developmental* or *stage-based* perspective on careers. In Chapter 3 we will present a model of career management that is designed to help individuals respond to the many challenges posed by these various perspectives and navigate their careers to help ensure success and satisfaction over the life span.

THE TRADITIONAL PERSPECTIVES ON CAREERS

The modern view of careers crystallized during the era of prosperity in the decades following the end of World War II. As the industrialized world experienced unprecedented economic growth, demand for human capital soared and individuals had an abundance of job opportunities.[1] Working under a relational psychological contract, wherein there was a presumption of mutual loyalty between the employer and employee, a career in the latter half of the 20th century was viewed as a relatively stable and consistent undertaking. Put simplistically, you took a job with a solid, respected employer; kept your "nose to the grindstone" and your mouth shut; enjoyed regular promotions that allowed for linear, upward advancement within the organization; and retired with a nice pension when you reached the age of 65. This idealized vision of a traditional "organizational career," wherein one expected *advancement and stability* within one's career, became an anachronism in the

1980s as large-scale corporations began shedding human resources in mass numbers as a means to increase competitiveness in a global economy. Beginning in the 1980s and accelerating in the 1990s, career paths within organizations became more unstructured and unpredictable because of the increasing likelihood that jobs would be eliminated, outsourced, or substantially changed to ensure that organizations could move in different strategic directions if necessary.[2]

Even with the uncertainty in employment and careers over the past three decades, the theme of *advancement* and *stability* has been present in many definitions of a career. Such definitions are somewhat limiting since they imply that a person is pursuing a career only if he or she exhibits steady or rapid advancement in status, money, and the like, essentially with just one or two employers. In addition, another aspect of this theme revolves around the career as a source of stability within a single occupational field or closely connected fields. In this context, we often hear of the "career soldier" or "career police officer," or we hear of a career "lifer" with a particular organization. Similarly, a person's pursuit of closely connected jobs (teacher, guidance counselor, private tutor) is thought to represent a career, whereas a sequence of apparently unrelated jobs (novelist, politician, advertising copywriter) violates a neat consistency of job content and would not constitute a career.

Even with the mass job losses of the past 30 years, the objective of achieving linear advancement and stability with a single organization remains a popular career goal for many if not most workers, although the opportunities for linear advancement with a single organization are not nearly as great as they were during the heyday of the organizational careers in the decades that immediately followed the end of World War II. Instead, today's workers are challenged by substantially less certainty in their careers along with diminished job security.[3]

Another traditional theme places an emphasis on the career as a *profession*. A profession is typically distinguished from an "ordinary" occupation based on the belief that a profession represents a more desirable career choice and involves work that is of high economic status, allows for a high degree of autonomy, and can provide a high level of compensation.[4] As examples, doctors and lawyers are thought to have "professional" careers, whereas clerks and machinists typically are not. This traditional emphasis on the career as a profession also appears to be rather limiting, since it suggests that one must achieve a certain occupational or social status for one's work activities to constitute a career. Indeed, many occupations and careers allow for such desirable outcomes as high prestige, income, and autonomy, but are not typically afforded professional status.

Related to the professional view, the selection of a career can also be seen as a *calling,* whereby one primarily works for the fulfillment that the job or profession brings into one's life.[5] In this sense, a person is "called" to a career based on a strong attraction to a particular profession, such that the nature of the work will satisfy the person's need for making the world a better place.[6] Professions typically associated with a calling are those where there is a helping or nurturing component to the work, although any type of a profession or work could be seen as based on a calling.

CONTEMPORARY PERSPECTIVES ON CAREERS: THE BOUNDARYLESS AND PROTEAN THEMES

The combined effects over the past three decades of the mass downsizings of numbers of workers, the resultant loss of job security, and the well-documented decline in loyalty between employers and employees have wreaked havoc on traditional organizational careers where the expectation of job stability, security, and advancement had been the norm. In addition, ongoing market pressures for organizations to be flexible in the deployment of human resources in order to stay competitive creates an environment where the psychological contract between employers and employees will remain primarily transactional, and a long-term linear career within a single organization will continue to be the exception rather than the rule. In organizations that adopt dominant transactional orientations, employees are presented with opportunities to remain employable, although not necessarily in their current organization, by developing new, more portable skills for continued professional development.

In reaction to this new world of work the nature of careers has changed, resulting in new ways of looking at careers and career management. These new conceptualizations recognize the need for individuals to be adaptable in their careers as they navigate the uncertainties that exist not only in the general business environment but within particular companies as well. The two most widely recognized contemporary theories of careers are the *boundaryless* and the *protean* concepts.

Boundaryless Career

The boundaryless career concept is based primarily on the writings of Michael Arthur and his colleagues that began in the mid-1990s.[7] A boundaryless career is representative of work life in modern organizations that place less emphasis on internal boundaries (such as hierarchical levels and functional partitions) and that require the passage across boundaries between the organization and the myriad of networks it establishes with other organizations and individuals.[8] In this sense, boundaryless careers are disconnected from a single employment setting and its existing career paths and are untethered from traditional organizational career arrangements.[9] Boundaryless careers, which are typically characterized by frequent interorganizational mobility, have been observed in countries other than the United States, such as New Zealand, the United Kingdom, and Japan,[10] and the boundaryless career concept has been applied to individuals pursuing global careers.[11]

The emergence of boundaryless careers is a function of changes in the worldwide economy (increased global competition and advances in technology) that have produced significant alterations in organizational practices, such as acquisitions, reorganizations, reductions in force, and the use of temporary employees, all within the context of an increasingly transactional psychological contract with employees.[12] In addition, personal and family characteristics can trigger the acquisition of career competencies and the adoption of a boundaryless career orientation. Attitudes toward family role participation, parental responsibilities, stage of family development, and spouses' commitment to their careers can all affect whether individuals are willing or able to adopt a boundaryless career philosophy.[13]

Because of ambiguities and unresolved issues in the literature, it is difficult to derive a consensual definition of a boundaryless career. We instead propose that the boundaryless career involves three different perspectives or themes that can be contrasted with the traditional career as described earlier. The first perspective of the boundaryless career is that it involves mobility patterns that depart from a traditional career whereby the individual pursued continuous advancement with a single organization. Much of the literature on boundaryless careers speaks to these "nontraditional" forms of boundary crossing, especially the movement to other organizations in the pursuit of new opportunities or a better match with job interests.

The second perspective on the boundaryless career is that it requires the use of competencies or strategies that are different from those used in a traditional career. As proposed by Michael Arthur and his colleagues, these career competencies necessitate looking outside the organization for identity (knowing-why), marketability (knowing-how), and the establishment of networks of information and influence (knowing-whom).[14] With these competencies the individual psychologically or physically crosses the boundary from one organization to another by pursuing job contacts or leads, expanding knowledge and skills, and establishing connections with a wide network of influential people outside the employing organization.

The third perspective on the boundaryless career involves the need for individuals to maintain a high degree of self-responsibility for their career choices and to follow personally meaningful values in making career decisions. In this sense, the boundaryless career means that individuals should be adaptable and proactive in managing their careers as a way to attain personally meaningful values and goals, especially in times of personal or organizational change. This perspective is in contrast with a traditional career where the individual looks to the organization to determine the career path to be followed.

Protean Career

The protean career concept is another emerging view of careers in the 21st century that actually predates the concept of the boundaryless career.[15] In his book *Careers in Organizations,* Douglas T. Hall described the protean career as managed by the individual rather than the organization, and guided by the search for self-fulfillment.[16] Named after the mythological Proteus, the Greek god who could change his shape at will, the protean career has been characterized as self-directed, flexible, adaptable, versatile, and initiated by the individual to achieve psychological success. In recent years, Hall and his colleagues have elaborated on the protean career, developed scales to assess protean career attitudes, and explored the implications of protean careers for individuals and organizations.[17]

There are thought to be two primary dimensions of a protean career that are, in actuality, quite similar to the elements of the boundaryless career.[18] First, a protean career is proactively *self-directed*. Individuals pursuing a protean career feel responsible for managing their career and take the initiative in exploring career options and making career decisions. Second, it is *values-driven* in that individuals make career decisions to meet their personally meaningful values and goals, resulting in feelings of psychological success, in contrast to striving to achieve values and goals imposed upon them by organizations and society. Moreover, the personal values and goals that protean careerists attempt to achieve are relevant to the "whole life space" or "life's work" rather than focused solely on employment.[19]

Boundaryless and Protean Career Conceptualizations: Similarities and Differences

Although the boundaryless and protean career concepts are occasionally linked together,[20] it is more likely that while they overlap one another, they are still unique concepts.[21] Nevertheless, the distinctions between the two concepts are somewhat elusive and depend upon how broadly one defines a boundaryless career. Symptomatic of the confusion is that both the boundaryless career and the protean career have been contrasted to a traditional organizational career.[22] If both of these career forms are thought to be the opposite of the organizational career, how are they different from one another? First, it makes sense to view the protean career as an orientation, attitude, or approach to a career rather than an actual structure of a career.[23] Indeed, several studies show that protean career attitudes are *not* strongly related to extensive interorganizational mobility preferences and behaviors.[24] Thus, while the protean career reflects a psychological orientation that produces specific career behaviors, the boundaryless career generally involves boundary-crossing behaviors that are produced by the views that individuals hold about the world.[25]

Regardless of these fine distinctions in their meanings, it is clear that the boundaryless and protean career conceptualizations reflect not only a fundamental shift in the way individuals view their careers, but also the behaviors and decisions that are required to manage a career successfully in the 21st century.[26] As we will discuss in Chapter 3 when we present the career management model, it is up to each individual to be proactive in taking charge of his or her career and in making career decisions that are personally appropriate. In this sense, we see the boundaryless and protean concepts as having a direct influence on the attitudes and actions necessary for successful career management.

SOCIAL INFLUENCES ON CAREERS

Although the selection, pursuit, and management of a career are seen, at least in Western cultures, as inherently individually based activities, there are many social institutions, structures, and networks that influence our careers.[27] Indeed, the social learning theory of careers posits that occupational choices result, in part, from planned and unplanned learning experiences that occur as we move through various social events and activities during our lifetimes.[28] At the most basic level, family interactions and background can have a pervasive influence on the long-term psychosocial development of the individual that, in turn, affects a wide range of factors associated with career choices and aspirations.[29] These factors can include individual characteristics such as personality, interests, values, abilities, and interpersonal skills, as well as attitudes and expectancies toward particular occupations.[30] Interpersonal and group experiences within other social organizations such as schools, community groups, sports clubs, and religious institutions can all have an influence on the career attitudes that develop during one's formative years.

Beyond the family, other social networks begin to exert a positive influence on a career as the person ages. For example, college groups and associations can create lifelong affiliations that can assist in employment and career advancement. Once a person starts working, professional organizations, trade unions, and industry groups can provide useful career support. In addition, organizations that one joins in the community, such as a membership in a golf or tennis club, can offer the opportunity to connect with influential members of the business community. Friendships that one develops with current or former coworkers can provide job leads and employment advice.

What each of these examples has in common is that they require the individual to "network" with other people to create interpersonal relationships that could positively influence the individual's career, either at present or in the future. Networking refers to the activities that establish and maintain relationships that can potentially provide information, influence, guidance, and support to individuals in their careers.[31] It is believed that by engaging in networks of relationships individuals develop social capital.[32] Social capital refers to valued resources that are available to an individual through relationships that exist within a social network.[33] In essence, social capital provides access to people of influence who can assist the individual in a number of career-related tasks, such as getting information on job openings with a particular company, obtaining an interview for a job that was not advertised, or receiving advice on career paths to pursue or avoid. In addition, as we discussed earlier, the use of networks and the building of social capital are identified as essential behaviors in achieving success in a boundaryless career environment. We will discuss networking and the use of social capital in more detail in Chapter 5 when we review all of the possible career strategies that individuals could deploy.

The Different Meanings of Career Success

The changing nature of careers at the dawn of the 21st century along with evolving social structures bring with them new ways of looking at career success. Career success is defined as the positive material and psychological outcomes resulting from one's work activities and experiences, with these outcomes including both objective and subjective components.[34]

From a more traditional perspective, career success has been viewed primarily in objective terms, which include such factors as total compensation, number of promotions, and other tangible trappings of accomplishment. Although these objective indicators of career success are certainly relevant, the pursuit of a boundaryless career places an emphasis on understanding career success from a subjective perspective. A boundaryless career is believed to intensify the need for using internal psychological and self-generated guides such as personal growth and continuous learning in defining one's career success.[35]

From this subjective side, career success is viewed as a function of the individual's perception of satisfaction with the job and with career progress. In addition, research has shown that such elements as time for self, job challenge, job security, social relationships, and a balance between one's career and personal life are viewed by business professionals as important indicators that their careers are successful.[36] These subjective dimensions get at the individual's perception of psychological success that goes beyond such external indicators of success as prestige, power, money, and advancement.[37]

Often, professional employees in large corporations see career success strictly in objective terms, where the speed of progression up the corporate ladder becomes an obsession. This narrower view of success can lead to career goals and actions that can be inconsistent with personal values and beliefs. Further, many highly successful managers and executives can experience feelings of personal failure, reflecting regret over having sacrificed family relationships and other affiliations in the ambitious pursuit of the objective form of career success.[38] In contrast, when career success is seen in subjective or psychological terms, the focus is on individual satisfaction with the career and how well it has met personal goals and expectations. The subjective view of career success can also be expanded to include such dimensions as the balance between one's work and personal lives or the ability to establish close interpersonal relationships. Adopting a broader meaning of career success can take some of the pressure off of upwardly striving middle managers and executives, since the focus of career goals and strategies is no longer exclusively on advancement, but encompasses various aspects of personal fulfillment.

Looking to the future, if individuals can adopt a boundaryless philosophy toward their careers and if they can accept a broader definition of the meaning of career success, then they would have a much better chance of managing their careers so that they are able to stay true to their beliefs and values.[39]

THE DEVELOPMENTAL OR STAGE-BASED PERSPECTIVE ON CAREERS

It has long been recognized that children pass through a series of rather predictable periods or stages that shape their personality, intelligence, and sense of morality as they mature.[40] In a similar sense, many researchers believe that adulthood also unfolds or develops in a relatively predictable manner, with the premise that each phase of adulthood has its own particular developmental tasks and life and career concerns that need to be addressed.[41]

Do careers in the 21st century really unfold in orderly stages of development? The answer to this question is uncertain. On the one hand, the answer could be no, given the changes in the business world over the past few decades, as described in Chapter 1. These economic, demographic, and global changes have all affected the orderliness of the ideal progression through career stages. Downsizings cause job loss resulting in career disruptions. Women and men in the workforce might wish to pause their careers to raise children. Many employees are returning to school to gain new skills. When individuals step out of the workforce, either voluntarily or involuntarily, gaps are created in their employment histories. Discontinuities in employment can have a negative impact on future income beyond that attributable to diminished work experience both for men and for women.[42] Undoubtedly, the evolving worldwide economy is having immediate and long-term effects on many individuals' progression through career and life stages, which might make the seamless progression between career stages an obsolete concept.

On the other hand, the answer to the above question could be yes. The experiences, needs, values, and situations of all individuals change over time as they age, which could make it appropriate to view a career as a series of relatively unique stages or phases. It is readily apparent that the career concerns and expectations of a 25-year-old management trainee are different from those of a 45-year-old manager or a 65-year-old executive. Individuals face a variety of career tasks and developmental issues at different life stages. Further, changes in the nature of career motivation are likely to occur over the course of an employee's life. An understanding of the tasks and developmental implications of different career stages can help individuals manage their careers more effectively and can help organizations manage and develop their human resources.

On balance, we believe that it is still important to understand the concept of career stages and to examine how these stages fit within the larger context of adult life development. In this section we consider several views of adult life development, providing brief descriptions of the pioneering work of Erik Erikson and Daniel Levinson and his colleagues. We then discuss briefly our view of career development and preview subsequent chapters on the specific stages of career development.

Adult Life Development

There is a commonly held stereotype that adulthood, especially old age, is synonymous with decline. In a youth-oriented culture it is not surprising that adulthood is often viewed (and feared) as a period of deterioration of physical, intellectual, and emotional functioning. Although various aspects of biological functioning undoubtedly decline during adulthood, the decline is generally quite gradual until very late adulthood. In addition, research on the psychological and physical functioning of individuals as they age demonstrates that stereotypes that inspire age discrimination are without merit; indeed, the majority of older workers are able to perform their work roles far beyond the typical age of retirement and well into later years in life.[43] In addition, research findings refute the assumptions that age changes precipitate declines in work performance or lead to an increase in workplace accidents or absenteeism.[44] In fact, older workers tend to be more loyal, have lower rates of absenteeism, and are generally more reliable than younger workers.[45]

But there is more to the study of adulthood than simply cataloging physical, intellectual, and psychological functions. There is a much broader question of concern: "Is there an underlying order in the progression of our lives over the adult years, as there is in childhood and adolescence?"[46] Historically, the most influential models of career development have proposed a series of stages that were closely linked to age. For example, Donald Super identified five stages—growth, exploration, establishment, maintenance, and decline—that were thought to capture individuals' work-related experiences from the years of childhood to retirement.[47] In addition, these models generally assume that individuals pursue a continuous linear career within one occupational type, perhaps one or two organizations, and without major disruptions or redirections. As we will discuss shortly, the movement over the past three decades away from stable, traditional careers can make it difficult to apply somewhat rigid age-based stages to modern careers that are subject to increased uncertainty and disruption.

Erikson's Approach to Life Development

One of the earliest and most influential writers on life development, Erik Erikson, proposed that people progress through eight stages of psychosocial development (Table 2.1).[48] Each

TABLE 2.1

Erikson's Eight Stages of Development	
Stage of Development	*Age*
1. Basic trust versus mistrust	Infancy
2. Autonomy versus shame and doubt	Ages 1 to 3
3. Initiative versus guilt	Ages 4 to 5
4. Industry versus inferiority	Ages 6 to 11
5. Identity versus role confusion	Puberty and adolescence
6. Intimacy versus isolation	Young adulthood
7. Generativity versus stagnation	Middle adulthood
8. Ego integrity versus despair	Maturity (late adulthood)

SOURCES: Based on material from the following: Erikson, E. H. (1963). *Childhood and society.* New York: W. W. Norton; Adams, G. R. (2006). Erikson's theory of development. In J. H. Greenhaus & G. A. Callanan (Eds.), *Encyclopedia of career development* (pp. 295–298). Thousand Oaks, CA: Sage.

stage poses a crisis of sorts and, depending on the outcome of the stage, provides the setting for either growth or arrested development. For example, at the first stage of development, the helpless infant is totally dependent on others for its nurturance and survival. Under favorable circumstances, the infant will develop a sense of trust in parents and other people. With unfavorable conditions, the child will emerge with a basic mistrust of the world that may be difficult to reverse throughout life. At each stage of development, the ratio of positive and negative experiences determines the nature of the outcome.

The last three stages of Erikson's model are most relevant to adulthood and careers. The major task of early adulthood is the development of intimacy, a deep commitment to other people and groups. Failure to develop and maintain intimate relationships can bring a sense of isolation to the young adult and impair his or her ability to love. As a person approaches middle adulthood, the development of generativity (literally, guiding the next generation) becomes particularly important and can be accomplished through parenting and/or serving as a mentor to a younger colleague. Failure in this task can bring a feeling of stagnation in which no contribution or legacy is left to future generations. During late adulthood, people need to understand and accept the ultimate meaningfulness and limitations of their lives or risk ending life with despair.

Erik Erikson's major contributions to the study of life and career development are twofold. First, he proposed an underlying order in which certain key issues present themselves at critical parts of our lives. Although "success" at each stage does not guarantee permanent resolution of a conflict, "failure at an early stage jeopardizes full development at a later stage."[49] Second, he identified three key developmental tasks of adulthood—intimacy, generativity, and ego integrity—that are particularly relevant to an understanding of careers.

Levinson's Approach to Adult Life Development

The seminal work of Daniel Levinson and his colleagues plays a particularly significant role in the overall understanding of adult life development and in the delineation of career and life stages.[50] In the 1970s, Levinson's research team conducted interviews with 40 American-born men between the ages of 35 and 45. Each man in the sample (10 business executives, 10 university biologists, 10 novelists, and 10 industrial workers) was seen between 5 and 10 times, and the interview transcripts generated an average of 300 pages of text per man.[51] These biographical interviews attempted to reconstruct the story of each man's life from childhood to the present. After this initial study, Levinson conducted interviews with 45 women, also ranging in age from 35 to 45.[52] Fifteen women were homemakers, 15 were pursuing corporate careers in finance, and 15 were pursuing academic careers. Levinson and his associates conducted interviews similar to those of his male sample, generating reconstructions of the stages of the women's lives.

Levinson proposed that there are four eras of the human life cycle: preadulthood, early adulthood, middle adulthood, and late adulthood (Table 2.2). Each era includes alternating stable and transitional periods. In stable periods, which usually last six or seven years,

TABLE 2.2   Levinson's Eras of Development

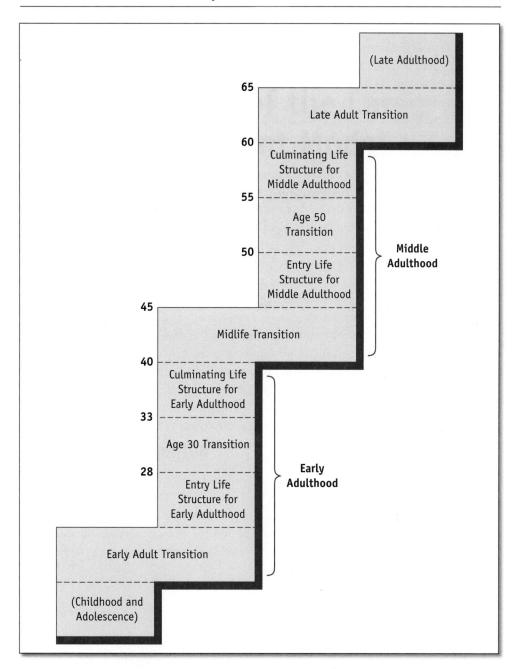

SOURCES: Based on a diagram originally included in *The Seasons of a Man's Life,* by Daniel J. Levinson et al. (1978). Updated to be consistent with terminology in Levinson's "A Conception of Adult Development," *American Psychologist, 41* (1986), 3–13.

people pursue goals to accomplish their significant life values. Stable periods are not necessarily tranquil, but they are stable in the sense that people attempt to create a desired lifestyle. Since no life structure remains appropriate forever, transitional periods, normally of four or five years' duration, are necessary to question and reappraise the established life structure and to consider making changes in various parts of one's life.

According to Levinson, early adulthood normally begins in the late teens and culminates in the mid-40s with the termination of the midlife transition. In the very beginning period of adulthood, people emerge from adolescence and try to create a niche for themselves in adult society. Young adults need to begin the process of separation from their parents, often leaving home and becoming less financially and emotionally dependent on their parents. They also need to take some tentative steps into early adulthood by imagining or even trying out an adult role in some manner.

Levinson considers the mid-20s to be a stable period in which the young person enters into the adult world, but faces two potentially conflicting tasks: (1) to explore adulthood by trying out different roles (e.g., jobs, relationships) while keeping his or her options open and (2) to settle down and create a stable life. Whereas some people emphasize the exploratory task and form no real commitments to people or organizations, others form relationships that are expected to endure well into the future. Whatever decisions are made in this period, there are bound to be flaws. People who emphasized options and exploration may begin to wonder whether they are capable of developing and maintaining meaningful relationships. People who emphasize stability and commitments to an occupation, a company, or another person may wonder whether these commitments were premature and overly constraining.

In Levinson's model, the late 20s and early 30s represent a transitional period that stimulates a reappraisal of one's current life. These first three periods comprise the novice phase of early adulthood in which one is struggling to become a "real" adult. A major task of this novice phase is to form, refine, and pursue a "Dream," a powerful view of how one wants to live one's life. The Dream frequently has occupational goals (e.g., becoming a rich and famous financier or becoming a world renowned scientist), but it can extend beyond work to one's role in family, community, or the larger society. During the mid-30s, the person has two major tasks: (1) to establish a niche in adult society in areas of life (work, family, leisure) that are central to the person and (2) to "make it"—that is, to advance along some timetable in an effort to build a better life. This period is primarily devoted to the pursuit of one's Dream and becoming a full-fledged adult.

According to Levinson, middle adulthood commences in the early 40s with the midlife transition period. During this time, the life that was pursued so intensely during the early adulthood period is reappraised, often with a great deal of turmoil and agony. Levinson and his associates concluded that 80 percent of the men and 85 percent of the women in their samples experienced a moderate or severe crisis during the midlife transition. Why do some people begin such a painful reevaluation during the early or mid-40s? Levinson points to the significance of three related factors. First, even modest decline in bodily functioning around age 40 may be interpreted as a loss of youthful vigor and may stimulate an increasing awareness of one's mortality. The opportunity to make a lasting contribution to the world can be threatened by the realization that one's life is half over. Second, a generational shift normally occurs in the 40s. People in their 20s and 30s are apt to view those in their 40s as members of the "older" generation. With the possibility of teenage children at this point and the likelihood of ailing or deceased parents, the person in his or her 40s feels pushed into senior status in the adult world and fears that youth (and all that it stands for) is largely completed.

Also, by the 40s, a person has experienced enough of life to assess progress toward the youthful Dream. A person who has failed to accomplish this Dream must deal with the failure and make some choices for the future. The person who has successfully climbed the ladder may begin to doubt whether the quest was worth it. The choices made in the 30s may have emphasized certain aspects of the self (e.g., success, achievement, power, competition) over others (e.g., friendships, nurturance, spiritual development).

Levinson speculates that the midlife transition is followed by a stable period in which a person must try to fashion a satisfactory life for the middle years. This period, in turn, is followed in the early 50s by another transitional period during which time the person works further on the issues raised and the new goals developed during the midlife transition. The late adult transition (age 60–65) terminates middle adulthood and begins late adulthood.

A key aspect of Levinson's model is the proposed existence of four eras of the human life cycle in which a number of stable and transitional periods enable the individual to work on the major developmental tasks of each era. Despite the plausibility of the model, a number of questions have become evident over the years. How closely are the eras and the transitional periods linked to age? Is the sequence of periods fixed or can people "skip" periods? How universal are the periods? Are these periods applicable to both men and women in American society?

First, Levinson believed that the periods are closely related to age. Although the participants in his samples showed some variation in the onset or termination of a period, the range was rather small, perhaps two years on either side of the average. Thus, Levinson believed that there is a close, but by no means perfect, correspondence between chronological age and period of life development for both men and women. Levinson also believed that each person goes through each period in a fixed sequence. This does not mean that a person actively or successfully deals with each developmental task in each period— only that the developmental tasks present themselves in a fixed order. The ability to generalize Levinson's model to all people in all societies has also been questioned. Although Levinson acknowledged that the answer to this question is unknown, he argued in favor of universal applicability. He cited literature from ancient Chinese, Greek, and Hebrew civilizations to support his view.

Perhaps the most intriguing issue in Levinson's model is the role of gender in adult life development. Daniel Levinson and his colleagues believed that women go through the same developmental periods as men, although some of the specific issues might differ between men and women. However, many women face a delicate "balancing act" between the pursuit of career progress and the demands of motherhood that makes the very nature of life development different for men and women. Consistent with this theme, Lisa Mainiero and Sherry Sullivan, in their pioneering work on the varied (or kaleidoscope) career paths and directions of women, found that women were more likely than men to make career transitions for family reasons and to achieve a more satisfying balance between work and family.[53] They also observed that women were more likely than men to experience employment breaks or interruptions and that women, as compared with men, take a more relational approach to their careers by basing work hour decisions on the potential consequences for other members of their family.[54] In this sense it is possible that the sequence of developmental issues is reversed for women and men. For many women, the early adulthood stage can involve a preoccupation with balancing career, family, and dual-career issues. Even the pursuit of career success for women in their 30s is coupled with concerns about balancing multiple life roles (if they are a parent) or about the ticking away of the "biological clock" (if they are childless). On the other hand, middle adulthood, when many men are reducing their involvement in work, can be a period of professional involvement and accomplishment for women as they become more independent and somewhat freer of family demands.[55]

It is our opinion that Daniel Levinson's model of life development continues to be relevant some three decades after his initial work was published. While career progression in the 21st century is more complex than in the 1970s, the notion of period-related developmental tasks still seems applicable to adulthood, and the alternating stable and transitional periods seems to permit continued growth and development throughout adulthood. Finally, the three eras of adulthood—early, middle, and late—offer a useful structure for examining career-related issues during one's lifetime.

STAGES OF CAREER DEVELOPMENT

In Chapter 1, we defined career development as an ongoing process by which an individual progresses through a series of stages, each of which is characterized by a relatively unique set of issues, themes, or tasks. While the concepts of life development and career development are compatible, there is a greater emphasis on work-related issues in career development models. This book views development of a career in terms of four stages. This view is based in part on the literature in career development and in part on Levinson's view of adult life development. The four stages of this model are summarized in Table 2.3 and are discussed below.

TABLE 2.3 Four Stages of Career Development

1. *Occupational and Organizational Choice*

   Typical Age Range: Initially 18–25; then variable

   Major Tasks: Develop occupational self-image, assess alternative occupations, develop initial occupational choice, pursue necessary education, obtain job offer(s) from desired organization(s)

2. *Early Career*

   Typical Age Range: 25–40

   Major Tasks: Learn job, learn organizational rules and norms, fit into chosen occupation and organization, increase competence, pursue career goals

3. *Midcareer*

   Typical Age Range: 40–55

   Major Tasks: Reappraise early career and early adulthood, reaffirm or modify career goals, make choices appropriate to middle adult years, remain productive in work

4. *Late Career*

   Typical Age Range: 55–Retirement

   Major Tasks: Remain productive in work, maintain self-esteem, prepare for effective retirement

Stage 1. Occupational and Organizational Choice

From a career perspective, the initial set of tasks in this stage are to form and refine an occupational self-image, explore the qualities of alternative occupations, develop at least a tentative occupational choice, and pursue the type of education or training required to implement the choice. The accomplishment of these initial career tasks requires considerable insight into one's own abilities, interests, values, and desired lifestyle, as well as the requirements, opportunities, and rewards associated with alternative occupational fields. Indeed, for young adults, choosing an occupation involves the formation of an image of oneself and an increased understanding of the world of work. The model of career management that will be described in Chapter 3 is based on continual exploration and discovery, and many people develop second or third occupational choices during the course of their work lives. Since occupational choices can occur at other stages, the tasks associated with occupational choice can reappear throughout one's lifetime. Chapter 6 focuses extensively on the occupational choice process.

Once an occupation has been selected, the second set of tasks in this stage focuses on selecting and entering an organization, and landing a job that can satisfy one's career values and utilize one's talents. The organizational choice and entry process can take several months to complete and often depend on the number of years of education one has pursued. Although the entry process is experienced initially by persons who are moving directly from school to their first career-related work assignment, one can enter a new organization at any age; therefore, the age range can be quite varied. Chapter 6 will elaborate on the tasks associated with the organizational choice and entry process. It will review how individuals choose organizations, consider several obstacles to a match between the individual and the organization, and suggest ways to manage the organizational entry process more effectively.

Stage 2. The Early Career: The Establishment and Achievement Phases

This career stage, which really encompasses two periods, reflects the dominant issues of early adulthood: finding a niche for oneself in the adult world and striving to "make it" along the chosen path. Having already selected an occupation and an initial job, a critical first task of the early career is to become established in one's career. The new employee must not only master the technical aspects of his or her job but must also learn the norms, values, and expectations of the organization. In this establishment period of the early career, the individual's major task is to learn about the job and the organization and to become accepted as a competent contributor to the organization; in other words, to make a place for his- or herself in the occupation and the organization.

It may seem odd that the early career can extend all the way up to age 40. But the entire stage, in our view, does reflect the early career in that the individual typically continues to pursue youthful aspirations, as yet unencumbered by the sometimes painful reappraisal of the midlife transition. Thus it is suggested that the dominant theme of the early career, becoming established and making it (however defined), can maintain itself in one form or another for a significant period of time. Chapter 7 will examine issues pertaining to the early career in considerable depth.

Stage 3. The Midcareer

An individual's midcareer is initiated by the midlife transition, which serves as a bridge between early and middle adulthood. A number of tasks and concerns characterize the midcareer years. First, the individual is likely to reappraise the lifestyle and demands that dominated his or her early career. Next, it is necessary to begin to form a lifestyle (with its career implications) to move fully into middle adulthood. Whether the new lifestyle is consistent with the prior one or constitutes a minor or radical departure, there are a number of specific work-related issues that confront the individual in midcareer.

Chapter 8 examines midcareer issues. Among the major concerns treated are the distinctive requirements of the midlife transition, the dynamics of midcareer change, the dangers of obsolescence, and the possibilities of midcareer plateauing. As with the other career stages, we will consider individual and organizational actions that can contribute to effective functioning during midcareer.

Stage 4. The Late Career

There are two major tasks that dominate this stage. First, the individual must continue to be a productive contributor to the organization and maintain his or her sense of self-worth and dignity. However, the maintenance of productivity and self-esteem is often hindered by changes within the individual and by society's bias against older people. Second, the individual in late career must anticipate and plan for an effective retirement, so that disengagement from work is not devastating to the individual and that the postretirement years are meaningful and satisfying. The issues that dominate the late career will be examined more thoroughly in Chapter 8.

Difficulties in Applying a Career Stage Perspective

We have traced four career stages and we have chosen to organize the career stages around typical—although approximate—age ranges. We are not claiming that this is the only or the best way to view career development, but it does seem to structure our knowledge about careers in a meaningful manner. Nonetheless, there are several factors that complicate the use of stages as a predominant method of viewing career progression. One issue concerning career stages is whether there is a true linkage of the stages to chronological age. First, it is important to recognize that all age ranges are approximations. The onset and termination of stages can vary. Thus, a high school graduate might accept a first full-time job at age 18, whereas a PhD graduate may take a first academic post at 27 or 28. Some approaches to career development define career stages on the basis of work activities, relationships, and psychological issues rather than on the basis of age. Despite the many valuable contributions of that approach, we take the position that age—or more generally, life experience—strongly shapes career aspirations, experiences, and concerns, and therefore plays a critical role in the identification of career stages.

A second issue concerns the assumption that the stages of a career cycle depict development in a "normal" career, that is, a career in which a person chooses an occupation at an early age and remains continually in the same career field (or in the same organization) for the duration of his or her work life. The idea of long and sequential career stages is based in large part on the assumed pursuit of traditional organizational careers that were prevalent when career stage theories were first proposed in the 1960s and 1970s. There is an emerging belief, as we move through the early part of the 21st century, that career stages or cycles currently are shorter in duration and reoccur periodically over the course of a person's career.[56] It is thought that career cycles are now compressed because of the frequent and dramatic changes or transitions associated with pursuing a boundaryless career.[57] Michael Arthur and his colleagues have identified three career cycles or "modes"—fresh energy, informed direction, and seasoned engagement—that are generally consistent with the early, middle, and late career stages, respectively.[58] Although fresh energy is typically displayed in the early career, informed direction in midcareer, and seasoned engagement in late career, Arthur and his colleagues demonstrated how individuals periodically "recycle" back to earlier modes as they change projects, jobs, employers, or occupations.[59]

What are the complications that arise from deviations from this "normal" or "ideal" career cycle? Consider the following illustrations:

- A 42-year-old woman accepts paid employment for the first time in nearly 20 years. Is she beginning her midcareer years or is she entering the establishment period of her early career?

- A 38-year-old banker pursues a promotion to senior vice president with a different bank. Is he deeply entrenched in the achievement period of his early career or is he beginning another organizational entry stage?

- A 55-year-old computer executive leaves Silicon Valley to become a novelist. Is he entering his late career or is he struggling to establish himself in the early career stage of his new literary pursuits?

These kinds of classification problems are inherent in all age-related theories of career development, but they may not be problems after all. Our aim is not merely to classify an individual into a particular stage but to understand how careers unfold and how people relate to work at different stages of their careers and lives. The newly employed woman primarily has to deal with the early career issues of socialization and establishment, but from the perspective of a 42-year-old. The 38-year-old banker does have to deal with the problems of organizational entry, but with the experience and concerns of a person who is advanced in his early career and is "on the move." The 55-year-old former computer executive does, in most respects, have to establish himself in his new career field, but from the vantage point of a man nearing late adulthood.

We should not bemoan these deviations from a neat classification system, because they reflect the rich diversity of careers and lives. In Table 2.4 we attempt to portray this diversity by linking the tasks of career development with the three eras of adulthood. Notice that the selection of an occupation, the entrance into an organization, the establishment of oneself in a new setting, and the striving for achievement in that setting occur most prominently in early adulthood. However, the selection of a different occupation or organization can occur during middle adulthood or late adulthood, necessitating renewed establishment and achievement concerns in the different career field or organization. Conversely, the tasks most closely aligned with midcareer and late career (reappraisal, remaining productive, preparation for retirement) may also occur to some extent during early adulthood. Perhaps our aim should be to understand the typical issues that people generally experience at each career stage, and then consider the possible variations that can occur at each stage. This approach will be followed in Chapters 6 through 8 when we delve more deeply into the different career stages.

TABLE 2.4 Relationship Between Career Development Tasks and Stages of Adulthood

	Stages of Adulthood		
Career Development Tasks	*Early Adulthood*	*Middle Adulthood*	*Late Adulthood*
Occupational/Organizational choice	XXX	XX	X
Early Career			
Establishment	XXX	XX	X
Achievement	XXX	XX	X
Midcareer			
Reappraisal	X	XXX	XX
Remain productive	X	XXX	XXX
Late Career			
Remain productive	X	XXX	XXX
Prepare for retirement	X	XX	XXX

NOTE: XXX Very Frequently; XX Frequently; X Occasionally.

SUMMARY

This chapter presented a number of different perspectives from which a career and career management can be viewed. Traditional organizational careers, wherein one strives for and expects job stability, security, and upward advancement, have been supplanted by careers that are far less certain. The boundaryless and protean career concepts represent contemporary perspectives on careers that take into account the increased uncertainty in people's work lives. These new ways of looking at careers recognize that individuals will likely work for multiple organizations (rather than just one or two organizations), that the nature of the psychological contract with their employer will probably be transactional (rather than relational), that the individual will be challenged to develop multiple skills that can be transported from one work setting to another, and that the individual (rather than the organization) has ultimate responsibility for his or her career management. This emphasis on flexibility and adaptability in the individual's career does not necessarily mean that the boundaryless career is the only or the dominant career model, but rather that an increasing segment of the population is likely to pursue a career with boundaryless characteristics.

(Continued)

(Continued)

This chapter also recognized that careers and career choices do not occur in a vacuum. Social institutions, such as a person's family and community groups, have a significant influence on the individual's interests, values, and preferences that eventually translate into specific career choices. Research on careers also recognizes the role that social networks play in career decision making and advancement. By engaging in these networks, individuals build social capital that facilitates connections with people of influence who can help the individual in various career-related tasks.

The boundaryless and protean career concepts expand the meaning of career success. Traditionally, career success was viewed primarily in objective terms, with such tangible outcomes as compensation level, job title, promotion record, and executive perks being seen as indicators of success. It is now recognized that career success also has subjective components that recognize an individual's feelings of psychological success. These subjective elements can include feelings of satisfaction with the individual's career accomplishments or with his or her total life. This expansion in the meaning of career success recognizes that individuals have multiple demands from both the work and nonwork spheres of their lives, and accomplishments in both should be taken into account when gauging success.

The research of Erik Erikson and Daniel Levinson suggests that the early, middle, and late stages of adulthood present somewhat different tasks and challenges that need to be addressed. Early adulthood is characterized by a preoccupation with establishing oneself as an adult and "making it" in the adult world. Middle adulthood often involves a reappraisal of one's life situation and a concern with making a lasting contribution to the world. In late adulthood, one needs to come to terms with the meaning and value of one's life. Possible gender differences in stages of life development were also considered.

Four stages of career development were identified: (1) occupational and organizational choice, during which time one develops an occupational self-image, explores alternative occupations, forms an occupational decision, and selects and enters an organization; (2) early career, in which one is concerned with establishing oneself in a career field and achieving competence and recognition; (3) midcareer, during which time one may need to reexamine the course of one's career and life and perhaps make adjustments for the future; and (4) late career, in which one needs to maintain a satisfactory level of productivity and self-esteem and plan for an effective retirement. These four career stages provide the structure for Chapters 6 through 8 of the book.

ASSIGNMENTS

1. Interview a friend, acquaintance, coworker, or relative who is in a different career stage than you are. What career-related tasks and activities is this person currently undertaking? What are the issues and concerns that are uppermost in his or her mind? In what ways are these issues and concerns consistent or inconsistent with the approach to life development and career development proposed in this chapter?

2. Chart the career histories of a male and a female friend, acquaintance, coworker, or relative. Are the two career histories parallel and similar to each other? Are they similar to Levinson's model? Do employment gaps exist in either career history? If so, ask if these employment gaps have had any effect on the individual's career.

DISCUSSION QUESTIONS

1. Using Levinson's model as a framework, in what stage of adult life development do you see yourself? What concerns are uppermost in your mind at this time? Are these concerns consistent with Levinson's model?

2. Some people experience a crisis during their early or middle 40s. What factors are responsible for a midlife crisis? Does everybody experience a midlife crisis? Why or why not?

3. Do you think everybody follows the same developmental path through adulthood? Is Levinson's model applicable to women as well as men? To single people as well as married people? To working-class adults as well as upper-middle-class adults? Why do you feel that way?

CHAPTER 2 CASE

Kevin at the Crossroads

By everyone's account, Kevin has the ideal life. At the age of 39 he has attained the title of Vice President of Corporate Planning for XO Engineering Services Inc. (fictitious name), a midsized engineering firm specializing in providing support for large-scale infrastructure projects around the world. Kevin has spent his entire professional career at XO.

At the age of 23 Kevin received his bachelor's degree in mechanical engineering from one of the top universities in the United States. While he looked at a number of engineering companies prior to graduation, he was most impressed with XO right from the start. By Kevin's estimation, XO was a progressive organization that had outstanding growth prospects and really seemed to care about its employees. During the interview process he was surprised by how many times he heard that XO was like a family. Many of the employees whom Kevin met during his site visit had spent their entire careers at XO, and some had been with the company for its entire 30-year existence. Another selling point in favor of XO was that its corporate headquarters was in a Virginia suburb right outside of Washington, D.C. Kevin had grown up in northern Virginia and really wanted to stay in the metro Washington, D.C., area. For all of these reasons, the choice of XO as an employer was a "no-brainer" for Kevin.

Kevin's Early Career

Kevin's work ethic, intelligence, and charisma were recognized by XO's senior management early in his tenure with the company. In every assignment and project, Kevin's superiors would give him glowing evaluations. Kevin's rise up the corporate hierarchy was meteoric, at least by XO's standards. He went from a junior to a senior engineering position in one year and to a project manager two years after that.

(Continued)

(Continued)

With XO's encouragement, Kevin had gotten an executive MBA from a top-notch business school in Washington. By the time he was 30, Kevin was an Assistant Vice President, and at the age of 34 he was promoted to Vice President of Engineering Services. At age 38 he was moved to his present position. His current salary and bonus now total more than $200,000 per year. He is financially well off and he knows that XO's senior management and board of directors see him as a future senior officer, maybe even the CEO someday. His decision to take a job with XO many years ago has paid off for Kevin. He is in a secure, stable career with a solid company and he has great prospects for further advancement.

Kevin's Nonwork Life

While an undergraduate, Kevin met and began dating Anne, a fellow student pursuing a degree in education. After three years of dating, they got married. While Kevin was starting his career at XO, Anne began teaching seventh grade English in a school district close to their home. The two-career relationship worked well, with both Kevin and Anne enjoying much success in their careers. And their dual incomes afforded them a comfortable lifestyle.

Kevin and Anne agreed that they wanted to have children as soon as they could. Two years after they got married they had their first son and two years later they had another son. Their two career relationship resulted in a fair number of child care challenges and stresses when the two boys were younger, but Anne's job meant that she could be counted on to get home in the afternoon and she had her summers off. Both Kevin's and Anne's parents lived relatively close by, and they took turns watching the boys when needed. Once the two boys started school, the child care challenges became less difficult to manage. With his career on the fast track, Kevin did not get too involved in child rearing activities—he just did not have the time. His job required him to travel about 30 percent of the time, so he was often away from home, and when he was at the corporate headquarters he usually put in some long hours.

As his sons got older Kevin became involved in helping coach their sports teams. Both boys enjoyed athletics, and they started playing baseball and football as soon as they were old enough. Kevin had played both sports in high school, and he was quite pleased that his sons gravitated to these two sports. Kevin really enjoyed coaching and he looked forward to the practices and games, not only because he could spend time with his two sons, but he also believed that he had a positive influence on all the players he coached.

Just recently, several parents approached Kevin about becoming the manager of the travel baseball team for the next season. The travel team, of which Kevin's older son was a member, consisted of the top players in that age group. Because of the higher caliber of play, the travel team usually practiced twice a week and also played two games per week. While Kevin was flattered by the invitation to manage the team, he knew that his job demands would make it impossible for him to consider the offer seriously. Nevertheless, he really did want to manage the team and found himself bitter that his job was getting in the way of something that he really wanted to do.

Kevin's Dilemma

For at least the past three months Kevin has been having a difficult time being motivated about his work. After 17 years at XO, the job is not as challenging as it once was and the same old routine has gotten to be a hassle. The regular travel overseas is the worst part since it takes him away from his family for several days at a time. When he is away he has a hard time focusing on his work—he just counts down the days to when he can get back home. His work has not really suffered yet, mainly because his technical skills are still sharp, but he worries that if he doesn't get his act together soon, his performance might begin to slip.

Deep down, Kevin really envies his wife and her career. He sees Anne's teaching and counseling of children as fulfilling work, at least when compared with engineering. And unlike Kevin, it seems as if Anne is always motivated by her work. She also gets to spend a much greater amount of time with their children than he does. When he daydreams, Kevin secretly wonders what it would be like to be a teacher. One of the local colleges has been running ads for a program that would allow individuals who already have a bachelor's degree to get a teaching degree with only a year's worth of coursework. And he sees listings in the local newspapers for math and science teachers. Kevin is certain he would be a great teacher with his technical skills and all of his real-world experience.

His daydreams often fade quickly though, especially when he considers all that he would be giving up if he were to change careers. For one thing, his starting salary as a teacher wouldn't even be a third of what he is making as an executive with XO. Plus, if he were to leave XO now, he would be leaving a tremendous amount of potential future income "on the table," so to speak, given his chances for further promotions and compensation increases with XO. Longer-term, if he were to leave XO before he hit the age of 50 he would also forgo a substantial amount of pension income in his retirement. He hasn't spoken with Anne about his daydreams, and even if he did discuss the idea with her he isn't sure how she would react. She seems happy with the current situation and the successes they have achieved together. To willingly take a significant step backward in their household finances might not sit too well with her.

While in the midst of one of his daydreams, Kevin was brought back to reality by a knock at his office door. It was the CEO of the company and he wanted to know if Kevin was free for lunch that day. Kevin wasn't sure if the invitation to lunch was good thing or not—after all, his boredom in his work might have finally caught up with him. To Kevin's surprise, the lunch with the CEO wasn't negative at all; in fact it should have been looked at as good news. The CEO explained to Kevin that XO's senior officers, with the blessing of the Board of Directors, had decided to make a major expansion of the company's operations into South America. Kevin knew that the expansion was possible, given that he had actually made the formal proposal to the Board. While XO already had an office in Brazil, this new strategy would significantly expand operations in that country and throughout the region.

The purpose of the lunch was to gauge Kevin's interest in taking over the expanded operations in South America. The CEO explained how much confidence he and the Board of Directors had in Kevin and that he was the clear-cut choice to head this mission. The CEO hinted that if he were successful in this venture, he would

(Continued)

(Continued)

be the heir apparent to the CEO position in two or three years. Of course, the move would mean a promotion to the Senior Vice President level and a major increase in compensation. The CEO further explained that Kevin would need to move to Brazil, but the expatriate assignment would likely be for only two years. The CEO asked Kevin to think about the offer and also discuss it thoroughly with Anne. He asked Kevin to get back to him in a week or so. The company needed to move quickly, because if Kevin wasn't interested, they would likely go through an external search for the position.

After the lunch, Kevin sat at his desk in stunned silence. As he was about to leave and head home, he remembered that he had to go directly to the football field for his younger son's practice that evening—the team has a big game this weekend and they need Coach Kevin to help get them prepared.

Case Analysis Questions

1. Based on the definition and the description of the boundaryless perspective of careers as provided in this chapter, do you think Kevin has adopted this approach to his career? Why or why?

2. Do you think Kevin sees himself as successful in his career? Why or why not?

3. What social factors are influencing Kevin's career choices? How big a role should social factors play in the career decisions of an individual? Should they play a role?

4. Do you think Kevin's age and the fact that he is at midcareer are having an effect on his "daydreaming" and the questioning of his future career direction? Why or why not?

5. If Kevin sought your help, what advice would you give him in terms of the management of his career? If you had to make a prediction, what career choices do you think Kevin will make?

CHAPTER 3

A Model of Career Management

To manage a career is to make a decision or—more accurately—a series of decisions. Should you pursue a career in information technology, marketing, or accounting? Should you accept a position with a major corporation or obtain a graduate degree instead? Should you move into general management or stay in a staff position? Should you accept a transfer to manage a subsidiary in a foreign country? How might a job change affect your spouse or significant other's career? How can you obtain employment after an unexpected job loss? Will a transition into a new career at midlife be a lifesaver or a disaster? If you pursue "early retirement," will you do volunteer work or start your own company?

Although these illustrations are all unique in some respect, they do possess a basic similarity: they all require active career management and decision making. As was stated in Chapter 1, if we do not actively manage the direction of our career, then we leave our career up to chance or whim. In today's less certain business environment, we need to be proactive and responsible for our careers. Career management is the process by which individuals can make reasoned, appropriate decisions about their work life. It is also an approach to problem solving that can be used to address a wide variety of career decisions.

In this chapter, we will discuss a model of career management. First, an overview of the model and the research that forms the basis of the model are presented. Next, the value of using the career management process in a continual manner is articulated. Finally, four indicators of effective career management are outlined.

In Chapters 4 and 5 we will delve more deeply into the career management process and emphasize the pragmatic application of the model to career decision making. These chapters will include specific guidelines to apply the career management model, as well as learning exercises to practice the skills required by the model.

AN OVERVIEW OF THE CAREER MANAGEMENT MODEL

In the social sciences, a model is a picture or representation of reality.[1] A model contains a set of variables that are related to each other in a specified manner so that we can better understand some piece of the world. The model of career management considered in this book is normative in nature; that is, it describes how people should manage their careers. Not everybody manages a career in this fashion, but the activities represented in the model can lead to desirable outcomes for the individual. The reasons for this assumption will become clear as the model unfolds.

The career management model is portrayed in Exhibit 3.1. Before defining the key components in a formal sense, the career management cycle is introduced with a brief example.

A young chemical engineer is pondering her future in her company. Although she enjoys her position as a staff engineer, a career in management has intrigued her for a while. She could lay low and follow the company's "plan" for her. However, she decides to take a more active role in the management of her career. She has some decisions to make.

EXHIBIT 3.1   Model of Career Management

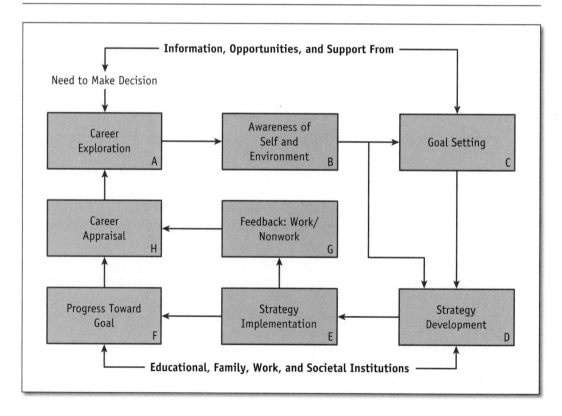

The first step in the career management model indicates that the engineer should engage in career exploration (Box A in Exhibit 3.1). That is, she should begin gathering information. She might collect information about herself (what she enjoys doing, where her talents lie, the importance of work in her total life), about alternative jobs inside or outside the organization (what does a plant manager really do, anyway? what are the salaries of veteran chemical engineers?), and about her organization (or other organizations) as a total system (is it possible to move from staff to line in this company? how do you get promoted around here?).

Career exploration, if conducted properly, should enable the engineer to become more fully aware of herself and her environment (Box B). She ought to gain insight, for example, into her values, interests, and abilities in both her work and nonwork lives. She should become more aware of job options and their requirements, and of opportunities and obstacles in the environment.

A greater awareness of herself and her environment can help the engineer choose a career goal or goals to pursue (Box C). First, greater self-awareness should prompt the engineer to set reasonable conceptual goals. A *conceptual goal* represents a general summary of the nature of the work experiences or outcomes the individual intends to attain, without specifying a particular job or position. In this sense, the conceptual goal is a manifestation of the individual's significant values, interests, and preferences. For example, the engineer might have a conceptual goal to attain substantial managerial responsibility as a means to influence corporate direction, but the conceptual goal does not specify a particular position.

In contrast, greater awareness of the work environment should assist in the setting of operational goals. An *operational goal* translates the conceptual goal into a specific or targeted job and is based on the individual's understanding of the internal and external work environments. To extend the above example, the engineer might have a longer-term operational goal to be the Assistant Vice President of Technical Support, which would satisfy her conceptual need to exert managerial responsibility. Of course, she could have interim operational goals that could take her to the assistant vice president level. She might first set a more reasonable operational goal of being a team leader for a high-profile engineering project. Or she might have a short-term goal to remain in her current position for the foreseeable future as a means to gain more practical experience and to build a record of accomplishment.

The establishment of realistic conceptual and operational goals can facilitate the development (Box D) and implementation (Box E) of a career strategy, that is, a plan of activities designed to attain the desired career goal. For example, if the engineer's goal is to become the Assistant Vice President of Technical Support, she might enroll in one or more management development seminars sponsored by the company, encourage her boss to assign her more managerial tasks in her present position, and learn more about the operation of the entire plant.

The implementation of a reasonable career strategy can produce progress toward the stated conceptual and operational career goals (Box F). If the engineer chooses a wise plan of action, she is more likely to attain her goals than if she did not pursue a strategy or developed an inappropriate strategy.

The implementation of a career strategy can provide useful feedback to the person. This feedback, in conjunction with feedback from other work and nonwork sources (Box G), can enable the engineer to appraise her career (Box H). The additional information derived from career appraisal becomes another vehicle for career exploration (see the arrow from Box H to Box A) that continues the career management cycle. For example, the engineer may discover that she has performed poorly on the newly acquired managerial portions of her job. This appraisal might lead the engineer to consider changing her goals; she may no longer wish to enter management. Or she may retain the goals but revise the strategies (see the arrow from B to D). For example, she might choose to pursue a graduate degree in management.

In sum, the career management cycle is a problem-solving, decision-making process. Information is gathered so individuals can become more aware of themselves and the world around them. Goals are established, plans or strategies are developed and implemented, and feedback is obtained to provide more information for ongoing career management.

Individuals who follow this approach to career management do not live in a vacuum. As indicated by the border around Exhibit 3.1, the usefulness of exploration, goal setting, strategies, and feedback often depends on the support received from various people and organizations. For example, internship and counseling programs provided by colleges; performance appraisals, self-assessment workshops, and mentoring and training programs offered by work organizations; and advice, love, and support from families can all contribute to effective career management.

The successful application of this career management model depends both on the individual and the organization. It involves an exchange of information among employees, current and potential employers, coworkers, friends, and families. Individuals must be willing to take on the task of being proactive and responsible for their careers. It takes effort to gather the information needed to make appropriate career decisions. Studies have shown that individuals who receive social support from family and friends feel more secure and are better able to progress in their career development.[2]

Organizations must also be willing and able to share information with employees, to make the necessary resources available, and to support employees in their attempts to manage their careers. Subsequent chapters will consider what individuals and organizations can do to stimulate career growth and effective career management.

THEORY AND RESEARCH ON THE CAREER MANAGEMENT PROCESS

In this section, we examine the theory and research that form the conceptual base for the model of career management. We will discuss, in turn, career exploration through career appraisal, defining key terms, offering a rationale for each component of the model, and summarizing relevant research.

This model is based on the assumption that people will be more fulfilled and more productive when their work and life experiences are compatible with their own desires and aspirations. People are more satisfied with their career choices and jobs when their work experiences are consistent with their values, interests, personality, abilities, and lifestyle preferences.[3] Performance in a career is enhanced when the job requires the application of skills and abilities that the individual possesses.[4] For these reasons, the career management model attempts to optimize the compatibility or "fit" between individuals and their work environments.

Career Exploration

Career exploration is the collection and analysis of information regarding oneself and the environment that foster the career management process.[5]

Most people need to gather information so they can become more keenly aware of their own values, interests, and abilities, as well as the opportunities and obstacles in their environment. It is assumed that the more extensive and more appropriate the career exploration, the more likely people will become aware of different facets of both themselves and the world of work.

Why does career exploration promote awareness? First, people may not know themselves nearly as well as they think they do. For example, they may not have a clear understanding of what they really want from a job or from life. Perhaps they haven't given it much thought, or possibly past decisions were guided more by what others wanted for them than what they wanted. People often need to collect the necessary data to increase awareness in these areas.

Moreover, people's insights into their talents may be incomplete. They may never have thought, for example, that success as the advertising manager of the high school yearbook was a reflection of their persuasive and interpersonal skills, or that accomplishments on a special task force at work reveal substantial leadership qualities. Oftentimes, individuals hold rigid ideas about appropriate work roles based on their gender; therefore, they may allow biases, rather than factual data, to determine what they think their abilities are.

In addition, individuals may on occasion overestimate strengths in certain areas and judge themselves to be more talented than they really are. Conversely, some people may persistently underestimate their competence. For these reasons, career exploration can provide an individual with a more complete and accurate picture of himself or herself. The ability to be self-aware, that is, one's ability to reflect on and accurately assess one's demonstrated behaviors and skills in the workplace, has been linked to effective job performance.[6]

In a similar vein, knowledge of different occupations, organizations, and career opportunities can also benefit from an active exploration of the environment. It is known, for example, that people can develop expectations about jobs and organizations that are not realistic. Again, a thorough exploration of the world can help clarify alternatives and options, and aid adaptability.

Types of Career Exploration

It is helpful to think of career exploration in terms of the type of information that is sought. For example, self-exploration can provide a greater awareness of personal qualities (see Table 3.1). People may come to possess a deeper understanding of the activities they like and dislike (interests) and their unique individual persona (personality). They may examine how much challenge (or security, money, or travel) they want from a job (work values). As noted earlier,

TABLE 3.1   Types of Career Exploration

Self-Exploration	*Environmental Exploration*
• Interests	• Types of occupations
• Talents	• Types of industries
Strengths	• Necessary job skills
Weaknesses	• Job alternatives
• Work values	• Company alternatives
Job challenge	• Impact of family on career decisions
Job autonomy	
Security	
Work–life balance	
Money	
Working conditions	
Helping others	
Power or influence	

self-exploration can also provide substantial information about strengths, weaknesses, talents, and limitations. Finally, self-exploration can provide a better understanding of the balance of work, family, and leisure activities that best suit a preferred lifestyle.

Environmental exploration, as the name implies, helps one learn more about some aspect of the environment. For a student (or someone considering a career change), environmental exploration is likely to be occupationally focused. What does a systems analyst really do? What skills are required for a career in electrical engineering? What is the difference between a career in private or in public accounting?

For employed people, environmental exploration might be oriented more toward alternative jobs within a particular organization or industry. In this context, exploration can provide information on one's current job or alternative future jobs. For what jobs would I qualify in two to three years? What experiences are needed to move from my current line position to a particular staff assignment? Is my current career path likely to come to a dead end within a few years?

Environmental exploration can also help a person learn more about alternative organizations or about one particular organization in more depth. For someone in the job market, whether by choice or necessity, such exploration may provide information about the relative merit of working in one industry versus another or about the likelihood of career advancement in one company versus another. Environmental exploration can also provide employees with information about their current organization. Who in the organization is willing and able to be my sponsor? Who really gets rewarded in the organization? What training and development opportunities are available to me?

Another important aspect of the environment for many employees is their family. For example, knowing your spouse's willingness to relocate might help you to make a decision to pursue career opportunities 2,000 miles away. Therefore, environmental exploration can also provide useful information about a family's needs and aspirations, a spouse's career values, and about the relationship between one's work life and family life.

The Impact of Career Exploration on Career Management

Research suggests that career exploration has a beneficial effect on career management. The most immediate consequence of career exploration is an enhanced awareness of self and environment. A number of studies demonstrate that as individuals engage in more career exploration, they become more aware of themselves and their chosen career.[7] In a similar vein, certain forms of career exploration can increase the amount of information people acquire during the job-search process.[8]

Research also indicates that career exploration can help people develop career goals, although it is likely that the focus and the quality of the exploration, rather than its mere quantity, facilitate goal setting.[9] Moreover, individuals' occupational decisions tend to be more appropriate or satisfying when their decisions are preceded by extensive career exploration.[10]

Research has also demonstrated the usefulness of career exploration for people pursuing job prospects.[11] Students who engage in extensive exploration generate more job interviews and offers, obtain higher salary offers, and develop more realistic job expectations. Career exploration can also help people develop more extensive career strategies and perform more effectively in job interview situations.

In short, career exploration can help people become more aware of themselves and the world of work. They are "ready" (or vocationally mature enough) to handle the formidable task of formulating career goals and decisions, and are able to develop strategies necessary to accomplish significant goals. This does not mean that career exploration is either easy or guaranteed to provide profound and useful information. It does suggest, however, that career management can be more effectively conducted if it is based on a solid foundation of accurate information.

The purpose of this section was to examine the meaning and relevance of career exploration. Specific career exploration techniques will be presented in Chapter 4.

Awareness

Awareness is a relatively complete and accurate perception of one's own qualities and the characteristics of one's relevant environment.

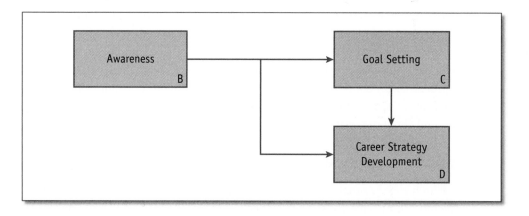

In our model of career management, a thorough awareness of self and environment enables a person to set appropriate career goals and to develop appropriate career strategies. As such, awareness is a central concept in career development.

Indeed, it would be difficult to set realistic goals in the absence of an accurate view of self and work. How can one set a realistic goal to become an actuary, for example, without a clear picture of the duties, requirements, and rewards of actuarial positions as well as an accurate assessment of one's talents and interests in those relevant areas? To extend this illustration farther, how can a person reasonably decide whether to remain an actuary or move into a general management track without clearly understanding his or her motives and abilities that might help or hinder a career in management?

This does not mean that people are always aware of themselves and their options when they set a goal or make a decision. In fact, we can all think of many career decisions that were based on stereotyped, biased, or distorted information. The point is that goals are likely to be more appropriate and more realistic when they are based on an accurate picture of self and environment.

Support for this notion comes from several sources. Researchers have found that students who reported extensive awareness of their values and their chosen field tended to establish more satisfying occupational goals than those who were relatively unaware of self and career field.[12] Information and awareness are likely to enhance the presence and clarity of career plans. Furthermore, information acquired about oneself or one's environment can help one develop realistic job expectations and attain higher levels of job satisfaction. Thus, research evidence suggests that awareness can have a positive effect on career management.[13]

Career Goal

A career goal is a desired career-related outcome that a person intends to attain.

One of the most consistent research findings in the organizational behavior literature is that employees who are committed to specific, challenging task goals outperform those who do not have goals or have a weak commitment to established goals.[14] The advantage of establishing a career goal is that a person can direct his or her efforts in a relatively focused manner. Research has found that once goals are in place, complementary behaviors and attitudes that reinforce these goals occur.[15] For example, a sales representative who sets an operational goal to become the regional marketing manager can begin to plan a strategy around attainment of the goal. Without an explicit goal, a plan of action is difficult to develop.

In our view, a career goal need not imply a promotion or an increase in salary. Certainly, an appropriate career goal may be a lateral move within the same or a different organization. In fact, a career goal does not have to involve a job change at all. A staff engineer's goal may be to remain in the same position while increasing technical skills and job responsibilities.

Up to a point, the more specific the operational career goal, the greater the likelihood of developing an effective strategy to achieve the goal. For instance, a financial analyst whose operational goal is to become a department manager within three years can ask what training or educational experiences, job assignments, and visibility will help to attain that position. Although many writers on career management discuss the virtues of goal setting, there is little research in the area of career goals. There is some evidence that a specific career goal can lead to greater optimism about one's career and that a higher degree of commitment toward one's goal can allow for the development of an extensive career strategy.[16] Indeed, clear career goals and plans have been associated with increasing levels of career effectiveness, career resilience, job involvement, and successful job search.[17] Edwin Locke and his associates have conducted extensive investigations as to why certain individuals perform better than others. These researchers have found that individuals are motivated to perform better when they set challenging but achievable goals.[18] In Chapter 5, we will examine in more detail the characteristics of different types of career goals and specific techniques for developing realistic and effective goals.

Career Strategy

A career strategy is a sequence of activities designed to help an individual attain a career goal.[19]

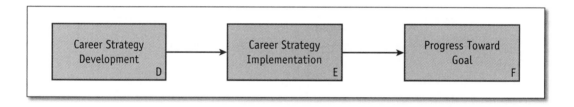

Organizations develop explicit strategic plans that enable them to pursue their goals successfully, and the same principle of strategic planning is applicable to individual career management. Much of the research on career strategies can be traced to Melville Dalton's seminal observation that managers' advancement within a manufacturing plant seemed less influenced by their formal education or years of service than by such "strategic" behaviors as joining a prestigious social or political organization.[20] Eugene Jennings's classic analysis revealed that highly mobile managers developed rather conscious strategies to move into the "executive suite," and successful managers took an active part in managing their careers and did not rely on the "loyalty ethic" of dutiful hard work, uncritical subordination to superiors, and undying respect for the corporate community.[21] While this loyalty-based approach may have worked in the past, today's companies require employees with the right experiences and career competencies, not merely longevity in the company.

Research has sought to identify the kinds of strategies employees use (or think they should use) to improve their chances of career success. An examination of these studies suggests that there are several general types of career strategies. These strategies include competence in one's present job, putting in extended hours, developing new skills, developing new opportunities, attaining a mentor, building one's image and reputation, and engaging in organizational politics.[22]

A more detailed discussion of these specific strategies along with guidelines for development of career strategies are provided in Chapter 5.

Career Appraisal

Career appraisal is the process by which people evaluate and reconsider career choices and then use this feedback to facilitate further planning.[23] The career appraisal process is portrayed in Exhibit 3.2. In work, as in all of life, people need to know how well or poorly they are doing.

EXHIBIT 3.2   Career Appraisal Process

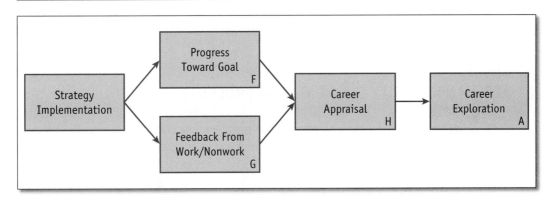

Constructive feedback enables people to determine whether their goals and strategies still make sense. Career appraisal, which enables a person to monitor the course of a career, represents the adaptive, feedback function of career management.

Feedback can come from a number of different sources. The very act of implementing a career strategy can provide feedback regarding work and nonwork lives. For example, spending weekends in the office (extended work involvement) can provoke praise from a boss and hostility from a family. Participating in a training session or developing a close mentor relationship can teach people valuable lessons about themselves as well as about jobs and organizations. In addition, feedback about progress toward specific goals can be obtained from a superior in a coaching or performance appraisal session, from peers, or from other significant persons. The information derived from career appraisal closes the career management cycle by becoming another piece of exploratory information that can enhance one's awareness of self and environment.

As noted earlier, the career appraisal process may lead to a reexamination of career goals. The feedback one obtains from work or nonwork sources can reinforce or lead to modification of a goal. An enthusiastic response to a training seminar or an outstanding performance review on a new project, for example, may convince an employee that his or her goal to reach the next management level remains desirable and feasible. Disappointments in the outcome of such activities, on the other hand, could prompt a person to shift goals.

Career appraisal can also affect strategic behavior. For example, in the course of a performance feedback session, an employee and his or her superior may conclude that additional formal training is unnecessary, but that greater exposure to key managers through a new work assignment is essential. In this case, the goal remains intact, but the strategy is revised. One's ability to monitor and revise career strategies has been found to lead to greater career mobility—including more cross-company promotions and more within-company promotions.[24]

In short, career appraisal provides a feedback loop that perpetuates career exploration and the entire career management cycle. The usefulness of feedback for learning and performing tasks has been repeatedly demonstrated in the literature. Feedback's function as a self-corrective mechanism is equally applicable to the management of careers.

CAREER MANAGEMENT AS AN ONGOING PROCESS

There are a number of reasons why career management should be a regular, ongoing process. First, since work is such a central part of life, a satisfying career can promote feelings of fulfillment, whereas a string of poor career decisions can have a devastating effect on a person's sense of well-being. In addition, it is not easy to develop a deep understanding of our place in the world of work. Goals are often unrealistic, and strategies are frequently ill conceived. Without continual, conscious, active career management, past errors might very well be prolonged and repeated.

Complicating the matter further, people often continue their commitment to a prior decision—even as they face repeated failure and frustration—to prove to themselves and others that their initial decisions were correct.[25] Such people may fool themselves into believing their past failures will be reversed and their prior efforts will therefore be justified. These individuals may actually create alternative explanations, or further self-justifications, as to why their initial decisions were correct. Active career management on an ongoing basis, including feedback from many sources, is necessary as a way to avoid digging deeper holes from which one may never emerge.

Furthermore, changing environments demand ongoing career management. In developing new business strategies, organizations substitute new missions for old, wiping out old career paths in favor of new mobility channels. As was discussed in Chapter 1, technological changes, reorganizations, downsizings, and mergers and acquisitions can all affect a person's career within a particular organization. Employees who are not sensitive to the implications of such changes in the environment may find themselves unaware of their options.

People change as well. Goals that were so important during one time of life may require reexamination in later stages. Parts of jobs that were exhilarating at age 30 may be tedious or even aversive at 50. New talents and values can emerge with age, maturity, and experience. Changing family situations can provide constraints and opportunities to careers. Again, those who are insensitive to changes in themselves will be missing a chance to make career decisions that are more compatible with current values and lifestyle preferences.

For these reasons, career management should be a continual, problem-solving process. This is not to say that people must constantly be conducting self-assessment activities or revising their goals or strategies every week or every month. It does indicate that people should generally be attuned to changes in themselves and the environment. As will be seen in subsequent chapters, there are periods when active career management is particularly critical. The choice of a college major and an initial career field, the job-search process, the decision to remain specialized or to broaden one's experiences, the reaction to job loss, and the decision to reevaluate involvements in work and family roles all require accurate information, realistic goals and plans, and an openness to feedback from the environment.

INDICATORS OF EFFECTIVE CAREER MANAGEMENT

How can people tell whether they are managing their careers effectively? Since career management is a problem-solving, decision-making process, it is tempting to examine the outcomes of career decisions at a particular point in time to assess the effectiveness of career management practices. One could, for example, look at advancement in title or responsibility, or level of job performance to gauge the effectiveness of career management.

These temptations should be avoided because, at least in the short run, career advancement and job performance are merely outcomes (although important ones) that do not necessarily reflect the process by which the outcomes were reached. They do not address the dynamics of career decision making.

Since career management is an ongoing, adaptive process, a snapshot view of a person's performance, status, or mobility does not necessarily reveal the manner in which the career has been managed. Following are four indicators of effective career management that can serve as a review of the career management model itself.

1. Effective career management requires a *deep knowledge of oneself and an accurate picture of the environment.* Some people have little insight into themselves and alternatives in the work environment. Without such knowledge, one may be fortunate enough to fall into a job that meets one's needs and permits the use of valued abilities. Over the long run, however, one cannot count on luck alone. A career is composed of many decisions during the course of a person's life. Accurate knowledge about self and environment enables a person to take an active role in making appropriate career decisions.

2. Effective career management requires the *development of realistic conceptual and operational goals* that are compatible with one's values, interests, abilities, and desired lifestyle. While gaining accurate knowledge about self and the environment is a necessary process, it is not enough for effective career management. This knowledge has to be translated into a decision to pursue particular goals. That is, one's goals, if accomplished, should have a reasonable chance of meeting one's personal needs. There is a tendency for some people, especially college students making initial career plans, to choose career goals that others (parents, spouses, professors, supervisors) think are appropriate, regardless of whether the goals meet their own needs. It is the compatibility or fit of goals and accomplishments with personal needs and values that characterizes effective career management.

3. Effective career management requires the *development and implementation of appropriate career strategies.* It is one thing to develop valid career goals; it is another to attempt to accomplish these goals according to a plan. Again, some people may, on occasion, achieve goals without any conscious strategic plan, but such good fortune is not likely to recur regularly. Since careers require many diverse types of decisions to be made over the long haul, skills in the development and implementation of career strategies are essential for effective career management.

4. Perhaps most important, effective career management requires a *continual feedback process* that permits adaptation in the face of changing circumstances. No one possesses totally accurate information about oneself or the environment, especially when people and the world are in a state of change. Moreover, goals and strategies may need fine-tuning or even a major overhaul. At different points, we all feel stuck in our careers, or feel as if we have hit a career plateau or roadblock. A situation like this may help us to realize that our career plans are inappropriate in light of the dynamically changing work environment. It is not incomplete awareness or even inappropriate goals or strategies per se that signal

ineffective career management. The real problem is a person's inability to recognize these difficulties and do something constructive about them. Effective career management, therefore, is a striving process in which imperfect information and decisions are replaced by better (yet still imperfect) information and decisions.

For these reasons, it is not easy to assess the effectiveness of a person's career management practices. Certainly, the external trappings of "success" tell us little about the accuracy of a person's information or the appropriateness of his or her goals and strategies. Nor does a person's apparent satisfaction with his or her work tell the whole story since people can become "satisfied" by meeting other people's needs. Rather, effective career management represents a process of using information and insight to attain outcomes capable of satisfying personally meaningful values and aspirations.

At this juncture, the reader may wonder whether we are advocating a purely "rational" approach to career management. In a very real sense, our career management model is based on rational thinking and actions. We recommend that individuals explore themselves and their environment in a systematic manner, select career goals and strategies in a conscious way, and pay close attention to changes in themselves and the world around them. A rational approach to career decision making can be useful, and a proactive, self-confident orientation to career management can reap benefits for the individual.

Nevertheless, to say that career management should be rational and systematic does not mean that it is mechanical, unemotional, or clear-cut. Career management is, by its very nature, a "messy" endeavor. Information is never complete, awareness is difficult and can come in fits and spurts, and goals and strategies may have to be revised many times before they make sense. Most significantly, unanticipated events in our personal and professional lives can cause major career disruptions and obviate even the best laid plans. Accordingly, individuals should not become robots when managing their careers, and "gut" feelings should, at times, take precedence over techniques and procedures.

Please keep these thoughts in mind when you examine the specific guidelines for applying the career management model in Chapters 4 and 5, and when you work on the learning exercises throughout the book. View the guidelines as just that—guidelines—rather than as unbending rules. Look for incremental advances in awareness, not instant insight. Accept the fact that you will make mistakes and will occasionally have to take two steps backward before progress is experienced. And most important, remember that career management is, at its core, a learning experience. Learning is occasionally rapid but is more often sporadic. It is often exciting but is frequently frustrating, and it is usually hard work. So relax, be patient with yourself, ask for support from those around you, and enjoy the process.

SUMMARY

This chapter presented a model of career management and developed a rationale for each component in the model. Career exploration, the driving force of the model, involves the collection and analysis of career-related information. This information can increase awareness of personal qualities (interests, values, personality, talents, and lifestyle preferences) as well as the environment (the world of occupations, jobs, organizations, and family).

Awareness of self and environment enables people to set realistic career goals. The development of conceptual and operational career goals can help individuals choose and implement appropriate career strategies designed to help them attain these goals. However, no particular strategy is likely to be effective in every situation. Hence the need for ongoing career appraisal in which career-related feedback is acquired and used. Such feedback can help people reexamine the effectiveness of their strategies and the appropriateness of their goals.

Because people and environments can change over time, career management should be an ongoing process. Four indicators of effective career management were identified: knowledge of self and the environment; the development of career goals that are consistent with values, interest, talents, and desired lifestyle; the development and implementation of appropriate career strategies; and a continual feedback loop that permits adaptation in the face of changing circumstances.

ASSIGNMENT

Interview a friend (perhaps a classmate or a coworker) about his or her career management activities. Has your friend engaged in career exploration? What is his or her level of awareness of self and environment? Has your friend set a career goal? Developed a career strategy? Why or why not? What should he or she be doing next?

DISCUSSION QUESTIONS

1. Why is career exploration such a critical component of career management? How, if at all, can people develop insights into themselves and their environment in the absence of deliberate attempts to seek information? What career exploration activities have you undertaken in the past year? In the past three years? How successful have they been?

2. Should career management be primarily a rational, systematic process? What are the advantages and disadvantages of adopting a highly rational approach to career management?

3. Why is it important to monitor and appraise your career? Why should career appraisal be conducted periodically? How frequently should you conduct a career appraisal? How do individuals and environments change in ways that can influence a person's career? What role does family play in career appraisal?

CHAPTER 3 CASE

Michele Terry the Aspiring Banking Executive

Michele Terry is a 45-year-old manager of marketing services at Federal Bank (fictitious name), a medium-sized financial institution. The fact that some of the staff she once hired have been promoted above her in recent years is a daily reminder that Michele's longtime ambition to become an executive vice president at Federal Bank is not likely to be fulfilled. Her recent performance appraisal meetings with her 40-year-old superior, an assistant vice president, left no doubt in Michele's mind about Federal's plans: She will most likely retire at her current level.

In fact, the handwriting had been on the wall for more than five years. During this time, Michele re-examined her original goal. How important was it for her to become an executive vice president with the bank? Her conclusion was that it was still a personally important goal. As a result, Michele had at least 15 interviews during the past five years with other banks. In each case, she got a polite but negative response. All of the institutions were hiring MBAs, and Michele had only a bachelor's degree. More important, Michele was competent enough but did not have sufficiently varied experiences in the financial services industry and did not seem to project the image of an officer, let alone an executive vice president. In a state of dismay, she also spoke with officers of other institutions in the financial services industry. The reactions to these inquiries were all similarly negative.

Last year, several conversations with Federal's officers and her husband convinced Michele to give up her dream of becoming an executive vice president at the bank. It was simply out of the question. Although there was a chance of further advancement, Michele concluded that it was slim. In the meantime, Michele reexamined why she always wanted to become a senior officer at the bank. In addition to money and status, she wanted the opportunity to affect broad policies to make inroads in the services that banks could provide to the community. Therefore, she concentrated on broadening the scope of her current position by looking for ways to influence the bank's approach to community reinvestment. Michele enrolled in several training seminars on community reinvestment and convinced her boss that she should chair a task force on new market development. She also began to serve as a mentor to several of Federal's younger managers, helping them get their careers established and perhaps avoid some of the mistakes she may have made earlier in her career.

On the home front, Michele seems more relaxed than she has been in quite some time, and she is better able to enjoy her family. She has encouraged her husband to switch to a more personally satisfying career field, has freely given him advice and support, and seems to enjoy the success her husband is beginning to experience in his rejuvenated career. Michele is also spending more time with her children and her infant grandchild and has rekindled her interest in the local political scene.

(Continued)

(Continued)

Michele's most recent performance appraisal was outstanding. Although she doesn't put in nearly so many weekends and evenings as she had in the past, her job performance has not suffered. On the contrary, her marketing group is working on several innovative projects, the task force she heads is making real progress, and she is deriving great pleasure from her relationships with several of the bank's younger managers. Although Michele is periodically frustrated over her lack of advancement, she is a respected contributor at the bank and, little by little, is coming to terms with her disappointment.

Case Questions

1. Identify the specific career exploration activities that Michele undertook to gather information about herself (her values, needs, abilities, interests, and desired lifestyle) and her environment (different jobs, employers, industries, their families)? What could she have done to acquire more information?

2. Does Michele currently have conceptual and operational career goals? If so, what are they? If not, explain why you believe that Michele does not currently have career goals.

3. What specific career strategies did Michele implement? Were they effective? Why or why not?

4. To what extent has Michele received useful feedback regarding her career? Should Federal Bank have been more proactive in helping Michele manage her career? What could the Bank have done to help her?

5. If you were advising Michele, what recommendations would you give her to help her effectively manage her career going forward?

Applications of the Career Management Model

A Guide to Career Exploration

Chapter 3 presented a model of career management and provided a theoretical rationale for each component of the model. This chapter will take a pragmatic look at career exploration, the driving force of the model. In particular, we will identify the underlying principles of career exploration, discuss exploration activities used in organizations, provide the reader with opportunities to participate in career exploration activities, and offer guidelines for successful career exploration. Chapter 5 will examine the remaining components of the career management model—goal setting, strategy development, and career appraisal.

TYPES OF CAREER EXPLORATION

Career exploration refers to the collection and analysis of information on career-related issues.[1] As noted in Chapter 3, it can provide information about one's own qualities (self-exploration) as well as information about the environment: occupations, jobs, organizations, and families. The purpose of career exploration is to help the individual develop a greater awareness of self and the environment so that realistic goals can be established and appropriate strategies developed. Exploration activities have become more critical in recent years as increased uncertainty and reduced job security mandate that individuals be adaptable and flexible in their approaches to career management. Knowing yourself and understanding the work environment can help you set reasonable and meaningful goals and can prepare you for career changes, regardless of whether these alterations are planned or not. Indeed, the ability to be prepared for career change and disruptions is the essence of managing the "boundaryless" career, as we discussed in Chapter 2.

Self-Exploration

When one engages in self-exploration, information is sought about a variety of personal qualities and attitudes that are relevant to career decision making. These qualities can include values, interests, personality factors, talents or abilities, lifestyle preferences, and any weaknesses or shortcomings. To develop an accurate career identity and set meaningful career goals, it is essential to understand what one wants from work and nonwork roles and what skills and abilities can be brought to (or developed in) the work environment. The intended outcome of the self-exploration process is self-awareness, or the attainment of a relatively complete picture of one's individual qualities.[2] Given the importance of self-exploration and self-awareness to the career management process, we will examine values, interests, personality, abilities, and lifestyle preferences in more detail.

Values are the beliefs about the qualities of human life or the types of behavior that an individual wants to attain.[3] They highlight individual differences in preferences for the rewards, payoffs, or other aspects of a job or a career.[4] People tend to set values in priority order and use them as a way to explain, coordinate, and justify behaviors.[5] It has been proposed that there are six primary life values: theoretical, economic, aesthetic, religious, social, and political.[6] While some people might place a high value on helping others (social) or gaining power (political), others are more concerned with creating beauty in the world (aesthetics) or discovering knowledge (theoretical). Each person probably has a unique combination of values that are personally significant. Understanding one's value structure can provide considerable insight into career aspirations. To take an extreme example, a person with strong material and political values is unlikely to be happy in an occupation that pays poorly and provides little opportunity to exercise leadership qualities.

As shown in Table 4.1, Shalom Schwartz identified 10 value types that are relevant to the work domain.[7] People may differ substantially in the importance they place on different values such as power, tradition, and security. Moreover, occupations and specific jobs vary in the extent to which they satisfy these values. It is not surprising that people tend to be more satisfied with jobs in which they have an opportunity to attain their significant work values.

TABLE 4.1   Illustrations of Work Values, Interests, and Abilities

Work Values[a]	Interests[b]	Abilities[c]
Power	Realistic	Cognitive
Achievement	Nature & agriculture	General intelligence
Hedonism	Computer hardware & electronics	Verbal reasoning skills
Stimulation	Athletics	Logical reasoning skills

Work Values[a]	Interests[b]	Abilities[c]
Self-direction	Protective services	Memory
Universalism	Mechanics & construction	Writing skills
Benevolence	Investigative	Reading skills
Tradition	Science	Psychomotor
Conformity	Mathematics	Precision of movement
Security	Medical science	Manual dexterity
	Research	Finger dexterity
	Athletics	Reaction time and speed
	Artistic	Athleticism and coordination
	Visual arts & design	Sensory
	Counseling & helping	Visual
	Performing arts	Auditory
	Culinary arts	Perceptual
	Writing & mass communications	Stimuli response
	Social	Physical
	Teaching & education	Muscular strength
	Social sciences	Cardiovascular endurance
	Health care services	Movement quality
	Religion & spirituality	
	Human resources & training	
	Enterprising	
	Politics & public speaking	
	Entrepreneurship	
	Marketing & advertising	
	Sales	
	Management	
	Conventional	
	Office management	
	Law	
	Taxes & accounting	
	Finance & investing	
	Programming & information systems	

NOTES: a. Items from: Schwartz, S. E. (1999). A theory of cultural values and some implications for work. *Applied Psychology: An International Review, 48,* 23–47.

b. The 30 Basic Interest Scales included in the Strong Interest Inventory arranged by the six Holland Interest Types. Taken from Donnay, D. A., Thompson, R. C., Morris, M. L., & Schaubhut, N. A. (2004). *Technical brief for the newly revised Strong Interest Inventory assessment.* Palo Alto, CA: Consulting Psychologists Press.

c. Adapted from Rotundo, M. (2006). Abilities. In J. H. Greenhaus & G. A. Callanan (Eds.), *Encyclopedia of career development* (pp. 1–5). Thousand Oaks, CA: Sage.

Career planning programs encourage individuals to examine their values carefully. People can learn about their values by analyzing their life history, identifying the kinds of career decisions they have made, and examining the reasons behind these decisions. Often, such informal analyses are supplemented by more structured value inventories.[8]

Interests refer to likes and dislikes attached to specific activities or objects.[9] Interests, therefore, are expressions of what a person likes to do, and are derived from such factors as values, family life, social class, culture, and the physical environment.[10] While they are reflective of values, interests are attached to particular tasks or activities. For example, two people might each value the expression of creativity in their work. While one person might have strong scientific interests and the other might be interested in literary activities, both sets of interests can serve the broader creative value for each person. Understandably, people who choose career fields that are compatible with their interests tend to be more satisfied than those whose chosen career is incompatible with their interests, and congruence between interests and career choice is related to subsequent satisfaction and tenure in the job.[11]

John Holland identified six general interest orientations that reflect one's personality, values, and preferred lifestyle.[12] Holland's theory assumes that vocational interests are an important expression of personality and that the six orientations correspond with specific personality factors.[13] The six orientations, which are collectively referred to as the RIASEC hexagon and are similar to the primary life values described earlier, include: *r*ealistic, *i*nvestigative, *a*rtistic, *s*ocial, *e*nterprising, and *c*onventional. Individuals who have a realistic orientation tend to be more practical and task oriented, while investigative types are more scientific, scholarly, and research oriented. Artistic people prefer unstructured situations, where creativity and self-expression are possible. Individuals in the social category are more humanistic, personal, and value oriented, and show skill in interpersonal relations. An enterprising designation indicates a preference for entrepreneurial, managerial, and goal-centered activities. Finally, the conventional style reflects an orientation toward structure, tradition, and detail.

In the 1920s, Edward Strong of Stanford University developed an inventory of interests that reflect specific occupational preferences. Strong believed that interests supply something that is not disclosed by ability or achievement.[14] They point to what individuals want to do and what they consider satisfying. Today's version of the Strong Interest Inventory (SII) includes descriptions of a person's interests in 30 basic areas.[15] The 30 basic interests can be grouped according to Holland's six occupational orientations described above.[16] Table 4.1 lists the interests according to occupational orientation. The SII provides information on the similarity of one's interests to those of members of more than 244 different occupational types. Use of the SII and other assessment instruments as tools for individual self-exploration will be discussed later in this chapter.

One's basic *personality* is another area of self-exploration that can influence career choices. Personality refers to relatively stable psychological characteristics that embody such elements as thoughts, emotions, interests, habits, and behaviors.[17] Significant prior research has shown that there are five basic personality factors.[18] The five factors are typically classified as extraversion, agreeableness, conscientiousness, emotional stability, and openness to experience.

1. *Extraversion* indicates the degree to which a person seeks interpersonal stimulation. Individuals with a high degree of extraversion are drawn to seek social situations where they can interact with others. Individuals scoring low on this dimension are described as more introverted, quiet, and reserved.

2. *Agreeableness* signifies individual characteristics such as likeability, kindness, courteousness, and nurturance. Individuals scoring high on this dimension are described as amicable, cooperative, sensitive, caring, and interested in helping others. Individuals scoring low on this dimension can be described as more self-centered and inwardly focused.

3. *Conscientiousness* refers to the cluster of individual traits relating to achievement, dependability, and persistence. Individuals scoring high on this personality trait tend to be organized, follow rules and norms, and are persistent in goal-directed behavior. Individuals scoring low on Conscientiousness are comparatively irresponsible, undependable, and less organized.

4. *Emotional stability* refers to an individual's tendency to remain calm and centered. Emotionally stable individuals are typically relaxed, self-assured, and calm.

5. *Openness to experience* describes individual differences in tolerance for and an attraction to the unfamiliar. Individuals who score high on this dimension are described as being imaginative, creative, and insightful. They prefer complexity and change over familiar and stable situations. In contrast, individuals who score lower on this factor are described as more conventional, down to earth, and less imaginative.

In general, these "Big Five" dimensions serve as the basis for personality questionnaires that are used by individuals for gathering self-information and by organizations for personnel selection, employee development, and individual assessment. We will discuss some of the well-known personality tests later in the chapter.

A person's *abilities* are another significant component to be taken into account in career management. Abilities (or talents) refer to the aptitudes, capacities, or proficiencies (Table 4.1) that allow an individual (sometimes with proper training and development) to perform a wide range of tasks.[19] Accordingly, they can set constraints on our potential accomplishments, and it is clearly necessary to consider our abilities and talents when making career decisions. Unfortunately, many people choose occupations or jobs that either require abilities they do not possess or do not take advantage of the talents they do have. Therefore, many career planning programs provide the opportunity for participants to assess their own strengths and weaknesses. Abilities and talents can be appreciated by reviewing accomplishments in school, work, and other parts of our lives.

Values, interests, personality, and abilities are interrelated in several respects.[20] First, as indicated above, interests are rooted in deeper values. But it is also true that interests are related to abilities.[21] People come to enjoy activities at which they excel. Through practice, they may also become more proficient at those activities they enjoy. Therefore, although it may be convenient to separate values, interests, personality, and abilities, at some point they must be appreciated as a coherent whole. Edgar Schein's concept of a *career anchor* probably comes closest to capturing this notion.[22] Schein introduced the concept of the career anchor to recognize different forms of orientation toward work. A career anchor is a cluster of self-perceived talents, motives, and values that forms the nucleus of a person's occupational self-concept. An anchor also can provide the basis for career choices, since a person is likely to make job and organizational selections that are consistent with his or her own self-image. It is only through a number of years of work experience and many reality tests that a person can fully clarify and understand his or her career anchor. Using his long-term research on Sloan School of Management (Massachusetts Institute of Technology) alumni, Schein identified the following eight career anchors:

Technical/Functional Competence anchor, in which the primary concern is the actual content of the work. Employees who hold this anchor typically want to remain within their technical/functional area (e.g., finance, human resources, marketing).

General Managerial Competence anchor, in which the major goal is general line management rather than a particular functional area within the organization. For individuals who possess this anchor, the dominant concerns are the integration of the efforts of others, accountability for total results, and the tying together of different functions in the organization.

Autonomy/Independence anchor, in which the primary concern is with freeing oneself from organizational rules and restrictions in favor of a career in which one can decide when to work, on what to work, and how hard to work. People with this anchor would be willing to turn down a promotion in order to retain autonomy.

Security/Stability anchor, in which long-term career stability is the underlying drive. The need for security may be satisfied by remaining in the same organization, the same industry, or the same geographical location. People with this anchor generally prefer stable and predictable work.

Entrepreneurial Creativity anchor, in which the major goal is to create something new, involving such demands as overcoming obstacles, running risks, and the achievement of personal prominence. People with this anchor want the freedom to build and operate their own organization in their own way.

Service/Dedication anchor, in which the primary concern is to achieve some valued outcome, such as improving the lives of others, perhaps by working in a "helping" occupation.

Pure Challenge anchor, in which the primary work demands involve solving seemingly unsolvable problems or surmounting difficult obstacles. Individuals with this anchor primarily seek novelty, variety, and challenge in their work.

Lifestyle Integration anchor, in which the dominant theme is achieving balance in all the major sectors of one's life. Specifically, individuals with this anchor would want harmonious integration of family and career activities.

Consideration of Needs Outside of Work

As important as work is for many people, it is only one of many significant roles in life. What type of family life do you want? In what way can you express your spiritual needs? How can community or leisure activities satisfy your basic values? How important is climbing the corporate ladder and making a large sum of money in your total life? In short, what type of lifestyle is most desirable?

A thorough analysis of nonwork involvements is critical for a number of reasons. First, it is likely that some basic values may be difficult or impossible to satisfy through work. Second, some career fields or jobs can take so much time or emotion that little is left for private lives. To make appropriate career decisions, the importance and variety of nonwork interests and values need to be examined. For example, a parent strongly devoted to coaching his or her child's soccer team would find a job requiring extensive travel frustrating. Third, the importance of nonwork and leisure activities can fluctuate over the course of a person's life. People must be sensitive to such changes to make career decisions that are consistent with as many parts of their lives as possible.

The relationship between work and nonwork lives is treated in detail in Chapter 10. For now, it is important to recognize that an accurate picture of work and nonwork aspirations should produce an awareness of a *desired lifestyle* that the individual wishes to attain; that is, a satisfying pattern of work and nonwork involvements. An understanding of a desired lifestyle requires answers to the following questions:

What are my significant life values?

What kinds of activities do I like/dislike?

What are my talents, and which ones are significant and personally meaningful?

Which of my values, interests, and talents are best met in the world of work?

Which of my values, interests, and talents are best met outside of work?

How can I achieve a balance of work and nonwork involvements to find expression for my most significant values, interests, and talents?

Beyond these questions, individuals also must take into account their leisure interests as they make career choices. Leisure interests are an important component in developmental models of career decision making and vocational choice, and occupational health psychologists have recognized the importance of leisure interests to mental and physical health and overall life satisfaction.[23] Research has identified four different leisure categories, including artistic and intellectual pursuits (e.g., gardening, cooking, crafts, writing, and dancing), competition and sports (e.g., card games, team sports, and individual sports), social (e.g., partying, shopping, and socializing with friends), and outdoors (e.g., hunting, fishing, camping, and adventure sports).[24] It is obvious that the passion for a particular leisure activity will play a substantial role in career choices. As a simplistic but clear example, someone who enjoys surfing and is devoted to it would likely be unhappy in a job far away from an ocean.

TECHNIQUES FOR EFFECTIVE SELF-EXPLORATION

There are a number of specific techniques designed to enhance self-awareness, all of which require the collection of data or information about ourselves, the organization of that data into meaningful and understandable themes, and the interpretation of these themes in light of their implications for career decision making.

Collection of Data

The first step in self-assessment is to gather data on one's values, interests, personality, abilities, lifestyle preferences, and leisure pursuits. Techniques for gathering information and the sources of data are both quite varied. Overall, the techniques and sources can be broken down into four general categories: individual assessment instruments, integrated career planning approaches, organizational programs, and informal means of assessment.

Individual Assessment Instruments

There are, literally, hundreds of assessment instruments available to assist individuals in gaining a better understanding of themselves. A few of the more prominent and most widely used for self-exploration purposes are discussed below. For a fuller discussion of each of these assessment instruments, please refer to the publisher's own documentation. Summaries of each instrument are also available in the *Encyclopedia of Career Development,* edited by Jeffrey H. Greenhaus and Gerard A. Callanan, and published by SAGE Publications in 2006. Also note that nearly all assessment instruments must be administered and interpreted by professional counselors.

Assessment of Values

The *Rokeach Value Survey* consists of two lists of values (18 in each list).[25] Individuals rank the values on each list on the basis of how important each one is as a guiding principle in their life. The first list covers "terminal" values, or those values that relate to what one wants out of life, while the second list consists of "instrumental" values that relate to ways of behaving in the world. A significant aspect of this instrument is the relative ordering of the values, in that individuals must rely on their own internal value system to guide them in the choices they make.

The *Work Values–Revised* (SWVI–r), as originally developed by Donald Super, attempts to measure the relative importance of a number of work values thought to be most important in career choice and development.[26] A total of 12 work values are assessed, and individuals are provided with a profile showing the 12 values listed in rank order of importance. The SWVI–r is available exclusively online at www.kuder.com, with keyboard administration and instantaneous scoring and reporting. The Web site also provides a linkage with the work values embodied within various occupations.[27]

Originally developed in 1931, the *Allport–Vernon–Lindzey Study of Values* (SOV) is a long-standing tool for the assessment of work values.[28] The SOV identifies six value orientations, including theoretical (discovery of truth), economic (that which is useful), aesthetic (form and harmony), social (love of people), political (power in all realms), and religious (unity of life). Respondents are asked to react to questions describing various familiar life situations. The SOV measures the relative strength of each of the six value orientations based on the answers to these questions. In reaction to difficulties and limitations with the earlier versions of the SOV, a new fourth edition was created and published in the *Journal of Vocational Behavior* in 2003.[29] The properties of the new and the earlier editions of the SOV were found to be almost identical.

Assessment of Interests

The *Strong Interest Inventory* (SII) is perhaps the best known of the tools available to isolate interests and related occupations.[30] The SII consists of 291 questions that measure various dimensions related to one's vocational interest pattern. Output from the Strong consists of three related sections—General Occupational Themes, Basic Interest Scales, and Occupational Scales. The General Occupational Themes are based on the six basic vocational interest orientations of Holland as discussed earlier in this chapter. The 30 Basic Interest Scales from the SII (see Table 4.1) measure the strength and consistency of the individual's interests in specific areas, such as investigative or artistic activities. The Occupational Scales reflect the degree of similarity between the individual's interests and those of women and men employed in 244 different occupations. Thus, the SII attempts to link an individual's fairly broad interest orientation (one of the six Occupational Themes) with the somewhat more specific interests (one or more of the Basic Interest Scales) and with specific occupational titles. Detailed information on the SII is available at www.cpp.com.

The *Self Directed Search* (SDS) and the *Vocational Preference Inventory* (VPI) are two other occupational assessment instruments, developed by John Holland, that are used extensively in individual self-exploration.[31] Both of these instruments are conceptually similar to the Strong in that they are based in part on the notion that well-adjusted and satisfied individuals within specific occupational fields possess common psychological characteristics, interests, and preferences. All three instruments—the SII, the VPI, and the SDS—attempt to measure one's pattern of interests and then link it to specific occupations that are satisfying to individuals with the same interest pattern. Also, like the SII, the VPI and the SDS utilize Holland's six major interest orientations as the link between individual characteristics and specific occupations. Detailed information on the SDS and the VPI is available at www3.parinc.com.

The *Fundamental Interpersonal Relations Orientation-Behavior* (FIRO-B) is an assessment tool that looks at how an individual's needs affect his or her behavior toward other people.[32] The FIRO-B offers insights into a person's compatibility with other people, as well as related individual characteristics. In essence, the FIRO-B assesses three interpersonal needs as follows:

1. Inclusion, or the extent of contact and prominence an individual seeks and wishes from others

2. Control, or the extent of power or dominance that a person seeks or wishes from others

3. Affection, or the amount of closeness that a person seeks and wishes from others

The FIRO-B measures the extent to which an individual wishes to express each of these needs and the extent to which an individual is comfortable in receiving another person's expressed need. Detailed information on the FIRO-B is available at www.cpp.com.

The *Kuder Career Search* was originally developed by Frederic Kuder and first published in 1939.[33] The current version of the instrument measures a respondent's interests in six different areas, including Arts/Communication, Business Operations, Outdoor/Mechanical, Sales/Management, Science/Technology, and Social/Personal Services. The Kuder system also uses a "person match" that allows individuals to be electronically matched with persons who have similar interest profiles. The test-taker can then read mini-autobiographies of the person with whom they are matched to get an idea of the requirements of the job held by that person. The variety of job titles represented in the database for the matching process allows the test-taker to investigate multiple career possibilities. Detailed information on the Kuder Assessment Tests is available at www.kuder.com.

The *Campbell Interest and Skill Survey* (CISS) was developed by David Campbell and was published in 1992. It is intended to measure self-reported interests and associated skills.[34] In a fashion similar to the Strong Interest Inventory, the CISS contains seven interest orientation scales (influencing, organizing, helping, creating, analyzing, producing, and adventuring) that roll up from 25 basic scales. The seven interest orientations are conceptually similar to the six RIASEC dimensions from John Holland. The instrument also includes 60 occupational scales that tie into the 25 basic scales. Detailed information on the CISS is available at www.pearsonassessments.com.

Assessment of Personality

The *Myers-Briggs Type Indicator* (MBTI) was developed by a mother and daughter team, Katherine Briggs and Isabel Myers. Based on the work of Carl Jung, a Swiss psychiatrist, the MBTI provides a useful measure of personality by looking at eight separate personality preferences that all people use at different times.[35] The eight types are organized into four bipolar scales. The four preferences that are identified as most like you (one from each scale) are combined into what is called a type. Included among the four personality dimensions are how a person energizes, how a person perceives information, how a person makes decisions, and a person's lifestyle preference. For the energizing scale, the two categories are extraversion and introversion. Extroverts have an affinity for drawing energy from the outside world of people, activities, or things. Introverts draw energy from their own internal world of ideas, emotions, or impressions. The two perception categories are designated as sensing and intuition. Sensing individuals prefer to gather information through the five senses by noticing what is actual. Intuitive individuals gather information through a "sixth" sense and notice what possibilities are available. The decision-making dimension includes thinking and feeling orientations. Thinking types prefer organizing and structuring information to make decisions in a logical fashion. Feeling types prefer to make decisions in a personal and value-oriented way. For the lifestyle preference, the two types are judgment and perception. The judgment type prefers living a planned and organized life, while the perception type prefers spontaneity and flexibility. The four bipolar scales result in 16 possible personality types.

Like the SII, the MBTI can be a useful mechanism for the assessment of personal characteristics and the determination of one's preferred work environment. Using the MBTI in conjunction with the SII, the individual is provided with information on personality type, interests, and possible work environments and occupations.[36] Detailed information on the MBTI is available at www.cpp.com.

The *Sixteen Personality Questionnaire* (16PF) was originally developed by Raymond Cattell in 1949.[37] Now in its fifth edition, the 16PF measures 16 personality dimensions as follows: levels of warmth, reasoning ability, emotional stability, dominance, liveliness, rule consciousness, social boldness, sensitivity, vigilance, abstractedness, privateness, apprehension, openness to change, self-reliance, perfectionism, and tension. The 16 factors can be further grouped into five global personality categories: extraversion, anxiety, toughmindedness, independence, and self-control. The full 16PF questionnaire consists of 185 items. In terms of career planning, the 16PF can be used to create a Personal Career Development Profile.[38] This profile allows individuals to gain greater insight into personality as it relates to personal and career interests. The profile consists of six sections detailing one's patterns for problem solving, coping with stressful conditions, interpersonal interactions, organizational role and work patterns, and career activity interests and lifestyle considerations. As with the MBTI, the 16PF is used extensively in organizations as a tool to help employees assess interests and preferences and ultimately manage their careers. Detailed information on the 16PF is available at www.pearsonassessments.com.

The *Minnesota Multiphasic Personality Inventory-2* (MMPI-2) is a 567-item personality measurement instrument set up in a true-or-false format.[39] The original version of the MMPI was published in 1943 and was initially used for clinical screening. It contained 10 scales for measuring personality dimensions, primarily dealing with psychoneurotic concerns. In 1989, development of the revised (or second) version of the MMPI was completed. While the new version contains the same scales, there were changes in interpretation of some scales and items were updated. The MMPI-2 is the most widely used and researched test of adult psychopathology. It is primarily used by clinicians to assist with the diagnosis of mental disorders and the selection of appropriate treatment. However, the MMPI-2 can also be used in career assessment in a number of ways, including measuring the degree of emotional adjustment and general personality functioning.[40] Detailed information on the MMPI-2 is available at www.pearsonassessments.com.

The *California Psychological Inventory* (CPI) is an assessment tool that measures personality and personal style.[41] Originally published in 1956, the CPI consists of 434 items and measures 20 dimensions of personality. A number of special-purpose scales are included with the CPI, including managerial potential, work orientation, and leadership. The CPI has been used in a number of career development applications, including career decision making and maturity.[42] Detailed information on the CPI is available at www.cpp.com.

Assessment of Abilities and Talents

The *General Aptitude Test Battery* (GATB) was developed by the U.S. Employment Service, a division of the U.S. Department of Labor, for employment service counseling and placement by various agencies of the U.S. government. The GATB is designed to measure cognitive, perceptual, and psychomotor skills.[43] It is one of the most frequently used tests and is unequaled in the size of its occupational data base. The GATB consists of 11 timed tests that measure nine abilities, including verbal ability, arithmetic reasoning, computational skill, spatial ability, form perception, clerical perception, motor coordination, manual dexterity, and finger dexterity. The basic aptitudes and capabilities measured by the GATB can be compared with occupational aptitude patterns that have been established for hundreds of different occupations.

The *Armed Services Vocational Aptitude Battery* (ASVAB) is the most widely used multiple-aptitude test used in the United States and is given to all applicants to the U.S. military.[44] The ASVAB is designed to measure nine knowledge and skill sets, including general science, arithmetic reasoning, word knowledge, paragraph comprehension, auto and shop information, mathematics knowledge, mechanical comprehension, electronics information, and assembling objects. Combinations of these skill sets can be used to measure other categories of abilities, such as general intelligence.

The *Bennett Mechanical Comprehension Test* (BMCT) is designed to assess aptitude in comprehending mechanical applications in realistic situations.[45] Originally developed in 1940, the BMCT looks at practical problem-solving ability, the application of physical laws, and various mechanical operations. The current BMCT has standard results for such activities as engineering, installation, maintenance and repair, automotive, aircraft or general mechanical positions, transportation or machine operators, skilled trades, and others. Detailed information on the BMCT is available at www.harcourt-uk.com.

In summary, value surveys, interest inventories, personality measures, ability tests, and other assessment tools can be particularly helpful for career counseling, both with young people making an initial career choice and with adults dissatisfied with their present work and/or considering a career change. Nonetheless, psychological tests and assessment instruments have limitations. Accordingly, the results of these tests should be used as discussion guides and as a reference for theme identification and future decision making. They are not intended to be, nor should they be used as, the conclusive answer to one's career direction.

INTEGRATED APPROACHES TO SELF-EXPLORATION

There are a number of sophisticated and integrated vocational assessment methods that are designed to further individual growth with regard to career planning and decision making. While most of these systems have as a central focus one or more of the primary assessment instruments discussed earlier in this chapter, the ultimate goal is to take the individual through the process of self-exploration to the point of having a higher degree of certainty over a college major or possible career paths. Integrated self-exploration programs can be offered through different venues, including a classroom, a counselor's office, a career resource center/placement office, an Internet Web site, or the Human Resources department of an organization.

Computer-based career support systems allow efficient and personalized access to self-exploration information.[46] These programs fulfill a number of career management needs, including information on various career topics, personality and skills assessment, listings of job vacancies, and career decision-making support. Most Internet-based career support systems are available for free or for the cost of a basic registration. The widespread availability of personal computers with Internet connections has made computer-based career assistance a practical and available tool for helping individuals in the career exploration and development process.

Curricular-based programs incorporate many aspects of career planning, including self-assessment, in a classroom setting. Most curricular programs are designed to span a number of weeks as the client builds a better understanding of self and the work environment over time. In addition, many schools and universities offer a career course for academic credit where students use an entire semester of study to gain a better understanding of themselves and the career management process.

Individuals should be careful not to choose a career direction prematurely, based solely on the results of an integrated career planning program. As with individual assessment instruments, these programs should be used as one of several aids for gaining a better understanding of one's personal preferences and needs. They certainly should not be used as the definitive guide to career selection.

ORGANIZATION-SPONSORED SELF-EXPLORATION PROGRAMS

For working adults, one of the most effective methods for gaining a better understanding of interests and abilities is through career management assistance programs offered at work. In an ideal sense, organization-sponsored programs should have benefits both for the individual employee and for the company.

Various researchers have noted a number of organizational career management tools that can enhance the self-knowledge of the working adult.[47] These programs include individual self-assessment through such activities as career-planning workshops, career workbooks, and organizational career assessment centers. These self-exploration programs offered by organizations will often use, as part of the total package, one or more of the commercial assessment instruments described earlier in this chapter. A brief profile of each technique is offered below:

Career-Planning Workshops. These use a structured, interactive group format where participants formulate, share, and discuss with each other personal data concerning such factors as strengths, weaknesses, values, and other personal information.[48] The ultimate goal of the workshops is for individuals to take personal responsibility for their careers by setting realistic career goals and implementation plans to achieve the goals.

Career Workbooks. These are intended to fulfill the same basic objectives as a group career workshop, but do so in an individual, self-directed fashion rather than on a participative, interactive basis. The workbooks use a series of exercises and reference materials to guide employees through the individual assessment process. Also, the workbooks are designed to be completed by the individual alone and are self-paced.

Assessment Centers. These centers were traditionally used to assess employee career potential, wherein the focus was primarily on quantifying the promotability of selected employees. In today's business world, these centers play multiple roles ranging from the assessment of personality traits and job-specific competencies to group exercises where individuals receive feedback on observed competencies and real or potential weaknesses. In this sense, the results from assessment center ratings can be used for career decision-making and employee development purposes.[49]

In addition to the above programs, working adults have other options for obtaining self-information through the organization. For example, periodic performance appraisals and supervisory feedback can offer insight into personal strengths and weaknesses, and that can add to the employee's exploration process. Many of the more prominent executive development programs use the 360 degree evaluation technique that provides feedback to the individual from a wider perspective. This fuller perspective, which includes assessments from superiors, subordinates, and peers, can give more extensive information on personal strengths and weaknesses, especially in the work role.[50]

INFORMAL SELF-EXPLORATION

A variety of informal techniques is open to individuals in their self-exploration journey. For example, one popular approach includes the following data-gathering devices:[51]

1. A Written Interview: a personal life story including educational experiences, hobbies, work experiences, significant people in one's life, changes and turning points in life, key decisions, and projections into the future

2. A 24-Hour Diary: a blow-by-blow account of two 24-hour periods, one on a weekday and the other on a weekend

3. Lifestyle Representation Collage: a narrative and pictorial portrayal of one's life

Other informal self-assessment programs have included such activities as

1. Ranking significant work values

2. Analyzing "peak" (high and low) experiences in life

3. Developing a present and future obituary notice

4. Analyzing one's current job satisfactions and dissatisfactions

5. Describing an ideal job

6. Fantasizing about one's future life

There are also several self-help books and other media that are available commercially that are designed to assist individuals in better understanding themselves.

It is also important to share informally the results of one's exploration activities with other trusted individuals as another means of gaining additional personal insight. These other individuals might include parents, spouse or significant other, other family members, close friends, coworkers, and supervisors.

Learning Exercise 1 appears in the Appendix on p. 93. It includes activities designed to help you collect self-related data. Although you may examine Exercise 1 at this stage, it is recommended that you finish reading Chapter 4 before you begin the exercise.

Theme Identification

Information is most useful when it is organized into coherent, understandable units. Therefore, it is necessary to make sense out of the data supplied by various inventories, exercises, and essays. You will need to ask what you have learned about yourself and whether there are consistencies that cut across the different data-gathering devices. You need to discover, in other words, what themes have emerged from the data.

A significant theme (such as "I want to get my own way" or "I need to work cooperatively with other people") can combine values, interests, personality, and abilities into meaningful wholes. The identification of themes is an inductive process. Much like a detective, the individual scrutinizes the specific data for clues about what it is saying, draws preliminary hypotheses about the presence of certain themes, and tests the data further to confirm or reject the hypotheses.

The following steps may be helpful in identifying themes:

1. Thoroughly examine each data-generating device for the presence of themes. Underlining key words or phrases is a helpful technique.

2. Look for data across different data-generating devices that support or refute the presence of a theme. The more consistently the theme emerges from the data, the more likely the theme is important.

3. Label the themes in as descriptive a fashion as possible.

4. Assess the accuracy and importance of the themes. How much data support the theme? In how many different devices has the theme been identified? How much, if any, contradictory evidence has been found? (The fewer the contradictions, the more accurate the theme.)

Theme identification is clearly an active process, but it is rarely simple and straightforward. This is understandable, since the results of self-exploration activities may prove insufficient, inconclusive, or contradictory. Further, self-assessment, as a process of uncovering personality and psychological attributes, could produce feelings of anxiety and doubt. Nonetheless, the results of exploration activities are important and necessary in the setting of career goals and in the management of one's career. Thus, self-exploration must be conducted, even though the process may at times be uncomfortable.

Learning Exercise 2 is included in the Appendix on p. 103. It provides an opportunity for you to identify themes that emerged from the data collected in Exercise 1. Although you may examine Exercise 2 at this time, it is recommended that you finish reading Chapter 4 before you begin the exercise.

Environmental Exploration

Self-exploration is an essential ingredient in effective career management because it provides the information that is needed to answer a number of related questions: What do I find interesting? What are my strengths and weaknesses? What rewards are important to me? What do I want from my work and nonwork lives?

But self-assessment represents only half of the equation. Careers are embedded in occupations, jobs, and organizations. It is through interaction with the work environment that values are met, talents are utilized, and interests are stimulated. Moreover, work environments differ in the extent to which they are compatible with a person's particular pattern of values, interests, and abilities. Prior research has shown that compatibility between the person (interests, abilities, preferences, etc.) and the work environment has a strong influence on such outcomes as job satisfaction, tenure, and career success.[52] In addition, research supports the "gravitational" view of employment, which states that individuals will, over the course of their labor market experiences, try to seek out jobs that are compatible with their values, interests, and abilities.[53] That is, individuals seek positions for which there is good person–work environment fit. Accordingly, self-awareness needs to be accompanied by an active exploration of one's environment.

Although there are many facets to the environment, four are particularly important in career management: *occupations, jobs, organizations,* and *families.* The aim of environmental exploration is to learn enough about these facets to make decisions about occupational fields, career paths, and different organizations. Effective environmental exploration should enable a person to identify the setting in which he or she is most likely to meet significant values and to find expression for interests, abilities, and a preferred lifestyle.

The most relevant facet of the environment will depend on the type of decision that is required in a particular situation. A student who is questioning the choice of a major or a midcareer employee who is dissatisfied with a career choice might need to focus on exploring alternative occupational fields. From a different perspective, a college senior who is about to graduate is probably going to need to know about entry-level jobs in different organizations.

Regardless of the particular decision to be made, individuals need to explore the potential of a match between a particular environment and desired work/lifestyle. To accomplish that task, environments need to be understood in light of the information derived from self-exploration. A bridge should be built between self-exploration and alternative environments. This section of the chapter considers how such a bridge can be constructed. Specific applications of these principles to the choice of an occupation, organization, and career path will be discussed in subsequent chapters.

Table 4.2 summarizes the types of information relevant to each subenvironment. First of all, occupations differ in the particular tasks that need to be performed. Physicists and social workers, for example, engage in different activities. These activities have implications for a person's values, interests, and abilities. Someone who values intellectual stimulation, creativity, and independence, has interests in scientific activities, and has conceptual skills might be drawn to a research career in theoretical physics. Someone who strongly values social welfare, enjoys working closely with other people, desires variety in work, and has strong interpersonal skills may find a career in social work more attractive. Knowledge of occupationally related tasks is basic to linking self-assessment to career decisions.

In addition to task differences, occupations frequently differ in context or environment. Economic rewards, such as income and job security, are not equally distributed across all occupations. Similarly, the physical setting of the work, the degree and type of interaction with other people, and even the dress code can vary substantially from one occupational field to another.

Because occupational fields require different tasks, provide different rewards, and permit different physical and social settings, they often have implications for different lifestyles. Two particular lifestyle considerations that should be examined are an occupation's time demands and its associated stresses and strains. Extensive time commitment to a job and/or exposure to extremely stressful work environments can produce conflicts between one's work life and other life roles. Therefore, occupations that require an extraordinary time involvement (e.g., extensive travel, seven-day work week) and are highly stressful may be incompatible with a lifestyle that attempts to achieve a balance between work and family or leisure activities.

TABLE 4.2 Illustrative Information Relevant to Environmental Exploration

Occupations	Jobs
Task activities	Task variety
Ability/training requirements	Task significance
Financial rewards	Ability/training requirements
Security	Financial rewards
Social relationships	Security
Physical setting	Social relationships
Lifestyle considerations	Physical setting
Time commitment to work	Lifestyle considerations
Work stress	Time commitment to work
	Work stress
	Amount of independence/autonomy
	Relation of jobs to other jobs
Organizations	Families
Industry outlook	Spouse's career aspirations
Financial health of organization	Spouse's emotional needs
Business strategies	Child(ren)'s emotional needs
Career path flexibility	Other family members' needs
Career management practices/policies	Family's financial needs
Size and structure	Family's desired lifestyle
Reward system	Family stage
	Self and spouse career stage

Table 4.2 also summarizes the type of information relevant to jobs and organizations. Notice first the similarity between occupational information and job information. Since a job (e.g., market research analyst) is merely a vehicle for pursuing an occupation (e.g., market

research), the similarity in information needs is understandable. However, a thorough occupational exploration does not preclude the need for additional job exploration. To illustrate, design engineers in one company do not necessarily perform the same activities with the same rewards as those in another company. Therefore, exploration focused on jobs and positions within particular organizations is essential.

In addition, notice that several additional pieces of information are relevant to job exploration. First, job autonomy can vary substantially between organizations or even between two units of the same organization. Sales representatives in two different companies may have essentially the same duties, but more autonomy in decision making may be granted in one company than in the other. This is particularly important to identify since autonomy can satisfy one's values for intellectually stimulating, independent, and creative work. Second, it is critical to examine the relationship between a particular job and other jobs in the same or different organizations. Some jobs, in effect, are "dead end" in that movement to other jobs is extremely limited. Some jobs, in other words, provide more options than others.

It should be clear by now that nearly all jobs are inextricably connected to organizations. Therefore, whether one is entering a first full-time job or is currently employed, it is important to realize that

1. The outlook of the industry or industries served by an organization can affect career possibilities.

2. The financial health of the organization can place limits on career opportunities.

3. The company's business strategy affects the type of human resources required and, therefore, the nature of career opportunities.

4. An organization's size and structure can affect mobility opportunities.

5. Organizations differ in the extent to which they support career management through such practices as training and development programs, performance-appraisal systems, job posting, and career seminars.

6. Organizations differ in the degree to which they provide flexible career paths that enable employees to move in a number of different career directions.

7. Organizations differ in the importance they place on various financial, social, and intrinsic rewards. Some companies, for example, may pay high salaries but offer few opportunities for challenging work.

In short, the culture, outlook, and financial health of an organization affect the nature of specific career opportunities. Business plans and strategies, assumptions about people, and reward systems all have significant consequences for career management. In reality, the exploration of jobs and organizations is naturally intertwined in career decision making. For example, a graduating MBA normally examines alternative jobs and organizations at the same time. A student interviewing for a sales position in Company A and one in Company B needs to examine the two jobs in detail as well as the characteristics of the two companies. Similarly, a manager considering his or her future in an organization needs to consider alternative jobs within that organization as well as in different organizations.

Techniques for Effective Work Exploration

Essentially, the exploration of the work environment can be broken down into two categories—the external and the internal.[54] Exploration of the external work environment involves the gathering of information on specific occupations, jobs, organizations, and industries. Students just entering the workforce and employed adults interested in locating a job with another organization would engage in exploration of the external work environment. It is important to recognize that external environmental exploration has been helped immensely in recent years by the Internet. Substantial amounts of industry, organizational, and occupational information now resides on the World Wide Web.

Information on specific occupations and occupational classes is available from a number of sources. First, it is important to recognize that a number of occupational classification systems exist that use various schema for grouping jobs and job data.[55] Experts use accumulated knowledge about the realm of jobs and sophisticated statistical techniques to create hierarchies of jobs and positions that take into account such factors as required skill and knowledge levels, work functions, job titles, and other related information. A few of the key occupational classification systems are listed here:

- The *Standard Occupational Classification* (SOC) was developed by the U.S. Department of Commerce. It serves as the single classification system for all occupations in the U.S. economy, including public, private, and military jobs, and is used by all federal agencies as the basis for the collection and reporting of jobs data. The SOC contains a hierarchy of occupations, moving from 23 general occupational groups to 96 more distinct groupings to 449 broad occupations to 821 detailed occupational titles.

- The *Occupational Information Network* (O*NET) is an online resource that provides detailed, research-based descriptions of 974 occupations using a total of 275 potential job characteristics and descriptors.[56] The O*NET is available as a database, an interactive Web site, and as a reference tool. The descriptors include worker characteristics (interests, values, and abilities of the typical worker), worker requirements, occupational requirements, and training and education needs. The O*NET is seen as the most comprehensive resource for occupational information.

- The Department of Labor's *Occupational Outlook Handbook* (*OOH*) is the most widely used source for occupational information.[57] The *OOH* describes job duties, work activities, qualifications, and projected openings for 270 occupations, which account for about 90 percent of the jobs in the U.S. labor force. While still available in text form, the *OOH* is available on the Internet, which allows for a more detailed and interactive sharing of occupational information.

- The *Monster Occupational Classification* (MOC) system is an example of an occupational classification structure developed by a private (nongovernmental) organization.[58] Established by the popular online job posting Web site www.Monster.com, this system uses a tailored version of the Standard Occupational Classification system as the means to organize job seekers' résumés by job titles.

- Many other reference materials are available in bookstores, libraries, and over the Internet that describe specific jobs and occupations. In addition, popular interest inventories as described earlier in this chapter include connections to specific occupations associated with various interest profiles.

Information on different organizations and industries is also available from multiple sources. For example, a company's Web site typically includes a description of the organization, corporate philosophies and goals, possible career paths, and job application procedures. In addition, an organization's annual report offers information on financial performance, key decision makers within the company, and the products and services the company provides. Outplacement and career-counseling firms also provide information on different companies as part of the services they give to their clients. More broadly, profiles and summaries of particular industries are available through the North American Industry Classification System (NAICS) and through other sources. In a less formal sense, one's family, friends, and former coworkers employed in different companies and industries can provide substantial information on occupations and contacts that might not be available through formal sources. In addition to those sources listed above, public libraries in several states have Career Information Centers that offer extensive client-centered activities that include the provision of occupational information and advisement/counseling.[59]

Internal work exploration involves the gathering of career-related information within one's own firm. There are a number of organizational career development tools that could be utilized to gather data on jobs and opportunities within one's organization. These include job posting programs, career ladders/career path planning, career resource centers, and in-house seminars and workshops. Other employees, including mentors and other supportive relationships, can also provide information on jobs and opportunities within other departments and subsidiaries owned by the company.

Learning Exercise 3 is included in the Appendix on p. 106. It provides an opportunity to practice environmental exploration. Although you may examine Exercise 3 at this time, it is recommended that you finish reading Chapter 4 before you begin the exercise.

Whether the primary focus is on gathering information about occupations, jobs, or organizations, it is essential to understand the needs and feelings of family members. Understanding the family's emotional and financial needs, career aspirations, and desired lifestyle is necessary if one wants to integrate work and nonwork lives. As Chapter 10 will show, the most significant source of information about the family's needs is the family itself—people need to talk and listen to the important people in their lives.

Understanding One's Preferred Work Environment

Once a set of themes is identified and confirmed and related environmental exploration has been conducted, it is necessary to address the significance of the findings for career management. An effective self-assessment should help people become more aware of the kinds of work experiences that will be personally meaningful and interesting, will meet their significant values, and will allow them to use those abilities and talents that are important to them. In addition, exploration of the work environment should lead to an understanding of occupations, industries, and geographic regions that hold promise. In short, self-assessment and environmental exploration should enable one to develop a portrait, however tentative, of a preferred work environment.

A statement about a preferred work environment is a summary of what you have learned from the exploration process. Based on the analyses of the themes that emerged from your self-assessment, you should try to identify the type of work environment that seems most compatible with your own qualities. The preferred work environment summary should touch on the following issues:

1. What types of tasks or activities are most interesting to you? For example, do you enjoy analytical activities, mechanical tasks, helping others, or scientific projects?

2. What abilities and talents do you wish to use in your work? Interpersonal? Quantitative? Creative? Writing skills?

3. How much freedom and independence do you want in your work?

4. What type of working relationship with other people do you prefer? Do you prefer working alone or with other people? How do you feel about exerting power or influence over other people?

5. What type of physical work setting is desirable (e.g., factory, office, outdoors)?

6. What is the role of money and security in your life?

7. How important is work in your total life, and what relationship do you desire between your work and other parts of your life?

8. What types of occupations and industries best fit your values, interests, personality, abilities, and preferred lifestyle?

Learning Exercise 4 is included in the Appendix on p. 109. It provides an opportunity to develop a statement about your preferred work environment. Although you may examine Exercise 4 at this time, it is recommended that you finish reading Chapter 4 before you begin the exercise.

Overcoming Obstacles to Career Exploration: A Set of Guidelines

Despite the logical role of career exploration in the career management process, it should not be assumed that exploration is always effective. That is, it does not always produce an enhanced awareness of self and/or the environment. Following is a list of potential obstacles to effective career exploration and guidelines for overcoming them.

1. Incomplete Exploration. Career exploration sometimes does not provide a sufficient amount of information to be useful. In other cases, a person may participate in little or no exploration, despite a recognized need for information. There are at least three reasons for inadequate exploration: complacency, hopelessness, and fear.

First, people may complacently accept the status quo. If they uncritically accept their course in life, there is no need to collect additional information. One explanation for this complacency is that people do not see the significance of career decisions. They often do not understand that a decision does have consequences in terms of future rewards and enjoyment.

Furthermore, some people attach such little importance to the work role that career exploration and career decisions are not going to make much difference in their lives. An uncritical complacency with things as they are or as they might be is unfortunate because decisions have to be made regardless of participation in career exploration. Students still have to choose majors, graduates still have to choose jobs, and even the most indifferent employees have to make decisions about their work lives.

Even if employees are not complacent, they may forgo career exploration if they perceive it to be useless. For example, research has found that managers who perceive few mobility opportunities in their organizations participate infrequently in career exploration.[60] In addition, people who believe that they have little control over their lives may engage in inadequate exploration. Unfortunately, this aversion to career exploration creates a vicious cycle in which decisions made by others (by default) reinforce the view that control over one's fate is impossible.

Finally, fear may block an active approach to career exploration. People who fear that their exploration will fail to provide useful information may avoid risking such failure and simply not pursue exploration activities. Those with low self-esteem may fear confronting their own weaknesses and thereby reduce their participation in exploratory activities.

Even among those who initiate career exploration, it may be tempting to bring exploration to a premature halt to gain a sense of security.[61] This may be a false sense of security, however, since exploration may raise issues that take time to understand or resolve. Therefore, one key ingredient to successful career exploration is the ability to tolerate a certain amount of ambiguity and frustration. Sometimes it is important to be persistent in career exploration.

Integrated and organizationally based career planning programs, as described earlier, can often provide information and support to overcome these forms of resistance to career exploration. Interactions with other more experienced career planners can help participants

- Realize career-related choices have a significant effect on the course of their lives; decisions do matter

- Recognize that they can exert sufficient control over their careers to make career exploration worthwhile

- Understand that fear of the unknown is natural but should not stifle their attempts to understand themselves and their environment

2. Coerced Exploration. Despite the need to acquire additional information, coercion is not a useful stimulant to successful exploration. While pressure from a manager, relative, or friend might be sufficient to initiate participation in a career exploration program, people tend to learn and change when the motivation comes from within and when there is a personal commitment to the learning process.

3. Random and Diffuse Exploration. This is exploration that is unfocused and does not build on the results of prior exploration activities. Effective exploration requires skill and practice. Therefore, some instruction in these skills through classes or workshops would help many people develop a more systematic approach to career exploration. This does not mean that career exploration, or career management in general, requires constant participation in formal programs, but rather that some initial, structured experience would be helpful in developing the appropriate skills.

4. Ineffective Forms of Career Exploration. As this chapter has shown, people committed to career exploration have choices to make about the manner in which they will seek information. Should they see a counselor, speak to family members, attend a career workshop, seek part-time employment, contact professional organizations, or pursue some of these activities in combination?

There is not sufficient evidence at this point to indicate which of these (or other) exploratory activities are most effective for a particular person in a specific situation. Research does suggest, however, that the most potentially useful exploratory activities are not necessarily the ones that are engaged in the most frequently.[62] It is likely that some people pursue the most easily accessible or the most comfortable exploratory activities and shy away from those that are more difficult to pursue or are more threatening. Although this is a natural, understandable tendency, it may result in a false sense of security.

Perhaps the most critical task is to estimate the likelihood that a particular activity will meet your informational needs. Although there is no easy solution to this problem, it is important not to equate ease with quality. Again, a structured experience can help provide guidance on the most useful, constructive forms of exploration.

5. Defensive Self-Exploration. In self-exploration, people need to obtain information from an activity and process it accurately and constructively. Clearly, some people are better able to accomplish this task than others. In particular, highly anxious people may not profit extensively from self-exploration.[63] It has been suggested that such people, when facing career decisions, focus on their own anxious feelings rather than on the information at hand. Therefore, people who are anxious about themselves or their careers may react defensively to threatening self-related information; may ignore, distort, or misinterpret the information; and may generally not utilize career exploration effectively. In terms of career decision making, highly anxious people may feel compelled to reach a premature or hastily contrived decision, or may avoid the decision entirely.[64]

The solution to this problem would seem to involve reducing feelings of anxiety to the point where they do not interfere with productive exploration. Fortunately, stress management programs have been found to stimulate exploratory behavior. It is also possible that group-oriented career planning workshops can help people become less anxious in career decision-making situations.

6. Exclusion of Nonwork Considerations. Effective career exploration requires attention to all segments of life. The time and emotion spent at work can affect the quality of one's family or personal life. Too many people fail to examine the implications of work-related decisions for other parts of their lives. Occupations are chosen, jobs are sought, and promotions are accepted without consideration of the consequences. Work, family, community, leisure, and religion all need to be examined and incorporated into career planning programs. Fortunately, these lifestyle issues are increasingly being included in structured career planning programs. The career exploration exercises included in this chapter periodically remind you to consider the impact of work experiences on other significant parts of your life.

Self- and Environmental Exploration: A Reciprocal Relationship

Career exploration provides an awareness of self and environment that enables a person to set valid, realistic career goals. Although the discussion has separated self-exploration and environmental exploration, in practice they are connected in several respects.

First, a particular exploratory activity may provide useful information about both self and environment. For example, a student who accepts a part-time or summer position as an accounting intern may not only learn about the work life of an accountant but may also test the compatibility of his or her abilities and interests with the field of accounting.[65] A performance-appraisal review with a boss not only can provide information about one's performance and progress in the organization, but can also suggest alternative opportunities for future mobility in the organization. Therefore, individuals need to be sensitive to the full range of information that can be acquired through a particular activity.

Second, there is a reciprocal relationship between self-exploration and environmental exploration; each can and should influence the direction of the other. For example, it is reasonable to engage in a certain amount of self-exploration before extensively exploring the environment. Self-awareness of interests, values, abilities, and lifestyle preferences can guide one's search for information regarding an occupation, job, or organization. Self-awareness also provides a framework for environmental exploration. Extensive environmental exploration without sufficient understanding of self is likely to be aimless and random.

However, since gaining self-awareness is often a fragmented process, it is impractical to attempt to complete the task of self-insight before commencing an assessment of the environment. Moreover, environmental exploration may highlight the need to engage in additional self-exploration. For example, a job search might reveal that a job in one organization requires much more extensive travel than a similar job in a different organization. This piece of information might stimulate the person to consider the impact of travel (positive or negative) on his or her desired lifestyle.

In reality, people need to use self-exploration to direct environmental exploration and vice versa. The more one learns about oneself, the more likely that certain questions about the environment become relevant. In a similar fashion, the more information that is acquired about an occupation, a job, or an organization, the more one has to think about the relevance of that information for one's own values and aspirations.

SUMMARY

Career exploration can be directed toward learning more about oneself and gaining knowledge about the environment. Self-exploration requires the collection of information about values, interests, personality, abilities, and desired lifestyle; the organization of this information into meaningful themes; and the identification of the implications of these themes in terms of the kind of work environment that is most likely to satisfy important values, provide interesting tasks, utilize individual talents, and provide a desired lifestyle.

Environmental exploration can help us learn more about different occupations, organizations, and industries as well as our family's needs and desires. The two forms of exploration, self and environmental, can reinforce each other by suggesting different areas in which we need to collect additional information. Learning exercises are included at the end of this chapter to provide the opportunity to practice career exploration.

A number of obstacles to effective career exploration were discussed in this chapter, including incomplete exploration, coerced exploration, random and diffuse exploration, ineffective forms of exploration, excessive defensiveness, and exclusion of nonwork considerations. Suggestions were made for overcoming each obstacle.

Now that you have finished reading Chapter 4, it is time to complete Learning Exercises 1, 2, 3, and 4, which are included in the Appendix beginning on p. 93. Be thoughtful and patient in the completion of these Exercises. You will refer to them as you complete later chapters in this book.

ASSIGNMENTS

1. Take a few moments to reflect on the things you like to do, the things you believe are important, your preferences, your competencies, and your weaknesses. On a separate sheet of paper, prepare a list of what you see as your interests, values, talents, and weaknesses. You can use the information provided in Table 4.1 to help guide you in the preparation of the list. Ask a friend, family member, or colleague to review your list and give you feedback on whether or not they see it as an accurate reflection of you. Ask them to explain any differences they see. How do you think the list you prepared and the feedback you received could help you in your career management process?

2. Take a few minutes to carefully review each of the descriptions of the eight career anchors, developed by Edgar Schein, that were presented earlier in this chapter. Once you have read each description, think about which one best fits you and your orientation toward work. Identify why you think this career anchor best describes you. Which career anchor describes you the least and why? How might you be able to use this information on career anchors in your self-exploration process and in theme development?

DISCUSSION QUESTIONS

1. What are the differences among values, interests, personality, and abilities? How does understanding these factors help us manage our careers effectively?

2. How important is work in your total life? What makes you feel that way? Has the importance of work in your life changed in recent years? Do you think it will remain the same in the future? In what ways could your desire for a specific type of lifestyle affect your career decisions?

3. Is career exploration worth the effort? Since the world can change so rapidly, isn't the information collected through career exploration going to be irrelevant and/or outdated?

4. Reexamine the six obstacles to effective career exploration. Which of them have you experienced in the past? How can you overcome these obstacles in the future?

CHAPTER 4 CASE

Joe Francis the Sales Executive

At age 39, Joe Francis should have been pleased. In fact, he has been proud of his rapid rise to the position of Vice President of Sales at Infotek (fictitious name), an established computer software development firm. Having started as a sales representative at Infotek upon graduation from college, Joe's sales performance at the district and regional levels was legendary. However, his promotion to the vice presidency came as a surprise. He did not seek the position, always preferring sales to pencil pushing and administration. But it was hard to turn down the promotion with its hefty salary increase and the other executive perks.

Although he has not complained to anyone, Joe has had gnawing doubts about his work. For one thing, he has had strong reservations about the quality of Infotek's products. He has found it increasingly difficult to get enthusiastic about software systems that fall short of personal and industry standards. Joe's comments to the Research and Marketing departments have fallen on deaf ears. In fact, he has offered suggestions in a number of areas that the company seems unwilling to consider seriously. In addition, his fears about getting drowned in paperwork and administration have been realized. Joe has been bored for quite a while. Moreover, although the travel was fun initially, the seemingly constant business trips of the last few years have left him tired, irritable, and with little time for his family.

Joe has had to suppress many of these feelings. After all, his salary and bonus reach well into six figures. His family has expensive consumption habits, two of his children are nearing college age, and his family wants a larger summer house at the lake. He doesn't dare even discuss his feelings with his family, who have become pretty accustomed to "the good life."

(Continued)

(Continued)

Joe dreads going to work, but believes that he must do it for the sake of his family. He's unhappy much of the time but has been pleased with his status in the company. Anyway, Joe has found that the traveling isn't so bad after four stiff drinks on the flight. For the sake of his wife and kids, Joe had decided he would stay put for the next 15 or 20 years until early retirement.

Case Analysis Questions

1. What specific career exploration activities has Joe undertaken to gather information about himself (his values, needs, abilities, interests, and desired lifestyle) and his environment (different jobs, employers, industries, their families)? What should he have done to acquire more information?

2. How much insight does Joe currently have about himself and his environment?

3. Is Joe successful in his career? Do you think if Joe conducted more extensive career exploration, it would lead to more positive career outcomes for him?

4. If Joe sought your help, what advice would you give to help him manage his career effectively? If you had to make a prediction, where do you think Joe will be in his career five years into the future?

Appendix

Learning Exercises 1 Through 4

Each learning exercise involves a different aspect of career exploration. By investing time in these exercises, you can develop and practice critical career exploration skills. We recommend that you use a separate notebook in which to write your responses to these exercises. A separate career management notebook provides the flexibility to add more information to an exercise at a later point. It is recommended that you reread the appropriate chapter section before beginning each exercise. Although it may be possible to complete all exercises in one sitting, it is less tiring and more effective to allow some time for reflection in between them.

LEARNING EXERCISE 1. SELF-EXPLORATION: DATA COLLECTION

Learning Exercise 1 contains a number of activities designed to provide self-assessment data. Be as thorough as possible in answering all questions. Remember that the more you write, the more self-assessment information will be available for you to interpret.

Learning Exercise 1.A: An Autobiography

Here you are today—a college undergraduate or graduate student, an employee with substantial work experience under your belt, or someone ready to reenter the job market after an absence of several years. Think of all the yesterdays that made you what you are today.

Given all that you know about yourself, write an autobiographical story that traces your history up to now. Divide the story into chapters, each chapter should cover a five-year period, starting with birth to 5 years old, 5 to 10 years old, and so on. In each chapter, try to answer the following questions if they are relevant: Who were the important people in your life and why were they important? What was your family life like at the time? What were your school experiences like and how did you react to school? What were your work experiences like and how did you react to work? Did you develop hobbies and interests, and what did you like about them? To what extent did your parents influence the activities you've pursued and the choices you've made? How have other family relationships shaped your experiences? What happened to you during this period that changed the course of your life?

Write as much as you can about each question. Don't worry about whether these chapters have anything to do with your career—you'll find that out later. If you are in doubt about whether or not to include something, include it. The more you write, the better.

Learning Exercise 1.B: Focus on School

Now identify your favorite and least favorite courses and subjects, those subjects in which you did best and worst, and significant extracurricular activities (e.g., sports, music, clubs) in which you participated.

Junior/Senior High School

Favorite Courses   *Least Favorite Courses*

————————————   ————————————

————————————   ————————————

————————————   ————————————

————————————   ————————————

Courses in Which You Did Best   *Courses in Which You Did Worst*

————————————   ————————————

————————————   ————————————

————————————   ————————————

————————————   ————————————

Extracurricular Activities

————————————————————————————————————

————————————————————————————————————

————————————————————————————————————

————————————————————————————————————

College

Favorite Courses   *Least Favorite Courses*

————————————   ————————————

————————————   ————————————

————————————   ————————————

————————————   ————————————

Courses in Which You Did Best   *Courses in Which You Did Worst*

_____   _____

_____   _____

_____   _____

_____   _____

Extracurricular Activities

_____

_____

_____

_____

What do your responses tell you about your interests and particular strengths and weaknesses?

_____

_____

_____

_____

_____

_____

Learning Exercise 1.C: Focus on Work

Think about the BEST JOB you ever had. It could be your current job or a prior job, and either part-time, full-time, or temporary.

What do (did) you like most about the job? Be specific in terms of tasks, people, and other aspects.

_____

_____

_____

_____

_____

_____

What do (did) you dislike about the job? Again, be specific.

_____

_____

_____

_____

_____

On what specific tasks or projects did you accomplish something significant? Why were you able to accomplish it?

_____

_____

_____

_____

_____

_____

On what specific tasks or projects did you not perform as well as you would have liked? What was the reason?

_____

_____

_____

_____

_____

_____

Now think of the WORST JOB you ever had. It could be your current job or a prior job, and either part-time, full-time, or temporary.

_____

_____

_____

_____

_____

_____

What do (did) you dislike most about the job?

_____

_____

_____

_____

_____

What do (did) you like about the job?

_____

_____

_____

_____

_____

On what specific tasks or projects did you accomplish something significant? Why?

_____

_____

_____

_____

_____

_____

On what specific tasks or projects did you not perform as well as you would have liked? What was the reason?

_____

_____

_____

_____

_____

_____

Now describe your conception of an IDEAL JOB. What would it be like? Be specific in terms of the kinds of tasks, other people, rewards, and anything else that is important to you.

_____

_____

_____

_____

_____

_____

_____

_____

Next rank the following 10 factors in terms of how important each is to you for a career-related job. Enter a 1 next to the factor that is most important to you, a 10 next to the least important factor, a 2 next to the second most important, a 9 next to the second least important, and so on until you have ranked all 10 factors.

How important is it that your job . . .

____ Permits you to work on a wide variety of tasks?

____ Gives you the opportunity to help others?

____ Provides you with a great deal of independence in deciding how the work gets done?

____ Enables you to make a great deal of money?

____ Offers you a secure future?

____ Gives you the opportunity to develop friendships at work?

____ Has pleasant working conditions?

____ Enables you to work with a supervisor who is competent and supportive?

____ Provides you with power and influence over other people?

____ Gives you a feeling of accomplishment?

Indicate any other job factors not listed above that are important to you.

_____

_____

_____

_____

_____

_____

Learning Exercise 1.D: Life Roles

How important are different parts of your life? Rank the following five life roles from 1 (most important) to 5 (least important).

___ Your career

___ Your religious and spiritual life

___ Your family life

___ Your participation in community service activities

___ Your leisure and recreational pursuits

Explain why each of these life roles is important (or unimportant) to you:

Your career:

_____

_____

_____

_____

_____

_____

Your religious and spiritual life:

_____

_____

_____

_____

_____

_____

Your family life:

_____

_____

_____

_____

_____

_____

Your participation in community service activities:

_____

_____

_____

_____

_____

_____

Your leisure and recreational pursuits:

_____

_____

_____

_____

_____

_____

LEARNING EXERCISE 2. SELF-EXPLORATION: THEME IDENTIFICATION

Now that you have generated data about yourself in Learning Exercise 1, and perhaps have gathered other self-assessment information, the next step is to derive a set of themes based on your data. Review the steps for identifying themes presented in Chapter 4. You should be able to identify at least five themes from your data—if you have more than five themes, that is fine; just write down all of the themes that you have along with the supporting evidence. Jot down your preliminary thoughts first, and then list your final set of themes along with supporting evidence.

Theme 1:

_____

_____

_____

Evidence:

_____

_____

_____

_____

_____

_____

Theme 2:

_____

_____

_____

Evidence:

_____

_____

_____

_____

_____

_____

Theme 3:

_____

_____

_____

Evidence:

_____

_____

_____

_____

_____

Theme 4:

_____

_____

Evidence:

_____

_____

_____

_____

_____

Theme 5:

_____

_____

_____

Evidence:

_____

_____

_____

_____

_____

_____

Other Themes:

_____

_____

_____

_____

_____

_____

LEARNING EXERCISE 3. SUMMARY OF PREFERRED WORK ENVIRONMENT

As indicated in this chapter, a preferred work environment (PWE) is a summary of the work experiences you find desirable; for example, the kinds of tasks you find interesting, the talents you wish to express, the importance of autonomy and freedom on the job, and so on. Reexamine your responses to Learning Exercises 1 and 2 and write down a comment for each component of the PWE listed below. For example, under tasks and activities, you might write, "I enjoy working on tasks that are technical in nature and that require a great deal of analysis."

Components of PWE comment(s):

_____

_____

_____

_____

_____

_____

Tasks and activities most interesting to you:

_____

_____

_____

_____

_____

_____

Significant talents you want to express at work:

_____

_____

_____

_____

_____

_____

Importance of independence and autonomy on the job:

_____

_____

_____

_____

_____

_____

Work relationships (Work alone? With others? Supervise?):

_____

_____

_____

_____

_____

_____

Physical work setting:

_____

_____

_____

_____

_____

_____

Importance of money:

_____

_____

_____

_____

_____

_____

Importance of job security:

_____

_____

_____

_____

_____

_____

Relationship between work and other parts of life:

_____

_____

_____

_____

_____

_____

Other components of preferred work environment:

_____

_____

_____

_____

_____

_____

LEARNING EXERCISE 4. ENVIRONMENTAL EXPLORATION

You can practice environmental exploration by completing either Learning Exercise 4.A or 4.B. If you are not currently employed, you should complete exercise 4.A, which will give you an opportunity to explore occupations. If you are employed, you might find exercise 4.B (job exploration) more useful. Examine the exercises before you decide which one to complete.

Learning Exercise 4.A: Occupational Exploration

Choose an occupation about which you would like to learn more. Maybe it is one you are considering pursuing. Or perhaps you are pretty sure you want to pursue a certain occupation and would like to examine it in more detail. If you are completely undecided about an occupation at this time, read Chapter 6 (especially "Development of Accurate Occupational Information") to help you decide which occupation to explore in this exercise. Write down the name of the occupation you have chosen to explore.

_____

_____

_____

Review the preferred work environment (PWE) statement you constructed in Learning Exercise 3. Then look at the suggested sources of occupational information described in Chapter 4. Using as many sources as possible, collect information relevant to each component of your PWE in relation to the occupation you have chosen to explore. Summarize the information and the sources (so you can reexamine the raw data) in the format shown on the following pages. Remember to use as many different sources of information as you can.

Name of Occupation:

_____

_____

_____

_____

_____

Components of the PWE	Relevant Information About Occupation	Information Source
What tasks and activities are performed?		
What talents are required? Do you possess them or can you learn them?		
What type of working relationships with other people are likely?		
What is the physical work setting?		
How much money can be earned in the long term and short term?		
How much job security is likely?		
Effect of pursuit of occupation on family, leisure, religion, community		
Other significant issues (job prospects, opportunities for mobility, etc.)		

Learning Exercise 4.B: Job Exploration

If you are employed, choose a job in your organization other than the one you currently hold. It could be a job you expect to enter next or a job you would like to learn more about. Write down the job title:

_____

_____

_____

Review the preferred work environment (PWE) summary you constructed in Learning Exercise 3. Consider the following sources of information about a job: a written job description, the suggested sources of occupational information described in Chapter 4, your supervisor, employees who hold or previously held the job, members of the Human Resources department, and people who hold or held a similar job in a different organization. Using as many sources as possible, collect information relevant to each component of your PWE. Summarize the information and the sources (so you can reexamine the raw data) in the same format shown below. Remember to use many different sources of information.

Components of the PWE	Relevant Information About Job	Information Source
What tasks and activities are performed? _____		
What abilities are required? Do you possess them or can you learn them? _____		
How much freedom and autonomy can be obtained? _____		
What types of working relationships with other people are likely? _____		

(Continued)

(Continued)

Components of the PWE	Relevant Information About Job	Information Source
What is the physical work setting?		
How much money can be earned in the long term and short term?		
How much job security is likely?		
Effect of pursuit of job on family, leisure, religion, community		
Other significant issues (prospects of being offered job, usefulness of job for desired career path, etc.)		

Applications of the Career Management Model

Goals, Strategies, and Appraisal

In this chapter we focus on career goal setting, career strategy development, and career appraisal. As in the previous chapter, we will stress the pragmatic application of the career management model. Additional learning exercises are provided in the Appendix at the end of this chapter to help the reader develop and practice key career management skills. We also offer guidelines for effective goal setting, strategy development, and career appraisal.

CAREER GOAL SETTING

We all know or have heard stories of individuals who declared that they were going to be a millionaire by the time they were 30. Or perhaps we know someone who expressed a strong desire to become a senior executive of a corporation, or a top trial lawyer, or a surgeon. Most children begin projecting careers for themselves at young ages—"I'm going to be a police officer" or "I'm going to be a ballet star." Even older adults on the verge of retirement will often set plans to open their own business or perhaps get involved with some type of volunteer work.

The common theme in these examples is the setting, however tentative or ill defined, of career goals. A goal has been defined as the object or aim of one's actions. The usefulness of goal setting is based on the belief that goals regulate human action.[1] Goals can affect behavior and performance in a number of ways.[2] First, they can spur high levels of effort. Second, they can give focus or direction to effort because a specific goal provides a particular target toward which to strive. Third, goals can produce high levels of persistence on a task. Fourth, a specific goal can help one develop a useful strategy for accomplishing the task. Finally, because of their concrete nature, goals provide opportunities for feedback on task performance. We define a career goal as a desired career-related outcome that a person intends to attain.

Even with the acknowledged positive attributes, one can question, especially in this era of downsizings and economic uncertainty, whether career goal setting is still a relevant exercise. Some researchers have argued that with the current unsettled environment, goal setting is futile at best, and harmful at worst. Under this view, the work world is seen as so uncertain that setting any kind of goal is useless, with the person setting the goal subject to bitterness and disappointment. Further, it has been stated that career goals promote rigidity in terms of actions and strategies, when what is really needed is flexibility in being able to pursue other options or career directions.

In our view, career goal setting is, in most cases, a useful and productive process. As we noted, goals provide direction and they serve as a benchmark against which progress can be measured. In addition, the presence of a career goal, in and of itself, should not cause inflexibility in the management of one's career. The career goal is simply a descriptive target toward which one aims; it does not specify how one gets to the desired end-state. Further, goals can, and should, change as conditions dictate.

Even though career goals have beneficial aspects, there are times when the setting of goals can be counterproductive. Later in this chapter we will discuss how *not* setting career goals is an appropriate response when one does not have sufficient knowledge to make an informed decision.

With the preceding introduction as background, this section will examine several components of career goals, discuss the career goal-setting process, and provide a set of guidelines for effective goal setting.

Components of Career Goals

A career goal can be viewed in two fundamental ways: by its conceptual and operational components and by its time dimension.

Conceptual Goal Versus Operational Goal. A conceptual career goal summarizes the nature of the work experiences one intends to attain without specifying a particular job or position. It should reflect the person's significant values, interests, personality, abilities, and lifestyle preferences. For example, an individual's conceptual goal may be to hold a marketing job that involves extensive research and analysis, offers a great deal of responsibility, is broad and varied in pace, requires interaction with a variety of clients, does not chronically interfere with family responsibilities, and is situated in a small, growth-oriented company in a warm weather climate. This conceptual goal addresses the nature of the task, interpersonal and physical settings, and total lifestyle concerns. The conceptual career goal should also take into account the intrinsic enjoyment one derives from goal-related experiences. In this sense, conceptual goals are expressively appropriate to the extent to which their accomplishment permits a person to engage in enjoyable, fulfilling, and satisfying work activities; use his or her valued talents at work; and experience a satisfying lifestyle.

On the other hand, an operational career goal is the translation of a conceptual goal into a specific job or position. In addition, the operational career goal should also embody an instrumental element in the sense that the accomplishment of the operational goal can lead to (or is instrumental in) the attainment of a subsequent goal. In the example described above, the operational goal may be to attain the position of marketing research manager at Company X, and the attainment of the goal of marketing manager may enable a person to achieve his or her next goal of vice president of marketing. For another individual, an operational goal might be to remain in his or her current position for the foreseeable future. It is important to realize that an operational goal is simply a vehicle for meeting an underlying conceptual goal. And it is helpful for career goals to be stated in both conceptual and operational terms.

Short-Term Versus Long-Term Career Goal. Career goals have a time dimension in that one can distinguish between a short-term and long-term focus. Of course, what is considered short versus long is rather arbitrary and is likely to vary depending on a number of factors. Normally, a short-term goal is one that has a more immediate focus, perhaps *one to three years,* whereas a long-term goal is generally considered to have a time frame of *five to seven years.* Table 5.1 illustrates hypothetical short-term and long-term goals for an assistant manager in a Human Resources department.

TABLE 5.1 Short-Term and Long-Term Goals for an Assistant Human Resource Manager

	Short-Term Goal	*Long-Term Goal*
Conceptual	More responsibility for administering human resources operation	Involvement in human resource planning activities
	Broad exposure to all facets of human resources	Involvement in corporate long-range planning
	More interaction with line management.	Involvement in policy development and implementation
Operational	Manager of Human Resources within 2–3 years	Director of Corporate Human Resources in 5 years

Development of Long-Term and Short-Term Conceptual Goals

Ideally, the first step in setting a career goal is to identify a long-term conceptual goal. As an outgrowth of the self-exploration and assessment process, the long-term conceptual goal takes into account the person's values, interests, abilities, and expectations and should reflect the themes that represent the individual. It should, therefore, touch on job duties, degree of autonomy, type and frequency of interaction with other people, the physical environment, and lifestyle concerns. A long-term conceptual goal is, in effect, a projection of one's preferred work environment into a specific five- to seven-year time frame. Ask yourself what type of job duties, activities, rewards, and responsibilities you would like to experience in the long-term future.

Next, consider a short-term conceptual goal. Remember, the short-term conceptual goal should support the long-term one. To derive a short-term goal from a long-term goal, one should ask the following kinds of questions: What type of work experiences will prepare you to attain the long-term goal? What talents need to be developed or refined? What type of visibility is useful to reach a subsequent goal? These questions raise strategic issues. That is, the decision to pursue a particular short-term goal because of its value in attaining the long-term goal is an illustration of a career strategy.

But a short-term conceptual goal should display the qualities one hopes to express in work. Quite apart from its value as a stopping point, it must be viewed in terms of its capacity to provide important personal rewards, interesting and meaningful tasks, and the possibility of a desired lifestyle. As with the long-term goal, a short-term objective should be consistent with the significant elements of one's preferred work environment. For example, as shown in Table 5.1, the Assistant Human Resource Manager's short-term conceptual goal involves gaining more responsibility, exposure, and interaction as a means to fulfill the long-term conceptual of being involved in long-range planning and implementation of human resource and corporate strategy.

Development of Long-Term and Short-Term Operational Goals

An operational goal is the translation of a conceptual goal into a specific job or position. Environmental exploration is required to convert conceptual goals into operational ones: What specific occupation (or job or organization) will provide an opportunity to meet your significant values, interests, abilities, and lifestyle requirements (i.e., your conceptual goal)?

There is no automatic formula that can (or should) dictate the selection of an operational goal. Your judgment (with input from trusted others) about the desirability and practicality of each operational goal should be your guide. You should, however, attempt to estimate the likelihood that a particular operational goal will enable you to satisfy the significant elements of your conceptual goal. For example, as shown in Table 5.1, the Assistant Human Resource Manager's long- and short-term operational goals involving upward movement in title in the Human Resources department (the operational goals) are designed to allow for the attainment of greater responsibility and the exertion of greater influence in setting corporate policy (the conceptual goals). Thus, by examining these estimates for one or more operational goals, you can begin to assess the appropriateness of each operational goal.

The conversion of a goal from conceptual to operational terms clearly cannot be conducted in a vacuum. Instead, extensive information is required to assess the activities and rewards associated with each operational goal. This information cannot come simply from introspection. The individual needs data, much of which can be provided by the employer or potential employer. The role of the employer in providing such assistance is treated in subsequent chapters. Through the career appraisal process (discussed later in this chapter), the accomplishment or non-accomplishment of a goal can serve as an additional piece of career-related information.

Are Long-Term Career Goals Necessary?

The goal-setting process assumes it is possible to develop long-term conceptual and operational goals. However, it is not always feasible to project five to seven years into the future with any sense of accuracy or confidence. In such cases, the person should attempt to formulate at least a partial conceptual goal, even if it is somewhat vague and even if it cannot be associated with a specific operational goal at the present time. Consider the following example.

> Jose, who is 28 years old, hopes to work in an environment where he can help others, work with clients as individuals and in group settings, and develop educational programs for the community, all in a work environment where weekend and evening work could be kept to a minimum. This constitutes his long-term conceptual goal.
>
> Extensive environmental exploration indicates that a position in social work will likely enable Jose to achieve his conceptual goal. This long-term operational goal (to become a social worker) is admittedly vague, but the vagueness is appropriate at the present time. What type of social work position is most suitable for him? Should he work with children, adults, or a wide range of age groups? Should he work in a hospital, a school, a mental health clinic, or industry? At this time, these factors are unknowns.
>
> As vague as his long-term goal is, it can enable Jose to develop an appropriate short-term conceptual goal: to acquire the relevant education, experiences, and credentials to become a qualified social worker. His short-term operational goal is equally relevant: to obtain a master's degree in social work within two to three years.

Jose's experiences illustrate that one does not always have to develop a highly specific and elaborate long-term goal to develop a sensible short-term goal. It is important to think through the long-term future, develop a sense (however tentative) of what combination of work and lifestyle seems appropriate, and develop a short-term goal that is most consistent with this future, however hazy.

One can think of many situations in which a long-term goal is vague or uncertain. A mechanical engineer does not know whether she would like to remain in an engineering position or move into general management within five years. An accountant does not know whether he should remain at the firm in which he currently works or start his own small CPA practice. An upper-level manager is still uncertain whether the rewards of being a company president outweigh the costs. The engineer, the accountant, and the manager may not have formulated clear, certain long-term goals at this point, but they will be better able to identify short-term goals and appropriate strategies if they examine the long-term future and alternative options than if they have not given any serious thought to such issues.

Learning Exercise 5 appears in the Appendix beginning on p. 149. It provides an opportunity to practice developing career goals. Although you may examine Exercise 5 at this time, it is recommended that you finish reading Chapter 5 before beginning the exercise.

Overcoming Obstacles to Goal Setting: A Set of Guidelines

Like career exploration, the goal-setting process is not without obstacles. Ultimately, the quality of a career goal depends on whether the achievement of the goal is compatible with the individual's preferred work environment and whether the goal can be realistically achieved. Listed below are a number of obstacles to effective goal setting and suggestions for overcoming them.

Goals That Belong to Someone Else. The achievement of a career goal is meaningless if the goal does not meet your needs and values, if the tasks are not interesting to you, and if the talents needed to be successful are not possessed and valued by you. It is your work, your career, and your life.

Yet some people seem to base career decisions on pleasing someone else—a parent, a professor, a spouse, or a boss. They place little value on meeting their own needs and rely on others to decide what is appropriate for them. In what is probably an unconscious process, such people, in effect, say, "I'm not important, I don't know what's best for me," or "I don't really deserve to get my own needs met." Ultimately, such people may choose occupations or jobs that don't take advantage of their own abilities and that are not personally interesting or rewarding. In the long run, such goals, even if accomplished, will produce frustration and alienation rather than fulfillment and growth.

The solution to this problem is twofold. First, people must be in touch with their own values, interests, abilities, and lifestyle preferences. Second, they must recognize the importance of meeting goals that are compatible with these qualities. Regarding the first point, virtually all self-assessment procedures provide opportunities for awareness of personal characteristics. Autobiographical statements, value clarification exercises, and analyses of life experiences hopefully enable the individual to separate personal abilities and desires from others' wishes and values and from society's expectations.

The more difficult task is acting constructively on this awareness. Career-planning programs can go only so far. Perhaps the ultimate answer is feeling good enough about yourself to pursue goals that are relevant to your own personal aspirations and values. Discussions with family, friends, and colleagues about the importance of meeting personal needs would be a significant first step.

Goals That Exclude Total Lifestyle Concerns. Many people pursue a career goal without regard for its impact on other parts of their lives. It is only after marital difficulties or a personal tragedy that some people recognize the relationship between work life and private life. Many people in midcareer become particularly aware of the trade-offs between work responsibilities and family or leisure activities. Nevertheless, work and nonwork roles interact at all phases of a person's life.

The effective career manager anticipates the interrelationships between work and nonwork and sets career goals consistent with a desired total lifestyle. As noted earlier, many career planning programs include considerations of lifestyle. But it is still easy to focus so narrowly on job challenges, rewards, and prestige that family, religious, leisure, and community roles are virtually ignored. It takes a conscious effort to retain a total lifestyle perspective in career goal setting.

Goals That Fail to Take Into Account One's Current Job. A career goal (either short term or long term) need not involve job mobility. Any particular job is merely a vehicle for the satisfaction of more basic values (i.e., the conceptual goal). If goals are first stated in conceptual terms, then the current job's capacity to meet these values can be thoroughly examined. Often, successful career management is based on understanding the conceptual goal and the ability to use the current job to achieve that goal.

On too many occasions, however, individuals focus so narrowly on pursuing other jobs that they ignore their current job as a source of career growth and satisfaction. This myopic preoccupation with mobility could be a serious problem in today's work environment where promotions or lateral moves are in short supply or where such moves, if attained, have serious negative consequences for family or leisure activities (e.g., where another job requires relocation or extensive travel). A number of approaches to career planning include an examination of the ways in which one's current job can be improved, perhaps through increased responsibility or a greater variety of projects. This requires a constructive interaction between the career planner and his or her supervisor. This is a healthy focus that can be usefully incorporated into many career management activities.

Goals That Are Overly Vague. It is well understood that specific goals are generally more useful than vague goals. Because they present a particular target toward which to strive, specific goals can direct one's efforts more efficiently than vague goals. In addition, a specific goal offers a greater opportunity for feedback since progress toward the goal is easier to detect.

Consider the vague conceptual goal "to do things that are interesting to me." It would probably be more useful to specify what kinds of activities are considered personally interesting, for example, working with detailed statistics, writing reports, or meeting frequently with colleagues and clients. A set of specific conceptual goal elements can be more easily translated into an operational goal than a vaguely stated conceptual goal. Moreover, stating a conceptual goal in specific terms forces a person away from generalizations and toward a deeper understanding of his or her aspirations.

There are also advantages to setting a specific operational goal. It is difficult to compare a vague operational goal to one's conceptual goal. To "move into marketing" is probably too vague to be helpful since different marketing jobs may match one's conceptual goal to varying degrees. An operational goal "to become a market research analyst" is more specific and more useful because its connection to the underlying conceptual goal is more explicit and the path to the goal is more easily determined. As noted earlier, however, it might not be possible or desirable to develop a highly specific long-term goal in many circumstances. Perhaps the litmus test to determine whether a goal is specific enough is to examine whether it provides enough information to guide your behavior in a useful way.

Preoccupation With Instrumental Elements of an Operational Goal. Despite its many advantages, a specific operational goal can create tunnel vision. In the quest to accomplish a specific goal, people could forget why they wanted to reach the goal in the first place. They may also become so committed to a course of action that they resist new information that runs counter to the value of the goal. Perhaps most important, striving for a sequence of goals, each of which is designed to accomplish a subsequent goal, can rob people of the enjoyment of the here and now. In effect, people can be driven and tyrannized by the desire to reach some end-state. Preoccupation with the destination, in other words, can make the voyage joyless.

This possibility presents a dilemma. On the one hand, an operational career goal can enhance future career growth and satisfaction. However, a specific operational goal can, in some circumstances, detract from the intrinsic satisfaction of the present. Perhaps the solution is to maintain an equal concern for the expressive qualities of a goal, allowing one to focus both on concrete accomplishments and on the enjoyment that those accomplishments should bring.

Consider the case of an engineering school graduate who, early in his career, set his sights on the presidency of a large manufacturing organization. Every job assignment, every promotion, every transfer was chosen for its instrumental value. His commitment to this operational goal was so strong that he could not allow himself the luxury of reexamining its importance. Nor could he stop to ask whether all of the intermediate goals and accomplishments were enjoyable, satisfying, and fulfilling, or whether they played havoc with the rest of his life. Mortgaging the present for the future is a risky business.

A healthy concern for the expressive, intrinsic quality of career goals is therefore an essential part of career management. This requires an ongoing focus on conceptual goals. There is nothing inherently satisfying about a company presidency or any other operational goal. The tasks, activities, opportunities, and rewards associated with an operational goal, however, can be intrinsically satisfying. A simultaneous concern for present satisfaction and future direction is critical. This can only come from an ongoing assessment of oneself and the environment.

Goals That Are too Easy or too Difficult. It has been argued that feelings of psychological success are essential for individual development and satisfaction.[3] Feelings of psychological success are experienced by accomplishing tasks that are challenging and meaningful. Therefore, career goals that are too easy are unlikely to provide a real sense of accomplishment and success. Whether a goal is directed toward one's current job (e.g., to improve in certain areas) or attaining a different job, it must be challenging enough so that the achievement of the goal produces feelings of real success.

Goals that are too difficult, on the other hand, are unlikely to be accomplished. The inability to reach a desired goal can bring a deep sense of frustration and failure. There is a fine line between a goal that is challenging and one that is virtually impossible. Detecting the fine line requires insight into one's own talents, the ability to develop new talents, and opportunities and obstacles in the work environment. Therefore, when selecting an extremely difficult goal, one should understand the risks involved and be willing to assume those risks.

Inflexible Career Goals. Although goal setting is intended to be a flexible process, flexibility is often lost in practice. For one thing, people can become highly committed to a course of action to which they have devoted significant time, energy, and emotional involvement.[4] Second, the orientation toward the future built into goal setting tends to emphasize the end result and make it an "objective reality" that an individual might find difficult to question. Moreover, since change can be hard for most people, a thorough reexamination of career goals and a possible change in career direction could be particularly threatening.

Yet as we've stressed previously, flexible goals are essential to effective career management and are at the heart of the boundaryless career perspective. Since the work milieu and people inevitably change over time, goals that have been appropriate in the past might no longer be valid at present or in the future. In today's turbulent economic world, the setting of a concrete long-term career goal might not be advisable. Indeed, because of employment uncertainty in nearly all companies, individuals may find flexibility in the setting and changing of career goals to be a more appropriate action. For example, jobs and career paths may disappear or change as organizations restructure or develop new strategic plans, thereby leaving inflexible employees out in the cold. Similarly, technological and structural changes can give birth to new career routes that may require revisions in an individual's career goals.[5] In the broadest sense, people need to learn from their work and life experiences so that career goals can remain relevant and realistic. Career appraisal, discussed in a later section of this chapter, is the process by which learning and feedback provide flexibility to career management.

INABILITY TO SET CAREER GOALS: CAREER INDECISION

Although we have suggested that career goal setting is a critical part of the career management process, for many people, both students and working adults, the selection of a career goal is a difficult (or even impossible) task. *Individuals are considered career undecided if they have either not established a career goal or if they have set a career goal over which they experience significant uncertainty or discomfort.*[6] Since the selection of a career goal is viewed as a paramount task in the career management process, one would presume that the presence of career indecision would be both unsettling and detrimental to career success. As this section will show, however, career indecision should not be viewed as necessarily inappropriate, just as career decidedness (i.e., the selection of a career goal) should not be viewed as necessarily appropriate. It has been estimated that 10 to 30 percent of college students could be classified as undecided, but in many cases this state of career indecision is part of the normative developmental process.[7]

Given the importance of understanding career indecision, this section will discuss three related topics: the underlying causes and sources of career indecision, the existence of different types of career indecision, and the possible actions that could be taken to allow individuals to become career decided.

Causes and Sources of Career Indecision

Research on the career indecision of high school and college students found a variety of underlying reasons why individuals could not select a specific occupation or career goal.[8] In general, this research identified four sources of career indecision: lack of information about oneself, lack of information about the work environment, lack of self-confidence in decision making, and the presence of psychological conflicts.

Our research, which studied a large sample of managers and professionals, identified seven sources of indecision that were somewhat more refined than those listed above:[9]

1. *Lack of Self-Information* reflects the individual's insufficient understanding of his or her interests, strengths, values, and lifestyle preferences.

2. *Lack of Internal Work Information* reflects insufficient knowledge of career opportunities and job possibilities within one's own organization.

3. *Lack of External Work Information* reflects insufficient knowledge of opportunities outside of one's organization, including other occupations, companies, and industries.

4. *Lack of Decision Making Self-Confidence* reflects insufficient self-assurance in making career-related decisions.

5. *Decision-Making Fear and Anxiety* reflects decisional paralysis resulting from fear and anxiety over making a career decision.

6. *Nonwork Demands* reflect individual conflicts between personal career desires and nonwork (e.g., family) pressures.

7. *Situational Constraints* reflect individual career constraints produced by financial strain, age, and years invested in a given career direction.

In general, the first three sources—lack of self-information and the lack of information on the internal and external work environments—reinforce the discussion in Chapter 4, which stated that an awareness of self and the work environment is an essential requirement in career decision making. In contrast to the information-related sources that could be resolved with increased exploration, the lack of self-confidence and decision-making fear and anxiety may reflect more deep-seated personality dispositions and psychological conditions. Finally, nonwork demands and situational constraints could place limitations on personal career choices and desires and may either impair the setting of a career goal or cause substantial uncertainty or discomfort over a selected goal. Exhibit 5.1 contains a series of items, adapted from a more extensive instrument we developed, that can help you assess where you stand on the seven career indecision sources.[10]

EXHIBIT 5.1   Selected Items for the Seven Sources of Career Indecision

Source of Career Indecision[a]	Illustrative Item[b]
Lack of Self-Information	"I know exactly what I want most from a job (e.g., a lot of money, a great deal of responsibility, travel)."[c]
Lack of Internal Work Information	"I have a good understanding of where my organization is heading in the next five to ten years."[c]
Lack of External Work Information	"I have a good grasp of what career opportunities might exist for me with a different employer."[c]
Lack of Self-Confidence	"I am confident that I can make career decisions that are right for me."[c]
Decision-Making Fear and Anxiety	"The idea of making a career-related decision frightens me."
Nonwork Demands	"Family pressures conflict with the direction that I would like my career to follow."
Situational Constraints	"The number of years I have invested in my current career prevents me from considering other careers that hold more appeal."

NOTES: a. Sources identified in Callanan, G. A., & Greenhaus, J. H. (1990). The career indecision of managers and professionals: Development of a scale and test of a model. *Journal of Vocational Behavior, 37,* 79–103.

b. Items scored on a scale of 1 (Strongly Disagree) to 5 (Strongly Agree).

c. Item is reverse scored.

Types of Career Indecision

Past research on the career decision making of students indicated two forms of career indecision. "Being undecided" was viewed as stemming from limited experience and knowledge, whereas "being indecisive" was seen as reflecting a more permanent inability to make a career decision.[11] The "being undecided" type was later termed developmental indecision, while the "being indecisive" type was termed chronic indecision. In our study of managers and professionals, we also found support for the existence of developmental and chronic indecision.[12] Developmentally undecided employees were younger, had limited knowledge about the internal and external work environments, and experienced extensive nonwork demands. The chronically undecided group was comparatively older than their developmentally undecided counterparts. In addition, they lacked sufficient self-information, had lower self-confidence, displayed more extensive decision-making fear and anxiety, and experienced extensive situational constraints.

Our research also isolated two other types where managers had selected a career goal.[13] Borrowing from the typology developed by Irving Janis and Leon Mann,[14] we were able to isolate a hypervigilant type and a vigilant type of career decidedness. The hypervigilant group had selected a career goal, but their profiles indicated that the decision might have been made with insufficient information and/or was hastily contrived due to pressure and anxiety. On the other hand, the vigilant group had likewise selected a career goal, but their profile showed that the decision was made in a well-informed manner with low levels of stress and anxiety.

Brief examples might help clarify the differences among the four types:

1. Annie is a 35-year-old internal audit manager for a consumer products company located in New York. After nearly 12 years with the firm she is dissatisfied with her present responsibilities and believes her chances for further advancement within the organization are limited. Moreover, the "rat race" of the big city has started to wear on her and her family. Consequently, Annie is not really sure what she wants to do with her career. Annie has taken the Myers-Briggs Type Indicator and other assessment instruments that show she has an entrepreneurial personality. In fact, managing her own business has quite an appeal for Annie. She has also begun to look at a couple of interesting business ventures back in her home state of Mississippi.

2. Sanjay is a 27-year-old sales representative for a paper products company. He has held four different jobs in the six years since he graduated from college with a degree in business administration. Sanjay cannot seem to set goals for himself, and he still is not sure about what type of career he should pursue. Making decisions has always been difficult for Sanjay since he becomes anxious and "tenses up" whenever the need to make a commitment arises. Right now, Sanjay

is unsure of how to go about selecting a longer-term career goal, but he is certain that his current sales position is not for him.

3. Jennifer is 26 and has just completed law school. Her whole family is excited about her future career as a lawyer. Her father, who is an attorney himself, is especially pleased that his daughter has decided to follow in his footsteps. Unfortunately, amid the euphoria and hoopla over her graduation, Jennifer is beginning to think that she may have been prematurely "pushed" into selecting the legal profession as a career. Jennifer's parents put undue pressure on her to enter law school. They were visibly upset when her two older brothers decided not to pursue legal careers, and Jennifer did not wish to disappoint her parents again. Because of her quick selection of law as her vocation, Jennifer never really explored her own interests and values and didn't look at other possible occupations. At present, her life is full of stress since she is concerned about her future happiness as a lawyer.

4. At age 48, Dan is as happy as he has ever been. As a high school math teacher, Dan enjoys the chance to work with young people and he really does like teaching such subjects as algebra and geometry. Although Dan has been teaching for only four years, he is pleased that he made the "tough" decision to get out of his former career as a systems analyst. Dan is certain that his satisfaction with teaching is a function of the painstaking and thorough job he did of selecting it as his career goal. Dan took the time to reexamine his interests and values. He knew he loved to work with numbers and apply logical thinking, but he also liked working with young people. With some exploration, he learned that the local school district had a shortage of qualified math teachers. After discussing his thoughts with his fiancée and receiving her encouragement, Dan decided to try to become a teacher. Once he received his teaching certificate, Dan was set. He hasn't regretted the move.

It should be clear that these four scenarios represent the different types of career indecision. In the first case, Annie could be described as developmentally undecided since she doesn't have a career goal but is actively exploring her interests and opportunities. On the other hand, Sanjay could be considered chronically undecided given his ongoing inability to set career goals and his associated high level of anxiety. In the third case, Jennifer is representative of the hypervigilant type. Her decision to pursue a law career was made prematurely, and she did not consider her own interests, abilities, and talents. She chose to pursue the career that would please her parents, but not herself. Dan represents the vigilant type. His decision to pursue the teaching of math as his career goal was the product of a thorough assessment of his interests and lifestyle preferences, as well as the work environment.

As these examples show, the usefulness and appropriateness of setting a career goal depends on the circumstances. There are times when the selection of a career goal is beneficial (as with Dan), and there are times when it is useless or even harmful. For an individual such as Annie, who lacks sufficient decision-making information, being developmentally undecided is an appropriate state and, as reflected in the case of Jennifer, being prematurely decided is an inappropriate state. Career goals should not be set until the individual is sufficiently aware of self and the environment and is confident that the goal is capable of providing compatibility with personal qualities.

Possible Steps to Becoming Career Decided

As stated in Chapter 4, the key activity that precedes the setting of a career goal is exploration. Individuals should engage in various forms of career exploration to enhance awareness of themselves and their environment. This heightened awareness of self and environment should enable individuals to set realistic career goals that are compatible with their personal qualities and preferred work environment. Certainly, being developmentally undecided is an appropriate condition as long as you are in the process of learning more about yourself and your environment. For those who tend to be chronically undecided, the accumulation of additional information may be helpful, but it might not be enough to allow the selection of a career goal. In the chronic case, individuals must find ways to break the "paralysis" brought on by the high degrees of unproductive fear and anxiety and of situational constraints. Career counseling programs and other activities that reduce debilitating stress and anxiety and improve self-confidence could prove useful in overcoming chronic indecision. Other career planning activities as described in Chapter 4, such as career workshops and the informal sharing of personal feelings and beliefs, could serve to reduce stress and promote exploration behavior and career goal setting. It should be noted that the complete elimination of decision-making anxiety and stress may not be advisable. Some degree of stress and anxiety can in fact facilitate, and provide the incentive for, needed career exploration behavior.

For those who are decided on a career goal, the key consideration is whether the selection was made in a well-informed fashion (the vigilant type), or was conducted in a tense and hasty manner (the hypervigilant type). The premature selection of, and commitment to, an inappropriate career goal could have unfavorable consequences. Our research found that those managers who made a premature selection of a career goal held less favorable work attitudes and experienced more extensive life stress than managers whose career goal selection was more vigilant in nature.[15] Hypervigilant individuals should be encouraged to reexamine their career decisions to assess whether their choices are truly consistent with their abilities, interests, and aspirations.

In summary, the important lesson to be learned from the discussion on career indecision is that the selection of a career goal is not positive or negative per se, but is dependent on the circumstances surrounding the selection. Being undecided about one's career because of a lack of sufficient information (i.e., developmentally undecided) is appropriate. In contrast, being career decided but ignoring one's true interests and talents, could prove to be a source of dissatisfaction for the individual, and could cause unfavorable work outcomes for the employing organization. In an ideal sense, all career decision making should be performed in a "vigilant" fashion, wherein the career goal is selected with substantial knowledge and awareness. In this regard, schools and organizations should strive to offer programs that encourage vigilant career decision making.

IMPLICATIONS OF GOAL SETTING FOR ORGANIZATIONS AND THEIR EMPLOYEES

Employees who set career goals in a vigilant manner—based upon insights into themselves and their alternatives as well as a balanced concern for their present and future—should have the greatest likelihood for productive and satisfying careers.[16] Organizations can promote a vigilant approach to career goal setting in a number of ways.

Facilitate Self-Awareness. Reasonable and appropriate career goals are unlikely to be developed without a foundation of accurate information regarding one's talents, values, interests, and lifestyle preferences. Organizations can promote self-awareness by providing career counseling and sponsoring career planning activities. However, considerable self-insight can also be derived from everyday work experiences within organizations. Effective performance appraisal and feedback systems, education and training activities, temporary assignments, job changes, and an expansion of the current job can all serve as potential learning experiences. Employees can gain from these activities most effectively when they have an opportunity to discuss the insights they have acquired with other knowledgeable people, especially their own manager.

Facilitate an Awareness of the Environment. Extensive information about the environment is necessary to set realistic and appropriate career goals. What rewards are associated with a market research position? How much travel is required for a product manager in this company? What skill areas are most critical for success as a sales manager? What is this company going to look like in 1 to 2 years or in 5 to 10 years?

An organization can promote an awareness of the environment by providing employees with access to key information about alternative jobs in the organization, such as duties, responsibilities, required skills, travel, and time commitment pressures. This requires that the organization itself understand the *behavioral* requirements of different jobs and career fields so that this information can be provided to employees. In addition, the organization should communicate its mission, structure, and culture to employees who are trying to determine the presence of a fit between the organization's needs and their needs.

In today's decentralized environment, it is likely that many employees will move outside their functional areas for their next jobs. Networking—through either formal or informal corporate sponsorship—encourages employees to broaden their horizons with regard to setting future career goals. An alternative is to provide exposure through ad hoc groups or task forces as well as temporary positions or lateral moves. These opportunities provide a flexible approach for employees to learn about other areas and functions of the organization. Such activities have been found to be particularly helpful for women and minorities who might be less likely than white males to have had effective sponsorship.

Encourage Experimentation. Much learning about oneself and the environment comes from active experimentation. People can learn a great deal from trying on new roles. A financial analyst or a salesperson contemplating a move into management should be encouraged to incorporate managerial responsibilities into his or her current job, perhaps through a special assignment or project. Experimentation can also take the form of seeking information from previously unfamiliar sources. Speaking with a counselor about a career dilemma, joining a support group for newly transferred employees, attending a seminar on marketing in the financial services industry, or enrolling in a graduate course or program can all stimulate an employee to think about his or her future from a different perspective.

Respond to Chronic Indecision. Our prior suggestions are based on one rather critical assumption: that the undecided employee simply needs to learn more about himself or herself, the environment, or alternative courses of action—that is, the employee is "developmentally" undecided. Perhaps recent changes in an employee's work situation, family pressures, or career interests triggered a reevaluation of his or her future. Or changes in the individual's personal life (aging and feelings of mortality), work environment (merger or acquisition, change in corporate strategy), or family environment (empty nest, spouse career aspirations) have produced major uncertainties regarding career aims. Career indecision in the face of such changes suggests that an adaptive, developmental process is helpful in achieving career decidedness.

However, as noted earlier, some employees may be indecisive about making a career decision because of an extraordinarily high level of anxiety and stress surrounding the decision-making process. Managers should learn to recognize when indecision about a career goal represents a kind of chronic indecisiveness and paralysis. Observations about prior career moves might be helpful in this respect. In addition, discussions with the employee about his or her career attitudes might reveal a considerable degree of stress about making a career decision. The employee might be reluctant to make any career decision for fear of making a poor one. The employee might claim that more information is needed to make a decision (more testing, more counseling, more course work), when in reality no amount of additional information is likely to move the employee closer to a decision.

We are not suggesting that managers become therapists, but rather that they probe the basis for employees' indecision and recommend appropriate courses of action. For example, since chronically undecided employees tend to be anxious and lack confidence in their decision making, they might benefit from career counseling on a one-to-one basis as a supplement to company-sponsored workshops. Since chronically undecided individuals may also manifest high levels of life stress, a critical aspect of counseling is to determine whether part of the problem involves a need for a more comprehensive form of support, such as financial management skills or stress reduction, before undertaking any career goal setting. In short, simply providing more information to chronically undecided employees may not be enough.

Discourage Career Hypervigilance. Hypervigilant employees tend to make career decisions in a reactive mode without adequate time for reflection, preparation, and thinking through their options and alternatives. Often this results in a decision that is not compatible with the employee's values, talents, and interests, thereby setting up a cycle of dissatisfaction or failure. For such individuals, getting away from everyday pressures and concerns to have proper time to reflect is critical. Effective career management programs that enable these employees to distinguish between the different dimensions of career goals can be particularly helpful. As they reflect on what may be truly fitting choices and goals, some combination of seminars, workshops, computer-based programs, and individual counseling may be especially useful.

Benefits to the Organization. While it might be desirable for employees to set realistic career goals, there has to be some tangible benefit for the organization to promote such activities. One major incentive for an organization to encourage career goal setting is that its employees learn to take responsibility for their careers. A second advantage is that when employees become involved in career goal setting they are likely to become more highly skilled and more useful to the organization.

Moreover, many career goal setting programs include analyses of employees' skills not only by the individuals themselves but by their superiors and/or peers as well. Understanding how others view their strengths and weaknesses further encourages employees to improve, particularly when these views do not threaten their self-concept. Taking stock of one's plans can aid in determining what types of training and development activities are needed. Such activities should be viewed in a positive light as they frequently result in more highly skilled employees. And in the event of a downsizing, the employee has a "skills portfolio" to take along to another job or another organization.

For these reasons, career goal setting is often in the best interest of the employee and the organization. Although there are certainly risks to the individual (e.g., disappointment) and the organization (the potential loss of talented individuals), we would argue that the advantages justify the risks. As with any development program, support from the organization's top management is necessary for success. Of particular importance is the creation of a work climate where individuals feel safe enough to engage in career goal setting. All too often in today's business environment, employees are not willing to openly voice an interest in career goal setting out of a belief that showing an interest in future career plans calls into question their loyalty to their present position and boss. In other cases, senior executives make positive statements about career issues while their managers ignore them in practice.

In our view, it is important for companies and their managers to show a strong commitment to continued employee development through career planning. Even under turbulent conditions, employees should be expected to consider options and alternatives. Often, however, managers believe that while they are encouraged to develop their employees, they themselves are forgotten. Therefore, it is important for organizations to promote career management across the various hierarchical levels of the organization. The best way to ensure this is to incorporate subordinate career growth into each manager's reward system. In light of our previous discussion, the most appropriate criterion to apply is *not* whether the subordinate has set a career goal or is ready for a promotion but whether the subordinate is being encouraged to explore himself or herself and the environment and is being provided with useful feedback, guidance, and support.

Finally, it is important for organizational managers to recognize the need for consistency between the strategic needs of the company on the one hand and the career management practices used by the firm on the other. More precisely, an organization's business strategies and other competitive factors normally will dictate the type and level of individuals who are employed. The career management practices described in this chapter can help fulfill these human resource needs by linking individual aspirations with organizational staffing responsibilities.

Knowledge of individual career goals can also aid senior organizational managers in the critical task of succession planning. Individuals with career goals that fit the demands of top management positions can be targeted and groomed for these posts. Thus, a company can take advantage of the embedded knowledge of its existing personnel by deploying them in areas and in jobs that mesh with individual aspirations in the form of career goals. Without knowing individual differences, organizations are apt to make unwarranted or haphazard job assignments.

In summary, we believe that organizations and their employees can benefit from well-designed and -maintained career management programs. We have articulated how career goals that are the product of a thorough assessment of one's own interests, abilities, and lifestyle preferences, as well as an examination of the work environment, can produce positive work attitudes. We also stated that career goals that are set without benefit of this thorough assessment can be counterproductive. Organizations that implement career management programs to help individuals explore themselves and their work environment can reap rewards in the form of potentially more productive employees and a more efficient matching of employee desires with corporate human resource requirements.

DEVELOPING CAREER STRATEGIES

The concept of the boundaryless career is, in large part, based on the idea that individuals must be adaptable and flexible in the actions they pursue and the changes they make in the management of their careers. It also reflects the notion that the "single" organizational career, with job security taken for granted, is no longer viable.[17] Indeed, recent research has shown that careers are increasingly dominated by mobility between firms rather than within one particular firm. Employees in the United States and other parts of the industrialized world who are just entering the workforce or who are early in their careers are likely to be employed by seven or more employers over their work lives. This fact is not surprising, given that traditional job ladders and career paths have been dismantled at many companies. With this environment, it becomes even more critical for individuals to be proactive in their career management. Specifically, individuals must set career goals and pursue career strategies that give them the greatest chances of personal and professional success.

We define a *career strategy as any behavior, activity, or experience designed to help a person meet career goals.*[18] A career strategy represents a conscious choice by an individual as to the type of investment he or she is willing to make in attempting to reach career objectives. Ideally, people pursue a particular career strategy based on the expectation that it will give them the greatest chances of achieving personal and professional success. Career strategies are activities designed to help a person meet career goals. They involve conscious individual choices as to which human capital investments to make and which to avoid.[19]

Types of Career Strategies

As mentioned in Chapter 3, research suggests that there are seven broad types of career strategies that individuals can use to enhance their chances of career success and fulfillment. The seven strategies include attaining competence in the current job, putting in extended work hours, developing new skills, developing new opportunities at work, attaining a mentor, building one's image and reputation, and engaging in organizational politics. Table 5.2 presents a brief summary of the career strategies.

Attaining competence in the current job is a basic career strategy, given that organizations make promotion decisions, at least in part, on an employee's present performance. In addition, the skills acquired or honed in one job might be essential for performance in another job either with one's current employer or with another organization. The concepts underlying the protean and boundaryless career philosophies make it necessary for individuals to have relevant skills at the times when those skills are required by employers. Focusing on developing abilities in a current job can improve an individual's chances for employability in the future.

Putting in extended hours either at the work site or at home is a popular career strategy, especially in the early career when an employee is proving himself or herself to the company.

TABLE 5.2   Major Career Strategies

I.   Attaining Competence in the Current Job

Meaning: The attempt to perform effectively in one's current job.

II.   Putting in Extended Hours

Meaning: The decision to devote considerable amounts of time, energy, and emotion to one's work role. It is often considered a contributor to competence in the present job. It might also interfere with family and personal life.

III.   Developing New Skills

Meaning: The attempt to acquire or enhance work-related skills and abilities through education, training, and/or job experience. It is intended to help one's performance on one's current job or could be used on a future job.

IV.   Developing New Opportunities at Work

Meaning: Actions designed to have one's interests and aspirations known to others and to become aware of opportunities that are consistent with those aspirations.

V.   Attaining a Mentor

Meaning: Actions designed to seek, establish, and use relationships with a significant other to receive or provide information, guidance, support, and opportunities. Although a major function of the mentoring process is to receive (or give) information, the mentoring relationship goes beyond the mere exchange of information and has a deeper emotional meaning.

VI.   Building One's Image and Reputation

Meaning: The attempt to communicate the appearance of acceptability, success, and/or potential for success. It also can include the acceptance and completion of high-profile assignments that build one's reputation within the organization.

VII.   Engaging in Organizational Politics

Meaning: The attempt to use flattery, conformity, coalition, and trading of favors and influence as a means for attaining desired outcomes. It can include overt and covert actions, such as sabotage and other self-serving behaviors, that raise one's standing in the organization, possibly at the expense of others.

Working beyond normal hours can enhance performance in one's current job and can signify to the organization that one is committed to the job and capable of taking on large volumes of work. This is not to suggest that extended work involvement is always necessary or even useful. We all know of organizations where many employees are present evenings and weekends because it is expected, not necessarily because any real work gets accomplished. Putting in extended work hours can also result in negative consequences over the longer term given that extra work hours during evenings and weekends might impinge on the time a person can spend on family or personal activities.

Developing new skills is a career strategy that involves the acquisition or enhancement of work abilities that either improve performance in the present job or will be required in a subsequent position. Michael Arthur and his colleagues refer to this strategy as "knowing how."[20] They note that skill development can involve formal occupational training as well as experiential learning. Skill development can include such activities as participation in training seminars, degree or nondegree university programs, or attendance at a leadership development workshop. Employees can also develop skills by acquiring additional responsibilities on their current job, by working with an experienced colleague, or by joining occupational associations that sponsor continuing education. In essence, a commitment to skill development and lifelong learning helps ensure that a person's work abilities and knowledge are kept relevant with present work demands (and thereby transferable to other organizations).

Developing new opportunities at work comprises a number of more specific strategies that are designed to increase one's career options. As an example, self-nomination is a frequently observed strategy that involves the willingness to inform superiors of accomplishments, aspirations, and desired assignments. Self-nomination is intended to enhance one's visibility and exposure to those in more senior positions within the organization, which can bring recognition, special assignments, and sponsorship. Another relevant career strategy under this category is networking. In their typology, Arthur and his colleagues refer to this career strategy as "knowing whom."[21] Networking involves the identification of and communication with a group of relevant acquaintances and friends who can provide information, advice, and support regarding career opportunities.

Developing new opportunities at work has traditionally been seen in terms of progress within a specific organization, that is, in terms of intraorganizational mobility. In today's environment, however, with the virtual elimination of the relational psychological contract between employer and employee, this strategy should be viewed more broadly. More precisely, individuals should work on cultivating opportunities both in the internal and in the external labor markets. Depending on one's career stage, actively seeking out opportunities in the external labor market can prove beneficial, especially in terms of compensation.[22]

Attaining a mentor as a career strategy has received considerable attention in recent years. Mentoring can be defined as relationships between junior and senior colleagues, or between peers, that provide various developmental functions.[23] The mentoring role can be filled by a variety of individuals, not by just one person. A mentor can provide coaching, friendship, sponsorship, and role modeling to the younger, less experienced protégé. In the process, the mentor can satisfy his or her need to have a lasting influence on another person's life. Frequently viewed as a career strategy for both mentor and protégé, the mentoring relationship will be examined more closely in Chapter 7.

Building one's image and reputation is a career strategy in which the individual attempts to convey an appearance of success and suitability. For example, being married, participating in community activities, and dressing properly can provide a positive public image that can bring career rewards. While this type of strategy is not necessarily important in all or most situations, past research has found that significant numbers of employees make the investment in image building because of the perceived high value to career advancement.[24] Building one's work reputation is an important strategy because it is presumed that an individual's past experiences and accomplishments bode well for future performance. Thus, a focus on building a strong work reputation can improve a person's employability regardless of the employer.[25] One can build a positive reputation by accomplishing such tasks as engineering a turnaround of an unfavorable work situation or by showing leadership on a particular assignment.

Related to the strategy of building one's image and reputation is the concept of impression management. Impression management is the process by which people attempt to influence the images that others have of them and involves many strategies that individuals use in trying to be seen in a certain way or to create a particular impression in others' minds.[26] It reflects the basic human motive to be viewed favorably (and to avoid being viewed unfavorably) by others. The need to manage impressions is especially high when the impression one makes is critical for attaining career outcomes, and the more people want certain outcomes the more likely they are to manage impressions in an effort to obtain them.[27] For example, job applicants and those seeking promotions would typically engage in impression management activities as a career strategy to achieve an operational career goal. Although a number of impression management behaviors have been identified by various researchers, William Turnley and Mark Bolino cite the following five strategies as the ones that are most often used in terms of assertive actions:[28]

1. *Ingratiation,* where individuals seek to be viewed as likable by doing favors for others, agreeing with others, or flattering others

2. *Exemplification,* where people seek to be viewed as dedicated by being a good role model and going beyond the call of duty

3. *Intimidation,* where individuals seek to appear dangerous by making threats or signaling their power to punish or create pain and discomfort

4. *Self-promotion,* where individuals hope to be seen as competent by playing up their abilities and accomplishments

5. *Supplication,* where people seek to be viewed as needy or in need of assistance by "playing dumb" or advertising their shortcomings and weaknesses

Another concept related to the strategy of building one's image and reputation is the development of social capital. Social capital is defined as the potential resources derived from an individual's interpersonal relationships and the valued resources available from the within the organization of that network of relationships.[29] The establishment of social capital is a way to gain valuable information about an organization or a job opening that otherwise might not be readily available, create trust between members in the social network, raise one's status relative to peers, and open opportunities for advancement or a job shift. Building and then tapping into social capital can provide a number of positive career outcomes and allow for the fulfillment of career goals. Of course, relationships in the social network need to be nurtured in order to create trust and open communication between the members. In this sense, individuals need to pay attention to and invest in the social connections, both inside and outside of the work organization, that can lead to the creation of social capital.

Engaging in organizational politics includes activities that also fall under the tactic of impression management as described previously. Organizational politics cover such diverse activities as agreeing with or flattering one's supervisor, advocating company practices, not complaining about rules or regulations, and forming alliances or coalitions with others in the organization. More extreme and often personally unacceptable political practices can include sabotaging another person's work or spreading rumors about a colleague. In many organizations, becoming involved in organizational politics and engaging in impression management activities are career strategies that are necessary for career advancement, although certain behaviors might be viewed as unethical or reprehensible. Nonetheless, regardless of the personal acceptability, engaging in organizational politics is a career strategy that is used regularly.

Research on the effectiveness of various career strategies suggests that developing a variety of skills and having a diverse number of work experiences significantly improves one's chances of meeting career goals and attaining career success. Other research has found that the use of such strategies as self-nomination and networking contribute to an individual's career success. The usefulness of a particular career strategy is dependent on a number of factors, including the nature of the job, the type of the industry, and the culture and norms of the particular organization. Indeed, a career strategy that might be successful in one case, might not work in another.

Guidelines for the Development of Career Strategies

Overall, the research on career strategies seems to suggest the following:

1. There is no "one best" strategy that is equally effective in all situations.

2. The effectiveness of a particular strategy depends on the nature of the career goal. A person striving to reach the presidency of an organization, for example, is likely to benefit from different strategies than one whose goal is to become an engineering project manager.

3. The effectiveness of a particular strategy depends on the organization's norms and values. For example, some organizations may encourage secrecy and political machinations, whereas others may reward openness and collaboration.

4. Individuals should not limit themselves to one single strategy but should engage in a variety of strategic behaviors.

5. Strategies should be used not only to reach a career goal but also to test one's interest and commitment to a goal. For example, the strategy of developing new skills by taking a graduate course in cost accounting might indicate to the individual that a goal of attaining a management position in financial management is (or is not) appropriate depending on how the individual reacts to the course. In this way, planning can be viewed as a process of learning more about ourselves and the environment.

6. Career strategies should reflect steps to be taken, as well as areas to be avoided. Individuals should pursue "positive" career strategies that lead to career success, while avoiding "negative" or inappropriate strategies that could cause career failure.

It is impossible (and undesirable) to specify in advance each and every component of a career strategy. An essential part of the career management process is "learning by doing." As a person begins to develop and implement a strategy, additional strategic behaviors may become more obvious than they were before the process began. In this section, we propose a five-step process for developing a set of career strategies.

1. Reexamine your long-term goals. Make sure you understand what the goals represent in terms of desired activities, rewards, and lifestyle (conceptual goal) and why the particular occupation or job (operational goal) is appropriate for meeting the conceptual goal.

2. Identify behaviors, activities, and experiences that will help you reach long-term goals. Two questions need to be raised regarding each element of a career strategy: Will it help you attain your goals? Regardless of its usefulness, do you want to engage in that behavior?

One first needs to estimate the potential usefulness of a set of activities. The most useful sources of information are discussion and observation. Conversations with others in the organization, for example, may provide helpful information and dispel myths about certain strategies (e.g., that everyone must follow the same career path to a particular job).

Usually, a person can profit the most from conversations with others who have substantial experience in the organization, such as a superior or a more established colleague. Since there can be an element of rivalry between superior and subordinate that prevents information sharing in some circumstances, a mentor is sometimes the more appropriate source of information about the potential usefulness of certain career strategies. In fact, the establishment of a mentor relationship is itself a career strategy. Nonetheless, formal feedback from superiors through such activities as performance appraisal and participative goal setting can serve to identify career strategies and developmental activities.

Consider as an example the case of Beth, a 28-year-old manager in the accounting department of a medium-sized insurance company. At the age of 22, Beth received a bachelor's degree in accounting from a large state university. After working two years in the billing department of a hospital, Beth accepted an accounting analyst position with the insurance company. In her four years there, she advanced quickly, assuming the position of manager at a comparatively young age. She enjoys working at the insurance company, and her longer-term goal is to be a vice president by age 35. During her annual performance review Beth asked her supervisor, the officer in charge of the department, what actions she could take to facilitate further advancement. Her supervisor willingly offered several ideas. First, he told her that the company normally filled officer positions with employees who had earned an MBA. In addition, the supervisor stated that officers generally would have to show competence in a variety of skills and should have a fairly broad range of experience in other departments within the organization. Finally, he stated that working on assignments that would give her exposure to the firm's senior management would help her chances for promotion. With this information in hand, Beth set about to develop specific career strategies, including enrollment in an MBA program, monitoring the company's job postings to increase awareness of opportunities in other departments, and requesting high-profile assignments that would give her a chance to work with senior management.

The second issue involves a person's decision to engage in a strategic behavior regardless of its apparent usefulness. Some behaviors may help attain one element of a career goal but interfere with the attainment of other elements. For example, frequent job changes and accompanying relocations may enable a person to acquire useful experiences and skills but may interfere substantially with family life. Therefore, the effectiveness of a particular career strategy must be judged in a holistic sense.

Moreover, certain strategies may be useful but personally distasteful. Forming political alliances, making oneself look good at the expense of a colleague, and loyally supporting an organization's questionable practices may violate ethical and/or religious values. A career strategy cannot be viewed in simply utilitarian terms.

One should emerge from this process with a relatively small list of critical and acceptable strategic plans, and with statements of purpose and approximate time frames if possible. Table 5.3 presents a statement of hypothetical career strategies for a person seeking advancement in a Human Resources department.

3. Examine short-term goals. In particular, examine the fit between short-term goals and long-term goals. In light of long-term career strategies, do your short-term goals still appear instrumental to the attainment of your long-term ones? If not, you may want to revise your short-term goals to improve the fit.

4. Identify behaviors, activities, and experiences that will help you attain the short-term goals. As with step 2, potential usefulness and personal acceptability should be twin criteria by which a strategy is evaluated. Develop a small list of critical and acceptable strategic plans for accomplishing short-term goals.

TABLE 5.3 Statement of Career Strategies for an Assistant Human Resources Manager

Strategies to Achieve Long-Term Goal of Director of Corporate Human Resources		
Activity	Purpose	Time Frame
Perform effectively on current job	To remain productive, grow on job	Ongoing
Receive promotion to Manager of Human Resources	To gain competence, experience, and visibility in company	2–3 years
Receive MBA degree with specialization in human resources	To gain specialized knowledge and credibility	3–4 years
Strategies to Achieve Short-Term Goal of Manager of Human Resources		
Activity	Purpose	Time Frame
Perform effectively on current job	To remain promotable, grow on job	Ongoing
Take beginning courses in MBA program	To gain greater knowledge of labor relations	0–6 months
Discuss career goals with supervisor	To make supervisor aware of career aspirations, obtain feedback and suggestions	0–6 months
Obtain information on possible Human Resources Manager opening in company	To assess likelihood of achieving short-term goal	0–6 months
Contact search firm	To assess likelihood of achieving short-term goal in another company	6–12 months
Attempt to initiate quality of work–life program in conjunction with current Human Resources Manager and operations	To enhance productivity, develop relationships with line management, gain experience in quality of work life	1–2 years

5. Combine the lists of strategies for short-term and long-term goals. It is likely that strategies designed to attain both types of goals are particularly critical and should remain at the top of the combined list. Keep the list manageable by ordering the strategic activities in a logical time sequence.

The planning and implementation of a career strategy is not nearly as mechanical as this five-step process might suggest. First, the five steps overlap somewhat in time. It is artificial to separate discussions about goals, long-term strategies, and short-term strategies. Second, strategies cannot always be specified in advance. One may have to implement one part of a strategy to determine the next step. The important outcome of this process is an appreciation of how different strategies relate back to your significant goals. The essential ingredient in this process is openness to information and willingness to reexamine and possibly revise goals and/or strategies; in short, to monitor and appraise your career.

Learning Exercise 6 appears in the Appendix on p. 154. It provides an opportunity to practice developing a career strategy. Although you may examine Exercise 6 at this time, it is recommended that you finish reading Chapter 5 before beginning the exercise.

CAREER APPRAISAL

If career management is to be a flexible, adaptive process, there must be some way for people to adjust to new information about themselves and/or the environment. Career appraisal serves this function. We define career appraisal as *the process by which career-related feedback is gathered and used.*

The feedback obtained through career appraisal has two specific functions. First, it can test the appropriateness of a particular career strategy. Is the strategy effectively moving a person closer to his or her goals? Second, feedback can test the appropriateness of a goal itself. Is the career goal still relevant and attainable?

Consider the situation of a 36-year-old high school history teacher who has become increasingly bored with his job. After extensive self-assessment, he has concluded that he should seek work in an educational setting that is more varied than his current position, that offers the opportunity for greater financial rewards, and that takes advantage of his skills in working with people on an individual basis (the conceptual goal). After reading materials on careers in education and talking with a number of people in the field, his conceptual goal is translated into a specific operational goal: he intends to move into secondary school administration within the next three years.

The teacher's strategy was two-pronged. First, he applied for admission to a part-time master's program in educational administration at the local university. Completion of the graduate program would enable him to be certified in administration and eligible for future openings in administrative positions. Second, he obtained permission to represent his school at local and state conferences and parent–teacher organization activities. The latter strategy was designed to give him a broader perspective on his school's operations. Actually, his strategy was developed as much to test his interests and talents in administration as to prepare him for his future career shift.

The teacher's graduate school experiences were enlightening. After one semester, he realized he was less interested in administering a school (he hated the courses in budgeting, personnel, and curriculum development) than in helping kids on an intensive one-on-one basis. Several psychology electives in the second semester reinforced his recent discovery. As a result of these revelations, he has applied to a doctoral program in school psychology.

As the teacher's experiences indicate, career appraisal reflects the problem-solving nature of career management. With an effective appraisal process, career management becomes a learning experience in which one looks for signs that either confirm or disconfirm prior decisions. These signs are pieces of information that close the career management cycle by re-instigating career exploration. The teacher's disillusionment with his initial master's program was the result of a strategic experience that heightened his awareness of his own interests as well as the day-by-day duties of a school administrator. It was this awareness, gained through strategy-based exploration, which enabled him to revise his goal in a more suitable direction.

Types and Sources of Information Derived From Career Appraisal

An individual open to his or her environment can acquire a great deal of information relevant to goals and strategies. Although information cannot be pigeonholed so neatly, career-related feedback can conveniently be classified in terms of the following:

1. *The Conceptual Goal.* What has the individual learned about values, interests, talents, and desired lifestyle? Is this information consistent or inconsistent with the person's conceptual goal? For example, the history teacher's strategic experiences essentially reinforced his conceptual goal of greater variety, opportunities for more money, and more individualized work with other people.

2. *The Operational Goal.* What has the individual learned about the appropriateness of the operational goal? Is a match still possible between the conceptual goal and the operational goal? Put another way, is it still believed that the targeted job is compatible with the conceptual goal? Note that the history teacher's most significant conclusion was that a career in school administration would not necessarily meet his values and interests.

3. *Strategy.* What has the individual learned about the appropriateness of the strategy? Is it working? Does the individual experience a sense of progress toward the goal? If the goal involves gaining additional competencies in the current job, has it been reflected in favorable performance appraisals? If the career goal involves a different job, does the organization still view the person as a viable candidate for the job? In the teacher's case, he realized that although his strategy was appropriate for his initial goal, it would have to be revised if he were to pursue a career in psychology. His application to a doctoral program in psychology was the first step of this revised strategy.

Feedback regarding goals and strategies can come from a variety of sources. One source consists of social interactions with other people who have either observed the person's behavior or undergone similar experiences themselves. Supervisors, subordinates, mentors, clients, family members, friends, and acquaintances would fall into this category.

A second source of feedback resides in observing the work and nonwork environments. A salesperson losing three consecutive sales can gain insights into his or her job performance. Production rates, quotas reached, and patents established can all provide useful information. So can the observation that five of your colleagues (but not you) have received recent promotions. The observation of an improved or deteriorated family life can also be a significant environmental cue.

People can also serve as their own source of feedback. Judgments about one's own performance can be independent of what other people in the environment can communicate.

Guidelines for Effective Career Appraisal

Successful career appraisal requires the individual to be vigilant in detecting as early as possible when a strategy is or is not working as expected. This early warning orientation is likely to be more helpful than simply carrying a strategy to completion before examining its usefulness. The ongoing feedback effort suggested in the career management model requires a more or less consistent monitoring of activities and their consequences.

Ongoing career appraisal can be aided by considering the following guidelines:

1. The most basic principle, and perhaps the most difficult to follow, is the willingness to see the world clearly and to make revisions in goals and strategies when appropriate. An "escalation effect" can occur when people persist in a course of action despite its lack of success. People are sometimes willing to continue their commitment to a "losing cause" to justify to themselves and others that their prior decision was sound. This practice is inconsistent with effective career management, which requires people to incorporate new data and revise prior decisions when necessary. Therefore, we suggest the following:

    • Be honest with yourself. If things are not working well, seriously consider the possibility that either your prior decisions were faulty or circumstances have changed.

    • Be less concerned with having to justify your prior decisions to others.

    • Be willing to appear and perhaps be inconsistent at times. Although persistence and consistency of action are generally valued in our society, they can be dysfunctional if carried to the extreme.

2. Use your career strategies to provide benchmarks of accomplishments. Statements of strategies should include purposes and desired outcomes. Test the usefulness of the strategies against these specific benchmarks. Usually, strategies are neither completely appropriate nor totally useless. The establishment of benchmarks can help identify specific strengths and weaknesses of a particular strategy.

3. Strategies are as much learning opportunities as they are vehicles for accomplishment. Periodically review the appropriateness of career goals in light of any new information you have acquired. Studies of executives have shown that successful managers are able to learn from their experiences and make necessary adjustments in their career goals and strategies.

4. If you are employed, structure your interactions with your supervisor to acquire desired information. Come into a performance appraisal meeting with your own agenda to supplement (not replace) your supervisor's. What can you learn from your manager about your current performance, your strengths and weaknesses, and the organization's needs that will help you appraise your goals and strategies? What should your manager know about your aspirations that will help him or her provide useful feedback?

5. Share experiences and feelings with trustworthy people. Frank discussions among peers can be beneficial to all parties. First, others may see parts of you that are hidden to yourself. Second, verbally articulating goals, desires, reservations, and strategies may help clarify your own feelings. Third, others may be willing to share their own successes, failures, and revelations that bear on your circumstances.

   In effect, try to form a network that provides mutual feedback, guidance, support, and stimulation. In doing this, choose colleagues with whom you can communicate freely. Since it is often difficult to reveal sensitive career matters, the members of the network need to build trust and openness, a climate that takes time and patience to develop. Whether such a network is offered and sanctioned by the organization or whether it takes place informally is less important than the members' willingness to share and help each other.

6. Seek feedback from nonwork sources. Work and nonwork lives, as we have repeatedly argued, affect one another. Not only do work decisions affect family lives, but family situations (e.g., spouse's career needs) can affect work lives. For example, one part of a person's career strategy might be to demonstrate competence and loyalty by working extraordinarily long hours. It might initially have been assumed that these work hours would not adversely affect family

relationships. After some time, however, it is necessary to examine the accuracy of that assumption. Since a person can easily misperceive a family's feelings and attitudes, candid sharing of information is often necessary to balance work and nonwork activities.

CAREER MANAGEMENT: A BLEND OF FORMAL AND INFORMAL ACTIVITIES

It might appear that the career management process is highly structured and formal. There are group sessions to attend, autobiographies to write, goals to list, and exploratory interviews to conduct. Must it require an endless stream of seminars and forms? Career management does have its structured side. Formal programs include vocational counseling and/or testing, career planning seminars or workshops, and self-administered career planning exercises. Of course, many programs combine these activities in various ways.

Career management activities, however, need not always be formally organized, structured programs. Indeed, any activity that is pursued to develop or act upon career-related information is a form of career management. For example, one can learn about one's interests and strengths through course work (how many pre-med students switch majors after the first course in organic chemistry?); part-time or full-time work experiences; conversations with colleagues, family members, and friends; or conscious introspection and reflection.

Since career management is an ongoing process, informal activities are probably more potent in the long run. It is not feasible (or even desirable) to buy another workbook or join another seminar every time you face a significant career decision. What you need to learn are the skills for translating your daily experiences into learning opportunities. A formal program can frequently provide these analytical skills.

As shown in Table 5.4, career theorists suggest three types of reassessment activities that vary in formality and intensity. Perhaps it is easy to see the usefulness of a year-end assessment of accomplished and unaccomplished goals and satisfying and dissatisfying experiences. It may be less obvious, but periodic reassessments can also be useful, since they roughly coincide with the time frames for short-term and long-term goals, respectively.

But the real importance of career management lies in a way of thinking. The core of effective career management is a mental set, an awareness of one's own concerns as well as environmental opportunities and constraints, an alertness to changes in self and environment, and a willingness to make conscious decisions and plans to revise them accordingly. This philosophy of active career management should serve as a foundation for lifelong participation in formal and informal activities.

TABLE 5.4   Periodic Career Management Activities

Activity	Intensity	Frequency	Sources of Input and Help
General evaluation of year's performance and of satisfaction with various aspects of life Any problems?	1–2 day's worth of work	Once a year	Organization-initiated formal performance appraisal Conversations with important people in your life
Analysis of changes in you and your opportunities; are changes needed?	Up to one week's worth of work, at one time or spread out over a few months	Every 3–4 years	Three- to 7-day career planning seminars Conversations with important people in your life
Major reassessment of self and opportunities	Of the magnitude described in this book	Once every 7–10 years	Assessment centers Career counselors Three- to 4-month university programs Conversations with important people in your life

SOURCE: From Clawson, J. G., Kotter, J. P., Faux, V. A., & McArthur, C. C. (1992). *Self-assessment and career development* (p. 425). Englewood Cliffs, NJ: Prentice Hall.

SUMMARY

Career exploration paves the way for the establishment of career goals. A career goal should not focus exclusively on a specific job or position but should be conceived more broadly in terms of desired work experiences. A career goal should also (a) focus on the intrinsic enjoyment derived from work experiences, (b) include total lifestyle concerns, (c) take into account one's current job as a source of satisfaction and growth, (d) be sufficiently challenging and flexible, and (e) be capable of meeting one's own needs and values, not other people's expectations. A general procedure was outlined for establishing career goals, and learning exercises are provided to practice this procedure.

Career indecision was defined as the inability to select a career goal, or subsequently to experience significant uncertainty or discomfort over a selected goal. A variety of factors can cause career indecision, including insufficient self-awareness, a lack of information on the internal and external work environments, low self-confidence, decisional fear and anxiety, nonwork demands, and situational constraints. Different types of career indecision and decidedness have been observed, indicating that the appropriateness of being undecided or decided is a function of the underlying circumstances. Individuals should strive to achieve vigilance in their career decision making, such that their career goals are selected confidently and patiently, and are based on sufficient knowledge of self and the work environment.

Career strategies are actions designed to help individuals attain their career goals. The development of a career strategy is itself a learning experience that encourages individuals to reexamine their career goals and identify key behaviors, activities, and experiences that can help them reach their goals. It is helpful to specify the purpose of each part of a career strategy and an approximate time frame for accomplishment. Observation as well as conversation with peers, managers, and other knowledgeable people can help people devise reasonable plans. A learning exercise is provided to practice career strategy development.

However reasonable a career strategy may appear, it is essential to monitor and appraise its effectiveness. As a strategy is implemented, the individual should ask whether the initial goal still makes sense and whether the strategy still appears capable of helping in the achievement of the established goal. Individuals should be willing to revise goals and strategies when necessary.

Career management is a blend of formal and informal activities that should be pursued throughout one's working life. Periodic reappraisals of career accomplishments and aspirations are useful. The heart of active career management is a willingness to assume responsibility for one's career, take the necessary steps to influence the course of one's career, and make revisions in plans and strategies when appropriate.

Now that you have completed reading Chapter 5, it is time to begin Learning Exercises 5 and 6, which can be found in the Appendix on p. 149.

ASSIGNMENT[30]

Think about where you will be in your career and your life five years into the future. Create a list of the jobs that you think you will have, the additional skills you might develop, and the further education you will pursue. Using this list, prepare a résumé for yourself that reflects where you believe you will be in five years. Once you have prepared the résumé, share it with someone in your family and with a close friend. Ask them for their insight as to whether the résumé is an accurate portrayal of where they think you will be in five years. If their opinion is different from yours, can you determine why? How might this information factor into your present and future career decision making?

DISCUSSION QUESTIONS

1. Why is it not advisable to focus primarily (or strictly) on the operational/instrumental qualities of a career goal?

2. Career goal setting as described in this chapter emphasizes rational analysis of conceptual and operational goals. Should emotions and "gut-level feelings" also play a role in goal setting? Why do you feel that way?

(Continued)

(Continued)

3. Have your career decisions and aspirations been based primarily on your own needs and values, or have you been heavily influenced by other people's hopes and expectations for you? What can you do to ensure that future career decisions are guided by goals that are personally meaningful to you?

4. Why can career goals easily become rigid and inflexible? Have you ever continued to pursue a goal that no longer makes sense? Why? Why are inflexible goals inconsistent with the model of career management presented in this book?

5. Do you think that you are presently experiencing career indecision? If you are, what do you see as the primary cause(s)? If you are career decided, do you consider yourself vigilant or hypervigilant? Why?

6. Although some strategies may help you achieve your career goals, they may be unacceptable to you on other grounds. What factors should be taken into account when judging the personal acceptability of a career strategy? Have you (or someone you know or have read about) pursued, avoided, or abandoned a career strategy that was personally unacceptable? What were the consequences of this decision?

7. Why is career appraisal such an important part of the career management process? Do you think that career appraisal inevitably leads to a change in career strategies or goals? Why or why not?

CHAPTER 5 CASE

Kimberly the Graduating College Student

Kimberly was starting to get worried. In less than two months she would be graduating from college and she wasn't even close to finding a full-time job for after graduation. The problem was that Kimberly didn't really know what job or company would be right for her. She had developed a résumé and a standard cover letter, but what good were they when she had no idea where to send them? She was really questioning her decision to major in business management. As her advisor had told her, a degree in management didn't really qualify her for any specific position. She envied her friends who majored in accounting. They all seemed to know exactly what jobs they wanted and for what companies they wanted to work—in fact, many of them already had jobs lined up.

Kimberly had gone to a few of the on-campus interviews that were hosted by the university's Career Center, but most of the companies were looking for financial sales professionals and she didn't think that she had the aggressive personality that these companies wanted. It wasn't as if she didn't have "people" skills, but the high pressure world of financial sales was just not right for here. With 18 credits in her final semester, Kimberly was finding it difficult to devote time to her job search and to start looking into opportunities for interviews off campus.

Kimberly was a solid B student who did much better in her junior and senior years than she did early in her college studies. She really liked her management courses, especially the ones dealing with individual behavior and leadership. She had also taken a course in industrial and organizational psychology that she found interesting. In the back of her mind, Kimberly even thought about switching majors to psychology and perhaps pursuing a career in that field. One thing she knew was that she didn't want a job where she had to deal with numbers—she had really struggled with her math and statistics courses and she wouldn't be happy in that type of job. She also wanted to find a job close to where she grew up. She really valued the relationships she had with her family and friends and would never want to take a job that would force her to move to another geographic area. One reason she chose to go to the local state university was so she could continue to live at home and commute to school.

For the last three years Kimberly had worked as a waitress at a chain restaurant located near the campus. About a year ago she had been promoted to an assistant manager and given responsibility for running the restaurant during her scheduled shifts. The job was demanding, but it had given her firsthand management training. Kimberly had done so well in the assistant manager's position that the chain offered her a full-time position upon her graduation. Once she graduated, the company would send her for training and then would assign her to a full-time management position at a restaurant in the area. They also had a nice benefits package, including full tuition reimbursement for graduate courses. Kimberly thought that she might want to get an MBA sometime in the next few years and would want to work for a company that paid for graduate coursework.

Although she liked working at the restaurant and the management responsibilities that came with it, Kimberly had never seen it as a "career-oriented" or professional job—it was just something she did to earn money to pay for her college expenses. Besides, her parents were expecting her to get a job with a major corporation so that she could get on the fast track to advancement. They probably wouldn't be too thrilled with their daughter taking a job as a restaurant manager, especially after the thousands of dollars they had invested in her education. But Kimberly wasn't convinced that a job with a big corporation would be right for her either. She dreaded the thought of ending up in "cube world" for several years as she tried to climb the corporate ladder. Kimberly had never been the type of person who could "sit still" for long periods of time; she needed to be on the move. That is why she thrived in the fast-paced environment of the restaurant.

Kimberly was in a quandary over where to turn for advice. She didn't think her family would be of much help, and most of her friends were in the same boat as she was. The university's Career Center was good at coordinating job interviews, but they didn't seem that interested in working with individual students. She tried to think of family friends who might be able to set her up with an interview at a company in the area, but she was coming up empty. Kimberly knew she needed some guidance, and soon. The queasy feeling she got in her stomach when she thought about her future was not going away until she was set on her career choice.

(Continued)

(Continued)

Case Analysis Questions

1. Do you think that Kimberly is experiencing career indecision? Why or why not? Based on the definitions and descriptions of the four subtypes of career indecision and career decidedness, what category do you think best describes her?

2. Do you think Kimberly has any career goals at this point? If you think she does, what are her goals?

3. Do you think Kimberly has begun formulating any career strategies? If you think she has, what are her strategies?

4. Do you think Kimberly has done enough self- or environmental exploration to make informed career decisions? What other information about herself or the work environment should she be seeking at this point in her college career? To whom (or where) could she go to get help and advice on her career options?

5. If Kimberly sought your help, what advice would you give her in terms of the management of her career?

Appendix

Learning Exercises 5 and 6

LEARNING EXERCISE 5. GOAL SETTING

So far, you have developed a summary of your preferred work environment (PWE) (Learning Exercise 3) and have begun to explore the relevant work environment (Learning Exercise 4). In Learning Exercise 5, you will practice the development of career goals. Before you begin, reread the discussion of career goal setting in this chapter. Remember that your long-term goal need not be very precise at this time. Simply be as specific as you can.

The first step is to develop a long-term (five to seven years) conceptual goal. In formulating it, try to address all of the significant elements of your PWE. List the elements of your long-term conceptual goal below and consult Learning Exercise 3 to verify that all of the important elements of your PWE are incorporated in the long-term conceptual goal.

Elements of the Long-Term Conceptual Goal

1.

2.

3.

4.

5.

6.

The next step is to convert the long-term conceptual goal listed above into long-term operational goals. (See Table 5.1 for an example.) First, in the space below, list (from the preceding section) all of the elements of the long-term conceptual goal. Then choose two operational goals (occupations or specific job positions) in which you think you might be interested. Identify them in the space provided.

Significant Element of Long-Term Conceptual Goal	Long-Term Operational Goal	
	A	B

Next, list all of the positives (advantages) and negatives (disadvantages) you can think of regarding the operational goals you have identified.

Long-Term Operational Goal A

Positives

1.

2.

3.

4.

5.

6.

Negatives

1.

2.

3.

4.

5.

6.

Long-Term Operational Goal B

Positives

1.

2.

3.

4.

5.

6.

Negatives

1.

2.

3.

4.

5.

6.

If you are still not sure which (or if either) operational goal is appropriate for you, do not be concerned. The important thing is that you are thinking about your long-term future and have identified goals for further thought and action.

The next step is to identify a short-term (one to three years) conceptual goal. Reexamine the summary of your PWE as well as your long-term conceptual and operational goal analyses. To formulate a short-term conceptual goal, answer the following question: What type of work, educational, and other experiences and responsibilities would help prepare you to attain the long-term conceptual and operational goals? List the elements of your short-term conceptual goal below.

Elements of the Short-Term Conceptual Goal

1.

2.

3.

4.

5.

6.

Now, convert your short-term conceptual goal into operational goals. As before, list all significant elements of your short-term conceptual goal, and choose two alternative short-term operational goals.

Short-Term Operational Goal A

Positives

1.

2.

3.

4.

5.

6.

Negatives

1.

2.

3.

4.

5.

6.

Short-Term Operational Goal B

Positives

1.

2.

3.

4.

5.

6.

Negatives

1.

2.

3.

4.

5.

6.

If you are still not sure which short-term operational goal is more appropriate for you, it may be necessary to examine one or both goals in more detail. That is, part of your career strategy would include plans for additional data gathering.

LEARNING EXERCISE 6. CAREER STRATEGY DEVELOPMENT

In this exercise, you will develop strategies to help you attain your stated career goals. Reread the guidelines for the development of career strategies in this chapter and reexamine Tables 5.2 and 5.3 for illustrations of career strategies. Then, follow the five-step process described in this chapter and enter the relevant information below.

Strategy to Achieve Long-Term Goal (Goal = _____)

Activity	Purpose	Time Frame

Strategy to Achieve Short-Term Goal (Goal = _____)

Activity	Purpose	Time Frame

Now, combine the lists of strategies for the short-term and long-term goals. Keep the final list manageable by ordering the strategic activities in a logical time sequence. What should evolve from this activity is an overall plan of action—what you will be doing, why, and when. Describe this plan below.

_____

_____

PART II

Stages of Career Development

Occupational and Organizational Choice

This chapter examines two critical steps in the career management process. The first part of the chapter discusses several different views on the occupational choice process, primarily focusing on the ways in which people go about the task of finding an occupation. After reviewing the theory and research on occupational choice, we then examine several obstacles to the occupational choice process, and we offer recommendations for improving the process. Once an occupational field is selected, the next step is finding a job. Thus, the second part of the chapter discusses organizational entry, or the manner in which job seekers assess and choose prospective employers, and vice versa. This discussion of organizational entry explains the process by which individuals cross the boundary from outside to inside an organization; it reflects the movement into such entities as businesses, schools, or the armed forces.[1] The organizational entry process consists of two simultaneous activities. On one hand, individuals assess organizations to determine which one is most likely to meet their career needs and values. On the other hand, organizations assess candidates' qualifications so they can select those with the highest likelihood of succeeding in the firm. Just as candidates make decisions about organizations, organizations make decisions about job candidates.

OCCUPATIONAL CHOICE

Take a moment to consider the following four scenarios:

- Jessica is a 22-year-old woman who has just accepted her first full-time position upon graduation from college. As a newly hired junior accountant at an industrial products company, Jessica is finally about to embark on her career. She is hopeful that her college degree in accounting and her summer internship jobs have prepared her well for this new position.

- Tom is a 34-year-old commercial lending officer for a large bank who has just tendered his resignation after 11 years with the firm. Tom determined that his career in banking, while thus far financially rewarding, wasn't turning out the way he expected. In Tom's view, the bureaucracy of the bank imposed needless constraints and restrictions, and its overly cautious approach to lending went against his entrepreneurial spirit. Moreover, with the spate of mergers in the banking industry, Tom wasn't sure about his prospects for keeping his job in the future. Consequently, Tom adjusted his career goals and has accepted a new job as a sales representative for a small pharmaceutical company.

- Wilma is a 46-year-old woman whose youngest child just started high school. After some hesitation, Wilma has decided to re-enter the workforce full-time. While she wasn't sure what job she should pursue, Wilma was certain she wanted to work in an environment where she could demonstrate her computer skills. After taking computer certification classes, she began her job search. Two months later, Wilma landed a position as a web master for a small company.

- Antonio is a 58-year-old man who was told three months ago that his job as a production supervisor at a specialty chemical company was being eliminated in a cost-cutting move. Working with the outplacement firm that his former company provided, Antonio assessed what he wanted to do with the rest of his career until he would retire in 10 years or so. After considering all of his options, Antonio accepted a position as head of plant operations at a local hospital.

What these cases represent are four distinct examples of people choosing occupations and specific jobs. While it is generally accepted that occupational choice is a key activity in the early phases of career development, these examples show that the dynamics of occupational selection can be relevant at each career stage. The experiences of Jessica, Tom, Wilma, and Antonio illustrate that the choice of an appropriate occupation (either initially or as a career change) is a pivotal task in the career management process, one that can take place, really, at any point in one's life.

Are you in the process of selecting an occupation? If you are, are you confident that you will make the right decision, or do frequent doubts enter your mind? Do you know where to turn for information and insight? Have you thought about how to select an occupation from among competing alternatives?

THEORIES OF OCCUPATIONAL CHOICE

An occupation is a group of similar jobs found in several establishments.[2] This definition distinguishes a specific job in a particular organization (e.g., a marketing research analyst at Procter & Gamble) from the broader notion of an occupation (marketing research). Therefore, we can think of such diverse occupations as accounting, pharmacy, computer engineering, and the ministry, each of which has a somewhat unique set of requirements and rewards.

A comprehensive review of the theories of occupational choice is beyond the scope of this book and is available elsewhere.[3] Instead, we present four significant themes that can help us understand the manner in which people make occupational choices and appreciate the variety of psychological, social, economic, and cultural factors that enter into occupational decisions:

1. Occupational choice as a matching process

2. Occupational choice as a developmental process

3. Occupational choice as a decision-making task

4. Occupational choice as a function of social and cultural influences

For each theme, we will review the relevant research, highlight important findings, and illustrate its significance to our model of career management.

Occupational Choice as a Matching Process

Most theories of occupational choice contend that a person, consciously or unconsciously, chooses an occupation that "matches" his or her unique set of needs, motives, values, and talents. One of the earliest approaches to occupational choice, the so-called trait and factor theory, is perhaps most explicit in this regard. According to this view, a person would be expected to identify his or her abilities, needs, interests, and values; select appropriate career goals; and then choose an occupation thought to be most compatible with these goals.

The work of John Holland is the most well-known and influential theory that views occupational choice as a process of matching occupations and people.[4] Holland's theory proposes that people express their personalities in making an occupational choice, and individuals can be classified in terms of their similarity to the six personality types that were described in Chapter 4. Recall that these types included realistic, investigative, artistic, social, enterprising, and conventional. Each personality type is characterized by a common set of activity preferences, interests, and values. For example, as Table 6.1 indicates, enterprising personality types perceive themselves as adventurous, ambitious, and energetic, whereas conventional types see themselves as efficient, obedient, practical, and calm.

Holland proposes that occupational environments can also be classified into these six categories. Each environment is dominated by a particular personality type and reinforces those qualities possessed by that type as noted above. Moreover, Holland classified specific occupations into the same six environments as he had classified the personality types. For example,

TABLE 6.1 Illustrations of Holland's Typology of Personality and Occupations

---

I. *Realistic*

Personal characteristics: Shy, genuine, materialistic, persistent, stable

Sample occupations: Mechanical engineer, drill press operator, aircraft mechanic, dry cleaner, waitress

II. *Investigative*

Personal characteristics: Analytical, cautious, curious, independent, introverted

Sample occupations: Economist, physicist, actuary, surgeon, electrical engineer

III. *Artistic*

Personal characteristics: Disorderly, emotional, idealistic, imaginative, impulsive

Sample occupations: Journalist, drama teacher, advertising manager, interior decorator, architect

IV. *Social*

Personal characteristics: Cooperative, generous, helpful, sociable, understanding

Sample occupations: Interviewer, history teacher, counselor, social worker, clergy

V. *Enterprising*

Personal characteristics: Adventurous, ambitious, energetic, domineering, self-confident

Sample occupations: Purchasing agent, real estate salesperson, market analyst, attorney, personnel manager

VI. *Conventional*

Personal characteristics: Efficient, obedient, practical, calm, conscientious

Sample occupations: File clerk, CPA, typist, teller

NOTE: The entries are selected illustrations. For a complete classification, see Holland, J. L. (1985). *Making vocational choices: A theory of vocational personalities and work environments.* Englewood Cliffs, NJ: Prentice Hall.

realistic occupations include engineering and construction work, investigative occupations include the physical and biological sciences, artistic occupations include music and art, social occupations include teaching and the ministry, enterprising occupations include public relations and advertising, and conventional occupations include administrative work.

One of John Holland's major assumptions is that individuals will seek out work settings that allow them to showcase their skills and abilities, express their interests and values, and take on relevant assignments.[5] In addition, it is expected that people's stability in an occupational area will depend on the fit or match between personality type and occupational environment. For instance, social personality types who find themselves in electrical engineering (an investigative occupation) could become dissatisfied with the occupation and might choose another occupation more consistent with their social orientation. Research has found that congruence between personality and occupational environment can lead to such favorable outcomes as higher job satisfaction, improved job stability, and increased job involvement.[6] In addition, a mismatch between one's personality and occupational choice could be a reason to pursue a career change.

In general, traditional or classic views on the matching of individuals with occupations are based on the notion of "supplementary" congruence, or the matching of individuals with environments in which they are similar to people already in those environments.[7] However, some researchers have noted the possibility of a "complementary" congruence, wherein personality characteristics and abilities of the individual can serve to complement personal characteristics and abilities already present in the work environment.[8] In this sense, the strengths of the individual might fill a void in a given work environment and thereby improve overall group performance.

Donald Super's extensive work is also based on the notion of a match between individuals and occupations. The key concept in his model is the person's self-concept, "the individual's picture of himself, the perceived self with accrued meanings."[9] Our self-concept, in other words, consists of attributes we believe we possess: our abilities, personality traits, needs, interests, and values.

Super believes that an occupational choice enables a person to play a role appropriate to the self-concept. People implement their self-concept in developing an occupational choice; that is, they select an occupation that is compatible with significant parts of their self-concept. In effect, people develop a self-concept, develop images or beliefs about a series of occupations, and take steps to enter the occupation that is most compatible with their self-concept. Indeed, a great deal of evidence supports the notion that people prefer and choose occupations that are compatible with their self-concept.[10]

Occupational Choice as a Developmental Process

Although evidence indicates that people match or implement their self-concept in choosing an occupation, one's selection of an occupation does not take place at a single point in time. The decision to become a pharmacist, for example, does not begin and end when a high school junior or senior decides to attend a pharmacy college.

The choice of an occupation can be considered a developmental process that evolves over time. For one thing, the decision to pursue a particular occupation is really a series of decisions that span a significant portion of one's life. The pharmacist-to-be may have decided to participate in the fifth grade science fair, to take an accelerated mathematics program in junior high school, to join the chemistry club in high school, and to seek summer employment at a local pharmacy. A number of educational and vocational decisions and activities culminate in an occupational choice.

Second, as Donald Super and others have indicated, one's self-concept is formed, clarified, and modified over an extended period of time. It takes time and experience for talents to emerge and for interests and values to crystallize. Time is also required for people to learn about the world of work. Misinformation is hopefully replaced by more accurate perceptions as we learn about different occupations and jobs. Potential occupations are pursued or discarded as new information becomes available to the child, adolescent, young adult, and mature employee.

For these reasons, it is proper to view occupational choice as an unfolding, gradual, evolving process. As we indicated earlier in this chapter with the examples of Jessica, Tom, Wilma, and Antonio, the need to make occupational choices can occur throughout the life cycle. Likewise, the gathering of information and the gaining of personal insights relevant to one's occupational choice can occur through the various career stages.

People learn about themselves and the work world through exploratory behavior. Childhood, adolescence, and the high school and college years provide time for maturation. Our self-concept becomes more stable, clearer, and more realistic. For example, part-time and summer employment provide substantial opportunities for reality testing—a firsthand look at ourselves. By waiting tables, clerking, selling, or repairing, we not only can test our talents and interests, but we also can learn what it is like to work outside the home. In addition, the completion of temporary work assignments, including internships, cooperative education programs, and apprenticeships, is designed to help students develop an accurate self-concept, gain a realistic understanding of various career fields and organizational environments, and allow a check for fit between individual characteristics and the demands of different jobs.[11] In our earlier example, Jessica's selection of accounting as an occupation was a product of her developing as a person, learning from earlier job-related experiences, and knowing her likes, dislikes, and special competencies.

Lifelong learning and personal development have become the mantras of the workplace. Adults continue to gain personal insights over the later stages of the life cycle. We constantly reassess ourselves and our achievements in relation to our career goals. Incongruities between expectations and reality can lead to changes in career goals and alterations in occupational preferences. From our earlier examples, Tom's decision to make a midcareer change by leaving the banking profession and making another occupational choice reflected his dissatisfaction with his work environment and his desire to express his entrepreneurial personality.

Transitions and changes in life roles can also necessitate the making of occupational choices. Our example of Wilma, who returned to work after the demands of caring for younger children had diminished, is representative of an occupational choice that resulted from a change in a life role. Finally, organizational actions can force a change in one's occupational field. Downsizings, mergers and acquisitions, and business failures can serve to make new career goals and an associated occupational choice a necessity. Loss of one's job, as given in the example of Antonio at the beginning of the chapter, is a powerful if not overwhelming inducement to seek a new occupation.

Occupational Choice as a Decision-Making Task

We have seen how occupational choice can be viewed essentially as a developmental process in which experiences and increasing maturity enable a person to develop, modify, and clarify the self-concept, gain further insights into the world of work, and attain a match between a chosen occupation and one's self-perceived interests, abilities, needs, and values.

Given a set of alternative occupations, how does one choose which occupation to pursue? According to the career management model presented in Chapter 3, a person should engage in career exploration, acquire a greater awareness of self and of alternative occupations, and develop a career goal. In the context of occupational choice, the operational career goal is to enter a particular occupation. But this does not explain *how* individuals select a particular occupational field. How, for example, does one determine whether finance or marketing will provide a better match? What psychological process guides one in the selection of a particular occupational field?

A number of models of vocational decision making have been developed to address this very issue.[12] Although there are several differences among them, most are based on some form of psychological decision theory where it is generally assumed that individuals use compensatory or trade-off approaches in which unfavorable aspects of a given job are offset by the favorable elements of the job.[13] Under one view, occupational choice could be based on a rational, deductive, and programmed decision-making process wherein people choose courses of action that are expected to produce desirable consequences.[14] With this decision-making approach, the individual becomes aware of the desired outcomes or rewards that are expected to emanate from a job (e.g., advancement opportunities, salary, or interesting work) and then assesses the value of these job outcomes. The individual then searches to identify occupations that would provide the valued job outcomes. The individual, armed with these data, would then systematically choose the occupation that had the highest desirability. However, finding an occupation attractive is not the same as choosing to enter an occupation. There may be many attractive occupations (e.g., professional athlete, politician, brain surgeon) that we ultimately reject for one reason or another. Perhaps we believe we do not have the right mix of talents for a particular occupation or that our financial resources (or our patience) are not adequate for the extensive training required. Thus, the individual assesses the likelihood of actually getting into the identified occupations. In other words, we are most likely to pursue an occupation that we not only find attractive but also have a decent chance of entering.

Do people really choose occupations in such a rational, calculative manner? Do people compare occupations on a long list of job outcomes and choose occupations that maximize the likelihood that they will obtain desirable outcomes and avoid undesirable outcomes? Our occupational preferences and decisions do seem to be guided by our desire to seek maximum rewards from work. However, a competing view of occupational decision making suggests that occupational choice is neither as rational nor as systematic as we have described previously. Individuals, when confronted with real-life choices, often use decision-making strategies wherein the first option that fulfills minimally acceptable standards on specific occupational attributes is chosen. This "unprogrammed" or noncalculative approach means that people do not initially assess a job on a long list of outcomes but rather focus on one or two significant outcomes. Jobs that fail to reach an acceptable level on these significant outcomes are rejected from further consideration, even if they would provide many other desirable outcomes. The jobs that survive this cut would not be compared to one another, but rather are placed on an "active roster" of acceptable alternatives. From this active roster, the person often makes an "implicit" decision (unknown even to the self) to favor one alternative over the others, based on just one or two outcomes.

There has not been sufficient research to draw sound conclusions about the relative usefulness of the rational/programmed and the unprogrammed decision-making approaches to occupational choices, although recent research seems to indicate the efficacy of structured, rational decision-making strategies as a way to improve the quality of the decision.[15] Even though the jury is still out, both approaches share one important principle, namely, that choices are based on perceptions of different occupations or jobs. Whether the choice is based on one or two critical outcomes or on a longer list of outcomes weighted by value and importance, beliefs about an occupation's ability to provide these outcomes determine occupational preferences. If beliefs and perceptions are unrealistic, occupational decisions are likely to be faulty. If a person is mistaken in his or her view that a certain occupation will provide interesting work activities, that person will be disappointed and disillusioned in the job. The implications of these unmet expectations will be discussed in detail later in this chapter.

Social and Cultural Influences on Occupational Choice

As we discussed in Chapter 2, our careers and career decision making are shaped considerably by social influences. Since behavior is a function of the person and the environment, the choices we make are reflections of our personal characteristics and the environment in which we live. The occupational choice process is no exception to this general rule.

Most of the research on occupational choice seems to focus on the person as an active agent in the formulation of occupational plans and decisions. Certainly, our model of career management emphasizes what one can or should do to plan, manage, and appraise a career. Much of the psychologically oriented theory and research discussed so far considers personal goals and intentions, awareness, information seeking, and strategy development as key influences on occupational decision making.

However, there are other approaches to the study of occupational choice and decision making. In particular, the sociological approach to careers reflects the idea that circumstances beyond the individual's control can exert considerable influence on the course of his or her life and occupational choices.[16] Undoubtedly, the environment—both past and present—plays a major role in occupational decision making. A person's past environment includes family of origin, social class, income, and place of residence. The present environment includes the economic, political, and cultural climate in which a person lives.

First, consider the ways in which a child's social background can influence his or her orientation to the work world. Although the United States may be less class conscious than other cultures, there can be distinct lifestyles associated with membership in different socioeconomic classes. Social class and economic status not only affect the availability of resources for one's career choice, but also affect the network of attitudes, customs, and expectations one may experience.[17]

Studies have shown that differences in values and attitudes, especially occupational and educational aspirations, can be attributed to one's socioeconomic status.[18] Accordingly, a parent's occupation can determine the kind of people met and admired during childhood. Growing up as a child of a physician is likely to expose one to different role models than growing up as a child of a firefighter—not better or worse, but different. Selective exposure to different adults can stimulate widely different occupational aspirations. In addition, social status and access to economic resources can influence the career decision making self-confidence of individuals, such that someone who grows up in a more affluent environment might have a comparatively higher degree of confidence in his or her occupational choices.[19]

Moreover, social class can affect the values we hope to attain at work. A father or mother who has lived through some unstable time (a strike or extended layoff, lapses in continued employment caused by downsizings, or the Great Depression) may encourage a child to value security above all else in a job. A college professor or scientist may encourage a life of study and research, a social worker or physician a life of service, and an entrepreneur a life of competition. This is not to say that a child automatically adopts a parent's work values, but that the opportunity to identify with parents and internalize their values is certainly present.

One's family background has a significant effect on occupational choice and aspirations.[20] Parents' occupations can influence the development of their children's interests and skills in certain areas, particularly regarding the choice of white- or blue-collar jobs. An automobile mechanic's son or daughter is likely to get an early introduction to the world of "things" and mechanical operations. A doctor's daughter may accompany her mother to the office or hospital and develop an interest and ability in working with people in emergency situations. In addition, parents' occupations affect family income. A wealthy family can provide the resources to pursue special hobbies and perhaps develop some latent interests and skills. Financial resources also make it easier for the child to attend college and perhaps graduate or professional school.

Parents' occupations and income can also influence the type of neighborhood in which a family lives. A place of residence is influential because it determines whom we meet and with whom we interact in our daily lives. Because of their residents' backgrounds and values, neighborhoods differ in their emphasis on athletic achievements, academic attainments, and occupational success. Peer pressure among children can work to encourage or discourage educational accomplishments and aspirations.

In addition to the cultural norms of a particular social class or neighborhood, the geographical location of one's residence can affect occupational decisions. Young people growing up in a city may have little knowledge of the life of a forest ranger, and someone from a tropical climate might not seriously consider a career in ski resort management. These geographical considerations do not pose insurmountable barriers (a Miami-bred college student at a New England university could develop an interest in and proficiency at skiing), but they do restrict a view of what constitutes a feasible career.

Beyond the influences of family, social class, and geography, career decisions are also made in the context of the larger society and culture within which one lives.[21] In addition, economic conditions and consumer preferences promote certain industries and occupations over others. The growth in many service industries is a result of increased consumer buying power and preference for a more leisurely lifestyle. Technological changes create positions that were unheard of just a few years before. The role of "accidents" in career decision making must not be forgotten. If you hadn't attended that political rally, you never would have met your fiancé, who couldn't have introduced you to his cousin, who wouldn't have asked you to go to the conference in social planning, which ultimately stimulated your interest in public administration. These kinds of "random" accidental events occur all the time and can easily influence the course of our lives.

In summary, one's social background can stimulate or suppress certain skills, values, and abilities. Social class has been found to be related to beliefs about one's ability and control over a situation, as well as the importance of work to one's identity.[22] One's social background provides or withholds financial resources and, to a large extent, determines the people who will play a major role in one's early life. Moreover, the cultural environment reinforces certain values, legitimizes certain career aspirations, and places occupational decisions in a larger economic, political, and technological milieu. In short, the environment can influence how people view themselves, their future, and the world of work.

GUIDELINES FOR EFFECTIVE OCCUPATIONAL DECISION MAKING

Despite our position that occupational choice is a matching process, observation and common experience tell us that many people do not necessarily choose occupations that are compatible with their talents, values, and interests. Some choose occupations that fail to utilize their talents, that provide for little satisfaction of their needs and values, and that involve job duties in which they have little or no interest. In this section, we apply the career management model by examining several factors that can contribute to the choice of an appropriate occupation.

Development of Self-Awareness

Self-awareness is the cornerstone of effective career management. In the absence of a deep understanding of one's values, interests, personality, abilities, and preferred lifestyle, one would require considerable luck to fall into a compatible occupation. The major obstacles to the development of self-awareness were discussed in Chapter 4. At this time, it is appropriate to consider your degree of self-awareness. Review your responses to Learning Exercises 1 (data collection), 2 (theme identification), and 3 (preferred work environment) provided at the end of Chapter 4. Do the themes still make sense to you? Is your preferred work environment summary consistent with these themes? Does your summary touch on all eight of the elements listed in Exercise 3? If not, ask yourself why certain elements are missing.

Learning Exercise 7 appears in the Appendix on p. 193. It provides an opportunity for you to revise or complete your preferred work environment statement. If you believe you need more information in certain areas, indicate how you can go about obtaining the information. Consider the possibility of seeing a vocational counselor, taking tests, reading materials on self-assessment, and speaking to friends, relatives, spouse, colleagues, coworkers, or professors. Remember that self-exploration is a process; it is never really completed. Therefore, a periodic appraisal of your preferred work environment can be helpful.

Development of Accurate Occupational Information

Self-awareness needs to be combined with a satisfactory understanding of alternative occupations. However, lack of relevant work experience, stereotypes of occupations, and unfamiliarity with certain occupational fields all detract from development of a solid base of occupational information.

Actually, there are two related steps in occupational exploration. The first is to identify a number of occupations that may be potentially compatible and satisfying. Then, collect more in-depth information on each occupation. Obviously, one can go back and forth between the two steps, but some form of screening is necessary, if for no other reason than time and information overload. As was discussed in Chapter 4, effective screening of various occupations can be accomplished by consulting sources that provide information on a wide range of occupations. Once some initial screening has been conducted, it is possible to collect more extensive information on a smaller number of occupational alternatives. Again, an understanding of one's preferred work environment can help focus one's information search.

Other people in one's social network, such as counselors, professors, friends, relatives, and work associates, can provide information on specific occupations. In addition, personal or family contacts can frequently identify individuals who are currently employed in a particular occupation and are willing to share their experiences and opinions. Seminars, which can also provide useful information on specific occupations (e.g., "Careers in Advertising"), are often sponsored by student groups (e.g., the Society for the Advancement of Management), counseling offices, and professional associations. Finally, work experience, which has frequently been mentioned as a source of information about oneself and the world of work, is also helpful. For students, cooperative work assignments, internships, and part-time or summer jobs can be explored for potential employment possibilities. In addition, a student can attempt to arrange an "informational interview" with an individual in a career or a company in which the student is interested. An informational interview is requested and arranged by the student as an informal way to gain information about a prospective job or company without the pressure of trying to sell oneself, as in a formal interview process.[23] The student can use the informational interview as a way to gain knowledge about the company and its business lines and, in a preliminary way, test for a fit with a particular job or the organization as a whole.

Effective Goal Setting

One of the most significant components of the career management process is the development of realistic and appropriate career goals. In the context of occupational choice, the goal is to enter a specific occupational field. Assuming that a person has conducted sufficient self- and occupational exploration, how should he or she decide from among alternative occupations?

Learning Exercise 5, included at the end of Chapter 5, provided an opportunity for you to develop long-term and short-term operational goals. If you identified specific occupations in Exercise 5, this would be a good time to reexamine the ratings you gave and the advantages and disadvantages you listed for each occupation. If you did not identify specific occupations in Exercise 5, you should do so at the present time. On separate paper, list the elements of your conceptual goal (long term or short term), identify two occupations in which you have some interest, and then list the advantages and disadvantages of each occupation.

The choice of an occupation is, at the end, a subjective, emotional experience. No absolute criteria are available to determine what represents a "good" career choice. No easy, automatic formulas exist (or should exist) to eliminate the subjective element. However, a systematic collection and analysis of relevant information can provide a realistic data base in making such decisions.

Development of Career Strategies

Once a career goal is selected, we need to identify strategic behavior, activities, and experiences that facilitate goal accomplishment. The twin criteria by which strategies should be chosen are their potential usefulness and their personal acceptability. Moreover, one important function of a strategy is to enable a person to test the viability of his or her career goals. In this case, strategies can help to confirm or disconfirm the wisdom of an occupational choice. Regardless of which strategies are used, it is important to understand the purpose of each activity, sequence the activities, and establish timetables for completion. Again, it is necessary to be flexible in developing and implementing a career strategy. No list of strategies should ever be considered final. Even if goals remain the same, specific strategic behaviors should be added or deleted as necessary. Most important, people should take advantage of the feedback and appraisal functions of strategies. Periodically ask yourself whether your chosen occupation still makes sense to you. If the evidence is consistently and convincingly negative, be prepared to change your course of action—or pay the price somewhere along the line.

Learning Exercise 8 appears in the Appendix on p. 194. If a strategy to enter an occupation (or change occupations) is relevant to you at the present time, use Learning Exercise 8 to formulate the strategy.

ORGANIZATIONAL CHOICE: THE PROCESS OF ENTERING AN ORGANIZATION

Once a person has settled upon a particular occupation, the next step is to find a job and successfully gain entry into an organization. As with occupational choice, organizational choice involves trying to find a match between the individual, in terms of his or her values, interests, abilities, and lifestyle preferences; a job, in terms of required skills and aptitudes; and an organization, in terms of its mission, products, culture, and geographic location of the job. Organizational choice and entry is a multistage process involving activities undertaken by the individual job seeker (such as researching a company, preparing a résumé and cover letter, lining up professional references, etc.) and simultaneous efforts by the organization (posting or advertising available job openings, participating in job fairs, establishing appropriate screening tools, etc.).[24]

Past research has identified four phases in the organizational entry process, with each phase having different but related tasks for the job candidate and the hiring organization.[25] The four stages are *recruitment, selection, orientation,* and *socialization. Recruitment* is defined as the process of mutual attraction between the individual and the organization. At this stage, the individual locates information on job sources and firms, while the organization is concerned with finding and attracting job candidates. *Selection* involves the process of mutual choice. Individuals in this phase must deal with job interviews, assessments, and making choices among job offers. For the hiring organization, the key task is an assessment of candidates for future job performance and retention. *Orientation* is defined as the period of initial adjustment once the person has actually entered the organization. For the individual, this means coping with the stress of entry, while the organization must attend to the emotional and information needs of newcomers. The last stage, or *socialization,* is termed the process of mutual adjustment. During this phase, the individual moves through typical work stages and experiences various successes. The organization employs socialization techniques and tactics to influence newcomers' behavior and ensure their assimilation into the organization. This chapter will cover the recruitment and selection processes, and Chapter 7 will discuss orientation and socialization.

The ultimate objective of organizational entry is to attain a match between the individual and the organization. The candidate's capabilities and the job's requirements must match, as should the individual's needs and the organization's rewards or reinforcements. The capability–job requirement match can affect the level of job performance an employee attains, whereas the need–reinforcement match can influence the level of job satisfaction an employee experiences.[26] Both matches affect the contribution a new employee makes to his or her organization.

Consequences of a mismatch can be severe. From the employee's perspective, a mismatch can produce dissatisfaction and disappointment, can be a threat to self-esteem, and might result in a decision to pursue another job in a different organization. From the organization's point of view, poor performance can detract from the organization's effectiveness, and extensive turnover can be costly since replacements need to be recruited, selected, trained, and developed into productive employees.[27] For these reasons, it is important to understand the dynamics of organizational entry, including how individuals choose jobs in organizations, the role of expectations in the organizational entry process, and the steps individuals and organizations can take to increase the likelihood of successful organizational entry.

THEORIES OF ORGANIZATIONAL CHOICE

The basic approaches an individual can take when deciding on an employer are similar to those used in occupational choice. Specifically, job candidates are attracted to an organization that is most likely to provide desirable outcomes and they avoid those organizations that would likely result in undesirable outcomes. In one sense, the job seeker could take a programmed approach to organizational choice by rationally and systematically gathering all relevant information during the recruiting process and then using this information to estimate the likelihood that alternative employers will provide the desired set of outcomes. The individual then rationally and systematically assesses the desirability or value of each potential outcome from alternative employers. Thus an individual would be expected to make the most logical choice by accepting a job offer from the firm that is most compatible with one's values, that is, the one most likely to provide such positive outcomes as interesting work, pleasant working conditions, advancement opportunities, and others.

In contrast with this rational (or programmed) approach to organizational choice, a job candidate could be considerably less thorough or systematic in the selection process. According to this alternative (or unprogrammed) view, candidates initially become attracted to organizations that are acceptable according to just one or two critical outcomes (not a long set of outcomes), develop an implicit (often unconscious) choice of an organization, and then engage in perceptual distortion in favor of the organization they have already implicitly chosen.[28] Organizational choice, in this view, is based on the subjective perception that an organization can provide a satisfactory opportunity to attain just one or two highly significant outcomes. For example, research has shown that an organization's "corporate image" has a strong influence on an individual's choice to pursue employment with that organization.[29]

Which approach, programmed or unprogrammed, more accurately describes the organizational choice process? Although research has supported the efficacy of both types of decision making, one can argue that the more thorough the search and the greater the number of outcomes and organizations considered, the greater the likelihood of a favorable match and success in the job search process.[30] Perhaps the most relevant question is not which type of job search is more typical, but which type is more beneficial for the individual and the organization. It should not be surprising that a programmed approach with a thorough search for extensive information enables a candidate to be more confident and satisfied with the organizational entry process.

The Role of Expectations in Organizational Entry

The basic approaches to organizational choice reflect a matching process in that people choose jobs that will satisfy significant values. In effect, candidates develop expectations about an organization's capacity to provide valued outcomes. These expectations guide people toward or away from various job opportunities. Thus, a person's attraction to a certain job is based on the expectations that the job will provide such desirable outcomes as interesting work and autonomy on the job. Whether accurate or not, these expectations strongly influence a person's choice of jobs in organizations.

Yet job expectations—for interesting work, advancement opportunities, financial security, and the like—may not be realized when a candidate actually enters the organization as a new employee. There is evidence that expectations of both college educated and non–college educated individuals concerning their jobs tend to be unrealistically inflated upon organizational entry. Moreover, the more abstract the topic (e.g., opportunity for personal growth), the more unrealistic are the applicants' expectations. New employees often experience "reality shock," a sense of disillusionment, disappointment, and dissatisfaction upon discovering that the reality of the job and the organization do not quite match their preconceived expectations.

Several typical expectations held by job seekers as they embark on their job search are identified in Table 6.2, along with the true realities of being a new employee. It is not

TABLE 6.2   Comparisons of Expectations and Experiences

A Recruit May Expect That . . .	A New Employee May Experience That . . .
1. "I will have a great deal of freedom in deciding how my job gets done."	1. "My boss pretty much determines what I do and how I do it."
2. "Most of my projects will be interesting and meaningful."	2. "It seems like I have an endless stream of trivial, mundane tasks."
3. "I will receive helpful, constructivefeedback from my boss."	3. "I really don't know how I am doing on the job."
4. "Promotions and salary increases will be based on how well I do my job."	4. "Promotions and money are tight, and they appear to be based on factors other than my performance."
5. "I will be able to apply the latest techniques and technologies to help the organization."	5. "People resist adopting my suggestions, even though the old ways are antiquated and inefficient."
6. "I will be able to balance my work and family responsibilities without much difficulty."	6. "My job and family responsibilities often interfere with one another."

suggested that all candidates hold these expectations or that all new employees experience the same realities. However, there is certainly an opportunity for a gap between naive expectations and day-to-day job experiences.

Development of Unrealistic Expectations

What happens when expectations prove to be unrealistic? It has been argued that candidates who hold such expectations become dissatisfied when faced with the realities of a job and, ultimately, may choose to leave the organization.[31] For example, if a job candidate is told during the interview process that working extended hours or on weekends is rarely required, but then finds out after accepting a job that long hours are the norm, that person will likely be dissatisfied, disillusioned, and tempted to leave the organization. The reasons for the devastating effect of unrealistic expectations will be examined in a later section. For now, assume that recruits who hold unrealistic expectations about a job and organization will, at the very least, be surprised when they confront a reality on the job that does not confirm their expectations, and this surprise may be accompanied by dissatisfaction and disillusionment if the job experiences are generally undesirable.[32]

If we assume for the moment that unrealistic expectations can have a negative effect on new employees, we need to pose certain questions: Why do people develop unrealistic expectations? Where do these expectations come from? Why do they end up being unrealistic? We attempt to answer these questions by identifying a number of factors that can lead to unrealistic expectations.

Career Transitions

Perhaps the most fundamental explanation for unrealistic expectations is that the path from the job-seeker role to the employee role represents a career transition. A *career transition* is a period in which a person either changes career roles (interrole transition) or changes orientation to a current role (intrarole transition). For example, when a person leaves school and enters a work organization (an interrole transition), there are many differences between the old and the new settings: differences in tasks, required behaviors, norms, and expectations. Indeed, the lives of students and employees are vastly different. Even a job change within the same organization or from one organization to another represents a career transition, although the differences in settings may not be as severe as those between student and employee roles.

In short, many new employees, whether coming directly from school or from another organization, have to face a set of demands with which they may be unfamiliar. New employees must confront such experiences as reliance on other people (bosses, peers, customers), low levels of freedom and autonomy, extensive resistance to changes they might suggest, too much or too little job structure, and the politics of organizational life.[33] The organization is not typically going to change to accommodate a new employee. Often times, close supervision, mundane tasks, little responsibility, and tight controls are an organization's way of ensuring the satisfactory performance of new, untested employees.

Organizations' policies and practices might explain the nature of the job experiences a new employee must confront, but might not deal with the employee's expectations. Why do so many people expect to have considerable freedom in a job, to get promoted in a short time, to be appraised and counseled by a supportive, caring boss, and to obtain challenging, meaningful, and rewarding assignments? Where do people get such ideas in the first place? To answer this question, several other critical influences on unrealistic expectations must be explored.

The Recruitment Process

Even though organizations commit substantial resources to recruiting, the recruitment process has often been viewed as the most significant source of unrealistic expectations. In essence, it is claimed that organizations often portray jobs in overly optimistic terms, thus inducing unrealistic expectations on the part of the job candidate. To understand why this occurs, one must appreciate that the organization's goal is to attract qualified candidates. To keep qualified candidates interested in the organization, recruitment often focuses on "selling" the organization. This is done by presenting incomplete or overly flattering accounts of what it is like to work in the organization.

For instance, even a cursory examination of recruiting brochures or corporate Web sites illustrates how companies emphasize the positive: challenging and exciting work, rewards based on job performance, good opportunities for promotion, and timely, constructive feedback from your boss. Of course, there is the question of whether organizations can deliver on these promises. Even if they could, these descriptions omit some of the less flattering qualities that characterize almost any job in any organization. The dependence on the use of brochures and their overly positive message is a key source of unrealistic expectations.

This is not to say that organizations deliberately lie, but in their effort to put their best foot forward, they can easily slant their presentations in favor of positive information. Moreover, employees responsible for recruitment often have little direct line experience in the organization. Accordingly, they might also believe these glowing accounts of the organization and, in the process, pass on these unrealistic expectations to job candidates.

Of course, individual candidates have their own goal during recruiting: to keep the organizations interested in them so they may select the most appropriate organization for which to work. To keep an organization interested, candidates are likely to emphasize their strengths and omit potential weaknesses or reservations. This all amounts to a "mutual sell" in which each party (the candidate and the organization) may be reluctant to reveal less desirable qualities.

These goal conflicts are hardly conducive to an open, complete sharing of information during recruitment and selection. As a later section of this chapter will show, organizations can choose to modify their recruitment practices to offer candidates a "realistic job preview" that is intended to convey a more complete, accurate picture of the organization than traditional recruitment normally permits.

Organizational Stereotypes

Many candidates hold images and stereotypes of certain companies or industries even before they have had extensive contact with the organization. For example, research has found that job candidates hold specific stereotypes of small companies that differ substantially from those of big firms.[34] In addition, candidates can hold highly specific images of particular companies. Job candidates perceive a company's image in terms of its job opportunities, products, labor relations posture, administrative practices, geographical location, pay practices, and financial performance. Moreover, the image of a company is an important factor in a candidate's decision to pursue a job with that company.[35]

In a sense, then, stereotypes of images breed expectations. Since stereotypes are, by definition, partially incomplete or inaccurate, the resulting expectations may not be particularly realistic. A candidate who holds a stereotype about Company X ("Great reputation. People are promoted quickly. Good money and lots of challenge.") may not bother to test out these assumptions during recruiting or may not believe any piece of discrepant information a company may provide.

Educational Process

Specific coursework at the college or graduate level often does not sufficiently prepare students for the reality of the work world. For example, technically oriented courses in engineering or business rarely dwell on the problems inherent in working within an organizational structure as a new employee. Moreover, many colleges try to instill in their students a sense of pride in themselves and an ardent enthusiasm for their chosen career field. Under these conditions, it is not surprising that many graduates emerge with an unrealistic picture of what they will face in their first job. Such disillusionment may be particularly severe when employers deliberately hire overqualified job candidates. It is almost inevitable that such employees will see themselves as underutilized.

Lack of Prior Work Experience

Job candidates without extensive prior work experiences may be particularly susceptible to the development of unrealistic expectations. Job candidates with a variety of prior work experiences are more likely to engage in a more thorough information search during recruiting than candidates without such experience. Presumably, varied work experiences teach people that all organizations are not the same; hence the need for obtaining more information about each potential employer.

Self-Delusion

So far we have considered the effects of the environment (recruiting, education, work experience) on the development of unrealistic job expectations. We also must consider the possibility that some people fool themselves into believing what they want to believe. The strong positive relationship between a person's values and his or her expectations suggests that people come to expect job characteristics they want to experience.

Why the tendency to fool ourselves during a job search? First, candidates who are initially attracted to a job may distort or ignore negative information because they do not want to be confronted with anything unfavorable about a job they have already decided they prefer. Also, candidates with few alternative opportunities may hear only the positives of a job that they believe they might ultimately be forced to take.

Distortions also may be due to the feelings of dissonance or tension people experience after having reached an important decision. When individuals make a choice, they normally reject one alternative in favor of another. They may then engage in distortion or selective attention to convince themselves of the wisdom of their decision. In the process, however, they set themselves up for disillusionment since the overly glowing picture of the chosen organization could not be matched by the realities of the first year of employment. Thus, one source of unrealistic expectations is our own natural tendency to see the world through rose-colored glasses, that is, to see it as we would like it to be.

Organizational Choice and Entry in Later Adulthood

In Chapter 2 we discussed the view that specific age ranges can demarcate career stages. The organizational entry stage, and the challenges associated with it, normally would be experienced in the earliest period of adulthood, or in the time frame of 18 to 25 years old. Of course, the need to make career changes or job switches, either by choice or by circumstance, makes the issues surrounding organizational entry relevant at any age. Thus, while an individual may be in the middle or late adulthood stages in a chronological sense, he or she could be looking for a new job or accepting a new position, thereby facing the demands of recruitment, selection, orientation, and socialization that come with organizational choice and entry. The important distinction is that older adults confront these demands from a different, more experienced perspective. In other words, recruitment, establishment, and socialization are still important tasks for older adults, but they are addressed in what is hoped is a wiser and more mature fashion. Consider the following example:

> Sharon never thought she would have to prove herself again. After all, in the first 22 years of her career, she had built a record of significant accomplishment—several promotions, ultimately to the level of Vice President for Planning and Development; a salary of $170,000; an executive MBA degree from a top school; a recognized leadership position in the organization, with admiration from her peers and subordinates alike; and the opportunity to help map her company's future. In the 23rd year, Sharon's fast track rise came to an abrupt end. Her company was purchased in a hostile takeover and the new company saw Sharon's position as expendable. At the age of 46 Sharon found herself out of a job. Working with an executive search firm, Sharon put together a new résumé and pursued several promising leads. With few managerial- and executive-level jobs available, Sharon found the competition to be intense for the open positions that fit her background and experience. Sharon made sure she was well prepared for each interview by researching each prospective company extensively. After several months of job search, Sharon accepted the position of Business Planning and Forecasting Manager for a small automotive products retailer. The salary and status were comparatively much lower than her previous job, but Sharon was convinced that her new employer was a good match for her.

Even though Sharon is in middle adulthood, she was forced to "cycle back," by confronting the variety of tasks associated with finding a new employer and gaining entry. In this sense she was like a graduating college student looking for a first professional position. She had résumés to prepare, companies to research, questions to ask, and offers to assess. But Sharon approached these tasks from a more mature perspective. Her 23 years of corporate experience had provided extensive knowledge of her own talents and interests, as well as an understanding of the inner workings of business organizations. Accordingly, she was clear on the type of work situation she wanted, and she also knew which conditions to avoid. Because of her experience, Sharon was less prone to developing unrealistic expectations about her new job. Thus, while Sharon was forced to endure the rigors of organizational entry, she was able to manage the process as a mature adult.

ORGANIZATIONAL ACTIONS DURING THE ENTRY PROCESS

Organizations have three major tasks to accomplish during the organizational entry process. First, they need to attract talented and qualified candidates into the applicant pool and keep them interested in the organization. Second, they need to attract candidates in such a way as to minimize the development of unrealistic job expectations on the part of the candidates. Third, they must assess candidates accurately and extend offers to those who are likely to succeed in the organization. Organizations use a multitude of techniques, to varying degrees, in the attraction, recruitment, assessment, and selection processes.[36] This section discusses several approaches that organizations can use to attract and select candidates in an effective, realistic manner.

Attraction of Job Candidates

Certainly, organizations will not be able to staff themselves properly unless they can induce talented candidates to enter and remain in the recruitment process. Research on recruitment has identified a number of issues that have significant implications for organizations.[37]

Impact of the Recruiter. For many candidates for managerial, professional, and technical positions, the first formal contact with the organization is with the recruiter, and the first activity is the screening interview. Listed below are a few of the desirable qualities of this initial interaction between the candidate and the organization.[38]

First, candidates' reactions to interviews are most positive when the recruiter is perceived as knowledgeable. Recruiters who are familiar with the candidate's background and understand the organization and job qualifications in detail are viewed favorably. Given the straightforward nature of this fact, it would seem surprising that recruiters are often perceived as unprepared and/or unknowledgeable. However, the lack of interview preparation and knowledge may be a function of the way organizations train and prepare their recruiters. Many large and small companies fail to offer recruiter training programs or ensure that their recruiters are properly prepared prior to beginning their recruitment assignments.

In addition to adequate knowledge and preparation, recruiters' behavior during the interview affects candidates' attitudes.[39] Recruiters who ask relevant questions, answer candidates' questions accurately, and discuss career paths and job qualifications produce positive responses from candidates. Finally, the perceived qualities of the recruiter play a prominent role in the interview setting. A warm, enthusiastic, perceptive, and thoughtful recruiter understandably affects the recruit's reactions affirmatively.

Although there is no direct evidence on the frequency of poorly conducted interviews, it is clear that interviews can cause negative reactions among job candidates. One possible explanation for this phenomenon is recruiters' apparent lack of awareness of job candidates' values, needs, and aspirations. In addition, recruiters can often overestimate or underestimate the significance that individuals attach to specific aspects of the job and the organization. It seems unlikely that recruiters can present favorable information on topics of special significance to candidates if they misjudge the importance of these topics.

The implications of these findings are clear. Organizations need to pay sufficient attention to the initial interview process to ensure that proper information about the organization is presented to candidates. To present this information satisfactorily, recruiters need to understand candidates' concerns better, develop a deeper knowledge of the organization, and project a positive, concerned image. Careful selection and training of recruiters is certainly one place for an organization to begin.

Follow-Up Activities. Upon completion of the initial screening interview with a candidate, organizations decide whether to carry the process to the next step (normally a site visit) or to terminate the relationship with the candidate. Often, job candidates hold unrealistic expectations regarding the selection process,[40] including the time it takes for an organization to make a go/no-go decision on whether to continue the recruitment process. Organizations can take three weeks or more to make a decision on a potential employee, depending on the number of interviews to be conducted as well as the number of layers of management approval that are required to further the recruitment process. Clearly, many companies could profit by shortening the lag time between the interview and the go/no-go decision and, at the very least, should indicate during the initial interview what the time lag is likely to be.

The organization should also pay close attention to the site visits for candidates who survive the initial screening. Positive attitudes regarding the visit have been associated with the opportunity to meet with supervisors and peers, to ask questions and to have them answered frankly, and to receive sufficient information about the job and the company. Candidates should also be informed about the specifics of the on-site activities in advance of the visit. Research has found that positive evaluations by job candidates of the site visit and the location and the "likableness" of the host increased the probability that a candidate would accept a job offer.[41]

Organizations must also be mindful of how they handle the job offer. Candidates held more positive attitudes toward offers when the organization contacted them after the offer to provide additional information, was open to candidates' questions, and was willing to discuss specific terms of employment.

In summary, organizations can take more effective steps to attract candidates during the recruitment process. The importance of the recruiter and the initial interview cannot be overemphasized. Also influencing the candidates' attitudes toward the organization are the manner in which the site visit is planned and the way in which the job offer is extended. All of these activities contribute to the image an organization projects to the public. The fact that an organization's image and reputation can attract or repel potential candidates is a reminder of the importance of the recruitment process.

Realistic Recruitment

The preceding section examined ways for organizations to project an attractive image to job candidates. However, as previously discussed, an organization's image can be "too positive" if it is not based on reality. Since the recruitment process is one source of candidates' unrealistic job expectations, it is a prime target for reexamination and possible revision.

Realistic recruitment means presenting candidates with relevant and undistorted information about the job and the organization, even when this information might be seen as negative or unflattering to the hiring organization.[42] The vehicle through which realistic information is conveyed to candidates has been called the realistic job preview, or RJP. As the term indicates, an RJP presents job candidates with a balanced, realistic picture of the job and the organization, and with a preview of the positive and negative aspects of the job. An RJP may be presented through a company's Internet Web site, films, booklets, lectures, or one-on-one discussions. An RJP is often contrasted with a traditional job preview (TJP), wherein the organization paints an overly optimistic (and hence unrealistic) picture of the job and its requirements.

The presentation of realistic information to job candidates should reduce the level of voluntary turnover among candidates who ultimately join the organization. Several arguments have been advanced to support such a position. First, realistic previews lower candidates' expectations to more appropriate levels—expectations that are more likely to be met on the job.[43] Employees whose expectations have been met tend to be satisfied with their jobs, and satisfied employees are less likely to quit than are dissatisfied employees. According to this "met expectations" view, RJPs function by deflating initial expectations so that new employees experience little disappointment, disillusionment, and dissatisfaction when they confront reality.

A second explanation views a realistic preview as presenting a dose of reality about the job, which allows for the development of coping strategies that can help the new employee deal with the potentially disappointing and dissatisfying aspects of the job. For example, candidates who learn during recruitment that a job requires a great deal of close supervision may prepare themselves by rehearsing how they would deal with close supervision or perhaps by convincing themselves that close supervision may not be so terrible after all. In either case, RJPs should help new employees develop successful coping activities.

A third explanation is that RJPs convey an air of honesty to job candidates. This can have two effects. First, candidates may admire and respect an organization that is candid enough to "tell it like it is." This attitude can bond a new employee to the organization and reduce the likelihood of turnover. In addition, candidates who accept a job after receiving an honest disclosure of its negative qualities will become committed to the job and organization because they believe they made their decision with full knowledge of the facts and without coercion or distortion on the part of the organization.

Fourth, it has been suggested that realistic previews offer candidates a basis to self-select out of the recruitment process. In other words, they should enable candidates to determine whether a job will meet their significant values. Faced with an accurate, balanced portrayal of a prospective job, some candidates might choose to reject a job offer because they don't perceive a match between their needs and values and the organization's rewards and opportunities.

Do Realistic Job Previews Work?

The major objective of realistic recruitment is to reduce voluntary turnover among new employees. Therefore, a fair test of RJPs' effectiveness is to compare the turnover rates of new employees who received an RJP during recruitment with a comparable group who did not. Several reviews have evaluated the overall effectiveness of RJPs.[44] Such studies suggest that RJPs can reduce turnover significantly, which can provide considerable savings to organizations who have to recruit, select, and train fewer new employees to replace those who terminate. However, there are two caveats. First, RJPs do not significantly reduce turnover in every case. If the retention rate of a job is low because of its undesirable qualities, then even an RJP is not likely to reduce turnover.[45] Thus, the impact of RJPs on turnover can vary from setting to setting. Second, there is little evidence to support any of the four mechanisms (met expectations, coping, air of honesty, self-selection) that presumably explain the effectiveness of RJPs. Taken together, these two problems indicate that it is not fully understood when and why RJPs are effective. In addition, research has shown that when job candidates face a choice between an RJP-based job or a TJP-based job prospect, a significantly larger proportion will choose the TJP-based job, assuming all other factors are equal.[46] However, other research has found that an RJP-based job with higher compensation than a comparable TJP-based job resulted in the RJP-based job being viewed as attractive as the traditionally previewed job.[47] Thus, compensation can be used as a mechanism to mitigate the potential negative effect on job attractiveness that results from an RJP.

There are a number of circumstances or contextual situations in which RJPs are likely to be most effective. First, when job candidates can be selective about accepting a job offer they feel less compelled to accept a job because alternative employment is available. The presence of alternative job choices allows the self-selection mechanism of an RJP to operate. In contrast, people who see few alternative opportunities may distort or discount negative information during recruitment, thus rendering a RJP less effective. Second, when job candidates would have held unrealistic expectations in the absence of an RJP, then a realistic preview can be an eye-opener. Third, an RJP is of value when job candidates would have had difficulty coping with the demands of a job accepted in the absence of a realistic preview. Finally, the effectiveness of an RJP increases when the information presented to the prospective employee touches on topics that are significant or relevant to the candidate. If RJPs are to foster self-selection and effective coping behavior, they must include topics that are relevant to a wide variety of job candidates.

In conclusion, realistic job previews are potentially valuable ingredients in an organization's recruitment program. Not only might they reduce turnover among new employees, they can present an image of the organization as an honest, caring employer. Moreover, the concept of the RJP is not limited to new hires. It can be extended to situations in which employees are faced with a promotion, job transfer, and/or geographical relocation. In each of these situations, a realistic forewarning of future circumstances may be helpful to the individual and the organization.

Regardless of an organization's recruitment practices, some reality shock is inevitable. There are many sources of unrealistic expectations other than organizational recruitment. Organizational entry is a career transition, and there are going to be some unpleasant surprises and required adjustments. The first 6 to 12 months on a new job challenge the new employee and the organization. These challenges will be examined in more detail in Chapter 7.

Assessment and Selection

Once prospective job candidates have been attracted and realistically recruited, the next step for the organization is final assessment and selection. This section will discuss briefly the process by which organizations assess and select their employees. More extensive treatments of this topic are available in other published works.[48]

In the selection of individuals for employment, organizations first attempt to achieve a match or fit between the knowledge, skills, and abilities of the individual and the specific requirements of the job. In addition, some recruiters are also assessing the fit between the job candidate and such broader organizational factors as strategy, culture, and corporate values.[49] Ideally, organizations should use selection techniques (and make actual selections) that are based on the accomplishment of both match-ups. In this sense the "total" person is selected, one who is hired not only to meet the challenges of a particular job, but also to "fit" with the work and cultural environment of the organization.

In contrast to the "total" person view of hiring, some prominent organizations have begun to challenge the precise matching approach in selecting individuals for employment. Some firms make hiring decisions using a single criterion (or a limited number of criteria) such as the degree of conscientiousness or level of intelligence.[50] While there can be arguments for using a limited number of criteria in making hiring decisions (e.g., the simplification of the assessment process), we continue to believe that the total person strategy of matching individual to organization is the most appropriate approach to ensure longer-term satisfaction for the individual and the hiring organization. Nonetheless, it is obvious that individual intelligence and character do play a critical role in most, if not all, hiring decisions and have been found to be consistent predictors of individual job performance.[51]

Overall, the selection of individuals whose abilities and personal characteristics match the job and the work environment can have positive consequences for the organization in terms of lower turnover and a more involved and committed workforce.[52] Thus, it is in the organization's (and the individual's) best interests to utilize selection methods that serve to ensure a proper person–environment fit.

INDIVIDUAL ACTIONS DURING THE ENTRY PROCESS

From an individual's perspective, the primary aim of organizational entry is to obtain a job that is reasonably consistent with his or her preferred work environment. In this regard, an individual can take certain steps to improve the likelihood of a positive outcome and an appropriate adjustment to a new work role.[53] This section considers five major tasks people need to confront during organizational entry, including the development of self-awareness, the identification of prospective employers, the use of effective job interview behavior, the assessment of organizations, and the choice an organization for which to work. In each task area, there are guidelines for effectively managing the organizational entry process.

Development of Self-Awareness

It should be clear by now that effective career management decisions rest on a foundation of self-awareness. It is impossible to evaluate jobs and organizations without understanding one's personal values, interests, and talents. Research has shown that self- and environmental exploration not only help individuals who are seeking an initial career-oriented job evaluate alternative organizations, but also assist more seasoned employees who might be seeking reemployment after a job loss.[54] At the organizational entry stage, candidates will be exposed to information about different organizations. This information can be used to assess alternative organizations and to help a candidate clarify his or her own preferred work environment.

Identification of Prospective Employers

There are a number of sources for job leads, including college placement offices, unsolicited direct applications, personal contacts, advertisements in newspapers and journals, personnel agencies and search firms, Internet employment Web sites, and corporate Web sites. Much has been written about each source and its relative advantages and disadvantages.

Although college placement offices are a widely used source of job leads for college students, the importance of personal contacts cannot be underestimated. For professional, managerial, and technical employees, personal contacts often provide the most useful information about potential employers. There exist two broad types of personal contacts: (1) family members, friends, and social acquaintances and (2) work contacts such as present or past bosses, colleagues, and teachers. As we discussed in Chapter 2, people's social capital allows them to use personal contacts within a "social network" to learn of job openings or to put them in contact with others who might know of openings.[55] That is, they know many people who are either aware of job openings or know others who are.

Normally it is more difficult for younger people to use personal contacts because their social networks are not as extensive as those of older, more experienced people. Nevertheless, it is never too early to begin to establish networks and build social capital. Part of the challenge is identifying potential sources of information. Faculty members, fellow students, relatives, and friends of the family may all possess useful information. Participation in campus clubs and student professional organizations also may provide job leads and future contacts. However, meeting people is not enough. They also have to communicate their needs, values, and aspirations so others are aware of their desires. This requires an assertive posture that is essential to all aspects of career management.

In recent years, corporate Web sites and Internet recruitment have become key mechanisms for the attraction, application-filing, testing, and assessment of prospective job candidates.[56] Web sites provide an efficient way to deliver a company's recruitment message and basic information about corporate strategy and mission, and they also allow interested job candidates instant access to open positions. And when combined with electronic employment screening,[57] corporate Web sites let companies quickly identify individuals for further assessment and simultaneously eliminate those who do not meet the basic requirements for the position. For the job candidate, corporate Web sites provide a wealth of information.

Effective Job Interview Behavior

Just like an organization, a job candidate has multiple goals during recruitment. Candidates need to make a favorable impression to receive a job offer, and they must gather useful information about companies so they can assess alternatives. Sometimes these goals can conflict with one another. This section will examine impression management, and the next will turn to accurate assessment of jobs and organizations.

Although companies scrutinize candidates' educational and work experiences and often administer psychological and integrity tests, the most widely used assessment procedure is the personal interview. Therefore, job candidates should be aware of the factors that contribute to a successful interview. In general, interviews are judged most effective when the interviewee knows about the company, has specific career goals, asks good questions, is socially adept, and is articulate. These five factors seem to reflect two underlying dimensions of interviewee behavior: preparation/knowledge and effective interpersonal communication skills.

The first dimension underscores the need for candidates to conduct thorough research on the organization. There are many possible information sources. In addition to commonly available documentation (e.g., newspaper articles, annual reports, and corporate Web sites), these sources include potentially useful people, such as friends, family members, members of professional and social organizations, and people with contacts or who know people with contacts.

People who work in the company of interest can be particularly helpful. It is recommended that job candidates conduct information interviews with such people, that is, interviews that are designed to obtain useful information, not necessarily to obtain a job.[58] Moreover, candidates should enter these interviews with questions that are relevant to their preferred work environment. A relatively clear understanding of desired tasks, rewards, and opportunities should enable a candidate to identify many of the relevant features of an organization and its jobs.

The second dimension, effective interpersonal communication skills, reflects social skills and articulation. Although there is no guaranteed way to become articulate and socially adept, candidates can work toward reducing their anxiety so that their positive qualities can emerge during the interview. Employment interviews are anxiety-provoking situations for most people. They are somewhat unpredictable and can play a major role in one's career. However, the literature suggests a number of ways to reduce anxiety to appropriate and manageable levels:

- Know yourself. People who know what they want can be more relaxed during an interview and can respond more naturally and effectively to questions about career goals and expected contributions to the organization.

- Research the company thoroughly and prepare salient questions to ask.

- Participate in programs designed to enhance interview skills, job search focus, and assertiveness. Many such programs are available through college placement offices or organizationally sponsored training activities.

In short, adequate planning and preparation for interviews can make a candidate more relaxed and effective in recruitment situations.

Assessing Organizations

To make a realistic job choice, a candidate needs to assess organizations carefully and systematically. A useful organizational assessment requires the collection and analysis of data from varied sources. Table 6.3 lists several different types of information that would be helpful in organizational assessment and interview preparation.

It may be difficult to obtain such data for two reasons. First, candidates may be so preoccupied with making a positive impression and obtaining a job offer that they don't seek information or pay attention to information that is provided. Second, organizations may be unable or unwilling to provide some important pieces of information.

Job candidates can overcome these potential obstacles in several ways. First, they should be conscious of their own motives and goals during recruitment. They must recognize that their desire to impress a company may possibly distract them from their task of collecting

TABLE 6.3 Types of Information for Organizational Assessment and Interview Preparation

1. Line(s) of business conducted by the organization

2. Size of the organization

3. Structure of the organization

4. Outlook of the industry(ies) in which the organization does business

5. Financial health of the organization

6. Organization's business plans for the future

7. Location of the organization's headquarters and major facilities

8. Availability of training and development opportunities

9. Promotion and advancement policies (e.g., promotion from within)

critical information. Candidates must understand that it is possible to impress and assess simultaneously. Indeed, companies may not even be impressed with candidates who fail to ask significant and perceptive questions.

Second, candidates must see the connection between their preferred work environment and the assessment of an organization. Otherwise, the questions they ask may turn out to be irrelevant or trivial. Candidates should review their preferred work environment summary before each interview and identify the specific information they will need to assess the compatibility of the organization with their values, interests, talents, and desired lifestyle.

Third, candidates should understand the most appropriate data collection techniques. Observing prospective supervisors and colleagues in their work environment can give some clues about their competence, cooperativeness, and attitudes toward the organization and each other. Even if one's observations cannot provide conclusive evidence, they can suggest areas to be pursued with direct questioning. In other words, take advantage of the site visit to understand the people, the organization, and the facilities.

In addition, it is important to understand that the way in which a question is asked can affect the impression you make and the likelihood that you will obtain useful information. Members of the organization are human beings who can become defensive if they believe the questions are personally threatening or embarrassing. Therefore, questions should be asked in a sensitive, nonthreatening manner. Table 6.4 gives a set of example questions that might be used during the interview process by a job candidate for a financial analyst position.

A fourth obstacle for a job candidate to overcome is an overload of information at the completion of an interview or a visit to an organization. To prevent information loss, candidates should complete a brief log immediately after a recruitment interview to record their

TABLE 6.4   Sample Questions Asked by Interviewee

Target Job: Financial Analyst

Sample Interview Questions

1. What is the role of a financial analyst in this company?
2. What training opportunities are available?
3. Do financial analysts work on a variety of projects at one time?
4. How much responsibility and independence do financial analysts have in their work?
5. What technical support is available?
6. What long-term career opportunities are available for financial analysts?
7. How are salary increases and promotions determined?
8. How much travel is involved?

---

reactions to the interview as well as objective data such as the time and place of the interview and the interviewer's name.[59] Items on the log should be tied to the important elements of one's preferred work environment (e.g., "Will the job take advantage of my talents?" "Is there likely to be sufficient autonomy on the job?" "Are there training opportunities?"). Not only would this practice help one assess alternative organizations, it also would permit one to identify issues for which further information is needed. In addition, job candidates should ask for business cards from the individuals they meet during the interview process or the site visit. Business cards can help prevent information loss, provide key contact data such as phone numbers and e-mail addresses, and be a guide to the position titles of the people who conducted the interviews.

Choosing Organizations

Like the choice of an occupation, the selection of a job with a particular organization should not be a mechanical "by the numbers" decision. Nor should it be speculative or unsystematic. On the basis of one's preferred work environment, one should identify a set of desirable and undesirable outcomes, and then estimate the compatibility of each alternative job with each outcome. Some job offers (or potential job offers) may be discarded quickly, whereas others may require more information and a more thorough analysis of the data.

Of course, if the individual has only one job offer, then it might be difficult to "discard" that job since there might not be an alternative that is readily available. In this case, the job offer and the organization have to be evaluated based on other possibilities and whether the job seeker can afford to wait longer to see if another, perhaps more attractive, offer is forthcoming. Accepting a job offer simply because it is the only one available might set the person up for longer-term disappointment if that job and organization do not fit with individual interests, values, and abilities.

Evaluating alternative jobs on the basis of expected outcomes and other criteria should stimulate one to think about values and aspirations and the likelihood that competing jobs will meet preferences. Lists of advantages and disadvantages of each job can also help a candidate to visualize the relative attractiveness of each alternative. There is a subjective, emotional element in job choice that should not be suppressed. Although this book emphasizes the systematic collection and analysis of information, the decision to accept one job over another also has to "feel" right. One should not rely too heavily on other people's views of one's needs and values. Although it is important to obtain input from a wide variety of people, it is a candidate's needs and values that must be met, not other people's visions of what one should want from work.

SUMMARY

Four themes capture much of the thinking and research on the occupational choice process: (1) occupational choice is a matching process in which individuals seek an occupation that is consistent with their talents, values, interests, and desired lifestyle; (2) occupational decisions evolve over time as people develop and refine their knowledge of themselves and the work world; (3) occupational choice is a decision-making task in which people evaluate the likelihood that alternative occupations will provide desirable outcomes; and (4) individuals' occupational decisions are influenced by their social background and the current economic, political, and technological environment.

Self-awareness, the cornerstone of career management, is a necessary ingredient in effective occupational decision making. In addition, people need to develop a solid base of information to screen alternative occupations for potential appropriateness. The choice of an occupation from a set of alternatives should maximize the compatibility of the chosen occupation with one's conceptual goal. Career strategies particularly relevant to occupational choice include competence in current activities, self-nomination, networking, and seeking guidance.

Organizational entry is the process by which a job candidate moves from outside to inside an organization. Its objective is to attain a match between individual talents and needs and a job's demands and rewards. Candidates develop expectations that guide their selection of jobs and organizations. Often, however, these expectations prove to be unrealistically inflated. The development of unrealistic job expectations can be due to a radical career transition (e.g., moving from school to work), the recruitment process itself, stereotypes that candidates hold about particular organizations, the nature of candidates' prior educational and work experiences, and candidates' natural tendency to see things as they would like them to be, not necessarily as they are. New employees can become disillusioned and dissatisfied if they see that the reality of the job doesn't live up to their lofty expectations.

Organizations should develop recruitment techniques that attract candidates effectively. At the same time, organizations should consider developing realistic recruitment procedures in which candidates are given a balanced picture of the job—both the positive and the negative features. Under certain conditions, realistic recruitment can reduce dissatisfaction and turnover among new employees.

Individuals also need to manage the organizational entry process. In particular, candidates should understand their own preferred work environment, develop networks to identify prospective employers, develop or refine job interview skills, conduct accurate assessments of organizations, and make job choices based on sound information and self-knowledge.

ASSIGNMENTS

1. Think about an organization into which you were hired. List the characteristics of the organization that you evaluated before you made the choice. In making the choice did you consider just one or two important characteristics of the company (as with unprogrammed decision making), or did you evaluate more thoroughly a longer list of salient characteristics (as with programmed decision making)? In retrospect, were you satisfied with the organizational choice you made? Do you think your approach to decision making influenced your subsequent satisfaction with the organizational choice you made? Explain why or why not.

2. Interview your parents and/or other relatives to understand how your family background can influence (or has already influenced) your career choices. Think back to when you were growing up. Consider such factors as your parents' aspirations, the income of your family, the neighborhood(s) in which you grew up, the sports you played, and the religious training you have had. Try to trace the significance of these factors to your current career plans. What influence (if any) has your spouse or others from your peer group (siblings, friends, or colleagues) had on your career choices?

DISCUSSION QUESTIONS

1. Do most people choose occupations that match their talents, values, interests, and desired lifestyle? What are some obstacles to establishing such a match?

2. What is the role of emotion or "instinct" in deciding on an occupation? What weight should be given to a formal, rational analysis of a job versus a more subjective, emotional appraisal?

3. What can you do to develop realistic expectations about a job in which you are interested? Identify as many sources of information as possible.

4. To what extent have your educational and/or prior work experiences given you a realistic picture of what it would be like to enter a new organization? How could colleges and universities help individuals develop more realistic job expectations?

5. What are the advantages that accrue to organizations that practice realistic recruitment? Are there any risks involved? In your prior attempts to seek employment, did organizations provide you with a balanced, realistic picture of the job and the organization? What were your reactions to the recruitment procedure?

6. Why is an understanding of one's preferred work environment so critical to effective job search and organizational entry? What does a job candidate risk if he or she lacks self-insight in this area?

7. What can you learn about a job or an organization by visiting its facilities? How can you prepare for a visit to maximize the amount of useful information you receive? How can you assess whether a prospective employer will fit with your preferred work environment (PWE)?

CHAPTER 6 CASE

Natalie the Retail Manager (Part A)

Natalie graduated from a large state university with two important possessions—a combined marketing and management degree and high aspirations. She believed that her education, abilities, and ambition would lead to a rewarding career in management. As she interviewed with several companies for her first postgraduate job, it seemed that retail organizations offered the best opportunity for a quick rise to the management ranks. Also, retail firms seemed to give her a good chance to apply her dual majors. The fast track program offered by Enigma,[60] a chain of upscale department stores, was especially intriguing to Natalie. The program included an intensive training course for aspiring managers combined with challenging on-the-job assignments. The recruiter told Natalie that those selected for this program could expect an unencumbered rise to upper management. Natalie was also impressed by what she had seen in the literature the recruiter had used to describe Enigma's proactive development programs and corporate culture.

Natalie was so pleased with her choice of Enigma as her first employer that in all the excitement she didn't get much of a chance to talk to her parents or friends about it. Also, the preparations for graduation and the end-of-year parties didn't leave much time for her to check into Enigma as an employer. In Natalie's view, the recruiter gave her a fairly balanced overview of the company. One month after graduation, Natalie began the three-month course that blended textbook learning with real-life, store-based training at the company's Dallas headquarters.

Natalie found the training course to be quite demanding. Substantial emphasis was placed on individual initiative and accomplishments, often pitting trainees against one another in business simulations. Natalie thought the emphasis on individual action to be somewhat strange since the recruiter had stressed that Enigma's success was based on teamwork and esprit de corps. Although she was in a class with 40 other trainees, Natalie found it difficult to make friends with her cohorts. The rigors of the training and the emphasis on individual competitiveness left little time or inclination for personal bonds to be established. Near the end of the training period Natalie received her first performance evaluation. The instructors saw her intelligence and technical skills as strong points, but also noted that she needed to be more decisive, become more sensitive to customer needs, and develop a "killer instinct" when dealing with employee behavior difficulties. Even though the training wasn't exactly what she had expected, Natalie still believed that she was well prepared for a regular store assignment.

After completion of the training course, Natalie was filled with confidence as she began her career as an assistant manager at one of Enigma's busiest and most profitable stores in an east coast suburban location. While the competitiveness of the training course was a surprise, she looked forward to the assignment because it was close to her parents' home and it was within easy driving distance to major metropolitan areas. As an assistant manager, Natalie was given significant responsibility for the Housewares department. She was told that her duties covered all aspects of the department, including inventory control, customer service, staff scheduling and hiring, and merchandise presentation. It was explained to Natalie that her "normal" work week would be Tuesday through Saturday, from

9:30 a.m. to 6:30 p.m., but that Enigma's culture dictated that the managers see their responsibility to their stores as being 24 hours a day, seven days a week.

One Year Later

Natalie has really begun to dread these visits to the doctor's office. The regular migraine headaches she developed from the very beginning of her time at Enigma were bad enough, but now the heartburn and stomach distress are almost unbearable. While she sat in the doctor's office, Natalie began to reflect on the past year at Enigma. The first six months had been really overwhelming. It took her a while to comprehend Enigma's use of a Darwinian "survival of the fittest" approach to employee development and retention. She had been thrown into the Housewares department with virtually no advance preview of the workings of the operation or the personnel. When she did meet with her boss in the afternoon of her second day, Natalie was told, for the first of many times, that this is a "sink or swim assignment, so you better dive in and start swimming."

The staff in Housewares included a mixture of full- and part-time employees. Generally, the full-time staff members were assigned to Housewares on a permanent basis, while part-timers could be assigned to any department in the store, depending on such factors as absenteeism or promotional campaigns. From the start of her assignment, Natalie felt a sense of hostility toward her from three full-time staff members, each of whom had been with Enigma for more than five years. Natalie believes that the hostility, which had subsided somewhat just in the last few weeks, resulted from two factors. First, the longer-tenured staff resented her being given the job of assistant manager without having paid any "dues" on the front lines of the department. Second, nearly all of the staff at the Enigma store had a negative view of management, primarily because of what were seen as Enigma's abusive demands and "factory-like" approaches to the supervision of its employees.

Natalie could accept the first factor since it was true that she was out of college for less than six months and she was supervising people who had been with the store for many years. Natalie was dismayed over the second factor, but saw its validity. During her recruitment, Enigma portrayed itself as a progressive and caring organization that was concerned about the quality of life of its employees. Yet the three-month training program and her work experiences clearly pointed to a different organization, one that saw its employees as nothing more than human capital that could be used up and then replaced. Horror stories (and turnover) were commonplace. Employees were regularly called upon to work ridiculous hours or abandon personal plans at the last minute because they were needed at the store. Also, the managerial culture dictated that employee difficulties were dealt with in an aggressive and dispassionate way. The abusive attitude toward the staff and the culture were troubling to Natalie because they went against the grain of her personality. She had always viewed herself as a friendly and caring person, but the store demanded that she think and act differently or risk being seen as not a team player.

Natalie's relationships with her boss and her fellow assistant managers were strained, to say the least. The competitiveness that was fostered in the training program carried over into operations of the stores. Natalie's boss, a woman in her mid-30s, was overtly ambitious, and she had no qualms about telling everyone who would listen that her goal was to be a vice president and regional manager by the time she was 40. The boss appreciated the contributions of the people who worked for her, but only to the extent that they could be instrumental in taking

(Continued)

(Continued)

her to the next level. Natalie believed that if she showed too much ambition or in any way tried to question the established procedures or culture, she would be seen as a threat and labeled a maverick and not supportive of the management team or Enigma's mission. So Natalie learned to implement changes and improvements in her department in a quiet fashion. Also, she tried to create a new culture within Housewares that encouraged teamwork as a way to improve performance. Through her efforts, Housewares had shown steady performance gains, and by the end of Natalie's first year, it was one of the top two departments in the store.

When it came to her relationships with her contemporaries, Natalie continued to find it difficult to create any sort of personal or emotional ties with the 11 other assistant managers. The encouragement of individualistic behavior, brought on by the store's penchant for interdepartmental performance comparisons, created a working environment where everyone was most concerned with his or her own performance, not the performance of the store in total. This environment also led to a variety of political behaviors being used, from backstabbing to outright sabotage. Although it took a little while, Natalie caught on to the self-serving games and had learned how to act when confronted with political behaviors.

In her personal life, it was tough for Natalie to engage in any social activities, let alone find an intimate relationship. She had been putting in 70-hour workweeks throughout her first year with Enigma, and the grueling schedule left little time for leisure or exercise. She realized that her health problems were partly attributable to a lack of outside interests that could have served to reduce stress. Just within the last two months, Natalie has vowed to spend more time in activities outside of work. She joined a health club and started socializing more with family and friends.

Despite all the tribulations of the past year, Natalie believed that she had grown in the managerial position at Enigma. The work culture wasn't real positive, and she still felt some residual hostility from her subordinates, but she had learned to cope and had actually been successful in putting her own imprint on the workings of her department and the store. After six months on the job she had wanted to quit, but now, even with the migraines, the heartburn, and the advice of her doctor to find a less stressful job, she thought she would stick it out for a while longer. (Part B of the Natalie case is at the end of Chapter 7.)

Case Analysis Questions

1. Critique the process Natalie went through in her selection of Enigma as an employer. Do you think the selection of Enigma was right for her? What could she have done differently in her job search?

2. Do think Enigma was right in the approaches it used to recruit Natalie? Should an employer have a moral obligation to always use realistic recruitment?

3. Do you believe that the "survival of the fittest" approach that Enigma used in developing its managers was an appropriate strategy? Do you think Natalie should have been more forceful in trying to correct managerial and cultural wrongs that she observed?

4. Do you agree with Natalie's decision to "stick it out for a while longer" with Enigma after she had been on the job for a year? Should Natalie have been more proactive in considering other employment options at this point in her career?

Appendix

Learning Exercises 7 and 8

LEARNING EXERCISE 7. REEXAMINATION OF PREFERRED WORK ENVIRONMENT (PWE)

Reread your responses to Learning Exercises 1, 2, and 3 before completing Exercise 7.

Component of PWE	Is PWE Accurate?	Is PWE Complete?	Where Can You Get More Information?
What tasks do you find interesting?	Yes No	Yes No	
What talents do you want to use?	Yes No	Yes No	
How much freedom and independence do you want?	Yes No	Yes No	
What type of relationships with others do you want?	Yes No	Yes No	
What physical work setting do you prefer?	Yes No	Yes No	
How important is money?	Yes No	Yes No	
How important is security?	Yes No	Yes No	
How important is balance of work, family, and leisure?	Yes No	Yes No	

LEARNING EXERCISE 8. FORMULATION OF CAREER STRATEGY TO ENTER CHOSEN OCCUPATION

Please list the activities necessary, the purpose of these activities, and the time frame needed to complete each one. Realize that the formulation of a strategy should occur for each occupation that you may be considering. Be thorough in listing your needed activities.

Activity	Purpose	Time Frame

CHAPTER 7

The Early Career Stage

Establishment and Achievement

In previous chapters we discussed the process of selecting career goals and choosing (or targeting) a job and an organization. This chapter examines the two dominant themes of the early career—establishing oneself in a career and then striving for additional achievement—and offers guidelines to advance career management at this stage.

In any new job, the first charge is literally to become established. There is much to learn in this phase. One must become accustomed to the day-to-day routine and must demonstrate mastery of new assignments. Acceptance by one's colleagues and bosses is another important consideration. In short, the hope is that one can become competent, productive, and satisfied in the new occupation and/or organization. Of course, it may take several years to determine whether competence, productivity, and satisfaction are attained. Once the establishment phase has passed, the next stage is achievement.

Having gained a measure of self-confidence and acceptance through the establishment phase, the next major task of the early career is to increase one's level of achievement and to contribute to one's employer (or employers). Several questions arise at this point. Should an employee move from his or her current functional area to another department? Should one make preparations to assume a managerial role? Are there sufficient opportunities at one's company to pursue a number of different options? If not, what high-level opportunities are available at other companies? This second phase of the early career typically reflects a concern for, if not a preoccupation with, achievement and accomplishment. Of course, the pursuit of career achievement and accomplishment has become more complicated over the past several years as companies have taken a more "transactional" approach to hiring and upward mobility and as individual careers have become more "boundaryless." Disruptions brought on by corporate mergers and downsizings also make it difficult for individuals to follow a standard path toward achievement of career goals.

Table 7.1 identifies changes that typically occur during the course of the early career. Employees early in their tenure with an organization tend to be somewhat dependent on

TABLE 7.1 Changes During the Early Career

Establishment Themes	Achievement Themes
Fitting in	Moving up
Dependence	Independence
Learning	Contributing
Testing competence	Increasing competence
Insecurity	Self-confidence
Seeking approval	Seeking authority

the organization for guidance and also exhibit a need for security. However, as these same individuals gain more years of experience, they become more confident, assertive, dominant, independent, and achievement oriented and less concerned with gaining approval from others. In addition, their achievement and self-fulfillment needs become more prominent. As individuals mature in the early career, they do so not in a vacuum, but develop a sense of self through competency in developing relationships with others.[1] In time, both the Establishment and Achievement themes enable men and women in the workplace to become competent contributors.

Although it is impossible to pinpoint the timing of the transition from establishment to achievement, such a shift is likely to occur. This fact does not suggest that neophyte employees care little about achievement, nor are veteran employees unconcerned about learning and gaining acceptance and security. We recognize that more senior individuals who are starting out in a new job might be concerned with establishing themselves in the new company while their peers of the same age might be more concerned with achievement. Thus, the relative emphasis on establishment and achievement can fluctuate during the course of the early career.

THE ESTABLISHMENT PHASE

A person beginning—or redirecting—his or her career is traveling in foreign territory. An unproven commodity at this point, the new employee needs to answer at least some of the following questions.[2] Will the job give me an opportunity to test myself? Will I be considered a worthwhile employee? Will I be able to maintain my individuality and integrity? Will I be able to lead a balanced life? Will I learn and grow? Will I find the work environment stimulating and enjoyable? Will I "fit in" after being out of the workforce for several years raising my children? The employee at this point is a newcomer to the organization and has not yet acclimated to the organization psychologically. Therefore, there is a strong need to become accepted as a competent, contributing member of the firm, while exhibiting positive work habits and attitudes and establishing effective relationships with coworkers.[3]

At the same time, the organization must ensure that the new person learns how to perform the job and how to fit into the company. Fitting in requires more than a mastery of task skills. It also requires learning how the organization operates, what actions are rewarded or punished, and the organization's values, culture, and social network. New hires and others in the establishment phase generally are the most receptive to information about the company and the ways they can make a contribution to it. Organizations were once concerned about the employee *assimilating,* yet the concept of mutual *acceptance,* where both employee and employer favorably receive the other, is equally important.[4]

Just as a person growing up learns about society's values and norms (e.g., thrift, honesty, cooperation), so too must the newcomer learn how to function in the organization. Organizational socialization can be defined as "the process by which an individual learns appropriate attitudes, behaviors, and knowledge associated with a particular role in an organization."[5] It is generally believed that those who are well socialized into a firm are more likely to stay and develop their careers within the organization. This is true because the socialization process allows the employee to learn the functions and hierarchy of the organization and become indoctrinated in the organization's culture.

An organization's culture can be defined as

> a pattern of basic assumptions invented, discovered or developed by a given group
> as it learns to cope with its problems of external adaptation and internal
> integration that has worked well enough to be considered valid and, therefore, is
> to be taught to new members as the correct way to perceive, think, and feel in
> relation to those problems.[6]

Socialization of new organizational members is the primary mechanism by which an organization can ensure the stability and perpetuation of its culture. Thus, proper socialization has an influential role in the longer-term survival of the firm since it serves to ensure continued adherence to the norms, values, and essential mission of the enterprise. By creating an environment of mutual acceptance, the organization has properly socialized recruits and allowed them to be integrated into their new work environment.[7]

In essence, socialization is a learning process wherein the individual moves or changes from a former role (perhaps that of a college student, stay-at-home parent, or employee in a prior organization) into the new role of employee in the current organization. Evidence suggests that well-designed socialization processes can positively influence individual motivation, job and career satisfaction, income, job involvement, and organizational commitment.[8] Consequences of these positive influences include enhanced individual and organizational performance, and lower levels of employee turnover.

From the new employee's perspective, successful socialization is critical because it is difficult, if not impossible, to be competent and accepted without learning about and adjusting to the organization. Socialization is also essential to organizations. After all, organizations have histories and procedures that have been tested by time and tradition, and have ongoing work groups with established norms and priorities. Somehow, the newcomer must learn how to operate within an organization's established cultural system to become successful.

Content Areas of Socialization

Based on a review of the socialization literature and research, Georgia T. Chao and her colleagues identified six content areas of socialization.[9] The six areas represent the possible outcomes an organization would expect to result from the socialization process.

1. Performance proficiency: the extent to which the individual has successfully learned the tasks involved on the job

2. People: the extent to which the individual has established flourishing work relationships with organizational members

3. Politics: the extent to which the individual has been successful in gaining information regarding formal and informal work relationships and power structures within the organization

4. Language: the extent to which the individual has learned the profession's technical language as well as the acronyms, slang, and jargon that are unique to the organization

5. Organizational goals and values: the extent to which the individual has learned the organization's culture, including informal goals and the values espoused by organizational members, especially those in powerful or controlling positions

6. History: the extent to which the individual understands and appreciates the organization's traditions, customs, myths, and rituals, as well as the personal backgrounds and work histories of important or influential organizational members

Well-designed socialization programs attempt to address most if not all of the six content areas as listed above. Organizations can facilitate socialization through building a strong culture that then disseminates (either formally or informally) consistent lessons for newcomers. Organizations interested in attracting and retaining the best talent should purposively manage the socialization process.[10] Nonetheless, a substantial amount of socialization takes place informally as individuals observe and monitor the behavior of others in the organization and as they are exposed to the inner workings of their employer.

Stages of Organizational Socialization

A number of researchers have proposed that socialization follows a sequence of stages as presented below.[11]

Stage 1. Anticipatory Socialization. The socialization process begins informally, even before the employee joins the organization on a full-time basis. Career choices are based initially on rough ideas of what a career will be like. Individuals gather these ideas from books, television shows, or Internet searches. Or they may be learned vicariously through interactions with others (family, teachers, and friends). Job candidates enter the recruitment process with specific expectations about organizational life and their future career. As discussed in Chapter 6, the major concern at this early career stage is that these expectations are realistic, so that individuals have a reasonable chance of meeting them and of utilizing their talents.

Formal anticipatory socialization programs can include internships, apprenticeships, cooperative educational assignments, and informational interviews. These programs provide positive developmental experiences for individuals entering the work world. Research has found that such assignments improve career decision-making self-efficacy, strengthen one's self-concept, allow one to acquire job-related skills, and allow students a significant advantage in gaining full-time employment upon graduating.[12]

Stage 2. Entry/Encounter. The recruit begins employment and encounters a new environment. In fact, the environment is not only new, but may depart radically from the newcomer's expectations in many ways. This early learning environment includes a sense-making process, as the newcomer reconciles unmet expectations with the new reality of the job.[13]

There are also enormous learning requirements for the recruit. There are new tasks to learn, new relationships to cultivate, new work groups to enter, and new policies and procedures to grasp. In short, one needs to "learn the ropes." Organizational newcomers should recognize the need to take an active role in learning the work processes and culture of their new company. These learning activities can be both formal and informal in nature. Often, informal lessons may reinforce formal procedures, or they may influence individuals in directions that are not sanctioned by the firm.[14]

Organizations realize that newcomers have a great deal to learn. Often, this recognition is couched in terms of "breaking in" the new recruit. Although it is debatable whether the treatment of people deserves the same term as applied to a new pair of shoes, it cannot be denied that substantial learning must take place during this early period of employment. But how do newcomers learn the ropes? Either consciously or unwittingly, organizations attempt to socialize newcomers in a variety of ways. Socialization tactics used by organizations can be broken down into two types: institutionalized and individualized. Institutionalized socialization consists of common programs and training experiences that are formally presented to all (or nearly all) new organizational members. On the other hand, individualized socialization consists of unique activities and learning experiences that are specifically targeted to one person. Listed below are some of the common organizationally sponsored socialization techniques.

1. *Recruitment* can be defined as activities engaged in by the firm with the purpose of attracting potential employees; these potential employees may be internal or external recruits. Recruitment is considered a socialization technique because it enables organizations to select candidates whose talents and values are most compatible with the organization's requirements. In addition, realistic recruitment can be used to set candidates' expectations to more appropriate levels. Realistic recruitment involves presenting the job in both a positive and negative light, thereby reducing the degree of reality shock experienced. Realistic recruitment usually offers information to the recruit that is important in order to complete job assignments, and is not widely known to those outside the firm.[15]

2. *Training* activities are designed to provide instruction on job-related tasks and to orient the newcomer to the organization's goals and practices. Through planned learning programs, newcomers develop their competencies in order to perform to the best of their abilities. Training and development activities have evolved from one-on-one apprenticeship programs, to programs that blend classroom instruction, systematic job instruction, team building, simulation, Web-based or computer-based individualized instruction, and satellite videoconferencing, among others. Research suggests that when companies offer a variety of newcomer training options, employees are able to choose the method that best fits their development needs.[16]

3. *Debasement experiences* are also used to socialize the newcomer.[17] In one version, "sink or swim," the employee is given a difficult assignment with little guidance or support. Organizations may also provide an "upending experience" by assigning tasks that are trivial or insoluble, thereby making it clear to the new employee that the organization is in control. Milder forms of debasement might include hazing and scut work designed to put newcomers in their place right from the start. Most people have played (or will play) the gofer role (go for coffee, etc.) that often befalls the lowest and newest person in the hierarchy. Regardless of the specific form, debasement strategies are intended to shake the newcomer's confidence so that the organization can influence or reshape his or her behavior. Successful completion of debasement strategies may be followed with initiation ceremonies and rites of passage that indicate the newcomer is no longer a rookie, but is now a full-fledged member of the organization.[18]

4. *Reward and control systems* also provide socialization experiences to the newcomer. New employees learn what an organization values by observing what activities or outcomes are rewarded. Objective market and financial indicators are used to monitor employees' accomplishments in such areas as increasing sales, improving profits, and serving as agents for change. Performance appraisals and promotions normally are related to progress along preestablished dimensions.

Organizations can involve multiple raters or sources of information (otherwise known as 360 degree feedback) when giving performance appraisals. This type of appraisal provides data from a variety of both internal and external constituents (customers, coworkers, supervisors, and subordinates). One goal of 360 degree evaluations is to eliminate the subjectivity associated with one person (the supervisor) assessing the employee. Rather, a variety of views are gained, thereby giving the employee a holistic appraisal that one hopes offers specific opportunities for growth.[19]

Stage 3. Change and Adjustment. We have seen how newcomers encounter the reality of a new work environment and are subject to pressures to adapt to these realities. In what ways do they change as a result of encountering this new environment? Put another way, how do they know if the socialization process has been successful? Research suggests that change and successful adjustment can take a number of forms:[20]

1. Has the employee learned the job? It is essential that task demands be sufficiently mastered so that the newcomer performs successfully and dependably and feels successful in the job role.

2. Has the employee been integrated into the work group? Successful integration requires an appropriate level of mutual trust and acceptance so the group can operate effectively. The recruit must typically adjust to the group's established practices, norms, and values. For example, a group that emphasizes cooperation and good-natured kidding is likely to put pressure on a new member to adopt these behaviors.

3. Has the employee achieved an acceptable level of role clarity? Can he or she handle the ambiguities and conflicts inherent in the organization? Conflicts may arise between work and outside life (family or leisure activities) and between the demands of the work group and other groups in the organization. The successful resolution of these conflicts is an important learning task for newcomers.

4. Has the employee learned how to work within the system? Working within the system means dealing with one's manager and peers, overcoming resistance to new ideas, accepting initially low levels of responsibility, and understanding the

reward system. Interestingly, experienced employees can learn much about their own roles and the organization when they socialize newcomers.

5. Does the employee understand and accept the organization's values? Is the recruit, for example, beginning to act, think, and feel like an integral part of the company? In other words, is the newcomer's self-concept changing to be more in line with the organization's values? Have the culture and norms of the organization been successfully transmitted? This is, in fact, the heart of the socialization process.

Edgar Schein distinguished pivotal or essential values (e.g., belief in free enterprise, acceptance of organizational hierarchy) from relevant values that are desirable but not absolutely essential for employee acceptance (e.g., dress codes).[21] One sign of unsuccessful socialization is a new employee's rejection of an organization's values and norms, either pivotal or relevant. Newcomers who react with such "rebellion" are unlikely to survive in the organization, unless their talent level is so high as to make their "rebellious" behavior tolerable.

Schein also suggests that the blind acceptance of all values produces a level of conformity and sterility that can be disastrous for the individual and the organization. For example, newcomers who accept all values of an organization may become so tied to the system that they are incapable of making needed changes in the organization when they develop more influence later in their career. In line with this view, several researchers have found that the type and intensity of a newcomer's organizational socialization experiences can detract from individual innovation.[22]

Another response, what Schein calls creative individualism, is the most desirable outcome of the socialization process. In this case, pivotal values and norms are accepted, but the less essential ones may be rejected. By retaining portions of their own identity, such creative individualists should be able to make the most innovative contributions to the organization over time. While accepting the core goals and values of the organization, creative individualists are able to question some of the organization's less useful qualities and can effect changes in these qualities as they acquire more influence in the system.

Mutual Acceptance and the Psychological Contract

Successful socialization is signified by a sense of mutual acceptance. The individual accepts the organization by sustaining high levels of involvement, motivation, and commitment and by deciding to remain with the organization for the present time.

Simultaneously, the organization accepts the newcomer as a trusted and valued member. Having survived the initial trials and obstacles, the individual has, to a certain extent, proven himself or herself in the eyes of the organization. Veteran employees signify their acceptance of the newcomer in a number of ways: by providing a positive performance appraisal, more challenging assignment, promotion, or substantial salary increase; by introducing the newcomer to crucial social knowledge about the organization and its people; and by involving him or her more extensively in group interactions. Without being accepted into the work group, the newcomer is unlikely to be fully involved with the organization. The process of assimilation and acceptance enables all parties to be full organization members focused on achieving the organization's goals.[23]

Mutual acceptance also shows an initial approval of the psychological contract between the individual and the organization. Psychological contracts are the implied agreements between employer and employee that serve to specify the contributions an employer believes are owed to the organization, as well as the inducements the employee believes are owed in return from the organization.[24] As we noted in Chapters 1 and 2, there exist two forms of psychological contracts: relational and transactional. The "traditional" view of careers assumed a relational contract between employer and employee involving a high degree of commitment to the relationship by both parties. In contrast, a transactional contract is more short term in nature and is predicated on performance-based pay, involves lower levels of commitment by both parties, and allows for easy exit from the agreement. A transactional contract is economic and extrinsic, and usually remains stable and observable over the length of the relationship.[25]

Historically, the relational psychological contract provided security to the organization and to the individual worker through the formation of this unwritten social bond between the employer and employee. From this perspective, adherence to the relational psychological contract made life simple and predictable for the employing organization and the individual. More precisely, the relational psychological contract promised security and the possibility of advancement in exchange for the employee's singular commitment to the organization.[26] For example, upon entering an organization, an individual may have expected that in exchange for hard work, good performance, and loyalty, the organization would provide increasingly interesting and challenging work, substantial salary increases, and rapid advancement. Thus, the organization expected the employee to make many personal and family sacrifices for the good of the company in exchange for steady advancement and the promise of job security.

Even with the shift from relational to transactional psychological contracts, the employee and the organization still go through the process of testing one another. This testing puts each party in a better position to evaluate the viability of its expectations. The individual has a better sense of the organization's responses to his or her efforts, and the organization has a better idea of what it can expect from the employee. However short lived, mutual acceptance represents a tentative approval of continued employment, or a ratification of the psychological contract. What follows is an example of mutual acceptance.

> Sarah started work in the budget department of a large department store chain a little more than a year ago. She was impressed with the company right from the start—everyone inside and outside of her department made her feel welcome. After two months with the company Sarah's career got a boost, although she didn't see it that way at the time. Specifically, the senior budget analyst who was in charge of tracking the company's capital expenditures and assessing future spending plans resigned suddenly. With no one else available to fill the void, Sarah stepped in and assumed the role. As a junior analyst with limited work experience, Sarah found the job of simultaneously learning the capital budgeting system and dealing with day-to-day expenditures to be extremely stressful. Her prior work experiences helped, and Sarah was determined to succeed. Sarah performed so well that the company promoted her to budget analyst after only six months and she received a 10 percent raise. Time and again her company's management has commented on her outstanding work. She has been identified as someone who can advance rapidly and she has been given added responsibilities. Sarah enjoys her work and socializes frequently with the other people in her department. After one year she is really committed to the company and, from all indications, the company is committed to her.

This case provides an example where mutual acceptance is an outcome of the socialization process. But there are many situations in which a bad match is recognized by the individual and/or the organization—a violation, in a sense, of the initial psychological bond. Perhaps the individual did not live up to the organization's expectations, or the organization did not provide the kind of work setting the individual expected. In such situations, employees may become less productive and less satisfied, and may ultimately choose to leave the organization. In those cases, mutual acceptance does not occur, and a mutually satisfying psychological contract is never established.

Continuing Tasks of Establishment

Mutual acceptance does not really terminate the establishment period. Rather, it provides some concrete feedback to the individual and the organization. Schein identified four other general issues that must be addressed during this phase.[27]

First, the employee must continue to improve on the job. If a new assignment or promotion is granted, the employee needs to demonstrate continued capability at higher levels of complexity and responsibility.

Second, the employee normally develops competence in a specialization area (e.g., marketing, engineering, information systems) that will serve as a foundation for the future career. Businesses generally expect their managers to be specialists in their early career, regardless of whether they ultimately want to move into a more general management position.

Third, the employee must continue to learn how to work effectively as a less experienced member of the organization. The employee is still relatively new and may not receive all of the autonomy he or she would like. In essence, employees must appreciate their status and must continue to learn how to work effectively within the constraints of the organization.

Fourth, employees should reassess their talents, values, and interests in light of their recent work experiences. There should be sufficient insight at this point to reevaluate the appropriateness of the chosen occupation and the opportunities within the organization. Decisions to remain or leave the career field and the organization need to be made.

Floundering: Learning Through Experience

The establishment period can evolve within one occupational field and one organization. However, there may also be considerable struggle and trial before a person finds a suitable line of work and a compatible organization in which to pursue the chosen work. People in their 20s may experience a "Quarterlife Crisis" when they graduate from college and confront the process of choosing a career, determining where they will live, carving out social relationships, and attempting to manage money. This period can indeed be rocky, especially when a young person has trouble finding a satisfying job. Young adults need to understand that part of the adjustment to adulthood is getting comfortable with one's self-identity—which in actuality is a process that continues throughout one's entire adult life.[28] Therefore, many people may try to establish themselves a number of times before they find a satisfying connection to the work world.

Consider the situation of Reginald, an MBA student, whose route to graduate school at age 30 demonstrates the tortuous path many people follow to establish a suitable career direction.

Reginald was an undergraduate management major who had given little thought to the kind of career he ultimately wanted. Because of limited job prospects, he accepted a position as a claims adjuster in a large insurance company, as an opportunity to learn about himself and the world of work. In time, he acquired the technical and interpersonal skills that made him a successful adjuster—so successful that after three years he was offered a promotion to claims supervisor. This promotion opportunity forced Reginald to consider whether he really wanted a career in claims. Realizing that he wanted more autonomy and financial rewards than his current career path could offer, he declined the promotion and left the company shortly thereafter.

Reginald next accepted a sales position with a national manufacturer of office copiers. He quickly knew he had made the correct decision. He enjoyed sales immensely and became one of the top producers. However, a number of disturbing policy and personnel changes (including the promotion of a less-qualified peer) convinced him that this was not the kind of company where he could grow and develop.

Reginald changed employers so he could pursue what was crystallizing as a natural career goal—to become a sales manager at a progressive company. He accepted a district sales manager position for a distributor of copiers. Although he performed well in this position, he thought the company's management style was too authoritarian.

At age 26, Reginald wondered if he could ever find the kind of company that would suit his values and career goals. He quit his position and went to work for a former boss, who was now regional manager at an office products firm. Although he started out as a sales representative, Reginald was promised the position of branch manager at the end of six months, when the current branch manager was to leave. Unfortunately, the job went to someone else, another old friend of Reginald's boss.

Disillusioned and bitter, Reginald quit the office products firm and, along with four other aspiring entrepreneurs, founded an Internet-based marketing organization. He looked forward to testing his skills in marketing and selling an innovative service. After six months, though, clients were few and expenses drained the company's cash flow. Hope was rapidly vanishing.

In the midst of his risky business venture, Reginald began to establish a serious romantic relationship and was now considering marriage. He became more concerned with stability in his career and his life. After one year of slow growth and an uncertain future, Reginald cut his ties with the company he had helped to form.

Seeking a more stable career direction, Reginald accepted a sales position with an audiovisual production company. He performed well in this position and, for the first time in his career, worked closely with marketing people. After six consecutive months of reaching his sales quota, however, Reginald was fired in a cost-cutting move.

Reginald was plagued with self-doubt. Was he unlucky or was he a failure? Was he unrealistic in his career goals or did he just have a series of bad breaks? Two months short of his 30th birthday and nine months before his wedding, Reginald was desperate. He called up friends to get a better handle on different career opportunities. He scanned newspapers for employment openings. Disillusioned with his experiences in sales, he listened with interest and excitement when his fiancée suggested he consider a career in marketing. Having spoken to a number of people, he was optimistic that marketing would satisfy his career interests. But he also learned that an entry-level position in marketing often required either prior marketing experience or an MBA degree.

With some trepidation, Reginald returned to graduate school to pursue an MBA on a full-time basis. He joined the MBA Society, a student-run group, and attended a "mentoring" session in which alumni spoke to students about career opportunities in different fields. Conversations with an alumnus eventually led to a summer internship in the marketing department of a large, prestigious consumer products company. Having just successfully completed the internship, Reginald finally feels that he has direction in his career. At the age of 30, his establishment as a marketing professional is just beginning.

This case illustrates the difficulties some people have in establishing their career. Finding a fit is not always easy. Career indecision, unrealistic expectations, personal shortcomings, lack of self-insight, organizational turmoil, and economic fluctuations can introduce considerable uncertainty and frustration into careers and lives.

On the positive side, however, people can learn from their experiences. Researchers at the Center for Creative Leadership in Greensboro, North Carolina, examined the lives and work experiences of executives as they developed through their careers.[29] Their studies have documented the important role that career difficulties, hardships, and traumas can have in promoting individual development. These hardships can include business failures and mistakes, career setbacks (e.g., demotions, missed promotions, dissatisfying jobs), subordinate personal or performance problems, and personal difficulties (e.g., divorce, work–family conflict, illness or death of a loved one or coworker). Successful responses to these career challenges can be shown in a number of ways, including a greater degree of sensitivity to others, recognition of one's personal limits, awareness of the need for balance between work and family life, acceptance of the need to take charge of one's career, and the development of coping strategies.[30]

No experience is really wasted, although it may appear so at the time. What Reginald had going for him was a considerable degree of self-insight, a determination to make his career work, a willingness to leave situations that no longer seemed tenable, and a strong belief that he could influence the course of his career. These traits will serve Reginald well throughout his career, even though they were found through difficult experiences early in his career.

ORGANIZATIONAL ACTIONS DURING ESTABLISHMENT

Effective Recruitment

Discrepancies between job expectations and the realities of the organization can inhibit a new employee's adjustment to the organization. As we discussed in Chapter 6, realistic recruitment procedures can play a significant role in helping newcomers establish themselves in their career and forge a healthy, candid relationship with the firm.

In addition, there is a tendency for organizations to select overqualified candidates for some positions because it is easier to choose the most qualified individuals than the best qualified. It is also easier to examine credentials than real job qualifications. Thus, college graduates might be sought to fill positions demanding a high school diploma, and MBAs are recruited for positions that require a bachelor's degree. In some instances, these high qualifications are justified because they are required for future jobs to which the employee might ultimately be promoted. In the meantime, however, many of these highly qualified newcomers may believe that their talents and training are underutilized in their first job and may leave (or become alienated) before they have had a chance to establish themselves. To avoid underutilization in these situations, organizations should provide the newcomer with sufficiently challenging, responsible tasks to maintain high levels of motivation and involvement.

Effective Orientation Programs

The first few days or weeks in an organization can be particularly critical in orienting the newcomer to the work environment. Effective orientation programs, now often called "onboarding" programs, can help new employees become part of the organization and inform them about the organization's policies, benefits, and services. Research has identified the following functions of new orientation/onboarding programs:[31]

- Introduction to the company

- Review of important policies and practices, including benefits and services

- Benefit plan enrollment

- Completion of employment forms

- Review of employer expectations and development of accurate employee expectations

- Introduction to peers and facilities

- Introduction to the new job

- Introduction of mentors

- Follow-up feedback session after initial orientation

Orientation or onboarding programs are designed to provide the newcomer with all the vital information (regarding people, processes, and technology) so that the person becomes integrated quickly into the organization.[32] Information that the organization sees as important for the newcomer to know immediately can include a review of company policies, practices, and benefits. Orientation programs also help the newcomer understand the organization's culture and the role the individual plays in making the company effective. The information provided should be responsive to newcomers' specific questions and needs, such as information on job-related questions or on particular career paths. Therefore, some portion of an onboarding/orientation program should involve small-group discussions and one-on-one sessions, where more attention can be devoted to individual concerns. For example, orientation programs can work to combat high levels of anxiety that new employees may experience. This support should be offered anywhere from the first few weeks to the first year. Finally, the program should offer follow-up by going through a checklist provided by Human Resources that identifies all the information that is essential to be shared with the newcomer. Honest feedback on the onboarding/orientation program should be solicited at this time.

Early Job Challenge

Most employees desire and expect high levels of challenge and responsibility on a new job, but many organizations are hesitant to provide early challenge and instead exercise tight supervision and control until newcomers are more experienced, skilled, and trusted.

However, when early job challenge is provided to new employees, the results can be quite beneficial and long lasting. Even pre-entry opportunities lead to positive experiences for newcomers. Interns who are given challenging job assignments note higher organizational commitment and loyalty when they join the organization full-time. Research has found that job challenge and job significance promote higher job satisfaction and the motivation for employees to learn their new job. Thus, individuals who perceive their jobs as challenging are more satisfied and respond by working harder and more creatively.[33]

Providing early challenge enables a new employee to internalize high work standards. A recruit who is exposed to substantial challenge learns that the organization is demanding, that it expects people to assume responsibility for decisions, and that it holds people accountable for results. As newcomers come to appreciate this emphasis on challenge, responsibility, and accountability, they will accept these standards as their own and will act in ways consistent with these standards.

It is also well documented that other people's expectations affect our behavior.[34] When supervisors expect their subordinates to handle additional challenge, they build more challenge into the job; offer help, encouragement, and support; and find that their optimistic predictions are confirmed by their subordinates' accomplishments—a self-fulfilling prophecy in action. Described below is an example of how PepsiCo provides early job challenge.[35]

> At PepsiCo, Inc., early job challenge is a key activity in grooming managerial and executive talent. PepsiCo's goal is to capture and convey the excitement of being part of a dynamic, results-oriented company, with powerful brands and world-class people. A career in the PepsiCo organization is intended to be an accumulation of challenging experiences over the course of many years—with each experience contributing to the growth of the individual and organization. The objective is to match great talent with important opportunities to build our business.
>
> Early in their career, individuals usually stay with one division, but are rotated through a multitude of varying assignments. The recruits are presented with significant work demands right from the start and are expected to perform to exacting standards. While for many the PepsiCo program can be demanding, those who survive receive exceptional rewards. Certainly, the PepsiCo approach is not for everyone. Some individuals may be slower starters or may need a higher degree of nurturance. Nonetheless, the PepsiCo program supports the view that early job challenge and demanding assignments can be pivotal in career development and advancement.

Douglas Hall proposed that employees who accomplish sufficiently challenging tasks experience a sense of psychological success (an internal feeling of being successful) that raises their self-esteem and sense of competence, increases their career involvement, and spurs them on to want even more challenge.[36] Hall's psychological success model explains how "success breeds success"—by giving employees a real opportunity to develop a positive self-image and to define success in their own subjective terms. Providing new employees with meaningful, challenging work right from the start may require the organization to reexamine its assumptions about recruits as well as its established traditions. Organizations also may have to reevaluate the most effective way to train recruits, perhaps moving in the direction of pre-entry programs like internships. Indeed, evidence suggests that the use of internships has grown substantially in recent years.

Organizations should not permit their stereotypes to interfere with early career growth. There is some evidence, for example, that women may be assigned to less challenging tasks than men, especially when the organization has had little experience working with women (or other underrepresented groups) in certain job classifications, or when the person making the assignment is male. These differences in early career experience may account for the wage and intrafirm mobility differences experienced by women.[37] The message should be clear: if women or other groups of employees are initially given less challenging assignments, their career growth may be unfairly stunted.

Frequent and Constructive Feedback

Although performance appraisal and feedback are important at all stages of career development, they are particularly crucial during the establishment years because of the newcomer's need to become competent and accepted. It is not enough to assign challenging tasks. Newcomers have to know how well (or poorly) they are performing on these tasks. Feedback must be frequent enough so that employees can make changes in their behavior on an ongoing basis to maximize learning. Moreover, if the feedback is positive, it can serve as a powerful source of praise and reinforcement. Also, performance feedback sessions provide an opportunity for supervisors and subordinates to discuss their assumptions and expectations about each other—to clarify the psychological contract.

But feedback must be administered in a constructive, supportive manner if it is to be effective. Employees tend to hold two simultaneous yet conflicting needs.[38] On one hand, they want honest feedback; they want to hear the truth. On the other hand, they also want to hear only good news to protect their sense of self-esteem and to receive extrinsic rewards.

Sometimes feedback is so negative and devastating that an adversarial and defensive relationship is created between supervisor and subordinate. In other cases, supervisors are so concerned about being "kind" that they provide no useful feedback to the subordinate. Perhaps most frequently, supervisors are so uncomfortable with performance appraisal that they simply avoid the process altogether.

As we noted earlier in the chapter, organizations can improve the appraisal and feedback process by using the 360 degree feedback technique. This allows the new employee to understand that the appraisal process is in fact for employee development, rather than for punitive reasons. Such efforts involve developing more useful performance appraisal forms, encouraging newcomers to engage in self-appraisal, extending the appraisers to include peers and others in and outside the organization, training supervisors in providing feedback, and separating discussions of performance feedback from discussions of salary and promotion decisions.

The First Supervisor: A Critical Resource

A newcomer striving for competence and acceptance requires what Douglas Hall called "supportive autonomy"—sufficient challenge and autonomy to develop a sense of psychological success and a supportive environment in which to make mistakes, learn, and grow.[39] The newcomer's supervisor can play a major role in providing supportive autonomy.

Subordinates have a number of task and personal needs that the manager can fulfill at different career stages. It takes a certain type of manager to play the roles of coach, feedback provider, trainer, role model, and protector in an accepting, esteem-building manner. Managers must be personally secure and unthreatened by subordinates' training, ambition, and values. In effect, managers should be viewed as the career developers of their subordinates and should be trained and rewarded for fulfilling this role.

Drew is an experienced retail manager in a large home goods store. He manages a group of 15 retail salespeople. He recently had two new salespersons join his group and it is obvious that the two newcomers have different needs as they try to become acclimated to their new retail environment. One newcomer, Doris, a mother of three, is in her early 40s. She had worked in another retail store for 11 years before she stopped working to raise her children. The other newcomer, Craig, is in his early 20s and recently graduated from a local university with a degree in Design and Merchandising. He has had relatively few work experiences, except for the summers when he worked part-time in a retail setting. Drew immediately saw Doris as a peer, but quickly recognized that he needed to coach Doris through the process of adjusting to the work setting and learning the intricacies of the company's computer systems. He has advised her to be patient as she becomes reacclimated to full-time work and as she learns specific tasks. In contrast, Drew has been more directive with Craig. He has tried to temper Craig's excitement about his new job, keep him focused on the tasks at hand, and help him to manage his time more wisely. As an enlightened manager, Drew consciously adapts his leadership style to meet the needs of his subordinates. Even though both Doris and Craig are newcomers, they have different needs given their levels of work experience.

Encouragement of Mentor Relationships and Other Supportive Alliances

Mentoring can be defined as relationships between junior and senior colleagues, or between peers, that provide a variety of developmental functions.[40] The establishment of a relationship with a mentor is thought to be one of the critical events of early adulthood, and finding a mentor or sponsor is seen as a major developmental task of the early career.[41]

The term *mentor* can be traced to Greek mythology in which Odysseus, absent from home because of the Trojan Wars, charged his servant Mentor with the task of educating and guiding his son Telemachus. In fulfilling this obligation, Mentor, through the wisdom provided by Athena, acted variously as teacher, coach, task-master, confidant, counselor, and friend.[42] In this historical sense, the mentor–protégé relationship was comprehensive (it involved educational, occupational, physical, social, and spiritual development) and was based on a high degree of mutual affection and trust. In a similar vein, as illustrated in Table 7.2, mentors fulfill both career and psychosocial functions.

TABLE 7.2   Mentoring Functions

Career Functions (primarily enhance career advancement)	Psychosocial Functions (primarily enhance sense of competence and effectiveness)
Sponsorship	Role modeling
Exposure and visibility	Acceptance and confirmation
Coaching	Counseling
Protection	Friendship
Challenging assignments	

SOURCE: Adapted from Allen, T. D. (2006). Mentoring. In J. H. Greenhaus & G. A. Callanan (Eds.), *Encyclopedia of career development* (pp. 486–493). Thousand Oaks, CA: Sage.

Most mentoring relationships are established when the protégé is in his or her early career, and some relationships may involve the protégé's immediate supervisor. A survey of executives revealed that over 75 percent of the respondents reported having had at least one mentoring relationship during their career.[43] Other studies have shown that individuals who had experienced a mentor relationship were earning more money at an earlier age, were better educated, and were more likely to follow a career plan than those who had not established a relationship with a mentor. In fact, research has consistently indicated that mentoring is related to a variety of positive work outcomes, including higher degrees of career and organizational commitment, recognition, satisfaction, career mobility, and compensation.[44] In addition, research has found that the positive outcomes of having a mentor are independent of gender or level in the organization. And mentoring lowers work and nonwork stress. Thus, mentoring can have a positive effect on individuals' job/career outcomes.[45]

Most people would readily agree that employees striving to establish their career would benefit from coaching, support, exposure to senior executives, sponsorship, and identification with a successful role model. The question is whether they need one mentor or a constellation of mentors to fulfill all of these roles. It is not clear that a single individual must fulfill, or is capable of fulfilling, all of the functions in the traditional sense. Current mentoring research suggests that protégés establish a developmental network of mentors, so that mentoring functions can be provided from a variety of sources. Under the assumption that not every mentor can provide advice and support with the same intensity, the developmental network provides protégés with a range of sources from which they can receive career support, emotional closeness, and important information. It has already been indicated that the first supervisor is a critical career developer of the new employee, as a coach, trainer, and feedback provider. Others in the constellation could include subordinates, peers, and customers, who may also provide job-related feedback, career strategy information, and emotional support.

Organizations can stimulate such diverse relationships by making it easier for newcomers to interact with these multiple benefactors. Discussion groups, seminars, and social gatherings are among the vehicles that can be used. Further, organizations can promote access to other types of career management and assessment mechanisms to achieve understanding and growth among newer staff members who may not have access to a mentor.[46] These activities, which could serve either as a supplement to, or as a substitute for, a formal mentoring program, should include career counseling and coaching, 360 degree feedback, and other forms of assessment.

Companies with formal mentoring programs have observed several benefits, including socialization of the protégé; better understanding of the organization's mission, values, structure, and informal systems; increased organizational communication; increased competence, motivation, and performance; greater organizational commitment and improved retention of new hires; identification of management talent; and enhanced diversity within the organization.[47] However, the "engineering" of relationships goes against the spontaneous and mutual attraction that normally characterizes mentoring alliances, and formal programs can cause anxiety and discomfort among participants, can create pessimism about career prospects for those not chosen to participate, and can overemphasize a single supportive relationship when in reality a constellation of developmental alliances is more enriching. The evidence to date suggests that the individual benefits received from formal mentoring relationships do not compare to the benefits received from informal relationships. However, the most important ingredient in formal relationships is the quality of the relationship, so organizations need to develop mechanisms to allow mentors and protégés to develop mutually supportive bonds.[48]

Because the upper echelons of corporate America are still dominated by a white male majority, much has been written about the perceived and actual difficulties of women and minorities in finding and maintaining a mentor during the early career years.[49] We discuss these challenges for individuals and organizations in Chapter 11 when we focus on managing diversity.

INDIVIDUAL ACTIONS DURING ESTABLISHMENT

Although the organization can take certain actions to facilitate the employee's career establishment, it is, as always, the individual who has the ultimate responsibility to manage his or her career effectively. Following are some steps individuals can take.

Career Exploration and Goal Setting

During the establishment years, it is essential that new employees understand their developmental needs. Similarly, newcomers should understand that this period is a time of mutual testing. Both the individual and the organization are assessing the presence or absence of a match. Without a conscious awareness of these issues, it is unlikely that useful information will be acquired and appropriate decisions made. It is, therefore, crucial for new employees to use their assignments, performance reviews, day-to-day observations, and informal relationships to learn more about themselves and the organization. With this knowledge and information, individuals should be willing and able to adjust career goals as necessary. Career management is a dynamic process, and one's goals can change as new insights are gained and organizational realities become clear.

Career Strategies: Influencing the Environment

Although the establishment period often requires the individual to adjust to the demands of the new environment, the newcomer is not a passive victim at the complete mercy of the organization. In fact, newcomers can play an active role in the ultimate success of the socialization process. Newcomers with a strong sense of self-competence can adopt active strategies and coping responses to understand the organization's culture and influence the environment.[50]

Since information and help do not always come when they are most needed, an assertive strategy is often required. Such an approach might include the following activities:

- Initiate discussions with your supervisor on ways to increase the level of challenge, responsibility, and variety in your job.

- Initiate discussions with your supervisor regarding your recent performance. If the feedback is not sufficiently specific or critical, politely but firmly seek greater detail.

- Analyze your supervisor's needs and discuss ways in which you can help your supervisor become more effective in his or her job.

- Seek information from peers who are in a position to observe your performance.

- Participate in formal programs to learn as much about the organization as possible.

- Read literature on the organization and seek answers to your questions.

- Develop informal contacts in the organization that can provide you with information, insights, and accumulated wisdom about the organization.

- Be prepared to share your perceptions and opinions with others. Mutual information sharing is more likely to sustain relationships than one-sided communications.

- Try to learn where the organization is heading and what skills it will require in the future.

- Reexamine the compatibility between your values, interests, and talents and the values, requirements, and opportunities in the organization.

One of the ways these strategies can be implemented is through employee networks. Networks are groups of employees organized (either formally or informally) to provide individual members with information about the company, allow employees to feed information back to the company, and encourage career management activities. One company that has sponsored formal employee networks is Avon Products, Inc. Avon believes that part of its corporate social responsibility is to provide avenues by which the employee can develop herself. Avon advocates workplace diversity and strives to create an environment that values and encourages the uniqueness of each employee. Avon is committed to creating a culture that supports employees as they balance their many, and sometimes competing, work and personal responsibilities. Around the globe, it has several internal networks including a parents' network, a Hispanic network, a black professional association, an Asian network, and a gay and lesbian network. The networks act as liaisons between employees and management to bring voice to critical issues that impact the workplace and the marketplace.[51] Certainly, early career stage employees would benefit both personally and professionally from participation in such networks.

THE ACHIEVEMENT PHASE

At some point during the early career, the concern with acceptance and "fitting in" subsides and striving for achievement and authority takes precedence. The shift from establishment to achievement is neither fixed in time nor abrupt, although it seems that a certain degree of security and acceptance may trigger achievement striving. It is also significant to recall that a large portion of the achievement period coincides with the period in adult development where the need to accomplish achievement-oriented goals becomes particularly strong.[52]

The achievement phase has been referred to as an "advancement" stage by several researchers, presumably because the desire for vertical mobility (i.e., promotions) is so strong. The term *achievement,* rather than advancement, is used here because it is a broader concept that can encompass many different forms of accomplishment. Achievement can mean different things to different people, and given the lack of quick vertical mobility for many employees, is a more relevant concept today.

Indeed, with wide variations in career aspirations, orientations, and patterns, the meaning of achievement, accomplishment, and success rests on the individual's career orientation and personal definitions. Further, compatibility between career orientation and job setting produces higher levels of job satisfaction, career satisfaction and organizational commitment, and a lower intention to leave an organization.[53] Conversely, incompatibility can result in higher degrees of dissatisfaction and a corresponding desire to leave the particular work setting. Consider the following example.

> As Arun has discovered, there is a fine line between being in a satisfying work environment and a dissatisfying one. For the last four years, Arun has worked in a department where the manager encouraged his people to be independent minded. The manager wanted his staff to be able to complete their assignments from start to finish based on their own knowledge and judgment, with the freedom to suggest and implement changes when they thought them necessary. Arun thrived in this kind of setting. He loved the independence and autonomy. It made him feel like a real contributor to the department's success. Unfortunately for Arun, a new manager took over the department five weeks ago. Since that time, Arun has seen a 180-degree turn in the way his work group is managed. New rules and procedures have been put in place requiring the daily monitoring of activities and accomplishments. On several occasions Arun has had to justify his routine decisions, and has even been criticized for not seeking approval from the different layers of management. Arun has found the meddling from above and the strict approval process to be disconcerting. If a turnaround doesn't happen soon, Arun is certain he'll have to look for another job.

There are a number of general issues that are the focus of concern to many employees during the achievement period:

1. To demonstrate continued, increasing competence in one's work assignments

2. To acquire additional levels of responsibility and authority in work assignments

3. To determine the most appropriate type of contribution one can make to oneself, the occupation, and the organization, such as whether to remain in a specialized function or to move into general management

4. To assess opportunities inside and outside the organization

5. To develop long- and short-range career goals consistent with one's career aspirations

6. To develop and implement strategies to attain one's career goals

7. To use values to drive career decisions and to be self-directed in making these decisions

8. To remain flexible and adaptive to changing circumstances

9. To understand that viable careers exist in and outside of "traditional" boundaries

10. To define for oneself what is meant by career success

ORGANIZATIONAL ACTIONS DURING ACHIEVEMENT

Provide Sufficient Challenge and Responsibility

During the establishment period, early job challenge enables newcomers to test their abilities and begin to make a real contribution to the organization. In the achievement period, employees have a greater urgency to enlarge their area of responsibility, to become more autonomous and independent, to "call the shots." Having spent a number of years learning and launching their career, employees are ready to acquire more responsibility.

Although additional responsibility can come through promotions and other forms of job mobility, the current job also can be used to this end. Jobs can be "enriched" to provide high levels of responsibility and autonomy and to permit the employee to keep learning, growing, and stretching. Employees also want meaningful tasks, and feel some significance in the work they do. The organization, especially the immediate supervisor, must consider ways to provide additional challenge and responsibility and must know its employees well enough to judge how much challenge they can handle. Participative goal setting, schedule and budget control, additional discretion on how jobs get accomplished, and participation in special assignments are all ways to enhance the level of challenge and responsibility. Providing feedback on tasks allows employees to have knowledge of their results, and enables them to adapt as needed to achieve set goals. In addition, job rotation, especially among early-career employees, has a positive influence on such career outcomes as promotability, salary progression, and overall job performance. Firms also gain from job rotation when there is uncertainty about employees and their skills because it allows both the firm and the employee to better understand what strengths the employee has and what learning needs to take place.[54]

Employees who aspire to higher-level management positions will need additional challenge and responsibility on their current job to groom themselves and test their capabilities for future positions. Moreover, added challenge and responsibility enable employees who wish to stay in their functional area or even on their current job to remain competent, motivated, and involved. An international study of leadership development practices found that carefully managed on-the-job assignments and skill assessments, not necessarily formal training, were key factors in allowing optimum individual development and growth.[55] The most respected leadership behaviors include the ability to "bring in the numbers," to take "a stand and make tough decisions," and to "mobilize a team." Other skills and experiences needed for achievement-oriented individuals include

- Strong interpersonal skills

- Passion for results

- Ability to bring out the best in people

- Having a network of mentors or personal coaches

Using the results from a number of studies on the developmental experiences of managers and executives, researchers from the Center for Creative Leadership identified 14 different components of managerial jobs that have important developmental consequences.[56] The 14 components of managerial jobs are shown in Table 7.3. As Table 7.3 indicates, the components are grouped according to whether they represent a job transition (a change in work role, job content, status, or location), the need to create change (such as starting an

TABLE 7.3 Developmental Components From Studies of On-the-Job Learning*

Development Task	Component
Job transitions	Line to staff
	Increases in job scope
	Radical job moves
	Changes in employers, status, or function
Creating change	Start-up operation
	Fix-it assignment
Assuming higher levels of responsibility	Organizational level
	Large-scale operations
Nonauthority relationship	Serving on task forces
	Making deals and coordinating among departments
Overcoming obstacles	Difficult boss
	Hardships
	Negative experiences
	Experience with crises and diversity

SOURCE: Adapted from McCauley, C. D., Ruderman, M. N., Ohlott, D. J., & Morrow, J. E. (1994). Assessing the developmental components of managerial jobs. *Journal of Applied Psychology, 79,* 544–560.

operation from scratch or engineering a turnaround), assuming higher levels of responsibility (moving to a job characterized by increased visibility and scope), exercising influence in nonauthority relationships (participating in projects or serving on a team where negotiation skills and coordination are required), and overcoming obstacles (dealing with difficult situations or adverse business conditions).[57] All of these assignments serve to increase the level of job challenge and stimulation afforded the individual employee.

Performance Appraisal and Feedback

The need to appraise performance never really ceases. Organizations must make a number of decisions about individual employees during their early career, decisions about promotability, training and development needs, and salary increases. These decisions are important not only for the so-called fast track manager, but for other managers and nonmanagers as well. In addition, employees continue to need ongoing performance feedback, especially as it relates to their career goals.

Construction of Realistic and Flexible Career Paths

In a traditional sense, a career path is a sequence of job positions, usually related in work content, through which employees move during the course of their careers. A standard career path for someone in marketing might involve the following positions: marketing representative, branch manager, a staff position at corporate headquarters, district marketing manager, regional marketing manager, and vice president of marketing. The identification of career paths can be helpful to organizations in planning their staffing needs and it can provide a structure for employees in planning their personal careers. Nonetheless, it is important to recognize that this traditional, standard view of career paths has been altered radically over the past two decades. The combined effects of mergers, downsizings, new technology, job restructurings, and new organizational designs either have eliminated (or mangled) career paths in many organizations or have made it difficult to formulate individual career plans that are based on a consistent path of jobs. As we have noted previously, these changes in the work environment dictate that individuals be more proactive, boundaryless, and protean in the ways they attempt to manage their movements along a career path that has the potential to shift (or be eliminated) at any given time.

The traditional approach to career path identification has been to examine the paths that employees have historically traveled in the organization. Like the marketing example just cited, these traditional paths tend to be oriented along functional or departmental lines and emphasize vertical motility. Although historically derived career paths may be useful, they tend to be overly narrow and constraining and are based on what has happened, not what might or should happen.

Instead of relying on history and tradition, an alternative approach develops paths based on similarity in required job behaviors and knowledge and skill requirements. The development of such career paths involves thorough analysis of job content, grouping of similar jobs into "job families," and identification of logically possible paths of progression among these job families. Cross-functional paths are also possible; they may leverage company or functional experiences into new environments.

This form of career path development is realistic in that various paths are defined by actual job behavior requirements, rather than by job title or tradition. This method provides an individual with flexibility in career mobility since one can more easily move across functional lines. Initially limited career mobility opportunities can be greatly expanded when career paths are analyzed according to their behavioral, knowledge, and skill requirements.

Stimulate Career Exploration

Many organizations sponsor workshops, seminars, discussion groups and counseling to aid the self-assessment process. Moreover, since much self-insight can be gained through ongoing job experiences, timely, constructive performance feedback and coaching sessions with a supervisor or other significant person is a useful ingredient in any self-assessment effort.

Organizations also can help employees gather information on alternative job opportunities. Effective job exploration requires up-to-date job descriptions that provide accurate information on job duties and behaviors, knowledge and skill requirements, demands, and rewards. However, information on jobs or career paths will not be useful unless it gets to the people who need it. Ideally, line managers should be provided with sufficiently detailed information on jobs and career paths to aid their subordinates' career planning efforts. Job posting programs and career days are other vehicles for disseminating job-related information. Today, many job postings are available on company intranets (available only to employees) or on the company Web site. These sites allow both employees and potential candidates to explore career options. An example of a company-sponsored job-posting Web site is provided below.

> The Johnson and Johnson organization (J&J), headquartered in New Brunswick, New Jersey, uses a company-wide job posting program called QuickConnect. On this Web site, all career opportunities and event information is listed. J&J prides itself on having a small company environment, especially concerning the employees' careers, yet operating within the bounds of a big company. The QuickConnect Web site also provides information on the company's business strategy and history, commitment to workforce diversity, organizational structure, shared values and credo, career path options, career development, and reward and compensation practices. Also, career opportunities are provided whether they are for seasoned professionals or for graduating students. J&J employees can manage their own career profiles on the site, thereby allowing potential hiring managers to find employees who might fit their needs. Leadership development programs are offered for soon-to-be-graduating MBAs with interest in the finance, human resource, international, or procurement management fields. Similarly, college seniors can identify opportunities within the financial, global operations, and information technology leadership development programs. These programs emphasize mentoring, cross-business experiences, interaction with senior management, training, and a wide variety of assignments to increase the candidates' learning potential.[58]

Exploration designed to understand the organization—its goals and strategies, future human resource needs, mobility opportunities, reward systems, and the like—can be encouraged and aided in a number of ways. Although much of this type of learning takes place informally through mentoring relationships, organizations can provide information on their business and human resource plans. Organizations should provide realistic information on mobility patterns, a sort of realistic career preview, so that employees' expectations are in line with the reality of the organization's environment. Lateral movement within firms may be a sound mobility strategy for development of new competencies. While once considered a "kiss of death" to one's career, downshifting, or movement down the hierarchy, is now being used by individuals who want to redirect their careers and need to learn necessary skills to prepare for another position.[59]

INDIVIDUAL ACTIONS DURING ACHIEVEMENT

A great deal of advice has been offered to employees who aspire to higher-level positions in organizations. Common to all of these guidelines is the need for individual initiative and self-determination—an active approach to career management. A number of potentially useful actions recommended in the literature are discussed below.

Set Realistic Goals

Goal-setting procedures were examined extensively in Chapter 5. At this time, it is important to remember that if the employee does not establish goals, the goals will likely be established (or assumed) by the organization to fit its own needs. Therefore, it is in the employee's best interest to reconsider established career goals (conceptual and operational) periodically, set new goals where necessary, and communicate these aspirations to the organization.

One important decision for many individuals is whether to remain in a specialized function within the organization or prepare to seek a general management position. The decision to contribute as a specialist versus a generalist should not be based only on the availability of positions in the current organization and other organizations, but also on the fit of the position with one's career orientation. Individuals who hold certain career orientations, such as a technical/functional career anchor, may wish to make their contribution as a specialist. Individuals who hold other orientations, the managerial competence anchor for example, may see more challenge and rewards in a general management position. The achievement period of the early career can be a critical time to examine these kinds of alternatives. An analysis of one's cumulative work experiences, discussions with one's supervisor and/or significant other, and participation in career-planning programs can help the employee assess his or her dominant career orientation.

Another issue to consider is that traditional advancement prospects, at least in a hierarchical sense, are comparatively far more limited in the current business environment. Intense competition, mergers and acquisitions, and the need to stay "lean and mean" are combining with the sheer number of people born in the baby boom generation to effectively restrict upward mobility opportunities. Due to these conflicting factors, achieving hierarchical success (i.e., promotion) is becoming more uncommon, but ways to achieve subjective career success are infinite.[60] Recognizing this fact is a key to setting realistic, achievable career goals. Indeed, individuals should be less concerned with upward advancement and instead appreciate both the diversity in career paths that may satisfy their needs and the skill sets required to pursue these paths. This diversity may involve planning and setting goals that include lateral moves, downward moves, higher degrees of specialization in a given function, and leaving the organization to join another organization or to start one's own business. The premise is that one's sense of accomplishment, satisfaction, and achievement can be gained in diverse ways, not only through promotions. We will discuss this concept further in Chapter 8 when we cover possible reactions to career plateauing and obsolescence.

Performance and Responsibility on the Current Job

It is often observed that mobile managers have learned to become a crucial subordinate to a mobile boss. Being crucial means demonstrating technical competence, of course, but it also means developing skills that complement the boss's skills and make the boss look good.

This strategy requires that subordinates understand their superiors' skills, needs, and aspirations. It has been observed that a boss's needs depend on his or her own career stage.[61] For example, a boss in the establishment period needs technical and psychological support from the subordinate, whereas one in the achievement period requires loyal followership that enhances the performance and reputation of the boss. Subordinates should understand their needs, their boss's needs, and the constraints under which the boss operates and establish a feedback and evaluation system for assessing the relationship between themselves and their boss.

Individuals also must recognize that the types of job experiences and the length of tenure in high-responsibility jobs can play a critical role in determining career performance and progress. As discussed in Chapter 5, career strategies should take into account not only those assignments that are important for future advancement, but also recognize that there are certain jobs that can cause untoward disruptions in career progress and thus should be avoided if possible. Awareness of dead-end jobs and "derailment" type assignments is a critical factor in successfully managing one's career.[62] Derailment, or the movement off an established track of upward mobility, normally represents a mismatch between the demands of the work situation and one's personal skills. While derailment is caused by a multitude of issues, individual and contextual factors that can lead to derailment include one or more of the following: problems with interpersonal relationships, a failure to meet business objectives, an inability to build and lead a team, and an inability to develop or adapt to a new work situation or demands. Derailed managers have been found to be less self-motivating and less focused on continuous learning.[63]

It is also important not to be trapped by narrow job descriptions. Employees can attempt to expand their jobs by volunteering to take on new assignments and responsibilities. Again, this demands an active stance on the individual's part. If further expansion is not possible and further learning is unlikely, it may be time to leave the position.

Mobility Paths

Employees with upward mobility aspirations should be willing to nominate themselves for future positions. But not all job changes are equally useful. Highly mobile managers must understand the most promising paths (and the related career strategies) that will allow them to achieve their goals. In addition, they apply the boundaryless and protean concepts of career management in that the career strategies they pursue for upward mobility are kept flexible enough to accommodate the inevitable twists and turns that are faced throughout their work lives.

While pursuing appropriate career strategies is critical to attaining career success, it is also important to recognize the role of individual personality in career management. A wide range of personality traits—for example, emotional stability, extraversion, proactivity, positive mood, and self-monitoring (awareness of social expectations and ability to modify behavior accordingly)—have been associated with various aspects of career success.[64] As Michael Crant has concluded from his review of personality and careers, "Our personality fundamentally shapes who we are, how other people view us, and the situations that we choose to enter. By better understanding who we are and identifying the various elements of our own personality, we can make better decisions about careers."[65]

Attaining Sponsorship

Support and sponsorship from bosses, mentors, and other influential people are often crucial to goal attainment. Although high visibility and exposure are necessary to attain sponsorship, they are not sufficient. The sponsored individual should also be a high performer and be loyal and trustworthy to superiors. That is, the individual helps the supervisor attain organizational goals, minimizes risks for the supervisor, and prevents potentially embarrassing outcomes. In short, such an employee is a crucial subordinate. Developmental relationships and support are especially critical during the achievement phase of one's career. As discussed earlier, employee development can be supported by a constellation of individuals, including mentors, superiors, peers, subordinates, and friends both inside and outside one's current organization.[66]

A Word of Caution

Many of the strategies discussed above have a "chess-like" quality in that they involve constant adjustments and frequent movement. Each move is made as a stepping stone to the next position. There is nothing wrong with this strategy as long as the jobs comprising this route to success are themselves satisfying and compatible with the person's needs and values. One must also determine whether career goals and strategies are consistent with the desired balance of work, family, and leisure activities. Extensive work involvement, intense competition, and frequent relocations may provide career success, but at the expense of personal failure on the home front.[67] Excessive levels of organizational and career commitment can have adverse consequences for both the individual and those around him or her. Stress and tension in social and family relationships and limited time for nonwork and leisure activities have negative consequences. The impact of work experiences on stress and quality of life will be examined in Chapters 9 and 10.

THE EARLY CAREER: A QUESTION OF TIMING

We have seen how the early career is initiated by a period of establishment followed by a dominant concern with achievement and accomplishment. We also positioned the early career within early adulthood (ages 25 to 40). It is in the era of early adulthood that socialization to work, launching a career, and settling down to pursue one's dream normally take place.

However, one must recognize that the establishment–achievement cycle can be triggered by a career transition any number of times during adulthood. All job changes require resocialization to a somewhat unfamiliar task and interpersonal environment. Such resocialization is probably prerequisite to subsequent achievement and innovation. Changing employers or career fields would undoubtedly require some form of resocialization and reestablishment, since the new environments would be as unfamiliar as the previous environment originally was.[68]

Moreover, establishment and achievement concerns can be reactivated during middle or late adulthood. Individuals in their 40s, 50s, and 60s who change jobs, employers, or occupations are faced with similar pressures to establish themselves in a new environment. One can only speculate whether the establishment and achievement pressures of these people are as severe, given their more extensive work and life experiences.

Recall our example of Sharon from Chapter 6. She had spent 23 years with one company, rising to the level of vice president for planning and development. At the age of 46 she was cut loose by her employer, and eventually found a new job (albeit with lower prestige and responsibility) as business planning manager for a small automotive products retailer. In beginning this new position, Sharon had to endure the demands of establishing herself as described earlier in this chapter, even though chronologically she was in midlife. She had new people to meet, new rules and procedures to follow, and a new culture to comprehend. She had to accept early job challenge and "hit the ground running" in order to prove her worth.

Thus, as this example indicates, the dominant themes of the early career, establishment and achievement, are not strictly limited to people in their 20s and 30s. It follows that the organizational and individual actions recommended in this chapter can also be applied to a wider group of people than those in their early career. Ultimately, it behooves individuals to understand their own developmental needs (whatever their age) and organizations to recognize the implications of these needs for the individual's career growth and the organization's effectiveness.

SUMMARY

The early career poses two major tasks for an employee: establishment and achievement. The initial task of the early career is to establish oneself in a career field; that is, to gain competence in the job, to learn the ropes in an organization, and, ultimately, to gain acceptance as a valued contributor. An organization attempts to socialize new employees by providing job-related training, rewarding desirable behavior and punishing undesirable behavior, and communicating and reinforcing its dominant values and norms through socialization. The new employee who has undergone successful socialization is competent on the job, is integrated into the work group, achieves a satisfactory level of role clarity, learns to work within the system, and internalizes the key values and norms of the organization.

Organizations can help new employees establish their careers by developing effective recruitment and orientation practices, offering important early job challenge, providing constructive performance feedback, and helping employees develop supportive relationships with their supervisor and other important members of the organization. At the same time, individual employees can engage in career exploration to understand themselves and their new environment, and can develop strategies to help them influence their work situation.

When a new employee becomes relatively secure and established in his or her career, the concern with fitting into the organization subsides, and the desire for increasing levels of achievement, authority, and responsibility takes over. During this period, the individual needs to maintain effective performance on the job, develop more insight into career orientation, set realistic career goals, understand the influence of different career paths and patterns on goal accomplishment, and attain support from others both inside and outside their organization. To help individuals with these tasks, organizations can encourage career exploration, provide challenge and responsibility on the job, construct realistic and flexible career paths, provide constructive performance appraisals, and help employees formulate career management plans.

ASSIGNMENT

If you are employed presently, take a few minutes to consider the programs your company offers to help employees become established during the early part of their careers. What programs, if any, are being used? How would you rate the effectiveness of these efforts in assisting employees with the tasks of establishment? If you are not employed currently, you may want to interview a close associate or relative about the programs at his or her organization. Or do some exploration on the Internet to see what different companies offer. Then answer the assignment questions given here.

DISCUSSION QUESTIONS

1. Why do organizations attempt to break in employees when they first join? Describe the major socialization practices used by organizations and relate them to experiences you have had as a newcomer. Identify the signs of a successful and an unsuccessful socialization experience.

2. Reexamine the example of Reginald, the 30-year-old MBA student, provided in this chapter. How effectively has he managed his early career? What, if anything, could he have done differently to shorten his period of floundering?

(Continued)

(Continued)

3. What are the advantages (and disadvantages) of providing a new employee with a challenging initial job assignment that provides considerable responsibility and autonomy? Why do many organizations have reservations about providing this type of assignment? What can organizations do to provide challenging, meaningful work to newcomers and, at the same time, address the reservations they hold?

4. Describe the significance of the mentor–protégé relationship. What functions does the mentor provide and how can they contribute to the development and growth of the protégé's early career? Do you agree with the proposition that mentoring functions can be provided by a number of individuals? Why or why not? What can individuals do who may not have access to a mentor?

5. Look at the eight career anchors proposed by Schein that are shown in Chapter 4. How would you characterize yourself in terms of these career orientations? How can employees gain greater insight into their career orientation? How would such insight contribute to more effective career management?

CHAPTER 7 CASE 1

Natalie the Retail Manager (Part B)

At the conclusion of Chapter 6 we provided Part A of the Natalie case. You may want to reread Part A of this case before reading Part B.

At the end of Part A, Natalie had just completed one year of employment with Enigma. After some uncertainty and soul searching, Natalie decided to stay with Enigma for a while longer. Part B describes Natalie's situation after five years with Enigma. (Remember, Enigma is a fictitious name and should not be confused with any real company.)

Five Years Into Her Career at Enigma

Natalie's career at Enigma is now at a crossroads. She is confronted with some tough decisions concerning both her professional and her personal lives. Enigma has recently offered her the chance to become the manager of its Seattle store. She would be given complete responsibility for the store operations, would receive a 40 percent salary increase, and could garner a sizable performance bonus after one year. While flattered by the opportunity, Natalie has other factors to consider. She is engaged to be married and the wedding date is just eight months away. Her husband-to-be has made it clear that he is not in favor of a move to the west coast. Besides, they had talked about starting a family in the next two years and a move to Seattle would take them far away from their parents and other relatives who would willingly satisfy any child care needs that might arise if they did have children.

Natalie needed some time to ponder her choices. The past four years at Enigma had been an emotional roller coaster. She had thought about leaving Enigma on several occasions, but had never "tested the waters." She always believed that the pros of staying with the company outweighed the cons. The extensive demands of the job had kept her busy, and the corporate culture still served to create unnecessary animosity and obstacles. But Enigma showed that they believed in her ability by promoting her a year ago to deputy store manager and by paying for her to attend a number of executive development programs. Most of her friends from college were still trying to move into an initial management position. They were amazed at the experiences Natalie had already encountered. Natalie had likened her situation to being in quicksand, the deeper she had gotten into Enigma, the harder it was to get out. In the back of her mind she often wondered whether other employers or another type of career would be a better fit for her and her aspirations. In fact, she often dreamed of becoming an entrepreneur by opening up a high-end housewares store. Five years of her life had been devoted to Enigma, five years of headaches, stress, and various political battles. But the five years of rewards had been there too: nice salary increases, bonuses, and a major promotion.

The west coast regional manager wanted an answer in two days. If Natalie didn't take the promotion, it would please her fiancé and her family, but she knew it would be difficult to get another opportunity to be a store manager anytime soon. If she did take the promotion, she was looking at escalating demands, with even more stress and headaches. Natalie believed that if she really pressured her fiancé he would, reluctantly, agree to move to Seattle. And she rationalized that they could always find some sort of child care arrangement out there when they did have kids. But she still hadn't ruled out the possibility of starting her own business. One way or another, this was the toughest decision she had ever faced in her life.

Case Analysis Questions

1. Is Natalie in the establishment or the achievement phase of her early career? What factors did you take into account in answering this question?

2. Identify all of the issues that Natalie needs to take into account in making this major career decision. How is Natalie's nonwork life influencing the decision that needs to be made? As an upwardly mobile manager in her early career, should Natalie even be concerned with these nonwork issues? Why or why not?

3. If you were in Natalie's shoes after five years with Enigma, what career and life choices would you be prepared to make? What are the most important factors that you considered in making your choices?

4. If you were to write a continuation to this case, what would you predict for Natalie for the future, say 10 or 15 years after her college graduation? Would it be a happy or an unhappy future?

CHAPTER 7 CASE 2

Claudia the Star Performer

Throughout Claudia's senior year in college, she was actively recruited by a number of firms. As one of the top business students in her graduating class, Claudia believed that she could be choosy in selecting an employer. One of her strongest selection criteria was whether the hiring firm would pay for her MBA. Claudia eventually settled on a research assistant position with a medium-sized commercial bank. The salary was competitive and the bank would reimburse her for her graduate work.

Holding true to her goal, Claudia immediately began pursuing her MBA, attending one of the premier business schools in the country on a part-time basis. After three years, and an investment of $45,000 by her company, Claudia received an MBA in finance with a minor in international business.

Unbeknownst to her employer, Claudia had signed up for several of the on-campus interviews that were being held for graduating MBA students. She was especially interested in the large investment banking companies that were actively recruiting on campus. She was also interested in relocating to New York City. It wasn't that Claudia was displeased with her commercial bank; in fact, the opposite was true—the bank had treated her quite well, giving her challenging assignments and two promotions. Claudia just wanted to determine her market value and gain some leverage with the bank. Also, a job with one of the top investment banking firms would allow Claudia to continue advancing in her profession, and pursue her lifelong dream of living in New York City and attending the theater frequently.

Claudia was pleasantly surprised when she received offers from two prestigious New York investment banks. Both offers represented a 50 percent increase over her present salary and would pay her relocation expenses. Both jobs would also allow her to use her experience and allow her to manage the firms' research department. Claudia believed she had no choice but to ask the commercial bank if it would match the offers. Of course, she knew that the bank, with its rigid pay structure, would be loath to give her that kind of an increase. And her manager was not leaving his post anytime soon. True to her expectation, the bank refused to match the offer but stated that she would receive a generous increase at her next performance review. Claudia, feeling as if the bank offered her little choice, resigned the next day.

Claudia felt only a little remorse upon leaving the bank, rationalizing that the open labor market was the efficient, capitalistic way. Claudia also felt that this might be a one-time opportunity to pursue both personal and professional interests while living in New York City. The bank's management was bitter that it had lost one of its star performers and saw a significant investment go down the drain. But this was not the first time the bank had lost a star performer to a competitor after the employee had received a graduate degree. Indeed, at the most recent meeting of its executive management committee, the bank was considering dropping all support for graduate school tuition reimbursement, reviewing instead whether hiring MBAs from the outside was a more prudent course of action.

Case Analysis Questions

1. As a star performer and one who wanted to continue achieving in her profession, was Claudia wrong in seeking additional responsibilities from another employer? What would you do, given her track record and MBA?

2. Do you think that Claudia acted ethically in quickly accepting the job from the investment bank? As an employee in the establishment phase of her early career, what alternatives should Claudia have considered in her pursuit of upward advancement? Should Claudia have given the bank a better opportunity to advance her in her career? Why or why not?

3. What are the economic implications for the bank? If you were a member of the executive management committee, what path would you have recommended at the meeting? How could the bank have better managed this important human resource?

CHAPTER 8

The Middle and
Late Career Stages

Career Challenges for Seasoned Employees

As we discussed in Chapter 2, the midcareer years roughly span the 15-year period between the ages of 40 and 55, whereas the late career stage includes those who are over the age of 55. Of course, as we also discussed in Chapter 2, these age ranges are somewhat arbitrary as corporate downsizings, individual uncertainty with regard to future income streams, and longer life expectancies have blurred the distinctions between the middle and late career stages and the move toward full retirement from work.

It is fortunate that a good deal has been learned about mid- and late career issues in recent years. The graying of America is no myth. Clearly, the aging of the baby boom generation, the roughly 78 million people born in the United States during the nearly 20-year period after World War II, will have a dramatic effect on work organizations, government institutions, and individual career management over the next several decades. Data from the U.S. Bureau of Labor Statistics (BLS) presents a vivid picture of the future labor force.[1] In the year 2000, the baby boom generation was in the age range of 36 to 54, and represented roughly 48 percent of the total civilian labor force in the United States. By the year 2010, with baby boomers aged 46 to 64, their percentage of the civilian labor force is projected to be approximately 37 percent. Moreover, as boomers likely begin to retire in large numbers after 2010, their percentage of the civilian labor force will drop dramatically. For example, by 2020, BLS projections have the baby boom workers (now aged 56 to 74) representing only about 20 percent of the labor force, a drop of 28 percentage points from the year 2000. Put a different way, the BLS projects that the number of baby boomers in the civilian workforce will drop by roughly 30 million workers during the 20-year period from 2000 to 2020. By the year 2030, baby boomers in the workforce are forecast by the BLS to total less than 10 million, or less than 6 percent of the civilian workforce.

The implications of these forecasts are clear. Individuals and organizations must become more attuned to the needs and experiences of mid- and late career employees. As fewer younger employees enter the labor force, as demands for skilled labor prevent organizations from offering early retirement options, and as financial pressures coupled with longer life expectancies force people to delay retirement, more and more senior employees are expected to continue as active members of the workforce, at least over the next two decades. These seasoned employees will have to make a number of significant decisions about the timing of retirement and the ways in which they would like to live their preretirement and retirement years.

In this chapter we will examine the middle and late stages of career development. We will consider the tasks and challenges posed by each of these two career stages, examine some typical concerns experienced by seasoned employees in these stages, and offer career management guidelines for organizations and individuals.

THE MIDDLE CAREER YEARS

The midcareer years pose two major career/life tasks. *Confronting the midlife transition* involves reappraising one's accomplishments relative to ambitions and dreams and reexamining the importance of work in one's life.[2] Moreover, many midcareer employees may have to learn to cope with the personal and professional stressors produced by the midlife transition. *Remaining productive* during midcareer requires employees to update and integrate their skills; exercise sufficient autonomy to express these skills; and develop new skills, such as the mentoring of younger colleagues.

Confronting the Midlife Transition

The midlife transition typically takes place between the ages of 40 and 45, according to Daniel Levinson. It can be triggered by a number of experiences: fear of lost youth and missed opportunities, awareness of aging and mortality, failure to accomplish significant career and life goals, the inability to achieve an acceptable balance between work and family commitments, and the need to shed youthful illusions that propelled the earlier portion of one's career and life. In essence, the individual at midlife is increasingly forced to reappraise and recognize that he or she has stopped growing up, and has begun growing old. The midcareer employee may also experience rivalries with more energetic, ambitious, and highly educated younger colleagues and may feel defensive and guilty about these hostile feelings. Technical or managerial obsolescence, common among midcareer employees, can add to these frustrations. The recognition that one may not advance further in the organization—that one has reached a career plateau—can undoubtedly intensify feelings of failure and cast a gloom over one's future career. In addition, many highly successful and mobile employees experience feelings of personal failure at midlife, reflecting the guilt and regret over having sacrificed family relationships and other affiliations in the ambitious pursuit of career success.[3]

It is no surprise, then, that many midcareer employees become restless. Although some people may make drastic occupational changes or pursue alternate lifestyles, many more are psychologically conflicted. Some may exhibit renewed energy toward new career pursuits; others may continue their direction toward fulfillment of longstanding goals; while still others may reduce their involvement in work and turn their attention and energies toward their families and themselves.[4]

We have painted a somewhat negative picture of the midlife transition. Indeed, Levinson and his colleagues concluded that 80 percent of the men and 85 percent of the women in their research experienced a crisis during this period.[5] However, other researchers have questioned whether the midlife crisis is universally experienced, arguing that feelings of frustration, mortality, and stress may occur at different times for different people, depending on their particular pattern of life experiences and the culture and point in history in which they live. Moreover, major sources of crises, such as the financial burdens, job loss, or illness or divorce, can occur anytime throughout adulthood.[6] In contrast to Levinson's findings, more recent studies involving thousands of middle-aged adults found that only 10 percent stated that they experienced a midlife crisis. Further, neuroscientists who have studied mental functioning have found that the human brain is more flexible and adaptable after the age of 40 than once thought. Studies suggest the right and left hemispheres of the brain become more integrated at midlife, and hence allow for greater creativity. The "use it or lose it" adage has been confirmed scientifically, suggesting that those who challenge themselves mentally throughout midlife continue to strengthen cognitive ability. In addition, better emotional regulation, increased wisdom and practical intelligence, and a strong sense of mastery are positive outcomes associated with midlife.[7] Thus, midlife is not universally seen as a period of trauma and change, and can be a positive time filled with growth and personal discovery.

What can be concluded about the midlife transition? First, the notion that people need to reappraise their lives as they enter middle adulthood is compelling. Coming to grips with this fact and making adjustments for the next era of life seem essential. Early adulthood and all that it entails—youth, feelings of immortality, dreams, and hopes—can never be relived. Whether these issues arise between the ages of 40 and 45, as Levinson and his colleagues proposed, or possibly later as others suggest,[8] is still uncertain. However, it seems reasonable that these issues should surface in the "early" part of middle adulthood.

Second, it is unclear whether the feelings that accompany midlife appraisal are so intense as to constitute a crisis. Perhaps it is sufficient to state that the entrance into middle adulthood raises certain issues that may produce a variety of emotional reactions regarding social, psychological, and physical domains. It is important that the entry into middle adulthood is begun with a reappraisal of accomplishments and life goals. This reappraisal enables individuals to find constructive ways to remain professionally and personally productive and fulfilled throughout their midcareer years. It also facilitates an assessment of the many emotions associated with midlife. Perhaps this period of transition and self-assessment allows for adaptation to a middle-age adult life role. Ways in which individuals and organizations can address the midlife transition will be examined later in the chapter.

REMAINING PRODUCTIVE: GROWTH, MAINTENANCE, OR STAGNATION?

The second major task of midcareer is to remain productive. For many, the middle career years are characterized by maintenance of the status quo, where individuals experience little motivation to start in new directions, possibly from a lack of opportunity within their employing organization. This period has been dubbed *middlescence* because it can be as frustrating and confusing as adolescence.[9] Millions of midcareer employees are dealing with middlescence as they try to find new meaning in work, while balancing the responsibilities of job, family, and leisure. While many people desire growth and development during midcareer, others enter a period of maintenance or begin to stagnate and decline, essentially "checking out" of the organization. Two midcareer experiences, plateauing and obsolescence, can affect midcareer productivity and trigger feelings of stress.

The Career Plateau

Realistically, everyone plateaus at one time or another. Although plateauing can occur at any career stage, it is particularly relevant to the seasoned employee. For that reason, we consider the career plateau as a central issue in midcareer.

A career plateau has traditionally been defined as the "point in a career where the likelihood of additional hierarchical promotion is very low."[10] Researchers have identified various types and reasons for career plateaus. When an individual is unable to rise further within an organization, that is, when the likelihood of additional hierarchical promotions is low, the person is viewed as "structurally" plateaued. When growth opportunities associated with increasing responsibility on one's current job become unavailable, the person is "content" plateaued.[11] It is reasonable to believe that a person might be plateaued in both ways, with no opportunities to move up the corporate ladder and with no opportunities for growth in the current job.

When an individual becomes plateaued, it is normal to look for reasons as to why the plateau has occurred. In a basic sense, firms may plateau the employee, or the employee may choose to be plateaued. Firms often have two main reasons for why they plateau an employee.[12] First, the organization may have *constraints* it is facing and therefore cannot allow the employee to advance farther up the hierarchy or cannot provide additional responsibilities associated with the current job. The employee might not be able to advance (structural plateau) due to the narrowing organizational pyramid, a poor economy and downsizing that may be occurring, inappropriate recruiting and staffing, or increased competition for similar jobs. The employee may also not receive increased job responsibilities (content plateau) because of inflexible job descriptions or unavailable training in new technology. In these scenarios, it is the actions or situations within the organization that result in the employee being plateaued. Second, the organization may negatively *assess* the value of the employee, and hence plateau him or her. An employee may not receive promotions (structural plateau) because management believes the individual lacks the necessary experience, interpersonal skills, work ethic, commitment, or political savvy needed for higher-level jobs. Or the employee might not receive greater job responsibility (content plateau) because he or she is "not ready," "can't handle it," or lacks the desire or necessary skills. These negative assessments of the employee, valid or not, cause the employee to be plateaued. So, organizations may plateau employees for organizational *constraint* or *assessment* reasons.

Seasoned employees may choose to be plateaued for *personal* reasons. This reason for plateauing may become more common as baby boom employees, many in dual career relationships, choose to stay in their current job instead of pursuing (or accepting) a higher-level job that requires additional responsibilities. The stress, travel, and potential relocation implications to, and interruptions of, one's nonwork life (family, health, or leisure) may outweigh the additional compensation or prestige that the new job might bring. Depending on the firm's culture, some employees may explicitly make known their personal choice to be plateaued, while others may send ambiguous signals to management. Although the choice to become plateaued can go against the grain of organizational expectations, employees can make a conscious decision to be plateaued for *personal choice* reasons.

Why is plateauing such a universal experience?

1. At the most basic level, the pyramidal structure of most organizations provides fewer and fewer positions at higher levels of the hierarchy. The higher one rises in the organizational structure, the fewer the number of positions that are available for further advancement. As the pyramidal structure becomes flatter, there are fewer management levels through which one might advance.

2. There is increasing competition for these few positions because of the glut of baby boomers reaching middle or senior levels of management at the same time and the downsizing of the corporate structures that has taken place over the past several years.

3. The degree of employee plateauing is exacerbated in organizations that are growing slowly, not growing at all, or contracting their operations and workforce. The outsourcing of jobs, either across state or country lines, has created more plateauing. Furthermore, a company's business strategy can affect the number and type of growth opportunities and hence the incidence of plateauing in certain career paths.

4. The virtual elimination of mandatory retirement can clog career paths and prevent younger employees from progressing in the hierarchy.

5. Changes in technology may close certain career paths or open new paths for which employees are not prepared.

6. Some employees may be more likely to plateau structurally because they are thought to be too valuable in their present position and hence must stay, lack technical or managerial skills to advance further, or lack career management skills required to develop a mobility-oriented career strategy.

7. As was stated in Chapter 7, a variety of factors can cause executives and others to become "derailed" off the fast track and end up plateaued. These factors include problems with interpersonal relationships, a failure to meet business objectives, a failure to build and lead a team, and an inability to change or adapt during a transition.[13]

8. As we noted above, the desire for a more balanced lifestyle has led an increasing number of employees to make the organization aware that they do not wish to be considered for further advancement or increased job responsibilities because of the potential conflicts with family or leisure commitments.[14]

What are the consequences of plateauing? There is evidence that many plateaued men feel like failures since they equate career success with masculinity. For some men, the sense of failure is tinged with guilt over the little time they have spent with their families during their pursuit of career success. Some women may feel betrayed if they have forgone marriage and/or family to concentrate on a career that now seems to be going nowhere. Plateaued employees might be stereotyped as "deadwood" and may be alienated within the firm. Other harmful psychological reactions include lower self-worth, lower skill assessment, and lack of acceptance by peers and supervisors due to perceptions of lower work contributions.[15]

It is not surprising that most individuals associate plateauing with negative outcomes. Plateaued employees can become less involved in their jobs and display decreased motivation in their work, especially if they believe that the organization has devalued their work contributions. Ultimately, these employees may exhibit deteriorated performance and cause a decline in the performance of their department and/or organization. After all, the most powerful incentives that have motivated performance to this point, the promise of further advancement or increased job responsibilities, are no longer a feasible reward for effective performance. Studies have shown that individuals who perceived themselves as career plateaued exhibited lower levels of satisfaction with their job, their career, and their personal development; experienced high levels of stress; and were more apt to leave their organization.[16]

Are negative outcomes inevitably linked to career plateauing? Given the relatively common occurrence of becoming plateaued, experiencing a career plateau may not be as embarrassing or stressful as it once was considered. Indeed, a leveling-off period (as represented by a career plateau) can have a positive influence on individual development and personal growth. Since a career plateau can represent a time of stability, plateaued individuals can master new work skills, pursue a more predictable family and personal life, and can replenish psychic energy.[17] They may also use this time to take stock of their position and recount their accomplishments. Plateaued employees may also take more interest and become more psychologically involved in their nonwork commitments, and gain pleasure in doing so.[18]

Consistent with these conclusions on the potentially positive aspects of career plateaus, researchers have observed that most employees adapt to their career plateau without too much trouble.[19] Whether due to a real change of values or simply a rationalization of their current situation, the job performance of these adaptable employees may not suffer greatly. Consider the following example.

Jan emerged from her annual performance review feeling numb. For the third year in a row she had received only a "good" rating—another indication that her promotion prospects were close to nil. It wasn't always like this for Jan. Earlier in her career she received "excellent" or "outstanding" evaluations and she was promoted every two or three years. She wasn't necessarily on the fast track, but she continued to advance at a steady pace.

In the course of her 25-year career, Jan could point to many accomplishments, both in her work and in her personal life. She had overseen the installation of a new automated system, had taken over an operation with poor performance and turned it around, and had made cost-saving recommendations to senior management that resulted in significantly reduced expenses. Moreover, Jan had obtained her MBA going part-time, had gotten married, raised two children, and gone through a divorce. Jan recently purchased her own home and is dating an executive at another company in town.

All in all she was pleased with her professional and personal development. But with her latest evaluation, Jan is uncertain what to do next. She realizes she won't be receiving more promotions, and she is feeling the heat from younger staff members and colleagues who are eager to move up the ladder. Being on a career plateau has been a stressful experience for Jan. She could look for another job, but she has no idea of her prospects. Besides, she has asked herself why she would want to trade her current job, with good pay and benefits, for another job where she would be an unknown commodity and would have to prove herself all over again.

After a period of time, Jan began to accept her plateaued state. She realized that not having to compete for higher-level positions had benefits. She now had more time for her children and was able to pursue other outside interests. She had time to work on decorating her new home, and even began using the company's exercise facilities. At work, Jan refused to let her situation have a negative effect on her performance. She decided to do the best job she possibly could. Also, Jan looked for ways to expand her knowledge of new computer applications, thinking this would increase her value to the firm. Eventually, Jan spoke with her boss about the prospects for a lateral move to another department in the company. She stressed that she wanted to go into an area where she could gain new experiences. Jan's boss welcomed the idea and said she would see what she could do, but she also encouraged Jan to keep her eye on the posting board for opportunities.

Four months after their meeting, Jan posted out of the department—she is looking forward to putting her newly acquired personal computer skills to good use. She believes she can continue to contribute to the firm and is excited that she will have the opportunity to learn more in this new position.

Unlike Jan, some plateaued employees are more prone to deteriorated attitudes and performance. A model that addresses this issue, shown in Table 8.1, classifies employees along two dimensions: likelihood of future promotion (i.e., likelihood of being structurally plateaued) and performance on their current job. Note that there are two kinds of structurally plateaued employees: the "solid citizens," who are still performing effectively in their current job, and the "deadwood," whose job performance is substandard. Although the solid citizens perform the bulk of the organization's work, managerial attention and concern are frequently directed toward encouraging and rewarding the fast track stars and punishing, shelving, or firing the deadwood. One major challenge for management, therefore, is to prevent solid citizens from becoming deadwood. Management actions relevant to this challenge will be considered later in this chapter.

TABLE 8.1   Model of Managerial Careers

	Likelihood of Future Promotion	
Current Performance	*Low*	*High*
High	Solid citizens (effective plateauees)	Stars
Low	Deadwood (ineffective plateauees)	Learners (Comers)

SOURCE: These categorizations are based on Ference, T. P., Stoner, J. A. F., & Warren, E. K. (1977). Managing the career plateau. *Academy of Management Review, 2,* 603.

Obsolescence

Like plateauing, obsolescence is not a uniquely midcareer issue, but it may be more pronounced and more devastating in midcareer than in earlier years.[20] Seasoned employees who cannot incorporate new developments into their work processes are susceptible to obsolescence, and could be considered by the organization as "past their prime." Obsolescence has been defined as the degree to which "workers lack the up-to-date knowledge or skills necessary to maintain effective performance in either their current or future work roles."[21] Personal changes that result from the midlife transition and other experiences could cause a reduced level of achievement orientation and a lower level of interest in work that, in turn, may adversely influence the desire to stay current in one's job.

Obsolescence has its root in change. Research has identified several factors that can lead to obsolescence, including environmental disruptions, individual characteristics, the nature of work, and organizational climate.[22] Environmental disruptions encompass shifts in competitive balance between organizations that are typically associated with changes in technology. In this case, the adoption of new technology by one company causes competing companies to adopt the same technology to stay competitive. Workers in those companies must learn the new technology or the worker (and the company) can face obsolescence. Several individual characteristics can also cause obsolescence. As one example, an employee's advancing age might reduce the desire to learn new skills or understand new technology. The nature of one's work, which encompasses the knowledge, skills, and abilities (KSAs) embodied in the job, can influence worker obsolescence. In this case, the KSAs change in such a way or so quickly that the employee cannot keep up. Finally, the organization's climate can also play a role in contributing to obsolescence. Organizations that allow a high degree of interaction and communication among colleagues and encourage participatory management styles tend to do a better job of keeping their workforces informed of new developments in their fields and related fields. In addition, organizational climates that encourage and reward professional growth and development, allow risk-taking behavior, and prize innovation usually discourage worker obsolescence. When workers see that the firm is rewarding advancement of knowledge, they typically direct their efforts toward keeping updated in their field.

As the prior discussion shows, both the individual and the work environment play a critical role in averting obsolescence. Obsolescence is less likely to manifest itself when jobs are challenging, when job reassignments are made periodically to maintain stimulation and avoid overspecialization, when people are given sufficient responsibility and authority on their job, when colleagues interact freely, and when organizations reward employees for keeping up to date by providing challenging work, promotions, and salary increases.[23] In fact, opportunities for continued learning and development on the job are probably the greatest deterrent to obsolescence. Suggestions for combating obsolescence will be examined in more detail in a later section of this chapter.

Career Change

The popular press, TV shows, and movies would have people believe that middle-age restlessness almost inevitably leads to major career changes. Vivid examples of urban business executives who open general stores in a rural community, engineers who become artists, or accountants who leave their firms to pursue a career in organic farming merely reinforce this view. Although many people in midcareer do shift career direction, career change is neither an inevitable product of the midlife transition nor is it limited to the midcareer years.

Career change has been viewed as movement into a different occupation that is not part of a typical career path or is not part of a path that represents increasing financial gains.[24] It is obvious that more and more people are willing to consider different career fields during their lives. Moreover, although some career changes involve minimal movement in job demands and lifestyle, others represent major transitions. Scholars suggest that a "trigger event" may not necessarily cause a career change, but trigger events may precipitate personal exploration and experimentation with ideas that may lead to career change.[25] Indeed, research has found that getting laid off is not necessarily a sufficient cause for one to change a career path, but rather leads individuals to consider another type of career path.[26]

What are the compelling reasons for people to make career changes? Although the number of reasons may seem endless, they can be grouped into general categories. First, there are several individual factors that can influence a career change. While individual elements like age, gender, health, interests, values, and skill transferability play a large role, researchers suggest that one's self-concept and professional identity may motivate one to deviate from an established career path. When individuals perceive that their job and their current sense of personal identity are no longer in balance, they may change careers to deal with the dissonance they feel. One's self-concept is not only a current state of being, but also a future state. Individuals' belief that their future possible self (or where they want to be) is disconnected from their current job may also precipitate a change in career.[27]

A personal dissatisfaction with one's current occupation or lifestyle can be a powerful stimulant to change. One source of this dissatisfaction is a lack of fit between current opportunities and significant needs, desires, or goals. The skills that individuals brought to a job may no longer be required. Or as individuals develop, they may find that their interests and preferences have changed such that they now conflict with their chosen career.[28] Also, dissatisfaction with one's life in general can have a significant influence on job satisfaction and the desire for career change.[29] Another individual factor is an underlying need for greater achievement and contribution beyond what the individual has done up to the point of the change. All of these individual factors can impact one's desire for career change.

There are also a number of environmental factors that can induce career changes. Certainly the loss of one's job, or even the threat of loss, can be a direct reason to change one's path, but there are many others. These additional environmental factors might include a technological change, economic forces, a corporate restructuring or downsizing, changes in a company's reward system, increased job demands, and alterations to family relationships.

In addition to these individual and environmental factors, there usually needs to be an *attractive alternative* to one's current situation in order for a career change to take place. The alternative would typically provide a better fit with one's needs, values, or abilities than the current occupation. For example, career changers frequently mention the opportunity for more personally meaningful work and a greater fit with personal values as important reasons for their changes.[30] Other factors associated with successful career change include *confidence* that the change can actually be made, the *belief* that one is in control of one's fate during the change, and the *presence of support* from one's social network.[31] In fact, career change can be positively influenced by social networks that offer referral opportunities for attractive career alternatives.[32]

In all, the individual and environmental factors described above help explain why midcareer people decide to change careers. Given the dynamic and complex life situation that midcareer employees face, there are a number of "healthy" reasons for changing careers:

- Reaching a career plateau

- Becoming obsolete

- Feeling misutilized or underutilized

- Recognizing that the original occupational choice was inappropriate

- Realizing that one's skill set might be best used in another occupation

- Appreciating that being satisfied is not determined only by financial wealth

All of these reasons relate in one way or another to a lack of fit between one's current career status and one's self-concept, which is then likely to increase one's dissatisfaction with the current role if action is not taken. Such feelings of dissatisfaction may intensify during midcareer when more general issues of aging, mortality, and missed opportunities are also surfacing. Before embarking on a midcareer change, people must understand their motives, their ideal self-concept, and the nature of the changes they will have to undergo if they decide to shift career direction. Career changers need to stay open to the range of job possibilities for which their experiences have qualified them, while remaining realistic about what they can achieve.[33] A career coach may serve the midcareer changer well. The career coach, or executive coach, can help to identify skills (or needed skills), develop career alternatives, and aid in career decision making.[34] Often, the career coach can help an individual to determine whether the benefits of jumping to a new career field outweigh the potential loss of stature and credits one has built with one's current company. Indeed, there are a number of obstacles to career change. These obstacles may be financial (a salary cut, loss of income in a new business venture, forgoing pension or health care benefits), time related (the time required to train for a different occupation), or psychological (the uncertainty and insecurity about becoming competent in a different field).

The next sections will consider more specific actions that organizations and individuals can take to resolve some of the midcareer issues discussed to this point.

ORGANIZATIONAL ACTIONS DURING MIDCAREER

We have reviewed the major developmental tasks of midcareer as well as the potential for plateauing, obsolescence, and career change. Next, we examine the actions that organizations can take to help employees manage their careers during this stage.

Help Employees Understand Midcareer Experiences

Before any organization can help employees understand their midcareer experiences, organizational managers must first appreciate the issues facing midcareer employees. In this way, organizations can avoid overreacting to employees who are having trouble adjusting to middle age and can offer useful programs to this cohort of employees. Moreover, educating managers on these issues can help improve the supervisor–subordinate relationship, especially when one or the other party is in midcareer. The organization must also recognize that there are likely to be considerable differences in how individual employees react to midcareer. Seminars and workshops can be used to educate upper-level managers on the importance of understanding midcareer dynamics, especially with so much of the workforce in midcareer.

Moreover, employees can cope more effectively with midlife transitions, plateauing, obsolescence, and restlessness when they understand that they are experiencing natural, normal reactions to a different career status. People need to work through these feelings to enter middle adulthood stronger and healthier. The failure to confront these feelings, doubts, and frustrations could produce even greater problems somewhere down the line. Seminars, workshops, and support groups can provide an opportunity for people to talk about their feelings and realize that they are not alone. Professional counseling or executive coaching might also be appropriate for some employees.

Provide Expanded and Flexible Mobility Opportunities

Because promotional opportunities may be limited during midcareer, alternative forms of career mobility can be used to keep midcareer employees stimulated, challenged, and motivated. *Career mobility* is a broad term that denotes all possible directional movements within one's career.[35] Lateral mobility may be particularly appealing to midcareer plateauees, especially when the moves do not involve geographical relocation. The judicious use of periodic mobility may prevent solid citizens from becoming deadwood and may deter obsolescence. Career mobility opportunities not only stretch and stimulate employees, but also might provide a different perspective on solving an organization's problems.

Lateral and even downward transfers are useful to the extent to which they bring additional challenge, skill utilization, and stimulation. Since extended time in one job can produce negative attitudes or stagnation, perhaps mobility in any direction, if handled properly, can promote positive attitudes and motivation. Remember, not all midcareer employees will experience a plateau. Many will hold realistic mobility aspirations and will need the organization's help in achieving these goals. Therefore, several of the organizational actions relevant to the achievement period of the early career—stimulation of career exploration, career pathing, and development planning, to mention a few—are also appropriate for the mobile midcareer manager.

Utilization of the Current Job

Although many midcareer employees may no longer expect advancement, their needs for achievement and autonomy can remain strong. An alternative or supplement to lateral mobility during midcareer is the improvement of the current job by building in more variety, challenge, and responsibility.[36] Participation in task forces, project teams, and temporary assignments can provide stimulation and recognition and should be welcomed by many in midcareer if the responsibilities do not cut too deeply into their personal and family lives. Providing sufficient challenge and responsibility throughout the midcareer years can be a primary deterrent to development of deadwood attitudes and behaviors.[37]

One factor that characterizes the work experience of solid citizens is the presence of clear job duties and agreed-upon performance objectives. Moreover, clear and accurate performance feedback is critical to maintain the high performance of plateaued employees, even though the absence of promotional opportunities may make these performance discussions unpleasant for the supervisor. Accurate performance appraisals, particularly 360 degree feedback, are also essential to detect the presence or potential for obsolescence.[38]

Encourage and Teach Mentoring Skills

In Chapter 2 we noted that the generativity need (to guide the next generation) is particularly strong during middle adulthood. Moreover, the long-term service and broad experience of many midcareer employees may make them particularly suitable to mentor younger colleagues. However, before midcareer employees can help others, they must understand their own feelings about their career and lives. Special lectures, group discussions, or coaching on midcareer issues can be developed to accomplish this. It is also likely that many midcareer employees will require some training on how to coach, counsel, and provide feedback as mentors.[39]

Training and Continuing Education

The use of training or retraining for plateaued or obsolescent employees has been suggested frequently in the literature,[40] although some management scholars have offered a rather critical evaluation of continuing education as a deterrent to obsolescence.[41] First, although organizations may formally support and endorse continuing education, participation in such activities is often discouraged and unrewarded by individual supervisors as it may be considered a distraction from formally assigned tasks.

Second, it is not clear that participation in continuing education, in and of itself, can really help avert obsolescence. Instead, continual job challenge and periodic job rotation are normally viewed as the most effective deterrents to obsolescence. Well-planned, demanding, and innovative continuing education programs can help if employees are counseled to enter the right program at the right time to meet their own needs and goals, and if continuing education supplements rather than replaces stimulating, challenging job assignments. Continuing education that is relatively short in duration and focused on more specific topics has a comparatively better chance of helping to lower the degree of employee obsolescence.[42]

One significant function of continuing education is preparing midcareer employees who wish to engage in a career change. Continuing education can serve as a catalyst that encourages employees to consider the possibility of a different career field at some point in their future. In this sense, educational benefits provided by the organization are used to help interested employees prepare themselves for a career shift. Organizations can then creatively encourage their "surplus" employees to take early retirement to pursue the alternative career field or perhaps become an entrepreneur.[43]

Broaden the Reward System

Many of the specific suggestions outlined here involve reexamination and expansion of the organization's reward system. Instead of focusing exclusively or primarily on promotions and increased compensation as the incentive for effective performance, alternative rewards should be considered by organizations.[44] Interesting and challenging jobs, stimulating reassignments, flexible work arrangements, recognition, praise, and financial rewards can all be used to maintain the effectiveness of employees experiencing midcareer plateaus. These steps can help prevent solid citizens from becoming deadwood.

Rewarding employees for lifelong learning and development, success in challenging jobs, and participation in appropriate continuing education programs are the most effective means for forestalling functional obsolescence. Offering mobility opportunities, providing the framework for becoming a mentor, and broadening the reward system to recognize a variety of contributions to the organization are other avenues by which midcareer employees can be engaged. Such approaches explicitly recognize the importance of long-term career performance, not simply vertical mobility through the hierarchy.

INDIVIDUAL ACTIONS DURING MIDCAREER

Self-assessment is critical in midcareer. In addition to exploring one's values, interests, and talents, it is essential to understand one's real feelings about middle age and any shifts in the relative priorities given to work, family, and self-development. Specifically, individuals should conduct periodic self-assessments and reappraisals to determine whether their interests, values, and skills are in line with their established goals and plans. This awareness should empower individuals to better recognize and utilize opportunities as they arise, and can allow a more proactive response to changes in the work environment. If the organization does not provide a mechanism to stimulate this reappraisal, then the employee must take the initiative through participation in formal career development programs or discussions with colleagues, friends, family members, or counselors.

An examination of alternatives involves exploration of work and family environments. In the work domain, reappraising career-related aspirations, reassessing one's current job for possible improvement, investigating lateral mobility opportunities, and adopting flexible work arrangements might be considered. Exploration of different occupations and organizations, as discussed in Chapter 6, also may be appropriate. Moreover, relationships with one's spouse and/or children might need to be examined, new priorities might need to be set, and more personal time might need to be allotted.[45]

Midcareer employees considering a career change not only need to understand their own motives and interests, but also must anticipate and examine the consequences of career redirection, especially if the redirection includes an entrepreneurial venture. Employees contemplating a midcareer change should consider (a) the impact of the change on their family, (b) the risk of severing relationships with friends and colleagues in the current organization, (c) the possibility of reduced status in the community as a result of the career shift, (d) the time it might take to build a reputation in the new field, and (e) the possibility of reduced income.[46] Potential midcareer changers should discuss these issues extensively with family members, friends, career coaches, and colleagues prior to making a commitment to a career change.

The goal-setting process during midcareer is not fundamentally different from other stages, although the goal itself may be less likely to involve hierarchical advancement. Of particular importance is the establishment of a conceptual goal that is not tied to a particular position. Success in managing one's career during midcareer is based on the ability to understand one's conceptual goal and to see the possibilities of satisfying that goal either in one's current position or in other jobs or career fields.

Career strategies or action plans, as always, must be tied to goals and tested for feasibility. The development of active, realistic strategies of any type requires an awareness of goals, a willingness to communicate those goals to others, and a talent for observation, listening, and analysis. Participation in special skill building sessions for those in midcareer might help promote a more active, realistic strategy for dealing with the issues raised in this chapter. Most important, perhaps, is the conviction that one can influence, to a considerable extent, the course of one's career at any period of development.

Dealing With Job Loss

Loss of one's job can be a traumatic experience at any point in the life cycle, but it may be especially difficult and damaging for persons in the midlife phase.[47] First, individuals in midlife may be vulnerable to periods of self-doubt and a questioning of competence and worth; job loss can only add to the magnitude (and trauma) of the questioning process. Second, individuals in midlife are most susceptible to financial strains, with a peak in such demands as household expenses, acquisition of material goods, planning for (or making) the payment of children's college tuition, and attempting to save for one's retirement. Again, the loss of one's job can only exacerbate the financial stress. Further, job loss can put strain on a marriage that may already be on shaky ground due to the pressures of the midlife transition.

There are a number of well-documented reasons (or combination of reasons) why individuals are terminated by their employers. The most common causes include poor performance of the individual, a corporate-wide downsizing, divestitures, unfavorable financial or economic conditions faced by the company, or a violation of company policy or some unethical behavior. It is important to understand that poor performance may not necessarily indicate employee incompetence. Rather, it may reflect such factors as differences of opinion on priorities and strategies, personality clashes, and organizational politics.[48]

Individual reactions to job loss can be varied, depending on such factors as financial resources, social contacts and status, the meaningfulness of the work in the individual's life, and the person's level of confidence and self-esteem.[49] In essence, job loss can disrupt the established equilibrium in various facets of one's life, including economic, psychological, physiological, and social.[50] Reflecting the disrupted life equilibrium, some outcomes of job loss may include reduced happiness, increased depression, mental and physical illness, increased anxiety, and disengagement. Conversely, for some people, job loss can be a growth experience. Even though it may not be viewed as a worthwhile occurrence at the time of dismissal, job loss can be a "blessing in disguise" because it can force people to reassess their interests and desires and look for new avenues for personal fulfillment.[51] Researchers have found that, regardless of one's initial financial and emotional state, the subsequent process of coping with job loss and landing a new job follows a predictable series of stages.

In the first stage, individuals experience an initial response to the loss of a job. Researchers have identified four different types of initial response.[52] First, the individual may feel a sense of shock and disbelief, even when warning signs were in place to signal the impending termination. People often assume that job loss "won't happen to them." A second type of initial reaction is anger at the company and its management for allowing the termination to occur. A third response is a sense of relief, as the uncertainty and stress of potential termination is finally lifted. Lastly, individuals may show signs of escapism by displaying little or no emotion and attempting to divorce themselves totally from the difficult situation.

After the initial reaction subsides, individuals move into the second stage, where they confront the tasks of becoming reemployed. The campaign to secure a new position involves a multitude of activities including preparing and mailing (or e-mailing) up-to-date résumés, drafting cover memos and letters of introduction, working with an outplacement firm, identifying former work associates who can serve as job contacts and leads, and practicing proper interview performance.[53]

For the majority of people, coping with job loss ends after the second stage, when a new work position is found. However, if the job search continues for an extended period, individuals may enter a third stage in which the frustration of not finding work results in vacillation about one's career, lingering self-doubt about one's abilities, and anger that can involve displaced aggression toward others.[54] If individuals do not become reemployed, a fourth stage can occur in which they experience such dismay over not finding a new job that they resign themselves to being unemployed and begin withdrawing from activities, including those aimed at finding work.[55]

From the above descriptions, it is clear that the second stage following job loss is the critical period for finding a new position. It is during this phase that one is likely to undertake a concerted job search effort. For this reason, it is important that the job seeker apply the career management concepts discussed throughout this book. More precisely, individuals should first conduct a thorough appraisal of interests, talents, and lifestyle preferences. Second, the individual should assess the work environment, gathering information on alternative jobs, companies, and industries. Coincident with the self- and work-exploration processes, individuals should set tentative goals on the types of position (or positions) toward which they would like to target their reemployment efforts. Strategies would then be set on how to go about landing a preferred job.

Of course, no set of actions, regardless of how practical they are, guarantees that one will find a job in a timely fashion. Nevertheless, it is important that the career management model be followed to at least ensure that the individual is doing everything possible to locate a new job that is consistent with his or her interests and preferences. The career management model provides the individual with the ability to focus on the "problem" of finding a new job while also establishing a mechanism for dealing with the emotional needs associated with reemployment as the individual seeks counsel and social support from friends and relatives. Both problem-focused and emotion-focused support are necessary for the individual to navigate the job loss situation successfully.[56]

There are a variety of actions that organizations can take to assist their employees in coping with job terminations. Basic programs include advance notification, severance pay and extended benefits, retraining, outplacement assistance, and counseling. Because of the social responsibility and legal consequences of job layoffs, organizational leaders should also ensure that the process is procedurally fair.[57] Further, in the case of an across-the-board downsizing, it is recommended that the organization attempt to dispel the inevitable self-blame that individuals might place upon themselves as a means to minimize the loss of self-esteem and confidence that is likely to occur.[58] Also, it is important that organization-sponsored interventions to assist laid-off workers attempt to enhance confidence and self-efficacy about finding another job. Clearly, individual confidence can have a positive influence on subsequent job search behaviors.[59] Research also suggests that when job search assistance and social support are provided by employers, job seekers report higher earnings with their new job, and usually acquire jobs more quickly than when that assistance is not provided.[60] In Chapter 13 we will provide further discussion on the approaches companies utilize in handling employee dismissals and layoffs.

THE LATE CAREER

Businesses cannot afford to cast off or take for granted their older workers. For one thing, there is a greater number of older workers now than ever before, and this trend will continue as the baby boom generation ages. Second, legislation, including the Age Discrimination in Employment Act (ADEA),[61] protects workers age 40 and older from discriminatory employment practices. Third, as worldwide economic growth and the attendant need for more labor continues, the resultant projected shortage of workers in the future will place a greater value on the older worker who can provide stability and continuity to an organization's workforce. Finally, it makes good and socially responsible business sense for companies to utilize all of their human resources fully. Ironically, even in the face of a growing labor shortage, the takeovers, restructurings, and other corporate actions have led many large organizations to "ease out" senior employees through early retirement programs. Many of these programs are designed to reduce fixed operating costs by inducing the retirement of older, more expensive workers and replacing them with lower-cost younger workers.[62] It is clear that the treatment of the older worker will be a major management issue facing employers for at least the next three decades as the entirety of the baby boom generation reaches retirement age.

From the individual employee's perspective, three developmental needs stand out during the late career. First, a handful of late-career employees must prepare themselves for senior leadership roles in their respective organizations. For the vast majority, however, the primary tasks of the late career are to remain productive and to prepare for effective retirement.[63]

Remaining Productive

Remaining competent and productive is important to the late-career employee. Few people wish to be "carried" as excess baggage, but there are several obstacles to remaining productive during the late career. For one thing, rapid changes in technology and organizations pose a threat of obsolescence, especially to older workers with limited education and skills.[64] Unless midcareer obsolescence is prevented or reduced, the situation can only get worse during the late career. This becomes even more devastating when changes in an organization's mission, structure, or technology eliminate jobs, career paths, or even whole functions.

Second, the plateauing process discussed earlier can have negative effects on the performance of late-career employees. Although a plateau may initially be reached during midcareer, a midcareer solid citizen who is bored, unrewarded, and/or unmotivated may well become late-career deadwood. In other words, obsolescence and plateauing may have their roots in midcareer but eventually produce increasing deterioration during the late career.

Maintaining effective performance during the late career also can be jeopardized by society's stereotypes and biases against older people, in general, and older workers, in particular. Older workers have typically (and erroneously) been viewed as deficient in several areas: productivity, efficiency, ability to work under pressure, ambitiousness, receptivity to new ideas, adaptability, versatility, and the ability to develop new skills.[65] However, research demonstrates that stereotypes that inspire age discrimination are without merit; indeed, the majority of older workers are able to perform their work roles far beyond the typical age of retirement and well into later years in life.[66] Indeed, there is no support for the presumption that increased age leads to ineluctable declines in work performance, increases in workplace accidents, or higher absenteeism.[67] As we noted in Chapter 2, older workers tend to be more loyal, have lower rates of absenteeism, and are generally more reliable than younger workers.

Despite the inaccuracy of age stereotypes, such biases can have a significant effect on how organizations treat and manage the older worker.[68] A number of management actions, as listed below, can be traced to the negative stereotypes and myths concerning older workers.[69]

- If older workers are seen as rigid and resistant to change, then organizations will be less likely to help them improve their performance.

- If older employees are perceived as less motivated to keep up to date with changes, then organizations will be less willing to invest time and money in skill development programs for them.

- If older employees are seen as less creative or innovative, then organizations are less willing to move them into a position requiring these qualities.

- If older employees are believed to be less productive, and organizations use only subjective appraisals of performance, then older employees will have low performance ratings.

These management assumptions can produce a self-fulfilling prophecy in which older workers, deprived of developmental experiences and mobility opportunities, never have the chance to disconfirm the original stereotypes. These inaccurate stereotypes can produce a negative attitude toward older workers that, in turn, can produce bias in such areas as personnel selection, performance appraisal, and assignment to training. Daniel Feldman suggests two reasons for these negative stereotypes: lower performance ratings of seasoned employees allow supervisors to give higher ratings to younger employees, thereby justifying the distribution of scarce financial resources to those younger employees; and supervisors are trying to block upward mobility of senior employees, thereby creating fewer rivals for themselves.[70] In either case, if older employees perceive that their supervisors devalue their contributions, they may experience reduced satisfaction, feelings of depression and help-lessness, and lower self-worth and self-esteem.

Organizations need to overcome these inherent biases and recognize the value of their older workers for a number of reasons. First, senior employees are less likely to take time off except when absolutely necessary. Second, seasoned employees are less likely to leave the organization voluntarily because of their well-paying jobs and good pensions, congru-ence between what they hope to get from their jobs and what they actually get, their satis-faction with their work and its tangible and intangible benefits, and their commitment to the organization. Thus, older workers can be dedicated, productive, and enthusiastic employees, but must be treated with dignity and respect and must be recognized for their value to the organization.

Preparation for Retirement

Retirement is a major career transition for most people because it can signify an end to 40, 50, or even 60 years of continual employment. Retirement is defined as the depar-ture from a job or career path, taken by individuals after middle age, where the individ-ual displays a limited or nonexistent psychological commitment to work thereafter.[71] While this definition seems straightforward enough, the recent proliferation of available part-time positions and changes in attitudes toward working longer can sometimes make it difficult to determine when someone is actually retired. In general, retirees can be differentiated from nonretirees based on the following: retirees tend to be older, usu-ally over the age of 50 years; they tend to spend less of their time working for pay; they are more likely to receive some income that is specially designated for retirees; and they tend to think of themselves as retired.[72]

Preparing for retirement involves deciding when to retire and planning for a satisfy-ing, fulfilling life upon retirement. However, the decision to retire has been complicated in recent years by government and corporate actions. On the one hand, the ADEA has vir-tually eliminated any mandatory retirement age. Essentially, the decision of when to retire is now a voluntary one for nearly all American workers. Changes in the Social Security system also can encourage employees to delay retirement. Older workers can begin tak-ing Social Security benefits as early as age 62, although the longer one waits to take money from the system, the larger the amount one receives per month. These actions provide older workers with greater latitude in the timing of retirement and the type of retirement they prefer.

Attitudes toward retirement are likely to be rooted in one's attitude toward work. Work ful-fills so many human functions and can be such an important part of one's identity that to leave the work role may be akin to leaving one's self-concept behind.[73] Work provides a niche in society and a feeling of usefulness and purpose, and it allows people the opportunity to fulfill their basic needs for affiliation, achievement, power, and prestige. Work also provides financial rewards and a structure that helps people organize their daily lives. For many people, these tangible and intangible benefits are not easy to give up. Indeed, many employees who find retirement unfulfilling often embark on a "post-career career."[74]

On the other hand, many employees relish the thought of retirement and look forward to days without the pressures of deadlines, supervisors, and long hours. It is important to understand why some people seem to adjust more favorably to retirement than others. Satisfaction in retirement has been linked with a variety of factors, including the extent to which the person had engaged in financial planning while still employed, the presence of a good pension, experiencing good health, anticipated pursuit of hobbies or travel, absence of an overly emotional involvement with one's job, the ability to structure one's day, involvement in volunteer work, and high levels of self-esteem.[75]

Retirement intentions can take different forms given the variety of situations in which older workers might find themselves. Retirement could occur at the "traditional" age of 65, or it may occur earlier or later, depending on individual circumstances. Seasoned individuals are also considering "refirement" or the reigniting of their passion and interests toward new career areas where they can make significant contributions and remain engaged in meaningful work, but on their own terms regarding the time and involvement they are willing to devote to work.[76] The following are descriptions of various retirement options available to seasoned employees.

Early Retirement

Over the past three decades the option for workers to retire "early" has become commonplace. Organizations offer early retirement packages as a way to reduce the size of the workforce and to effect cost savings in a less stressful manner than simple across-the-board reductions in staff. It is almost impossible to find one major corporation that has not offered some form of early retirement to its workers. For individuals, the decision to retire early could be prompted by having a skill set that is obsolete, being dissatisfied with one's job, or facing periodic or chronic health problems. Or early retirement might be induced if the worker wishes to spend more time with family, to travel, to do volunteer work, or to pursue other business interests. Or it could be that the individual has acquired enough financial resources that he or she is able to retire, or has received such a generous financial incentive from his or her employer that it makes sense to retire early.[77] While there is no consensus on a definition of early retirement, it is generally viewed as the decision to retire prior to the age at which one is eligible for full corporate pensions,[78] typically when one is in his or her mid-40s to late 50s in age.

Phased Retirement

Phased retirement normally means that an older worker remains with his or her employer while gradually reducing hours worked, with the reduced work time viewed as a step toward full retirement. This phased approach to retirement means that the employee typically reduces the amount of time spent on the job by working fewer hours per day, week, month, or year.[79] It also allows employees to reduce work activity gradually while still exercising skills developed at earlier points in the career.[80] Thus, long-tenured employees may be given the option to work fewer hours, have less responsibility, or both, as a stepping stone to full retirement.

From the organization's perspective, phased retirement allows valued employees to stay engaged within the company for a longer period of time than would be possible if only a standard retirement, with full disengagement from work, were available. In addition, phased retirement represents a form of social responsibility on the part of the participating organization since it signifies that the organization is willing to make accommodations for its employees in the form of progressive employment practices.[81]

Although phased retirement appears to be a win–win option for employers and employees, there are several potential drawbacks. First, organizations might be reluctant to offer phased retirement on an unconditional basis since it is likely that only certain employees approaching retirement would have the right mix of abilities and attitude to be meaningful contributors to an organization in a phased retirement arrangement. In addition, employers might be reluctant to offer phased retirement because of policies that require a minimum number of hours to be worked in a year and restrictions that are imposed by defined benefit pension programs that calculate benefits based on earnings attained in the final years of a career with the organization. To get around these restrictions, some employers offer a form of phased retirement called "retire–rehire." In this case, full-time workers officially retire from their firm and then return as part-time or temporary workers; the time interval between retirement and rehire can be a matter of days.[82]

Bridge Employment

An increasingly popular option for employers to attract older workers is to offer bridge employment. Bridge employment allows workers who have retired from a career-oriented job to move to a transitional work position, which thus allows a "bridge" between one's long-term career and the entry into total retirement from all work.[83] Bridge jobs normally involve a combination of fewer hours, less stress or responsibility, greater flexibility, and fewer physical demands. From the individual worker's perspective, bridge employment contributes to older adults' economic security by providing additional income and can also enhance emotional and physical well-being. In this sense, the bridge job is viewed as an opportunity to do something meaningful in one's life and to have control over one's work role. In addition, bridge jobs allow employees to focus on the meaningful aspects of their work without concern over hierarchical advancement or the other issues associated with job security and mobility.

ORGANIZATIONAL ACTIONS DURING LATE CAREER

Reasonable attempts to manage older workers require sensitivity to late-career issues on the part of the organization's top management and supervisory staff. This necessitates a clear understanding of the differences between the myths and realities of aging and recognition of the value differences among generations of workers.

Performance Standards and Feedback

Clear standards of effective performance should be developed and communicated to the older worker. When confronting low productivity among older workers, performance problems should be stated in clear behavioral terms, the consequences of continued ineffective performance should be identified, and options to improve performance should be explored.[84] Accurate, unbiased performance appraisals are essential to maintain effective performance and to document reasons for terminating an older worker if necessary.

Education and Job Restructuring

Many of the suggestions made to prevent or ameliorate midcareer obsolescence and to manage the midcareer plateaued employee are also relevant to the employee in late career. Ongoing learning opportunities, through the integration of stimulating, responsible job assignments and continuing education, can play a major role in the revitalization of the late-career workforce.

In order to combat the obsolescence of older workers, two key factors must be addressed. First, the employee must believe that he or she can assert control over the career and its development. Second, the employee must believe that the work he or she is doing is meaningful and making a positive contribution to society. Education, training, and job restructuring activities should have the following components: (a) a thorough assessment of employees' training and development needs; (b) the design of developmental experiences such as training for upgrading technical, managerial, and/or administrative skills; (c) a plan for redeploying workers to needed areas; (d) a review and evaluation of the program's effectiveness; and (e) long-range planning with the employees to identify future retraining needs.[85]

Development and Enforcement of Nondiscrimination Policies

The ADEA forbids age discrimination in such areas as hiring and placement, compensation, advancement, and termination. Nondiscrimination makes good business sense and protects organizations from costly litigation. Training managers on ADEA employment laws also makes good business sense and ensures that the organization is being socially responsible toward its older workers.

Development of Retirement Planning Programs

Retirement planning programs can smooth the transition between work and retirement. Typically, retirement planning programs cover such topics as the challenge of retirement, health and safety, housing, time management, legal issues, and financial planning. Some recommendations for successful retirement planning programs are given below:[86]

1. Retirement planning programs should focus on both the extrinsic and intrinsic aspects of retirement. Extrinsic elements include financial security, housing alternatives, and legal issues. Intrinsic factors associated with retirement include the various psychological issues related to disengagement from work. Some researchers have suggested instituting "realistic retirement previews" that provide a balanced, accurate picture of retirement.

2. Programs should be run in small groups that encourage two-way communication and provide opportunities for counseling. In this way, the social and psychological consequences of retirement can be discussed in a more candid fashion.

3. Ideally, participation in retirement planning programs should begin at least five years prior to the anticipated retirement of the employee to allow adequate time to address all issues. Counseling activities should also be available for a specified period of time after retirement.

4. Previously retired persons can be used as information resources and role models during retirement planning sessions.

5. Spouse participation in retirement planning programs can be quite beneficial and should be encouraged.

6. Organizations should consider offering special retirement planning programs for those employees who have an especially strong commitment to work. These employees may have a particularly difficult time dealing with the prospect of retirement.

7. Retirement planning programs should be designed to help maintain positive attitudes and performance among preretirees, allow the organization to retain desirable older employees, and educate older employees on the retirement options available to them (early retirement, phased retirement, and bridge employment). However, programs must be carefully evaluated to determine whether they are meeting the needs of the employees and the organization.

Establishment of Flexible Work Patterns

Undoubtedly, many organizations prefer that the more competent, adaptable late-career employees continue working beyond "normal" retirement age and that others take early retirement. A system of flexible work patterns may enable both of these aims to be met.

Competent employees nearing retirement age could be induced to continue employment if they had more options than simply remaining a full-time member of the organization in their current position. These options can include part-time employment, special consulting assignments, job sharing, flexible or compressed working hours, and job restructuring. Programs like phased retirement and bridge employment could also help organizations retain the services of highly valued older employees while unclogging career paths for younger workers.

The flip side of the retirement issue is the encouragement of less talented or less adaptable workers to take early retirement. Here, too, innovative programs may serve the needs of the employee and the organization. These innovations can include supplementing the reduced Social Security benefits for employees who retire before full benefits are given, cash bonuses, maintenance of fringe benefits until age 65, cost-of-living adjustments to pension benefits, and full pension benefits for early retirement.[87]

Hiring Seasoned Employees

The aging of the baby boom generation is creating a growing pool of retirement-age individuals looking for alternative working arrangements. Accordingly, employers have an opportunity to hire this pool as a means to fill current and future labor requirements. Organizations will need to develop creative approaches to attract and recruit these workers. At a minimum, these approaches should involve taking the company's recruitment message to the potential workers, using marketing techniques to highlight company programs, and establishing an internal work climate that is attractive to older workers. Several organizations have developed creative approaches to reach out to workers over the age of 50.

INDIVIDUAL ACTIONS DURING LATE CAREER

Active career management is no less significant during the late career than during earlier periods of development. The suggestions made to midcareer employees earlier in this chapter are equally applicable to those in late career. Moreover, given the presence of age stereotypes, there may be a number of obstacles that older workers face in acquiring more challenging and responsible assignments or lateral mobility opportunities. Therefore, an awareness of one's current career needs and an assertive career strategy are necessary to ensure an individual–organizational fit during the late career.

Like many other career issues, retirement planning should be conducted by the individual employee, whether or not the employer offers a formal program. In addition, we recommend that the approaches the individual uses toward retirement planning resemble the active approaches to career management as outlined throughout this book. Preretirees are encouraged to gather relevant information about their financial assets and expenses, preferred lifestyle, and social and psychological needs. The development of financial, social, and personal objectives and the identification of action steps are all a part of this planning process. Financial advice from experts should be sought. Various types of software and Web sites can also help individuals set plans for retirement. Overall, planning for retirement should involve as much concern and attention as the planning for earlier activities and events in the career.

Individuals making preparations for retirement should ask themselves a number of fundamental questions, such as: How might I live in retirement? What do I really care about? What is of value and worth? By probing interests and values in this fashion, preretirement employees can gain a clearer picture of what they wish to accomplish and the life they would like to have in their retirement years.

SUMMARY

The middle career years present employees with two major tasks—to confront the midlife transition and to remain productive in their work. The midlife transition serves as a bridge between early and middle adulthood. Triggered by an awareness of aging and a fear of lost youth, many employees need to reconcile their accomplishments in life with their youthful aspirations. Although midcareer employees may not necessarily experience a crisis during this period, some form of reappraisal of accomplishments and goals may be necessary to move into middle adulthood in a constructive, productive manner.

Productivity during midcareer can be hampered if employees realize that they have reached a career plateau in which future advancement opportunities or increases in job responsibility are unlikely. Although some midcareer employees react to the plateauing experience with frustration, guilt, and stagnation, others adapt by substituting other goals for vertical mobility. Midcareer employees may also fall prey to technological or managerial obsolescence and ultimately job loss if they lack sufficient up-to-date knowledge and skills to maintain effective performance on their job.

Organizations can promote effective career management during midcareer by (a) helping employees understand their midcareer experiences; (b) providing a variety of mobility opportunities, including lateral and downward transfers; (c) providing sufficient challenge and responsibility on the current job to maintain involvement and productivity; (d) providing training or retraining as a supplement to challenging job assignments; and (e) encouraging some midcareer employees to serve as mentors to their junior colleagues. Individuals need to develop insight into their values and motives, reassess their current career prospects, and establish a conceptual career goal that can be achieved in a variety of jobs.

(Continued)

(Continued)

The late career also poses some potential threats to employee motivation and performance. Not only might older employees have to deal with the aftermath of midcareer obsolescence or plateauing, but they may also have to contend with negative age biases that obstruct continued growth and development on the job. Moreover, the late-career employee must begin to consider a number of issues regarding retirement. A variety of postretirement job alternatives (volunteerism, phased retirement, or bridge employment) are available to the late-career employee.

Organizations can help late-career employees by (a) understanding their unique problems, (b) developing clear performance standards and offering concrete feedback, (c) providing job challenge and continual training to maintain motivation, (d) developing and implementing nondiscriminatory policies regarding older workers, (e) developing effective preretirement programs, and (f) establishing flexible work patterns for employees nearing retirement age. Individuals should maintain an active vigilance during the late-career years and should plan their retirement with care and attention.

ASSIGNMENT

If you are 40 years of age or older, take a few introspective minutes to consider your career and life history. Do you believe that you have gone through (or are going through) a midlife transition? If the answer is yes, what kinds of issues did you deal with (or are you dealing with) during the transition period? Describe the changes that you have undergone (in work, family, or personal life) as a result of the midlife transition. Did you (or do you) view this period of time as a "crisis"? Why or why not? If you do not believe that you have experienced a midlife transition, why not? How would you reconcile that with Levinson's theory as discussed in Chapter 2 and this chapter?

If you are younger than 40 years old, interview a friend, relative, or colleague who is in his or her mid- to late 40s or early 50s. Determine whether the person has gone through a midlife transition. If the answer is yes, what kinds of issues did the person deal with during the transition period? Describe the changes that the person has undergone (in work, family, or personal life) as a result of the midlife transition. Did the person view this period of time as a "crisis"? Why or why not? If the person does not seem to have experienced the midlife transition, why not? How would you reconcile that with Levinson's theory as discussed in Chapter 2 and this chapter?

DISCUSSION QUESTIONS

1. Defend or refute the following statement: "Reaching a plateau in the organization drastically reduces the productivity and satisfaction of employees." Describe the reasoning behind your position.

2. What characteristics distinguish a solid citizen from a deadwood plateaued employee in an organization? What can organizations do to prevent solid citizens from becoming deadwood? What forces may prevent organizations from taking these actions?

3. What triggers a desire to make a midcareer change, and what factors inhibit people from actually making such a change? When is a midcareer change an adaptive behavior and when do workers use it as a shield against their real problems?

4. What are some common stereotypes of the older employee? Do you think these stereotypes are generally accurate or inaccurate? How do stereotypes of aging affect the ways in which organizations manage their older employees?

5. Why do some older workers relish the thought of retirement while others dread the prospect of leaving their work life behind? What kind of planning should be conducted to prepare oneself for retirement? Why should retirement planning begin considerably before the anticipated retirement date?

CHAPTER 8 CASE

George the Banker

George did not know what to think. The walk to the train, the train ride, and the drive home involved no effort at consciousness. His world was in turmoil and he did not know whether to feel anger or relief, exhaustion or despair.

George had what most would consider a "good job": vice president in the accounting department of Obelisk Bank (fictitious name). Obelisk was a medium-sized regional bank with just over $4 billion in deposits. At 54 years of age, George had believed he would retire comfortably from Obelisk on his own terms and when he decided it was time. George had begun working at Obelisk nearly 23 years ago. After high school, he had spent four years in the marines, and then used the GI bill to get his bachelor's degree in accounting. After spending six years in public accounting, during which time he gained his CPA, George joined Obelisk as an assistant controller. His early career at the bank had progressed nicely, but he had held his current position for the past eight years. George was generally pleased with his work and his record of achievements, although since his mid-40s a vague sense of unfulfillment and even disenchantment had taken hold. He knew that the lack of an MBA prevented him from advancing, and he recognized that he had been passed over for promotion, in deference to much younger colleagues, twice within the past four years. He even half-heartedly entertained the notion of returning to school for his MBA, but age and a lack of real desire, he believed, precluded this.

George's older daughter was graduating from college this year and she was planning to attend graduate school in the fall. His younger daughter was entering college as well. George was proud to tell his coworkers how he was putting his two daughters through college. George's wife returned to work five years ago, managing a gift shop. Her salary was a nice addition to the family income, but it really didn't go very far in paying the bills. College tuitions were a real financial strain, and there were still

(Continued)

(Continued)

nine more years to go on the mortgage. As was the case with his father before him, George saw his primary life role as breadwinner of the family. For financial, emotional, and psychological reasons, George was nowhere near ready for retirement.

George had gone to work that morning as always. For the past three months, Obelisk had been abuzz with rumors that it was the object of a takeover by a large bank from another state. The bank's senior management had even written an open letter to the employees telling them, in no uncertain terms, that the bank wasn't for sale and that the management would resist any and all takeover bids. George felt encouraged by the letter to the employees. He personally believed that the bank's senior management would take whatever steps were necessary to keep the bank from being acquired.

George began to reflect back on one of the many maxims his high school football coach had told his players— "the worst hit in football is when you're blindsided, because you never see it coming and you really can't prepare for it." George now had a better appreciation than ever for his old coach's words of wisdom. In the late afternoon that day he had gotten a call from one of the secretaries in Human Resources that the head of HR needed to see him immediately. The message from the Senior VP of Human Resources was delivered bluntly. Obelisk was cutting costs as a means to stave off the takeover, and several officers were being targeted for dismissal. George was given two options. The bank either would "credit" him with an additional three years of service so he could take early retirement and earn the full defined contribution pension when he turned 59.5 years of age, or it would give him a severance package of one year's salary, six months of medical coverage, and three months of outplacement services. George was given until the next day to make a decision, but with either option, his last day at Obelisk would be on Friday, just three days away.

When George got home the house was empty. His two daughters were out and his wife was working until 10 o'clock that night. George rarely had a drink after work, but tonight was different. He eased back in his chair, sipped his drink, and thought. About 29 years ago, his college roommate had prodded him to join his firm. The salary was about the same, but they would pay for his MBA degree. Also, the chances to move beyond accounting and into more general management were strong. Twelve years ago, George's cousin had encouraged him to join her at her fledgling CPA firm. He could have come in as her partner, but the income was less certain and the benefits were nowhere near as good as they were at Obelisk. George networked extensively when he was younger, which had led to other solid job opportunities over the past several years. But each time he had a chance to move, he would remember what he would be giving up by leaving Obelisk. The bank was like a rock. And he knew two things—the bank offered security, and they would never let him go because he was too valuable. George became depressed as he grasped the reality that he had opted for security over opportunity every time.

George started feeling bitter. He had given his life to Obelisk, willingly working nights and weekends when necessary. He recalled the times he missed his daughters' school functions because he was so dedicated to the bank. He had never even taken more than one week of vacation at a time because he believed he was needed too much at the office to spare more than a week. George tried to figure out all the questions he needed to answer in the next few hours. They came to him quickly and in no logical order. How much is college tuition going to cost me over the next four years? How many more years am I going to live? Will my wife and I be able to travel the world like we had planned? What company would be willing to hire a 54-year-old accountant with a limited range of work experiences? Which severance package makes the most sense? Should I think about opening my own business? Should I hire a lawyer and hit Obelisk with an age discrimination lawsuit? Will my family think I'm a failure? Should we sell the house and move to something smaller?

George poured himself another drink. He heard the garage door closing and the familiar words "Hi honey, how was your day?"

Case Analysis Questions

1. How would you rate Obelisk's approach to the dismissal of George? What could or should they have done differently?

2. Why do you think George was blindsided by his dismissal? Do you think there was any way he could have seen the dismissal coming?

3. Why do you think George "opted for security over opportunity every time"?

4. Do you think George has a right to be bitter at Obelisk?

5. Should George take the early retirement option or the severance package? What do you see as the key issues for George as he decides what to do with his career in the short run and over the longer term?

6. If you were to make a prediction, what do you think George's career and life will look like five years into the future?

PART III

Contemporary Issues in Career Management

CHAPTER 9

Job Stress and Careers

The presence of job stress in the workplace is a major concern for both employees and organizational managers. Stress has taken an immense toll on the physical and emotional health of individuals, as well as the bottom lines of organizations. Indeed, stress can lead to such negative consequences as depression, burnout, physiological and psychosomatic illnesses, and low job satisfaction.[1] Each year, stress causes hundreds of billions of dollars in additional cost to American business due to increased absenteeism and turnover, employee burnout, lower productivity, higher medical costs, and worker compensation claims.[2]

The incidence and magnitude of stress experienced in today's business environment continue to escalate. Research indicates that large percentages of employees believe that their work-related stress is increasing and that this stress results in related physical symptoms such as fatigue, headaches, upset stomach, and muscle tension. Pressures emanate from several sources—long hours and poor communication at work, greater job demands with little control over one's work, conflicts with coworkers, personal financial worries, and the balancing of work and family lives.[3] Individuals must become more aware of the role of stress in their lives. Excessive levels of stress can seriously impair an employee's work performance and career success. Moreover, job stress will not go away by itself. One needs to understand the nature of job stress before it can be controlled. Finally, one needs to understand the support mechanisms that are available for coping with job stress.

In this chapter we examine the implications of job stress. First, we define stress and identify its sources and consequences. Then, we examine three particular sources of job stress that have been subject to much scrutiny—Type A behavior, career transitions, and bias in the workplace. In addition, we discuss job burnout and technology-induced stress/workaholism, both of which have been described extensively in the popular press. We conclude the chapter by offering ways in which individuals and organizations can deal personally with stress as they go through the process of managing their careers and their lives.

JOB STRESS: AN OVERVIEW

Stress involves an interaction between a person and the environment that is perceived to be so trying or burdensome that it exceeds the person's coping resources.[4] In a more basic sense, stress is aroused when a person is confronted with an opportunity, a constraint, or a demand.[5] An opportunity is a situation in which a person stands to gain additional gratification of his or her significant values or desires, as in a new work assignment or promotion. A constraint, on the other hand, threatens to block additional gratification; for example when a job promotion is denied. A demand threatens to remove a person from a currently gratifying situation, as when one is fired from a job.

A particular situation can simultaneously represent an opportunity, a constraint, and a demand. A new, challenging work assignment, for instance, may represent an opportunity to develop skills and acquire needed exposure, but it can also constrain one from spending more time with family, and can become a demand if it overloads one to the point that work effectiveness and satisfaction suffer. A situation—be it an opportunity, constraint, or demand—is stressful when it exceeds or threatens to exceed the individual's capacity to handle it.

For stress to be aroused, the individual must care about the particular outcomes of a given situation, but lack control over the circumstances or have a weak system of support.[6] If a person is indifferent toward future advancement within the work organization, then a new work assignment probably would not produce a significant amount of stress since the outcome (future advancement) does not hold a high degree of importance to the individual. Uncertainty, unpredictability, and fear of the unknown breed stress. If one knows for certain that a new job will be satisfying and stable, it will be far less stressful than if there is a degree of uncertainty about how satisfying the new job will be. In this sense, a person has to be emotionally involved in an uncertain situation for it to be stressful. Consider the case of Christie, a recent MBA graduate.

> Christie had spent several sleepless nights contemplating her first new product proposal before the executive management team of her employer. She had spent day and night for the last three weeks preparing the report and her presentation. She viewed the proposal as the first real test of her contribution to the organization, and if she succeeded, she would be considered as having managerial potential. Christie's presentation lasted 5 minutes and was followed by about 10 minutes of questions from the management team. Christie was thanked for making a fine presentation and was then dismissed from the meeting by the company's president. As she left the room, she felt cold and realized she was sweating profusely. She quickly went to the nearest women's restroom and in a release of tension, shook uncontrollably.

Christie's presentation represented an opportunity to test herself and impress the management team, but it also posed a threat to her self-esteem and her reputation within the company. Although she did not know how well the presentation would go, she cared deeply about the outcome because it was important to her future career with the company. Under these circumstances, it is understandable why Christie experienced a high level of stress that was manifested in such a physical way.

SOURCES AND CONSEQUENCES OF STRESS

Exhibit 9.1 presents an overview of the job stress process. This approach distinguishes environmental stressors from the perception of stress, from strain symptoms, and from the outcomes of stress.[7]

Table 9.1 identifies a number of potential environmental stressors. Stressors can be understood as "stimuli that evoke the stress process."[8] These stressors include factors within the work environment as well as factors outside the work environment. Stress can be produced by work situations that are ambiguous, overload (or underload) one's capacities, require extraordinary time commitments, or put one in the middle of two conflicting people or groups. Stress can have its roots in organizational policies or practices, in the demands of the job itself, and in the nature of the physical and social context of work. Individuals may become distressed due to the lack of career development opportunities, the lack of prestige associated with their job, the necessary time and travel associated with the occupation, or minimal occupational prospects for the future.

Research has found stressors that are hindrance oriented (e.g., organizational politics, red tape, role ambiguity) are negatively related to job performance, but challenge-oriented stressors (e.g., high workload, time pressure, job scope) motivate workers and can be positively related to job performance even as they evoke other strains such as fatigue and exhaustion.[9] Stress can also occur in the nonwork environment, where personal factors such as family finances, health concerns, and interpersonal relationships can create substantial burdens and pressures.[10]

The presence of an environmental stressor does not inevitably produce stress. It depends on how the situation is interpreted or appraised. Some people may not see a situation as particularly important, thereby reducing the level of perceived stress. For example, if Christie's career were not so important to her, the presentation would not have produced much stress. Or one may be so confident about one's ability to handle a situation that it is not viewed as threatening or uncertain. Therefore, what is perceived as stressful by one person may not be seen as stressful by another. An individual's characteristics, such as personality or coping ability, can help in perceiving and responding to stress at various levels. For example, those high in neuroticism (emotional instability) are likely to be less able to handle stressful situations because they tend to show more emotional reaction when distressed and use avoidance or denial as ways to cope with the stressful situation.[11]

EXHIBIT 9.1

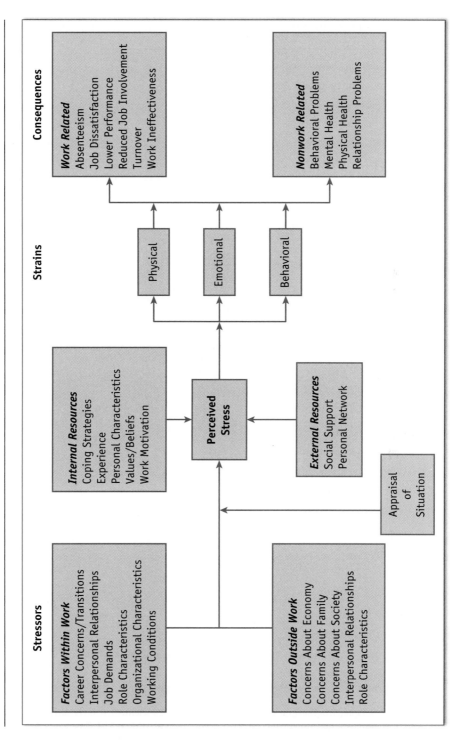

TABLE 9.1   Illustrations of Environmental Stressors

Career Concerns/Transitions

  Change of job, employer, location

  Obsolescence

  Career plateau

  Bias in the workplace

  Loss of employment

  Retirement

Interpersonal Relationships

  Conflict within and between groups

  Competition

  Inconsiderate or inequitable supervision

Job Demands

  Time pressure and deadlines

  Responsibility for people

  Repetitive work

Role Characteristics

  Role conflict: caught between conflicting expectations

  Role ambiguity: lack of clarity about expectations or performance

  Role overload/underload: too much or too little work

Organizational Characteristics

  Centralization, low participation in decision making

  Poor communication

  Pay inequities

Working Conditions

  Crowding

  Noise

  Excessive heat or cold

Nonwork Pressures

  Family/role conflicts

  Life changes, for example, divorce, illness or death of loved one, birth of child

  Worries about economy/current events

SOURCES: Adapted from several sources, including Brief, A. P., Schuler, R. S., & Van Sell, M. (1981). *Managing job stress.* Boston: Little, Brown; Spector, P. E. (2006). Stress at work. In J. H. Greenhaus & G. A. Callanan (Eds.), *Encyclopedia of career development* (pp. 771–778). Thousand Oaks, CA: Sage.

Certain personal characteristics can produce stress over and above the effects of particular environmental pressures. For example, highly anxious employees tend to experience high levels of stress regardless of the environmental conditions.[12] Other personal qualities, such as Type A characteristics (which we will discuss in more depth shortly), inflexibility, and intolerance of ambiguity can also heighten feelings of stress.[13] In addition, some individuals may simply have a personal disposition toward stress, whereby they experience stress regardless of the characteristics of the work situation.[14] The important point is that stress can be produced by a particular situation that is interpreted as threatening, as well as by a general personal tendency to perceive life circumstances as stressful.

In addition, the amount of control an employee has over a work situation can determine whether that situation produces extensive stress. Individuals who have control over the particular tasks they perform (the way they complete the tasks or the time or place at which the tasks are undertaken) may be able to avoid a stressful incident or perceive the incident as a challenge rather than a hindrance. Control may be particularly important on jobs that that are highly demanding.[15]

Perceived stress can produce a number of different strain symptoms. These strains may become manifest in a variety of physical, psychological, and behavioral outcomes (see Table 9.2). The impact of work stress on physical and psychological health is well documented. In fact, stress has been linked with cardiovascular disease, gastrointestinal disorders, susceptibility to viruses, overeating, drug and alcohol abuse, and other related health problems.[16]

TABLE 9.2 Illustrations of Strain Symptoms

Physical
> Short term: heart rate, galvanic skin response, respiration
> Long term: ulcer, blood pressure, heart attack
> Nonspecific: adrenaline, gastric acid production

Emotional
> Apathy, boredom
> Inattentiveness, loss of ability to concentrate
> Irritability
> Negativism

Behavioral
> Sudden change in use of alcohol
> Sudden change in smoking habits
> Sudden, noticeable weight loss or gain
> Difficult breathing

SOURCE: Taken from a longer list developed by Schuler: Schuler, R. S. (1980). Definition and conceptualization of stress in organizations. *Organizational Behavior and Human Performance, 24,* 115–130.

Of course, not everyone who experiences stress will develop these strain symptoms. Some people have a naturally high capacity to handle stress. In addition, effective coping skills can help protect people from the ravaging effects of extreme stress. Further, the availability of support from others can help keep stress within manageable bounds so that people do not experience such negative reactions to stressful situations. Coping strategies for stress will be discussed in a later section.

Extensive strain can reduce job involvement and productivity, and increase dissatisfaction, absenteeism, and turnover. In short, extensive work stress may not only prove dangerous to one's physical and emotional well-being, but may also produce dysfunctional consequences for the organization. Exposure to stress over a long period of time can be so debilitating that it has a significant impact on both health and productivity, and may result in burnout.[17] Moreover, research has found that excessive stress is strongly related to workplace harassment and violence.[18]

It is important to recognize that stress per se is not necessarily harmful. In fact, many researchers have concluded that a moderate level of stress enhances performance and health. Extreme levels of stress (low or high) can be distressful because they serve either to understimulate or overstimulate. Optimal levels of stress can be challenging and produce *eustress* (positive feelings and high involvement) rather than distress. Current thought suggests that management should encourage employees to consider challenges as eustress. This perspective could create a positive interpretation of the challenges presented and therefore minimize the distressful situation. Therefore, stress must be managed so that a proper balance is created, based on each employee's interpretation, that allows for optimum functioning for the individual and the organization.[19]

Type A Behavior as a Source of Stress

As noted earlier, personal needs, motives, and behavior patterns can produce stress. One such personality-related behavior pattern, known as Type A, is characterized by a hard-driving competitiveness, a sense of extreme impatience and time-urgency, the desire to live a fast-paced lifestyle, a preference for performing many activities simultaneously, and a constant striving for achievement and perfection.[20] In contrast, the Type B pattern has been characterized as having low or moderate levels of competitiveness, a higher degree of patience, and a less intense need for accomplishment and perfection. It is believed that the Type A pattern is produced by certain beliefs and fears that people hold about themselves and the world. For example, Type A individuals have higher perceptions of their intellectual ability, morality, and self-worth than Type B's. In addition, Type A's tend to base their sense of self-worth on their attainment of material success.[21]

On the positive side, Type A employees tend to be involved in their jobs and hold high levels of occupational success and self-esteem.[22] Moreover, they can be more productive than their Type B colleagues, largely because of their internal belief of self-competence, ability to juggle multiple projects, and tendency to develop high performance goals. On the other hand, studies of Type A personality have found that employees who exhibit this trait also experience comparatively higher levels of job stress and health-related problems such as coronary heart disease, and report lower job satisfaction and organizational commitment and higher turnover motivations.[23]

Programs have been developed to help Type A's alter their more harmful behaviors. Many of these intervention programs involve self-appraisal, a reorientation of one's philosophy of life, behavior therapy, and psychotherapy.[24] Might the reduction of Type A behavior, however, render the employee less productive on the job? Some researchers think not. Studies suggest that most intervention techniques can allow for alteration of the negative components of Type A behavior. Results indicate that interventions can achieve increases in the time devoted to relaxing with a related improvement in psychosomatic symptoms. The implications are that employees who successfully reduce their competitiveness and impatience, and who increase their control over pressing demands, can reduce the likelihood of poor health under stressful situations without impairing their level of job performance.

Career Transitions as a Source of Stress

Career transitions involve changes either in role characteristics—as when a person takes a first job, is promoted, or changes employers—or in orientation to a role currently held, as illustrated by alterations in attitudes toward a job due to changes in job duties, colleagues, or one's own behavior. All career transitions involve changes and contrasts between old and new settings. For example, a recently transferred and relocated employee has many adjustments to make: a new job, a new boss, a new group of colleagues, a new office, maybe even new work norms and expectations. There also is a different home in a different community, new neighbors, and, if there are children, new schools to enter and new friendships to form.

While career transitions usually require adjustments to new tasks, relationships, and expectations, do they really produce extensive stress? As was discussed in Chapter 8, one form of transition, job loss, has been linked to such strain symptoms as poor health, depression, insomnia, irritability, low self-esteem, and a feeling of helplessness. Beyond job loss, when do career transitions produce high levels of stress?

1. Undesirable career transitions are more likely to be stressful than desirable transitions. Most employees desire promotions and the salary increases that generally accompany them. As was indicated above, job loss and unemployment, on the other hand, can be devastating to one's financial security and sense of self-worth. Life transitions that have negative connotations produce more psychological distress. In fact, several researchers have discussed how individuals who see career plateauing as a "career failure" will experience job-related stress over time. Also, the reasons why employees plateau can affect the amount of

stress they experience. For example, individuals who choose not to pursue a promotion experience less stress than those who believe that they have plateaued because the organization didn't see them as worthy of a promotion.[25]

2. Career transitions that involve extensive changes, such as changing organizations or occupations or relocating to another geographic region can produce more stress and a greater need to cope than transitions that involve fewer or smaller changes.

3. Sudden, unexpected transitions may produce more shock and stress than gradual transitions. Also, uncertainty and fear over the effect of the transition can produce stress. Expected changes with more certain consequences allow the individual to prepare for the transition and develop more constructive coping responses.

4. Career transitions accompanied by other life transitions (e.g., marriage, divorce, birth of a child, serious illness in the family, financial hardship) are likely to be more stressful than career transitions unencumbered by other major life alterations.

5. Transitions that are forced on an individual may be more stressful than those under the individual's control. A forced transition is probably less desirable than a self-initiated one, and the timing of such a change may be beyond the control of the individual. Transitions can be more stressful when the individual cannot control the onset or duration of the stress-producing situation. Involuntary career transitions, such as the loss of one's job or the transfer to a different geographic area, can be stress-causing events.

In sum, transition-induced stress is likely to vary with the specific characteristics of the career transition, simultaneous life stresses, and the support and psychological resources available to the individual. Individual coping strategies can also help people deal with the changes and adjustments associated with transitions. A later section of this chapter will review the characteristics of effective coping behavior. Consider the following example that highlights the multifaceted nature of transition-induced stress.

Isabel was feeling overwhelmed and desperate for help. Three months ago she was unexpectedly promoted to quality assurance manager of her company. While the promotion was flattering, the time demands have been extraordinary. She has been putting in 70-hour work weeks, and there is no relief in sight. Compounding matters, Isabel's home and family life are in a state of flux. As the divorced mother of a three-year-old son, Isabel had relied on her mother to provide care for her child while she was at work. This child care arrangement was ideal for Isabel since it gave her flexibility to work as many hours as she needed without worry or guilt over the adequacy of supervision for her child. Unfortunately, two weeks ago Isabel received a call at work from the local hospital—her mother had a fall and had broken her hip. All at once, the stress in Isabel's life tripled—she had the demanding job, she lost the ideal child care arrangement for her son, and she had to find a way to care for her ailing mother. She feels like her head is about to explode and she just doesn't know where to turn. She has no other immediate family members in the area, and her friends are just as busy with their lives as she is with hers. She fears her new boss would be unsympathetic, and she is unaware of any programs at her company to help her deal with the crisis situation.

This example highlights the multifaceted nature of transition-induced stress. The promotion to the new job, with the excessive time demands on Isabel, represents, in and of itself, a stress-provoking career transition. On top of that, other events in Isabel's life are producing added stress and strain. At the moment, Isabel does not see a way out of her plight; that is, coping resources and support are not readily available to her. As we will discuss later in this chapter, more innovative organizations are attuned to the needs of their employees who, like Isabel, are undergoing significant career and life transitions with related stress. A number of programs are offered by employers to assist their employees with transition-related conflicts, and researchers have discussed how organizations can help employees who are undergoing stressful transitions.[26]

Employment Bias as a Source of Stress

A wide range of organizational and personal factors can produce job stress. It is also possible that employees can experience stress if they face bias and discrimination in their organization. Although it is not clear whether women and minorities experience more stress than other employees, there is significant evidence to suggest that certain organizational and societal conditions can be particularly stressful for these groups.

From a historical perspective, research has found that women in male-dominated fields, especially professional women, are exposed to four unique stressors over and above the more general ones men experience: employment discrimination, sex-role stereotyping, social isolation, and work–family conflicts.[27] In addition, many minority employees are subject to race stereotyping, restricted advancement opportunities, and social isolation. Several studies have reported the link between race discrimination and stress. Often, such perceived discrimination is related to lower organizational commitment and job satisfaction, and higher work tension. In order to reduce minority workers' stress, organizations must move toward a skills-based rather than a race-based culture, and should constantly challenge the interpersonal and institutional racism experienced by many minority employees.[28]

An employee exposed to bias, discrimination, and stereotyping becomes vulnerable to stress because of the lack of fit between talents/aspirations and organizational opportunities. An employee who occupies a token position is likely to feel alienated from the mainstream organization. And any "first"—for example, the first female or minority senior vice president in an organization—is likely to experience intense pressure and stress. These stressors include not just being the "first" to achieve a particular position, but also having to deal with the potential biases of one's peers. Maintaining high levels of performance can create additional stress as women, people of color, and homosexuals are usually watched closely to see if they are deserving of their new position. Stress can be experienced because the individual has become a role model for more junior minority group members in the organization.[29]

It is important to recognize that not all minorities face bias and isolation, and not all organizations stereotype and discriminate against their minority employees. Rather, the research suggests the potential for these stressors, and indicates the need for individuals and organizations to understand and modify these stressors when present. Undoubtedly, there is a need for additional research that focuses on the individual and organizational consequences of the stress experienced by minorities and women. Employment bias will be discussed more thoroughly in Chapter 11.

Burnout

The legendary football coach Dick Vermeil began his career in the National Football League (NFL) in 1976 as the head coach of the Philadelphia Eagles. Coach Vermeil enjoyed much success in Philadelphia. He was named the NFL's Coach of the Year in 1980, and in 1981 he led the Eagles into Super Bowl XV. Many people were surprised when Coach Vermeil suddenly retired after the 1982 season, citing burnout as the reason for leaving the coaching ranks.[30] Coach Vermeil eventually returned to the NFL in the late 1990s to coach the St. Louis Rams, where he guided that team to a Super Bowl victory in 2000. Over the past three decades expressions of burnout have been voiced by many other corporate, government, and sports figures who felt that the pressures of their work lives were creating such a high level of stress that they could not continue in their jobs.

Burnout is a psychological strain in response to chronic work stress.[31] Although initially it was thought that burnout was primarily associated with jobs with a high degree of human contact, such as those in the social services and health care sectors, it is now recognized that burnout is more widespread and can appear in many occupations and industries.[32] Burnout has been likened to job depression since emotional exhaustion is a symptom. Burnout has also been considered a problem of motivation because individuals suffering from this condition exhibit low engagement in their job. In this sense, burned out individuals often become unable to perform their jobs, mostly because of the powerlessness they experience as a result of burnout.[33] Like depression, burnout is a complex phenomenon that may occur for a multitude of reasons, and may manifest in a variety of ways.

Burnout consists of three interrelated components or psychological reactions.[34] First, continual contact with (and responsibility for) the problems of other people eventually produce a feeling of *emotional exhaustion*. Emotional exhaustion refers to feelings of being overextended and depleted of one's emotional and physical resources. To deal with the enervating features of their work, burned out workers become cynical and callous toward others and begin to *depersonalize* relationships with the people they serve, treating them more like objects and less like people. Increasingly, the burned out worker experiences a feeling of *low personal accomplishment* due to self-evaluations of incompetence resulting in a lack of achievement and productivity in work.[35]

Many of the causes of burnout are stressors encountered in the work environment: lack of rewards, of control, of clarity, of support, of fairness; a conflict of values; and an unmanageable workload. What enable these stressors to produce burnout are several personal characteristics: idealistic expectations, feelings of personal responsibility for failure, and predisposition to stress.[36] For example, an idealistic technology consultant who wants to complete a project within the prescribed deadline, and who enthusiastically expects to help his or her clients receive adequate resources from their organization to implement a new information system, may feel frustrated when the resources are not forthcoming. The consultant may also begin to believe that his or her personal shortcomings are somehow responsible for the organization's unwillingness to provide these resources. Burnout would occur when this situation pushes the individual beyond his or her ability to cope with the stress experienced.

The individual's predisposition to see the world in a positive or negative way is another personal characteristic that may induce burnout. The tendencies to perceive events with either positive or negative affectivity may influence one's perception of stress.[37] Individuals with negative predispositions have been found to experience high role stress and high emotional exhaustion and depersonalization, and to report low social support. They are also anxiety prone and tend toward job insecurity. Those with positive predispositions were found to report low burnout, high levels of personal achievement, high levels of organizational commitment and job satisfaction, and lower absenteeism and occupational injury.[38] Thus, the manner by which one views life events may increase (or decrease) chances for burnout.

Following are some common, identified signs of burnout:[39]

- *Negative emotions.* While we all experience negative emotions, burned out individuals are more anxiety prone and experience negative emotions more often, ultimately resulting in emotional fatigue.

- *Interpersonal friction and withdrawal.* When emotionally drained, burned out individuals have less empathy for those with whom they work and live. Communication with these individuals becomes strained, and burnout victims are apt to withdraw in order to cope. Burnout has a negative "spillover" effect in the work–family arena; workers experiencing burnout were rated by their spouses more negatively than those not experiencing burnout, and reported their job had a negative impact on their family.

- *Health suffers.* Burned out individuals typically suffer severe fatigue resulting in energy erosion. As emotional reserves become depleted, so does physical resilience. Burnout victims often experience disturbed sleep patterns, metabolic/endocrine changes, gastrointestinal disturbances, muscle tension, colds, headaches, and backaches.

- *Declining performance.* As burnout progresses, individuals become bored and find it difficult to be enthusiastic and productive in their work. Job dissatisfaction is common. Burned out individuals report low organizational commitment, high absenteeism and turnover, and greater intention to leave the job. Studies have found that nurses experiencing higher levels of burnout were judged by their patients to provide a lower level of patient care.

- *Substance abuse.* To cope with stress, burnout victims may find themselves drinking more alcohol or coffee, using more drugs (prescription or otherwise), eating more (or less), and smoking more often.

- *Feelings of meaninglessness.* Burnout victims tend to become apathetic—thinking "so what" or "why bother?" Enthusiasm is replaced by cynicism. Burnout has been associated with the feeling of alienation, as well as powerlessness, isolation, and self-estrangement.

Higher levels of burnout have also been related to increased violence in the workplace. Workers who described themselves as highly stressed or burned out experienced twice the number of incidents of physical or emotional harassment as those who were less burned out, while another study of police officers found a link between burnout and the use of violence against civilians.[40] Moreover, burnout can produce moodiness and withdrawal at home and high levels of burnout in one's spouse.[41] Burnout, therefore, can have harmful effects on employees, their families, and their work organizations.

Organizations concerned about this problem can attempt to change the environment that is responsible for the burnout. Managers need to realize that burnout is produced by high job demands, low control over the job, a lack of social support, and disagreements about values in the workplace.[42] Employees in jobs with a high proclivity for burnout who receive supportive and considerate supervision show a lower incidence of burnout. Also, employees who are reassured of their worth and value show reduced degrees of burnout and increased organizational commitment. In light of these findings, organizations, especially those with jobs that have high susceptibility for burnout, should ensure that supervisors and others in leadership positions be supportive of their personnel, and regularly acknowledge their value and worth. Organizational actions such as these can help prevent burnout from occurring.

In addition, organizations can help employees cope with the burnout they already experience. Employee assistance programs (EAPs) provide counseling services that focus on the prevention and/or remediation of occupational stress experienced by employees or members of their families. EAPs are currently considered one of the main vehicles for management to help employees deal with stress and burnout. These programs can have a positive effect on employee well-being and are perceived by employees as a desirable workplace resource.[43] Employers are also offering on- or off-site wellness/fitness centers, karate and yoga classes, massages, and outdoor volleyball and basketball courts to allow employees to burn off steam.[44] As one example, Lockheed Martin offers on-site "energy rooms" where employees can reenergize during their breaks by playing billiards, air hockey, or table tennis.[45] Obviously, these approaches are not mutually exclusive. Organizations should try to change their environment to reduce the likelihood of burnout and, at the same time, provide counseling and support to employees who experience burnout symptoms.

Technology-Induced Stress and the Potential for Workaholism

The increasing use of computer and communication technologies as common business tools has increased pressure on employees to be accessible to their employers 24 hours per day, seven days a week.[46] Such tools as laptop computers, cell phones, and PDAs (handheld personal digital assistants) allow employees to be connected to their offices at all times, and employers have become accustomed to having their employees available on a moment's notice. This "tethering" to the workplace, even during traditional nonwork hours, has the potential to produce significant amounts of stress. In addition, electronic tethering has also been linked to workaholism. People who show signs of workaholism have a compulsive need to work at the expense of everything else in their life. A *workaholic* has been defined as a person who is highly work involved, experiences low work enjoyment, and is compelled to work because of inner pressures.[47] It has been estimated that as many as 25 percent of U.S. employees meet this definition.[48]

Recent studies have found workaholism and burnout to be two separate and distinct concepts. Workaholics do not necessarily burn out, and differ from those who burn out on measures of hours worked, quality of social relationships, and perceived health.[49] Signs of workaholism are failure to use vacation time, refusal to stay home when ill, an inability to delegate work, and the tendency to seek control of group projects. Stress and work–life imbalance has been found in both men and women workaholics. The effects are felt not just by workers and their families but also by employers in terms of lost productivity, increased health care costs (especially for diseases that are aggravated by stress), and potential legal concerns, including disabilities and wage-and-hour issues. As with burnout, employees who experience workaholism need to learn coping techniques in order to create a balanced life and an equilibrium between work and leisure.

COPING, SOCIAL SUPPORT, AND STRESS

None of us can, or should, go through life free of stress. All people experience career transitions, some of them traumatic. Jobs may be pressure packed or routine and repetitive. Family circumstances, midlife reappraisal, job loss, and threats to health can all be stressful events. People who have survived life's trials are resourceful and have learned how to cope.

Coping behaviors enable individuals to avoid the harmful effects of stressful situations. Effective coping does not eliminate stress from our lives, but reduces it to manageable levels and prevents it from producing severe emotional or physical strain. Research has identified three broad categories of coping responses.[50] First, one can attempt to change the situation that produces the stress; in other words, reduce or modify the actual stressors. Table 9.3 presents illustrations of this problem-focused coping strategy. Seeking clarification of job standards, reducing workload, requesting advice from others, taking on more varied assignments, or changing jobs are all examples of coping responses designed to alter the environment or the person's role in it.

A second type of coping response changes the meaning of the stressful environment without necessarily changing the stressors themselves. This is known as cognitive restructuring or "self-talk." People can make a situation less threatening by cognitively reappraising it, making a comparison (favorable, of course) with others' conditions, focusing on the positive features of the situation, or changing work or life priorities to be more consistent with the

TABLE 9.3 Illustrations of Coping Behaviors Designed to Change a Stressful Work Environment

1. Attempt to eliminate burdensome parts of job	8. Seek job transfer
2. Attempt to add or better use staff to relieve pressures	9. Seek different organization or career field
3. Attempt to build more challenge or responsibility into job	10. Seek others' advice
4. Seek clarification of job duties	11. Attempt to upgrade job skills through education and/or experience
5. Seek clarification of career prospects	12. Attempt to resolve conflicts with supervisor, peers, and/or subordinates
6. Seek feedback on job performance	13. Participate in career-planning program
7. Seek more flexible work schedule	

situation in which they find themselves.[51] The plateaued manager who places a greater emphasis on community service than on further vertical mobility illustrates this technique.

A third form of coping attempts to manage the strain symptoms themselves. Relaxation techniques such as meditation or biofeedback, diaphragmatic breathing, yoga, physical exercise, and recreation can effectively reduce such physical strains as elevated pulse rate and blood pressure. Proper time management and journaling can help the individual to stay ahead of daily pressures. Finally, proper nutrition and regular prayer have been found to calm both mind and body.[52]

Research has not revealed a specific type of coping response that is universally effective. The usefulness of specific coping activities undoubtedly depends on many factors: the severity of the stress; the psychological, coping, and social resources of the individual; and the particular circumstances of the stressful situation. In effect, this is a contingency approach to coping wherein a repertoire of coping skills combined with positive attitudes toward oneself seem to be the most crucial factors in managing stress. Indeed, the field of positive psychology suggests that there are human strengths that can act as buffers against occupational stress. These buffers include such attributes as courage, optimism, interpersonal skills, faith, hope, honesty, perseverance, resilience, and perspective. Employees who use these positive thinking buffers report better psychological well-being and job performance. It appears that positive thinking and emotions assist individuals by enhancing their optimism and resiliency and buffering them against daily stress.[53] An appropriate combination of problem solving, cognitive reappraisal, and physical exercise/relaxation may be particularly useful in reducing stress.

Edgar Schein developed a four-step approach that is consistent with this contingency approach to coping.[54] Step 1 involves diagnosing the situation and correctly identifying the real source of the problem. In this step, one needs to understand whether the stress comes from work, family, personal concerns, or some combination of these sources. Step 2 involves self-assessment. It is essential to take (and make) the time to reflect on feelings and motives and to become familiar with blind spots or other defenses that shield people from an insightful understanding of themselves.

In Step 3, a coping response is selected. By talking with peers, family members, friends, neighbors, and community resources about problems and stresses and by establishing supportive relationships with others, one can choose an appropriate coping response. It is important to identify either an external coping resource (e.g., a confidant) or internal resource (e.g., personal characteristic such as hardiness) so that the appropriate coping response is selected. Coping resources aid the person in choosing a healthy response.[55] The chosen response may involve changing an aspect of the stressful environment, shifting one's priorities and the meaning of the environment, or managing the strain symptoms themselves. Finally, Step 4 involves understanding the effect (if any) of the coping response and making adjustments when necessary. Consider the following example.

Gene was scared. Over the past three months his health and physical well-being had gotten progressively worse. It started with recurring headaches and a nagging tightness in his back and shoulders. Over time, he experienced stomach distress, a shortness of breath, and chest pains. On top of it all, Gene had trouble sleeping, spending many nights just staring at the ceiling. The culmination of Gene's physical problems occurred one night while he was driving home from work, when he suddenly experienced an episode of tachycardia (a rapid heartbeat). He pulled off to the side of the road thinking his life was about to end. Eventually his heartbeat returned to normal, but the incident left him deeply concerned.

Gene called in sick the next day and saw his physician. He also began contemplating why these health problems were occurring. He concluded that his problems were the outcome of the stress he was experiencing in his life. He was recently transferred to another division of his company that, while not causing him to move his family, did double his commuting time. His commute now took one and a half hours each way. In addition to the demands of the new job, Gene has had to deal with turmoil at home. His 16-year-old son was having problems in school—skipping classes and being disruptive when he did attend. The principal of the school had threatened suspension unless his son's behavior changed. Gene was afraid his son's current difficulties might eventually lead to something far more serious.

Gene began thinking about what was causing his distress and what was really important in his life. His job allowed him and his family to live comfortably and gave them financial security, but the commuting and work demands left little time for leisure and family activities. In short, he concluded that the excessive time he gave to his job and its associated travel had a negative effect on his and his family's well-being. He decided to talk to his wife about his thoughts. She confirmed what he already knew—his job was causing physical and emotional harm. His introspection and the conclusions he reached left Gene feeling a bit more at ease.

Gene began discussing his options with his wife. They agreed that Gene's work was important to him, but his family's well-being was essential. They considered that a new job, especially one closer to home, might give Gene the opportunity to spend more time with his family. He also knew that he needed to pay more attention to his diet and to begin an exercise program. With the support of his family, Gene started looking for a new job, and he began playing tennis on a regular basis. Gene resolved that until he found a new position, he would devote as much time as he could to his son. By being there to listen to what his son had to say, Gene hoped to help his son through the emotional turmoil of being a teenager.

Overall, Gene recognized that he likely would be sacrificing financial rewards by taking a new job, but the anticipated reduction in stress and increased time for family and leisure activities would be well worth it.

This example highlights the effective use of the contingency approach to coping with stress. The physical manifestations of Gene's stress forced him to take time to evaluate his situation. This set the stage for Gene to go through a period of self-assessment, examining his values and goals. His self-assessment allowed him to change the meaning of various aspects of his life. While work was important, his well-being and that of his family were more important. He then selected coping responses—finding a new work position, improving his diet and getting more exercise, and vowing to allow more time for his family. Finally, Gene sought to understand the effect of his intended actions—trade-off between financial rewards and a lower level of stress.

Gene's story emphasizes the importance of other people as sources of information and support. Social support has long been recognized as an invaluable aid to individuals undergoing conflict and stress, and is considered a form of coping. Support from others can help reduce the stressfulness of the environment as well as protect individuals from the harmful effects of the stress that they do experience. In fact, individuals who reported high strain symptoms and high levels of social support reported lower health care costs than individuals who reported low strain symptoms. This finding suggests that individuals with social support systems may be better at coping and may interpret strains as eustress rather than distress.[56]

Support to help deal with stress can come from many sources, both informal (family, friends, coworkers) and formal (self-help groups, mental health or other professionals, and child care or other service providers). Researchers often distinguish four classes of supportive behaviors: emotional, instrumental, informational, and appraisal.[57] Definitions and illustrations of these four types of support are provided in Table 9.4.

TABLE 9.4   Four Types of Social Support

Type of Support	Meaning	Illustrations
Emotional	Empathy, caring, trust, love	Boss praises your effective performance
Instrumental	Behavior that directly helps person in need	Subordinate's improving performance relieves you of pressure
Informational	Information to be used by person to cope with problem	Coworker gives you advice on how to discipline a subordinate
Appraisal	Information that provides feedback to person	Boss gives you constructive feedback on your most recent assignment
		Close friend gives you her opinion of your interpersonal style

SOURCE: Types and meanings of social support based on House, J. S. (1981). *Work stress and social support*. Reading, MA: Addison-Wesley.

Again, no magic formula exists to identify the sources and types of social support that are most applicable to a specific situation. Understanding oneself, as well as the sources of stress and available resources, are necessary preliminary steps, but it is important to recognize that supportive relationships are not a one-way street. One has to be willing to give social support to receive it. Studies have found that the amount of social support received is strongly related to the amount of social support given, especially from spouses, family, or friends.[58]

Organizational Actions

Organizations have developed a variety of programs to reduce the level of employee stress. Using the distinction among the three types of coping responses, organizations can either alter the stressful environment, work with employees to change their interpretation of the environment, or help them manage their strain symptoms.

Illustrations of these approaches are shown in Table 9.5. Any particular program is likely to incorporate two or more of the coping strategies. For example, a program designed to

TABLE 9.5   Illustrations of Organizational Actions to Reduce Employee Stress

Reducing Stressors
   Eliminate racial/gender stereotypes, biases, and discrimination
   Redesign jobs to be more in line with employees' capabilities and interests
   Clarify employee expectations through goal-setting program
   Provide constructive performance feedback
   Build supportive work groups
   Train supervisors in interpersonal skills
   Eliminate noxious elements of physical working conditions
   Help employees with problem-solving/coping skills
   Develop flexible work schedules
   Develop programs for transitioned (e.g., relocated) employees

Changing the Meaning of Stressful Situations
   Offer counseling services to employees
   Run programs to ameliorate Type A behavior, burnout
   Run programs on time management
   Run social support groups for employees

Managing Strain Symptoms
   Provide relaxation programs (e.g., meditation)
   Provide facilities for physical exercise
   Provide counseling and medical treatment
   Provide comprehensive "wellness" programs

build supportive work groups may simultaneously try to change the stressful environment (by fostering constructive communication between individuals) as well as the meaning of the environment (such as understanding when competition is healthy and when cooperation is necessary).

Before any program is initiated, organizations must properly diagnose the extent and roots of employee stress. Such diagnoses may be organization-wide or may be applied to select groups of employees based on level (e.g., senior executives), job category (e.g., air traffic controllers), location (e.g., employees at a nuclear power plant), or other relevant criteria (e.g., minority employees). Organizational diagnoses can focus on the assessment of organizational stressors, the degree of employee strain, or employee characteristics that modify the strain symptoms. Organizations also need to be aware that techniques that work for one employee may not work for all employees.[59] Examples of each type of diagnostic activity are presented below:

Assessment of Organizational Stressors

- Objective indicators of stress (e.g., turnover, absenteeism, accidents)

- Standardized questionnaires that measure organizational conditions

- Observation/documentation of employee work load and job control

Assessment of Employee Strains

- Physiological measures (e.g., pulse rate, blood pressure)

- Medical checklists

- Burnout or anxiety inventories

Assessment of Employee Modifiers of Strain

- Coping mechanisms

- Social support

- Type A behavior pattern

In the fast-paced, global economy of the 21st century it is unlikely that the level of stress experienced by today's workers is going to be reduced or even stay constant. On the contrary, the pressures of modern life, with increasing work and family demands, portend escalating levels of stress. Therefore, organizationally sponsored programs that help employees cope with stress and burnout can be especially important, as shown in the following example.

IBM is a company that believes part of its corporate responsibility is promoting employee well-being. IBM's strategy for promoting employee health and well-being is global, but its programs are customized to address local needs and cultures. These programs include early diagnosis and disease prevention efforts, such as clinical screenings, immunizations, physical fitness activities, nutrition and weight counseling, and stress management. Other primary prevention efforts include ergonomics and injury/illness prevention programs. IBM also offers online health management programs in the United States. Employees can use the Virtual Fitness Center (VFC) to help make physical fitness a part of their daily lives. Accessible 24 hours a day, seven days a week, from any computer with Internet access, the VFC enables employees to set goals, track their activity and chart their success, and stay focused on fitness goals year-round. IBM's employee assistance programs (EAPs) are available to help employees manage the stress associated with work and life priorities. IBM offers EAPs in the United States and worldwide, and most recently in India, China, and Japan. IBM's Global Stress Management program includes a stress intervention Web site, online manager stress intervention training, and location-specific stress management resources. Should an employee have greater needs, IBM's health benefits programs provide services that specifically address mental health. Several IBM locations in Europe offer Team Well-being interventions, which help organizations or teams assess their specific causes of stress and take action to reduce them. For example, IBM Germany offers a stress management program that is adaptable to all types of work situations, with a particular focus on the needs of mobile workers. The program includes training for managers on how to help their employees cope with stress, as well as education for employees on managing stress. Offerings are available in person and on demand through the IBM intranet.[60]

SUMMARY

Stress is aroused when an individual faces an opportunity, a constraint, or a demand. A situation is likely to be most stressful when the outcome is uncertain but is important to the individual. Stress can be produced by a number of conditions in the work environment—organizational characteristics, job demands, low job control, the quality of interpersonal relationships, working conditions, and career concerns—as well as pressures arising outside of work. Since individuals have different needs, competencies, and perspectives, a situation that is stressful to one person may not be stressful to another. A high level of stress can manifest itself in physiological, emotional, and behavioral changes. It can ultimately lead to a decrease in job satisfaction, involvement, and performance, and an increase in absenteeism and turnover.

This chapter examined three particular sources of stress. The Type A behavior pattern, characterized by a hard-driving competitiveness and sense of time urgency, can be physically and emotionally destructive. In addition, career transitions (such as promotions, relocations, or terminations) can be stressful under certain conditions: when they require extensive, unwanted adjustments; when they are accompanied by changes in other parts of an individual's life; when they are unexpected and forced on an individual; and when the individual's coping and social support mechanisms are absent or ineffective. It was also suggested that stress is likely to be experienced by women and minorities who are exposed to bias and discrimination in their work environment.

Also examined was the concept of burnout, a stress reaction in which an individual in a highly charged work setting experiences emotional exhaustion, depersonalizes relationships with others, and begins to hold lower feelings of personal accomplishment. Burnout is most likely to be experienced by employees who initially held idealistic expectations about their job, who ultimately come to believe they are personally responsible for organizational failures, and who have a predisposition for stress.

People who survive stressful conditions have likely learned effective coping skills and/or have utilized supportive relationships with others. Since no single coping behavior is likely to be effective in all situations, individuals must learn to assess the situation and select appropriate responses. These coping responses may be directed toward changing the stressful environment, reappraising the environment, or reducing the resultant strain symptoms through such activities as relaxation and physical exercise. In a similar manner, organizations can help alleviate employee stress through a series of programs designed to change the stressful conditions, help employees adjust to the conditions, and/or reduce the negative strain symptoms.

ASSIGNMENT

Think about the types of work and nonwork stressors you may be experiencing. What symptoms have you encountered? How successfully have you coped with these stressors?

DISCUSSION QUESTIONS

1. Take a look at the descriptions of the four types of social support shown in Table 9.4. Provide examples of emotional, instrumental, informational, and appraisal support that you have received from others and that you have offered to others.

2. What levels of stress can you tolerate? What levels of stress are harmful to you (distress) and what levels of stress are beneficial (eustress)?

3. Investigate your company (or a company for which you are interested in working) to determine what types of stress management programs it offers. Are companies obliged to offer such programs? Would you work for one that did not? Why or why not?

CHAPTER 9 CASE

Sally the Stressed Saleswoman

Sally, 29 years of age, has been selling telecommunications equipment to manufacturers since she graduated from college nearly eight years ago. She is obviously good at her job. Not only has she consistently met or exceeded her sales quota, but her customers report that she is knowledgeable about her products and continually puts in long hours keeping tabs on their needs and providing valuable consulting to them. Sally's employer, GA Industries (fictitious name), recognizes her value to the organization and has rewarded her handsomely over the years.

The last few months have been rough on Sally. She seems to be tired all the time. She has had trouble shaking a monthlong cold, and, for the first time she can remember, she canceled an appointment with a customer because she just could not get herself out of her apartment that morning.

Sally has also been short tempered of late. Although it has not affected her sales volume yet, she has had to catch herself a few times from snapping at some thickheaded customers. How many times does she have to explain the same things to these people? But that cannot be the entire problem.

She has found herself getting into a lot of petty arguments with Steve, her fiancé. She just seems to be preoccupied with her job wherever she is. The plans for Sally and Steve's wedding have taken a back seat to her work, and their wedding date has been put off a couple of times, much to Steve's dismay. On top of this dilemma, Sally and Steve have had many discussions about where they will live, and if and when they will have children. They have not been able to come to agreement on these issues.

"Why am I so irritable?" Sally keeps asking herself. She is doing well and still finds her job interesting and challenging. It is true that her boss, Maria, GA's industrial sales manager, keeps poking her nose into Sally's business and giving her unneeded advice about how to handle customers. Maria wants her to put more pressure on several customers to purchase certain pieces of equipment they really do not need. Her customers would not tolerate a hard sell like that, but Sally will avoid that issue as long as she can. She hardly sees Maria nowadays, maybe once every other week, and she is usually too busy to talk to her. Sometimes Sally wonders what Maria really thinks of her. Fortunately, her customers tell her how good she is at her job.

Sally admits that she has been a little peeved at the company for expanding her territory six months ago. Not that she is uninterested in new business, but she cannot do a thorough job with such a large territory. And she's been finding herself out of town four, sometimes five, days a week. The larger territory has left Sally drowning in paperwork, and she is beginning to wonder how she can ever maintain a relationship with her fiancé when they hardly ever see each other anymore. And then there are the wedding plans . . .

But the job is so challenging. And GA is coming out with a new product line next week. The whole sales force has been attending weekend meetings for about four weeks to learn more about these new products. It is exciting to introduce a new product on the cutting edge. Sally just wishes she understood the new product line better. She has not been able to focus at the training classes, has not really understood the lectures at the meetings, and has been unable to make much sense out of the manuals. She probably should have taken a few more technical courses back in college. But that's water under the bridge.

Sally would like to talk to someone about her feelings. But who? Talking to her boss Maria is out of the question. She would think Sally was being ungrateful, and Maria is so self-focused she would not be able to relate to her. Sally is convinced that her family and her fiancé just wouldn't understand the situation. The other salespeople, she guesses, would be pretty uncaring. But she does need to talk to someone. And soon!

Case Analysis Questions

1. What evidence is there that Sally is experiencing job stress? What are the symptoms?

2. What conditions are producing Sally's stress?

3. How is Sally's job stress affecting her family and personal life? And are her family and personal life affecting her work?

4. If you were Sally, what would you do? Identify as many alternative plans of action as possible and indicate the advantages and disadvantages of each. Which plan(s) of action would you choose? Why?

5. What types of social support (as shown in Table 9.4) would Sally find most helpful: appraisal, instrumental, emotional, or informational? From whom should she seek such support? Why?

6. If you were the president of GA Industries and just heard Sally's story, what, if anything, would you do? Why?

The Intersection
of Work and Family Roles

Implications for Career Management

Work and family lives touch each other in so many ways.[1] Think of how your career responsibilities can affect your family and personal life; how a good (or bad!) day at work affects your mood at home, or the times you missed a child's music recital or a workout at the gym because of your job. Think also of how your family responsibilities can affect your career; for example, whether you are willing to spend countless evenings or weekends in the office rather than with your family or friends, and whether you are prepared to accept a relocation that jeopardizes your spouse's career or your children's friendships.

It is no wonder that work–family balance is a hot topic on the nation's social agenda, especially when organizational downsizings have left many of us with more work to do and fewer resources with which to do it. Articles on flextime, parental leave legislation, "mommy tracks," and child care arrangements filled the pages of the popular press and the professional journals in the 1980s and 1990s, and have continued with even greater frequency in the new millennium. Individuals and families are increasingly concerned with finding ways to juggle their work and family responsibilities.

Why has the need to balance work and family lives become more intense in recent years? First, many individuals are simultaneously pursuing a career and committed to a family relationship. Indeed, both spouses are employed in nearly 6 out of 10 married-couple families in the United States,[2] and other industrialized countries throughout the world are witnessing similar trends. The changing composition of the workforce is largely attributable to the increasing participation of women in paid employment. Consider the following statistics:[3]

- In 2005, 59.3 percent of all married women in the United States age 16 and older were in the workforce, compared with just 30 percent in 1960.

- Nearly 62.6 percent of all married women with children younger than six were in the workforce in 2005, compared with only 19 percent in 1960.

- The employment rate for married women with children ages 6–17 was 76.9 percent in 2005, nearly double the rate (39 percent) in 1960.

- Approximately 28 percent of the households with children under 18 were single-parent households; 82 percent of these were headed by women.

In addition, men are increasingly required to juggle their work and family lives. With their wives employed outside the home with greater frequency, more responsibility for home chores and child care falls on husbands, who then need to balance these responsibilities with their work demands. Moreover, a small but significant number of divorced men assume custody of their children and feel the crunch of extensive family and career commitments.

In addition to these demographic changes, advances in communication technology have increased the work pressures of employees in many organizations. The proliferation of PDAs, cell phones, and other forms of electronic communication often makes employees feel "on call" 24 hours and seven days a week at the whim of organizations that require their immediate action.[4] Recent studies indicate that more than 10,000 companies provide PDAs to their employees, 60 percent of the employees with cell phones or smart phones take the phones with them on vacation, and 20 percent are contacted by their employers while on vacation.[5]

Moreover, an increasingly global economy requires many employees to communicate with colleagues, suppliers, and clients in different parts of the world and consequently in different time zones. Making or taking a 3:00 a.m. telephone call from the United States to speak with a colleague in Asia during the colleague's normal work hours can put additional strain on an already harried businessperson and disrupt sleep patterns.

The combination of heavy work commitments and extensive family responsibilities has required individuals and families to cope effectively with the stresses of this demanding lifestyle. It has also posed a challenge to employers to develop "family responsive" policies and practices or risk losing their competitive edge in attracting and retaining talented women and men.[6]

This chapter examines the relationship between work and family lives. We will discuss the factors that produce conflict between employees' work lives and their family lives as well as the consequences of this conflict for employees, families, and employers. We will also consider the many ways in which work and family lives can strengthen and enrich one another. Next, we will discuss potential stresses in a two-career relationship and the ways individuals and couples can manage this stress. We will also identify actions that organizations can take to help their employees resolve their work–family challenges and actions that individuals can take to manage their careers in ways that take their work *and* personal lives into account.

WORK–FAMILY CONFLICT: WHEN WORK AND FAMILY ARE "ENEMIES"

There are many times when our work and family lives are in conflict with one another. Work–family conflict exists when pressures from work and family roles are mutually incompatible, that is, when participation in one role interferes with participation in the other role.[7] Sometimes our work responsibilities interfere with our family lives (known as work-to-family conflict), whereas at other times our family lives interfere with our work (family-to-work conflict).[8] We will use the term *work–family conflict* when referring to the general notion of conflict between work and family lives and use the more specific terms *work-to-family conflict* or *family-to-work conflict* when referring to the specific direction of the conflict or interference. Research has revealed three significant forms of work–family conflict: time-based conflict, strain-based conflict, and behavior-based conflict.

Time-based conflict occurs because the activities we pursue in life compete for a precious commodity—time. The time spent in one role generally cannot be devoted to the other role. Out-of-town business meetings or late evenings at the office can interfere with family dinners and children's parent–teacher conferences. It is simply impossible to be in two places at once. Time-based work-to-family conflict is likely to be most prevalent for employees who work long hours, travel extensively, frequently work overtime, and have inflexible work schedules. All of these work characteristics increase or fix the time at work that cannot be spent on family role activities.

Time pressures that arise from the family domain can also produce conflict. Employees who experience the most extensive family-to-work conflict tend to be married, have young children, have large families, and have spouses or partners who hold responsible jobs. All of these family characteristics increase the amount of time required to fulfill family role requirements, which can interfere with work-related activities.

Strain-based conflict exists when psychological strain produced within one role affects our functioning in another role. Work stressors can produce such strain symptoms as tension, irritability, fatigue, depression, and apathy, and it is difficult to be an attentive partner, a loving parent, or an understanding friend when one is depressed or irritable. Strain-based work-to-family conflict is likely to be most intense for employees who experience conflict or ambiguity within the work role; who are exposed to extensive physical, emotional, or mental work demands; whose work environment is constantly changing; and who work on repetitive, boring tasks. All these stressful conditions can produce a "negative emotional spillover" from work to nonwork.[9]

Of course, many sources of strain can arise from the family role as well. Individuals who experience difficulties with partners or children or receive little support and aid from their families may find that their family stress intrudes into their work life. It is difficult to devote oneself fully to work when preoccupied with a stressful family situation.

Sometimes behavior that is effective in one role is simply inappropriate in another role. It has been suggested, for example, that managers when at work are expected to be self-reliant, aggressive, detached, and objective. Family members, on the other hand, may expect that same person when at home to be warm, nurturant, and attentive. If people cannot shift gears when they enter different roles, they are likely to experience *behavior-based conflict* between the roles. Behavioral styles that employees exhibit at work (logic, objectivity, power, and authority) may be incompatible with the behaviors desired by their partners and children on the home front.[10] Partners and children do not appreciate being treated like subordinates!

Therefore, a variety of role pressures can produce work–family conflict. Some of these pressures demand excessive time commitments, others produce extensive stress, and many produce both. Where do these pressures come from? Some come from role senders, persons with whom we interact in our work and family lives. Bosses, colleagues, partners, and children are all role senders who place demands on us to finish projects, attend weekend meetings, wash the dishes, and paint the house. People tend to experience more conflict when there are strong penalties for failing to comply with these demands from work and family roles. If a boss insists that you attend a Saturday work meeting, and a partner refuses to change vacation plans by one day, you are caught between the proverbial rock and hard place. If either the boss or the partner permits latitude to deviate from expectations, there is room to maneuver.

However, many pressures to participate or excel at work or in family activities come not from other people, but from the expectations we place on ourselves—we become our own role senders. For example, Type A employees, as we discussed in Chapter 9, place tremendous pressure on themselves to work long hours and be highly successful. Not surprisingly, they experience more work–family conflict than Type B's.[11] In the family realm, the desire to be the "perfect" partner or parent can place pressure on us that goes far beyond any pressure that children or partners can muster.

The pressures people put on themselves depend on the importance or salience of the role to their self-concept. People for whom work is a central part of life are more demanding on themselves to participate fully and competently in that role, thereby exacerbating the degree of conflict. Those who are highly involved in both work and family are likely to experience the most conflict.[12] They want to be highly productive in their careers and be an attentive parent and partner, and they feel guilty if they cannot do both all the time. Consider the following three scenarios.

- Bill is a hard-working attorney in his early 30s, married, with two children. He is preoccupied with his career, working long hours, traveling extensively, and bringing work home most evenings and weekends. Despite his heavy work pressures and a young family, Bill does not feel intense work–family conflict. He is so concerned about his career that he hardly notices the family pressures that surround him. Since he often convinces his wife to make only minor demands on his time and emotion, he does not even see the impact of his work on his family life, or, if he does see it, it does not bother him deeply. It is not so much that his family is unimportant, but rather that it takes a back seat to his career.

- Malik, also married with two children, has a demanding, time-consuming career as an executive. Unlike Bill, however, Malik is quite concerned about spending time with his family and sharing experiences with his wife and young children. His career is important, but so is his family. Despite his best efforts to juggle work and family activities, Malik experiences chronic, intense work–family conflict. He cares so much about both roles that the tug on his time and emotion is almost inevitable.

- Rajan's situation is slightly different. He works as an accountant for a state government agency. Although he likes his job, Rajan's career is not a crucial part of his life. He works primarily to earn enough money to support his wife and two young children. He puts in a 40-hour week, actively avoids business travel, and almost never brings work home. His passions are his family, his home, and his hobbies. Rajan does not experience intense work–family conflict. His job leaves him sufficient time to pursue his real interests, and it doesn't drain him of his energy.

In these three scenarios, the husband's work–family conflict depends on the relative importance he attaches to his work and family roles. Who is most typical—Bill, Malik, or Rajan? Fernando Bartolome and Paul Evans observed that most young male managers were obsessed with their careers, enmeshed in their career success, and driven by a need to achieve that seemed to overshadow family life.[13] Family was important to these men, but they tended to take it for granted. Although men, in general, may not be as obsessed with their careers now as they were decades ago, there will still be individual differences in the importance of work based on employees' underlying life values and the nature of their career fields.

It is not a question of who is right and who is wrong. All three situations require trade-offs between work and family pursuits. Bill's career progress has been rapid and successful but not without cost—his family relationships. Malik gets a great deal of satisfaction from both work and family roles. However, his heavy involvement in both roles may leave him frustrated and wondering what kind of father/husband (or executive) he could have been if he had centered his life even more on his family (or work). Rajan's satisfaction with his family and home life also came at a price—lack of extensive career accomplishments—although he may be quite willing to pay that price. To understand the consequences of a trade-off, people must know what values are most important to them and must understand the risks they assume to pursue these values.

We intentionally described the experiences of three men to illustrate that males are not immune to work–family conflict and guilt. The initial belief that women inevitably experience more work–family conflict than men has not been consistently supported. Some recent research suggests that the heavy work responsibilities of many men interfere with their family lives, whereas the heavy family responsibilities of many women interfere with their work.[14] However, there are likely to be many exceptions to this trend, and it is fair to say that *anyone* (man or woman) who encounters extensive work and family pressures can experience conflict or interference between these roles.

Table 10.1 presents a scale that measures work–family conflict. Strong agreement with an item reflects a relatively high level of work–family conflict. Therefore, the higher the score the more extensive is the work–family conflict. Extensive work–family conflict can produce high levels of stress; detract from our satisfaction with our family, job, and life; and can produce physical or psychological health problems.[15] However, this does not mean that everyone who experiences work–family conflict will experience stress, dissatisfaction, and poor health. A certain level of conflict is inevitable in a society in which women and men are required to juggle work and family responsibilities. Problems are probably most pronounced when the level of work–family conflict is so intense that it exceeds individuals' capacities to cope with the conflict. We will discuss coping skills in a later part of the chapter.

TABLE 10.1   Inventory of Work–Family Conflict

Below are 12 statements about the relationship between your work life and your family, home, or personal life. Indicate your agreement or disagreement by placing the appropriate number in front of each statement:

    1 = Strongly Disagree

    2 = Disagree

    3 = Uncertain

    4 = Agree

    5 = Strongly Agree

Work-to-Family Conflict

    1. ____ My work schedule often conflicts with my family life.

    2. ____ After work, I come home too tired to do some of the things I'd like to do.

    3. ____ On the job, I have so much work to do that it takes away from my personal interests.

    4. ____ My family dislikes how often I am preoccupied with my work when I am at home.

    5. ____ Because my work is demanding, at times I am irritable at home.

(Continued)

TABLE 10.1 (Continued)

> 6. ____ The demands of my job make it difficult to be relaxed all the time at home.
>
> 7. ____ My work takes up time that I'd like to spend with my family.
>
> 8. ____ My job makes it difficult to be the kind of spouse or parent I'd like to be.
>
> *Family-to-Work Conflict*
>
> 9. ____ My family takes up time I would like to spend working.
>
> 10. ____ My personal interests take too much time away from my work.
>
> 11. ____ The demands of my family life make it difficult to concentrate at work.
>
> 12. ____ At times, my personal problems make me irritable at work.

SOURCE: Modification of a scale initially developed by Kopelman, R. E., Greenhaus, J. H., & Connolly, T. F. (1983). A model of work, family, and interrole conflict: A construct validation study. *Organizational Behavior and Human Performance, 32,* 198–215.

NOTE: Questions 1–8 refer to the extent to which work interferes with family, home, or personal life. Questions 9–12 refer to the extent to which family, home, or personal life interferes with work.

WORK–FAMILY ENRICHMENT: WHEN WORK AND FAMILY ARE "ALLIES"

Although many of us experience work–family conflict—sometimes rather intensely—we should not conclude that work and family are always at odds with one another. It is true that work and family lives may conflict with one another, but they may be allies as well.[16] Our discussion about work–family conflict emphasized how work and family can be enemies by interfering with one another and producing stress and dissatisfaction. In contrast, when they are allies, work can strengthen our family lives, and family experiences can improve our work lives. We refer to these beneficial effects of work and family on one another as work–family enrichment.[17]

Work–family enrichment takes place when resources acquired in one role are used to improve our performance and satisfaction in the other role. A resource is an asset that can be used to solve a problem or master a challenging situation. Participating in a role—family or work—provides opportunities to acquire resources from that role. These resources include the

- Development of *new skills*

- Development of *new perspectives,* by forming novel ways of looking at situations and solving problems

- Enhancement of our *self-confidence* as a result of performing well in our duties

- Accumulation of *social capital,* the network of relationships we develop with other people who provide us with information or advice and who can use their influence to help us reach our goals

- Acquisition of *material resource*s such as money and gifts

Imagine the resources we might acquire in our lives from our role as a family member, for example, a spouse or partner, parent, child, sibling, or in-law.

We might improve our problem-solving *skills* as we learn to work effectively with our spouse or partner to solve daily problems, our listening skills in helping our toddler communicate his or her needs to us, or our multitasking skills in juggling our many responsibilities to our children, neighbors, and spouses with our own personal needs.

Our experiences with our child or with a younger brother or sister might produce a *new perspective* on working with others, for example, to let people try to solve problems on their own at first, and not offer advice until it is requested.

We may become more *self-confident* as we master the challenges of taking care of a home, raising children, solving problems as a couple, or helping our parents with a knotty problem.

We may have access to the wisdom, advice, and direct support of a member of our nuclear or extended family as we accumulate *social capital* in our lives as family members.

We may even have access to financial resources such as a spouse's income, a parent's inheritance, or an in-law's generous gift.

It is not difficult to imagine how the resources acquired from our family role can be beneficial to our work lives. For example:

- The problem-solving and listening skills honed as a spouse or parent may make us more effective members of work teams.

- The new insight regarding the importance of letting people try to solve problems before offering advice may make us more effective supervisors or mentors at work.

- The self-confidence we have acquired as a result of solving a challenging problem at home may enable us to approach our tasks at work with more confidence and resilience.

- A knowledgeable family member may provide us with excellent career advice or even use his or her influence to help us land a new job or acquire a business loan from a local bank.

- A substantial gift or family inheritance could be used to bankroll a new business.

All of these examples illustrate family-to-work enrichment, instances where resources acquired in the family domain are successfully applied to our work lives. An important series of studies by Marian Ruderman and her colleagues has demonstrated how women managers' home and family experiences strengthen their professional lives.[18] When asked what aspects of their personal lives enhanced their professional lives, many women replied that the resources gained from nonwork experiences improved their functioning at work. The most frequently mentioned resources were improved interpersonal skills, psychological benefits such as self-esteem, emotional support and advice, and handling multiple tasks. In their follow-up study, the researchers found that the more psychologically committed the women managers were to their home roles the greater the task and interpersonal skills they exhibited at work.

Just as our family experiences can strengthen our work life, so too can the resources acquired at work enrich our family lives. For example:

- An employee uses the communication skills she acquired in a management development workshop to develop a closer and more supportive relationship with her sister.

- An individual applies a newly appreciated awareness of work team dynamics to suggest that his family begin to solve problems collectively as a group.

- A boost in self-esteem from succeeding on a challenging job assignment gives an individual the self-confidence to solve problems at home more effectively.

- Discussions with a colleague at work provide an employee with useful suggestions on finding suitable care for elderly parents.

- Sizeable salary increases are used to purchase such essentials as quality child care, education, and medical care for the entire family.

In summary, when our work and family lives jostle for our time and attention, we experience conflict and stress. On the other hand, when work and family strengthen each other, we experience enrichment in our lives. Nowhere is the opportunity for conflict—or enrichment—more apparent than in the daily lives of two-career families, who are constantly juggling their work and family responsibilities. We examine this increasingly popular lifestyle next.

THE TWO-CAREER FAMILY

The "traditional" household—employed husband, at-home wife, two or more children—currently represents only a small percentage of American families. Instead, there are a greater variety of lifestyles, including single-parent households, childless couples, "house-husbands" tending to the domestic front, and of course two-career families. We define a two-career couple as two people who share a lifestyle that includes an ongoing love relationship, cohabitation, and a work role for each partner.[19] Consistent with the definition of a career offered in Chapter 1, each partner in a two-career couple need not necessarily hold a professional or managerial job or a job that is emotionally absorbing.

Why has the two-career lifestyle become so prominent? Certainly, one attractive feature is the financial security derived from two incomes. Many couples believe they need two incomes to acquire and maintain a desired standard of living.

However, money does not tell the whole story. Each partner's quality of life can be enriched as well. From a woman's perspective, employment can satisfy a whole range of needs—achievement, challenge, variety, and power—that may not be fully satisfied in a homemaker role. A woman's employment can enhance her self-esteem and emotional well-being, especially if her job provides opportunities for challenging, interesting work.[20] A rewarding, satisfying job can contribute to the richness of a woman's life. Moreover, the pursuit of a career can promote an independence and self-sufficiency that is healthy in its own right and critical if the marriage ends through divorce or death of the partner.

From a man's perspective, participation in a two-career relationship often involves additional responsibility at home. A more extensive involvement in child rearing can provide a closer bond with the children and expand the enjoyment in a man's life. Since the husband in a two-career relationship is not solely responsible for the financial well-being of the family, he may feel less pressure to "succeed" and so have more freedom to leave a dissatisfying job.

The two-career lifestyle can also benefit the quality of the relationship between the two partners. Two-career relationships provide opportunities for a more egalitarian sharing of participation in family roles.[21] Moreover, the employment of both partners can increase their mutual respect as equals, bring them closer together, and make for a more interesting, compatible couple.[22]

Sources of Stress in the Two-Career Relationship

The preceding section does not imply that two-career relationships are stress free. Indeed, there are a number of significant issues that need to be faced in such relationships. This section examines these issues, recognizing that they are not equally relevant to all two-career couples. But first, consider the following situation.

Rob and Helen are business executives in their mid-30s with two young daughters. Although they love their jobs and are deeply committed to their family, Rob and Helen feel frazzled much of the time. Juggling business meetings, birthday parties, and trips to the pediatrician leaves them physically and mentally exhausted. They are also concerned with the quality of the family day care center their daughters attend.

> Rob and Helen experience occasional pangs of guilt. At times, Helen wonders whether she is as good a mother to her daughters as her own homemaker mother was to her. And although Rob is proud of Helen's accomplishments at the public relations firm where she works, he secretly wonders how long it will be before her salary outstrips his own. Rob and Helen feel guilty when they are not devoting enough time to their work, and feel guilty when they can't spend as much time with their children or with each other as they would like. Rob and Helen both wonder whether their careers will suffer as a result of their extensive family responsibilities, and they realize that their employers have done little to help them balance work and family.

This example highlights the many forms of stress that can be experienced in a two-career family. We now discuss the specific sources of stress in more detail.

Work–Family Conflict

We have discussed how extensive work and family demands can produce work–family conflict. Many individuals find that their work demands conflict with the responsibilities they are expected to assume at home. Challenging jobs, extensive travel, and long work hours can easily conflict with pressures and desires to participate in family activities. Nevertheless, women still bear the brunt of the responsibility for homemaking and child care. Although women have added another role to their lives—the work role—they have not typically restricted their involvement in home and child care roles to any substantial degree, and they may still take major responsibility for most household chores as well as raising the children. Moreover, even when husbands do increase their participation in these domestic roles, they are often seen as "helping out" rather than assuming primary responsibility for the activities.

In effect, two-career wives often work a "second shift" of home and family chores, with their "work day" only half over when they return home from their paid employment.[23] One study of two-career business professionals found that mothers spent on average more than twice the number of hours on home and child care activities as fathers did.[24] Even marriages that start out with an equitable sharing of home responsibilities often revert back to a gender-based division of labor after the birth of a child,[25] when the husband's career may take priority over his wife's.

The overload and stress experienced by two-career partners can threaten the relationship in several ways. First, as in the example of Rob and Helen, parents may experience guilt over not spending enough time with their children. Second, the couple may simply not have the time to nurture their own relationship. Work demands and children's needs leave partners with little time for each other. The absence of shared time can pose a threat to the romantic and emotional relationship and can estrange partners from one another. Third, family and work responsibilities frequently leave little time for individuals themselves. Time to relax, reflect, exercise, or pursue leisure activities does not come easily, if at all.

In short, partners in two-career relationships often lead hectic, frenetic lives, especially if there are children in the family. There are work pressures, carpools, overnight business trips, children's dance lessons, demanding bosses, housework—the list seems endless. The two-career lifestyle can be quite rewarding, but it is not easy.

Restricted Career Achievements

The two-career lifestyle may restrict or slow down an individual's career accomplishments. This is especially likely to occur for women. Many mothers reduce their career involvement in an attempt to alleviate the conflict they experience between work and family. Two-career mothers often cut back on the number of hours they work, turn down career development opportunities that would conflict with their family responsibilities, refuse promotions that require relocation, or put their career "on hold" by leaving the workforce for a period of time. In this respect, two-career mothers may incur a "family penalty" because their extensive family responsibilities limit their career progress.[26] This penalty is partly self-imposed because two-career mothers often "voluntarily" cut back on their career involvement in order to meet their family responsibilities. However, employers may also discriminate against mothers by restricting their investment in them—for example, by providing limited opportunities for mentoring and challenging job assignments—because of their belief that mothers are more committed to their families than to their careers.[27]

Of course, not all women necessarily experience a family penalty. In fact, a recent study of managers and executives found that women's psychological commitment to their role as spouse did not restrict their job performance. Moreover, their commitment to their role as mother was associated with *higher* levels of performance on their job.[28]

Whereas some mothers may experience a family penalty that impedes their career success, men often experience a "family bonus" that actually helps their career. One study found that fathers earned more money, reached higher levels in their organization, and were more satisfied with their careers than men without children.[29] Why? Because fathers experienced more autonomy on their jobs than did men without children. Although it is possible that the fathers in this study sought additional autonomy, employers may also have granted fathers more autonomy because they perceive them to be more responsible and stable than men without children.

Just as a family penalty is not experienced by all women, a family bonus is not necessarily experienced by all men. Men who are highly involved in their family lives—who believe that their family time is a critical part of their lives—may cut back on their involvement in work, just as many mothers in two-career families do.[30] Such men may switch careers, limit travel, and turn down promotions or relocations for family reasons.

The extent to which career achievements are restricted in two-career families may depend, in part, on the time commitments required in a particular career field. A man or woman may not experience obstacles to career progress in a field that has reasonable, predictable, and flexible hours. On the other hand, job performance and career progress may suffer in a field requiring extensive and inflexible work hours and heavy travel. In addition, career achievements may depend on the relative importance of each partner's career, each partner's commitment to the family, the availability of outside help for housework and child care, the support received from the partner, and the employer's flexibility in addressing work–family concerns.

Two-career couples often must decide whose career has priority at any particular point in time. Who stays home with a sick child? Who takes a few hours off to attend an afternoon parent–teacher conference? For whose job will the family relocate? The partner whose career takes priority will make fewer career accommodations and will pursue his or her career more intensely than the other partner. Traditionally, a man's career took precedence over his family responsibilities, whereas a woman's family responsibilities were expected to take precedence over her work. Generally, the rationale was that the husband's job was more important, more demanding, and provided a larger portion of the family's income. These assumptions may no longer be accurate.

Couples can handle the issue of career priorities in different ways. Phyllis Moen and her colleagues have examined the strategies that two-career couples use to allocate their time and commitment to different roles. They found that in the most typical strategy (called neotraditionalists), husbands were more highly invested in their careers than their wives, who were more invested in their families. However, the researchers noted that other strategies are certainly possible: wives more invested in their careers than husbands (crossover committed), both partners highly invested in their careers (dual committed), and neither partner highly invested in his or her career (alternative committed).[31] It is also likely that in some two-career relationships, the relative priority of each career shifts, depending on the needs and stages of each career. What is most important is not the eventual solution that is reached, but rather the process the couple uses to reach the solution. This process should involve openness, flexibility, and concern for the partner. At the very least, both partners must agree on the relative priority of each other's career or risk extensive strain in the marriage.[32]

Therefore, the pressures and constraints of a two-career relationship may impede the career progress of one or both partners, especially if career progress is defined as rapid mobility up the organizational ladder. However, researchers found that two-career professional women often experienced significant career accomplishments, although at a somewhat later stage in their lives than their single or childless counterparts.[33] It would not be surprising if the same trend holds true for men. In the long term, then, career accomplishments may not be seriously hampered, at least not in occupations and organizations that permit flexibility in the pace of career growth. We will discuss this issue further when we examine organizations' responsiveness to employees' work–family concerns later in this chapter.

Competition and Jealousy

The division of labor in the so-called traditional family makes for a neat, noncompetitive world. The man achieves competence in the work world, the woman masters the domestic demands, and comparisons of relative success in their respective ventures are unlikely. When both parties are employed, however, it is likely that one partner will ultimately become more "successful" than the other.[34] Forty percent of college-educated women earn as much or more than their husbands,[35] and in some cases a husband may be threatened if his wife's career success outstrips his own. Indeed, one study found that the better a women performs on her job, the lower her level of marital satisfaction, suggesting that her success at work might produce resentment by her husband.[36] Jealousies on the part of the man or the woman, if left unattended, can threaten the stability of the relationship.

The effect of a partner's career success on feelings of competition and jealousy probably depends on the orientations of the two partners. Perhaps the most intense feelings of competition and jealousy are experienced by individuals who place substantial importance on their own career success, yet are insecure about their sense of worth. Under these conditions, a partner's career accomplishments can be particularly threatening. We must add, however, that in extensive discussions with undergraduate and graduate business students, we have found few men or women who believed that a partner's career success would provoke intense feelings of competition or jealousy.

The Impact of Two-Career Status on Children

According to a *Fortune* survey of working parents conducted more than 20 years ago, a majority of men (55 percent) and women (58 percent) believed that "children of working parents suffer by not being given enough time and attention."[37] However, most of these same parents also believed that children benefit by having working parents as role models. Perhaps these findings reflected the ambivalence experienced by many two-career parents. A more recent national survey, however, reveals less ambivalence: 64 percent of men and 78 percent of women believe that an employed mother can have just as good a relationship with her child as a mother who does not work outside the home.[38]

Although individual studies have sometimes revealed beneficial or harmful effects of both parents' working on their children, the research literature as a whole suggests that a mother's employment (which for married couples usually translates into both parents' employment) has no consistent positive or negative effect on children's development. Ellen Galinsky of the Families and Work Institute persuasively argues that we should not view a mother's employment in "either/or" terms, that it is either bad or good for children. She concludes that "[i]t depends on the people and the circumstances of their lives. And what's right for one person may not be right for another."[39] Ultimately, the impact of a two-career lifestyle on children's adjustment probably depends on such factors as the quality of the parent–child relationship, the quality of child care, and the personal satisfaction of the parents.

QUALITY OF LIFE IN TWO-CAREER FAMILIES

Some of the potential advantages and risks associated with a two-career relationship have already been presented. How can families maximize the advantages and minimize the risks? Three closely related factors are particularly significant: social support, effective coping, and flexibility.

Social Support

We talked earlier about support from others as a resource that can help people improve the quality of their lives. Not surprisingly, individuals who receive extensive support from organizations and individuals tend to experience less work–family conflict and greater well-being than those who receive modest support.[40] In the context of a two-career relationship, support can enable husbands and wives to solve work and family problems effectively, and is strongly associated with partners' well-being.[41] Communication and mutual support are essential ingredients in a successful two-career relationship.[42] Two-career couples can benefit from a wide variety of supportive relationships.

Emotional support, especially from family members, is particularly important since the partners are involved in a lifestyle that requires compromises and can produce identity problems, jealousies, and guilt. Nearly 40 years ago, Robert and Rhona Rapoport spoke of the understanding and caring "facilitating husband" as a major contributor to the success of a two-career relationship,[43] a point of view that rings true to this day. However, men also need the support of an understanding partner. Indeed, support must be mutual, in that each partner must provide as well as receive support.

Since most two-career couples frequently experience novel situations, partners will benefit from information and advice on work- and family-related problems so that marital difficulties do not become too intense. Men need to contribute substantially in terms of action—home maintenance and child care being the primary areas—if there is to be balance and sharing in the relationship. Although hired help, another form of instrumental support, can substantially reduce conflict and overload, it cannot fully replace a mutually agreed upon and balanced sharing of responsibilities. Perhaps it is most important that two-career partners view their involvement and their spouse's involvement in home-related activities as fair and equitable.[44]

Finally, support can provide each partner with useful feedback. Partners may find it difficult to assess how well they are balancing work and family roles, whether the children are handling the situation satisfactorily, and how the relationship between the two partners is faring. Accurate, constructive feedback can serve as a confirmation of each partner's efforts and as a way to improve the functioning of the family unit.

Although support can and should come from a variety of sources, the support received from one's partner plays a special role because it reflects a commitment to the relationship. The relative emphasis placed on work and family by each partner may determine the degree of support each is willing to extend. Families in which at least one partner is strongly family oriented may be most able to balance work and family roles with minimal stress. A family orientation among husbands, for example, has been strongly associated with marital happiness, especially when the woman places a great deal of importance on her career.[45] Presumably, family-oriented husbands, who are willing to accommodate their careers to their family role, are less competitive and more supportive than their career-driven counterparts.[46]

Perhaps the most stressful and least supportive relationship is one in which both partners are highly involved in their careers and minimally involved in the family, yet both partners value a satisfying home and family life. Such relationships, described by Francine and Douglas Hall as "adversaries," may be threatened by constant conflicts over career priorities and division of labor in home and family tasks. As they state, neither partner "may be willing or able to make career sacrifices to facilitate the career of the other or to fulfill home and family roles."[47]

Coping With Work–Family Stress

Douglas Hall identified three strategies for coping with work–family conflict.[48] Using *structural role redefinition,* an individual reduces work–family conflict by changing role senders' expectations of responsibilities. An individual who arranges with the boss to leave work early on certain days or to limit the amount of work-related travel is altering other people's expectations. A woman who negotiates with her husband and children to do more work around the house or who hires outside help is reducing some of her domestic pressures. Structural role redefinition is an active, problem-solving approach to changing a part of the environment that is producing conflict and stress.

With *personal role reorientation,* the person changes expectations not by directly confronting role senders, but by changing his or her own conception of requirements. A woman who decides that standards for housekeeping can be relaxed and a man who gradually reduces his involvement at work are both reorienting the priority of certain tasks or roles to reduce their conflict.

With *reactive role behavior,* the individual tries to meet all expectations more efficiently. Getting up earlier, going to bed later, and managing one's time more efficiently are all attempts to "do it all." This strategy, so characteristic of the so-called Supermom, is mentally and physically taxing, fails to address the underlying conflicts, and is not generally successful.[49]

Perhaps what is most important is that individuals develop active coping strategies to alleviate work–family conflict and stress. One such approach to successful life management, called selection–optimization–compensation, emphasizes the importance of goals, strategies, and plans to overcome obstacles. Research has shown that individuals who engage in these behaviors experience low levels of stress and work–family conflict.[50] Time management, another self-management strategy, has also been shown to reduce work–family conflict.[51]

These coping strategies are individual responses to stressful situations. Couples also should develop collaborative coping strategies to solve the problems of the family unit as a whole, moving from a "me" orientation (self-interest, coercion, and suppression of conflict) to a "we" orientation (mutual goals, encouragement, a healthy expression of differences, and a willingness to compromise).[52] Hall and Hall offer many useful suggestions for how to achieve a "we" orientation in such areas as housework, parenting, and time management. But what works for one couple may not work for another; there is be no cookbook formula for success. However, what is applicable from one situation to another is the need to establish a climate of communication and problem solving. Hall and Hall suggested the following strategy to establish such a climate: talk about problems regularly, listen to your partner and express your own feelings, discuss goals and explore expectations, practice problem solving, and practice negotiating compromises.

These actions take time, skill, and practice, but they are essential if problems are to be identified and managed. Problem solving and compromise are necessary to prevent sex-role stereotypes or old behavior patterns from disrupting a couple's attempt to find fresh solutions to novel problems.

Flexibility

Satisfactory coping requires a great deal of flexibility on the part of all members of a two-career family, including the children. Seeing problems from another person's perspective and changing behavior or attitudes that are outmoded are hallmarks of effective coping. Rigid patterns of behavior, by definition, are not conducive to the resolution of stressful situations.

In Chapter 2 we discussed the notion of a protean career to illustrate the importance of flexibility. A protean career involves greater control over one's work life, in which career success is judged by internal standards (satisfaction, achievement, or a balanced life) rather than the traditional external standards of salary and promotions in an organizational structure. We can also speak of a protean relationship, which focuses on the growth and development of the partners, relatively unstifled by society's norms and expectations. The protean family is willing to adjust its relationship to meet the needs of family members, whether that involves remaining childless, living apart a portion of the time, or reversing the traditional sex roles within the relationship.[53]

The ability of two-career couples to adopt a more flexible lifestyle is often dependent on the policies and practices of their employers. Until recently, organizations did not see a need to help their employees balance their work and family roles. Fortunately, this attitude of neglect is changing. An organization's role in addressing work–family issues is examined in the following section.

ORGANIZATIONAL RESPONSES TO WORK–FAMILY ISSUES

Many, if not most, employers realize that it is in their best interest to help their employees balance their work and family lives. What used to be considered a "woman's issue" is increasingly recognized as an employee issue and a business necessity. What accounts for this shift in attitudes among the nation's largest employers?

First, more employees are struggling to balance their work and family responsibilities than in prior years. As discussed earlier, the emergence of the two-career lifestyle requires parents to coordinate their work demands with their family responsibilities. Although women face the most extensive pressures to juggle work and family demands, men are increasingly involved in home and child care activities, either by choice or necessity. In addition, a divorce rate that hovers around 50 percent has resulted in an increasing number of single-parent households, many of which are confronted by a steady stream of work and family pressures, with no partner to share the responsibilities. Moreover, employees are increasingly called upon to care for elder parents or other adult relatives.[54] One study revealed that 35 percent of U.S. employees in 2002 had elder care responsibilities, up from 25 percent five years earlier.[55]

In addition, employees' values are shifting to place a greater emphasis on quality of life. Indeed, employees are demanding opportunities to attain balance between their work and family, and a sizeable number are willing to make sacrifices in their careers to achieve a higher quality of life. More and more job seekers are raising the issue of work–life balance in their employment interviews. And substantial numbers of men and women are refusing promotions, relocations, and jobs with extensive pressure or travel because of the strains these positions would put on their family lives.

These changes in family and employment patterns, as well as shifts in employee values, are playing havoc with organizations' ability to staff themselves effectively, especially in light of the nation's shrinking talent pool. For one thing, organizations are losing the services of many talented young women managers and professionals who leave their jobs following the birth of a child. Many of these "career-and-family" oriented women want to continue their career but not with 50- to 60-hour weeks and extensive travel requirements.[56] Since employers have not typically provided an alternative work schedule for parents of young children, the employees often leave. This represents a substantial blow to employers who have invested time and money, and now face extensive recruiting and training costs to replace these valued employees.

The talent pool is not only shrinking, but it is increasingly female. It is projected that by the year 2014, nearly 60 percent of all women will be employed, and 47 percent of the workforce will be women. In addition, with increasing numbers of women receiving bachelor's, master's, legal, and medical degrees, employers find that many of their best and brightest job candidates are women. Extensive turnover among this group results in high costs and low productivity.[57]

In addition, mothers and fathers who remain in the workforce are often preoccupied with the difficulties of balancing work and family responsibilities. Moreover, excessive work–family conflict can produce high levels of absenteeism and extensive stress,[58] both of which can detract from an organization's productivity. Not surprisingly, a family-supportive work environment can improve employees' attitudes toward their work and their organizations.[59]

Despite the demographic changes in the workforce discussed in this chapter, employers usually run their operations on the assumption that the vast majority of managerial and professional employees will be willing to devote as many hours as necessary to complete a project, including evenings and weekends; will travel at the drop of a hat; and will relocate whenever it is to the advantage of the organization and the employee's career progress. Of course, this approach assumed that the managerial and professional workforce would be male, married to a homemaker, and therefore able to devote full time and attention to work.

Nobody likes to change assumptions, attitudes, and behaviors, especially if they have been working well for a long time. Employers are no exception. For many years, organizations had been slow to address work–family issues for a variety of reasons: they didn't know how to solve the problem, they were threatened by the demand for work–family balance that violates their "upward mobility ethic," they saw it as a "woman's issue," and they didn't see the payoff to the organization for addressing these issues.[60] However, this resistance to change is weakening as more companies experience difficulties attracting and retaining valued employees, and organizations see the benefits of implementing family-supportive practices. A study by the Families and Work Institute identified the leading reasons why employees initiated such practices. Topping the list were the desire to recruit and retain employees (47 percent), to support employees and their families (39 percent), and to enhance employee commitment and productivity (25 percent).[61] We now turn our attention to actions that organizations can take to help their employees balance their work and family lives.

Table 10.2 summarizes a variety of family-supportive policies and practices that have been adopted by organizations in response to the issues discussed in this chapter. We classify these organizational actions into three broad categories: dependent care, flexible work arrangements, and changing the organization's work–family culture.

TABLE 10.2   Examples of Family-Responsive Policies and Practices

Dependent Care

- Child care resource and referral
- Elder care consultation and referral
- Child care centers
- Discounts or vouchers for child care
- Sick child care
- Community involvement

Flexible Work Arrangements

- Part-time schedules
- Personal days
- Flexible work schedules
- Personal leaves of absence
- Job sharing
- Telecommuting (flexplace)
- Family, child care leaves
- Family illness days
- Flexible career paths and assignments

Changing Work–Family Culture

- Include commitment to work and family life in mission statement
- Emphasize job performance rather than hours spent at work
- Redesign work processes to be more compatible with employees' family and personal needs
- Provide work–family seminars and support groups
- Provide training to supervisors on dealing with work–family issues

Dependent Care

Concerns about the welfare of their children are keenly felt by working parents. In response to these concerns, employers have supported a wide range of child care programs. Only 17 percent of large companies surveyed by the Families and Work Institute in 2005 provided on-site or near-site child care centers for their employees' children; other forms of direct support for children include subsidies (discounts and vouchers) for private child care facilities and emergency assistance for sick children. Another widespread form of support is the administration of flexible spending accounts in which pretax dollars can be used to pay for child care services.[62]

The most popular—and probably least expensive—initiative is a resource and referral system that provides useful information and assistance to employees with a variety of child care needs. IBM created the first nationwide network of referral services that has been used by many other corporations.[63] Referral programs may also be supplemented by seminars, support groups, libraries, and newsletters. In addition, some employers are working with community groups to expand and improve a variety of child care services such as after-school programs, backup or "sick child care centers," and subsidies to family day care associations to increase the number of child care providers in family homes.

Although dependent care is often equated with child care, a growing area of concern is the care of elder relatives, most notably parents. With ever-increasing life spans, senior citizens are expected to make up 20 percent of the population by the year 2030.[64] In previous generations, nonemployed daughters and daughters-in-law often looked after their elders. Increasingly, these demands are being felt by employees who may not have the time, knowledge, or resources to help care for their loved ones.

As a result of these pressures, organizations are beginning to provide elder care support to their employees. This support can take the form of the flexible use of time to care for elders' needs, information about available services and policies, subsidies to defray the costs of elder care, and support groups through employee assistance programs. Not surprisingly, a recent survey revealed that companies are more likely to provide employees with time off to provide elder care (79 percent) than to provide direct financial support to employees to pay for elder care programs (6 percent).[65]

Flexible Work Arrangements

Flexible Work Schedules. As important as child care assistance can be to working parents, additional flexibility in the workplace remains a major priority for many employees. One of the early efforts in this regard was the establishment of flexible work schedules, which is offered by a sizable percentage of the companies in the 2005 Families and Work Institute survey. Flexible work schedules usually involve a core set of hours in which all employees must work (e.g., 10:00 a.m. to 3:00 p.m.) with a band of several hours around the core to provide flexible starting and leaving times. Additional flexibility may be provided by granting employees some control over when they take breaks, the shifts they work, and the number of paid and unpaid overtime hours they put in.

Since flexible work schedules offer employees some degree of control over their time, they can help employees reduce work–family conflict.[66] Although the results have not been uniformly positive, and the characteristics of the program must match the specific needs of the employees, flexible work schedules remain a central component of an organization's comprehensive approach to work–family issues.

Family Leaves. Another form of workplace flexibility is the opportunity to take a leave to care for children or other family members. Countries vary substantially in the extent to which they have initiated maternity leave legislation. In 1993, the United States passed the Family and Medical Leave Act (FMLA) that provides employees with up to 12 weeks of unpaid, job-protected leave for the employee's own medical condition or to care for a new-born or newly adopted child or a sick child, parent, or partner. This act applies to employees who work for organizations with 50 or more workers and who have been employed in the organization for at least one year, having worked a minimum of 1,250 hours within the prior 12-month period. Although more than 35 million employees have taken leaves since the passage of the FMLA, about 53 percent of the workforce is ineligible for FMLA leave, either because their employer is excluded from the act's provisions or because the employee doesn't meet the eligibility requirements of covered employers.[67] In addition to the federal statute, many states have passed parental and family leave legislation.

Moreover, in some instances the private sector has provided leaves that exceed the 12-week period mandated by the FMLA.[68] It appears that family leave programs can improve recruitment and retention, although there has not been substantial research conducted to confirm that. It is interesting that men have not generally taken advantage of parental leaves in great numbers, in part because they believe that it would hurt their careers.[69]

Part-Time Employment. In the 1980s and 1990s, Felice Schwartz created a storm in corporate, feminist, and academic circles when she advocated part-time employment options for women managers and professionals with young children.[70] Schwartz observed that many mothers were serious about their careers but also wanted to spend substantial time with their young children. When faced with the option of either full-time employment or no employment, many of these women quit their jobs altogether.

Schwartz urged employers to provide part-time employment in managerial and professional positions until the woman was ready to return to her full-time job. This part-time arrangement could be in effect from several months to several years. Schwartz further recommended a job-sharing program in which pairs of part-timers could be jointly responsible for a full-time assignment. Dubbed the "mommy track" by journalists, part-time and job-shared positions have been hailed by some as a viable option for young mothers (and fathers), and have been criticized by others as a form of second-class citizenship for women. It has often been observed that men have informally negotiated lower levels of work involvement during periods of heavy family responsibility without the stigma attached to part-time employment. In fact, relatively few men have opted for part-time employment so far.[71]

Is part-time employment a reasonable alternative for working parents? On the positive side, part-time employment can help women and men balance work with other parts of their lives. And it appears that the work attitudes of part-time employees are generally as positive as those of full-time workers.[72]

On the negative side, many part-time jobs do not provide health benefits. Moreover, from a career development point of view, it is feared that part-time employment, even for a brief period of time, signals to the organization a lack of serious commitment on the part of the employee. Perhaps it does have this connotation in some organizations that lack insight and experience regarding work–family issues. However, if the organization or its managers understand the work–family dilemmas experienced by many employees, provide challenging work during the period of part-time employment, and enable the employee to reenter the full-time workforce in a supportive manner if and when desired, then the long-term careers of individuals who opt for temporary part-time employment may not be seriously impaired. Therefore, employers must prevent stereotypes and self-fulfilling prophecies from limiting the contributions that women and men can make to the organization.

Flexible Career Paths. Beyond the establishment of part-time employment opportunities, organizations need to recognize more generally that an employee's career path can have significant implications for his or her family life. Many men and women are aware of the trade-offs involved in pursuing a fast track linear career path and want to pursue an alternative career direction. It is important for organizations to provide employees with alternative career paths that involve less immense time commitments and less extensive travel and to view these paths as viable and significant ways for employees to contribute to the organization. Organizations, in other words, should legitimize and reward alternative career directions for employees.

For example, a prominent certified public accounting firm recognized that its existing career progression system, involving very long hours, extensive travel, and a specified time frame for making partner, produced a high rate of undesirable turnover. Therefore, the firm developed alternative career tracks to achieve better retention of professionals, better service to clients, and more varied ways for employees to succeed. Under the new system, employees had the opportunity to develop expertise in multiple areas or choose to build an in-depth focus in a single function. They could develop these skills at a rate that was more compatible with their lifestyle, were not required to achieve partner status in a specified number of years in order to remain with the firm, and could contribute to the firm in significant ways even if they did not aspire (or had not developed the skills) to become a partner.[73]

Even employees on a fast track can be developed in ways that are less disruptive to their family lives. For example, companies can place a variety of facilities at a central location so employees can acquire a breadth of experience without the need to relocate. Companies can also use membership on task forces and special project assignments as an alternative to relocation, and employers that require overseas assignments can shorten these assignments to a matter of months rather than years. When relocation is essential, it is often critical that the organization support the career-oriented partner of the relocated employee. Such support could include career guidance, help in skill assessment and résumé preparation, and the waiver of policies prohibiting husbands and wives from working simultaneously for the same organization.[74]

Telecommuting, often called flexplace, permits work to be performed at a satellite office or, more typically, from home. Work-at-home programs, made more feasible with advanced computer technology, can give employees more discretion over their use of time to balance work and family demands. Telecommuting doesn't eliminate work–family conflict, and in fact may exacerbate stress at times because of the parents' physical presence at home and the feelings of social isolation. Nor does it eliminate the need for additional child care assistance. Nevertheless, telecommuting can still be a viable option for parents whose ability to juggle work and family is enhanced through their physical presence at home, and/or the substantial reduction in commuting times.[75]

Although research on the family-supportive practices discussed in this chapter has not been entirely consistent, there is considerable evidence that individuals experience less work–family conflict and more positive work attitudes when their employers provide more flexibility and control to their employees.[76] In addition, a number of studies have shown that organizations providing family-supportive programs tend to be productive and profitable.[77]

CHANGING THE ORGANIZATION'S WORK–FAMILY CULTURE

As important as the availability of family-supportive practices is, the practices are not likely to be used unless they are implemented in a supportive environment by understanding and flexible managers and supervisors.[78] In other words, the most family-supportive employers provide formal work–family programs within a culture that respects employees' family and personal lives. These organizations have revised their cultures to eliminate outdated assumptions that are not in tune with the needs of the contemporary workforce. Some cultural assumptions that need to be revised include the following:[79]

- "Keep your personal problems at home."
- "Put in long hours regardless of family responsibilities."
- "Travel when and where the organization dictates."
- "Relocate without concern for family needs."
- "Presence (at the workplace) equals performance."
- "Hours (worked) equal output."

The family-responsive organization replaces these assumptions with a more supportive culture. Central components of this culture are the recognition of the legitimacy of family and personal issues to all employees as well as the significance of work–life issues to the organization itself. Such a culture will stimulate an awareness of the potential for work–family conflict and will encourage discussion of the impact of the conflict on the employee and the organization. The organization will understand that many employees value both career and family and will develop policies and programs to mesh employees' values with the organization's need to be effective and competitive.

A family-responsive organization should establish an explicit corporate policy regarding work and family and communicate this policy throughout the organization. Some companies have incorporated work–family issues into their mission statements to reflect and reinforce their commitment in this area. Companies have also formed work–family groups or departments within the organizational structure whose primary function is to develop and administer the kinds of work–family programs discussed in this chapter.[80]

Since the supervisor is a critical link in administering policy, responsive employers have sponsored training to help supervisors react with flexibility to work scheduling and career planning. Organizations that have successfully changed their work–family culture also focus on measuring performance results rather than the number of hours or weekends spent at the office, or other symbols of organizational commitment. Perhaps most important, the responsive organization realizes that its actions can benefit its employees and give itself a competitive edge in the marketplace.

A recent corporate program consistent with many of the principles discussed in this chapter is Best Buy's initiative to change its culture from a focus on work hours and scheduling to an emphasis on the quality of the work performed by its employees. Best Buy, a retail organization headquartered in Minneapolis, Minnesota, refers to its initiative and new culture as ROWE, an acronym for Results Only Work Environment.[81] The ROWE initiative was deliberately *not* presented as a work–family or work–life program but rather as a way to achieve better performance for Best Buy by focusing on actual results rather than work time for all employees regardless of their family or personal situations. Work teams were tasked with designing ways to meet their work goals in a manner consistent with their own circumstances. The researchers described the transformation as follows:

> Teams transitioning from conventional time-based work practices to a ROWE arrangement aim to foster an environment where employees are free to complete their work whenever and wherever, provided they are productive, doing what works best to accomplish the tasks at hand, as well as each team's longer term goals. This type of working environment shifts the spotlight away from time-oriented measures of work success (how many hours a worker put in last week; how much time she spent on a given task) to a completely results-based appraisal of productivity and accomplishment. With the ROWE innovation, Best Buy aims to change the temporal organization of work, shifting to an environment where employees have the tools (ways to roll over phone calls, etc.) they need to accomplish their assigned objectives while simultaneously giving them the freedom to accomplish their tasks with whatever type of work schedule is best for them.[82]

Although the research on the ROWE initiative is not yet complete, the preliminary results are promising.[83] Over a six-month period, members of teams undergoing the ROWE initiative were compared to employees in other teams that had not yet experienced the ROWE culture change. Compared to these other teams, the ROWE team members (a) perceived more control over their time and more adequate time to accomplish their work; (b) reported aspects of greater health and wellness; (c) perceived the culture of Best Buy as more family friendly; (d) were more committed to Best Buy as a place to work; (e) were more satisfied with their jobs; (f) experienced less conflict between their work and family lives; (g) reported doing less low-value, unnecessary work in their jobs; and (h) held lower intentions to quit Best Buy.

CAREER MANAGEMENT AND THE QUALITY OF LIFE

This chapter has shown how our work and family lives are intertwined in many ways, some positive and others negative. We believe that most people's ultimate aim is to feel satisfied, effective, and fulfilled in those parts of their lives that matter to them.[84] When employees lament the work–family conflict they experience or the excessive imbalance in their lives, they are expressing a concern that they are not as satisfied, effective, or fulfilled in an important part of their life as they would like to be.

In part, the stress we experience in juggling our work and family responsibilities is due to the circumstances in which we find ourselves. We may work in jobs that demand much of our time and are stressful and exhausting at the same time that our families—spouse, children, or parents—require our attention and support. With that in mind, it is important to realize that the decisions we make in our everyday lives also affect the balance or imbalance we experience. We often work long hours because we want to, select occupations or career paths that are stressful, and choose to ignore or deny the pressures we experience, all the while not realizing the effects of such decisions on other parts of our lives. Career management, a proactive, problem-solving approach to work and life, can help individuals make decisions that are compatible with the type of lifestyle they want to live. Career exploration, goal setting, strategy development, and appraisal should focus not only on our work requirements but rather on our total life. Below we list some suggestions for achieving greater balance in life that are linked to our model of career management.

Career Exploration

- Assess the importance of work, family, community, and leisure roles in your life.
- Share your life priorities with your family.
- Understand the effect of your work experiences on your physical and psychological health.

- Be aware of the implications of different jobs, career fields, and career paths on your family and personal life.

Career Goal Setting

- Set a conceptual goal that incorporates your desired balance between work and other important parts of your life.

- Recognize that your conceptual career goal can be achieved in a number of different jobs.

- Pursue goals that have real meaning to you, not those that require you to live up to other people's expectations.

- Understand your family's view of your career goal.

- Understand how the achievement of your career goal would affect your family and personal life, and how your family situation might affect the likelihood of achieving your career goal.

Career Strategies

- Recognize the implications of specific career strategies (e.g., extended work involvement, rapid mobility, relocation) on your family and personal life.

- Discuss career strategies with significant people in your life before and during their implementation.

- Always consider the personal acceptability of a strategy as well as its instrumental value; avoid strategies that violate ethical or moral beliefs.

Career Appraisal

- Seek feedback from different people regarding various parts of your life.

- Discuss changes in personal and career values with family members.

- Examine the effects of career strategies on your work and nonwork lives on an ongoing basis.

- Be willing to admit mistakes and make changes to your career or family life if necessary.

Sometimes we experience intense work–family conflict and stress despite our best efforts. Perhaps we made decisions that, in retrospect, were not in our best interest. Or we did nothing to alleviate increasing pressures, mistakenly believing that they would subside by themselves and failing to seek support from other people who could have helped us. Eliminating work–family conflict is impossible for most of us, but keeping it within reasonable bounds is often possible if we understand why we experience intense conflict and stress and are committed to improving the situation.

We suggest the following four-step guide to action for individuals who are concerned about excessive work–family conflict in their lives. You will probably notice the resemblance between this guide and the proactive career-management process we have advocated in this chapter and throughout the book.

Step 1. Understand your priorities regarding career, family, and other life roles.

- If married or in a relationship, discuss, understand, and accept each other's priorities.
- Realize that because priorities can change over the life course, communication must be ongoing.

Step 2. Understand the nature of the conflict.

- Is work interfering with family, family interfering with work, or both?
- What factors are responsible for the conflict: Time pressures from work and family roles? Extensive stress at work or at home?
- Are *we* contributing to the conflict by virtue of the decisions we have made?

Step 3. Develop a plan and experiment with different approaches.

If work chronically interferes with family life, attempt to reduce the time pressures and/or stress at work in one or more of the following ways that make sense in your situation:

- Be open about your work, family, and personal needs at work and at home.
- Negotiate for a more flexible work schedule
- Redesign your job (e.g., reduce travel and/or weekend or evening work).
- Seek additional resources from work (e.g., extra staff).
- Seek emotional (understanding) and informational (advice) support from colleagues, friends, and family and be willing to provide support to others.
- Learn to cope more effectively with job stress.
- Seek a more compatible career path within the organization.

- Consider part-time or remote-location work.

- Change employer or career field.

If family life chronically interferes with work, attempt to reduce the time pressures and/or stress within the family:

- Be open about your work, family, and personal needs with family and friends.

- Seek a fair division of labor at home and consider the possibility of outside help (tangible support).

- Seek emotional (understanding) and informational (advice) support from family, friends, and colleagues, and be willing to provide support to others.

- Encourage family participation in career planning activities.

- Learn to cope more effectively with family stress.

Step 4. Monitor whether the plans are working and make changes as necessary; continue to experiment.

Active career management that incorporates work and nonwork issues is vital to enhancing one's quality of life. Open communication is a common element that cuts across all components of career management as well as our suggested four-step guide to action. People need to enlarge their scope of thinking—about work, family, and personal values—and discuss these issues with supportive people on a regular basis, not just when a crisis appears.

SUMMARY

Work and family lives affect each other in a variety of ways. Although the two roles are mutually supportive in many respects, there are times when they conflict. Three forms of work–family conflict were identified: time-based conflict, in which the time spent in one role interferes with the requirements of the other role; strain-based conflict, in which stress in one role affects experiences in the other role; and behavior-based conflict, in which behavior that is appropriate in one role is dysfunctional in the other role.

Also examined was the nature of two-career relationships in contemporary society. Despite its many rewards, a two-career relationship faces a number of potentially stressful conditions: extensive work–family conflict, gender identity problems, competition and jealousy between partners, negotiation of career priorities, and the possibility of somewhat limited or slow career progress. To manage these potential stressors, two-career couples need to learn effective coping behavior, utilize supportive relationships with other people, and remain flexible in their careers or family arrangements.

Organizations can respond to work–family issues by providing their employees with various forms of dependent care assistance. Employers can also provide more flexible work arrangements, including flexible work schedules, family leave, part-time employment, and opportunities for job sharing. They should also legitimize alternative career paths so that employees can contribute to the organization in a way that is consistent with their underlying values and lifestyle preferences. Employers' actions will be most effective if they develop a culture that understands and supports employees' attempts to balance their work and family responsibilities.

Employees need to manage their careers in the context of their overall quality of life. The career management process provided in this book can be used to address these kinds of issues. Exploration, goal setting, strategies, and appraisal all require communication about work and nonwork issues on an ongoing basis.

ASSIGNMENT

Complete the following questions and discuss them with someone significant in your life.

1. Are you as involved, effective, or satisfied in each of the following parts of life as you would like to be? Circle one response, yes or no, for each role in life.

Career	Yes	No
Family	Yes	No
Leisure	Yes	No
Community	Yes	No
Religion	Yes	No
Self-development	Yes	No
Other	Yes	No

If yes, what have you done to achieve this? If not, why are you not as involved, effective, or satisfied as you would like?

_____

_____

_____

2. Develop a plan or "experiment" to become more effective and satisfied with a part of your life.

_____

_____

_____

(Continued)

(Continued)

3. What do you need to do to become more involved, effective, and satisfied?

_____

_____

_____

4. How might it affect other parts of your life?

_____

_____

_____

5. Who can help you?

_____

_____

_____

6. How can you monitor your progress?

_____

_____

_____

DISCUSSION QUESTIONS

1. Develop a profile of the type of person most likely to experience extensive work–family conflict. Identify work pressures, family pressures, and personal characteristics most likely to produce work–family conflict.

2. You are likely to become a partner in a two-career relationship at some point in your life. Perhaps you are already. What might be the major sources of stress in the relationship? Do the stresses outweigh the potential advantages of a two-career relationship? Why or why not?

3. The kaleidoscope perspective on careers introduced and discussed in Chapter 2 suggests that men and women may approach their careers in somewhat different ways: men focus on personal goal achievement and make career decisions designed to enhance their career growth, whereas women focus on relationships and make career decisions that take the needs of their family into account. From your personal observation or experience, are men and women similar or different in how they approach their work and family lives?

4. Some people contend that children are the victims of a two-career relationship. Defend or attack that contention, giving the reasoning behind your position.

5. Two-career couples cope most effectively when they adopt a collaborative orientation rather than a "me-first" orientation. Explain how partners in a two-career relationship can develop a more collaborative orientation toward work–family issues.

6. Defend or refute the following statement: "Being successful in your career inevitably harms your family life." Provide the reasoning behind your position.

CHAPTER 10 CASE

The Prized Promotion

Doug Sanders is a 38-year-old plant manager for Johnson Electronics, a medium-sized company that manufactures computer components. He can't wait for dinner tonight to tell Lisa, his wife of 17 years, and Steve, his 15-year-old son, about his promotion.

It's been a long time coming, and Doug believes he richly deserves to be promoted to Vice President for Manufacturing at Johnson. He's been with the company for nearly 10 years, the first 5 as a mechanical engineer, and he has certainly paid his dues. For the past five years, since Doug was named plant manager, he has put in 12- and 13-hour days at the plant on a regular basis and is on emergency call 24 hours a day. Not to mention his willingness to fly to corporate headquarters in Denver whenever his boss thinks it is necessary. Besides, Doug's plant has reached new heights in productivity and profitability each year since he took over.

Doug is really looking forward to the new position. True, the hours are going to be just as long—if not longer—than his current job. But the 30 percent salary raise is nothing to sneeze at. Lisa can finally have her dream house! And Doug will have a lot more responsibility—he will finally be able to call the shots, at least as far as manufacturing is concerned. Doug suspects that the company is grooming him for even better things in the future. The relocation to headquarters in Denver is the icing on the cake. Doug and Lisa have always enjoyed their trips to Denver and Steve will be able to ski all the time.

Doug can't wait to break the news to the family tonight. He told Mr. Johnson that he would get back to him in a few days with a "definite yes" and a lot of plans have to be made in a hurry. Lisa will have to give notice on her job at the museum. She should be able to find something in Denver without much trouble. It's a bustling city that has culture on its mind.

(Continued)

(Continued)

The change will be good for Steve, too. Always a pretty good student, his grades—and his attitude toward school—have been slipping this past year. Doug realizes that he has been rough on Steve lately, putting on the pressure about grades, but the boy hasn't pushed himself hard enough. He can't afford any more screw-ups if he is going to have a shot at a top-notch university. Anyway, Doug has found from his own business experience that you've got to tighten the screws if you want to get the most out of people.

Doug thinks that the promotion is coming at just the right time. He has been pretty tense and preoccupied at home lately because of the union problems and the pressure for cost cutting. A change of scenery might be just what the doctor would order. Doug can't wait to see Lisa's and Steve's faces when he gives them the good news at the dinner table.

Lisa Sanders knows she has a lot to be grateful for. Doug is a good husband and father, and her son Steve is a really nice kid. Her family is very important to her and it was not easy for her to go back to work three years ago when Steve entered middle school. It wasn't that she particularly needed the money, but she wanted to accomplish something in addition to caring for Steve and Doug.

Lisa remembers that it was pretty difficult finding a job that matched her bachelor's degree in art history. She finally found a clerical position at the Art Museum and the rest is history. Although she doesn't consider herself to be ambitious, she welcomed the promotions that ultimately brought her to her current position, Assistant Director of the museum. She absolutely loves the job! She is doing what she enjoys the most—developing new cultural programs for the museum—the pay is pretty good, the hours are flexible, and most important, she is appreciated as a competent, creative, productive person. It feels very good. It's a "one in a million" job and she knows it.

Lisa can't wait to tell Doug about her newest project—her idea—that would make the museum more accessible to the elderly and the handicapped. Not that Doug would really appreciate the project. He knows little—and cares less—about art and hasn't shown much inclination to learn more about it in the past three years. Besides, he's been so preoccupied—no, obsessed—with his job recently that he doesn't seem to pay attention. He's always at the plant, and when he's home his mind is somewhere else. If his tension and moodiness keep up much longer, maybe Doug should see a doctor or something. Lisa thinks she should suggest that to him one of these days.

Lisa thinks lovingly about her son. Steve is bright, caring, and sensitive. It wasn't easy at first for him to adjust to Lisa's working, but he's become more independent and resourceful by necessity. He's doing OK, although adolescence can be a tough time for anyone. Actually, his grades have slipped a little lately—nothing serious—but he seems to find time for everything but studying. Maybe a little talk is in order to build up his self-confidence. He's always done so well in school. Lisa wishes that Doug wouldn't push Steve so hard about the studying. Putting too much pressure on Steve could easily backfire. Doug and Steve are at each other's throat—when they talk!

Lisa hopes that tonight's meal will be pleasant. Maybe Doug will be relaxed and will be interested in hearing about the museum project.

Steve Sanders is a high school sophomore and things are going pretty well. He has made a lot of real good friends and, probably for the first time in his life, Steve feels that he fits in at school. The teachers are tolerable, the kids are great, and he's got a new girlfriend, Lori. Steve loves his parents, although sometimes he thinks it is easier to love his mother than his father.

Steve thinks a lot about his dad. He's always at the plant and when he does come home he's usually angry—mostly at Steve. Steve feels that his father has been on his case since his last report card. It wasn't terrible but it wasn't as good as he's done and it certainly wasn't up to his father's standards. Steve considers himself a pretty good student who had a bad term. Steve knows he should work harder, but he can't stand it when his father gets on his back about school. He doesn't listen to Steve or want to know why Steve's grades started slipping or what problems he has. He just yells, probably like he yells at the workers in his plant.

Steve thinks about his mom a lot, too. He's really happy that she's doing so well at the art museum. She loves her job, but she always has time for his dad and him. Steve feels bad that his father never really seems interested in her job or spends much time with her. Steve realizes that his father doesn't have much time for him, either. Steve wonders whether that's the way it is when you're a big shot in the business world.

Steve is optimistic that things will start looking up again soon. He realizes that he's got great friends and parents who love him. And he has promised himself that he'll start hitting the books again.

The Dinner

Dinner was anything but pleasant! Doug was astounded at Lisa's and Steve's reactions to the news about his promotion. He thought they were downright hostile. Lisa was angry and shocked; this is the first she had heard that Doug was even up for a promotion. And Steve didn't know what to think, although he flatly told his parents that he's not moving, no matter what. After about an hour, they all started repeating themselves and figured that dinner was over.

They all left the dinner table in bewilderment and anger. But Doug promised to hold off making a firm commitment to Mr. Johnson. And Lisa promised to sleep on it and continue the conversation tomorrow morning. Steve didn't promise anything.

Case Analysis Questions

1. If you were Lisa or Steve, how would you have reacted to Doug's announcement of his promotion? Why?

2. If you were Doug, how would you have reacted to Lisa and Steve's anger and resistance? Why?

3. What could Doug have done differently in his conversations with his company and his family?

4. What does the Sanders' situation illustrate about the special challenges faced by two-career families?

5. What should the family do next?

CHAPTER 11

Managing Diversity

As the United States' workforce becomes increasingly diverse, so too will employers become more diverse.[1] Organizations that can manage their diversity effectively are likely to be more productive and competitive.[2] The significance of workforce diversity can best be conveyed by considering the following statistics and demographic forecasts:[3]

- By the year 2020, it is projected that people of color will make up about half of the U.S. workforce.

- In 2007, African Americans constituted an estimated 11 percent of the United States workforce, Asians nearly 5 percent, Hispanics 14 percent, and women 46 percent.

- In 2007, an estimated 21.7 percent of the U.S. managerial and professional workforce consisted of African Americans (8.4 percent), Asians (6.3 percent), and Hispanics (7.0 percent), and an estimated 50.5 percent of the managerial and professional workforce were women.

- In 2006, 63 percent of women with children younger than six were in the workforce.

- In 2010, all of the baby boom generation (the 78 million people born in the United States between 1946 and 1964) was over the age of 45, and by the year 2030, the entire generation will be over the traditional retirement age of 65.

- Worldwide competition requires organizations to be staffed with the most talented employees available.

- Large multinational corporations cross national boundaries in their operations, and the consumer behavior of women and minorities is critical to the competitiveness of many organizations.

The increasing diversity of the population and the workforce in terms of race, gender, age, religion, disability, and sexual orientation requires organizations to recognize their dependency on a more varied employee base. There is justifiable concern about organizations' ability to manage employees who are not only different from the traditionally dominant white male managerial base, but are also different from one another in many respects. In part, this concern is due to the career difficulties experienced by many minority group members, especially women and people of color. Without question, the election in 2008 of Barack Obama as the first African American president in U.S. history and the national political campaigns of Sarah Palin and Hillary Clinton in that same year underscore the progress in advancement and mobility achieved by African Americans and women over the last quarter century. Indeed, the number of women and people of color in management and executive positions has risen dramatically over the past three decades. Nonetheless, the progress in upward career mobility to the senior-most positions has been slow. This difficulty in rising above lower and middle management positions illustrates the presence of a glass ceiling or "an invisible but impenetrable barrier that prevents qualified women and people of color from advancing to senior management jobs."[4] The glass ceiling effect has been observed numerous times, including in an analysis conducted by the U.S. Department of Labor.[5]

Taylor Cox and Stacy Blake provide six arguments for why an organization can improve its competitive advantage through the effective management of its cultural diversity.[6] A brief summary of these six arguments is presented below:

1. *Cost Argument.* Organizations have managed women and minorities less effectively than they have managed white males. Therefore, organizations that are unable to manage an increasingly dominant part of the workforce will incur considerable additional costs that will detract from their productivity.

2. *Resource-Acquisition Argument.* Organizations that have the most favorable reputation for managing a culturally diverse workforce will attract the most talented women and minorities into their ranks.

3. *Marketing Argument.* Organizations that serve multinational or domestically multicultural consumers will benefit from a diverse workforce that brings a blend of insights and cultural sensitivities to the organizations' marketing efforts.

4. *Creativity Argument.* The representation of varying perspectives in a culturally diverse workforce should enhance the level of creativity in the organization.

5. *Problem-Solving Argument.* The availability of multiple perspectives in a culturally diverse workforce should enable problem-solving groups to produce high-quality solutions and decisions.

6. *System Flexibility Argument.* Organizations that manage diversity effectively become more fluid and flexible, which enables them to respond to environmental changes more quickly and efficiently.

Later in this chapter, we present our opinions on the strength of these arguments. But first, we examine barriers to fairness in organizations, identify programs and policies that organizations can provide to manage diversity effectively, and propose actions that individuals can take to manage their careers in a culturally diverse organization.

FAIRNESS IN ORGANIZATIONS

As noted earlier, one reason for the concern about organizations' ability to manage diversity is the suspicion that women and people of color are not growing in their careers to a degree commensurate with their talents. For example, although the number of women managers has more than doubled in 30 years, they hold fewer than 16 percent of the corporate officer positions in Fortune 500 companies and about 9 percent of the highest-ranking corporate positions in these companies.[7] The percentage of minority senior managers is also small, as witnessed by an Executive Leadership Council finding that "blacks held 460 of the 2,000 positions that are within four steps of chief executive at Fortune 500 companies."[8] If women and people of color faced substantial obstacles in reaching the upper echelons of their organizations in the past, how can organizations manage an increasingly diverse group of employees in the future?

An organization is acting fairly when its employment decisions (regarding such issues as hiring, pay, and advancement) are based on job-related criteria rather than an individual's membership in a population subgroup (e.g., sex, race, religion, age).[9] Conversely, discrimination occurs when organizational practices have a negative effect on the employment of subgroup members that is not based on job-related factors. Two types of discrimination have been distinguished: access discrimination and treatment discrimination.

In cases of *access discrimination,* subgroup members are less likely to be hired for a particular job than members of the dominant group despite the fact that they could have performed the job as effectively as members of the dominant group. For example, if bias in employment interviews disproportionately rejects talented women for a construction management position in favor of equally (or less) talented men, women (as a group) will have limited access to that particular job. Discrimination in hiring was the target of the early fair employment movement during the 1960s and 1970s.

Treatment discrimination occurs when the treatment of employees already in an organization is based on their status as a member of a subgroup rather than on their merits or achievements; that is, when such employees receive fewer opportunities than they legitimately deserve on the basis of job-related criteria. For example, minorities or women systematically excluded from key committee assignments or sponsorship opportunities experience treatment discrimination within their organization.

Although access discrimination has certainly not been eliminated, women and minorities have been entering managerial and professional positions in increasing numbers. Thus, a key issue is how fairly women and minorities are treated once they are in an organization. For this reason, we focus on understanding treatment discrimination in organizational settings.

Much of the concern regarding fairness is based on the more restricted career advancement historically experienced by minorities and women as compared to white men. Therefore, we will begin our discussion with career advancement and then move to an examination of those factors that may explain differences in career advancement between women and men as well as between minority and nonminority employees.

Career Advancement

"The glass ceiling limits opportunities for many minority workers to develop their careers and reach top management positions in corporate America."[10] One could argue that the limited representation of minorities in senior management is due to the fact that they entered the managerial pipeline later than nonminorities. Although this may explain a portion of minorities' restricted career advancement, it is unlikely that it is the sole explanation. Research suggests that white employees' promotions outstrip minorities' promotions even when the two groups have accumulated comparable levels of human and social capital. Thus, factors other than years of experience and education are necessary to explain the apparent glass ceiling.[11]

This is not to say that minorities are always at a disadvantage in their quest for upward mobility; some employers are as likely to promote people of color to senior positions as whites.[12] Nor can we say that a hostile environment necessarily stifles the aspirations of each and every minority manager in the same way. But, as a group, minorities have experienced more restricted advancement opportunities than whites.

The career advancement of women presents a similar picture. The small proportion of women at senior management levels suggests that many women do not move beyond jobs in lower and middle levels of management.[13] Moreover, Belle Rose Ragins, Bickley Townsend, and Mary Mattis suggest that many CEOs may not fully appreciate the barriers to advancement that women experience.[14]

Job Performance Assessments

Why have minorities and women experienced restricted career advancement? One possible explanation is that they perform less effectively in their current job assignments than white men. The research bearing on this issue presents a somewhat different picture for minorities than for women. Most of this research has examined differences in supervisory ratings of job performance as a function of the employee's sex or race. In general, women have been perceived to perform at least as effectively on the job as men and in some situations more effectively.[15] Therefore, it is unlikely that women's restricted advancement is due to the belief that they are ineffective on their current jobs.

Most of the research on race or ethnic differences in job performance and career advancement has examined white and black employees. Several quantitative reviews of studies observed a small but consistent tendency for black employees to receive lower job performance assessments than white employees.[16] Similar findings were observed in military and managerial samples, although the race differences in job performance ratings were again very slight.[17] In general, then, black employees receive somewhat lower job performance assessments than white employees, although race differences in performance evaluations may vary according to such factors as the particular racial groups compared, the aspect of job performance that is assessed, and the measures used to assess performance.[18]

Are assessments of job performance biased against minority employees? There is no simple answer to this question, although several streams of research suggest at least the potential for bias in some situations. One review of the research found that white raters rated whites higher than they rated blacks, whereas black raters rated blacks higher than they rated whites.[19] The tendency to give higher performance ratings to same-race subordinates can harm minorities, since the majority of supervisors (and hence performance evaluators) in most organizations are white. This study also found that race differences in job performance ratings were more substantial in organizations where blacks made up a very small proportion of the workforce. One explanation is that blacks in small numbers are "put under the microscope" in the assessment of their job performance.

Bias in the evaluation of job performance could take another form as well. One study found that black managers who performed successfully on their jobs weren't given as much "credit" for their success as white managers. When white managers succeeded, their bosses were likely to attribute this success to the managers' ability. However, when black managers succeeded, their bosses were less likely to attribute this success to the managers' ability and were more likely to attribute it to the help and assistance the managers received from other people.[20] The bosses, in effect, discounted black managers' success by attributing it to forces outside the manager. We don't know whether this form of bias is widespread, but when it does occur, it can have a detrimental effect on the careers of blacks because most organizations would prefer to promote individuals who succeed by virtue of their talents.[21]

In summary, there is some evidence that the job performance of black employees is assessed somewhat lower than the job performance of white employees. It is difficult to determine how much of this difference reflects true differences in job performance and how much represents bias in the evaluation process. Nevertheless, we believe that organizations should carefully scrutinize their performance evaluation systems to ensure that they are not biased against any group.

Lost Opportunities

What factors other than job performance evaluations restrict career advancement? It has been suggested that women and minorities receive fewer opportunities to exert authority on their jobs, develop effective supportive relationships within the organization, and become part of the informal network of friendship, power, and influence. Exclusion from these resources represents "lost opportunities" for women and minorities to develop job-related skills and establish important career contacts.[22] These lost opportunities, which may be reflected in the absence of an influential mentor or the assignment to mundane tasks, can reduce the work effectiveness of women and minorities over time and can diminish their opportunities for further growth, development, and advancement.

Authority. There is some indication that women and minorities report less authority and power in their jobs than white men.[23] It has been suggested that women and minorities are often assigned to jobs that permit less authority and discretion, and are underrepresented in line career paths.[24] However, at least one study found that race and sex differences in power and authority persisted even when women and minorities were in jobs comparable to those of white men.[25] If women and minorities do possess limited authority in their job, their opportunity to develop new skills and exercise political clout is likely to be diminished.

Exclusion From Informal Networks. It is often suggested that some of the most critical decisions affecting employees' career accomplishments are made over lunch, during the cocktail hour, or on the golf course. Historically, women and minorities have been excluded from these informal activities, and have been less accepted by their organization than were white men.[26] Although overt exclusion is less likely to occur in modern organizations, isolation from informal networks of information and power, when it occurs, can restrict the career opportunities of women and minorities.

The Establishment of Mentor Relationships. In Chapters 5 and 7 we emphasized the importance of mentoring and other developmental relationships to an individual's career. At this point, we add that it is important to understand the complex role of gender and race in high-quality developmental relationships.[27] Although it has been asserted that women and minorities have a difficult time finding a mentor or sponsor, a number of studies indicate that they are no less likely to have had a mentor than white men.[28] Perhaps it is not so much a question of the establishment of a mentor relationship but rather the nature and quality of the relationship.

Because of the sheer numbers of white men in most organizational hierarchies, many minorities develop cross-race mentoring relationships (i.e., they have a white mentor) and many women have cross-sex mentoring relationships (a male mentor). Moreover, although cross-race relationships tend to provide career support to the protégés, they may provide less psychosocial support than same-race relationships.[29] Cross-race relationships may add certain complications that inhibit the development of minority employees. A recent model of racial dynamics in developmental relationships illustrates the many factors that determine success in such relationships, including the culture of the organization, the way the mentor and protégé deal with racial issues, and the level of trust in the relationship.[30]

Despite these concerns, evidence suggests that those managers of color who advance the farthest in an organization share one characteristic—a strong network of mentors and powerful corporate sponsors who offered long-term, close, developmental support.[31] Mentoring for minorities is a necessity in organizations today. The following is an example of an African American protégé who used mentoring to benefit his career.[32]

Ed Beasley didn't have many African American role models to turn to as he ascended the government administration ladder, but he has benefited greatly from mentors both black and white. As assistant to the city manager in Flagstaff, Arizona, in 1988, Beasley's boss and mentor, then president of the statewide city managers' association, helped convince officials in the smaller town of Eloy to interview Beasley for an interim city manager spot. "Even though I didn't have the title or experience, it gave me the opportunity to show what I could do," recalls Beasley. After six months in the job, he had the "interim" label removed, making him the state's youngest city manager at age 28. Today, 46-year-old Beasley is city manager for Glendale, Arizona's third largest city. He is responsible for a $670 million annual budget.

One of just a handful of black city managers in the nation, he's played a critical role over the past three years in winning deals to build a $350-million multipurpose sports facility that hosted the 2008 Super Bowl and will house the NFL Arizona Cardinals. He was also influential in getting the recently completed, state-of-the-art arena for the NHL's Phoenix Coyotes, which will host the NHL All-Star Game in future years.

During the hectic months before the opening of the 17,500-seat Coyotes arena, Beasley often found himself on the phone with two mentors: one a city manager in another state and the other a corporate chief financial officer in Arizona. There were public doubts about whether the arena would open in time for the start of the hockey season, whether Glendale had the capacity as a city to pull it off, and if the mixed use facility would actually be used at such. Beasley felt pressured but needed to stay focused. "[Mentors] are people who, when I get into a critical situation, I will ask for guidance," says Beasley. "I could pick up the phone and say, 'Here's the track I'm going down. Do you see anything here I'm missing?'" Their nonconfrontational questioning, both across a desk and over the phone, helped him work through his own doubts about the process. With the guidance and support of his mentors, Beasley was able to open these facilities successfully.

Cross-sex developmental relationships also seem to provide the protégé with less psychosocial support than same-sex relationships, although the results are not entirely consistent in this regard.[33] It appears that cross-sex developmental relationships are more challenging than same-sex relationships because of the possibility of gender stereotypes and the potential misinterpretation of a relationship as sexual.[34] Nevertheless, we note that in our class discussions, women MBA students with male mentors have spoken overwhelmingly favorably about the mentoring they have received.

Tokenism. A token is a member of a particular subgroup that constitutes a very small percentage (perhaps 15 percent or less) of a population in an organization.[35] The impact of token status on women and minorities can be substantial. Tokens are highly visible because they are perceived to be different from members of the dominant group. This heightened visibility and attention can produce performance pressures because the token's performance is scrutinized more carefully than the performance of nontokens.[36] Under these conditions, every performance problem experienced by a token may be magnified in the eyes of the organization's management. In addition, women and minorities may feel substantial stress because their accomplishments not only affect their own careers but may also influence management's attitude toward other women and minorities in the organization.

Token status can isolate women and minorities from the mainstream organization as differences between tokens and nontokens become exaggerated. This isolation can exclude tokens from informal social networks and make it difficult for them to attract a mentor or sponsor.[37] Moreover, the isolation of tokens from informal groups and their representation in such small numbers can reinforce existing stereotypes held by the dominant group, since there are not enough direct experiences with tokens to counteract the stereotypes, and negative stereotypes can cause decrements in tokens' job performance.[38]

A MODEL OF ORGANIZATIONAL FAIRNESS

We have seen that the career advancement of women and minorities has often lagged behind that of white men. It is important to reemphasize that the restricted career opportunities discussed in this chapter are not experienced by all women and minorities, and they are not experienced to the same degree in all organizations. In this section, we explore the reasons behind unfairness in organizational settings.

Exhibit 11.1 presents a model of organizational fairness that explains the reasons why women and people of color may experience restricted career advancement opportunities.

EXHIBIT 11.1   Model of Organizational Fairness in Career Advancement Opportunities

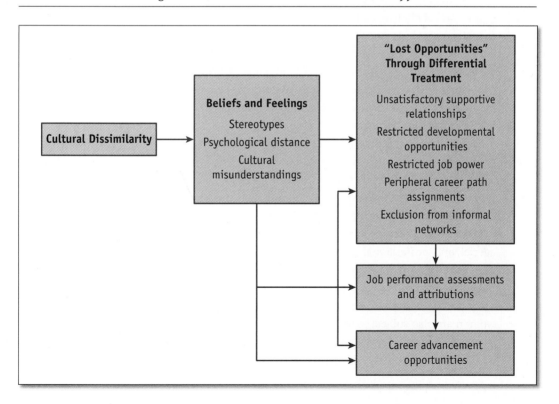

The model indicates that cultural dissimilarities between groups in organizations produce stereotypes, feelings of psychological distance, and cultural misunderstandings. These beliefs and feelings, in turn, can result in differential treatment for women and minorities compared to white men. Differential treatment represents lost opportunities for women and minorities to develop job-related talents, which can detract from job performance and eventually dampen career advancement prospects.

Stereotypes

A stereotype is a preconceived perception or image one has of another person based on that person's membership in a particular social group or category. We may believe that Mary, an accountant, is logical and organized because we believe that accountants in general are logical and organized. We may perceive John, a social worker, to be compassionate and fair minded because we perceive social workers to possess these characteristics. Of course, not all stereotypes are so flattering. For example, we may believe that investment broker Susan is unethical and engineer Brad is narrow minded because we perceive brokers and engineers to be unethical and narrow minded, respectively.

Moreover, the actions we take in response to our stereotype can ultimately confirm the stereotype. For example, because of our belief that members of a particular group are lazy, we may not provide an individual from that group with attention or encouragement or with a great deal of challenge and responsibility on the job. The individual might respond to this lack of support by not appearing to care about the organization and by not expending much effort on the job. This reaction might well reinforce our original perception of the individual as lazy. Although neither party's actions necessarily operate at a conscious level, their consequences are quite real. Negative stereotypes can produce biased assessments of members of targeted groups and can play a role in decisions regarding promotions, salary increases, and job assignments.[39]

Unfortunately, negative attitudes, stereotypes, and prejudice based on an individual's race or sex have not disappeared in contemporary society.[40] Historically, social stereotypes have been a significant obstacle to the careers of black managers[41] and the most difficult stereotypes to combat are those that malign a minority employee's ability and qualifications.[42]

Sex-characteristic stereotypes also persist in contemporary society. Women are thought to possess a number of qualities that are seen as incompatible with success in many managerial and professional positions. For example, whereas men are often perceived as aggressive, dominant, and independent, women are likely to be perceived as compassionate, understanding, and warm.[43] As a result of these stereotypes, women may be passed over for a job that is perceived to require "masculine" characteristics.[44] As we observed in Chapter 10, women are also subject to sex-role stereotypes regarding the priorities they attach to their career and family responsibilities. Many men (and some women) believe that women should be primarily responsible for home and child care activities. As a result of these beliefs, women with extensive family responsibilities may be stereotyped as less committed than men to their work and the organization.

Psychological Distance

Cultural similarity produces feelings of psychological closeness between people in a relationship, whereas dissimilarity in cultural background and experiences may produce a feeling of psychological distance.[45] It is possible that white men feel more psychologically distant from women and minorities than they do from other white men.

Psychological distance can provoke mistrust and even fear because of the belief that people who are different from us are more difficult to understand and therefore more difficult to predict.[46] For example, if we feel different and distant from a person, we may not understand what motivates the person or how to influence the person. In organizational settings, supervisors often form an in-group of trusted and favored subordinates and relegate subordinates who are mistrusted to out-group status. It is possible that the placement of an individual into an out-group is attributable in part to the psychological distance a supervisor feels toward that individual.[47]

Note that stereotypes can create psychological distance, and psychological distance can reinforce existing stereotypes. If we stereotype a subordinate as lazy or ineffective, we may accentuate the differences between that individual and ourselves, ascribe the individual out-group status, and provide few opportunities for the individual to demonstrate his or her strengths. The individual may assume (quite accurately) that he or she is not valued, and therefore show little initiative or interest in improving job performance. This understandable reaction is likely to be interpreted as a lack of interest in work, which will reinforce our initial stereotype, increase our feeling of psychological distance, and result in a self-fulfilling prophecy.

Cultural Misunderstandings

As a result of cultural differences, stereotypes, and psychological distance, there are many opportunities for people to misunderstand each other. For example, a man may perceive a woman's willingness to cooperate with a stubborn colleague as a sign of weakness and accommodation rather than the strength and resolve it may actually represent. A supervisor unfamiliar with Asian culture might misinterpret the modesty and deference of an Asian as a lack of confidence or even as a lack of talent, rather than as a sign of respect for another person based on cultural norms. Cultural misunderstandings can be exacerbated by language differences that produce tension and conflict.

Perhaps the most serious consequence of stereotypes, psychological distance, and cultural misunderstandings is the tendency to discount the present or future contributions of persons who come from different backgrounds. If one believes that members of a particular group are unqualified, that women are not sufficiently aggressive, that an employee's language or cultural differences pose insurmountable obstacles, or that mothers of young children are not committed to their careers, one will be unwilling to invest the time and the organization's resources to develop these individuals and groom them for additional responsibility.

An organization's unwillingness to invest time and resources in particular groups of employees can take several forms—assignment to less significant career paths, exclusion from informal networks within the organization, reluctance to encourage the exercise of power and authority on the job, assignment to fewer tasks or projects designed to build skills or visibility, and provision of less extensive sponsorship or mentorship opportunities. These actions (or inactions) represent lost opportunities for women and minorities to gain valuable experience and exposure. An accumulation of lost opportunities over time can diminish the employee's talents or dampen motivation, both of which can reduce job performance.

We have been emphasizing the stereotyping, psychological distancing, and misunderstanding by white men because they generally possess the most power in organizations. However, it is also possible for women and people of color to stereotype white men, misunderstand their intentions, and experience psychological distance from them. We will return to this issue when we discuss organizational and individual actions that can be taken to manage diversity.

In summary, cultural differences within an organization can produce stereotyping, feelings of psychological distance, and misunderstandings. These beliefs and feelings may result in lost opportunities for women and minorities to cultivate developmental relationships and acquire needed skills and experiences. Not only may lost opportunities erode job performance over time, but stereotyping, distancing, and misunderstandings can bias the assessment of the job performance of women and minorities. Perceptions of ineffective performance and low potential, real or imagined, can curtail the career advancement of women and minorities.

Although diversity is most closely associated with race and sex, other dimensions of diversity are significant in contemporary organizations. For example, organizational diversity may be viewed in terms of differences among employees in age, religion, national culture, language, sexual orientation, and disability status, and significant diversity issues can also revolve around line–staff interactions and functional differentiation, such as engineering versus marketing or production versus sales.[48] Although the specific concerns will vary depending on the dimension of diversity being considered, there are common elements as well—different backgrounds and perspectives, stereotyping, distancing, and misunderstandings.

IS DIVERSITY INHERENTLY VALUABLE?

Broadly speaking, there are two schools of thought regarding why organizations should be concerned about managing diversity. According to one approach, the world and the workplace are becoming increasingly diverse. Since this trend is inevitable, it behooves the organization to cope with this new demographic reality. Therefore, organizations must hire and develop the most talented individuals from all backgrounds in an effective and fair manner. It is not a question of whether diversity is inherently desirable or undesirable, but rather it is a fact of life. This approach is most consistent with the cost and the resource acquisition arguments presented earlier in the chapter.

The second approach, which goes beyond the demographic necessity of becoming more diverse, asserts that organizational diversity is healthy and beneficial in its own right. This approach, which is most consistent with the marketing, creativity, and problem-solving arguments, assumes that employees from different cultural groups bring different strengths and perspectives to the organization that can enhance its effectiveness. For example, it has been suggested that because of their unique socialization experiences, women view situations differently than men. For example, because women are more attuned to social relationships, they may be more likely than men to involve colleagues and subordinates in a collaborative manner, share power and information, and include others in decision making.[49] The implication is that women possess special qualities and skills (e.g., communication, cooperation, emotionality, intimacy) that provide different perspectives on the management of organizations.[50] In a similar vein, it has been suggested that because racial and ethnic minorities have experienced the world differently than the dominant cultural group, they can bring different views, approaches, perspectives, and understandings to the solution of organizational problems.[51]

Are women and people of color substantially different from white men in how they view work-related tasks, approach problems, and relate to other people? In our view, the research does not provide a definitive answer to this question. Studies comparing men and women in managerial and professional careers have often revealed considerable similarity in personality, work-related values, and behaviors. Although this does not mean that men and women react identically in all situations, it does call into question the assumption that women in managerial roles *necessarily* bring different strengths and perspectives to the organization than men bring. In fact, it is likely that there is considerable variation in talents and perspective within each sex group. What is apparent, however, is that there are many women who bring special strengths and perspectives to an organization not necessarily—or only—because of their sex but rather because of their intelligence, education, training, and unique work and life experiences.

Similarly, it is not clear that people of color *necessarily* have unique perspectives on work-related issues by virtue of their race. However, even if there are not consistent and substantial race differences in managers' perspectives or behaviors, it is clear that there are many minority employees who bring special strengths and perspectives to an organization not necessarily—or only—because of their race but rather because of their intelligence, education, training, and unique work and life experiences.

The "different perspective" approach has been viewed critically by Stephen Carter, who states,

Viewpoint, outlook, perspective—whatever word is used, the significance is the same. We have come to a point in the evolution of our ways of talking about race when it is not only respectable but actually encouraged for public and private institutions alike to make policy based on stereotypes about the different ways in which people who are white and people who are black supposedly think.[52]

Carter suggests that this view can put pressure on minorities (and we would add women) to represent the "minority perspective" (female perspective) to see things the way minorities (women) see things. This approach, in our view, runs the risk of replacing old race and gender stereotypes with new and different perspective stereotypes.

Conclusion

We do not claim that women and racial minorities are the same as white men in how they define issues and problems, see the world, or interact with other persons. However, we are not convinced at this time that there are substantial and consistent differences in perspective between women and men or between different racial or cultural groups. Moreover, although several studies illustrate the potential advantages of sexually or racially diverse work groups, a recent quantitative review of the research found that groups with a substantial amount of "bio-demographic" diversity (e.g., sex, race, ethnicity, age) did not perform more effectively than groups more homogeneous along these lines.[53] We agree with Roosevelt Thomas, who observed that

> many individuals believe that there is richness in diversity that you can't get from a homogeneous workforce. This may be true, but it's not necessary to support managing diversity. Whether there is a richness or not, managers will have employees with significant differences and similarities. The compelling case for managing diversity lies in the fact that diversity is a reality—or soon will be. By focusing on the richness, you risk suggesting that the manager has a choice.[54]

Our skepticism regarding group differences in perspective does not detract at all from what we see as an organizational imperative to manage diversity effectively. Organizations desperately require talent, and talent is distributed amply across different groups. Organizations simply cannot afford to ignore the talents and contributions of employees because of their sex, race, religion, age, physical disability status, or sexual orientation. It is in the best interest of the employee, the organization, and society for all talent to be identified, developed, and rewarded.

Moreover, it is also apparent that there are sufficient cultural differences in language, customs, and experiences that can lead us into the trap of stereotyping and misunderstanding other people. Biases, conscious or not, run deep, and what is unfamiliar is often denigrated.

We need to understand different groups and cultures to acknowledge our similarities and to appreciate our differences. We also need to understand our stereotypes and their effects on our behavior as well as on the behavior of others with whom we interact.

Whether or not there is inherent value in diversity, there is value in mutual understanding and respect, and there is certainly value in ensuring that all employees have the opportunity to demonstrate their talents and be rewarded for their accomplishments. With these thoughts in mind, let us consider ways in which organizations can manage diversity.

ORGANIZATIONAL ACTIONS

Characteristics of the Multicultural Organization

A multicultural organization "seeks and values all differences and develops systems and work practices that support the success and inclusion of members of every group."[55] Table 11.1, which identifies the key elements of a multicultural organization, is adapted from the work of Taylor Cox.[56] Let us examine each element of a multicultural organization before discussing specific programs and policies that organizations can implement to manage diversity.

TABLE 11.1   Elements of a Multicultural Organization

  I. Elimination of Access Discrimination
 II. Mutual Accommodation
III. Elimination of Treatment Discrimination
 IV. Structural Integration
  V. Minimal Intergroup Conflicts
 VI. Responsiveness to Work–Family Issues

SOURCE: These elements are based extensively on Cox, T. H. (1991). The multicultural organization. *Academy of Management Executive, 5*(2), 34–47, with some modifications and additions.

Elimination of Access Discrimination

As noted earlier in this chapter, access discrimination occurs when members of a particular subgroup are disproportionately excluded from joining an organization by virtue of their subgroup membership rather than job-related factors. Applicant qualifications, not race, sex, religion, national origin, sexual orientation, age, physical disability status, or any other nonperformance-related factors, must determine hiring decisions. An organization cannot even begin to utilize its human resources fully if it hires (or fails to hire) people on the basis of irrelevant factors.

Mutual Accommodation

We observed in Chapter 7 that the socialization process encourages new employees to learn and accept the organization's assumptions, norms, values, and expectations—in short, to assimilate into the organization's dominant culture. We stressed that organizations possess established ways of accomplishing tasks—what should be done, how it should be done, and by whom it should be done—and that employees must adapt to the most crucial of these expectations to become accepted and successful.

Socialization has generally been viewed as a one-way street in which employees adapt and assimilate into the organization's culture. However, a multicultural organization realizes that members of cultural groups in today's society may not be willing to assimilate fully into the organization's culture.

Moreover, it may not be in the best interest of the organization to demand full assimilation. If members of different groups do possess different views and perspectives (an assertion we consider an important proposition rather than an established fact), then organizations should encourage members of different groups to retain their uniqueness. Total accommodation to an organization's culture could reduce the contributions that members of different groups can make to the organization.

Of course, employees from diverse cultural backgrounds must assimilate and accommodate to some degree. They must accept the mission of the organization and many of its most cherished norms and values. But the organization needs to accommodate the social and cultural norms of its employees. As Roosevelt Thomas has observed, "All companies will and should require some individual adaptation. The challenge is to ensure that the prescriptions are essential to the integrity of the organization and not unnecessarily restrictive."[57]

Elimination of Treatment Discrimination

As we discussed earlier, an organization can intentionally or unwittingly discriminate against members of subgroups. Employees who are excluded from informal networks and those who experience restricted developmental opportunities, limited power, and peripheral career path assignments may prematurely plateau in their careers. These experiences diminish the opportunities for learning, skill development, and career contacts, and can dampen job performance and career advancement prospects.

The multicultural organization understands the potential for treatment discrimination. It recognizes that discrimination not only impedes the progress of individual employees, but also prevents them from maximizing their contributions to the organization. Therefore, multicultural organizations develop mechanisms that aim to eliminate bias and discriminatory treatment, including "reverse discrimination."

Structural Integration

Structural integration refers to the representation of cultural groups at all levels and functions within the organization.[58] In many instances, members of some cultural groups are clustered at the lower levels of the organization, often reflecting the effect of the glass ceiling. In some instances, women may be disproportionately represented in human resource departments, blacks or Hispanics in community relations, Asians in technical positions, and so on. Of course, there is nothing wrong with pursuing careers in human resources, community relations, or technical fields if these areas are consistent with employees' career goals. However, when there is a systematic overrepresentation of subgroup members at different levels or functions, it is essential to determine the factors that are responsible for these patterns of career achievement.

The multicultural organization strives to ensure that members of all groups are at levels and in jobs that are commensurate with their talents and consistent with their aspirations. Artificial obstacles to full representation in different parts of the organization—stereotypes, bias, or indifference—must be removed.

Minimal Intergroup Conflicts

As Taylor Cox has noted, "Conflict becomes destructive when it is excessive, not well managed, or rooted in struggles for power rather than the differentiation of ideas."[59] Culturally diverse organizations are susceptible to potential conflicts between different cultural groups. Language difficulties, stereotyping, mutual misunderstanding, and resentments of perceived preferential treatment can also exacerbate intergroup conflict.

The multicultural organization recognizes the difference between healthy conflict (clash over ideas) and unhealthy conflict (clash over lifestyles or cultures). Moreover, the multicultural organization takes steps to ensure that unhealthy intergroup conflicts are minimized, and that those conflicts that occur are dealt with quickly and effectively so they don't fester into more extensive and damaging conflicts.

Responsive to Work–Family Issues

As we discussed in Chapter 10, a significant source of diversity in contemporary organizations is the substantial representation in the workforce of women (and increasingly men) who are concerned with balancing their career involvement with family activities and responsibilities. This concern is reflected in excessive turnover, a refusal to accept assignments or promotions, as well as extensive feelings of conflict and stress. The multicultural organization acknowledges the connections and conflicts between work and family, and seeks to create a culture that legitimizes work–family issues and helps employees balance their involvements in different life roles.

ORGANIZATIONAL APPROACHES TO THE CHALLENGES OF DIVERSITY

We have presented a portrait of the multicultural organization in its idealized form. Very few organizations, if any, have achieved this ideal level of multiculturalism. Nevertheless, some progress has been made, and employers can learn from the experiences of other organizations that have begun this effort. Before we discuss specific programs and policies, it would be helpful to describe three general approaches to the challenge of diversity: affirmative action, valuing differences, and managing diversity.[60]

Affirmative Action

Affirmative action is a public policy whose goal is to eliminate systematic bias against members of underrepresented groups by requiring an organization "to take proactive steps toward ensuring that the demographic characteristics of its workforce are consistent with the demographic characteristics of the labor markets in which it recruits."[61] Only organizations with 50 or more employees and that conduct business with the United States federal government are required to submit written affirmative action plans, although other organizations can develop voluntary plans.

Affirmative action organizations whose workforce contains proportionately fewer women and/or minority group members in certain jobs than are available in the labor market are required to take "affirmative" steps to reduce the disparity. Affirmative action does not require organizations to develop quotas in hiring or promotions but rather action plans, goals, and timetables to ensure progress toward achieving a better representation of the workforce to the labor market.

Roosevelt Thomas believes that affirmative action, born during the civil rights movement of the 1960s, was based on five assumptions:[62]

1. Adult, white males make up something called the U.S. business mainstream.

2. The U.S. economic edifice is a solid, unchanging institution with more than enough space for everyone.

3. Women, blacks, immigrants, and other minorities should be allowed in as a matter of public policy and common decency.

4. Widespread racial, ethnic, and sexual prejudice keeps them out.

5. Legal and social coercion are necessary to bring about the change.

According to Thomas, these five assumptions may no longer be valid. First, because of the demographic shifts we have discussed, the "mainstream" is already diverse. Second, the economy is anything but stable, and it has forced organizations to become more competitive and to seek talent from all segments of society. Third, the major problem is no longer getting women and minorities into organizations, but rather utilizing their capabilities fully throughout the organization. Fourth, blatant prejudice on the basis of color and sex has been replaced by concerns about education and perceived qualifications. Finally, coercion is less likely to play a dominant role today. Beliefs in high productivity and competitiveness are the motivating forces to the challenge of diversity.

Although affirmative action has been successful in many respects, it is unlikely to solve the long-term needs of organizations and employees in and of itself.[63] It is the object of strongly held (and varying) views by different groups in society and is increasingly under legal attack.[64] As organizations change their focus toward ensuring the full contributions of all members of a diverse organization, additional approaches are required.

Valuing Differences

This approach goes beyond "meeting the numbers" of affirmative action by attempting "to encourage awareness and respect for diversity within the workplace."[65] Through various types of educational and training activities, the valuing-differences approach attempts to improve interpersonal relationships in a diverse organization by achieving one or more of the following objectives:[66]

- An understanding and acceptance of differences among people
- An understanding of one's own feelings toward people who are different in some respect
- An understanding of how differences among people can be an advantage to an organization
- Improved working relationships between people who are different from one another

Thomas points out that valuing-differences activities can help improve the quality of relationships between employees and can reduce blatant forms of prejudice and discrimination. However, since an understanding and acceptance of diversity are not sufficient in and of themselves to maximize the contributions of all employees, a third approach—managing diversity—is also called for.

Managing Diversity

In Thomas's view, "Managing diversity is a holistic approach to creating a corporate environment that allows all kinds of people to reach their full potential in pursuit of corporate objectives."[67] He believes that the need to manage diversity is derived from the following questions:

> Given the competitive environment we face and the diverse work force we have, are we getting the highest productivity possible? Does our system work as smoothly as it could? Is morale as high as we would wish? And are those things as strong as they would be if all the people who worked here were the same sex and race and nationality and had the same lifestyle and value system and way of working?[68]

ORGANIZATIONAL PROGRAMS AND POLICIES

We now turn to a discussion of programs and policies that organizations can use to manage diversity. Some of these programs are derived from affirmative action because the need to ensure equitable access to organizations has not yet disappeared. Other programs involve valuing differences because special efforts are often required for employees to understand their feelings about people who are different. But taken together, the programs represent a set of actions designed to manage diversity as Thomas has used the term: a comprehensive attempt to change the culture of an organization so that all employees can contribute to the productivity and profitability of the organization. Table 11.2 identifies key components of a comprehensive process to manage diversity.

TABLE 11.2   Components of a Comprehensive Diversity Management Program

---

   I. Communication Regarding the Meaning and Importance of Diversity
   Expanded meaning of diversity
   Mission statement
   Orientation

  II. Unbiased Hiring Systems

 III. Identification of Critical Diversity Issues
   Assessment of organizational culture
   Ongoing research
   Diversity task forces

  IV. Diversity Training: Valuing Differences

   V. Language Policy and Programs

  VI. Sexual Harassment Policy

VII. Full Utilization of Career Systems

Career planning

Mentoring and other supportive relationships

Developmental experiences

Proactive promotion planning

Ongoing monitoring of all systems

VIII. Family-Responsive Programs and Policies

Dependent care

Flexible work arrangements

Legitimize work–family issues

IX. Leadership and Accountability

Communication Regarding the Meaning and Importance of Diversity

In order to manage diversity effectively, an organization must understand what constitutes diversity in its world, and must signify the importance of managing diversity to the internal and external environment. Central to Thomas's views is the recognition that diversity goes beyond race and gender. Diversity includes all significant differences in the experiences, perspectives, and backgrounds of different groups within an organization's workforce. Many organizations experience difficulties establishing cooperative relationships between the line and staff functions, or between manufacturing and sales, or between older and younger employees. These difficulties may limit the contributions that certain segments of the workforce can and should make. Organizations should determine the relevant dimensions of diversity that need to be managed successfully.

Having established the meaning of diversity for its purposes, an organization must signify to all its stakeholders—for example, employees, board of directors, stockholders, suppliers, and customers—that it is committed to managing diversity. As we saw in Chapter 10, a number of companies have included statements regarding work–family balance in their mission statements. In the same spirit, the incorporation of a statement regarding diversity in its mission statement would communicate an organization's serious commitment in this area.

Orientation programs represent an important vehicle for an organization to communicate significant elements of its culture to newcomers in the workplace. Orientation sessions can be used to inform new employees about the meaning and significance of diversity in the organization, and can begin to lay the foundation for positive attitudes toward diversity.

Unbiased Hiring Systems

Organizations must constantly guard against discriminatory hiring practices. Not only is it illegal to discriminate against members of "protected" groups, but it is also unwise from a business perspective. As noted many times, an organization cannot afford to exclude effective employees from its workforce, and talent, motivation, and commitment are found in all groups within society, irrespective of race, sex, religion, national origin, age, sexual orientation, and physical disability status.

For these reasons, organizations must engage in aggressive recruiting practices to locate the most talented applicants from all groups within society. Then they must scrutinize each part of the hiring process—application blanks, interviews, psychological tests—to ensure that they are valid and nondiscriminatory. A comprehensive treatment of hiring systems can be found elsewhere.[69]

Identification of Critical Diversity Issues

It is recommended that organizations seeking to manage diversity conduct an assessment of their culture.[70] An organization's culture includes its assumptions about people, its norms and values, and its expectations regarding what people should do and how they should do it. For example, the following assumptions and beliefs may not be conducive to the effective management of diversity:

- "It's production that counts around here—not people."

- "There's only one way to do things—our way."

- "To be successful, you have to show how you're better than your colleagues."

- "Employees' family problems are not our concern."

- "Loyalty to the organization means doing what you're told to do without question."

Companies can assess their culture by administering surveys, conducting interviews, and observing what goes on in the organization. A culture assessment can help to identify sources of bias and can determine what elements of the culture might have to be changed to create opportunities for all employees to develop in their careers and contribute effectively to the organization.

In addition to a culture assessment, ongoing research into management practices and employee attitudes can help organizations identify problems associated with a diverse workforce. Employee surveys can cover a wide range of topics relevant to diversity: perceptions of advancement opportunities, usefulness of human resource practices (e.g., performance appraisal, mentoring), supervisor–subordinate relationships, and organizational reward systems. Focus groups can be conducted in which small groups of targeted employees (e.g., women, older employees) can share their perceptions regarding the organization and the practices that have helped and hindered their career growth; useful information can also be obtained from diversity task forces or committees.

Diversity Training and Learning

Diversity training programs are designed to enhance "the awareness, knowledge, and interpersonal skills required to work successfully with others who are different from oneself."[71] These programs frequently include presentations, role-playing activities, team-building experiences, and videos. Diversity training should not be a standalone activity that replaces other diversity initiatives. Nevertheless, it can be a valuable process that enables employees to hold more positive attitudes toward diversity in general, increase their knowledge about diversity issues, understand the basis for racial and gender stereotyping, and perhaps develop the skills necessary to work more effectively with others from different backgrounds.[72]

A deep commitment to diversity learning is demonstrated by Sodexo, Inc., a leading provider of food- and facilities-management services that has more than 110,000 employees in the United States and, as Sodexo Alliance, more than 324,000 employees in 76 countries worldwide.[73] Because diversity and inclusion are central elements of Sodexo's business strategy, they are incorporated in all business and human resources initiatives and policies. One important aim of Sodexo's program is to enhance diversity competencies at all levels throughout the organization. These competencies include understanding the business case for diversity and inclusion, establishing and sustaining a diverse and inclusive work environment, utilizing diversity as a competitive advantage though the effective management of an increasingly diverse workforce, and securing and retaining diverse clients, customers, and partnered relationships with women- and minority-run businesses.

To achieve these competencies, Sodexo delivers numerous learning programs from the top management level (where diversity programs are conducted at senior management team meetings) to individual managers (who take an eight-hour introductory course on commitment to diversity and inclusion) and work teams (who can receive a customized learning program based on their unique needs, for example, selling to a diverse client base). Sodexo believes that its diversity learning initiatives have contributed to its effectiveness and growth.

Language Policies and Programs

Companies can experience difficulties that arise from multiple languages spoken in the workplace. Employees who do not speak English may misunderstand a supervisor's directive and may resent the fact that others in the organization have not taken the trouble to learn their native language. English-speaking employees, on the other hand, may resent the difficulties and inconveniences imposed by employees who do not communicate well (if at all) in English.

Organizations need to understand the difficulties stemming from language differences, and must be willing to provide flexible solutions. As one example, Roosevelt Thomas recommends that an organization that employs predominantly Hispanics asks, "Is there is a compelling business reason for these workers to speak English? Does the nature of their work require it? Is it too much to ask me to speak English and Spanish?"[74] In fact, some companies that are staffed primarily by Hispanics have printed their publications in English and Spanish, conducted meetings in both languages, and administered employment tests in Spanish.[75]

Sexual Harassment Policy

Sexual harassment is a form of sex discrimination in violation of Title VII of the Civil Rights Act of 1964. The Equal Employment Opportunity Commission has adopted the following definition of sexual harassment:

> Unwelcome sexual advances, requests for sexual favors, or other verbal or physical conduct of a sexual nature constitute sexual harassment when submitting to or rejecting such conduct is an explicit or implicit term or condition of employment; submitting to or rejecting the conduct is a basis for employment decisions affecting the individual; or the conduct unreasonably interferes with an individual's work performance or creates an intimidating, hostile, or offensive working environment.[76]

Clearly, sexual harassment is a serious situation for all parties involved in the action. Not only does the target (usually but not necessarily a woman) suffer a personal indignity, but the target's job satisfaction, career development, and health may deteriorate as well.[77] Moreover, the harasser is subject to severe disciplinary action, including termination, and the employer may be liable for the actions of its employees.

It is likely that the most effective deterrent to sexual harassment is the knowledge that it will not be tolerated in the workplace. A strong sexual harassment policy statement that defines sexual harassment, indicates its seriousness, and specifies the consequences for the harasser is necessary. However, the credibility of the policy will be sustained only if the employer investigates complaints swiftly and seriously and enforces the disciplinary action warranted.

Although perhaps not as well-known as sexual harassment, age harassment is a violation of the Age Discrimination in Employment Act of 1967 and the Civil Rights Act of 1964. Harassment on the basis of race, religion, or national origin is also a violation of the Civil Rights Act of 1964. Clearly, any form of harassment is inconsistent with an appreciation of diversity and can perpetuate a culture of disrespect and mistrust.

Full Utilization of Career Systems

We have seen throughout this book that career growth is enhanced when employees actively manage their careers and when organizations provide support in the form of performance appraisal and feedback systems, mentoring, training and development programs, job design, developmental assignments, and promotion planning. By managing diversity, organizations attempt to create a culture in which all employees can benefit from such support and grow in their careers, and in which individuals are not disadvantaged because of their cultural background. As Roosevelt Thomas has observed, "Managing diversity is a comprehensive managerial process for developing an environment that works for all employees."[78]

Why do special attempts have to be made to ensure that some individuals are not disadvantaged in their pursuit of career growth? We have discussed the potential challenges that women and minorities may experience in a mentoring relationship, the potential for bias in the evaluation of job performance, and how negative stereotypes may prevent a manager from providing critical opportunities for learning and development to subordinates. Whether or not the organization has intentionally favored one group over another, these lost opportunities can hamper the careers of affected individuals. Therefore, organizations should take steps to ensure that support and career opportunities are available to all employees through some or all of the following activities:

- Monitor the progress of all employees to determine whether the careers of women, people of color, and members of other underrepresented groups are disadvantaged in some respect.

- If it is discovered that the careers of some groups of employees are not flourishing relative to other groups, determine answers to the following questions:
  - Do employees perceive the organization's culture to be unsupportive and an obstacle to their career development?
  - Is the performance appraisal system biased?
  - Are some groups of employees provided with fewer opportunities to develop their skills through formal training or on-the-job stretch assignments?
  - Are some groups of employees less likely to be mentored or less likely to be in an effective mentoring relationship?
  - Are some groups of employees less likely to be considered for promotions or special projects despite performing effectively on their jobs?

- Address problematic responses to the questions raised above by revising career development systems (performance appraisal, training and development, mentoring) to ensure inclusion and fairness.

- Hold ongoing discussions among senior managers to ensure that career systems are working for everyone and that the accomplishments of all employees are recognized and rewarded.

Effective diversity initiatives seem to have several qualities in common. First, top management is committed to diversity and is actively involved in the process. Second, the companies are systematically tracking women and minorities to ensure that they are provided with useful developmental opportunities and to assess their progress in the organization. Indeed, one primary aim of such efforts is to make sure that talented candidates for promotion are not overlooked in the decision-making process.

Family-Responsive Programs and Policies

In Chapter 10, we discussed the need for organizations to help their employees to balance their work and family lives, and we proposed three types of programs that organizations can provide:

1. Dependent care (e.g., on-site child care, elder care)

2. Flexible work arrangements (e.g., part-time employment, job sharing)

3. Culture change to legitimize work–family issues

The reader may wish to review the material on work–family interaction discussed in Chapter 10 in the broader context of managing diversity.

Leadership and Accountability

A lack of commitment and responsibility on the part of an organization can be a major impediment to the successful management of organizational diversity.[79] Taylor Cox and Stacy Blake provide the following assessment of the role of organizational leadership in managing diversity:[80]

Top management support and genuine commitment to cultural diversity is crucial. Champions for diversity are needed—people who will take strong personal stands on the need for change, role model the behaviors required for change, and assist with the work of moving the organization forward. Commitment must go beyond sloganism. For example, are human, financial, and technical resources being provided? Is this item prominently featured in the corporate strategy and consistently made a part of senior level staff meetings? Is there a willingness to change human resource management systems such as performance appraisal and executive bonuses? Is there a willingness to keep mental energy and financial support focused on this for a period of years, not months or weeks? If the answer to all of these questions is yes, the organization has genuine commitment. If not, then a potential problem with leadership is indicated.

Effective leadership must be found in lower and middle management levels as well as in senior management. Leadership at all levels requires

- An understanding of the importance of managing diversity to the productivity of the organization and an appreciation of the similarities and differences between members of different cultural groups.

- An ability to manage a diverse group of subordinates. Interpersonal skills are crucial in most leadership roles. Effective leaders have to understand human behavior, communicate accurately, listen carefully, provide feedback constructively, and build commitment among followers. These skills are even more crucial when subordinates come from diverse backgrounds. Training programs designed to improve interpersonal skills should be a significant component of a program to manage diversity.

- An accountability for results. Managers throughout the organization will take their responsibility for diversity seriously when their performance in this area is recognized and rewarded. For example, companies committed to managing a culturally diverse workforce effectively should incorporate into managers' performance appraisals the managers' accomplishments in developing the performance and careers of women and people of color (as well as white men) and in working effectively with culturally diverse teams.[81]

MANAGING DIVERSITY: OPPORTUNITIES AND COMPETENCE

This section examines two additional questions regarding the diversity management process: (1) Should there be "special programs" for targeted groups within the organization? (2) Should organizations practice "preferential treatment"? Each question is complex, controversial, and politically sensitive, and neither question has an easy answer.

We have indicated throughout this chapter that the aim of the diversity management process is to enable all employees to contribute to the organization and reap the benefits of their accomplishments. Recall Roosevelt Thomas's observation that managing diversity helps an organization's management systems work for everyone. In an attempt to accomplish this aim, many organizations have developed programs for targeted groups, for example, a mentoring program for black managers or a career planning program for women professionals. In addition to creating a potential "backlash," special programs can feed existing stereotypes by making it appear that certain individuals or groups would not have succeeded without this special help. Are programs targeted for select groups consistent or inconsistent with a philosophy of managing diversity?

On the one hand, it can be argued that if mentoring is so important, all employees (not just minority managers, for example) should be provided with an opportunity to participate in a mentoring program. Similarly, if career planning activities are vital to success, all employees (not just women professionals, for example) should be provided with career planning opportunities. To do otherwise, it is suggested, would be unfair to one group—white men—and would put this group at a disadvantage.

On the other hand, it is asserted that special programs are needed because the existing systems that have worked for white men—performance appraisal, developmental assignments, promotion planning, sponsorship—are not as available or are not as effective for other groups in the organization. It is suggested that bias, stereotyping, and neglect have historically excluded many women and minorities from the formal and informal systems that have served white men so well for so many years. According to this view, targeted programs are designed to level the playing field, not to give any group an unfair advantage.

In a sense, the argument boils down to whether the current practices and systems within organizations do work for women and minorities. One can point to the increasing representation of women and minorities throughout organizations and conclude that special programs are no longer needed, and in fact are more divisive (pitting "us" against "them") than they are helpful. However, one can also point to the frustration and alienation experienced by many women and minorities who believe that the organization is not providing sufficient opportunities for them to grow in their careers. The restricted opportunities may not be intentionally planned but can be very real in their consequences: the informal contacts not made at an unwelcoming golf club, the meetings to which one is uninvited, the early morning "power breakfasts" that are unattended by women who get their children off to school.

It is our belief that organizations must determine whether their practices and systems are currently effective for diverse groups. A combination of survey research, focus group interviews, observation, and deep soul searching should provide insight into this issue. If it is concluded that current systems are effective for all groups, perhaps no special programs are needed. On the other hand, if it is concluded that certain groups are disadvantaged by the current practices, then the organization has two options. One option is to provide programs or practices to all employees within a given job category (e.g., all middle managers) and to ensure that no one is excluded from the program or practice by virtue of his or her membership in a subgroup. The second option is to provide programs especially targeted for selected groups. It is our opinion that the first option is the preferable long-term goal. However, targeted programs may be useful initially, especially if the group has special needs, or if the organization is concerned that the needs and the contributions of the group will simply not be recognized in a general program.

A second and related issue concerns the perceived preferential treatment in career development and advancement accorded to women and minorities. We emphasize "perceived" because it is difficult to determine objectively the extent to which preferential treatment (often referred to as "reverse discrimination") is practiced.[82]

Companies committed to affirmative action often set goals for the hiring or promotion of women and minorities. Given the powerful effect of goal setting on task performance, the establishment of affirmative action goals is not unreasonable in and of itself—goals motivate action and often produce success. However, some observers believe that goals quickly become "quotas" and ultimately lower standards of job qualifications and job performance. We do not want to enter this fray, in part because "standards" are not always easily measured and because biases and stereotypes themselves can interfere with the objective assessment of standards.

Nevertheless, it is important to reemphasize that most diversity advocates (and apparently a large segment of the public) firmly believe that decisions about hiring, training, development, and promotions must be made on the basis of competence rather than race, sex, or other social groupings. Managing diversity is entirely consistent with the ideology of meritocracy. Roosevelt Thomas has persuasively suggested that merit has three components: task merit (capability to perform a task), cultural merit (capability to conform to the organization's culture), and political merit (capability to receive the endorsement of a powerful sponsor). He believes that people who are "different" from the organization's power base often possess task merit but are not perceived to possess cultural merit or political merit. Moreover, all individuals, including (or especially) white men, have benefited from political assistance in their careers. "Managing diversity simply calls for the manager to ensure that cultural and political realities do not advantage or disadvantage anyone because of irrelevant considerations."[83]

Therefore, competence is and should be the major criterion for decisions affecting the careers of all employees. A key challenge in managing diversity is to provide sufficient support to all individuals so that competence can be developed, and to provide sufficient attention to all individuals so that competence can be recognized and rewarded.

INDIVIDUAL ACTIONS

A number of writers have recommended strategies that minorities or women can follow to achieve success in diverse work organizations.[84] In this section, we suggest actions for *all* employees pursuing careers in culturally diverse organizations based on the career management approach emphasized throughout this book.

Awareness of Self and Environment

- Understand the stereotypes you hold about members of other cultural groups. Be willing to admit that you (like all people) may hold preconceived biases against people who are different from you.

- Understand other people, including those from cultural backgrounds different from yours. Understand similarities and differences among cultures.

- Recognize that there is considerable variation in ability, interests, values, and personality within each cultural group.

- Understand situations from other people's (and other groups') perspectives.

- Understand your current organization's culture and its view of diversity. When seeking a new job in a different organization, assess its culture and view of diversity.

- Understand what it takes to be successful in your current work environment.

Career Goal Setting

- Set career goals that are personally meaningful to you.

- Avoid setting career goals based on race or gender stereotypes unless they also are compatible with your talents, values, and interests. Pursue your vision of success and don't be constrained by what women (or men, or whites, or people of color) are supposed to want.

- Communicate your goals to others inside and outside your organization.

Career Strategies

- Establish a broad network of social relationships inside and outside your organization.

- Don't compromise personal values in pursuing career goals.

- Be assertive in managing your career and in seeking new experiences and opportunities to develop new skills.

- Don't give up your uniqueness or cultural identity in trying to achieve success.

Career Appraisal

- Be willing to modify your attitude toward other people or groups as a result of your ongoing experiences with them.

- Be willing to change your own behavior toward people who are "different" from you.

SUMMARY

The workforce of the future will become increasingly diverse. It will include more women, minorities, and immigrants. Because of these demographic changes and the need for increased global competitiveness, it is extremely important for organizations to manage diversity effectively. Organizations need to understand the reasons why members of different subgroups may experience restricted career opportunities. Stereotypes, feelings of psychological distance from people who are "different," and cultural misunderstandings can have subtle but important consequences for career achievement. Employees subjected to stereotyped attitudes may have difficulties establishing or maintaining supportive relationships, may not be provided with sufficient opportunities to develop or demonstrate their competence, may experience limited power on their jobs, and may be excluded from important informal networks of contacts and support. These "lost opportunities" can have negative effects on employees' job performance and on their prospects for career advancement.

An organization seeking to manage diversity effectively should develop a vision of multiculturalism that is central to the organization's mission and communicate that vision to all of the organization's constituencies; eliminate discrimination in hiring; identify the most salient issues that interfere with effectiveness in the diverse work environment; provide opportunities for employees to understand and appreciate differences among people; address significant language conflicts; develop and implement an effective sexual harassment policy; ensure that its career policies and systems do not give unfair advantage or disadvantage to members of different cultural groups; develop family-responsive programs and policies; and exercise consistent leadership and accountability for diversity throughout the organization.

ASSIGNMENT

Interview an individual (e.g., a friend, classmate, or coworker) who is not of the same sex or race as you are. Ask this individual about his or her values, career goals, and strengths and weaknesses. Then have the individual interview you on the same topics. Discuss the extent to which this individual's career experiences/career plans and your career experiences/career plans have been influenced by your respective cultural backgrounds.

DISCUSSION QUESTIONS

1. Examine Cox and Blake's six arguments regarding why the effective management of diversity can improve an organization's competitive advantage. Which arguments do you find most convincing and least convincing? Why?

2. To what extent do you believe that women and minorities experience the "lost opportunities" indicated in Exhibit 11.1: unsatisfactory supportive relationships, restricted developmental opportunities, restricted job power, peripheral career path assignments, and exclusion from informal networks? Do you think the experiences of women differ from the experiences of members of racial/ethnic minority groups? Why or why not?

(Continued)

(Continued)

3. What stereotypes, if any, do you hold regarding members of the other sex? What stereotypes, if any, do you hold regarding individuals from different racial or ethnic groups? How accurate are these stereotypes and how do you think they were formed? What stereotypes do you think others hold of members of your sex and race/ethnic group? How accurate are these stereotypes?

4. Do you believe that a work group or organization that is culturally diverse (in terms of the sex and racial/ethnic composition) is more effective than a culturally homogeneous group or organization? Why or why not?

5. Can discrimination be eliminated from the workplace? Why or why not? What should employers do to eliminate or reduce workplace discrimination? How much progress has been made in eliminating workplace discrimination in recent years? What do you predict for the next 5 to 10 years?

CHAPTER 11 CASE

Dave the Aspiring Executive (Part A)

Dave began reflecting on the progress of his career over the past 12 years at the Xtel Corporation (fictitious name). He remembered how, early on, he received a great deal of support and assistance from Xtel, but those days seem to be gone.

In the 1980s, Xtel had instituted a program with two basic goals in mind: to help inner-city minority youths gain access to a college education and to create a ready pool of minority college graduates to help Xtel satisfy affirmative action hiring goals. Under the program, Xtel would pay the college tuition of the minority students in exchange for a commitment to work summers for the corporation and to accept employment with the firm after graduation for a minimum of two years. Xtel would accept four new participants into the program each year, so that a maximum of 16 students would be active at any one time.

Dave had always shown outstanding ability in math, winning awards in grade school and high school for his proficiency. During his junior year in high school, Dave began looking at colleges in the area. He set his sights on the Ivy League school in the city. At the same time, Dave's high school guidance counselor told him about Xtel's assistance program. Dave applied immediately to the Xtel program, sending in a brief background statement, a sketch of his career interests, two letters of recommendation, and the newly arrived acceptance letter from the Ivy League school. After two months, Dave received a letter from Xtel stating he had been accepted into their program.

At college, Dave majored in computer science and did exceptionally well. He joined the Black Student Organization at the school and also worked for the college radio station. During his summer internships, Dave worked in a number of different departments at Xtel, mainly assisting in the development of computer applications in each function. Dave was impressed with the fact that even though Xtel was a Fortune 200 company, it was still caring for its employees—Dave had expected Xtel to be more impersonal in its treatment of employees.

In the middle of his senior year Dave began discussing with Xtel's staffing manager where he would be working when he graduated. Dave was pleased that his first job would be in the audit department, working as a computer systems auditor. After two months of full-time work at Xtel, Dave had gotten a call from one of his former professors who inquired about his progress. During their conversation, she encouraged Dave to begin thinking about graduate school. With his grades, the professor was certain that Dave would have no trouble being accepted into the Ivy League school's Master of Science program in computer science. Dave sent an e-mail to Xtel's head of Training and Development seeking company support for his pursuit of the master's degree—he was pleased that Xtel encouraged his attendance and also offered tuition reimbursement. Dave finished the degree in two years, again doing exceptionally well in his studies.

In his first five years at Xtel, Dave progressed rapidly, rising to the level of audit manager at the age of 28. Over this period, he had received challenging assignments and had even made a presentation to a committee of the company's Board of Directors. Now in his early 30s and with a wife and a young son, Dave was interested in continuing his advancement at Xtel, mainly to provide a nice income and financial security for his family. He hoped to be an officer within a year. But Dave was getting a subtle message from Xtel's upper management that maybe he had advanced as far as he could at Xtel—he wasn't receiving the challenging assignments or support anymore, and his latest performance review cryptically indicated the need for broader-based experience. One particular example of the lack of support stood out. Dave had thought that attendance at one of the premier executive management programs would be beneficial as a career advancement strategy. But Xtel refused to support Dave in this endeavor, indicating that they had already identified those individuals who would be attending executive programs. Of course, Dave knew that Xtel had never sent a minority to any executive management program.

Dave had never believed that his race had any influence on his treatment or career progress at Xtel, but he was beginning to wonder. Dave had seen Xtel's newly published five-year goals for affirmative action placement. He noted that the five-year objective for minority representation at the junior officer level had already been achieved. All at once Dave began to feel a little used. He questioned whether his progress at Xtel was truly a reflection of his ability and contributions, or was it more a function of helping to fulfill Xtel's affirmative action targets at successive levels in the hierarchy? He did find it interesting that the affirmative action targets were managed closely, with minority representation in a given grade usually hitting right on the target.

Dave thought about his situation for some time, contemplating his next step. His skills and educational background made him highly marketable. After a while, Dave decided to meet with Xtel's Vice President of Human Resources to discuss career prospects. At the meeting Dave stated his strong desire to move up to the officer level within a year; after all, some of his less qualified contemporaries had already reached that level. The lukewarm response Dave received from the vice president gave him a clear message—his career at Xtel was in a holding pattern. Dave concluded it was time for a change. (Part B of Dave the Aspiring Executive is located at the end of Chapter 12.)

(Continued)

(Continued)

Case Analysis Questions

1. If Dave had the opportunity, what questions—if any—should he have asked the president of the Xtel Corporation regarding his recent treatment?

2. Do you believe that the Xtel Corporation has discriminated against Dave on the basis of his race? Why or why not?

3. To whom—inside or outside Xtel—could Dave have gone for social support? What types of support would have been most helpful: appraisal, instrumental, emotional, or informational? Why?

CHAPTER 12

Entrepreneurial Careers

Just about everyone has, at one time or another, fantasized about owning his or her own business. A great many people actually make the fantasy a reality by becoming an entrepreneur. Indeed, the last three decades have seen an explosion in the pursuit of entrepreneurial careers. According to the U.S. Census Bureau, new business "births" in the United States have grown from 541,000 new business births in 1990 to 629,000 births in 2004.[1] In addition, the total number of business establishments has grown steadily from 6.2 million in 1990 to 7.4 million in 2004.[2] In the mid-1990s, 7.6 percent of Americans (approximately 14 million people) had started new businesses, generating two thirds of all new jobs. By 2005, the proportion had reached 11.5 percent, with more than 23 million people starting new businesses or managing firms less than four years old.[3]

Part of the fantasy of being an entrepreneur includes the potential for wealth that may go along with this career choice. Entrepreneurs own nearly one third of all wealth in the United States, and their median net worth is more than four times that of non-entrepreneur households. *Forbes Magazine's* annual list of the 400 Richest People in America reports that a great majority (upwards of 80 percent) were entirely self-made. It appears that entrepreneurship pays!

Entrepreneurs are agents of change. They play an important role in the overall welfare of society by spurring economic growth, creating new jobs, and serving as role models for future generations of entrepreneurs. Over the past three decades, as the payrolls of Fortune 500 companies have declined significantly, entrepreneurial organizations have created tens of millions of jobs. These small but growing organizations have fueled the American economy, and have made many entrepreneurs wealthy in the process. By 2007, entrepreneurs were responsible for more than 50 percent of the gross domestic product (GDP) in the United States and accounted for 75 percent of new private-sector job creation. New businesses continue to enter the economy at fast rates, both in developed countries and in developing ones. Developed countries have seen average new business entry rates of more than 10 percent a year, while developing countries have seen an average of between 7 and 8.5 percent.[4]

Why the burgeoning interest in entrepreneurial careers? Answering this question is not an easy task—the reasons are almost as varied as the number of entrepreneurs. They can range from seeking freedom from the corporate rat race to inheriting a business from a long-lost relative; from having a passion for a certain product or activity to taking advantage of favorable economic conditions. Whatever the factors involved, the decision to become an entrepreneur represents an appealing career choice to many people, and the interest in entrepreneurship continues to grow. In this chapter, we present an in-depth examination of the unique aspects of the entrepreneurial career. First, we define entrepreneurship and consider the various factors that lead individuals to seek entrepreneurial careers. Next, we review the social and educational support available to current and aspiring entrepreneurs. We then review the career experiences and the challenges faced by women and minority entrepreneurs. We conclude the chapter with suggestions for managing the entrepreneurial career that are linked with the career management model presented in this book.

ENTREPRENEURSHIP: AN OVERVIEW

There exist in the literature a variety of definitions for the terms *entrepreneur* and *entrepreneurship,* each reflecting a distinct perspective on the topic. The 19th-century economist John Stuart Mill identified "risk bearing," or the ability to accept and take risks, as the characteristic that distinguishes an entrepreneur from an organizational manager.[5] Another economist, Joseph Schumpeter, saw entrepreneurship as simply the "creative activity of an innovator."[6] From his perspective, innovation is the distinguishing characteristic.

In an attempt to define entrepreneurship, research has identified five relevant schools of thought, each taking a somewhat different perspective on the term:

1. The "Great Person" school views entrepreneurs as having unique inborn, intuitive abilities to successfully run an enterprise.

2. The "Psychological Characteristics" school views entrepreneurs as having unique values, attitudes, and needs that drive them to be in charge of a firm.

3. The "Classical" school views entrepreneurs simply as innovators.

4. The "Management" school views entrepreneurs as organizers and managers of an economic venture.

5. The "Leadership" school views entrepreneurs as leaders of people.[7]

Several additional views of entrepreneurship follow[8]

6. It involves the identification, exploitation, and pursuit of an opportunity, or fulfillment of a need one perceives in the business environment.

7. It involves uncertainty, risk, and creative opportunism.

8. It requires a wide range of skills capable of enhancing and adding value to a targeted niche of human activity.

9. It covers a wide range of activities such as creating, founding, financing, adapting, and managing a venture.

10. It is the process of creating something different by valuing resources in a novel fashion; devoting the necessary time and effort; assuming the accompanying financial, psychic, and social risks; and receiving the resulting rewards of monetary and personal satisfaction.

11. It necessitates risk taking and innovation by the individuals who establish and manage a business for purposes of profit and growth.

The consistent themes in these views are creativity, innovation, and risk-taking propensity. Taking all of these notions into account, we define entrepreneurship as *managing a business of one's own that requires personal sacrifice, creativity, and risk taking, to create something of value.* This definition combines the relevant aspects of prior definitions covering ownership, innovation, novelty, risk taking, and creative opportunism—themes that the literature consistently applies to the term *entrepreneurship.*[9]

CHOOSING AN ENTREPRENEURIAL CAREER

There are a number of factors that make an entrepreneurial career distinct from the more traditional career where one is employed by an organization. First, entrepreneurial careers are marked by a substantially higher degree of personal commitment to the success of the firm since the career and the business are intertwined. In this sense, the career is the business and the business is the career. Success or failure in one domain is directly tied to success or failure in the other. Thus, as we've indicated, the entrepreneurial career involves a substantially higher degree of risk—of personal failure, monetary loss, and career turbulence. Indeed, while new business incorporations continue to rise, the failure rates on new U.S. business ventures are significant. One study followed new start-up firms that came into existence in 1998 and tracked their existence through to 2002. Sixty-six percent of the tracked firms were in business after two years, and 44 percent were in existence after four years.[10] While these statistics indicate that entrepreneurial efforts are risky, savvy entrepreneurs do have a fairly good chance of having their businesses survive.

Another factor that makes the entrepreneurial career unique is the lower degree of structure, predictability, and support as compared to what an employer would provide. Of course, for some, structure and predictability are the exact reasons to avoid an organizational career.

But for others who are unprepared, the lack of corporate infrastructure and support systems can be discomfiting.[11]

A third distinguishing factor is that those in entrepreneurial careers must possess a greater tendency toward action and innovation. Specifically, the nature of entrepreneurial firms is that decisive actions are required to respond to changing market conditions. By extension, the entrepreneur, as the person in charge, must show the ability to respond quickly to environmental change. In contrast, life in an organizational career is slower paced. In many large organizations, entrenched bureaucracies with risk-averse layers of management normally do not allow, nor do they necessarily reward, quick and innovative decision making.

A fourth distinctive element of the entrepreneurial career is that the entrepreneur performs a number of functional roles simultaneously. More precisely, the entrepreneur can be involved with operations, marketing, accounting, human resources, and planning functions all at the same time. Conversely, those in an organizational career typically play one functional role at a time, and the chance for organizational managers to have multifunctional influence is limited.

With the comparatively higher risk for personal and financial failure, the more extensive demands, and the lack of structure and support, one could ask why so many individuals would throw caution to the winds and embark on an entrepreneurial career. Research points to several general factors that can influence the choice of an entrepreneurial career.[12] These factors include seeking autonomy and independence, specific personality characteristics and psychological conditions that predispose one to an entrepreneurial career, environmental conditions, a passion for a specific product or activity, and the presence of role models. We will explore each of these factors in depth.

Autonomy and Independence

In their study of the values expressed by the members of the baby boom generation, Douglas T. Hall and Judith Richter found the "need for autonomy" and a "questioning of authority" to be prominent.[13] One could argue that all employees, regardless of their ages, value a certain degree of autonomy and independence in their work. Autonomy and independence imply that the individual experiences a substantial amount of freedom in his or her job—freedom of choice in decision making, freedom of expression in work, freedom from close supervision, and freedom from the bureaucratic process. With autonomy, the individual can implement his or her self-concept and live out important values.[14] Entrepreneurship allows for self-determination, financial independence, and acting on the belief that there is a "better way" of doing something.[15] Pursuing an entrepreneurial career is one of the primary ways that individuals can find an outlet for their autonomy and independence needs.

Early research on entrepreneurs indicated that they often have trouble responding to authority figures, showing an unwillingness to submit to authority, feeling uncomfortable working under it, and consequently needing to escape from it.[16] Many entrepreneurs who drop out of traditional corporate jobs do so because of a lack of freedom in decision making and of meddling from more senior executives. Indeed, several studies have found the goals of autonomy and independence to be the primary motivators, for both men and women, among those who started or purchased a business.[17]

From the prior discussion it is clear that the desire for autonomy, independence, and freedom are significant motivators for many entrepreneurs. Being one's own man or woman by owning and managing a business is an alluring proposition, one that more and more aspiring entrepreneurs worldwide are acknowledging.[18]

Personal Characteristics

A number of researchers have proposed that entrepreneurs possess certain personality and psychological characteristics, traits, and attitudes that predispose them to the undertaking of, and success in, business ventures of their own. In this sense, it is believed that current and future entrepreneurs have common personalities and background factors that allow them to embark more easily on an entrepreneurial career.

Need for Achievement. David McClelland first proposed that need for achievement is an important psychological characteristic of entrepreneurs. According to McClelland, those high in need for achievement exhibit three main behavioral traits: they take personal responsibility for finding solutions to problems; they set moderate performance goals and take moderate, calculated risks; and they desire specific feedback concerning performance.[19] Several studies have investigated the linkage between need for achievement and entrepreneurship, with most of this research finding that achievement motivation does serve as a prevalent predictor of entrepreneurship.[20] Of course, a high need for achievement is characteristic of many successful leaders, not just entrepreneurs. Clearly, there is enough evidence to suggest that a high need for achievement may influence an individual's decision to become an entrepreneur.

Internal Locus of Control. Individuals with an internal locus of control believe they can largely control their environment and their fate through their own actions and behaviors. In theory, those who believe they alone can control their destiny may be more likely to become, and be successful as, entrepreneurs than those who do not. However, locus of control has shown an inconsistent relationship with entrepreneurial behavior. Similar to need for achievement, an internal locus of control is generally associated with successful people, not just entrepreneurs. Research has concluded that a comparatively higher internal locus of control may differentiate entrepreneurs from the larger population, but not necessarily from managers in large organizations.[21] Research does suggest that there is a strong relationship between internal locus of control and success as an entrepreneur.[22] Thus, an internal locus of control may serve as another underlying factor that influences the undertaking of and success in an entrepreneurial career.

Tolerance for Ambiguity. Research has shown that the ability to accept and deal with conflicting and uncertain situations and to handle multiple, ambiguous assignments does appear to distinguish the entrepreneurial personality from non-entrepreneurs.[23] Studies support the view that entrepreneurs have a greater capacity to tolerate uncertainty in their lives than do organizational managers.[24] A high tolerance for ambiguity in one's life is also associated with Type A behavior, so it's not surprising that many entrepreneurs are also classified as Type A's.

Risk-Taking Propensity. In discussing the definition of entrepreneurship, we noted that a willingness to take risks is a common element in describing the entrepreneur. While several studies have found entrepreneurs to be more likely to take risks than organizational managers,[25] a few have found mixed results regarding risk-taking propensity as a personality trait of entrepreneurs.[26] However, some researchers now suggest that while entrepreneurs are more aggressive and risk oriented in their decision making than managers in large organizations, this may not be evident to entrepreneurs since they often perceive comparatively lower risk in a given situation.[27] Specific cognitive biases, such as overconfidence, an illusion of control, and the use of limited (but positive) information, tend to influence the entrepreneur's perception of risk.[28] It has also been suggested that entrepreneurs have such a strong belief in their ability to influence business outcomes that the possibility of failure is perceived as relatively low.[29] Therefore, given similar situations, the entrepreneur is likely to perceive lower levels of risk than the non-entrepreneur. It may be more insightful to view entrepreneurs as capable risk managers whose natural abilities tend to defuse what non-entrepreneurs might view as high-risk situations.

Entrepreneurial Self-Concept. As we discussed earlier in this book, individuals can have certain orientations toward work that reflect their personal motives, values, and talents. These orientations, known as career anchors, are the manifestation of an individual's self-concept or image in his or her career choice.[30] One of the career anchors described by Edgar Schein is entrepreneurship, where the individual's "primary concern is to create something new, involving the motivation to overcome obstacles, the willingness to run risks and the desire for personal prominence in whatever is accomplished."[31] The entrepreneurship anchor also reflects a desire to have freedom and autonomy to build the organization and create the business into the entrepreneur's own self-image. In effect, the entrepreneurship career anchor takes into account the prior personality traits discussed thus far—need for achievement, an internal locus of control, a tolerance for ambiguity, the willingness to bear risks, and desire for autonomy and control. The entrepreneurship anchor also suggests an individual's belief in his or her own abilities, a drive toward innovativeness, a tolerance for stress, and a proactive (take-charge) personality.[32]

Demographic and Background Factors. A number of studies have been conducted to see if entrepreneurs could be differentiated from non-entrepreneurs based on a variety of demographic characteristics including parents' occupation, parents' socioeconomic status, and birth order of the entrepreneur. As with virtually any career choice, one's parents can play an important role in influencing the decision. But with the selection of an entrepreneurial career, influence from one's parents can be especially salient. The father or mother may play a powerful role in establishing the desirability and credibility of an entrepreneurial career for the offspring.[33] Another background factor that appears related to the selection of an entrepreneurial career is being the firstborn child in the family. Research has found that the firstborn is most likely to receive special attention as well as opportunities for the development of self-confidence.[34] This heightened level of self-confidence and self-esteem may allow the individual to view entrepreneurship as a viable career alternative.[35]

Research has found that entrepreneurs tend to be better educated than the general population and come from families where parents owned a business.[36] In addition, several researchers have pointed out the positive influence that prior business experience can have on the success of entrepreneurial firms, and how a lack of experience can lead to business hardship and failure.[37]

As this section has shown, trying to get a handle on what constitutes a typical entrepreneur in terms of personality traits and background characteristics is a difficult, if not impossible, task. There is a high degree of diversity in the backgrounds of entrepreneurs and their impetus for starting a business. Research has suggested that any attempt to identify characteristics of the "typical" entrepreneur is inherently futile.[38] Indeed, entrepreneurs are innovative and idiosyncratic, and tend to be so unique that they cannot easily be categorized.[39] Nonetheless, prior research has given us insights into what makes the entrepreneur tick, at least in a general sense. We can conclude that entrepreneurs generally show a need for autonomy and independence, have a high achievement motivation, view themselves as being quite capable and able to determine their own destiny, have the ability to handle multiple assignments and ambiguous situations effectively, are willing to take risks, and may have been favorably influenced by their parents and others in their social network. While these same characteristics are commonplace among many successful people, entrepreneurs and non-entrepreneurs alike, it is apparent that entrepreneurs as a group consistently possess this combination of traits. As Edgar Schein indicates, the entrepreneurial self-concept, which includes innovation, need for autonomy and independence, risk-bearing ability, and creativity, seems to predispose certain individuals to embark on an entrepreneurial career.[40] It may be that any one of these aspects of the entrepreneurial self-concept, in conjunction with the right environmental conditions, predisposes an individual to become an entrepreneur.

Environmental Conditions

Becoming an entrepreneur can also be influenced by a number of environmental conditions and experiences. We will consider three prominent environmental factors: job loss, work dissatisfaction, and favorable business conditions.

Job Loss. Over the past three decades, waves of corporate downsizings and mergers caused millions of workers to experience the loss of their job (or jobs, in the case of multiple episodes of job loss). For many of these displaced employees, starting (or acquiring) their own firm represented a worthwhile career option. Studies have shown that as many as 15 to 20 percent of the managers who lose their jobs choose to become entrepreneurs.[41] It should not be surprising that employees who are the unwitting victims of downsizings and restructurings, and who still have unique competencies and a motivation to achieve, start their own firms. Being discharged from an organization may provide the final impetus for aspiring entrepreneurs. Also, individuals who are terminated may vow never again to become a pawn in a large organization's chess game. Of course, deciding to become an entrepreneur after being discharged from an organization should be done only after a thorough analysis of all available options. Given the uncertainties, the sacrifices, and the risks involved, the entrepreneurial career is not for everyone. Entering into a business venture without proper planning and insight can only compound the personal toll that started with the loss of one's job.

Work Dissatisfaction. In addition to job loss, another form of "negative displacement" that can influence the undertaking of an entrepreneurial career is job dissatisfaction.[42] Research has shown that dissatisfaction with their most recent previous job is a major reason for entrepreneurs to begin their own firms. Indeed, extreme dissatisfaction can push aspiring entrepreneurs from their previous place of employment and can also serve to convince them that no other form of employment represents an acceptable alternative.[43] Assuming the individual's perception to be true, the only viable solution would be to own your own firm (i.e., be your own boss).

As was the case with job loss, using work dissatisfaction as the primary (or sole) reason for becoming an entrepreneur may lead to difficulties. Based on the career management model we have discussed throughout this book, aspiring entrepreneurs need to explore their interests, values, and lifestyle preferences and then examine whether having their own business will satisfy these personal needs. If the decision to become an entrepreneur is not based on a thorough self-evaluation, but instead represents a knee-jerk reaction to an onerous work situation, then the individual is likely destined for personal unhappiness and further disappointment. Work dissatisfaction may contribute to the choice of an entrepreneurial career, but it should never be the sole deciding factor.

Favorable Business Conditions. Over the past three decades the desire to become an entrepreneur has been spurred by generally favorable business conditions and opportunities. As we move through the early part of the 21st century, several trends are continuing to drive new business ventures.[44] First, the steady increase in international trade over the second half of the 20th century has changed the world's economy, opening up both new consumer markets and previously untapped productive capacity. Globalization has thus created vast opportunities for new business. Second, the revolution in information and communications technology has "shrunk the world" and enabled entrepreneurs to create new businesses and to reach suppliers and customers worldwide, with little upfront capital. Today's reality is that the capabilities afforded by personal computers and other office technology products give the entrepreneur working at home the power of a big business.

It is apparent that a number of environmental, economic, and technological factors have combined to provide fertile ground for the undertaking of a business of one's own. Nonetheless, it is still important to recognize that the decision to become an entrepreneur should be the product of thorough analysis, covering personal desires, as well as conditions in the business environment.

OTHER FACTORS THAT ENCOURAGE ENTREPRENEURIAL CAREERS

Beyond the various individual characteristics and environmental elements that we have highlighted, there are several other well-known reasons why individuals are prompted to pursue an entrepreneurial career. Three of the most widely recognized reasons include a passion for a product or service, the presence of an entrepreneurial role model (or models), and the potential for a bridge career to maintain involvement in the workforce.

Passion for a Product or Service

Some people embark on an entrepreneurial career because of a personal zeal for a specific type of product or activity. Thus, someone with a passion for cooking may decide to open a restaurant or perhaps start a catering business. There are many examples of people who turned their passions into successful businesses. Nuts Are Good! Inc., was established because of its owners' love of almonds and peanuts. Another family, who had a passion for the safety of their children, developed P'kolino, multipurpose, modular furniture products that are designed to grow with the child and fit into the decor of a home.[45]

The allure of a certain activity can be a strong motivator for entrepreneurs. Often, the product or service represents an extension of the individual's self-concept, wherein the individual identifies so closely with the product or service that the provision of such becomes a natural career choice. Consider the following example:

When Al was employed in corporate finance he would often find himself daydreaming about wood-working—he could almost smell the scent of freshly sawed oak in his office. On other occasions, Al would be penciling sketches of a new dresser he could make, or maybe a coffee table. On nights and weekends, you could always find Al working away in his woodworking shop (which doubled as his garage), turning out carefully crafted wood products. He never made a profit on his creations, charging his friends and family only the cost of the raw materials he used. Al loved woodworking so much that the creation itself, and the admiration of his customers, was satisfaction enough.

Al liked working for the corporation. He had majored in accounting as an undergraduate, and had gotten his MBA in finance. Solving complex financial questions and preparing business plans were stimulating to him. But woodworking continued to be his first love—it was in his blood. His father was a carpenter and he passed on to Al a passion for creativity with wood. Al had never seen woodwork-ing as a vocation, only as a hobby to relieve the stress of the corporate world.

After 10 years in corporate finance, Al began seeing woodworking in a new light. The demand for his creations was more than he could fulfill. Comparable wood products at commercial establishments were selling for double and triple what Al charged. Also, Al's corporation was the subject of takeover rumors—the grapevine said that Al's department would be one of the first to go if a merger did take place. Al began talking seriously to his wife about starting his own woodworking business. They con-cluded that her job as head of corporate research for an investment banking firm would cover them financially while the business was getting started. They spent time looking for commercial real estate properties to rent to set up the shop. Once they found the proper location, they spent $20,000 on equipment and tools. The merger finally occurred at Al's company, and he was happy to resign, take his severance package, and become a full-fledged entrepreneur. Al and his wife took out advertise-ments in upscale magazines, approached local interior designers for referrals, and used their friends and families to spread the word of their nascent business to other potential customers. They took orders by mail, by phone, and over their Internet Web site. After three months in business, the demand for Al's wood products was exceeding his capacity and he was now thinking about hiring an assistant. Personally, Al is happier than he has ever been. The time pressure and demands are intense, but he is doing what he loves. He is wondering why he didn't start the business sooner.

This vignette, while fictional, identifies the process many fledgling entrepreneurs go through as they begin their new ventures. There are literally hundreds of real stories about entrepreneurs who have become successful by following their passion for a product or service.

Presence of Role Models

In Chapter 6 we discussed the influence of social forces on the selection of an occupation. Specifically, we advanced the view that parents, other family members, and friends can serve as important role models and mentors in making career decisions. Prior research sup-ports this view, finding that social support is related positively to the perceived desirability of starting a business.[46] The key question is this: Does having an entrepreneurial role model encourage the selection of an entrepreneurial career? The answer to this question appears to be yes—when entrepreneurial role models engage potential entrepreneurs in various professional activities (such as an employment relationship or discussions about business ventures), the potential entrepreneur's desire to own a business is increased.[47] Perhaps the most important role models for budding entrepreneurs are parents. Several studies have found that either the father or mother, working in an entrepreneurial venture, helps to establish the entrepreneurial career as a desirable and credible career alternative for their children.[48]

A special case of parental influence on the undertaking of the entrepreneurial career concerns the encouragement of the children of entrepreneurs to enter the family business. Often, entrepreneurial parents see their children as the future standard-bearers of the company, the ones who can carry the company on for future generations. In a poll of 500 family-owned companies, the first concern of entrepreneurial parents is planning for estates, taxes, and wealth, while the second major concern is planning for ownership transfer. Interestingly, fewer than one in three family businesses survive to the second generation, and a mere 12 percent survive to the third generation.[49] For many children of entrepreneurs, the decision to enter the family company is uneventful and free of stress, due to a desire to carry on the family legacy and build upon the efforts of one's parents. In this case, the children feel unthreatened, free to choose the career goals they desire. But for others, the decision to join and help run the family business can be a stressful experience, as the need to assert independence from the family unit clashes with parental pressure to enter the family enterprise. The pressure to be employed by the family firm would likely be highest when the individual is emerging from the school years when his or her formal education is complete. But at this time, the individual is in the process of entering the adult world, confronting the psychological conflict that results from the need to be one's own person versus the pull of the safety and security of the family.

The issue of succession, that is, who will run the family-owned business after the owner steps down, is often a point of contention. While the owner's sons and daughters are groomed to take over the family business, daughters of owners can sometimes be considered "invisible successors" with their major responsibility being the passing of family traditions and history on to the next generation.[50] However, as more women are becoming chief executives of major public corporations, many more daughters are taking over family businesses. Consider the following two examples:

> In 1956, Joe Hardy founded 84 Lumber along with his two younger brothers and a friend. They bought a tract of land in the rural town of Eighty Four, Pennsylvania, with the idea of starting a no-frills, low-overhead lumber yard focused on selling to contractors. In 1993, Joe's daughter, Maggie Hardy Magerko, took over as president. In her first year in the position, the company broke the billion-dollar sales mark. By 2007, sales netted more than $4 billion. Her net worth is estimated to be around $2 billion, making her one of the richest people in the United States.

> Abigail Johnson, heir to the largest mutual fund family, Fidelity Investments, became president of the company's mutual fund division in 2001, and now runs the employer services division, which administers payroll and employee stock plans. Abigail is following in her father's (Ned Johnson III) footsteps, and currently states her net worth as $15 billion, making, her one of the richest people in the United States.[51]

Regardless of the level of pressure one feels from family, the process of considering whether to enter the family business should follow the career management model presented earlier. The individual should thoroughly assess personal values, interests, talents, and lifestyle preferences and assess the work environment (both within and outside the family firm) to have sufficient knowledge to determine the most appropriate career goals. One's decision to enter the family firm should be made only if it is consistent with personal desires and fits with conditions in the internal and external work environments.

In summary, it does appear that parents can play an influential role in encouraging their children to pursue entrepreneurial careers. Once one becomes an entrepreneur, the role of parents, mentors, and other alliances may diminish considerably. The nature of the entrepreneurial career is such that decisive individual action is paramount. While social support may aid in the decision to become an entrepreneur, advice and intrusion from the social network may actually inhibit the entrepreneur from taking required actions.

Entrepreneurial Bridge Careers

In Chapter 8 we discussed how bridge employment allows workers who have retired from a career-oriented job to move to a transitional work position that provides a bridge or link between one's long-term career and the entry into total retirement from all work. With millions of baby boomers leaving their full-time careers over the next 30 years, it is likely that many will see an entrepreneurial career as a viable form of bridge employment.[52] These new entrepreneurs may hire other retirees to work for them, thus establishing "gray businesses" made up of older workers. Depending on the business and industry one is in, entrepreneurial careers can offer a flexible work environment that would be appealing to retirees and potential retirees who are looking at bridge employment opportunities.[53]

SUPPORT FOR THE ENTREPRENEURIAL CAREER

Coincident with the surge in entrepreneurial activity is the emergence of a variety of support mechanisms. These mechanisms include social networks and alliances, training and education programs, publications, and Internet Web sites. In addition, the U.S. Small

Business Administration has a number of programs designed to provide support for entrepreneurs.[54] This whole infrastructure of support for the entrepreneur has grown up in correspondence with the rapid increase in entrepreneurial activity. Let us briefly consider each type of support.

Social Networks and Alliances. Entrepreneurs can be helped by a number of different social groups and mutual-benefit organizations. Social networks operate at two different levels. Informal alliances include business support from friends and relatives. Formal assistance can come from such larger organizations as community groups, state or governmental agencies, ethnic institutions, religious associations, fraternal organizations, and other small business associations. Supportive alliances, such as those providing for cooperative buying arrangements, trade groups, joint venture capital raising activities, and community professional advice, provide help for potential entrepreneurs. An entrepreneur can easily access supportive alliance resources through the Internet. Some examples follow:

- Cooperative buying groups can be found through the National Cooperative Business Association's Web site (www.ncba.coop), where they offer comprehensive education, co-op development, communications, public policy, member services, and international development programs. On the NCBA Web site, MainStreet Cooperative Group (www.mainstreet.coop) assists start-up businesses by using a cooperative model to help them attain the necessary size and structure to have recognized purchasing and market power in their industry.

- The National Center for Women & Information Technology (www.ncwit.org) formed its Entrepreneurial Alliance to address the causes and possible interventions concerning the small number of women involved in starting businesses, filing patents, and transferring technology in the information technology field. The Entrepreneurial Alliance brings together representatives from more than 20 established entrepreneurial organizations, as well as national experts in research related to women and information technology entrepreneurship, who understand the factors associated with entrepreneurial success and are working as change agents to enable more women to succeed as entrepreneurs.

- The National Collegiate Inventors and Innovators Alliance (NCIIA) fosters invention, innovation, and entrepreneurship in higher education as a way of creating commercially viable and socially beneficial businesses and employment opportunities in the United States. The program was founded on the premise that invention and innovation are essential components of entrepreneurship, vital to the nation's economic future, and should be part of higher education curriculum.

The NCIIA works with colleges and universities to build collaborative experiential learning programs that help nurture a new generation of innovators and entrepreneurs with strong technical and business skills to make the world a better place (see www.nciia.org). The Collaborative for Entrepreneurship & Innovation (CEI) at Worcester Polytechnic Institute in Worcester, Massachusetts, is an example of a university-wide entrepreneurship program funded in conjunction with NCIIA (see www.wpi.edu/Academics/Depts/MGT/CEI/About/index.html).

- Connecticut Venture Group (CVG) is a voluntary professional organization that is committed to connecting leading venture investment professionals with high-growth emerging companies. The CVG's mission is to assist the development of these high growth enterprises through the promotion of capital formation in Connecticut (see www.cvg.org).

- StartupNation is another Web community (www.startupnation.com) that offers a wide variety of information, both in written articles and in episode podcasts, which are available via Internet radio and video. Members of the StartupNation community are small business experts who speak frequently at entrepreneurial forums and act as resources for top media venues nationwide.

Alliances increase the entrepreneur's likelihood of making contact with other entrepreneurs, of getting the necessary advice, and most important, of making contact with potential venture capital providers. Venture capital clubs meet regularly across the country. Venture Associates lists all venture capital clubs throughout the United States, with four clubs currently existing in Canada, Israel, Mexico, and Taiwan.[55] The first venture club was the Connecticut Venture Group, which started with 6 members back in 1974, currently has 400 members, and is the model for over 100 organizations around the world.[56]

A city's Chamber of Commerce can also help entrepreneurs and their businesses. Practically every city or metropolitan region has a Chamber of Commerce. For example, the Savannah, Georgia, Area Chamber of Commerce, which was established in 1806 as a trade association, is one of the oldest Chambers in the United States and has been in continuous operation since the founding date. Over the years, it has expanded from narrow interests in the mercantile community to a broader scope including business and professional communities. It has also expanded its scope from just the city of Savannah to include the entire Savannah area and surrounding communities. The Chamber now encompasses the coastal regions, and deals with the affairs of the state, national, and international entities that affect the Savannah area.[57] Local Chambers of Commerce are listed at www.chamberof commerce.com. This national Resource Directory has listings of Chambers of Commerce, Better Business Bureaus, Convention and Visitors Bureaus, and regional Occupational Health and Safety Administration (OSHA) offices.

Training and Education Programs. Colleges and universities recognize the importance of, and student demand for, educational programs in entrepreneurship. The provision of entrepreneurship education programs has grown to more than 2,200 courses at over 1,600 U.S. institutions. There are approximately 300 endowed entrepreneurship positions at U.S. colleges and universities, more than twice the number that existed in the mid-1990s. There are also over 100 established and funded centers devoted to entrepreneurial education.[58] Endowed professorships and funded centers provide an anchor for entrepreneurial education within a university. Many entrepreneurship programs were started when successful entrepreneurial alumni funded initiatives focused specifically on helping students learn about starting and running businesses. Foundations like The Ewing Marion Kauffman Foundation provide grants to organizations and universities to further entrepreneurial studies. The Kauffman Foundation was established in the mid-1960s by the late entrepreneur and philanthropist Ewing Marion Kauffman. Based in Kansas City, Missouri, the Kauffman Foundation is the 30th largest foundation in the United States, with an asset base of approximately $2 billion. The vision of the foundation is to foster "a society of economically independent individuals who are engaged citizens, contributing to the improvement of their communities." In service of this vision, and in keeping with its founder's wishes, the Foundation focuses its grant making in two areas: advancing entrepreneurship and improving the education of children and youth.[59]

Courses in entrepreneurship are extremely popular among students. At Babson College in Massachusetts, every business student takes a foundation course involving a yearlong entrepreneurial immersion in which students establish and run an actual business funded by the College. Profits from the business support a charitable project, which the students coordinate. Arthur M. Blank, cofounder of The Home Depot, established the Center for Entrepreneurship at Babson, where the mission is to advance entrepreneurship education and practice through the "development of teaching, research, and outreach initiatives that inspire entrepreneurial thinking and cultivate entrepreneurial leadership in all organizations and society."[60]

Approximately 175 business schools offer MBA programs in entrepreneurship. Graduate schools like Northwestern University, the University of Illinois at Urbana-Champaign, and Stanford University report between 10 and 54 percent of their graduates expressed an interest in starting a business.[61] Many business school graduates not only perceive business ownership in a positive light, but also see becoming an entrepreneur as a long-term career goal.

Courses and programs in entrepreneurship at the university level are designed to meet career and training needs of essentially two groups: traditional undergraduate and graduate students interested in an entrepreneurial career, and nontraditional students such as practicing and potential entrepreneurs who may pursue a graduate education. Content of the courses and programs can vary somewhat from school to school, but in general they cover traditional business subjects (e.g., marketing, finance, accounting, management), combined with a specific focus on the start-up of a business venture. Courses may spotlight starting new firms, small business management, venture capital sourcing, new product development, idea protection, venture plan writing, and financing. Entrepreneurial skills are developed in negotiation, leadership, creative thinking, and technological innovation classes.[62]

Universities and colleges can also pool their efforts to achieve a degree of synergy in serving the needs of entrepreneurs. An example of a cooperative effort is given below:

> The Global Consortium of Entrepreneurship Centers (GCEC) was founded in 1996 through the efforts of the University of Maryland and the Kauffman Foundation. The intent of the organization is to provide a coordinated vehicle through which participating members can collaborate and communicate on specific issues and challenges confronting university-based entrepreneurship centers. The sharing of information helps established entrepreneurship centers as well as emerging centers work together to develop programs and initiatives, and to collaborate and assist each other in advancing, strengthening, and celebrating the contributions and impact of these centers for entrepreneurs. The GCEC current membership totals 200 university based entrepreneurship centers.[63]

Publications and Web Sites. Recognizing the heightened interest in entrepreneurial careers and the trend in new business formations, the publishing industry has moved forcefully to supply related literature. Indeed, there exists a variety of periodicals, journals, magazines, books, and Web sites that cover such topics as owning your own firm and being successful once you become an entrepreneur. These publications play an important role in advancing the understanding of entrepreneurship by providing advice on starting and/or managing a business venture and giving realistic previews of what one will encounter in an entrepreneurial career. Entrepreneurial-based Web sites have also proliferated over the past two decades. A widely used tool is the Entrepreneur.com Web site where a Resource Center provides access to written publications, government resources, podcasts, and weblogs or blogs.

CHARACTERISTICS AND EXPERIENCES
OF FEMALE AND MINORITY ENTREPRENEURS

In earlier sections of this chapter we discussed two different views of entrepreneurial career selection—as a product of certain personality and psychological characteristics and as a function of environmental influences. Much has been written over the past few decades concerning whether female and minority entrepreneurs possess the typical entrepreneurial personality profile (i.e., need for autonomy and independence, high need for achievement, risk-taking propensity, internal locus of control, tolerance for ambiguity) and social learning experiences (i.e., entrepreneurial parents, encouragement, and support) as men and nonminorities. The following sections will discuss the entrepreneurial experiences of women and people of color.

Female Entrepreneurs

While the overall growth in new business formations has been exceptional, the growth in female-owned businesses has been especially impressive. For the past two decades, women-owned firms in the United States have continued to grow at nearly two times the rate of all firms (42 percent vs. 24 percent). More than 10 million firms in the United States are owned by women, employing nearly 13 million people, and generating close to $2 trillion in sales. These women-owned firms account for over 40 percent of all privately held firms. Women of color own 2.4 million firms, employing 1.6 million people, and generating nearly $230 billion in sales annually. Between 1997 and 2006, the number of privately held firms owned by women of color grew five times faster than all privately held firms (120 percent vs. 24 percent).[64] Paralleling the rise in female-owned firms, many studies have investigated female entrepreneurs. Several questions emerge from a review of this literature.

Are women entrepreneurs characteristically different from either their male counterparts or female managers in organizations?

In general, research has found few, if any, differences between female entrepreneurs and either their male counterparts or organizational managers in terms risk-taking propensity, need for achievement, innovativeness, desire for autonomy, internal locus of control, and a proactive personality. Management practices are also largely similar between the genders. Women appear to have no specific difficulties gaining information, and they network similarly to men. Women's level of education, level of prior work experience, borrowing and financing routes, and their degree of venture planning conducted have also been found to be similar to men's.[65] Therefore, characteristics and experiences of female entrepreneurs are similar to those of men.

What are the underlying reasons why women enter an entrepreneurial career?

As was just discussed, female entrepreneurs do not appear to display any major differences in personality or psychological characteristics compared to either their male counterparts or female organizational managers. One could therefore ask whether there are other special factors or circumstances that underlie the entrepreneurial career selection of women. Two factors seem to dominate women's selection of entrepreneurial careers: escaping the corporate rat race and the limitations of the "glass ceiling," and balancing work and family responsibilities.[66]

It has long been documented that women choose to leave the corporate workforce due to the dissatisfaction and discrimination they continue to experience due to the glass ceiling.[67]

It may be that women who reach the executive ranks realize that the "old boy's network" still prevails, or they are not content once they achieve executive status due to the stressors constantly impacting their daily professional lives and the trade-offs they have made to achieve success. Regardless, the fact remains that career choices for high-achieving women within traditional organizations are often quite limited.[68] In Jeremy Main's view, "entrepreneurship seems to suit women particularly, partly as an antidote to discrimination they encounter in corporations. Creating their own businesses offers an escape."[69] Indeed, Anne Fisher found that 23 percent of the women she interviewed noted frustration with the "glass ceiling at a big company" as the impetus for starting their own businesses.[70] Recognizing the slow progress to the top, it is no wonder that many achievement-oriented women opt out of corporations to run their own firms, where success is more a matter of one's own abilities and hard work.

Another factor that can influence women in the choice of an entrepreneurial career is the desire to combine career aspirations and the role of wife/mother/caretaker. A recent study by the Small Business Administration found that women are more likely than men to start a business as a means to achieve work–family balance. Women entrepreneurs appear to work fewer hours and invest less time in the development of their businesses than men. Men may work more hours because their goal is usually to earn money and because they face fewer demands for their time. Women's goal is usually to support themselves financially while managing other, nonwork demands. Women tend to devote more hours to caring for children, parents, and the household.[71] Other studies found a significant motivator for many young women's choice of an entrepreneurial career was to escape the double shift of being primarily responsible for the household while managing a full corporate workload.[72] In this sense, the less restrictive entrepreneurial career offers a greater opportunity for flexibility in scheduling work hours, and work location, thus allowing more time for family demands.

Not surprisingly, women entrepreneurs are comparatively more likely than men to choose to work part-time because they want to accommodate their work and caretaker roles simultaneously. Of course, combining entrepreneurship with extensive family time can have a downside in that work–family conflict and time demands may diminish the success of the enterprise. Research has noted the need to resolve the time-related conflicts brought on by family demands in order for female-owned firms to be successful. It has been cautioned that work–family conflict, a real concern for the woman entrepreneur, can be particularly troublesome in the lean initial years in the life of the firm.[73]

Thus, it appears that the relationship between entrepreneurship and family obligations is paradoxical. On the one hand, the generally greater personal freedom offered by entrepreneurship can allow individuals flexibility in allotting time to family commitments. But on the other hand, entrepreneurial success usually carries with it escalating demands that can diminish the amount of time the entrepreneur can spend with his or her family. Yet, some evidence suggests that women entrepreneurs are more satisfied with their careers than are men.[74] It may be that those woman entrepreneurs who resolve work–family conflict make choices on the relative importance of the different spheres of their lives and are satisfied with those choices.

Are there limiting factors in the career choices of female entrepreneurs?

As we discussed in Chapter 6, women generally tend to make career choices and select occupations from a narrower range of alternatives than do men. Consistent with this view, it has been found that women tend to have a lower overall preference for entrepreneurship than men, and women entrepreneurs tend to be concentrated in mainly retail and personal service firms and are less likely to be in manufacturing and high technology. Women start businesses that are less growth oriented and less driven by opportunity. According to some researchers, women tend to work in certain occupations and industries because they are more socially acceptable for women.[75]

Recent statistics support both the growth in the number of female entrepreneurs and their limited choice of industry. From 1976 to 2002, the percentage of self-employed women increased nearly 12 percentage points, from 26.8 percent to 38.6 percent.[76] Statistics from a 2002 U.S. Census Bureau report indicate that of the approximately 6.5 million female-owned businesses that existed at that time, approximately 30 percent were service organizations, 15 percent were in retail trade, 16 percent were in the health care and social assistance sector, and 8 percent were in real estate. However, women-owned businesses in "nontraditional" business sectors remained few, with about 3 percent in construction and 3 percent in mining and manufacturing.[77]

The reasons for limited entrepreneurial career choices among women are varied. It has been suggested that cultural conditioning, social learning, a lack of encouragement and role models, and low self-confidence can channel women away from an entrepreneurial career. On average, women start businesses that are smaller than those started by men. The smaller scale may be due to low self-confidence or the lack of access to larger-scale business opportunities and the financial resources necessary to develop them. Women are also more likely to set limits beyond which they do not want to expand their businesses to ensure that they do not adversely affect their family and personal lives. Social norms about the role of women, the shortage of female role models, and the greater household burdens faced by women lead female entrepreneurs to face more start-up problems.[78] Among female entrepreneurs, the most consistently noted difficulties include access to credit, inability to delegate responsibility and authority to subordinates, and conflicts between work and family/personal lives.[79]

Regardless of the potentially limiting factors that they face, female entrepreneurs generally possess a number of positive qualities. These qualities include high energy levels, skill in influencing others and gaining consensus, and a high degree of pragmatism in their business decisions.[80] Most women who pursue entrepreneurial careers seek challenge and the opportunity for self-determination.[81] Women find job and professional satisfaction in running their own businesses, and place great importance on relationships in their workplaces.[82]

As this chapter has discussed, all current and aspiring entrepreneurs face a variety of challenges, limitations, and difficulties in launching and operating their businesses. However, it appears that female entrepreneurs must confront a unique set of hurdles primarily because of societal influence and cultural conditioning. Fortunately, as more and more women become successful entrepreneurs, it is expected that the identified limitations and barriers will diminish.

Minority Entrepreneurs

Even with the burgeoning interest in entrepreneurial activity overall, only a limited amount of research attention has been given to the characteristics and experiences of minority entrepreneurs. This fact is surprising given the significant growth in minority-owned businesses overall and as a percentage of all companies. According to data from the U.S. Census Bureau, in 2002, 18 percent of American businesses were owned by minorities, totaling approximately 4.1 million businesses.[83] This number is more than double the number of minority-owned businesses in 1992 (1.97 million businesses), and 37 percent higher than in 1997 (3 million businesses).[84] In 2002, minorities owned nearly 18 percent of all businesses, up from 14.4 percent in 1997 and 11.4 percent in 1992. In 2002, Hispanics, African Americans, and Asian Americans owned 7 percent, 5 percent, and 5 percent, respectively, of all U.S. businesses, compared with 4 percent, 4 percent, and 3 percent, respectively, in 1992.

Similar to those owned by female entrepreneurs, minority-owned firms tend to be concentrated in service and retail trade businesses, with approximately 35 percent of minority-owned firms in the service sector, 17 percent in retail trade, 28 percent in the health care and social assistance sector, and 9 percent in real estate. In contrast, minority-owned firms in "nontraditional" business sectors remains low, with about 5 percent in construction and 13 percent in mining and manufacturing.[85]

The personality characteristics and motivations of minority entrepreneurs are similar to those of nonminorities. Several researchers have found the need for achievement to be the primary motivator among minority owners for starting their own firm. Other related factors such as independence, being one's own boss, and financial success were also rated as important motivators among minority business owners. In terms of background and environmental factors, minority role models and family role models are influential for people of color when starting a business and gaining access to key markets.[86] For many minority entrepreneurs, extensive support can come from mutual-benefit associations that are centered on racial or ethnic ties. Strong ethnic networks can provide aid in the form of venture capital, lines of credit, market and/or product information, a ready customer base, training opportunities, and the regulation of competition. Minorities often use their own personal savings, or that of family and friends, to start their businesses.[87] Many groups have followed this model of strong ethnic solidarity and assistance to achieve entrepreneurial success.

As with female entrepreneurs, one of the most important factors that lead people of color into entrepreneurial careers is treatment discrimination and bias in the corporate business environment. Indeed, real and perceived closure of upper-level management positions to minority employees can cause frustration and a reduced level of commitment to the corporation. Thus, the lack of access in the corporate world can be a motivator in the undertaking of an entrepreneurial career. Consider the following example:

> Roberta has been a top real estate executive at a large fast food franchiser for the past 15 years. Starting at the lowest levels of the managerial hierarchy after college, she rose to her current level through her talent and a great deal of hard work. In fact, Roberta has been so involved in her job that she has had little to no personal life.
>
> Roberta's personnel evaluations are always excellent, and she has been told that the next high-level job to open up will be hers. However, Roberta realizes that she has been in her current job for the past two years, and recently one of her white male counterparts received the promotion to Chief Operating Officer that she was expecting to receive. When she inquired as to why she was not even offered an interview for the job, Roberta was told that her counterpart had more experience and had a better working relationship with the CEO. Roberta was angered by these comments. She had been the one to put this fast food chain literally "on the map" by expanding the operation on the east coast over the last 10 years. And while she was rewarded financially for her efforts, she wanted to receive the position for which she had worked so hard.
>
> Roberta began to think that her talents might be better suited if she ran her own company. There are many discount drug chains, food stores, and other retail outlets that need to negotiate real estate deals throughout the east coast. Roberta knew the territory and had contacts in every state. She had been a contract negotiator many times, and she enjoyed the thrill those negotiations entailed. Roberta began considering a career as a freelance real estate negotiator, and looking for the opportunity to pursue such a career as an entrepreneur.

In total, it appears that minority entrepreneurs possess personality characteristics and face demands and concerns that are similar to those of entrepreneurs in general. Unfortunately, minority entrepreneurs also face additional challenges that must be overcome, including built-in racism and bias, possibly a singular focus on their own ethnic customer base, an inability to attract a larger customer base, possibly less business experience and availability of financing, and other barriers to business establishment and success. As with female entrepreneurs, the elimination of these barriers can be accelerated through greater self-determination among current and future minority entrepreneurs, combined with increased social and educational support for minority enterprises.[88] It must be recognized that minority entrepreneurs not only play a growing and increasingly important role in the economic vitality of the world's economy as a whole, but also are crucial to the economic development of many growing communities across the United States.

SELECTING AND MANAGING THE ENTREPRENEURIAL CAREER

Throughout this book we have underscored the need for a systematic and informed approach to career management. Selection of an entrepreneurial career, while admittedly somewhat different from the choice of an organizational career, should still be based on a thorough analysis of personal desires and characteristics as well as a detailed review of conditions and expectations in the work environment. In addition, the setting of entrepreneurial career goals and the establishment of related career strategies should be a function of the information gained from the assessment of personal desires and environmental conditions. Throughout one's entrepreneurial career, regular reappraisal should occur regarding whether key expectations and goals are being fulfilled. Let us consider each of these steps in more detail.

Self-Assessment. In Chapter 4 we discussed the view that self-awareness is critical in choosing career goals that are compatible with one's interests, values, and lifestyle preferences. Previously discussed assessment instruments, such as the Strong Interest Inventory, have separate categories that indicate whether an entrepreneurial self-concept or theme is present. As one example, Edgar Schein notes that the major goal of the entrepreneurial/creativity career anchor is to create something new, involving such demands as overcoming obstacles, running risks, and achievement. People with this anchor want the freedom to build and operate their own organization in their own way.[89] This description closely parallels the typology of the entrepreneur that we advanced earlier in the chapter.

In addition to gaining insight into the more personal issues of one's self-concept and psychological characteristics, aspiring entrepreneurs also need to ask themselves more fundamental questions concerning business success. The following lists a number of these questions:[90]

- Is my business idea good enough?
- Do I have the management skills needed to succeed?
- How important is money to me?
- Can I live with the risk of owning my own business?
- What will be my family's reaction to my becoming an entrepreneur?

The interlocking nature of the entrepreneur's career and the business itself dictates that the individual's assessment of interests, needs, and chances for success becomes an assessment of the business's interests, needs, and chances for success.

Assessment of the Work Environment. As with the gathering of self-information, the accumulation of knowledge about the work environment takes on a broader meaning for the aspiring entrepreneur. Thus, a personal analysis of conditions in the business environment becomes a wider assessment of expected conditions that one's hypothetical company would face. In this sense the individual's assessment of the work environment can represent an environmental analysis for the company, covering expectations on financing and economic conditions, changes in demographics, market preferences, legal and regulatory issues, technological advancements, and a host of other factors. The choice of an entrepreneurial career, and the selection of the type of business to own, should take into account the knowledge gained through this environmental review.

Setting Career Goals. Individuals who see themselves in an entrepreneurial career should set career goals that reflect this aspiration. Operational goals for an entrepreneurial career would likely indicate expectations for personal success and achievement of the firm. In this way, personal career goals and business objectives intersect. But entrepreneurial career goals can also be conceptual, reflecting one's significant values and the intrinsic enjoyment gained from the entrepreneurial experience.

Many times, entrepreneurs take a circuitous route to business ownership. As with any career selection, it may take a relatively long period of time to fully understand one's likes and dislikes, interests, special talents, and aspirations. Also, the realities of the business environment may change rapidly, or may become apparent only after several years of experience. The experiences of many successful businesspeople often reflect the trial-and-error approach. An example is Joseph Segel, founder of QVC, the Franklin Mint, and over 20 other companies.[91]

Another well-known example of the trial-and-error route to an entrepreneurial career is John Paul Jones DeJoria. As chairman of the John Paul Mitchell Systems company, Mr. DeJoria is a highly successful entrepreneur. But his route to the chairmanship of the Beverly Hills–based maker of hair care products and beauty aids was certainly not routine. From 1964, when he got out of the Navy, to 1980, when he cofounded the John Paul Mitchell Systems company, Mr. DeJoria held (and then was fired from or quit) a long list of sales jobs. He began his career working for such large corporations as Savin and Time, but didn't last in either job because he didn't see eye to eye with either company's management. Indeed, he quit Savin because he disliked wearing neckties on his sales calls. After his time with the large corporations, Mr. DeJoria became a door-to-door salesperson, selling such products as life insurance, encyclopedias, and medical linens. In 1971, Mr. DeJoria landed a job with Redken Laboratories, selling shampoo through hair salons, but left after a short period. He held additional jobs in the beauty business but didn't last in any of them. At one organization, his commission schedule had him making more money than the person who owned the company. Finally, in 1980, Mr. DeJoria came to the conclusion that the only boss for whom he could work was himself. That year he teamed with a Scottish hairdresser named Paul Mitchell to found the John Paul Mitchell Systems company. Working in a more free-wheeling environment of self-determination, he flourished. His company experienced many consecutive years of double-digit sales increases. Today, the privately held John Paul Mitchell Systems has annual salon retail sales approaching $1 billion, and the company produces over 90 products. These products are sold through 25 distributors within the United States to approximately 90,000 hair salons and schools. Globally, the company works with distributors in 75 countries that supply thousands of hair salons. Even though he has received lucrative offers from public corporations to buy John Paul Mitchell Systems, Mr. DeJoria refuses to sell. He has also branched out into other successful entrepreneurial ventures, including nightclubs, liquor, energy, a motorcycle dealership, and grooming products for pets. Mr. DeJoria revels in his celebrity status and enjoys the lifestyle that successful entrepreneurship allows. After years of struggle and floundering, John Paul Jones DeJoria was able to achieve success and satisfaction in an entrepreneurial career.[92]

Development of Career Strategies. Some of the career strategies that we discussed in Chapter 5 do not necessarily have direct relevance to the entrepreneurial career. For example, such strategies as image building and organizational politics would most likely be unnecessary for the entrepreneur. More appropriately, the entrepreneur's career strategies would reflect the strategies of the company, such as an expansion of the product line or perhaps a move into another geographic market. Other strategies that we discussed are appropriate for the entrepreneur. Competency in one's job (in this case as a business owner), extended work involvement, skill development, and opportunity development would all be relevant career strategies for the entrepreneur. Additional strategies that could have instrumental value include the development of business relationships with other firms, locating access to capital and financing sources, and the utilization of social networks and support groups.

Career Appraisal. Once an entrepreneurial career is undertaken, regular reappraisal should occur. Assessing one's career accomplishments in light of established goals and strategies could lead to the conclusion that no changes are necessary, or that some fine-tuning is required, or that wholesale alterations in career goals and strategies are mandatory. For the entrepreneur, feedback on career progress can be immediate and crystal clear, since progress in the business venture should track closely with the success of the entrepreneur's career. Often, but not always, failure of the business portends a lack of achievement in meeting the entrepreneur's career goals, especially if the career goals are focused on the success and accomplishment of the enterprise. Of course, if one's career goals or strategies are centered on gaining hands-on business experience or learning about financing options, then the time in the entrepreneurial career is well spent, regardless of the success of the firm. Further, the entrepreneur should assess the effect that business ownership has (either positively or negatively) on family responsibilities. In any case, the entrepreneur should periodically reappraise his or her career to see if important needs are being met. If they are not, then changes may be warranted–perhaps even leaving the world of entrepreneurship!

It is interesting to note that research shows only limited differences between entrepreneurs and salaried organizational members in terms of job attitudes and career outcomes. Not surprisingly, a study found the self-employed valued autonomy more than organizational employees did. Self-employed individuals also report significantly higher levels of satisfaction with job challenge, supporting the view that entrepreneurs may experience greater degrees of stimulation and vibrancy in their lives brought on by the constant demands of the company. However, there were essentially no differences between entrepreneurs and salaried employees for such outcomes as job and life satisfaction, satisfaction with free time, professional commitment, degree of comfort at work, satisfaction with financial rewards, satisfaction with coworkers, and the number of psychosomatic complaints.[93]

In summary, we believe that the process of managing the entrepreneurial career is essentially the same as that for an organizational career. The aspiring (and current) entrepreneur needs to attain a thorough understanding of self and the work environment, set realistic and informed career goals, develop career strategies to fulfill these goals, and regularly reappraise progress and personal fulfillment.

SUMMARY

The past several decades have seen a worldwide explosion of interest in entrepreneurial careers. Political changes, economic turbulence, corporate restructuring and downsizing, employee discontent with life in a large corporation, and a host of other factors are all influencing the expansion of entrepreneurship.

This chapter explored several topics relevant to the entrepreneurial career. Prior definitions of entrepreneurship have focused on the themes of creativity, innovation, and risk-taking propensity. Taking these themes into account, we defined entrepreneurship as managing a business of one's own that requires personal sacrifice, creativity, and risk taking, to provide an innovative new product or service to the market.

Becoming an entrepreneur means experiencing a career that is quite different from the traditional organization-based notion. The entrepreneurial career is marked by extensive personal commitment to the success of the firm, acceptance of lower degrees of structure and predictability, an orientation toward action and decisiveness, the simultaneous performance of multiple roles, and a willingness to accept risk. Because of these distinctive features, entrepreneurs find substantial challenge and stimulation in their work, but also must confront the precarious nature of business ownership.

Past research has questioned whether the selection of an entrepreneurial career is more a function of personal traits and characteristics, or a product of environmental influence, or perhaps a combination of both. Such

(Continued)

(Continued)

personal factors as the need for autonomy and independence, the need for achievement, an internal locus of control, a tolerance for ambiguity, a risk-taking propensity, an entrepreneurial self-concept, and various demographic/background factors have been found to have a positive influence on the choice of an entrepreneurial career. Of course, these same characteristics are present among many successful people, entrepreneurs and non-entrepreneurs alike. But they do give a fairly distinct picture of the common traits that constitute a "typical" profile of the entrepreneur.

In addition to personality characteristics, a number of environmental conditions can work to direct people toward an entrepreneurial career. In this chapter we concentrated on three such factors—job loss, work dissatisfaction, and favorable business conditions. We discussed how a passion for a particular product or service, and the need for bridge employment, can be strong motivators in the undertaking of business ownership. We also reviewed how the presence of role models and/or mentors has been shown to have a positive effect on the pursuit of entrepreneurship. Having a successful entrepreneurial role model, whether it is parents, relatives, or friends in the community, can often encourage entrepreneurial effort.

The national and worldwide surge in entrepreneurial activity has brought with it the establishment of social networks and alliances, training and education programs, Web sites, and publications that are all designed to assist the aspiring and existing entrepreneur to deal with the challenges of business ownership and provide a realistic preview of what can be expected from the entrepreneurial career.

In line with the general trend, entrepreneurial activity among females and minorities has grown considerably during the past three decades. While the personal motivations and background factors of female and minority entrepreneurs are consistent with entrepreneurs in total, they must also confront and overcome a variety of unique challenges. These include built-in discrimination and bias, social learning, cultural conditioning and lack of financial capital that may discourage entrepreneurial activity, lower self-efficacy regarding entrepreneurship, and, in the case of women, additional role demands regarding family commitments.

As with any career choice, the decision to become an entrepreneur should follow the career management model as outlined in this book. Specifically, entrepreneurial career goals should be based on a thorough understanding of individual interests, talents, values, and preferences, as well as information on the work environment. The entrepreneur should then set career strategies that will help achieve the established career goals. Finally, career reappraisal should be conducted regularly to ensure that relevant needs and expectations are being met.

ASSIGNMENT

Interview someone who owns his or her own business. Determine the factors that led this person into an entrepreneurial career. How successful is the person's enterprise? To what factors does he or she attribute this level of success? What are the rewards and stresses the person experiences in his or her entrepreneurial career? If the individual is a woman or person of color, what hurdles did she or he experience in the start-up of the business?

DISCUSSION QUESTIONS

1. Do you think you would be successful and happy as an entrepreneur? Why or why not?

2. Do you believe that there is a "typical" entrepreneurial personality? Why or why not?

3. How does the entrepreneurial career differ from an organizational one? How do these differences influence the setting of career strategies among entrepreneurs?

4. How can social learning and cultural conditioning influence the choice of an entrepreneurial career? What role do one's parents play in the choice?

5. What special career challenges do women and minority entrepreneurs face in launching and operating their businesses? What actions can women and people of color take to overcome these challenges?

6. What types of social support are available to current and aspiring entrepreneurs? How do colleges and universities contribute to the level of entrepreneurship across the country?

CHAPTER 12 CASE

Dave the Aspiring Executive (Part B)

At the conclusion of Chapter 11 we provided Part A of this case. If you haven't done so already, please read Part A of this case before reading Part B. At the end of Part A, Dave had just met with the Vice President of Human Resources of Xtel Corporation concerning his chances for future advancement with the company. The clear message he received was that his career at Xtel was in a holding pattern. Dave concluded it was time for a change. (Remember, Xtel is a fictitious name and should not be confused with any real company.)

While in graduate school, Dave had become friendly with a fellow student who was interested in developing and marketing software that could be used to help control production operations. Dave had been intrigued with the prospects for the software, especially since he saw its potential application at Xtel Corporation. Dave decided to give his friend a call to see what progress she had made. Dave also sought the advice of one of his neighbors who had experience in financing business start-ups. Working part-time on nights and weekends, Dave and his partners were able to finalize the software and put together a realistic business plan. They sought and received financing for their venture from a local commercial bank. Once they lined up their first client, Dave felt confident enough to resign from his position at Xtel Corporation. The resignation was tendered with mixed emotions. He felt a sense of gratitude and loyalty to Xtel for the financial support they had given him, but he was also disturbed by the treatment he received during the latter part of his career.

(Continued)

(Continued)

In any event, Dave is enthusiastic about his prospects as an entrepreneur. He is confident that he and his partners have tapped into a potentially lucrative market. He is strongly motivated to make the venture succeed and achieve financial security for his family.

Case Analysis Questions

1. Given his many years in an organizational career with a large corporation, do you think that Dave will be in for a rude awakening now that he has become an entrepreneur? Why or why not? What differences in experiences do you think he will encounter in his entrepreneurial career as opposed to his organizational career?

2. What qualities does Dave have that will help him in his entrepreneurial venture? Does Dave have any shortcomings that might limit his success as an entrepreneur?

3. Now that Dave has embarked on an entrepreneurial career, to whom should he turn for personal and professional support, advice, and assistance?

Career Management in Work Organizations

The Role of Strategic Human Resource Management Systems in Career Management

The dynamic and competitive environment faced by nearly all businesses requires that organizations be flexible and innovative to ensure their survival. The contingency view of organizational management holds that a company's strategic direction, structure, internal systems, culture, and leadership approaches should be consistent with the requirements and challenges of the external environment and the expectations of multiple stakeholders in the organization.[1] Early views of human resource management (HRM) systems concentrated primarily on functional activities such as recruiting, training, and personnel benefits. Today the role of HRM is strategic, with plans and initiatives involving human resources tied directly to the organization's strategic plans as a means to gain competitive advantage.[2] Indeed, a fit between a firm's HRM strategy and its business strategy is associated with the effectiveness of HRM practices, labor productivity, and the firm's success.[3] Several studies have found that organizations that integrate HRM systems with their strategic direction display lower turnover and increased levels of productivity, organizational commitment, job satisfaction, and corporate financial performance.[4]

Therefore, HRM systems, including workforce planning and staffing procedures, performance management and reward systems, career management and diversity programs, and training and development efforts, need to be consistent with the strategic plans of the firm. For example, a company with strong growth objectives requires a steady supply of qualified, motivated, and talented human resources to support the business expansion, and its human resource and career management systems should reflect this corporate strategy. In the case of a firm whose strategic direction includes downsizing and the shedding of businesses, the HRM system and related career programs may be more concerned with outplacement, helping employees identify their interests and career goals, and assisting them with the process of finding a new job.

In this chapter, we discuss a model of an integrated strategic HRM system that depicts how career management is embedded in this system to improve overall organizational effectiveness. We describe the key functional human resource areas and how career management is rooted in these activities, provide examples of corporate programs that position their human resource systems to support individual career development, and discuss how a firm's HRM systems can support its organizational strategic plans as well as individual employee development.

INTEGRATION OF CAREER MANAGEMENT WITHIN STRATEGIC HRM SYSTEMS

HRM systems represent the organization's mechanisms for forecasting its human resource needs and for recruiting, selecting, training, developing, appraising, promoting, rewarding, and communicating to its people. Career management and human resource systems are linked or integrated to the extent to which they help each other meet individual and organizational needs. To be most effective, career management programs need to be supported by all human resource functions. Many researchers have called for human resource managers to create a model that incorporates career management, career development, and performance management processes within the confines of the corporate human resource strategy.[5]

Ralph Christenson, a former Vice President of Human Resources at Hallmark Cards, developed a comprehensive model of a strategic HRM system that weaves various functions of career management throughout its five fundamental components.[6] As shown in Exhibit 13.1, the five fundamental components for managing talent, as shown within the oval, are Workforce Planning and Staffing, Learning and Development, Performance Management, Employee Relations, and Organizational Development. Christenson notes that Diversity is an important function that cuts across all others, and hence is shown as a building block of the five principal functions. Other building blocks include the various strategic and tactical actions that are necessary components of the work of the human resource professional.

These fundamental HRM components dovetail with the broader strategies undertaken by an organization. The strategic view of human resources includes the notion that talent is the engine that creates all organizational value. Given that perspective, human resources need to be directly connected to the business strategy so that customer needs can be met.[7] Therefore, the firm's human resources need to be linked to the firm's core competencies, its vision, strategies, priorities, and goals. Similarly, the firm's vision and strategies are informed by the business environment (e.g., customers, industry competitors, governmental regulations, and local and global economies) within which it operates. The relationship among these components is influenced by factors both within and outside the firm, and the

EXHIBIT 13.1   Strategic Human Resource Framework

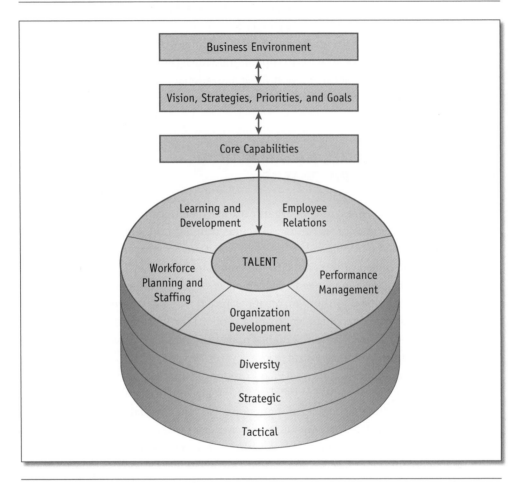

SOURCE: Adapted from Christensen, R. (2006). *Roadmap to strategic HR: Turning a great idea into a business reality* (p. 112). New York: AMACOM.

HR professional needs to understand and act within this framework to supply appropriate personnel who can optimize organizational performance. In fact, some researchers have suggested that human resource executives redirect their attention from internal staffing needs to the requirements of external stakeholders.[8] This shift allows the focus to move from the firm's human resource plans being developed in a vacuum to the development of a human resource strategy that emphasizes customer input. Thus, customer needs, organizational plans, and unique competencies determine whom the firm employs and how they are developed. As Christenson states, "Everything that the HR organization does should be focused on leveraging those human competencies to create capabilities that allow the organization to win with its strategy in the marketplace."[9] In this sense, Christenson's model focuses on leveraging the firm's human talent for competitive advantage.

STRATEGIC HUMAN RESOURCE PROCESSES

In the following sections we consider four of the main functions of Christenson's model that are directly associated with individual and organizational career management: Workforce Planning and Staffing, Learning and Development, Performance Management, and Employee Relations. Table 13.1 identifies each of the four major functions as well as the related tasks that are associated with human resource development and career management. Examples of corporate human resource systems that support individual career development are also offered.

TABLE 13.1 The Functional Work of Strategic Human Resource Management

Function	Workforce Planning and Staffing	Learning and Development	Performance Management and Rewards	Employee Relations
Key Human Resource Management Activities	*Workforce Planning:* • Future workforce demands • Staffing plans • Transitions plans *Staffing:* • Recruiting • College relations	• Employee development • Succession planning • Orientation programs • Competency development • Leadership development • New employee orientation	• Performance objectives and measures • Benefits programs • Human resource information systems (HRIS)	• Coaching and counseling • Work–life programs • Employee morale

Workforce Planning and Staffing

This function focuses on fulfilling the current staffing needs of the organization and projecting future requirements. Both current and future assessments are based on the strategic needs of the firm. Workforce planning and staffing also include processes whereby the firm attracts, integrates, and retains talent. We will discuss several processes important to workforce planning and staffing, specifically forecasting future workforce demands, staffing and transition plans, recruiting, and college relations.

Forecasting Future Workplace Demands. Once a firm has determined its strategic direction, it must assess the level and type of human resources needed to fulfill strategic expectations. As Manuel London states, "[H]uman resource planning requires analyzing employees' current skills, the skill levels needed by the business in the future, and the availability of those needed skills in the internal and external labor market."[10] If talent is really the engine that creates value, then identifying and hiring the right talent is the essence of strategic human resource management.

A number of factors are relevant to human resource forecasting, including an external environmental forecast (industry trends, demographics, and external workforce supply), an internal capabilities analysis (are the necessary skill sets available), and finally a future workforce forecast. The workforce forecast would include an analysis of the number and types of jobs available, the skills required, and a gap analysis that would indicate how the firm would move from the current workforce to a future workforce.[11] Once the supply of workers is identified, the level of required training is specified and the type of organizational structure and reporting relationships are articulated.

In determining the types of resources needed, organizations have a basic choice of selecting (or "buying") their personnel from the external labor market or developing (or "making") their personnel from the internal labor market. The buy or make decision is one that virtually all organizations face. The organizational decision as to whether selection or development is the appropriate strategy depends on the availability and accessibility of people with the right skills in the external labor market compared to the feasibility of developing current employees.[12] It must be stressed that depending exclusively on either the external or the internal labor pool can create problems. Hiring solely from external labor markets reduces opportunities for existing employees and thus weakens their commitment to the organization, whereas hiring exclusively from within may limit the number of fresh ideas brought into the organization and restrict an organization's ability to move rapidly in a different strategic direction.[13] While some experts have suggested a specific ratio (e.g., four to one) of internal to external hiring, Peter Cappelli has provided a number of questions that organizations must answer (e.g., for how long will the organization need the talent? how essential is it for the organization to maintain its existing culture?) to determine the appropriate mix of buying and making talent.[14]

Organizational Staffing. If a firm has determined that the internal system cannot fully supply the required talent, selection from the external labor market is necessary. It has been suggested that staffing is a critical management function because the quality of the people hired by the organization is the single greatest determinant of the firm's effectiveness. In effect, staffing allows a company to buy its needed competencies from outside the organization.[15]

In Chapter 6, we discussed organizational selection and staffing from the individual's perspective, covering such topics as interviewing, recruitment, and choice of job and organization. When organizations go through the staffing process many of the steps are the same, albeit from a different perspective. As a first step, the organization determines, through the human resource forecasting process, the number and types of employees it needs to hire.

The number of required employees is dictated by expected expansion and related resource needs, as well as actual and expected turnover among existing staff at all levels and in all functions within the company. The type of employee needed is related to the skill level, professional experience, and abilities required by the jobs to be filled. It is obvious that openings in entry-level positions would require a different set of skills and experiences than senior-level positions.

Once the number and type of resources are determined, or as open positions arise through turnover and internal transfer, the organization then has several options in terms of the actual hiring approach to be used. College recruiting, unsolicited inquiries, advertisements, executive search firms, internal staffing/placement, postings on the company's Web site, and personal recommendations or nominations are various ways for job candidates to become known to a hiring company.

After a pool of candidates is identified, the next step in the staffing process normally is the interview. Usually, the interviewee will first meet with a representative of the firm's human resource department who will conduct a general screening. Next, the candidate will be interviewed by one or more members of the hiring department. Once the interviewing phase is complete, the hiring area assesses all the candidates, rank orders from most to least qualified, and then makes its offers. These basic steps are followed regardless of the level in the organization that is being filled.

David Ulrich and Dave Lake offer a number of key factors to consider in the external sourcing of job candidates.[16] The organization needs to consider the degree of professional experience that is required. In particular, it must review the trade-off between hiring at the entry level, where candidates usually lack extensive experience but are more malleable in terms of new work ideas and approaches, versus hiring at a higher level, where candidates usually have more experience but could be less flexible or adaptive in reaction to new methods. Ulrich and Lake suggest that companies expand the pool of talent that is considered. Companies should pay particular attention to achieving diversity in their hiring to meet the challenge of the global marketplace. Serious consideration of multiple candidates and the use of multiple interviews will allow hiring managers to receive information from a variety of sources when interviewing candidates.

In addition to the influence of the firm's strategic plan, environmental trends and general business conditions also affect staffing from the external market. Factors such as the available labor force, population demographics, social trends, economic conditions, government regulations, and legislative actions may all influence the type and quality of potential employees who are available to the corporation. Downsizings and reorganizations have also changed the available labor market, in most cases creating a greater employee pool. Yet at the same time, these transitioned workers may not have the necessary skills for new jobs made available by changing trends (e.g., technological innovations).

Hence, honest self-appraisal and "re-skilling" may be necessary for these workers to find their way back into gainful employment.[17]

Transition Plans. One of the great tests of the human resource function, and the leadership of the firm, is to determine how employees should be transitioned into different jobs, or out of the company entirely, when the strategy requires changes in the workforce. Factors like a weak economy or excess human resources may necessitate the need for downsizing. Changes in technology or business strategy may also require different skills in the workforce. All of these situations create financial consequences to the organization and its human resources.[18] The organization must respond in a way that delicately addresses both its financial condition and employee morale.

Transitions may take the form of redeploying human resources.[19] Redeployment is an option that may be used for two basic reasons: to improve the skill levels and broaden the experiences of certain personnel and to respond strategically to changing business conditions. In the former case, the movement of employees is a planned developmental technique to gain more seasoned staff. For example, a company with extensive international interests may want its fast track employees to take one or more tours of duty in overseas operations so that they gain a multinational perspective. In the latter case, redeployment is used as a strategic response to a shift in business conditions resulting from internal or external factors. For example, the closing of a plant in one geographic location to take advantage of a better business climate in another geographic area is a strategic decision that may necessitate the redistribution (and relocation) of key staff.

When business conditions call for drastic action, organizations may need to eliminate individual positions or whole units to improve competitiveness. From the organization's view, displacing staff is normally a difficult decision, one that some companies try to avoid at all cost. For example, 3M has implemented assistance services that identify employees who are in transition to help them develop the career skills required to investigate other areas within 3M or jobs outside the company. In addition, 3M has an internal Web site that advertises current positions for which transitioned employees can self-nominate.[20] In keeping with their traditions and founding values, IBM and Hewlett-Packard have gone to great lengths to avoid staff layoffs. Both companies have tried to hold to that credo even during difficult times. Although IBM and Hewlett-Packard have faced business contractions, they have attempted to minimize layoffs by using such techniques as internal transfers, lateral and downward shifts, shortened workweeks, and early retirement.[21] All organizations must recognize the disruptions of human life and the threat to self-esteem that redeployment and displacements can cause. To state the obvious, unnecessary or poorly planned transitions are not only inefficient, but can lead to alienated, unproductive workers.

Recruiting. Chapter 6 discussed the tendency of many employers to present themselves in an overly favorable light during the recruitment process. It was noted that job candidates who develop unrealistic expectations are likely to experience "reality shock" upon entering the organization. This can contribute to employee dissatisfaction and turnover. Realistic recruitment, where candidates receive a balanced, accurate view of the prospective job and the organization, is designed to reduce levels of reality shock, dissatisfaction, and turnover.[22] The following is a description of a program that attempts to create a realistic recruitment process both for the recruit and the organization.

> The Vanguard Group, one of the world's largest investment management companies, faces a challenge of maintaining a staff of employees who understand their jobs, the company and its culture, and the fast-paced market within which the company works. While the company understands that most external job candidates are entertaining multiple job offers, it expects recruiters to accurately portray the job opportunities within the organization. Vanguard also recognizes the need for efficiency in the hiring process—from initial contact with the candidate to the extension of an offer.
>
> Vanguard's key to recruiting success is the development of interview teams that work with the manager making the hiring decision. The manager is ultimately responsible for the new hire, and therefore is asked to put together a customized interview team based on the position for which the company is recruiting. The interview team normally is composed of employees with the most direct knowledge about the position and who can provide multiple perspectives regarding the job. Job candidates are introduced to the interview team and are encouraged to use the team as a mechanism to learn about the job. Experience shows that job candidates learn more about the open position from the team than they would from the hiring manager alone. The team can also learn a lot about the candidate and whether the recruit will fit the job description and, more broadly, Vanguard's culture. Vanguard's goal is to select recruits the team agrees will be a good fit for the company. In consultation with the interview team, this recruiting process permits the hiring manager to make a quick offer. Vanguard believes this process to be efficient and allows for the hiring of the best people ahead of the competition.[23]

Case interviews and behavioral event interviews are two methods that attempt to create a realistic situation in which the candidate is asked to respond. In a case interview, applicants are presented with a business issue facing a company and are required to analyze the situation and propose a solution to the problem. In a behavioral event interview, applicants are asked to think back to a particular challenge they faced in a prior job and describe how they handled the situation. The content, creativity, deductive reasoning, and commonsense nature of the responses can indicate to recruiters the candidate's ability to perform in a given work environment. Companies such as J. P. Morgan and Microsoft have also become famous for the "wacky" questions they ask recruits. Microsoft's two most famous questions are "How much water flows through the Mississippi each day?" and "How many tennis balls are there in the U.S.?" These questions may be interspersed with questions based on work-related scenarios that inquire about the recruit's behavior in a given situation, for example, "A client wants to do such and such . . . What do you do?"[24]

Interview techniques such as these may appear at first to provide the interviewer with more information than the interviewee. However, these techniques, particularly behavioral event interviews, provide recruits with the opportunity to present their values and also give them the ability to learn more about the values and culture of the organization. As indicated in the examples given above, the recruit is permitted to ask questions about the type of customers with whom the position would interface, how the company maintains customer satisfaction, and finally about the overlap between departments that serve a particular customer (e.g., customer service, accounting, credit). This information can clarify the relationships the company has with its clientele, how departments interact to serve the customer, and can provide the candidate with a framework to decide if this is the type of company for which he or she could work.

In addition, organizations can encourage employees to refer friends, family members, and acquaintances for upcoming job postings. Employee referrals can be a particularly successful way to recruit new employees because the employees are often knowledgeable about the job, department, work group, and company, and individuals are likely to trust and understand what their friends and colleagues tell them about potential job opportunities. Companies also benefit because employee referrals tend to yield motivated workers who fit well in the work environment. The downside of using employee referrals exclusively is that these sources may present some diversity implications if they tend to reach few members of minority groups.[25]

While there are a variety of techniques that may be used for offering candidates realistic recruitment, the overarching purpose is to give accurate information about the company and the posted job. Research suggests that realistic recruiting aids in organizational attractiveness, commitment, and retention.[26] The presentation of realistic information on jobs and careers to candidates and employees remains a positive approach to integrating individual and organizational needs.

College Relations and Anticipatory Socialization. Chapters 6 and 7 described the process by which individuals enter work organizations and become socialized into their new work roles. It was noted that anticipatory socialization begins even before the newcomer joins the organization on a full-time basis. During this stage, values and talents are clarified and expectations are formed. One of the major tasks of this stage is the development of accurate, realistic expectations about one's chosen career field, and, more generally, about the world of work. In addition, anticipatory socialization practices can help companies gain a positive recruiting image and ensure an available pool of talented newcomers. The most well-known of the anticipatory socialization programs—internships and cooperative educational experiences—allow companies to establish relationships with colleges and universities and provide prospective employees with the chance to test out the prospective employer.

A number of large companies, including Aetna Life Insurance Co., Allstate Insurance Co., Boeing Co., Kodak, Hewlett-Packard, and Procter & Gamble use internships to achieve more efficient recruitment and staffing.[27] Hewlett-Packard employs anywhere from 500 to 700 interns annually, offering health benefits and relocation assistance. At Procter & Gamble (P&G), it is advantageous to start within an internship program because P&G is strongly committed to promoting its people from within, although gaining acceptance into an internship program is competitive.

Cooperative education is another vehicle that can be used to facilitate the transition from school to work. The following briefly describes the cooperative education program at Drexel University, one of the largest and most successful programs in the United States.

> At Drexel University, cooperative education provides an opportunity for the student to integrate classroom theory and practical work experience. Drexel calls this unique learning experience the "Co-op Advantage." Drexel has been operating the co-op program since 1919. Students work at their co-op jobs for a six-month period, alternating with six months of classroom study. Cooperative education at Drexel is a degree requirement for most majors.
>
> Drexel graduates enter the workforce having had as many as three different positions within their field of study, which allows them to be familiar with job interviews, and often results in higher paying starting salaries. Students at Drexel work for more than 1,500 companies in 27 states and 12 foreign countries. Each year, more than 9,500 Drexel students are enrolled in the cooperative education program. The professional staff of the Steinbright Career Development Center (SCDC) effectively manages more than 4,000 student placements into co-op work experiences each year. Employers of Drexel co-ops include Comcast Corporation, GlaxoSmithKline, Johnson & Johnson, Lockheed Martin, PECO Energy, and DuPont.[28]

Cooperative education programs are designed to help students develop a greater sense of responsibility, maturity, and self-confidence, as well as a better understanding of other people, a more serious appreciation of their academic studies, and a more practical, realistic orientation to the world of work. The experience gained through cooperative work assignments can either reinforce students' original occupational choices or convince them to consider other fields of study. Many students return to a former cooperative organization for full-time employment upon graduation.

Companies stand to benefit from college relations activities. Cooperative education and internships provide a ready supply of candidates to consider for full-time employment. These students have already been exposed to the company's culture, have familiarity with the firm's facilities and equipment, and have been trained in specific functional areas. Anticipatory socialization programs also benefit the neophyte. Soon-to-be or newly minted graduates are provided with an opportunity to learn about themselves, their chosen career field, and working in general. Specific skills, both technical (e.g., marketing research) and interpersonal (working as a member of a group), can be learned, practiced, and reinforced by internship and co-op experiences. In all, anticipatory socialization programs such as these advance all parties toward their desired career goals.

Learning and Development

HR professionals spend significant time on the provision of learning and development programs for employees. Normally, the talent needs of a company change as it grows and transforms. Christenson suggests that the shelf life for many professional skills is approximately three to five years.[29] Therefore, organizations have a critical need to build their learning and development processes so that they can continually upgrade their workforce. Several important processes are part of learning and development, including employee development, succession planning, orientation programs, competency development, and leadership coaching. Employee development differs from competency development in that the former is a joint effort on the part of an employee and organization to enhance the employee's knowledge, skills, and abilities. Successful employee development requires a balance between an individual's career needs and goals, and the organization's need to get work done. Competency development is the systematic collection and analysis of data to determine what characteristics differentiate outstanding from average performers in an organizational job or role. Competency development has broader implications for organizational hiring processes, while employee development has employee career implications.

Employee Development. Organizations support their business strategies by developing their human resources to achieve greater levels of competence. In this sense, the company's current staff is viewed as a critical resource, one that is necessary to sustain organizational growth. An organization needs to invest in the development of these employees so that it gains the talent and skill sets necessary to achieve its goals.

Developmental activities can be grouped into two basic categories: education/training and on-the-job experiences. Education and training programs are generally formal activities that can take place either in the work setting or at an outside organization. To supplement the skills that employees bring to the job, corporate "universities" are often called upon to increase the organization's human capacities. One model of university training occurs when firms offer tuition reimbursement. Employees must be accepted by the college of their choice and complete required credits to graduate with either a baccalaureate or master's degree. In some cases, the employee's coursework is pursued via distance education techniques that may include the Internet, mail, and videos.[30]

Another option is to provide education portals to train employees. Companies work with traditional universities or training organizations to provide college courses online. Working in conjunction with universities, the company may create its own Web site (education portal) to provide students with a virtual campus complete with the company's logo and related information. This model of a corporate university "offers a seamless blend of courses designed by colleges, commercial training suppliers, and the company's own training staff."[31] Finally, corporate universities may follow a tailored training model in which universities and corporations work together to develop specific distance learning courses designed to address a company's development needs. In this case, firms can direct universities on which components of their standard curriculum should be offered to employees, and which components need to be developed to address talent and learning requirements. In addition, this partnership allows corporations to add their own input and information to the training materials.[32] Eighty percent of Fortune 500 companies either have or plan a corporate university, and about 2,400 corporate universities exist worldwide, a figure that is expected to reach approximately 37,000 by 2010.[33] The following are examples of corporate university initiatives at Motorola and Boeing.[34]

> Motorola considers education to be an employee right as well as a responsibility, and every Motorola employee must complete at least 40 hours of training a year. This usually takes place at Motorola University (MU), which is probably the best known and most widely benchmarked corporate university in the world. Both employees and Motorola customers take courses at MU. MU has expanded its offerings over the years. Initially, there was a functional curriculum, covering such areas as engineering, manufacturing, sales, and marketing. Within each area, specific courses deal with relational skills, technical skills, and business skills. MU also offered classes in remedial reading and math. The university serves to socialize Motorola's employees properly by imparting important cultural values and shared philosophies such as risk taking and teamwork.
>
> MU was also one of the first programs to institute virtual reality in manufacturing training. Specifically, MU uses virtual manufacturing labs to train line workers by modeling the equipment instead of using the actual equipment for training purposes. These labs can be used at any Motorola site via the company intranet and through CD-ROM programs. Today, given the global environment within which Motorola hires, improved language skills are now needed by employees. MU offers language training not only to employees but also to their spouses and other family members, in order to give the learners the chance to practice their skills.

> The Boeing Company provides education to its employees through its Leadership Center. A large component of Boeing's programs focuses on executive learning. Newly promoted supervisory personnel must complete a Web-based curriculum within 30 days. This training includes topics on company policies and procedures, finding available resources, and understanding fiduciary responsibilities. Entry-level managers spend one week at a local training site studying performance management, reviewing organizational strategies and structure, and learning state and regional laws and regulations that govern their industry. Boeing's large management team, consisting of over 2,000 executives and 24,000 managers, keeps the Learning Center booked. They are required to take core leadership courses at five specific turning points in their careers: when they receive their first management assignment, when they become a manager of managers, to prepare for executive responsibilities, as they begin their first days as executives, and when they assume the challenges of global leadership responsibilities. Boeing's primary means of evaluating the success of its Leadership Center is by conducting employee surveys on an annual basis.

In addition to raising the skill levels of their employees, these corporations view their universities as recruiting tools and as a way to retain the top graduates of their programs. Although investments in a corporate university are expensive, in these companies' view it is money well spent.

The second way that organizations can develop their employees is through on-the-job training or learning (OJT). Even with the heavy corporate investment in formal programs, most development and learning occurs through OJT experiences. Research suggests that if learning is going "to stick," training needs to be continuous and provide opportunities for practice and reinforcement. On-the-job learning experiences not only provide this type of learning environment, but also are cost efficient. Studies suggest that higher wage and productivity growth rates occur in firms with extensive OJT programs. In fact, the rate of return on investment for OJT programs targeted at college educated employees is more than 80 percent, and the training is portable across employers and industries.[35]

On-the-job learning is a critical method for organizations to prepare their employees for the future. Through the use of different assignments and multifunctional experiences, companies can ensure a steady supply of trained staff who understand the business and key strategic issues. Effective organizations integrate learning opportunities into all business functions and work experiences and make OJT learning part of every manager's job.[36] There are many different projects, assignments, and other activities that can serve as OJT developmental experiences paving the way for future advancement. To cite an old maxim, there is no substitute for experience. Individuals who have a relatively long tenure in a given job or function are often valuable employees because they normally have a full range of knowledge about various aspects of the position. These individuals might become inside consultants or mentors and be asked to share their knowledge with junior employees. It has also been argued that people in support functions—such as finance, human resources, information technology, and procurement—should strive to become internal consultants. They often possess technical expertise that can be shared with junior employees—helping the novice learn the ropes, and at the same time allowing the senior employee to show off potential management skills.[37] In this way, information sharing and organizational learning occur, and all parties, employees and their organization, benefit.

During the early career years, employees can also benefit from job challenge and the opportunity to experience a number of different assignments. Through job challenge and rotational opportunities, employees build a base of experience and develop a wider range of competencies that can positively influence career success in later years. Air Products and Chemicals, Inc., uses an innovative approach to encourage rotational work assignments during the early years of employment.[38] New employees are put in challenging assignments as a way to stimulate their personal and professional development.

Since its inception, Air Products and Chemicals, Inc., has encouraged recent college graduates to take an active role in the planning and development of their careers. This philosophy was formalized in 1959 with the establishment of the Career Development Program (or CDP), which allows individuals with finance, marketing, engineering, chemistry, or information technology undergraduate or graduate degrees to fulfill their immediate, individual career objectives while preparing for and defining the challenges and opportunities that lie ahead. The CDP is characterized by diversified movement and flexibility, while providing an environment where the individual has a real influence on the direction of his or her career from the very beginning. The long-term goal of the program is to help participants identify and begin to cultivate professional skills, interests, and potential to the best benefit of the individual and Air Products.

The CDP is not a structured training program. Instead, it challenges new employees with actual work experience and gives them a broad perspective on the company's operations and objectives. Participants develop their skills and interests through a rotation of three different assignments, lasting 10 to 12 months each, during the first two to three years of employment. Everyone takes an active role in influencing his or her career path. Positions are designed to give each person exposure to a variety of company activities and to provide a high degree of visibility among all levels of management. Individuals have flexibility in the choice of functional area, sequence, and, to a degree, duration of assignments. Assignments can cover such areas as engineering, research, marketing, manufacturing, information technology, finance, auditing, and purchasing.

The initial assignment is generally in a function that is compatible with the employee's education and experience as well as the opportunities available within the company. After becoming acclimated to Air Products, new employees are encouraged to take the initiative and explore future assignments through discussion with the Career Development Program supervisor, fellow program participants, supervisors, and coworkers. Individuals are expected to seek new challenges as interests develop, taking a proactive role in tailoring their own career paths. Employees typically complete up to three CDP assignments before moving into a regular position.

Many past and current leaders of Air Products, including the current chief executive officer, John McGlade, joined the company through the Career Development Program. The ultimate goal of the Career Development Program is to establish an optimal match between an individual's longer-term plans and opportunities within the company. Through the CDP, Air Products encourages a proactive, entrepreneurial approach to career planning.

Succession Planning. Well-run organizations recognize that they regularly need to replace executives and managers throughout the life cycle of the firm. Voluntary and involuntary turnover, retirements, and sickness or disability can force organizations to be prepared to fill open positions with qualified personnel. Succession planning refers to the efforts of the firm to select and develop future leaders who, in time, will replace current leaders.[39]

The process of finding high-potential employees who are prepared to take on greater responsibilities is a complex process. Research has shown that the following personal characteristics are minimally necessary in order for an individual to be considered for higher level positions in the future. In contrast, not having these traits might mean that the individual has a "fatal flaw" that would preclude advancement to leadership positions unless the problem area (or areas) is corrected.[40] These "high-potential" characteristics include

- Ability to learn from mistakes
- Ability to develop new skills
- Interpersonal competencies
- Openness to new ideas
- Willingness to take personal responsibility for results
- Ability to take initiative

Other leadership competencies organizations should consider when selecting high-potential employers include the following:[41]

- Ability to lead change
- Excellent communication skills
- Disciplinary expertise
- Ability to drive results and work hard
- High integrity and ethics
- Appropriate risk-taking behaviors

While several succession planning approaches have been observed, HR professionals typically use four models, either individually or in combination with one another.[42] First, firms may offer *job rotation* as an opportunity for the high-potential employee to learn skills over a variety of positions or assignments. Employees may be transferred to different functional areas (e.g., manufacturing, finance, logistics) so that they learn how each functional area works and interacts with other functions within the company. Job rotations in sales and marketing give the high-potential employee experiences working with customers as well. Using job rotation as a developmental experience allows the high-potential employee to see the firm from a broader perspective and hopefully gives the individual the knowledge to deal with future problems.

Another model that HR professionals use is to identify a specific *talent pool* from which to draw future leaders. This approach encourages the high-potential employee to develop his or her skills more broadly, including assignments on cross-functional teams, undertaking difficult jobs, using cutting-edge technology, and taking advantage of key networking opportunities.[43] While the strength of the talent pool model is the recruitment and development of high-potential employees, the "wait until the management job becomes available" approach to advancement can be problematic for the upwardly mobile employee. High-potential employees may leave for jobs in other companies or other companies may try to raid the talent pool. Nonetheless, companies like Lockheed Martin develop leadership training programs (in communications, engineering, finance, human resources, information systems, and operations) to encourage high-potential employees to become part of their resource base.[44]

Another approach to succession planning is to *buy talent* from the market when it is needed and available. This model is beneficial because the entire market can be scoured for the desirable skill set. It may be difficult to find just the right person from within a firm, especially when the strategy requires a move to a new business arena. However, there are risks associated with hiring from outside the organization. First, high-potential employees may believe that they are never good enough for high-level positions if the company always buys talent. Also, some have suggested that firms take a "buyer beware" approach to bringing in talent from the external market. Often when new, high-potential employees are hired from outside, they need to overcome a steep learning curve that might delay their full contribution to the organization, especially when the company's culture and work ethic do not mesh with expectations of the newcomer. Sometimes new hires are not what they claim to be, and after extraordinary investment, companies realize that they have not hired the person they thought they had.[45] Even with these potential pitfalls, it can make good sense to "buy talent" as a succession strategy, but only when a thorough interviewing process has screened potential employees.

The final succession planning model is what Jon Briscoe and Brooklyn Derr call the *smaller is better* method. Smaller is better emphasizes the job rotation and talent pool approaches mentioned above, but shrinks the size of the pool considerably to make it more selective.[46] This model stresses that only those high-potential employees who have the talent, desire, and interest in staying with the company long enough to make a leadership contribution are considered for future advancement. Obviously, this interest can be discovered only after thorough analysis and conversation with the high-potential employees. While this method runs the risk of "putting all of one's eggs in one basket," the level of employee commitment this model engenders can be significant.

Overall, succession planning is a vital responsibility of the HR function. By maintaining a full "depth chart" of high-potential employees, the firm is ready to position these employees in leadership positions as they become available. Investment by the organization in succession planning is crucial for long-term sustainability and growth.

Orientation Programs. Even if an organization practices realistic recruitment, new employees still have to adjust to a new environment when they enter the organization. Orientation programs not only help new employees become integrated into the work environment in a general sense, but can also address some specific problems experienced by newcomers in the organization. Presented below is a description of the well-known and documented orientation program used by Walt Disney World in Orlando, Florida.[47]

For a company like Disney, with extensive contact between customers and employees, it is imperative that the staff be knowledgeable, courteous, and always willing to meet the needs of the guests. To ensure that new recruits are properly integrated into this culture, Disney employs a three-day orientation program. The orientation program is known as "Traditions." The first day of employment at Disney World involves attendance at a full-day session that describes the history of the organization. The session emphasizes the four key values of the Disney culture—safety, courtesy, show, and efficiency. All employees are taught that they have a role in serving the guests and that they should observe how employees perform this role during a tour of the facilities. Service standards are explained and demonstrated to help empower the new employees. These standards help them make the day-to-day decisions without having to refer questions to management. On the second day of the orientation, the employees hear about the support systems, policies, and procedures within the company, with the primary focus on safety and benefits. The third day involves on-the-job training. The recruit is assigned to an experienced coworker who, during the next two days to two weeks, exposes the new employee to a series of experiences specific to his or her work role. These peer trainers are role models who work with supervisors to provide the coaching, feedback, and reinforcement needed to help the newcomer learn the job and acquire the Disney spirit.

Once trainees begin working, they are eligible for cross-utilization training. One example is volunteering to teach "Traditions." This gives employees the opportunity to practice presentation skills, work with groups, and become good candidates for other positions. Some 70 percent of the promotions at Walt Disney Attractions come from within. Disney attributes its ability to promote from within to the strong orientation program and its employees' affinity to the Disney culture. The strongest elements in the Disney culture are teamwork, leadership, and planning.

Firms with more specific employee learning needs can also benefit from well-designed orientation programs. Headquartered in Philadelphia, ARAMARK Corporation is one of the world's leading managed-services providers with more than 250,000 employees worldwide who serve clients in 19 countries.[48] ARAMARK's orientation program for new hires in human resources provides an example of integrating HR professionals into all areas of an operation. ARAMARK's orientation program is described below:[49]

Program participants, generally new college graduates, are selected on the basis of their general mental abilities and their interest in and fundamental knowledge about Human Resources. The first part of the program focuses on general business knowledge. New hires start with a one-month orientation that provides a fairly detailed look at ARAMARK as a company and its various divisions. This process involves meetings with and presentations by corporate HR vice presidents from all lines of business, and site visits to individual accounts to learn how the HR function works within and across divisions.

The second part of the program focuses on honing HR-specific competencies. After the first month-long exposure to ARAMARK, the new HR representatives are assigned to an HR vice president who is responsible for one line of business at ARAMARK's corporate headquarters. This part of the program provides an immersion into the division's day-to-day HR operations and offers opportunities to complete high-visibility projects that involve working directly with upper-level management. During this time, new HR representatives focus on learning the division policies and procedures for staffing, training and development, performance management, and employee relations.

The initial task in developing a successful orientation program is to identify the specific information, skills, and support required by new employees. The major strengths of the Disney and ARAMARK programs are accurate identification and articulation of a need—describing the corporate theme (outstanding customer service at Disney) or job function of a human resource representative (at ARAMARK) as well as a determination of how best to get the message across. These orientation approaches demonstrate how custom-made programs can be used to improve newcomers' understanding of the organization's core values and modes of operation.

Competency Development. Chapter 7 discussed how human development and career advancement can be facilitated through learning. Many have argued that career advancement is the responsibility of the employee, and advancement occurs when the employee enhances his or her knowledge base. Organizations can assist employees by becoming "knowledge creators," that is, by developing their human resources in ways that enhance the level of competencies and knowledge available to the company.[50] Strategic competency development focuses as much on how goals are achieved (capabilities, behaviors, and skills) as on what is achieved (results). This integrated focus equally raises the bar on overall performance requirements. Praxair, Inc., is an example of a firm using competencies to develop its personnel.[51]

Praxair is an industrial gases company, with 28,000 employees worldwide, serving customers in more than 30 countries.[52] Praxair believes that competencies increase the company's ability to communicate requirements beyond the basic skills for a particular job. Competencies also are being used as a common global base for other HR systems and processes, including selection, performance management, education and development, and succession planning processes. Competencies are also utilized for job profiling and employee selection process.

The firm distinguishes between essential competencies and functional competencies. Essential competencies are, by and large, consistent throughout Praxair on a worldwide basis. The ability to use technology, a strong work ethic, and quality service delivery are considered essential competencies. Functional competencies, in contrast, can differ by both job level and geographical location. Essential and functional competencies are reflected in the performance development program and are used to generate employee development plans. The firm has recognized that competency definitions can differ significantly by culture and that a heightened level of sensitivity is necessary when using United States–based competencies in other cultures.

This competency development example clarifies the processes organizations pursue so that they can continually develop their workforce. As the Praxair example shows, organizations can enhance both essential and functional competencies in their workforce, which improves job performance by placing the right employee in the right job, and aids in long-term employee career goal attainment. Firms invest in their employee development, succession planning, orientation programs, and competency development processes so that their financial investment in personnel is preserved.

Leadership Coaching. For-profit and nonprofit organizations in the 21st century rely more heavily on teams and networking, and "coaching and commitment cultures have replaced . . . command, control, and compartmentalization" structures.[53] Manfred Kets de Vries suggests that "every self respecting executive now demand[s] a coach."[54] Coaches allow leaders to function effectively and develop the leader's emotional intelligence and communication skills. Relatively few studies have systematically investigated the leadership coaching process, although early research tended to focus on ways to correct recognized deficiencies in managers and executives. More recent studies have looked more broadly at leadership coaching to include other outcomes, such as the facilitation of learning and the achievement of peak performance.[55]

Coaching is important not only for executives or senior managers but also for first-line supervisors.[56] In addition to improving leader performance, a case can be made that coaching behaviors enhance leader sustainability. Results posit that coaching with compassion promotes healing and growth in the leader that offsets the negative effects of stress associated with the leadership role.[57] Optimal coaching is designed to provide employees with the skills, resources, and support they need to do their best work. The goal of coaching is to help people successfully achieve their performance goals and their professional/career goals. Effective coaching should cover assessment and goal setting (for both performance and career management), action planning and implementation, and improvement processes. Given the positive outcomes, leadership coaching will continue to be a central developmental activity, especially as firms need to provide greater career opportunities to retain high-performing employees.

In total, organizations invest in their employee development, succession planning, orientation programs, competency development, and leadership development processes so that their financial investment in personnel is maintained and organizational performance is optimized.

Performance Management and Rewards

After organizations identify, recruit, and develop their employees it is necessary to establish an effective process to manage employee performance. Performance management is essential to ensure that organizational goals and outcomes are met. While performance management has its roots in compensation and formal recognition systems, it also includes the assessment of individual performance in light of strategic organizational goals. Processes to be reviewed in this section include performance objectives and measures, benefits programs, and human resource information systems.

Performance Objectives and Measures. Christenson states that in order for the human resource function to become a strategic partner with the rest of the organization, it needs to lessen its exclusive focus on compensation management and refocus its efforts on influencing employees to perform based on goals tied to desired individual and organizational outcomes.[58] Total performance management systems are designed so that (a) individual and organizational goals are aligned, (b) individual and organizational performance is consistent, (c) insight is provided into needed adjustments in performance and goals, and (d) critical input is provided for individual development planning.[59] To delineate actions further at the corporate, group, and individual levels, Christenson provides a framework for a total performance management system (one that is in practice at Hallmark). This framework is illustrated in Exhibit 13.2.

EXHIBIT 13.2   Total Performance Management System

	Setting Expectations for Performance	*Managing Performance*	*Recognizing Performance*
Corporate	• Translate corporate vision and strategy into measurements • Set objectives and metrics • Communicate expectations	• Track results and provide ongoing feedback and redirection on organizational performance	• Company-wide incentives • Executive incentives (short and long term)
Group	• Translate group vision and strategy into measurements • Set objectives • Ensure alignment and integration (management team) • Communicate expectations	• Track results and provide ongoing feedback and redirection on group performance • Ongoing public recognition for group performance	• Management incentives • Group-wide incentives
Individual	• Mutually agreed-upon exceptions and consequences • Development plans	• Ongoing dialog and coaching (open, honest, and two-way) • At a minimum, midyear and formal reviews	• Merit increases • Individual incentives • Spot awards • Celebrations • Praise

SOURCE: Adapted from Christenson, R. (2006). *Roadmap to strategic HR: Turning a great idea into a business reality.* New York: AMACOM.

One example of an individual performance management practice is 360 degree feedback. All employees, regardless of their level in the organization, need feedback so they can monitor and improve their job performance. Although this requirement is particularly critical during the early career, performance feedback is important throughout all career stages. Multisource assessment systems, commonly known as 360 degree feedback, are growing in popularity. As a developmental tool, 360 degree feedback allows for the gathering of performance information from multiple sources "in a circle" around the individual, including coworkers, customers, subordinates, supervisors, and peers on a work team.[60] If conducted properly, 360 degree feedback systems provide a full assessment of an individual's critical competencies, specific behaviors and skills, overall performance, and areas that require further development.[61]

Companies such as BP Amoco, Allied Signal, and Ford have used 360 degree feedback systems to help achieve strategic goals and carry out organizational change efforts. Multisource feedback systems support organizational performance in several ways. First, feedback helps the company identify the skills and competencies needed to meet business goals. Second, feedback received from those who work most closely with the employee allows the employee to understand his or her strengths and weaknesses. Finally, training programs and developmental opportunities can be offered so the employee can develop the needed skills and track his or her progress in applying the skills on the job.[62]

Such 360 degree feedback systems can improve leaders' performance and enhance their subordinates' work engagement and satisfaction as well as reduce their subordinates' intentions to quit.[63] It is impossible to develop realistic career goals in the absence of useful performance feedback on one's current job. Periodic performance management sessions that focus on specific job behaviors, in conjunction with more quantitative indices of accomplishment provided by 360 degree feedback, are most likely to improve current performance and build a solid foundation for future career growth.

Benefits Programs. Employee benefits are various forms of compensation provided in addition to normal wages or salaries to increase employees' security and well-being. Fringe benefits can include but are not limited to employer-provided (or employer-paid) housing, group insurance (e.g., health, dental, vision, life), prescription plans, disability income protection, retirement benefits, child care benefits, tuition reimbursement, sick leave, vacation (paid and nonpaid), and profit sharing. Other specialized benefits may include relocation, adoption assistance, transportation benefits, and wellness programs.

Another important program in an organization's portfolio of career management benefits is preretirement counseling. In Chapter 8 we discussed how the prospect of retirement can evoke a range of emotions with individuals who are approaching this decision. Many people often do not know what to expect in retirement and may be ill prepared for the financial and emotional demands that retirement brings. With the mass number of retirements coming from the baby boom generation over the next 20 years, it is likely that organizations will need to offer preretirement programs to this large cohort of employees.

Seymour LaRock offers a set of questions that should be answered when developing a preretirement counseling program or reviewing the adequacy of an ongoing program. Issues to be addressed include the following:[64]

- Who should be involved in preretirement planning?

- How extensive should the program be? Is the program to be a one-time effort for a special group in an early retirement incentive offer or is this to be an ongoing company program targeted at senior employees?

- Who should develop and present the program: company personnel or outside consultants?

- Who should attend the program? At what age should employees be invited to participate? Does the invitation also include the spouse? Should there be separate programs for union, salaried, or hourly employees?

LaRock suggest several topics that should be included and discussed as core components of a preretirement planning program:[65]

- Company-provided retirement benefits

- Social Security benefits and Medicare

- Company-provided postretirement healthcare and life insurance benefits (if available)

- Financial planning

Specialists from the employer's human resources department can lead these discussions and provide essential information on the employer's own programs. However, outside speakers might be necessary to cover more specific topics. In many communities, representatives from the local Social Security office are available to address this group of employees. In others cases, an attorney might be used to discuss such topics as wills or estate planning, or an insurance representative may be engaged to lead a discussion of life insurance and health insurance coverage. Smaller employers may want to tap into materials available from the American Association of Retired Persons (AARP). In the case of universities and nonprofit entities, a range of preretirement planning materials is available from Teachers Insurance and Annuity Association–College Retirement Equities Fund (TIAA–CREF).[66]

Other topics that may be covered in preretirement planning include psychological adjustments to retirement, maintaining a healthy lifestyle, and the use of leisure time specifically for travel or education.[67] Information on phased retirement or bridge employment (as we discussed in Chapter 8) may also be presented. As with the other human resource practices we have discussed, preretirement planning programs must be based on an assessment of employee needs and concerns. What is most crucial for one employee may not be especially important for another. Preretirement planning programs may not only ease the transition from work to retirement but may also influence the decisions of employees either to hasten or postpone retirement. Moreover, if such programs succeed in relieving the anxiety of employees nearing retirement, they might make the remaining years of employment more satisfying and productive. One study found that human resource professionals in organizations that have adopted preretirement programs noticed a halt in the productivity decline of workers as they neared retirement. When these workers were confident in their preparation for their next stage of life, they devoted their time on the job to work, not to worry.[68]

Human Resource Information Systems. Human resource information systems (HRIS) enable an organization to acquire, store, manipulate, analyze, retrieve, and distribute information relevant to its human resources to aid organizational decision makers.[69] HRIS have grown in popularity since the 1960s, and are used not only for administrative personnel–related tasks, but also for strategic and business decision-making purposes. Researchers point to five reasons why companies should use an HRIS:[70]

1. To increase competitiveness by improving HR operations

2. To produce a greater number and variety of HR-related reports

3. To shift the focus of HR from the processing of transactions to strategic HRM

4. To enable employees to view, verify, and correct personal information in the system

5. To reengineer the entire HR function of companies

The greatest benefits from the implementation of HRIS are the quick response and access to information, and the greatest barrier is insufficient financial investment in the system.[71] With increasing functionality, flexibility, and affordability, HRIS are used extensively in organizations of all sizes. One study found that the professional standing of HR professionals has been enhanced by the use of HRIS for strategic partnering.[72] In addition, HRIS can contribute to cost reductions, increased quality and customer satisfaction, and innovation.[73] Clearly, as firms move toward a more strategic approach to human resource management, HRIS will play a vital role in the growth of their HR management capabilities and in their future success.

Employee Relations

Employee relations covers a variety of programs that an organization offers its employees so that individuals can work more effectively, can better integrate work and family lives, and can sustain their efforts over time.[74] Several career management practices speak to employee relations and are reviewed below. These practices include coaching and counseling, work–life programs, and employee morale initiatives.

Coaching and Counseling. Coaching has been well documented as a useful career management approach that can be successful in improving the bottom-line performance of the organization. James Hunt and Joseph Weintraub state that coaching is "an effective means of developing a more capable workforce at all levels and creating a very competitive organizational culture, one that can successfully compete for human capital and achieve business results."[75] At an operational level, coaching can be defined as a career management technique that promotes "both individual development and organizational learning in the service of the organization's larger goals."[76] Coaching has been found to increase job satisfaction and to support personal development, organizational change, and stress management initiatives.[77] Our examples earlier in this chapter point out the effectiveness of coaching for new employees through orientation and for more senior employees through leadership coaching.

Work–Life Programs. Research shows that investing in work–life programs has less to do with corporate responsibility and more to do with bottom-line business performance. Theses programs can create a culture in the organization that helps men and women better meet the competing demands of work and interests outside of work. Employees who believe that there is a supportive workplace culture are more likely to report that the quality of their work lives is also high.[78] And some studies indicate that the availability of work–life programs can improve employee commitment and productivity and reduce stress, absenteeism, and turnover.[79] HR professionals need to consider generational differences in the design of work–life programs and monitor patterns of program usage for each group.[80] Chapter 10 presents an extensive discussion of work–life issues and initiatives.

Employee Morale. The essence of employee relations is the building of a strong relationship between employer and employee, a relationship maintained by a corporate culture that is conducive to helping employees stay motivated, loyal, and performing at a high level. Morale can be defined as the general outlook that employees display toward their work organization or unit.[81] High morale is associated with positive employee attitudes, heightened energy levels, reduced stress levels, and an overall sense of esprit de corps among the employees. To create or maintain a workforce with high morale, organizations should communicate honestly with employees on business conditions and the direction the company is taking. In addition, organizations should listen to their employees by asking for employee input and advice; this can yield creative solutions and provides employees with a much desired sense of control in uncertain times. The organization should also focus on positive results by celebrating and using positive reinforcement on a daily basis. Finally, organizations should offer a comprehensive benefits package that attends to the needs of the employee and his or her family. Creating a working environment that helps employees meet their long-term career goals improves morale and builds lasting loyalty to both the company and fellow employees.[82]

In sum, several career management practices can affect the quality of the relationship between employer and employee. Although coaching and counseling, work–life programs, and employee morale initiatives are a few examples, there are many other formal and informal managerial actions that assist in building relationships with employees. Even anticipatory socialization activities (discussed earlier in the chapter) can begin to build relationships with relatively new employees.

Diversity

Diversity within an organization is not just a specific program (like a diversity awareness activity), but rather is an integral part of all that is done in the human resource function. Diversity is part of the process to leverage the talent to build capabilities throughout the firm to compete in the marketplace.[83] As firms incorporate diversity issues into all HR functions, it is important to develop a comprehensive and integrated approach. As was discussed in Chapter 11, a comprehensive approach should (a) communicate the importance of diversity throughout the organization; (b) identify critical diversity issues within the organization; (c) eliminate discrimination not only in hiring but also in the progression of employees throughout their career; (d) develop appropriate policies and programs regarding sexual harassment, the use of different languages in the workplace, and work–life challenges; and (e) hold the leadership of the organization accountable for managing diversity effectively.

SUMMARY

An important consideration for all organizations is the implementation of human resource management systems that have a focus on career management. In order to provide a strong foundation for the achievement of a firm's strategic goals, HRM systems should be aligned with corporate business strategies. This chapter discussed a model of an integrated strategic human resource system that depicts how career management can help improve overall effectiveness. We described the key functional human resource areas (workforce planning and staffing, learning and development, performance management and rewards, and employee relations), and showed how career management is rooted in these activities. We also provided examples of corporate programs where human resource systems support individual careers and career management. We discussed how a firm's HRM systems can support its strategic business plans as well as individual employee development. Organizations can offer an array of programs that help their employees manage their careers throughout the life cycle. Recognizing that individuals at different career stages have varying career needs and challenges, companies can and should tailor their career management programs to meet the requirements of all their employees.

ASSIGNMENT

Choose an organization for which you have worked or one you can investigate. Identify the company's unique culture and describe the career management programs that it provides. Explain how the organization's culture has either helped or hindered the development of an effective HRM system and describe the type of culture that is ideally suited for an effective HRM system.

DISCUSSION QUESTIONS

1. What techniques can organizations use to ensure that their strategic direction and business plans are reflected in their human resource systems and career management programs?

2. To what extent should organizations be committed to developing and promoting their resources from within? Are organizations better off just hiring their resources from the external labor market? Which situations might warrant the internal development approach and which might warrant the external selection approach?

3. Do you think that the waves of employee layoffs that have occurred over the past three decades indicate a general lack of loyalty toward employees on the part of most organizations? How does the lack of job security and loyalty affect organizational philosophies regarding strategic human resource programs? What are the implications of your answers in terms of the management of your own career?

4. Do you believe that employers have a moral obligation to assist their employees in managing their careers? Why or why not?

CHAPTER 13 CASE

The Corporate Policy Change

Located in the beautiful Adirondack Mountains of upstate New York, Be Our Guest Family (BOGF) Resort was recently sold to an east coast hotel chain. Previously, BOGF (fictitious name) had been a family-owned business, and the owners treated all employees like an extended family. BOGF Resort is well-known for its friendly, top-notch accommodations. In the summer and fall, BOGF Resort offers families a variety of outdoor activities, including six tennis courts, an 18-hole golf course, a lake for boating and fishing, an indoor/outdoor pool, and horseback riding. During the winter and spring, downhill and cross-country skiing are the outdoor activities of choice at BOGF Resort. Other activities available throughout the year include bowling and an onsite movie theater. BOGF Resort also has four restaurants and a tavern.

Since BOGF Resort provides many amenities, it has a large year-round staff, many of whom have worked for the company for up to 15 years. In fact, BOGF Resort often hired members from multiple

(Continued)

(Continued)

generations of the same family. BOGF Resort has a focused mission that is made clear to all its employees—to provide a premium vacation experience to all who come to BOGF Resort. This means that the customer comes first. Employees are asked to do all they can to keep customer satisfaction high. This focus encourages customers to schedule return visits to BOGF Resort, and also to tell their friends about their vacations at BOGF Resort. BOGF Resort employees know that their town relies almost exclusively on the tourism generated by the resort, since few other substantial businesses are located in the immediate area.

BOGF Resort has a "home grown" mentality regarding the advancement of its human resources. Many of the hotel and restaurant managers grew up working summers as valets, house cleaners, and wait staff. This human resource policy was initiated by the small-town, privately held atmosphere of the BOGF Resort. This policy also allowed the employees to have a variety of experiences, and to learn firsthand what customers expect from a top-of-the-line resort. Many children of BOGF employees attend a local university that has a hotel administration major. This education allows the young adults to come back to their hometown to work. Yet, the acquisition of BOGF Resort will soon cause its human resource policies to change.

The Mansion Corporation (fictitious name), a well-known hotel and restaurant corporation, has recently purchased BOGF Resort. The Mansion's human resource strategies are dramatically different from those of the BOGF Resort. The Mansion attracts "star" quality employees from other hotels and provides them with high-level administrative positions. These positions may be offered at any one of a number of the Mansion's resort holdings. The Mansion is generous with offers of relocation packages to lure potential employees away from their current employer.

The Mansion's policy regarding human resource selection is more of the "buy" than the "make" approach. The Mansion fills its skill gaps by hiring needed personnel from outside the company. In fact, the Mansion has recently hired a CFO and Chief Technologist from competitors. Both employees and their families moved from the Midwest to the Mansion's headquarters in Virginia. Many of the hotel's general managers are from either top hotel or top restaurant chains. The general premise under which Mansion operates is that it is more cost efficient to bring in the "best and the brightest." This allows the Mansion to hire the skills it needs when and where it may need those skills. The Mansion plans to make this policy known to BOGF Resort's personnel as part of their Introduction to the Mansion's Human Resources Policies package. The Mansion corporate policies become effective in a few weeks. The Mansion does not intend to discuss the effect of this policy with BOGF employees unless asked.

Case Analysis Questions

1. What effect, if any, will the Mansion's policies have on current BOGF personnel?

2. What effect, if any, will the Mansion's policies have on the business strategies of BOGF?

3. How should the Mansion implement this new policy change at BOGF? How might the Mansion communicate this policy change? What types of career management systems are most compatible with the Mansion's human resource strategy?

4. If you were an employee of the BOGF Resort community, what might you do given this human resource policy change?

Closing Thoughts on Career Management

In this book we have shown how individuals face constant change as they move through the course of their careers. These changes come from a variety of sources—personal, environmental, and organizational. From the personal side, there are a number of factors that influence our careers. Just the process of aging produces changes in our perspectives on our careers. In most respects, for example, the concerns of a 25-year-old are vastly different from those of a 65-year-old. Beyond aging, behavioral scientists can point to a number of changes in individual attitudes and behaviors that have occurred over the past two decades. Some of these changes reflect cultural shifts in beliefs, whereas others are reactions to social forces. Perhaps the most significant cultural change affecting individuals is the heightened challenge of managing commitments to both work and family. Many two-career couples face new dilemmas in juggling work and family responsibilities, and, by necessity, members of these relationships must learn to balance two careers as well as extensive family responsibilities.

Individuals have also adapted to a new work environment that has evolved over the past several decades. Significant changes have occurred both in the way people are employed and in the types of jobs they hold.[1] The use of contract staff and temporary workers has jumped markedly over the past two decades as organizations have sought to become more efficient. For many individuals, working on a contingent basis has become a permanent way of life. In this new environment, standard jobs have been replaced by evolving work situations that require flexibility and adaptability on the part of the worker. Under the old environment, jobs were tailored or structured to reflect the abilities of the workers. In the new work landscape, the individual must be increasingly adaptable to the work situation.

These recent alterations in work organizations and in their approaches to staffing directly challenge the career competencies of affected workers. The result has been that the playing field for the individual managing his or her career has changed. As we discussed in Chapter 2 and throughout this book, this ever-changing work environment has dictated that individuals be "boundaryless" and "protean" in the way they manage their careers. Individuals need to be proactive in the acquisition of the career competencies of knowing-why (self-identity), knowing-how (portable job-related skills and career-related knowledge), and knowing-whom (broad networks of relationships). These competencies should help individuals navigate their increasingly uncertain careers to achieve personally meaningful goals and values.[2]

While organizations have been shifting their levels of and approaches to staffing, the workforce itself has seen dramatic changes over the past two decades. For example, the workforce is becoming more culturally diverse. The increasing proportions of women, racial minorities, immigrants, and older workers have put pressure on organizations to manage this diversity effectively. Workforce diversity also challenges employees to understand cultural similarities and differences and to work cooperatively with others who may have different values and perspectives. Career achievements could well depend on an employee's ability to thrive in a multicultural environment.

LOOKING TO THE FUTURE

It is difficult to predict with any certainty how the process of career management will evolve in the future. As we have discussed throughout this book, the ever-changing landscape of work and the constant increases in nonwork demands bring greater uncertainty into the process. Several environmental factors that are influencing career management currently will also present challenges in the future. For example, advancements in technology will affect the types and number of jobs that need to be filled. The application of new technology has the power to wipe out certain occupations while creating new ones. In addition, upgrades in communications technology will make it easier for workers to be "untethered" to a physical work location, but also will require them to become electronically tethered to their jobs seven days a week, 24 hours a day.

Demographic shifts, primarily the aging and retirement of the baby boom generation, will have a profound impact on the future supply of labor. As a consequence, younger workers are likely to have greater career opportunities over the next three decades as organizations look for ways to fill open positions. At the same time, older workers will need to assess their career options regarding alternative work situations, part-time employment, and retirement.

Responding to economic conditions and increased global competition, organizations will continue to make changes in their structures and staffing approaches, including the increased use of team-based structures, the deployment of a higher proportion of contract and contingent workers, and a willingness to empower all employees to make decisions and respond to customer and client demands.

The further globalization of business will create new career opportunities on a worldwide basis, with increased prospects either for an expatriation assignment or the permanent relocation to a host country. These overseas assignments will require employees to be more aware of, and adaptable to, foreign cultures and expectations. Of course, when an overseas assignment ends, the process of repatriation also brings with it a number of career challenges as the employee must re-assimilate back into the home country.

Finally, it is likely that nonwork demands will continue at a high level for the majority of workers. Family commitments, community involvement, and the likelihood of a two-career relationship will challenge workers to integrate and balance their work and nonwork lives. As we discussed earlier in this chapter and throughout this book, individuals need to stay vigilant in their career management approaches to respond to these future opportunities, challenges, and demands. Following are our recommendations for effective career management, both in the present and in the future.

EFFECTIVE CAREER MANAGEMENT

Regardless of the current and future challenges and uncertainties, career management as a problem-solving process does not really change in fundamental form. Information, insight, goals, plans, and feedback are essential at all career stages. Reflecting this view, we offer below our thoughts on several career issues that transcend a particular time or place.

First, effective career management requires individual initiative—an active, probing approach to life. It requires inquisitiveness about oneself and the world and a willingness to take action and appropriate risks. Career management is based on the belief that people can exert control over significant portions of their lives. Although total control is impossible, the willingness to explore, set goals, and develop and implement plans can make a difference in the quality of one's career and one's life. In this sense it is critically important that one establish a clear self-identity. Indeed, the primary building block for career success and fulfillment is the need for one's work to be consistent with one's self-identity. This maxim is even more relevant in the current environment of job instability, where one's personal needs can easily be overlooked. Establishment of a clear self-identity normally involves a process of self-exploration where individuals use standard assessment tools in conjunction with introspection and feedback from trusted others in their social network to understand better their interests, talents, and lifestyle preferences.

Second, people must appreciate the relationship between their work and nonwork lives. Career management efforts should be based on an awareness of life goals, not just career goals. Career goals and achievements affect (and are affected by) participation in the family, community, and leisure spheres of one's life. Even if people cannot "have it all," they can decide what they want and what trade-offs they are willing to make. Understanding the interplay between work and nonwork and discussing the impact of the delicate balance with other significant people are essential ingredients of career and life management.

Third, people must avoid succumbing to other people's definition of success for their lives. Many people pursue a specific career path to satisfy other people—parents, professors, friends, bosses, spouses, or perhaps some general notion of what one "should" do. Happiness and fulfillment, however, depend on satisfying one's own, not other people's, values and aspirations. Much of the recent popularity of entrepreneurial careers can be traced to individuals pursuing their own career interests, that is, being one's own man or woman. Nonetheless, this book has not advocated a hedonistic "me" attitude toward career management. Sacrifices and compromises are necessary if people are to live in a larger world, share their lives with other people, and become committed to a cause, a community, or an organization. Taking other people's or institutions' needs into account and trying to achieve mutually acceptable and beneficial solutions to career dilemmas are healthy actions. However, continually trying to please others at the expense of oneself can be destructive to one's sense of well-being.

Fourth, employees are responsible for maintaining (or attaining) a portfolio of skills that is transferable to other work situations and other employers. Individuals should ensure that they have the competitive skills to improve their chances of finding a new position when it is needed. In this sense, the individual would possess a set of what might be called portable competencies that could be applied in any number of organizations or work settings.

Related to the idea of a portable set of skills is the recommendation that individuals invest in lifelong learning to keep their skills relevant (and thereby transferable).[3] Continuous learning can take many forms. One category would involve pursuing additional schooling; another could include seeking out assignments that allow new competencies to be learned. A commitment to learning might also involve staying abreast of developments within one's current organization as well as other firms in the industry.

Finally, career management is not the exclusive domain of the elite. It does not belong only to the top executive, the upwardly mobile, the affluent, or the entrepreneur. Career management is for everyone who wants to enhance the quality of his or her life. Career management is not always easy, but, to paraphrase an old saying, nothing important ever is. Hopefully, this book has shown that effective career management is possible for people who are ready to take on the challenge.

At its core, career management is a personal process. Although organizational programs and practices can aid it immeasurably, only individuals, with the help of family members, friends, and colleagues, can develop insight into themselves and their environment, become committed to career goals and strategies, and accurately appraise the course of their careers and make necessary adjustments. Nothing can ever replace the commitment of the individual to the active management of his or her own career.

ASSIGNMENT

As we have indicated, it is difficult to predict what the future holds for career management. While recognizing the uncertainties, in this assignment you are asked to try to predict the future challenges that you will face as you go through the process of career management. Specifically, write a scenario of the future that depicts your view of how the work world will look in a decade. You should describe the related implications for your career and organizational career management systems. Your narrative could address such issues as the new career competencies you will need for achieving career success in the future, the role new technologies might play in helping you manage your career, the techniques that might be available to achieve better integration of your work and family lives, the effects on your career of continued international integration of work organizations and cultures, the career assistance strategies that organizations will use to help you grow in your career, and the degree to which you and your employers will see loyalty as playing a role in your respective decisions. Try to be as creative as possible in making your predictions about the future.

Endnotes

ENDNOTES FOR CHAPTER 1

1. As provided on its Web site (http://www.aomonline.org), the Academy of Management is a "leading professional association for scholars dedicated to creating and disseminating knowledge about management and organizations. Founded in 1936 by two professors, the Academy of Management is the oldest and largest scholarly management association in the world." As of 2007, the Academy is the professional home for *18,266* members from *102* nations.

2. Uchitelle, L., & Kleinfield, N. R. (1996, March 3). On the battlefields of business, millions of casualties. *New York Times,* p. 1.

3. Statistics available at the Bureau of Labor Statistics at http://www.bls.gov under the menu item Mass Layoff Statistics (MLS). The Web site states that the MLS program "collects reports on mass layoff actions that result in workers being separated from their jobs. Monthly mass layoff numbers are from establishments which have at least 50 initial claims for unemployment insurance (UI) filed against them during a 5-week period."

4. De Meuse, K. P., & Marks, M. L. (2006). Downsizing. In J. H. Greenhaus & G. A. Callanan (Eds.), *Encyclopedia of career development* (pp. 245–249). Thousand Oaks, CA: Sage.

5. Ibid.

6. Probst, T. M. (2006). Job security. In Greenhaus & Callanan, pp. 442–446.

7. U.S. Department of Labor, Bureau of Labor Statistics. News Release dated August 25, 2006, titled "Number of Jobs Held, Labor Market Activity, and Earnings Growth among the Youngest Baby Boomers: Results from a Longitudinal Survey." Available at http://www.bls.gov/news.release/pdf/nlsoy.pdf and at http://www.bls.gov/nls/y79r21jobsbyedu.pdf

8. Balogun, J., & Johnson, G. (2004). Organizational restructuring and middle manager sense-making. *Academy of Management Journal, 47,* 523–549; Schilling, M. A., & Steensma, H. K. (2001). The use of modular organizational forms: An industry-level analysis. *Academy of Management Journal, 44,* 1149–1168.

9. Offermann, L. R. (2006). Team-based work. In Callanan & Greenhaus, pp. 795–796.

10. Zaheer, A., & Bell, G. G. (2005). Benefiting from network position: Firm capabilities, structural holes, and performance. *Strategic Management Journal, 26,* 809–825.

11. Ashkenas, R., Ulrich, D., Jick, T., & Kerr, S. (2002). *The boundaryless organization.* San Francisco: Jossey-Bass; Bird, A. (1994). Careers as repositories of knowledge: A new perspective on boundaryless careers. *Journal of Organizational Behavior, 15,* 325–344.

12. Callanan, G. A. (2004). What would Machiavelli think?—An overview of the leadership challenges in team-based structures. *Team Performance Management Journal, 41,* 77–83; Offermann (2006).

13. Mills, P. K. (2006). Empowerment. In Greenhaus & Callanan, pp. 280–284.

14. Callanan (2004).

15. Offermann (2006).

16. Coyle-Shapiro, J. A. M. (2006). Psychological contract. In Greenhaus & Callanan, pp. 652–659; Robinson, S. L., Kraatz, M. S., & D. M. Rousseau. (1994). Changing obligations and the psychological contract: A longitudinal study. *Academy of Management Journal, 37,* 137–152.

17. Callanan, G. A., & Greenhaus, J. H. (1999). Personal and career development: The best and worst of times. In A. I. Kraut & A. K. Korman (Eds.), *Evolving practices in human resource management: Responses to a changing world of work* (pp. 146–171). San Francisco: Jossey-Bass; Coyle-Shapiro (2006); Robinson et al. (1994); Rousseau, D. M., & K. A. Wade-Benzoni. (1995). Changing individual-organization attachments: A two-way street. In A. Howard (Ed.), *The changing nature of work* (pp. 290–322). San Francisco: Jossey-Bass.

18. Coyle-Shapiro (2006).

19. Ibid.

20. Statistics available from the U.S. Census Bureau at their Web site at http://www.census.gov. Statistics list the U.S. dollar value of goods and services with data available as of March 2007.

21. Ibid.

22. Herr, E. L. (2006). Globalization and careers. In Greenhaus & Callanan, pp. 337–342; Tharenou, P. (2006). International careers. In Greenhaus & Callanan, pp. 398–404.

23. Selmer, J. (2006). Expatriate experience. In Greenhaus & Callanan, pp. 306–307.

24. Russell, J. E. A., & Redman, D. W. (2006). Technology and careers. In Greenhaus & Callanan, pp. 796–804.

25. Cappelli, P. (2006). Churning of jobs. In Greenhaus & Callanan, pp. 165–167.

26. Heet, J. A. (2006). Workforce 2020. In Greenhaus & Callanan, pp. 877–880.

27. Callanan, G. A., & Greenhaus, J. H. (2008). The baby boom generation and career management: A call to action. *Advances in Developing Human Resources, 10,* 70–85.

28. Dohm, A. (2000). Gauging the labor effects of retiring baby boomers. *Monthly Labor Review, 123,* 17–25; Peterson, S. J., & Spiker, B. K. (2005). Establishing the positive contributory value of older workers: A positive psychology perspective. *Organizational Dynamics, 34,* 153–167.

29. Michello, F. A., & Ford, W. F. (2006). The unemployment effects of proposed changes in Social Security's normal retirement age. *Business Economics, April,* 38–46; Toossi, M. (2006). Labor force projections to 2014: Retiring boomers. *Monthly Labor Review, 128,* 25–44.

30. Statistics available at the U.S. Department of Labor, Bureau of Labor Statistics at http://www.bls.gov under the menu item "Employment Characteristics of Families in 2007." Released on May 30, 2008. See also U.S. Bureau of the Census, *Statistical Abstract of the United States.* Washington, DC: Table 581, Labor Force Participation Rates.

31. Ibid.

32. Ibid.

33. Raskin, P. M. (2006). Single parents and careers. In Greenhaus & Callanan, pp. 741–742.

34. Statistics available from the U.S. Census Bureau at their Web site at http://www.census.gov. Statistics are listed in Table C2 under the heading "Household Relationship and Living Arrangements of Children Under 18 Years, by Age, Sex, Race, Hispanic Origin."

35. Barley, S. R. (1989). Careers, identities, and institutions: The legacy of the Chicago School of sociology. In M. B. Arthur, D. T. Hall, & B. S. Lawrence (Eds.), *Handbook of career theory* (pp. 41–65). Cambridge, UK: Cambridge University Press.

36. Ng, T. (2006). Career mobility. In Greenhaus & Callanan, pp. 127–130.

37. Collin, A. (2006). Career. In Greenhaus & Callanan, pp. 60–63.

38. Our definition of career management is similar to that provided by Gutteridge, T. G. (1986). Organizational career development systems: The state of the practice. In D. T. Hall & Associates (Eds.), *Career development in organizations* (pp. 50–94). San Francisco: Jossey-Bass.

39. Callanan & Greenhaus (1999).

40. Niles, S. G. (2006). Life-career rainbow. In Greenhaus & Callanan, pp. 470–473; Savickas, M. L. (2006). Career construction theory. In Greenhaus & Callanan, pp. 84–88; Sverko, B. (2006). Super's career development theory. In Greenhaus & Callanan, pp. 789–792.

41. Zytowski, D. G. (2006). Work values. In Greenhaus & Callanan, pp. 863–865.

42. Callanan, G. A. (2003). What price career success? *Career Development International, 8,* 126–133; Seibert, S. E. (2006). Career success. In Greenhaus & Callanan, pp. 148–154.

43. Zytowski (2006).

44. Schein, E. H. (1996). Career anchors revisited: Implications for career development in the 21st century. *Academy of Management Executive, 10,* 80–88; Schein, E. H. (2006). Career anchors. In Greenhaus & Callanan, pp. 63–69.

45. Baruch, Y. (2006). Organizational career management. In Greenhaus & Callanan, pp. 573–580.

46. Beutell, N. J. (2006). Organizational staffing. In Greenhaus & Callanan, pp. 602–606; Gowan, M. A., & Gatewood, R. D. (2006). Personnel selection. In Greenhaus & Callanan, pp. 634–638.

47. Wanous, J. P. (2006). Realistic recruitment. In Greenhaus & Callanan, pp. 672–675.

48. Hughes, T. (2006). Orientation. In Greenhaus & Callanan, pp. 606–608.

49. Callanan & Greenhaus (2008).

50. Godshalk, V. M. (2006). Career plateau. In Greenhaus & Callanan, pp. 133–138.

51. Noble J. G. (2006). Civil Rights Act of 1964. In Greenhaus & Callanan, pp. 169–170; Noble J. G. (2006). Civil Rights Act of 1991. In Greenhaus & Callanan, pp. 170–172.

52. Thomas, K. M. (2006). Diversity in organizations. In Greenhaus & Callanan, pp. 236–243.

53. Foley, S. (2006). Family-responsive workplace practices. In Greenhaus & Callanan, pp. 317–319; Friedman, D. E., & Johnson, A. A. (1997). Moving from programs to culture change: The next stage for the corporate work-family agenda. In S. Parasuraman & J. H. Greenhaus (Eds.), *Integrating work and family: Challenges and choices for a changing world* (pp. 192–208). Westport, CT: Quorum Books.

ENDNOTES FOR CHAPTER 2

1. Callanan, G. A., & Greenhaus, J. H. (1999). Personal and career development: The best and worst of times. In A. I. Kraut & A. K. Korman (Eds.), *Evolving practices in human resource management: Responses to a changing world of work* (pp. 146–171). San Francisco: Jossey-Bass.

2. Greenhaus, J. H., Callanan, G. A., & DiRenzo, M. (2008). A boundaryless perspective on careers. In J. Barling & C. L. Cooper (Eds.), *Sage handbook of organizational behavior* (Vol. 1, pp. 277–299). Thousand Oaks, CA: Sage.

3. Baruch, Y. (2006). Career development in organizations and beyond: Balancing traditional and contemporary viewpoints. *Human Resource Management Review, 16,* 125–138.

4. Kulick, R. B. (2006). Occupational professionalization. In J. H. Greenhaus & G. A. Callanan (Eds.), *Encyclopedia of career development* (pp. 563–567). Thousand Oaks, CA: Sage.

5. Wrzesniewski, A., & Tosti, J. (2006). Career as a calling. In Greenhaus & Callanan, pp. 71–75.

6. Ibid.

7. Arthur, M. B., Inkson, K., & Pringle, J. K. (1999). *The new careers: Individual action & economic change.* London: Sage; Arthur, M. B., Khapova, S. N., & Wilderom, C. P. M. (2005). Career success in a boundaryless career world. *Journal of Organizational Behavior, 26,* 177–202; Arthur, M. B., & Rousseau, D. M. (1996). Introduction: The boundaryless career as a new employment principle. In M. B. Arthur & D. M. Rousseau (Eds.), *The boundaryless career* (pp. 3–20). New York: Oxford University Press; DeFillippi, R. J., & Arthur, M. B. (1994). The boundaryless career: A competency-based perspective. *Journal of Organizational Behavior, 15,* 307–324; Tams, S., & Arthur, M. B. (2006). Boundaryless career. In Greenhaus & Callanan, pp. 44–49.

8. Arthur & Rousseau (1996).

9. Ibid.

10. Arthur et al. (1999); Jackson, C. (1996). Managing and developing a boundaryless career: Lessons from dance and drama. *European Journal of Work & Organizational Psychology, 5,* 617–628; Yamashita, M., & Uenoyama, T. (2006). Boundaryless career and adaptive HR practices in Japan's hotel industry. *Career Development International, 11,* 230–242.

11. Banai, M., & Harry, W. (2004). Boundaryless global careers. *International Studies of Management & Organization, 34,* 96–120; Cappellen, T., & Janssens, M. (2005). Career paths of global managers: Towards future research. *Journal of World Business, 40,* 348–360; Carr, S. C., Inkson, K., & Thorn, K. (2005). From global careers to talent flow: Reinterpreting "brain drain." *Journal of World Business, 40,* 386–398.

12. Greenhaus et al. (2008).

13. Ibid.

14. Arthur & Rousseau (1996); Arthur et al. (1999); DeFillippi & Arthur (1994).

15. Briscoe, J. P. (2006). Protean career. In Greenhaus & Callanan, pp. 649–652.

16. Hall, D. T. (1976). *Careers in organizations.* Glenview, IL: Scott, Foresman.

17. Briscoe, J. P., & Hall, D. T. (2006). The interplay of boundaryless and protean careers: Combinations and implications. *Journal of Vocational Behavior, 69,* 4–18; Briscoe, J. P., Hall, D. T., & DeMuth, R. L. F. (2006). Protean and boundaryless careers: An empirical exploration. *Journal of Vocational Behavior, 69,* 30–47; Hall, D. T., & Mirvis, P. H. (1995). The new career contract: Developing the whole person at midlife and beyond. *Journal of Vocational Behavior, 47,* 269–289; Hall, D. T., & Moss, J. E. (1998). The new protean career contract: Helping organizations and employees adapt. *Organizational Dynamics, 26,* 22–37.

18. Briscoe & Hall (2006).

19. Briscoe & Hall (2006); Mirvis, P. H., & Hall, D. T. (1996). Psychological success and the boundaryless career. In M. B. Arthur & D. (Eds.), *The boundaryless career* (pp. 237–255). New York: Oxford University Press.

20. Dowd, K. O., & Kaplan, D. M. (2005). The career life of academics: Boundaried or boundaryless? *Human Relations, 58,* 699–721; Hall, D. T., Briscoe, J. P., & Kram, K. E. (1997). Identity, values and learning in the protean career. In C. L. Cooper & S. E. Jackson (Eds.), *Creating tomorrow's organizations* (pp. 321–335). London: Wiley.

21. Briscoe & Hall (2006); Inkson, K. (2006). Protean and boundaryless careers as metaphors. *Journal of Vocational Behavior, 69,* 48–63.

22. Greenhaus et al. (2008).

23. Briscoe & Hall (2006).

24. Briscoe et al. (2006).

25. Inkson (2006).

26. Ibid.

27. Inkson, K. (2007). *Understanding careers.* Thousand Oaks, CA: Sage.

28. Krumboltz, J. D., & Jacobs, J. M. (2006). Social learning theory of career development. In Greenhaus & Callanan, pp. 756–759.

29. Jepsen, D. A. (2006). Family background and careers. In Greenhaus & Callanan, pp. 313–317.

30. Ibid.

31. Colakoglu, S. N. (2006). Networking. In Greenhaus & Callanan, pp. 536–537.

32. Ibid.

33. Adams, S. M. (2006). Social capital. In Greenhaus & Callanan, pp. 746–750.

34. Seibert, S. E. (2006). Career success. In Greenhaus & Callanan, pp. 148–154.

35. Colakoglu, S. N. (2006). *The relationship between career boundarylessness and individual well-being: A contingency approach.* Unpublished doctoral dissertation, Drexel University, Philadelphia.

36. Friedman, S. D., & Greenhaus, J. H. (2000). *Work and family—Allies or enemies? What happens when business professionals confront life choices.* New York: Oxford University Press.

37. Eby, L. T., Butts, M., & Lockwood, A. (2003). Predictors of success in the era of boundaryless careers. *Journal of Organizational Behavior, 24,* 689–708; Greenhaus, J. H. (2002). Career dynamics. In W. C. Borman, D. R. Ilgen, & R. J. Klimoski (Eds.), *Comprehensive handbook of psychology: Vol. 12. Industrial and organizational psychology* (pp. 519–540). New York: Wiley.

38. Korman, A. K. (1988). Career success and personal failure: Mid- to late-career feelings and events. In M. London & M. E. Mone (Eds.), *Career growth and human resource strategies* (pp. 81–94). New York: Quorum.

39. Callanan, G. A. (2003). What price career success? *Career Development International, 8,* 126–133.

40. Erikson, E. H. (1963). *Childhood and society.* New York: W. W. Norton; Freud, S. (1959). *Collected papers.* New York: Basic Books; Kohlberg, L. (1964). Development of moral character and moral ideology. In L. Hoffman & L. W. Hoffman (Eds.), *Review of child development research* (Vol. 1, pp. 383–431). New York: Russell Sage; Piaget, J. (1952). *The child's conception of number.* London: Routledge & Kegan Paul.

41. Cytrynbaum, S., & Crites, J. O. (1989). The utility of adult development theory in understanding career adjustment process. In M. B. Arthur, D. T. Hall, & B. S. Lawrence (Eds.), *Handbook of career theory* (pp. 66–88). Cambridge, UK: Cambridge University Press.

42. Schneer, J. A., & Reitman, F. (1990). Effects of employment gaps on the careers of M.B.A.'s: More damaging for men than for women? *Academy of Management Journal, 33,* 391–406.

43. Callanan, G. A., & Greenhaus, J. H. (2008). The baby boom generation and career management: A call to action. *Advances in Developing Human Resources, 10,* 70–85; Keene, J. (2006). Age discrimination. In Greenhaus & Callanan, pp. 10–14.

44. Keene (2006).

45. Peterson, S. J., & Spiker, B. K. (2005). Establishing the positive contributory value of older workers: A positive psychology perspective. *Organizational Dynamics, 34,* 153–167.

46. Levinson, D. J., Darrow, C. N., Klein, E. B., Levinson, M. H., & McKee, B. (1978). *Seasons of a man's life.* New York: Knopf.

47. Super, D. (1957). *The psychology of careers.* New York: Harper & Row; Super, D. (1980). A life-span, life-space approach to career development. *Journal of Vocational Behavior, 16,* 282–298; Sverko, B. (2006). Super's career development theory. In Greenhaus & Callanan, pp. 789–792.

48. Adams, G. R. (2006). Erikson's theory of development. In Greenhaus & Callanan, pp. 295–298.

49. Bischof, L. J. (1976). *Adult psychology.* New York: Harper & Row; quote is on page 32.

50. Levinson et al. (1978).

51. Levinson, D. J. (1986). A conception of adult development. *American Psychologist, 41,* 3–13; Levinson et al. (1978).

52. Levinson, D. J., & Levinson, J. D. (1996). *Seasons of a woman's life.* New York: Knopf.

53. Mainiero, L. A., & Sullivan, S. E. (2005). Kaleidoscope careers: An alternate explanation for the "opt-out" revolution. *Academy of Management Executive, 19,* 106–123; Mainiero, L. A., & Sullivan, S. E. (2006). *The opt-out revolt: Why people are leaving companies to create kaleidoscope careers.* Mountain View, CA: Davies-Black.

54. Ibid.

55. Bardwick, J. M. (1980). The seasons of a woman's life. In D. McGuigan (Ed.), *Women's lives: New theory, research, and policy.* Ann Arbor: Center for Continuing Education of Women, University of Michigan; Mainiero & Sullivan (2006).

56. Greenhaus (2002).

57. Arthur et al. (1999).

58. Ibid.

59. Ibid.

ENDNOTES FOR CHAPTER 3

1. Dubin, R. (1983). Theory building in applied areas. In M. D. Dunnette (Ed.), *Handbook of industrial and organizational psychology* (pp. 17–39). New York: Wiley.

2. Blustein, D. L., Prezioso, M. S., & Schultheiss, D. P. (1995). Attachment theory and career development: Current status and future directions. *Counseling Psychologist, 23,* 416–432; Turner, S., & Lapan, R. T. (2002). Career self-efficacy and perceptions of parent *support* in adolescent career development. *Career Development Quarterly, 51,* 44–55; Zikic, J., & Klehe, U. (2006). Job loss as a blessing in disguise: The role of career exploration and career planning in predicting reemployment quality. *Journal of Vocational Behavior, 69,* 391–409.

3. Walsh, W. B. (2006). Person–environment fit (P–E fit). In J. H. Greenhaus & G. A. Callanan (Eds.), *Encyclopedia of career development* (pp. 622–625). Thousand Oaks, CA: Sage.

4. Gatewood, R. D., & Field, H. S. (2001). *Human resource selection* (5th ed.). Fort Worth, TX: Harcourt College Publishers.

5. Zikic, J. (2006). Career exploration. In Greenhaus & Callanan, pp. 103–107.

6. Atwater, L. E., Waldman, D. A., & Brett, J. F. (2002). Understanding and optimizing multisource feedback. *Human Resource Management, 41,* 193–208; Fletcher, C. (2003). Assessing self-awareness: Some issues and methods. *Journal of Managerial Psychology, 18,* 395–404; Luthans, F., & Peterson, S. J. (2003). 360–degree feedback with systematic coaching: Empirical analysis suggests a winning combination. *Human Resource Management, 42,* 243–256.

7. Zikic (2006).

8. Ibid.

9. Sugalski, T., & Greenhaus, J. H. (1986). Career exploration and goal setting among managerial employees. *Journal of Vocational Behavior, 29,* 102–114.

10. Zikic (2006).

11. Ibid.

12. Singh, R. (2006). Self-awareness. In Greenhaus & Callanan, pp. 709–713.

13. Ibid.

14. Locke, E. A. (2004). Goal-setting theory and its applications to the world of business. *Academy of Management Executive, 18,* 124–125; Locke, E. A., & Latham, G. P. (2000). New directions in goal-setting theory. *Current Directions in Psychological Science, 15,* 265–268; Locke, E. A., & Latham, G. P. (2006). Building a practically useful theory of goal setting and task motivation: A 35 year odyssey. *American Psychologist, 57,* 705–717.

15. Locke & Latham (2006).

16. Greenhaus, J. H. (2006). Career goal. In Greenhaus & Callanan, pp. 107–109.

17. Ibid.

18. Locke (2004); Locke & Latham (2000, 2006).

19. Callanan, G. A. (2006). Career strategy. In Greenhaus & Callanan, pp. 146–148.

20. Dalton, M. (1951). Informal factors in career advancement. *American Journal of Sociology, 56,* 407–415.

21. Jennings, E. E. (1971). *Routes to the executive suite.* New York: Macmillan.

22. Callanan (2006).

23. Larson, L. M., & Bailey, D. C. (2006). Career appraisal. In Greenhaus & Callanan, pp. 69–71.

24. Kildiff, M., & Day, D. V. (1994). Do chameleons get ahead? The effects of self-monitoring on managerial careers. *Academy of Management Journal, 37,* 1047–1060.

25. Brockner, J. (1992). The escalation of commitment to a failing course of action: Toward theoretical progress. *Academy of Management Review, 17,* 39–61; Wong, K. F. E., & Kwong, J. Y. Y. (2007). The role of anticipated regret in escalation of commitment. *Journal of Applied Psychology, 92,* 545–554.

ENDNOTES FOR CHAPTER 4

1. Zikic, J. (2006). Career exploration. In J. H. Greenhaus & G. A. Callanan (Eds.), *Encyclopedia of career development* (pp. 103–107). Thousand Oaks, CA: Sage.

2. Singh, R. (2006). Self-awareness. In Greenhaus & Callanan, pp. 709–713.

3. Hartung, P. J. (2006). Values. In Greenhaus & Callanan, pp. 843–847.

4. Betz, N. E., Fitzgerald, L. F., & Hill, R. E. (1989). Trait-factor theory: Traditional cornerstone of career theory. In M. B. Arthur, D. T. Hall, & B. S. Lawrence (Eds.), *Handbook of career theory* (pp. 26–40). Cambridge, UK: Cambridge University Press; Super, D. E., & Bohn, M. J., Jr. (1970). *Occupational psychology.* Belmont, CA: Wadsworth.

5. Hartung (2006).

6. Allport, G. W., Vernon, P. E., & Lindzey, G. (1960). *Study of values: A scale for measuring dominant interests in personality.* Boston: Houghton Mifflin.

7. Schwartz, S. E. (1999). A theory of cultural values and some implications for work. *Applied Psychology: An International Review, 48,* 23–47.

8. Allport et al. (1960); Rokeach, M. (1973). *Nature of human values.* Palo Alto, CA: Consulting Psychologists Press; Super, D. E. (1970). *Work Values Inventory.* New York: Houghton Mifflin; Zytowski, D. G. (2006). Work values. In Greenhaus & Callanan, pp. 863–864.

9. Borgen, F. H. (2006). Interests. In Greenhaus & Callanan, pp. 393–396.

10. Ibid.

11. Betz et al. (1989); Oleski, D., & Subich, L. M. (1996). Congruence and career change in employed adults. *Journal of Vocational Behavior, 49,* 221–229.

12. Holland, J. L. (1997) *Making vocational choices* (3rd ed.). Odessa, FL: Psychological Assessment Resources; Shahnasarian, M. (2006). Holland's theory of vocational choice. In Greenhaus & Callanan, pp. 352–356.

13. Strack, S. (1995). Relating Millon's basic personality styles and Holland's occupational types. *Journal of Vocational Behavior, 45,* 41–54; Tokar, D. M., & Swanson, J. L. (1995). Evaluation of the correspondence between Holland's vocational personality typology and the five-factor model of personality. *Journal of Vocational Behavior, 46,* 89–108.

14. Dik, B. J. (2006). Strong Interest Inventory. In Greenhaus & Callanan, pp. 778–785; Strong, E. K. (1943). *Vocational interests of men and women.* Stanford, CA: Stanford University Press.

15. Donnay, D. A., Thompson, R. C., Morris, M. L., & Schaubhut, N. A. (2004). *Technical brief for the newly revised Strong Interest Inventory assessment.* Palo Alto, CA: Consulting Psychologists Press.

16. Ibid.

17. Crant, J. M. (2006). Personality and careers. In Greenhaus & Callanan, pp. 627–634.

18. Dilchert, S., Ones, D. S., Van Rooy, D. L., & Viswesvaran, C. (2006). Big Five factors of personality. In Greenhaus & Callanan, pp. 36–42.

19. Rotundo, M. (2006). Abilities. In Greenhaus & Callanan, pp. 1–5.

20. Ackerman, P. L., & Beier, M. E. (2003). Intelligence, personality, and interests in the career choice process. *Journal of Career Assessment, 11,* 205–218; Larson, L. M., Rottinghaus, P. J., &

Borgen, F. H. (2002). Meta-analyses of Big Six interests and Big Five personality factors. *Journal of Vocational Behavior, 61,* 217–239.

21. Randahl, G. J. (1991). A typological analysis of the relations between measured vocational interests and abilities. *Journal of Vocational Behavior, 38,* 333–350; Swanson, J. L. (1993). Integrated assessment of vocational interests and self-rated skills and abilities. *Journal of Career Assessment, 1,* 50–65.

22. Schein, E. H. (2006). Career anchors. In Greenhaus & Callanan, pp. 63–69.

23. Hansen, J. C. (2006). Leisure interests. In Greenhaus & Callanan, pp. 468–469.

24. Ibid.

25. Rokeach (1973).

26. Zytowski, D. G. (2006). Work Values Inventory. In Greenhaus & Callanan, pp. 865–866.

27. Zytowski, D. G. (2006). *Technical manual for Super's Work Values Inventory-revised,* Version 1.0. Available at http://www.kuder.com

28. Kopelman, R. E., & Rovenpor, J. L. (2006). Allport–Vernon–Lindzey Study of Values. In Greenhaus & Callanan, pp. 15–18.

29. Kopelman, R. E., Rovenpor, J. L., & Guan, M. (2003). The Study of Values: Construction of the fourth edition. *Journal of Vocational Behavior, 62,* 203–220.

30. Dik (2006).

31. Reardon, R. C., & Lenz, J. G. (2006). Self-directed search (SDS). In Greenhaus & Callanan, pp. 717–719; Taber, B. J. (2006). Vocational Preference Inventory (VPI). In Greenhaus & Callanan, pp. 849–851.

32. Hammer, A. L., & Schnell, E. R. (2000). *FIRO-B technical guide.* Palo Alto, CA: Consulting Psychologists Press; Schnell, E. R. (2006). FIRO-B. In Greenhaus & Callanan, pp. 321–322.

33. Toman, S. (2006). Kuder career assessments. In Greenhaus & Callanan, pp. 451–452.

34. Boggs, K. R. (2006). Campbell Interest and Skill Survey. In Greenhaus & Callanan, pp. 58–60.

35. Hammer, A. L. (2006). Myers-Briggs Type Indicator. In Greenhaus & Callanan, pp. 524–527; Hammer, A. L. (2004). *User's guide for the MBTI career report.* Palo Alto, CA: Consulting Psychologists Press.

36. Kummerow, J. E. (1991). Using the Strong Interest Inventory and the Myers-Briggs Type Indicator together in career counseling. In J. E. Kummerow (Ed.), *New directions in career planning and the workplace* (pp. 61–93). Palo Alto, CA: Consulting Psychologists Press.

37. Chernyshenko, O. S., & Stark, S. (2006). Sixteen Personality Factor Questionnaire (16PF). In Greenhaus & Callanan, pp. 743–746.

38. Walter, V. (2000). *16PF Personal Career Development Profile: Technical and interpretive manual.* Champaign, IL: Institute for Personality and Ability Testing.

39. Butcher, J. N., & Perry, J. N. (2006). Minnesota Multiphasic Personality Inventory-2 (MMPI-2). In Greenhaus & Callanan, pp. 505–507.

40. Ibid.

41. Fuqua, D. R., & Newman, J. L. (2006). California Psychological Inventory. In Greenhaus & Callanan, pp. 57–58.

42. Ibid.

43. Converse, P. D., & Oswald, F. L. (2006). General Aptitude Test Battery (GATB). In Greenhaus & Callanan, pp. 331–333.

44. Baker, H. (2006). Armed Services Vocational Aptitude Battery (ASVAB). In Greenhaus & Callanan, pp. 25–26.

45. Leuty, M. E., & Hansen, J. C. (2006). Bennett Mechanical Comprehension Test. In Greenhaus & Callanan, p. 33.

46. Khapova, S. N., & Wilderom, C. P. M. (2006). Computer-based career support systems. In Greenhaus & Callanan, pp. 191–193.

47. Baruch, Y. (2006). Organizational career management. In Greenhaus & Callanan, pp. 572–580.

48. Shivy, V. A. (2006). Career-planning workshops. In Greenhaus & Callanan, pp. 132–133.

49. Woehr, D. J. (2006). Assessment centers. In Greenhaus & Callanan, pp. 27–31.

50. Prochaska, S. (2006). Three-hundred-sixty-degree (360°) evaluation. In Greenhaus & Callanan, pp. 807–810.

51. Clawson, J. G., Kotter, J. P., Faux, V. A., & McArthur, C. C. (1992). *Self-assessment and career development* (3rd ed.). Englewood Cliffs, NJ: Prentice Hall.

52. Bretz, R. D., & Judge, T. A. (1994). Person-organization fit and the theory of work adjustment: Implications for satisfaction, tenure, and career success. *Journal of Vocational Behavior, 44,* 32–54; Walsh, W. B. (2006). Person–environment fit (P–E fit). In Greenhaus & Callanan, pp. 622–625.

53. Wilk, S. L., Desmaris, L. B., & Sackett, P. R. (1995). Gravitation to jobs commensurate with ability: Longitudinal and cross-sectional tests. *Journal of Applied Psychology, 80,* 79–85.

54. Callanan, G. A., & Greenhaus, J. H. (1990). The career indecision of managers and professionals: Development of a scale and test of a model. *Journal of Vocational Behavior, 37,* 79–103.

55. Bublitz, S. T., & Levine, J. D. (2006). Occupational classification systems. In Greenhaus & Callanan, pp. 554–558.

56. Hartman, R. O. (2006). Occupational Information Network (O*NET). In Greenhaus & Callanan, pp. 559–560.

57. Hartman, R. O. (2006). Occupational outlook handbook. In Greenhaus & Callanan, pp. 560–561.

58. Bublitz & Levine (2006).

59. Durrance, J. C. (1991). Kellogg funded education and career information centers in public libraries. *Journal of Career Development, 18,* 11–18; Tice, K. E., & Gill, S. J. (1991). Education information centers: An evaluation. *Journal of Career Development, 18,* 37–50.

60. Sugalski, T., & Greenhaus, J. H. (1986). Career exploration and goal setting among managerial employees. *Journal of Vocational Behavior, 29,* 102–114.

61. Callanan, G. A., & Greenhaus, J. H. (1992). The career indecision of managers and professionals: An examination of multiple subtypes. *Journal of Vocational Behavior, 41,* 212–231.

62. Greenhaus, J. H., Hawkins, B. L., & Brenner, O. C. (1983). The impact of career exploration on the career decision-making process. *Journal of College Student Personnel, 24,* 495–502.

63. Greenhaus, J. H., & Sklarew, N. D. (1981). Some sources and consequences of career exploration. *Journal of Vocational Behavior, 18,* 1–12.

64. Callanan & Greenhaus (1992).

65. Callanan, G. A., & Benzing, C. (2004). Assessing the role of internships in the career-oriented employment of graduating college students. *Education + Training, 46,* 77–83.

ENDNOTES FOR CHAPTER 5

1. Locke, E. A., & Latham, G. P. (2006). New directions in goal-setting theory. *Current Directions in Psychological Science, 15,* 265–268.

2. Latham, G. P., & Locke, E. A. (2006). Enhancing the benefits and overcoming the pitfalls of goal setting. *Organizational Dynamics, 35,* 332–340.

3. Mirvis, P. H., & Hall, D. T. (1994). Psychological success and the boundaryless career. *Journal of Organizational Behavior, 15,* 365–380.

4. Wong, K. F. E., Yik, M., & Kwong, J. Y. Y. (2006). Understanding the emotional aspects of escalation of commitment: The role of negative affect. *Journal of Applied Psychology, 91,* 282–297.

5. Cappelli, P. (2006). Churning of jobs. In J. H. Greenhaus & G. A. Callanan (Eds.), *Encyclopedia of career development* (pp. 165–167). Thousand Oaks, CA: Sage.

6. Callanan, G. A., & Greenhaus, J. H. (1990). The career indecision of managers and professionals: Development of a scale and test of a model. *Journal of Vocational Behavior, 37,* 79–103.

7. Foley, P. M., Kelly, M. E., & Hartman, B. W. (2006). Career indecision. In Greenhaus & Callanan, pp. 109–115.

8. Ibid.

9. Callanan & Greenhaus (1990).

10. Ibid.

11. Crites, J. O. (1969). *Vocational psychology.* New York: McGraw-Hill; Goodstein, L. D. (1965). Behavioral view of counseling. In B. Stefflre (Ed.), *Theories of counseling* (pp. 140–192). New York: McGraw-Hill.

12. Callanan, G. A., & Greenhaus, J. H. (1992). The career indecision of managers and professionals: An examination of multiple subtypes. *Journal of Vocational Behavior, 41,* 212–231.

13. Ibid.

14. Janis, I. L., & Mann, L. (1976). Coping with decisional conflict. *American Scientist, 64,* 657–667.

15. Callanan & Greenhaus (1992).

16. Greenhaus, J. H., Callanan, G. A., & Kaplan, E. (1995). The role of goal setting in career management. *International Journal of Career Management, 7,* 3–12.

17. Callanan, G. A., & Greenhaus, J. H. (1999). Personal and career development: The best and worst of times. In A. I. Kraut & A. K. Korman (Eds.), *Evolving practices in human resource management: Responses to a changing world of work* (pp. 146–171). San Francisco: Jossey-Bass.

18. Callanan, G. A. (2006). Career strategy. In Greenhaus & Callanan, pp. 146–148.

19. Barney, J. B., & Lawrence, B. S. (1989). Pin stripes, power ties and personal relationships: The economics of career strategy. In M. B. Arthur, D. T. Hall, & B. S. Lawrence (Eds.), *Handbook of career theory* (pp. 417–436). Cambridge, UK: Cambridge University Press.

20. Arthur, M. B., Claman, P. H., & DeFillippi, R. J. (1995). Intelligent enterprise, intelligent careers. *Academy of Management Executive, 9,* 7–20.

21. Ibid.

22. Brett, J. M., & Stroh, L. K. (1997). Jumping ship: Who benefits from an external labor market career strategy? *Journal of Applied Psychology, 82,* 331–341.

23. Allen, T. D. (2006). Mentoring. In Greenhaus & Callanan, pp. 486–493.

24. Barney & Lawrence (1989).

25. Arthur, M. B. (1994). The boundaryless career: A new perspective for organizational inquiry. *Journal of Organizational Behavior, 15,* 295–306.

26. Turnley, W. H., & Bolino, M. C. (2006). Impression management. In Greenhaus & Callanan, pp. 374–378.

27. Ibid.

28. Ibid.

29. Adams, S. M. (2006). Social capital. In Greenhaus & Callanan, pp. 746–750.

30. This assignment is adapted from an exercise originally developed by Laker, D. R., & Laker, R. (2007). The five-year resume: A career planning exercise. *Journal of Management Education, 31,* 128–141.

ENDNOTES FOR CHAPTER 6

1. Callanan, G. A. (2006). Organizational entry. In J. H. Greenhaus & G. A. Callanan (Eds.), *Encyclopedia of career development* (pp. 586–588). Thousand Oaks, CA: Sage; Wanous, J. P. (1992). *Organizational entry: Recruitment, selection, orientation and socialization of newcomers.* Reading, MA: Addison-Wesley.

2. Crites, J. O. (1969). *Vocational psychology.* New York: McGraw-Hill.

3. Pryor, R. G., & Bright, J. E. (2006). Occupational choice. In Greenhaus & Callanan, pp. 547–554.

4. Holland, J. L. (1966). *The psychology of vocational choice.* Waltham, MA: Blaisdell; Holland, J. L. (1985). *Making vocational choices: A theory of vocational personalities and work environments.* Englewood Cliffs, NJ: Prentice Hall; Holland, J. L. (1997). *Making vocational choices: A theory of vocational personalities and work environments* (3rd ed.). Odessa, FL: Psychological Assessment Resources; Shahnasarian, M. (2006). Holland's theory of vocational choice. In Greenhaus & Callanan, pp. 352–356.

5. Shahnasarian (2006).

6. Walsh, W. B. (2006). Person–environment fit (P–E fit). In Greenhaus & Callanan, pp. 622–625.

7. Super, D. E. (1963). Toward making self-concept theory operational. In D. E. Super, R. Starishevsky, N. Matlin, & J. P. Jordaan (Eds.), *Career development: Self-concept theory* (pp. 17–32). New York: College Entrance Examination Board.

8. Muchinsky, D. M., & Monahan, C. J. (1987). What is person–environment congruence? Supplementary versus complementary models of fit. *Journal of Vocational Behavior, 31,* 268–277.

9. Blustein, D. L., Kenna, A. C., Murphy, K. A., & Devoy Whitcavitch, J. E. (2006). Self-concept. In Greenhaus & Callanan, pp. 713–717; Sverko, B. (2006). Super's career development theory. In Greenhaus & Callanan, pp. 789–625.

10. Blustein et al. (2006).

11. Callanan, G. A. (2006). Anticipatory socialization. In Greenhaus & Callanan, pp. 20–21; Callanan, G. A., & Benzing, C. (2004). Assessing the role of internships in the career-oriented employment of graduating college students. *Education + Training, 46,* 77–83.

12. Phillips, S. D., & Jome, L. M. (2006). Career decision-making styles. In Greenhaus & Callanan, pp. 94–96.

13. Osborn, D. P. (1990). A reexamination of the organizational choice process. *Journal of Vocational Behavior, 36,* 45–60.

14. Sauermann, H. (2005). Vocational choice: A decision making perspective. *Journal of Vocational Behavior, 66,* 273–303; Singh, R., & Greenhaus, J. H. (2004). The relationship between career decision-making strategies and person–job fit: A study of job changers. *Journal of Vocational Behavior, 64,* 198–221.

15. Singh & Greenhaus (2004).

16. Osipow, S. H. (1983). *Theories of career development.* Englewood Cliffs, NJ: Prentice Hall.

17. Giscombe, K. (2006). Socioeconomic status. In Greenhaus & Callanan, pp. 759–761.

18. Ibid.

19. Thompson, M. N., & Subich, L. M. (2006). The relation of social status to the career decision-making process. *Journal of Vocational Behavior, 69,* 289–301.

20. Jepsen, D. A. (2006). Family background and careers. In Greenhaus & Callanan, pp. 313–317.

21. Fouad, N. A. (2006). Culture and careers. In Greenhaus & Callanan, pp. 214–220.

22. Brown, M. T., Fukunaga, C., Umemoto, D., & Wicker, L. (1996). Annual review, 1990–1996: Social class, work, and retirement behavior. *Journal of Vocational Behavior, 49,* 159–189.

23. Gonzalez, P. (2006). Informational interview. In Greenhaus & Callanan, pp. 387–389.

24. Callanan (2006); Wanous (1992).

25. Wanous (1992).

26. Ibid.

27. Griffeth, R. W., & Hom, P. W. (2001). *Retaining valued employees.* Thousand Oaks, CA: Sage.

28. Soelberg, P. O. (1967). Unprogrammed decision making. *Industrial Management Review, 8,* 19–29.

29. Gatewood, R. D., Gowan, M. A., & Lautenschlager, G. J. (1993). Corporate image, recruitment image, and initial job choice decisions. *Academy of Management Journal, 36,* 414–427; Kolenko, T. A. (2006). Organizational image. In Greenhaus & Callanan, pp. 588–589.

30. Saks, A. M. (2006). Multiple predictors and criteria of job search success. *Journal of Vocational Behavior, 68,* 400–415.

31. Wanous (1992).

32. Greenhaus, J. H., Seidel, C., & Marinis, M. (1983). The impact of expectations and values on job attitudes. *Organizational Behavior and Human Performance, 31,* 394–417; Schleicher, D. J., & Fox, K. E. (2006). Job satisfaction. In Greenhaus & Callanan, pp. 436–440.

33. Schein, E. H. (1978). *Career dynamics: Matching individual and organizational needs.* Reading, MA: Addison-Wesley.

34. Greenhaus, J. H., Sugalski, T., & Crispin, G. (1978). Relationships between perceptions of organizational size and the organizational choice process. *Journal of Vocational Behavior, 13,* 113–125.

35. Gatewood et. al. (1993).

36. Piotrowski, C., & Armstrong, T. (2006). Current recruitment and selection practices: A national survey of Fortune 1000 firms. *North American Journal of Psychology, 8,* 489–486.

37. Turban, D. B. (2006). Recruitment. In Greenhaus & Callanan, pp. 675–679.

38. Turban, D. B., Campion, J. E., & Eyring, A. R. (1995). Factors related to job acceptance decisions of college recruits. *Journal of Vocational Behavior, 47,* 193–213.

39. Chapman, D. S., Uggerslev, K. L., Carroll, S. A., Piasentin, K. A., & Jones, D. A. (2005). Applicant attraction to organizations and job choice: A meta-analytic review of correlates of recruiting outcomes. *Journal of Applied Psychology, 90,* 928–944.

40. Derous, E. (2007). Investigating personnel selection from a counseling perspective: Do applicants and recruiters' perceptions correspond? *Journal of Employment Counseling, 44,* 60–72.

41. Turban et al. (1995).

42. Wanous, J. P. (2006). Realistic recruitment. In Greenhaus & Callanan, pp. 672–675.

43. Buda, R., & Charnov, B. C. (2003). Message processing in realistic recruitment practices. *Journal of Managerial Issues, 15,* 302–316.

44. Wanous (2006).

45. Ibid.

46. Saks, A. M., Wiesner, W. H., & Summers, R. J. (1994). Effects of job previews on self-selection and job choice. *Journal of Vocational Behavior, 44,* 297–316.

47. Saks, A. M., Wiesner, W. H., & Summers, R. J. (1996). Effects of job previews and compensation policy on applicant attraction and job choice. *Journal of Vocational Behavior, 49,* 68–85.

48. Gatewood, R. D., & Feild, H. S. (2001). *Human resource selection* (5th ed.). Orlando, FL: Harcourt; Gowan, M. A., & Gatewood, R. D. (2006). Personnel selection. In Greenhaus & Callanan, pp. 634–638.

49. Bretz, R. D., Rynes, S. L., & Gerhart, B. (1993). Recruiter perceptions of applicant fit: Implications for individual career preparation and job search behavior. *Journal of Vocational Behavior, 43,* 310–327.

50. Behling, O. (1998). Employee selection: Will intelligence and conscientiousness do the job? *Academy of Management Executive, 12,* 77–86.

51. Le, H., Oh, I., Shaffer, J., & Schmidt, F. (2007). Implications of methodological advances for the practice of personnel selection: How practitioners benefit from meta-analysis. *Academy of Management Perspectives, 21,* 6–15.

52. Arthur, W., Jr., Bell, S. T., Villado, A. J., & Doverspike, D. (2006). The use of person–organization fit in employment decision making: An assessment of its criterion-related validity. *Journal of Applied Psychology, 91,* 786–801; Hoffman, B. J., & Woehr, D. J. (2006). A quantitative review of the relationship between person–organization fit and behavioral outcomes. *Journal of Vocational Behavior, 68,* 389–399; Saks, A. M., & Ashforth, B. E. (2002). Is job search related to employment quality? It all depends on fit. *Journal of Applied Psychology, 87,* 646–654.

53. Kammeyer-Mueller, J. D., & Wanberg, C. R. (2003). Unwrapping the organizational entry process: Disentangling multiple antecedents and their pathways to adjustment. *Journal of Applied Psychology, 88,* 779–794.

54. Zikic, J., & Klehe, U. (2006). Job loss as a blessing in disguise: The role of career exploration and career planning in predicting reemployment quality. *Journal of Vocational Behavior, 69,* 391–409.

55. Adams, S. M. (2006). Social capital. In Greenhaus & Callanan, pp. 746–750.

56. Cober, R. T. (2006). Internet recruitment. In Greenhaus & Callanan, pp. 406–409; Williamson, I. O., Lepak, D. P., & King, J. (2003). The effect of company recruitment Web site orientation on individuals' perceptions of organizational attractiveness. *Journal of Vocational Behavior, 63,* 242–263.

57. Philbrick, J. H., Sparks, M. R., & Arsenault, S. (2006). Electronic employment screening. In Greenhaus & Callanan, pp. 257–259.

58. Gonzalez (2006).

59. Clawson, J. G., Kotter, J. P., Faux, V. A., & McArthur, C. C. (1992). *Self-assessment and career development* (3rd ed.). Englewood Cliffs, NJ: Prentice Hall.

60. Enigma is a fictitious name and should not be confused with any real company.

ENDNOTES FOR CHAPTER 7

1. Bray, D. W., Campbell, R. J., & Grant, D. L. (1974). *Formative years in business: A long-term AT&T study of managerial lives.* New York: Wiley; Coy, D. R., & Kovacs-Long, J. (2005). Maslow and Miller: An exploration of gender and affiliation in the journey to competence. *Journal of Counseling & Development, 83,* 138–145; Hall, D. T., & Nougaim, K. (1968). An examination of Maslow's need hierarchy in an organizational setting. *Organizational Behavior and Human Performance, 3,* 12–35; Surrey, J. L. (1991). The self-in-relation: A theory of women's development. In J. V. Jordan, A. G. Kaplan, J. B. Miller, I. P. Silver, & J. L. Surrey (Eds.), *Women's growth in connection* (pp. 51–60). New York: Guilford Press.

2. Schein, E. H. (1993). *Career anchors* (2nd ed.). San Francisco: Jossey-Bass Pfeiffer; Schein, E. H. (2006). Career anchors. In J. H. Greenhaus & G. A. Callanan (Eds.), *Encyclopedia of career development* (pp. 63–69). Thousand Oaks, CA: Sage.

3. Dix, J. E., & Savickas, M. L. (1995). Establishing a career: Developmental tasks and coping responses. *Journal of Vocational Behavior, 47,* 93–107.

4. Myers, K. M. (2006). Assimilation and mutual acceptance. In Greenhaus & Callanan, pp. 31–32.

5. Chao, G. T. (2006). Organizational socialization. In Greenhaus & Callanan, pp. 596–602; quote is on p. 596.

6. Schein, E. H. (1990). Organizational culture. *American Psychologist, 2,* 109–119; quote is on p. 111.

7. Myers, K., & Oetzel, J. G. (2003). Exploring the dimensions of organizational assimilation: Creating and validating a measure. *Communications Quarterly, 51,* 438–457.

8. Bauer, T. M., Morrison, E. W., & Callister, R. R. (1998). Organizational socialization: A review and directions for future research. *Research in Personnel and Human Resource Management, 16,* 149–214; Chao (2006); Chao, G. T., O'Leary-Kelly, A. M., Wolf, S., Klein, H. J., & Gardner, P. D. (1994). Organizational socialization: Its content and consequences. *Journal of Applied Psychology, 79,* 730–743.

9. Chao et al. (1994).

10. Chao (2006).

11. Chao (2006); Wanous, J. P. (1992). *Recruitment, selection, orientation and socialization of newcomers.* Reading, MA: Addison-Wesley; Zottoli, M. A., & Wanous, J. P. (2000). Recruitment source research: Current status and future directions. *Human Resource Management Review, 10,* 353–382.

12. Callanan, G. A. (2006). Anticipatory socialization. In Greenhaus & Callanan, pp. 20–21; Chao (2006); Callanan, G. A., & Benzing, C. (2004). Assessing the role of internships in the career-oriented employment of graduating college students. *Education and Training, 46,* 82–89; Scholaris, D., Lockyer, C., & Johnson, H. (2003). Anticipatory socialization: The effects of recruitment and selection experiences on career expectations. *Career Development International, 8,* 182–197.

13. Chao (2006).

14. Chao (2006); Morrison, E. W. (1993). Newcomer information seeking: Exploring types, modes, sources, and outcomes. *Academy of Management Journal, 36,* 557–589; Morrison, E. W. (2002). Newcomers' relationships: The role of social network ties during socialization. *Academy of Management Journal, 45,* 1149–1160.

15. Turban, D. B. (2006). Recruitment. In Greenhaus & Callanan, pp. 675–679; Wanous, J. P. (2006). Realistic recruitment. In Greenhaus & Callanan, pp. 672–675.

16. Arthur, W., Jr., Bennett, W., Jr., Edens, P. S., & Bell, S. T. (2003). Effectiveness of training organizations: A meta-analysis of design and evaluation features. *Journal of Applied Psychology, 88,* 234–245; Heames, J. T. (2006). Training and development. In Greenhaus & Callanan, pp. 817–818.

17. Schein, E. H. (1978). *Career dynamics: Matching individual and organizational needs.* Reading, MA: Addison-Wesley.

18. Wanous (1992); Wanous, J. P., & Reichers, A. E. (2000). New employee orientation programs. *Human Resource Management Review, 10,* 435–451.

19. Eichinger, R. W., & Lombardo, M. M. (2003). Knowledge summary series: 360–degree assessment. *Human Resource Planning, 26,* 34–44.

20. Ashforth, B. E., & Saks, A. M. (1996). Socialization tactics: Longitudinal effects on newcomer adjustment. *Academy of Management Journal, 39,* 149–178; Feldman, D. C. (1981). The multiple socialization of organization members. *Academy of Management Review, 6,* 309–319; Schein, E. H. (1964). How to break in the college graduate. *Harvard Business Review, 42,* 68–76; Schein (1978); Wanous (1992).

21. Schein (1978).

22. Allen, N. J., & Meyer, J. P. (1990). Organizational socialization tactics: A longitudinal analysis of links to newcomers' commitment and role orientation. *Academy of Management Journal, 33,* 847–858; Jones, G. R. (1986). Socialization tactics, self-efficacy, and newcomers' adjustments to organizations. *Academy of Management Journal, 29,* 262–279.

23. Myers, K. K. (2006). Assimilation and mutual acceptance. In Greenhaus & Callanan, pp. 31–32; Schein (1978).

24. Robinson, S. L., Kraatz, M. S., & Rousseau, D. M. (1994). Changing obligations and the psychological contract: A longitudinal study. *Academy of Management Journal, 37,* 137–152.

25. Coyle-Shapiro, J. A. M. (2006). Psychological contract. In Greenhaus & Callanan, pp. 652–659; Robinson et al. (1994); Rousseau, D. M., & Wade-Benzoni, K. A. (1995). Changing individual-organization attachments: A two-way street. In A. Howard (Ed.), *The changing nature of work.* San Francisco: Jossey-Bass.

26. Nicholson N. (1996). Career systems in crisis: Change and opportunity in the information age. *Academy of Management Executive, 10,* 40–51.

27. Schein (1978).

28. Klemm, C. (2007). Quarter-life crisis hits those in transition to adulthood. *Knight Ridder Tribune Business News,* June 24, pg. 1; Robbins, A., & Wilner, A. (2001). *Quarterlife crisis: The unique challenges of life in your twenties.* New York: Putnam/Tarcher.

29. Lindsey, E. H., Homes, V., & McCall, M. W. (1987). *Key events in executives' lives.* Greensboro, NC: Center for Creative Leadership; McCall, M. W. (1988). Developing executives through work experiences. *Human Resource Planning, 11,* 1–11; McCall, M. W., Lombardo, M. M., & Morrison, A. M. (1988). *The lessons of experience: How successful executives develop on the job.* Lexington, MA: Lexington Books; McCauley, C. D., & Van Velsor, E. (2004). *The Center for Creative Leadership handbook for leadership development* (2nd ed.). San Francisco: Jossey-Bass; Ruderman, M. N., & Ohlott, P. J. (2002). *Standing at the crossroads: Next steps for high-achieving women.* San Francisco: Jossey-Bass.

30. McCall et al. (1988).

31. D'Aurizio, P. (2007). Onboarding: Delivering on the promise. *Nursing Economics, 25*(4), 228–229; Morel, S. (2007). Onboarding secures talent for the long run. *Workforce Management, 86*(12*),* 9; Smith, R. E. (1984). Employee orientation: 10 steps to success. *Personnel Journal, 63,* 46–48.

32. D'Aurizio (2007); Frear, S. (2007). *Comprehensive onboarding: Traction to engagement in 90 days.* Washington, DC: Human Capital Institute.

33. Dixon, M. A., Cunningham, G. B., Sagas, M., Turner, B. A., & Kent, A. (2005). Challenge is the key: An investigation of affective commitment in undergraduate interns. *Journal of Education for Business, 80,* 172–180; Morrison, R. F., & Brantner, T. M. (1992). What enhances or inhibits learning a new job? A basic career issue. *Journal of Applied Psychology, 77,* 926–941; Shalley, C. A., Gilson, L. L., & Blum, T. C. (2000). Matching creativity requirements and the work environment: Effects on satisfaction and intention to leave. *Academy of Management Journal, 43,* 215–223.

34. Driskell, J. E., & Mullen, B. (1990). Status, expectations and behavior: A meta-analytic review and test of the theory. *Personality and Social Psychology Bulletin, 16,* 541–553.

35. *Taste the success.* Retrieved February 5, 2008, from http://www.pepsico.com/PEP_Careers/TastetheSuccess/index.cfm; *Opportunities for new grads,* retrieved February 5, 2008, from http://www.pepsico.com/PEP_Careers/CampusSeeker/RecentGraduates/index.cfm

36. Hall, D. T. (2004). The protean career: A quarter-century journey. *Journal of Vocational Behavior, 65,* 1–13.

37. Mai-Dalton, R. R., & Sullivan, J. J. (1981). The effects of manager's sex on the assignment to a challenging or dull task and reasons for the choice. *Academy of Management Journal, 24,* 603–612; Ransom, M., & Oaxaca, R. L. (2005). Intrafirm mobility and sex differences in pay. *Industrial & Labor Relations Review, 58,* 219–237.

38. Porter, L. W., Lawler, E. E., & Hackman, J. R. (1975). *Behavior in organizations.* New York: McGraw-Hill.

39. Hall (2004).

40. Ragins, B. R., & Kram, K. E. (Eds.). (2007). *The handbook of mentoring: Theory, research, and practice.* Thousand Oaks, CA: Sage.

41. Schein (1978).

42. Ragins & Kram (2007).

43. Catalyst. (2004). *Women and men in U.S. corporate leadership: Same workplace, different realities?* New York: Catalyst.

44. Baugh, S. G., Lankau, M. J., & Scandura, T. A. (1996). An investigation of the effects of protégé gender on responses to mentoring. *Journal of Vocational Behavior, 49,* 309–323; Colarelli, S. M., & Bishop, R. C. (1990). Career commitment: Functions, correlates, and management. *Group & Organization Studies, 15,* 158–176; Dreher, G. F., & Chargois, J. A. (1998). Gender, mentoring experiences, and salary attainment among graduates of a historically black university. *Journal of Vocational Behavior, 53,* 401–416; Dreher, G. F., & Cox, T. H., Jr. (1996). Race, gender and opportunity: A study of compensation attainment and the establishment of mentoring relationships. *Journal of Applied Psychology, 81,* 297–308; Fagenson, E. A. (1989). The mentor advantage: Perceived career/job experiences of protégés versus non-protégés. *Journal of Organizational Behavior, 10,* 309–320; Godshalk, V. M., & Sosik, J. J. (2000). Does mentor-protégé agreement on mentor leadership behavior influence the quality of a mentoring relationship? *Group & Organization Management, 25,* 291–317; Scandura, T. A. (1992). Mentorship and career mobility: An empirical investigation. *Journal of Organizational Behavior, 13,* 169–174; Kirchmeyer, C. (2005). The effects of mentoring on academic careers over time: Testing performance and political perspectives. *Human Relations, 58,* 637–660; Turban, D. B., & Dougherty, T. W. (1994). Role of protégé personality in receipt of mentoring and career success. *Academy of Management Journal, 37,* 688–702.

45. O'Neill, R. M. (2002). Gender and race in mentoring relationships: A review of the literature. In D. Clutterbuck & B. R. Ragins (Eds.), *Mentoring and diversity: An international perspective* (pp. 1–22). Oxford, UK: Butterworth-Heinemann; Sosik, J. J., & Godshalk, V. M. (2000). Leadership style, mentoring functions received, and job-related stress: A conceptual model and preliminary study. *Journal of Organizational Behavior, 21,* 365–390; Tharenou, P. (2005). Does mentor support increase women's

career advancement more than men's? The differential effects of career and psychosocial support. *Australian Journal of Management, 30,* 77–110; Wallace, J. E. (2001). The benefits of mentoring for female lawyers. *Journal of Vocational Behavior, 58,* 366–391.

46. Dreher, G. F., & Dougherty, T. W. (1997). Substitutes for career mentoring: Promoting equal opportunity through career management and assessment systems. *Journal of Vocational Behavior, 51,* 110–124.

47. Benabou, C., & Benabou, R. (2000). Establishing a formal mentoring program for organizational success. *National Productivity Review, 19*(4), 1–8; Butyn, S. (2003). Mentoring your way to improved retention. *Canadian HR Reporter, 16*(2), 13–15; Gibbs, S. (1999). The usefulness of theory: A case study in evaluating formal mentoring schemes. *Human Relations, 52,* 1055–1075; Payne, S. C., & Huffman, A. H. (2005). A longitudinal examination of the influence of mentoring on organizational commitment and turnover. *Academy of Management Journal, 48,* 158–168; Perrone, J. (2003). Creating a mentoring culture. *Healthcare Executive, 18*(3), 84–85; Singh, V., Bains, D., & Vinnicombe, S. (2002). Informal mentoring as an organizational resource. *Long Range Planning, 35,* 389–405.

48. Baugh, S. G., & Fagenson-Eland, E. A. (2007). Formal mentoring programs. In B. R. Ragins & K. E. Kram (Eds.), *The handbook of mentoring at work: Theory, research, and practice* (pp. 249–272). Thousand Oaks, CA: Sage.

49. Blake-Beard, S. D., Murrell, A., & Thomas, D. (2007). Unfinished business: The impact of race on understanding mentoring relationships. In Ragins & Kram, pp. 223–248; McKeen, C., & Bujaki, M. (2007). Gender and mentoring: Issues, effects and opportunities. In Ragins & Kram, pp. 197–222.

50. Dix & Savickas (1995).

51. *Corporate responsibility: Making the world more beautiful.* Retrieved June 10, 2009, from http://responsibility.avoncompany.com/

52. Levinson, D. J., Darrow, C. N., Klein, E. B., Levinson, M. H., & McKee, B. (1978). *Seasons of a man's life.* New York: Knopf; Levinson, D. J., & Levinson, J. D. (1996). *Seasons of a woman's life.* New York: Knopf.

53. Igbaria, M., Greenhaus, J. H., & Parasuraman, S. (1991). Career orientations of MIS employees: An empirical analysis. *MIS Quarterly, 15,* 151–169.

54. Campion, M. A., Cheraskin, L., & Stevens, M. J. (1994). Career-related antecedents and outcomes of job rotation. *Academy of Management Journal, 37,* 1518–1542; Fox, M. L. (2006). Job design. In Greenhaus & Callanan, pp. 414–420; Ortega, J. (2001). Job rotation as a learning mechanism. *Management Science, 47,* 1361–1371.

55. Bernthal, P., & Wellins, R. (2006). Trends in leader development and succession. *Human Resource Planning, 29*(2), 31–41.

56. For an overview of the work of the Center for Creative Leadership, see McCauley, C. D. (2006). Center for Creative Leadership. In Greenhaus & Callanan, pp. 162–164; for research on the components of managerial jobs, see McCauley, C. D., Ruderman, M. N., Ohlott, P. J., & Morrow, J. E. (1994). Assessing the developmental components of managerial jobs. *Journal of Applied Psychology, 79,* 544–560.

57. McCauley et al. (1994).

58. *Career opportunities.* Retrieved February 20, 2008, from http://www.jnj.com/careers/global/career_advancement/index.htm

59. Kaye, B., & Farren, C. (1996). Up is not the only way. *Training & Development, 50*(2), 48–54.

60. Seibert, S. E. (2006). Career success. In Greenhaus & Callanan, pp. 148–154.

61. Baird, L., & Kram, K. E. (1983). Career dynamics: Managing the superior/subordinate relationship. *Organizational Dynamics, 11,* 46–64.

62. Kovach, B. E. (1989). Successful derailment: What fast-trackers can learn while they're off the track. *Organizational Dynamics, 18*(2), 33–48; Van Velsor, E. (2006). Derailment. In Greenhaus & Callanan, pp. 225–226.

63. Van Velsor, E., & Leslie, J. B. (1995). Why executives derail: Perspectives across time and cultures. *Academy of Management Executive 9*, 62–72; Yeh, Q. J. (2008). Exploring career stages of mid-career and older engineers—When managerial transition matters. *IEEE Transactions on Engineering Management, 55*, 82–94.

64. Crant, J. M. (2006). Personality and careers. In Greenhaus & Callanan, pp. 627–634; Seibert (2006); Levine, S. P. (2006). Self-monitoring. In Greenhaus & Callanan, pp. 729–730.

65. Crant (2006); quote is on p. 633.

66. Greenhaus, J. H., Callanan, G. A., & DiRenzo, M. (2008). A boundaryless perspective on careers. In J. Barling & C. L. Cooper (Eds.), *The Sage handbook of organizational behavior* (Vol. 1, pp. 277–299). Thousand Oaks, CA: Sage; Ragins & Kram (2007).

67. Gaultier, A. (2002). Paying the price: The high cost of executive success. *New Zealand Management, 49*(6), 34–38; Korman, A. K. (1988). Career success and personal failure: Mid- to late-career feelings and events. In M. London & E. M. Mones (Eds.), *Career growth and human resource strategies* (pp. 81–94). New York: Quorum.

68. Scholaris, D., Lockyer, C., & Johnson, H. (2003). Anticipatory socialization: The effect of recruitment and selection experiences on career expectations. *Career Development International, 8,* 182–197.

ENDNOTES FOR CHAPTER 8

1. Toossi, M. (2002). A century of change: The U.S. labor force, 1950–2050. *Monthly Labor Review, 125,* 15–28; Toossi, M. (2005). Labor force projections to 2014: Retiring boomers. *Monthly Labor Review, 128,* 25–44; Toossi, M. (2007). Labor force projections to 2016: More workers in their golden years. *Monthly Labor Review, 130,* 33–52.

2. Levinson, D. J., Darrow, C. N., Klein, E. B., Levinson, M. H., & McKee, B. (1978). *Seasons of a man's life.* New York: Knopf; Levinson, D. J., & Levinson, J. D. (1996). *Seasons of a woman's life.* New York: Knopf; Schein, E. H. (1978). *Career dynamics: Matching individual and organizational needs.* Reading, MA: Addison-Wesley.

3. Burke, R. J. (1999). Career success and personal failure feelings among managers. *Psychological Reports, 84,* 651–654; Nicholson, N., & de Waal-Andrews, W. (2005). Playing to win: Biological imperatives, self-regulation, and trade-offs in the game of career success. *Journal of Organizational Behavior, 26,* 137–154.

4. Arthur, M. B., Inkson, K., & Pringle, J. K. (1999). *The new careers: Individual action & economic change.* London: Sage; Gordon, J. R., & Whelan, K. S. (1998). Successful professional women in midlife: How organizations can more effectively understand and respond to the challenges. *Academy of Management Executive, 12,* 8–24.

5. Levinson et al. (1978); Levinson & Levinson (1996).

6. Cohen, G. (2006, January 16). The myth of the midlife crisis; It's time we stop dismissing middle age as the beginning of the end. Research suggests that at 40, the brain's best years are ahead. *Newsweek,* p. 82; Lachman, M. E. (2004). Development in midlife. *Annual Review of Psychology, 55,* 305–331.

7. Baltes, P. B., Staudinger, U. M., & Lindenberger, U. (1999). Lifespan psychology: Theory and application to intellectual functioning. *Annual Review of Psychology, 50,* 471–507; Cohen (2006); Lachman (2004); Lachman, M. E., & Bertrand, R. M. (2001). Personality and the self in midlife. In M. E. Lachman (Ed.), *Handbook of midlife development* (pp. 279–309). New York: Wiley; Magai, C., & Halpern, B. (2001). Emotional development during the middle years. In Lachman, pp. 310–344; Stewart, A. J., & Osgrove, J. M. (1998). Women's personality in middle age: Gender, history and midcourse corrections. *American Psychologist, 53,* 1185–1194.

8. Cohen (2006); Levinson et al. (1978).

9. Morison, R., Erickson, T., & Dychtwald, K. (2006, March). Managing middlescence. *Harvard Business Review,* pp. 78–86.

10. Ference, T. P., Stoner, J. A. F., & Warren, E. K. (1977). Managing the career plateau. *Academy of Management Review, 2,* 602–612; quote is on page 602.

11. Godshalk, V. M. (2006). Career plateau. In J. H. Greenhaus & G. A. Callanan (Eds.), *Encyclopedia of career development* (pp. 133–138). Thousand Oaks, CA: Sage.

12. Ibid.

13. Van Velsor, E., & Leslie, J. B. (1995). Why executives derail: Perspectives across time and cultures. *Academy of Management Executive, 9,* 62–72.

14. Godshalk, V. M. (1997). *The effects of career plateauing on work and non-work outcomes.* Unpublished doctoral dissertation, Drexel University, Philadelphia.

15. Bardwick, J. M. (1986). The plateauing trap. Toronto: Bantam Books; Godshalk (2006); Morison et al. (2006).

16. Allen, T. D., Russell, J. E. A., Poteet, M. L., & Dobbins, G. H. (1999). Learning and development factors related to perceptions of job content and hierarchical plateauing. *Journal of Organizational Behavior, 20,* 1113–1137; Chay, Y. W., Aryee, S., & Chew, I. (1995). Career plateauing: Reactions and moderators among managerial and professional employees. *International Journal of Human Resource Management, 6,* 61–78; Godshalk (1997); Lee, P. C. B. (2003). Going beyond career plateau: Using professional plateau to account for work outcomes. *Journal of Management Development, 22,* 538–551; Nachbagauer, A. G. M., & Riedl, G. (2002). Effects of concepts of career plateaus on performance, work satisfaction, and commitment. *International Journal of Manpower, 23,* 716–733.

17. Godshalk (2006).

18. Allen et al. (1999); Chay et al. (1995); Godshalk (1997).

19. Duffy, J. A. (2000). The application of chaos theory to the career-plateaued worker. *Journal of Employment Counseling, 37,* 229–236; Ettington, D. R. (1997). How human resource practices can help plateaued managers succeed. *Human Resource Management, 36,* 221–234.

20. Fossum, J. A., Arvey, R. D., Paradise, C. A., & Robbins, N. E. (1986). Modeling the skills obsolescence process: A psychological/economic integration. *Academy of Management Review, 11,* 362–374.

21. Kaufman, H. G. (2006). Obsolescence of knowledge and skills. In Greenhaus & Callanan, pp. 539–546; quote is on page 539.

22. Ibid.

23. Ibid.

24. Zimmerman, E. (2003, May 18). To veer in midcareer, away from the money. *New York Times,* p. BU13.

25. Ibarra, H. (2006). Career change. In Greenhaus & Callanan, pp. 77–82.

26. Kunda, G., Barley, S. R., & Evans, J. (2002). Why do contractors contract? The experience of highly skilled technical professionals in a contingent labor market. *Industrial and Labor Relations Review, 55,* 234–261.

27. Ibarra (2006); Khapova, S. N., Arthur, M. B., Wilderom, C. P. M., & Svensson, J. S. (2007). Professional identity as the key to career change intention. *Career Development International, 12,* 584–595.

28. Ibid.

29. Judge, T. A., Boudreau, J. W., & Bretz, R. D., Jr. (1993). Job and life attitudes of male executives. *Journal of Applied Psychology, 79,* 767–782; Judge, T. A., & Watanabe, S. (1993). Another look at the job satisfaction-life satisfaction relationship. *Journal of Applied Psychology, 78,* 939–948.

30. Zimmerman (2003).

31. Heppner, M. J., Multon, K. D., & Johnston, J. A. (1994). Assessing psychological resources during career change: Development of the Career Transitions Inventory. *Journal of Vocational Behavior, 44,* 55–74.

32. Ibarra (2006).

33. Strenger, C., & Ruttenberg, A. (2008). The existential necessity of midlife change. *Harvard Business Review, 86*(2), 82–90.

34. Chung, Y. B. (2006). Career coaching. In Greenhaus & Callanan, pp. 83–84.

35. Ng, T. (2006). Career mobility. In Greenhaus & Callanan, pp. 127–130.

36. Hall, D. T., & Richter, J. (1990). Career gridlock: Baby boomers hit the wall. *Academy of Management Executive, 4,* 7–22.

37. Ettington, D. R. (1998). Successful career plateauing. *Journal of Vocational Behavior, 52,* 72–88.

38. Eichinger, R. W., & Lombardo, M. M. (2003). Knowledge summary series: 360-degree assessment. *Human Resource Planning, 26,* 34–44.

39. Morison et al (2006).

40. Ibid.

41. Kaufman, H. G. (1995). Salvaging displaced employees: Job obsolescence, retraining, and redeployment. In M. London (Ed.), *Employees, careers, and job creation: Developing growth oriented strategies and programs* (pp. 105–120). San Francisco: Jossey-Bass.

42. Larwood, L., Rodkin, S., & Judson, D. (2001). Retraining and the technological productivity paradox. *International Journal of Organizational Theory and Behavior, 4,* 201–224.

43. Hall & Richter (1990); Morison et al. (2006).

44. Gordon, J. R., & Whelan, K. S. (1998). Successful professional women in midlife: How organizations can more effectively understand and respond to the challenges. *Academy of Management Executive, 12*(1), 8–24.

45. Ibid.

46. Morison et al. (2006).

47. Latack, J. C., & Dozier, J. B. (1986). After the ax falls: Job loss as a career transition. *Academy of Management Review, 11,* 375–392; McKee-Ryan, F. M. (2006). Job loss. In Greenhaus & Callanan, pp. 427–432; Wolf, G., London, M., Casey, J., & Pufahl, J. (1995). Career experience and motivation as predictors of training behaviors and outcomes for displaced engineers. *Journal of Vocational Behavior, 47,* 316–331.

48. Cascio, W. F., & Wynn, P. (2004). Managing a downsizing process. *Human Resource Management, 43,* 425–436; Latack & Dozier (1986); Marks, M. L., & deMeuse, K. P. (2005). Resizing the organization: Maximizing the gain while minimizing the pain of layoffs, divestitures, and closings. *Organizational Dynamics, 34,* 19–35.

49. Schneer, J. A. (1993). Involuntary turnover and its psychological consequences: A theoretical model. *Human Resource Management Review, 3,* 29–47.

50. Latack, J. C., Kinicki, A. J., & Prussia, G. E. (1995). An integrative model of coping with job loss. *Academy of Management Review, 20,* 311–342.

51. Blumenstein, R. (2004, July 20). Older executives find job losses often mean having to retire early. *Wall Street Journal,* p. B1.

52. Latack et al. (1995).

53. McKee-Ryan (2006).

54. Latack et al. (1995).

55. Ibid.

56. McKee-Ryan (2006).

57. Ibid.

58. Schneer (1993).

59. Eden, D., & Aviram, A. (1993). Self-efficacy training to speed reemployment: Helping people to help themselves. *Journal of Applied Psychology, 78,* 352–360; Marks & deMeuse. (2005).

60. Westaby, J. D., & NicDomhnaill, O. M. (2006). Outplacement. In Greenhaus & Callanan, pp. 608–609.

61. Scidurlo, L. (2006). Age Discrimination in Employment Act of 1967 (ADEA). In Greenhaus & Callanan, pp. 14–15.

62. OECD Economic Outlook. (2002). Increasing employment: The role of late retirement: Incentives for early retirement still exist, even after recent reforms. *OECD Economic Outlook, 72,* 146–151; Stoll, J. D. (2007, December 19). GM starts first phase of buyouts. *Wall Street Journal, 250*(144), A13.

63. Williams, C. P., & Savickas, M. L. (1990). Developmental tasks of career maintenance. *Journal of Vocational Behavior, 36,* 166–175.

64. Kaufman (1995, 2006).

65. Beehr, T. A., & Bowling, N. (2002). Career issues facing older workers. In D. C. Feldman (Ed.), *Work careers: A developmental perspective* (pp. 214–241). San Francisco: Jossey-Bass; Greller, M. M., & Simpson, P. (1999). In search of late career: A review of contemporary social science research applicable to the understanding of late career. *Human Resource Management Review, 9,* 309–347; Sterns, H. L., & Miklos, S. M. (1995). The aging worker in a changing environment: Organizational and individual issues. *Journal of Vocational Behavior, 47,* 248–268.

66. Keene, J. (2006). Age discrimination. In Greenhaus & Callanan, pp. 10–14.

67. Ibid.

68. Roscigno, V. J., Mong, S., Byron, R., & Tester, G. (2007). Age discrimination, social closure, and employment. *Social Forces, 86,* 313–334.

69. Feldman, D. C. (2006). Late career stage. In Greenhaus & Callanan, pp. 453–457; Greller & Simpson (1999).

70. Feldman (2006); Sterns & Miklos (1995).

71. Collins, G. (2006). Retirement. In Greenhaus & Callanan, pp. 693–696.

72. Talaga, J. A., & Beehr, T. A. (1995). Are there gender differences in predicting retirement decisions? *Journal of Applied Psychology, 80,* 16–28.

73. Mollica, K. (2006). Early retirement. In Greenhaus & Callanan, pp. 254–255.

74. Lancaster, H. (1997, August 5). Why retire at all? Here's how to launch a postcareer career. *Wall Street Journal,* p. B-1.

75. Hanisch, K. A. (1994). Reasons people retire and their relations to attitudinal and behavioral correlates in retirement. *Journal of Vocational Behavior, 45,* 1–16; Kim, S., & Feldman, D. C. (2000). Working in retirement: The antecedents of bridge employment and its consequences for quality of life in retirement. *Academy of Management Journal, 43,* 1195–1210; Lim, V. K. G., & Feldman, D. C. (2003). The impact of time structure and time usage on willingness to retire and bridge employment. *International Journal of Human Resource Management, 14,* 1178–1191; Schmitt, N., White, J. K., Coyle, B. W., & Rauschenberger, J. (1979). Retirement and life satisfaction. *Academy of Management Journal, 22,* 282–291.

76. Anonymous. (2004, May 24). The ReFirement Workbook assists organizations in engaging employees. *Business Wire,* pg. 1.

77. Mollica (2006).

78. Ibid.

79. Hutchens, R. (2006). Phased retirement. In Greenhaus & Callanan, pp. 638–640.

80. Ibid.

81. Callanan, G. A., & Greenhaus, J. H. (2008). The baby boom generation and career management: A call to action. *Advances in Developing Human Resources, 10,* 70–85.

82. Ibid.

83. Ulrich, L. B. (2006). Bridge employment. In Greenhaus & Callanan, pp. 49–51.

84. Eichinger & Lombardo (2003).

85. Kaufman (1995).

86. LaRock, S. (2000). Retirement planning programs should go beyond investment advice, especially for older workers. *Employee Benefit Plan Review, 55*(5), 16–18; Wotherspoon, C. J. (1995). Plan

now, enjoy later? A study of the use and effectiveness of formal retirement planning programs. *Benefits Quarterly, 11*(1), 53–57.

87. Collins (2006); Hutchens (2006).

ENDNOTES FOR CHAPTER 9

1. Ganster, D. C., Fox, M. L., & Dwyer, D. J. (2001). Explaining employees' health care costs: A prospective examination of stressful job demands, personal control, and physiological reactivity. *Journal of Applied Psychology, 86,* 954–964; Perrewe, P. L., & Ganster, D. C. (2001). *Exploring theoretical mechanisms and perspectives* (Research in Occupational Stress and Well Being, Vol. 1). New York: JAI; Spector, P. E. (2006). Stress at work. In J. H. Greenhaus & G. A. Callanan (Eds.), *Encyclopedia of career development* (pp. 771–778). Thousand Oaks, CA: Sage.

2. Clark, M. C. (2005). *The cost of job stress.* Retrieved June 25, 2009, from http://www.mediate .com/articles/clarkM1.cfm

3. Lambert, E. G., Pasupuleti, S., Cluse-Tolar, T., Jennings, M., & Baker, D. (2006). The impact of work-family conflict on social work and human service worker job satisfaction and organizational commitment: An exploratory study. *Administration in Social Work, 30*(3), 55–74; Schiff, L. (1997). Downsizing workplace stress. *Business and Health, 15,* 45–46; Spector (2006).

4. Lu, L., Cooper, C. L., Kao, S., & Zhou, Y. (2003). Work stress, control beliefs and well-being in Greater China: An exploration of sub-cultural differences between the PRC and Taiwan. *Journal of Managerial Psychology, 18,* 479–510; Spector (2006).

5. Kahn, R. L., & Byosiere, P. (1992). Stress in organizations. In M. D. Dunnette & L. M. Hough (Eds.), *Handbook of industrial and organizational psychology* (Vol. 3, pp. 571–650). Palo Alto, CA: Consulting Psychologists Press.

6. Christie, A., & Barling, J. (2006). Careers and health. In Greenhaus & Callanan, pp. 158–162.

7. Eulberg, J. R., Weekley, J. A., & Bhagat, R. S. (1988). Models of stress in organizational research: A metatheoretical perspective. *Human Relations, 41,* 331–350; Le Fevre, M., Matheny, J., & Kolt, G. S. (2003). Eustress, distress, and interpretation in occupational stress. *Journal of Managerial Psychology, 18,* 726–744; Lu et al. (2003); van Vegchel, N., de Jonge, J., & Landsbergis, P. A. (2005). Occupational stress in (inter)action: The interplay between job demands and job resources. *Journal of Organizational Behavior, 26,* 535–560.

8. LePine, J. A., Podsakoff, N. P., & LePine, M. A. (2005). A meta-analytic test of the challenge stressor-hindrance stressor framework: An explanation for inconsistent relationships among stressors and performance. *Academy of Management Journal, 48,* 764–775; quote is on p. 764.

9. Ibid.

10. Lu et al. (2003). Schaubroeck, J., & Ganster, D. C. (1993). Chronic demands and responsivity to challenge. *Journal of Applied Psychology, 78,* 73–85; Xie, J. L., & Johns, G. (1995). Job scope and stress: Can job scope be too high? *Academy of Management Journal, 38,* 1288–1309.

11. Bakker, A. B., van der Zee, K. I., Lewig, K. A., & Dollard, M. F. (2006). The relationship between the Big Five personality factors and burnout: A study among volunteer counselors. *Journal of Social Psychology, 146,* 31–50; Heppner, P. P., Cook, S. W., Wright, D. M., & Johnson, W. C., Jr. (1995). Progress in resolving problems: A problem-focused style of coping. *Journal of Counseling Psychology, 42,* 279–293; Van Heck, G. L. (1997). Personality and physical health: Toward an ecological approach to health-related personality research. *European Journal of Personality Research, 11,* 415–443.

12. Liu, C., Spector, P. E., & Shi, L. (2007). Cross-national job stress: A quantitative and qualitative study. *Journal of Organizational Behavior, 28,* 209–221; Lu, L. (1999). Work motivation, job stress and employees' well-being. *Journal of Applied Management Studies, 8,* 61–72.

13. Bakker et al. (2006); Burke, M., J., Brief, A. P., & George, J. M. (1993). The role of negative affectivity in understanding relationships between self-reports of stressors and strains: A comment on the applied psychological literature. *Journal of Applied Psychology, 78,* 402–412; Fortj-Cozens, K. (1992). Why me? A case study of the process of perceived occupational stress. *Human Relations, 45,* 131–141.

14. Jurison, A. C. (2000). *The effects of personality predisposition and job stress effects on sick leave usage in the Chicago Housing Authority.* Unpublished doctoral dissertation, University of Sarasota; Nelson, D. L., & Sutton, C. (1990). Chronic work stress and coping: A longitudinal study and suggested new directions. *Academy of Management Journal, 33,* 859–869; Scott, C. (2005). Helping employees become wellness CEOs. *Workspan, 48*(5), 76–83.

15. Spector (2006).

16. Bishop, G. D., Enkelmann, H. C., & Tong, E. M. W. (2003). Job demands, decisional control, and cardiovascular responses. *Journal of Occupational Health Psychology, 8,* 146–156; Cohen, S., Frank, E., Doyle, W. J., Skoner, D. P., Rabin, B. S., & Gwaltney, J. M. (1998). Types of stressors increase susceptibility to the common cold in healthy adults. *Health Psychology, 17,* 214–223; Ganster, D. C., Fox, M. L., & Dwyer, D. J. (2001). Explaining employees' health care costs: A prospective examination of stressful job demands, personal control, and physiological reactivity. *Journal of Applied Psychology, 86,* 954–964; Grunberg, L., Moore, S., & Anderson-Connolly, R. (1999). Work stress and self-reported alcohol use: The moderating role of escapist reasons for drinking. *Journal of Occupational Health Psychology, 4,* 29–36; Kamarck, T. W., Muldoon, M. F., & Shiffman, S. S. (2007). Experiences of demand and control during daily life are predictors of carotid atherosclerotic progression among healthy men. *Health Psychology, 26,* 324–332; O'Connor, D. B., Jones, F., & Conner, M. (2008). Effects of daily hassles and eating style on eating behavior. *Health Psychology, 27*(Supplement), S20–S31; Raynor, D. A., Pogue-Geile, M. F., Kamarck, T. W., McCaffery, J. M., & Manuck, S. B. (2002). Covariation of psychosocial characteristics associated with cardiovascular disease: Genetic and environmental influences. *Psychosomatic Medicine, 64,* 191–203; Schaubroeck, J., Ganster, D. C., & Kemmerer, B. E. (1994). Job complexity, "Type A" behavior, and cardiovascular disorder: A prospective study. *Academy of Management Journal, 37,* 426–439.

17. Baruch-Feldman, C., Brondolo, E., & Ben-Dayan, D. (2002). Sources of social support and burnout, job satisfaction, and productivity. *Journal of Occupational Health Psychology, 7,* 84–93; Halbesleben, J. R. B. (2006). Sources of social support and burnout: A meta-analytic test of the conservation of resources model. *Journal of Applied Psychology, 91,* 1134–1145.

18. Driscoll, R. J., Worthington, K. A., & Hurrell, J. J., Jr. (1995). Workplace assault: An emerging job stressor. *Consulting Psychology Journal: Practice and Research, 47,* 205–211; Schat, A. C. H., & Kelloway, E. K. (2003). Reducing the adverse consequences of workplace aggression and violence: The buffering effects of organizational support. *Journal of Occupational Health Psychology, 8,* 110–122.

19. Le Fevre et al. (2003); Quick, J. C., & Quick, J. D. (1997). *Preventive stress management in organizations.* Washington, DC: American Psychological Association.

20. Birks, Y., & Roger, D. (2000). Identifying components of Type-A behavior: "Toxic" and "nontoxic" achieving. *Personality and Individual Differences, 28,* 1093–1105; Jamal, M., & Baba, V. V. (2001). Type-A behavior, job performance and well-being in college teachers. *International Journal of Stress Management, 8,* 231–240.

21. McGregor, L., Eveleigh, M., & Syler, J. C. (1991). Self-perception of personality characteristics and the Type A behavior pattern. *Bulletin of the Psychonomic Society, 29,* 320–322; Ryan, R. M., & Brown, K. W. (2006). What is optimal self-esteem? The cultivation and consequences of contingent vs. true self-esteem as viewed from the self-determination theory perspective. In M. H. Kernis (Ed.), *Self-esteem issues and answers: A sourcebook of current perspectives* (pp. 125–131). New York: Psychology Press.

22. Jamal, M., & Baba, V. V. (2003). Type A behavior, components, and outcomes: A study of Canadian employees. *International Journal of Stress Management, 10,* 39–50; Ryan & Brown (2006).

23. Ganster, D. C., Schaubroeck, J., Sime, W. E., & Mayes, B. T. (1991). The nomological validity of the Type A personality among employed adults. *Journal of Applied Psychology, 76,* 143–168; Jamal & Baba (2003).

24. Cooper, C. L. (2006). The challenges of managing the changing nature of workplace stress. *Journal of Public Mental Health, 5*(4), 6–9; Quick & Quick (1997).

25. Frank, M. L. (2000). What's so stressful about job relocation? British researchers give some answers. *Academy of Management Executive, 14,* 122–123; Godshalk, V. M. (2006). Career plateau. In Greenhaus & Callanan, pp. 133–138; Joseph, J. (1992). *Plateauism and its effect on strain as moderated by career motivation and personal resources.* Unpublished doctoral dissertation, University of Iowa.

26. Herlihy, P. (1997, Spring). Employee assistance programs and work/family programs: Obstacles and opportunities for organizational integration. *Compensation and Benefits Management,* pp. 22–30; Latack, J. C., & Havlovic, S. J. (1992). Coping with job stress: A conceptual evaluation framework for coping measures. *Journal of Organizational Behavior, 13,* 479–508; Peterson, N., & González, R. C. (2000). *The role of work in people's lives: Applied career counseling and vocational psychology.* Belmont, CA: Wadsworth/Thomson Learning.

27. Nelson, D. L., & Quick, J. C. (1985). Professional women: Are distress and disease inevitable? *Academy of Management Review, 10,* 206–218.

28. Goldstein, B.P. (2002). Catch 22—Black workers' role in equal opportunities for black service users. *British Journal of Social Work, 32,* 765–778; Sanchez, J. I., & Brock, P. (1996). Outcomes of perceived discrimination among Hispanic employees: Is diversity management a luxury or a necessity? *Academy of Management Journal, 39,* 704–719.

29. Bell, E. L. J., & Nkomo, S. M. (2001). *Our separate ways: Black and white women and the struggle for professional identity.* Boston: Harvard Business School Press; Hackett, G., & Byers, A. M. (1996). Social cognitive theory and the career development of African American women. *Career Development Quarterly, 44,* 322–340; Lyness, K. (2006). Glass ceiling. In Greenhaus & Callanan, pp. 333–336.

30. *Dick Vermeil.* Retrieved June 6, 2008, from http://en.wikipedia.org/wiki/Dick_Vermeil

31. Halbesleben (2006).

32. Maslach, C., & Leiter, M. P. (2008). Early predictors of job burnout and engagement. *Journal of Applied Psychology, 93,* 498–512.

33. Potter, B. A. (1998). *Overcoming job burnout: How to renew enthusiasm for work.* Berkeley, CA: Ronin Publishing.

34. Greenhaus, J. H. (2006). Burnout. In Greenhaus & Callanan, pp. 51–52.

35. Cordes, C. L., & Dougherty, T. W. (1993). A review and integration of research on job burnout. *Academy of Management Review, 4,* 621–656; Halbesleben (2006); Halbesleben, J. R. B., & Buckley, M. R. (2004). Burnout in organizational life. *Journal of Management, 30,* 859–879; Maslach & Leiter (2008).

36. Jackson, S. E., Schwab, R. L., & Schuler, R. S. (1986). Toward an understanding of the burnout phenomenon. *Journal of Applied Psychology, 7,* 630–640.

37. Burke et al. (1993); Judge, T. A. (1993). Does affective disposition moderate the relationship between job satisfaction and voluntary turnover? *Journal of Applied Psychology, 78,* 395–401; O'Brien, A., Terry, D. J., & Jimmieson, N. L. (2008). Negative affectivity and responses to work stressors: An experimental study. *Anxiety, Stress & Coping: An International Journal, 21,* 55–83.

38. Cropanzano, R., James, K., & Konovsky, M. A. (1993). Dispositional affectivity as a predictor of work attitudes and job performance. *Journal of Organizational Behavior, 14,* 595–606; Iverson, R. D., & Erwin, P. J. (1997). Predictors of occupational injury: The role of affectivity. *Journal of Occupational and Organizational Psychology, 70,* 113–128; Iverson, R. D., Olekalns, M., & Erwin, P. J. (1998). Affectivity, organizational stressors, and absenteeism: A causal model of burnout and its consequences. *Journal of Vocational Behavior, 52,* 1–23; Latack, J. C., Kinicki, A., & Prussia, G. E. (1996). Response to "Negative affectivity and coping with job loss." *Academy of Management Review, 21,* 331–332; Mak, A. S., & Mueller, J. (2001). Negative affectivity, perceived occupational stress, and health during organisational restructuring: A follow-up study. *Psychology & Health, 16,* 125–137.

39. Åkerstedt, T., Kecklund, G., & Gillberg, M. (2007). Sleep and sleepiness in relation to stress and displaced work hours. *Physiology & Behavior, 92,* 250–255; Burke, R. J., & Greenglass, E. R. (2001).

Hospital restructuring, work–family conflict and psychological burnout among nursing staff. *Psychology and Health, 16,* 83–94; Jackson, S. E., & Maslach, C. (1982). After-effects of job-related stress: Families as victims. *Journal of Occupational Behaviour, 3,* 63–77; Leiter, M. P., Harvie, P., & Frizzell, C. (1998). The correspondence of patient satisfaction and nurse burnout. *Social Science & Medicine, 47,* 1611–1617; Leiter, M. P., & Maslach, C. (2000). Burnout and health. In A. Baum, T. Revenson, & J. Singer (Eds.), *Handbook of health psychology* (pp. 415–426). Hillsdale, NJ: Lawrence Erlbaum; O'Brien et al. (2008); Peterson, U., Demerouti, E., & Bergström, G. (2008). Work characteristics and sickness absence in burnout and nonburnout groups: A study of Swedish health care workers. *International Journal of Stress Management, 15,* 153–172; Potter (1998); Powell, W. E. (1994). The relationship between feelings of alienation and burnout in social work. *Families in Society, 75,* 229–235; Sonnenschein, M., Sorbi, M. J., & van Doornen, L. J. P. (2007). Electronic diary evidence on energy erosion in clinical burnout. *Journal of Occupational Health Psychology, 12,* 402–413; Vahey, D. C., Aiken, L. H., Sloane, D. M., Clarke, S. P., & Vargas, D. (2004). Nurse burnout and patient satisfaction. *Medical Care, 42,* 57–66; Zedeck, S., Maslach, C., Mosier, K., & Skitka, L. (1988). Affective response to work and quality of family life: Employee and spouse perspectives. *Journal of Social Behavior and Personality, 3,* 135–157.

40. Froiland, P. (1993). What cures job stress? *Training, 30,* 32–35.

41. Greenhaus (2006).

42. Lindblom, K. M., Linton, S. J., Fedeli, C., & Bryngelsson, I. L. (2006). Burnout in the working population: Relations to psychosocial work factors. *International Journal of Behavioral Medicine, 13,* 51–59; Maslach, C., & Leiter, M. P. (1997). *The truth about burnout.* Chichester, UK: Wiley.

43. Levine, M. (2006). Employee assistance programs. In Greenhaus & Callanan, pp. 271–272; Kirk, A. K., & Brown, D. F. (2003). Employee assistance programs: A review of the management of stress and wellbeing through workplace counseling and consulting. *Australian Psychologist, 38,* 138–143; Reynolds, S. (1997). Psychological well-being at work: Is prevention better than the cure? *Journal of Psychosomatic Research, 43,* 93–102.

44. McKee, S. (1995, September 5). Take it easy! Companies offer new ways for employees to beat job stress. *Peoria Journal Star,* p. C1.

45. *College students: Locations: Mid-Atlantic.* Retrieved August 25, 2008, from http://www.lockheedmartinjobs.com/college_locations_midatlantic.asp

46. Anonymous. (2007). Addicted to technology? There could be legal repercussions. *HR Focus, 84*(8), 1–3; Anonymous. (2008). Beware the dangers of workaholism. *HR Focus, 85*(1), 9.

47. Spence, J. T., & Robbins, A. S. (1992). Workaholism: Definition, measurement, and preliminary results. *Journal of Personality Assessment, 58,* 162–174.

48. Anonymous (2008).

49. Schaufeli, W. B., Taris, T. W., & van Rhenen, W. (2008). Workaholism, burnout, and work engagement: Three of a kind or three different kinds of employee well-being? *Applied Psychology: An International Review, 57,* 173–203.

50. Latack, J. C. (1989). Work, stress, and careers: A preventive approach to maintaining organizational health. In M. B. Arthur, D. T. Hall, & B. S. Lawrence (Eds.), *Handbook of career theory* (pp. 252–274). Cambridge, UK: Cambridge University Press; Latack & Havlovic (1992); Wallace, E. V. (2007). Managing stress: What consumers want to know from health educators. *American Journal of Health Studies, 22,* 56–58.

51. Neck, C. P., & Manz, C. C. (2007). *Mastering self-leadership: Empowering yourself for personal excellence* (4th ed.). Upper Saddle River, NJ: Pearson Prentice Hall; Latack (1989); Latack & Havlovic (1992); Wallace (2007).

52. Anonymous. (2007). Taking control of stress. *Harvard Health Letter, 32,* 3–4; McKee (1995); Wallace (2007).

53. Gianakos, I. (2000). Gender roles and coping with work stress. *Sex Roles, 42,* 1059–1079; Gianakos, I. (2002). Predictors of coping with work stress: The influences of sex, gender role, social

desirability, and locus of control. *Sex Roles, 46,* 149–158; Havlovic, S. J., & Keenan, J. P. (1991). Coping with work stress: The influence of individual differences. *Journal of Social Behavior & Personality, 6,* 199–212; Ong, A. D., Bergeman, C. S., Bisconti, T. L., & Wallace, K. A. (2006). Psychological resilience, positive emotions, and successful adaptation to stress in later life. *Journal of Personality and Social Psychology, 91,* 730–748; Siu, O., Chow, S. L., & Phillips, D. R. (2006). An exploratory study of resilience among Hong Kong employees: Ways to happiness. In Y. K. Ng & L. S. Ho (Eds.), *Happiness and public policy: Theory, case studies and implications.* New York: Palgrave Macmillan.

54. Schein, E. H. (1978). *Career dynamics: Matching individual and organizational needs.* Reading, MA: Addison-Wesley.

55. Latack, J. C., Kinicki, A. J., & Prussia, G. E. (1995). An integrative process model of coping with job loss. *Academy of Management Review, 20,* 311–342.

56. Latack et al. (1995); Manning, M. R., Jackson, C. N., & Fusilier, M. R. (1996). Occupational stress, social support, and the costs of health care. *Academy of Management Journal, 39,* 738–750.

57. See the pioneering work of James House in House, J. S. (1981). *Work stress and social support.* Reading, MA: Addison-Wesley.

58. Acitelli, L. K., & Antonucci, T. C. (1994). Gender differences in the link between marital support and satisfaction in older couples. *Journal of Personality and Social Psychology, 67,* 688–698; Jou, Y. H., & Fukada, H. (2002). Stress, health, and reciprocity and sufficiency of social support: The case of university students in Japan. *Journal of Social Psychology, 142,* 353–370.

59. Iverson et al. (1998); Quick & Quick (1984).

60. Adapted from the IBM corporate Web site. Retrieved June 11, 2008, from http://www.ibm.com/ibm/responsibility/people/wellbeing/promoting-health.shtml

ENDNOTES FOR CHAPTER 10

1. Eby, L. T., Casper, W., Lockwood, A., Bordeaux, C., & Brinley, A. (2005). Work and family research in IO/OB: Content analysis and review of the literature (1980–2002). *Journal of Vocational Behavior, 66*(1), 124–197; Greenhaus, J. H., Allen, T. D., & Spector, P. E. (2006). Health consequences of work-family conflict: The dark side of the work-family interface. In P. L. Perrewe & D. C. Ganster (Eds.), *Research in occupational stress and well-being* (Vol. 5, pp. 61–98). Amsterdam: JAI/Elsevier; Greenhaus, J. H., & Foley, S. (2007). The intersection of work and family lives. In H. Gunz & M. Peiperl (Eds.), *Handbook of career studies* (pp. 131–152). Thousand Oaks, CA: Sage; Greenhaus, J. H., & Parasuraman, S. (1999). Research on work, family, and gender: Current status and future directions. In G. N. Powell (Ed.), *Handbook of gender and work* (pp. 391–412). Newbury Park, CA: Sage; Greenhaus, J. H., & Powell, G. N. (2006). When work and family are allies: A theory of work-family enrichment. *Academy of Management Review, 31,* 72–92.

2. Annual Social and Economic Supplements, 1968–2006, Current Population Survey, U.S. Department of Labor, U.S. Bureau of Labor Statistics.

3. Statistics available at the Bureau of Labor Statistics at http://www.bls.gov under the menu item "Women in the Labor Force: A Databook (2006 Edition)"; see also Raskin, P. M. (2006). Single parents and careers. In J. H. Greenhaus & G. A. Callanan (Eds.), *Encyclopedia of career development* (pp. 741–742). Thousand Oaks, CA: Sage; statistics available from the United States Census Bureau at their Web site at http://www.census.gov.

4. Johnson, D. (2006). It's all a blur: Techno-stress, "negative spillover" & you (reports on handheld electronics usage). *Industrial Safety & Hygiene News, 5,* 6.

5. Frase-Blunt, M. (2001). Busman's holiday. *HR Magazine, 46,* 76–80; Rosato, D. (2003, June 6). Handy BlackBerry can be addictive. *USA Today,* p. E.13.

6. Greenhaus & Foley (2007).

7. Greenhaus, J. H., & Beutell, N. J. (1985). Sources of conflict between work and family roles. *Academy of Management Review, 10,* 76–88.

8. Frone, M. R. (2003). Work-family balance. In J. C. Quick & L. E. Tetrick (Eds.), *Handbook of occupational health psychology* (pp. 143–162). Washington, DC: American Psychological Association.

9. Evans, P., & Bartolome, F. (1980). *Must success cost so much?* New York: Basic Books; Greenhaus & Parasuraman (1999).

10. Greenhaus & Beutell (1985).

11. Burke, R. J. (2006). Type A behavior pattern. In Greenhaus & Callanan, pp. 828–831.

12. Frone, M. R., & Rice, R. W. (1987). Work-family conflict: The effect of job and family involvement. *Journal of Occupational Behaviour, 8,* 45–53.

13. Bartolome, F., & Evans, P. (1979). Professional lives versus private lives: Shifting patterns of managerial commitment. *Organizational Dynamics, 7*(4), 3–29.

14. Although some studies have found greater conflict among women than men, other studies report no sex difference in work-family conflict, or even greater conflict among men than women. See Byron, K. (2005). A meta-analytic review of work-family conflict and its antecedents. *Journal of Vocational Behavior, 67,* 169–198; Greenhaus & Parasuraman (1999).

15. Greenhaus, Allen, & Spector (2006).

16. Friedman, S. D., & Greenhaus, J. H. (2000). *Work and family—Allies or enemies? What happens when business professionals confront life choices.* New York: Oxford University Press.

17. Ibid; also see Greenhaus and Powell (2006). Although we choose to use the concept of work–family enrichment to refer to the positive effects that work and family roles have on each other, others have used similar concepts such as work–family facilitation and work–family positive spillover.

18. Graves, L., Ohlott, P., & Ruderman, M. (2007). Commitment to family roles: Effects on managers' attitudes and performance. *Journal of Applied Psychology, 92,* 44–56; Ruderman, M., Ohlott, P., Panzer, K., & King, S. (2002). Benefits of multiple roles for managerial women. *Academy of Management Journal, 45,* 369–386.

19. Hall, F. S., & Hall, D. T. (1979). *The two-career couple.* Reading, MA: Addison-Wesley.

20. Barnett, R. C., & Hyde, J. S. (2001). Women, men, work, and family: An expansionist view. *American Psychologist, 56,* 781–796.

21. Gilbert, L. A. (2006). Two-career relationships. In Greenhaus & Callanan, pp. 822–828.

22. Parasuraman, S., & Greenhaus, J. H. (1993). Personal portrait: The life-style of the woman manager. In E. A. Fagenson (Ed.), *Women in management: Trends, issues, and challenges in managerial diversity* (Vol. 4, pp. 186–211). Newbury Park, CA: Sage.

23. Hochschild, A. (1989). *The second shift.* New York: Viking.

24. Friedman & Greenhaus (2000).

25. Campbell, B. M. (1986). *Successful women, angry men.* New York: Random House.

26. Friedman & Greenhaus (2000).

27. Ibid.

28. Graves, Ohlott, & Ruderman (2007).

29. Friedman & Greenhaus (2000).

30. Ibid.

31. Moen, P., & Yu, Y. (2000). Effective work/life strategies: Working couples, work conditions, gender, and life quality. *Social Problems, 47,* 291–326.

32. Greenhaus, J. H., Parasuraman, S., Granrose, C. S., Rabinowitz, S., & Beutell, N. J. (1989). Sources of work-family conflict among two-career couples. *Journal of Vocational Behavior, 34,* 133–153.

33. Poloma, M. M., Pendleton, B. F., & Garland, T. N. (1982). Reconsidering the dual-career marriage: A longitudinal approach. In J. Aldous (Ed.), *Two paychecks: Life in dual-earner families* (pp. 173–192). Beverly Hills, CA: Sage.

34. Hall & Hall (1979).

35. Gilbert (2006).

36. Greenhaus, J. H., Bedeian, A. G., & Mossholder, K. W. (1987). Work experiences, job performance, and feelings of personal and family well-being. *Journal of Vocational Behavior, 31,* 200–215.

37. Chapman, F. S. (1987, February 16). Executive guilt: Who's taking care of the children? *Fortune,* pp. 30–37.

38. Bond, J. T., Thompson, C., Galinsky, E., & Prottas, D. (2002). *Highlights of the National Study of the Changing Workforce.* New York: Families and Work Institute.

39. Galinsky, E. (1999). *Ask the children: What America's children really think about working parents.* New York: Morrow; quote is on p. 6.

40. Ayman, R., & Antani, A. (2008). Social support and work-family conflict. In K. Korabik, D. S. Lero, & D. L. Whitehead (Eds.), *Handbook of work-family integration: Research, theory, and best practices* (pp. 287–304). Oxford, UK: Elsevier; van Daalen, G. (2008). *Social support, does it make a difference?* Oisterwijk, the Netherlands: BOX Press.

41. Friedman & Greenhaus (2000).

42. Gilbert (2006).

43. Rapoport, R., & Rapoport, R. N. (1971). Further considerations on the dual career family. *Human Relations, 24,* 519–533.

44. Gilbert (2006).

45. Bailyn, L. (1970). Career and family orientations of husbands and wives in relation to marital happiness. *Human Relations 23,* 97–113.

46. Parasuraman & Greenhaus (1993).

47. Hall & Hall (1979); quote is on p. 24.

48. Hall, D. T. (1972). A model of coping with role conflict: The role behavior of college-educated women. *Administrative Science Quarterly, 17,* 471–489.

49. Beutell, N. J., & Greenhaus, J. H. (1983). Integration of home and nonhome roles: Women's conflict and coping behavior. *Journal of Applied Psychology, 68,* 43–48.

50. Baltes, B. B., & Heydens-Gahir, H. A. (2003). Reduction of work–family conflict through the use of selection, optimization, and compensation behaviors. *Journal of Applied Psychology, 88,* 1005–1018; Wiese, B. S., Freund, A. M., & Baltes, P. B. (2002). Subjective career success and emotional well-being: Longitudinal predictive power of selection, optimization, and compensation. *Journal of Vocational Behavior, 60,* 321–335.

51. Adams, G. A., & Jex, S. M. (1999). Relationships between time management, control, work-family conflict, and strain. *Journal of Occupational Health Psychology, 4,* 72–77.

52. Hall & Hall (1979).

53. Ibid.

54. Neal, M. B., & Hammer, L. B. (2007). *Working couples caring for children and aging parents: Effects on work and well-being.* Mahwah, NJ: Lawrence Erlbaum.

55. Bond, Thompson, Galinsky, & Prottas (2002).

56. Schwartz, F. N. (1989, January–February). Management women and the facts of life. *Harvard Business Review,* pp. 65–76; Schwartz, F. N. (1992). *Breaking with tradition.* New York: Warner Books.

57. Table 570. Civilian Labor Force and Participation Rates with Projections: 1980–2014, U.S. Census Bureau; also, see Schwartz (1992).

58. Frone, M. R. (2006). Work-family conflict. In Greenhaus & Callanan, pp. 867–869.

59. Foley, S. (2006). Family-responsive workplace practices. In Greenhaus & Callanan, pp. 317–319.

60. Hall, D. T., & Richter, J. (1988). Balancing work life and home life: What can organizations do to help? *Academy of Management Executive, 2,* 213–223.

61. Bond, J. T., Galinsky, E., Kim, S. S., & Brownfield, E. (2005). *National study of employers.* New York: Families and Work Institute.

62. Ibid.

63. Friedman, D. E. (1990). Work and family: The new strategic plan. *Human Resource Planning,* *13*(2), 79–89.

64. Ibid.

65. Bond, Galinsky, Kim, & Brownfield (2005).

66. Byron (2005).

67. Gerstel, N., & Armenia, A. (2006). Family and Medical Leave Act (FMLA). In Greenhaus & Callanan, pp. 310–313.

68. Bond, Galinsky, Kim, & Brownfield (2005).

69. Powell, G. N. (1997). The sex difference in employee inclinations regarding work-family programs: Why does it exist, should we care, and what should be done about it (if anything)? In S. Parasuraman & J. H. Greenhaus (Eds.), *Integrating work and family: Challenges and choices for a changing world* (pp. 167–174). Westport, CT: Quorum.

70. Schwartz (1989).

71. Morrow, P. C. (2006). Part-time employment. In Greenhaus & Callanan, pp. 613–616; Powell (1997).

72. Ibid.

73. The discussion of Price Waterhouse is based on Connor, M., Hooks, K., & McGuire, T. (1997). Gaining legitimacy for flexible work arrangements and career paths: The business case for public accounting and professional services firms. In Parasuraman & Greenhaus, pp. 154–166; see also Callanan, G. A., & Greenhaus, J. H. (1999). Personal and career development: The best and worst of times. In A. I. Kraut & A. K. Korman (Eds.), *Evolving practices in human resource management: Responses to a changing world of work* (pp. 146–171). San Francisco: Jossey-Bass.

74. Driessnack, C. H. (1987). Spouse relocation: A moving experience. *Personnel Administrator,* 94–102; Rodgers, F. S., & Rodgers, C. (1989). Business and the facts of family life. *Harvard Business Review,* 121–129; Shellenbarger, S. (1992, January 7). Allowing fast trackers to stay in one place. *Wall Street Journal,* p. B1.

75. McCloskey, D. W. (2006). Telecommuting. In Greenhaus & Callanan, pp. 804–805; Riley, F., & McCloskey, D. W. (1997). Telecommuting as a response to helping people balance work and family. In Parasuraman & Greenhaus, pp. 133–142.

76. Greenhaus & Foley (2007).

77. Arthur, M. M. (2003). Share price reactions to work-family human resource decisions: An institutional perspective. *Academy of Management Journal, 46,* 497–505; Konrad, A. M., & Mangel, R. (2000). The impact of work-life programs on firm productivity. *Strategic Management Journal, 21,* 1225–1237; Perry-Smith, J. E., & Blum, T. C. (2000). Work-family human resource bundles and perceived organizational performance. *Academy of Management Journal, 43,* 1107–1117.

78. Allen, T. D. (2001). Family-supportive work environments: The role of organizational perceptions. *Journal of Vocational Behavior, 58,* 414–435; Brewer, A. M. (2000). Work design for flexible work scheduling: Barriers and gender implications. *Gender, Work and Organization, 7,* 33–44; Powell, G. N., & Mainiero, L. A. (1999). Managerial decision making regarding alternative work arrangements. *Journal of Occupational and Organizational Psychology, 72,* 41–56; Roehling, P. V., Roehling, M. V., & Moen, P. (2001). The relationship between work-life policies and practices and employee loyalty: A life course perspective. *Journal of Family and Economic Issues, 21,* 141–171; Thompson, C. A., Beauvais, L. L., & Lyness, K. S. (1999). When work-family benefits are not enough. *Journal of Vocational Behavior, 54,* 392–415.

79. Friedman (1990); Magid, R. Y. (1986). When mothers and fathers work: How employers can help. *Personnel,* 50–56.

80. Many companies refer to such organizational units and practices as "work–life" rather than "work–family" to be more inclusive of employees who may not have partners or children but do have a personal life.

81. The material in this section is based on Moen, P., Kelly, E., & Chermack, K. (forthcoming). Learning from a natural experiment: Studying a corporate work-time policy initiative. In A. C. Crouter & A. Booth (Eds.), *Work-life policies that make a real difference for individuals, families, and organizations.* Washington, DC: Urban Institute Press.

82. Moen, Kelly, & Chermack (forthcoming); quote from p. 11 of pre-copy-edited chapter.

83. Ibid.

84. Greenhaus & Foley (2007).

ENDNOTES FOR CHAPTER 11

1. Heet, J. A. (2006). Workforce 2020. In J. H. Greenhaus & G. A. Callanan (Eds.), *Encyclopedia of career development* (pp. 877–880). Thousand Oaks, CA: Sage.

2. Cox, T. H., & Blake, S. (1991). Managing cultural diversity: Implications for organizational competitiveness. *Academy of Management Executive, 5*(3), 45–56; Milliken, F. J., & Martins, L. L. (1997). Searching for common threads: Understanding the multiple effects of diversity in organizational groups. *Academy of Management Review, 21,* 402–433; Robinson, G., & Dechant, K. (1997). Building a business case for diversity. *Academy of Management Executive, 11*(3), 21–31; Thomas, K. M. (2006). Diversity in organizations. In Greenhaus & Callanan, pp. 236–243; Thomas, R. R., Jr. (1991). *Beyond race and gender.* New York: AMACOM.

3. Estimated workforce characteristics by race and ethnicity were extrapolated from Table 5 (Employment Status by Sex, Presence and Age of Children, Race, and Hispanic or Latino Ethnicity, March 2006) from the 2006 Annual Social and Economic Supplement, *Current Population Survey,* U.S. Department of Labor, U.S. Bureau of Labor Statistics; the workforce participation rate of women with children under six years of age was obtained from a 2008 news release (USDL 08-0731) of the U.S. Department of Labor, U.S. Bureau of Labor Statistics; also see Heet, Workforce 2020.

4. Morrison, A. M., & Von Glinow, M. A. (1990). Women and minorities in management. *American Psychologist, 45,* 200–222; quote is on p. 200.

5. Lyness, K. S. (2006). Glass ceiling. In Greenhaus & Callanan, pp. 333–337; Martin, L. A. (1991). *Report on the glass ceiling.* Washington, DC: U.S. Department of Labor. See also a more recent report of the Glass Ceiling Commission, *A solid investment: Making full use of the nation's human capital.* Federal Glass Ceiling Commission, Washington, D.C., 1995.

6. Cox & Blake (1991).

7. Litzky, B. E., & Greenhaus, J. H. (2007). The relationship between gender and aspirations to senior management. *Career Development International, 12,* 637–659.

8. Keller, E. (2007, February). *Companies say blacks in management give a competitive edge: New "diversity officers" recruit blacks to diversify workforce, boost profits.* Retrieved July 25, 2008, from http://www.america.gov/st/washfileenglish/2007/February/20070206172244berehellek0.3748896.html &h=200&w=168&sz=12&hl=cs&start=18

9. Avery, D. R. (2006). Racial discrimination. In Greenhaus & Callanan, pp. 667–671; Derous, E., & Ryan, A. M. (2006). Religious discrimination. In Greenhaus & Callanan, pp. 686–690; Gutek, B. A. (2006). Sex discrimination. In Greenhaus & Callanan, pp. 730–734; Keene, J. (2006). Age discrimination. In Greenhaus & Callanan, pp. 10–14.

10. Thomas (2006); quote is on p. 240.

11. Avery (2006); Lyness (2006).

12. Powell, G. N., & Butterfield, D. A. (1997). Effect of race on promotions to top management in a federal department. *Academy of Management Journal, 40,* 112–128.

13. Lyness (2006); for a study that found no sex difference in promotions to senior management, see Powell, G. N., & Butterfield, D. A. (1994). Investigating the "glass ceiling" phenomenon: An empirical study of actual promotions to top management. *Academy of Management Journal, 37,* 68–86.

14. Ragins, B. R., Townsend, B., & Mattis, M. (1998). Gender gap in the executive suite: CEOs and female executives report on breaking the glass ceiling. *Academy of Management Executive, 12*(1), 28–42.

15. Greenhaus, J. H., Parasuraman, S., & Wormley, W. M. (1990). Effects of race on organizational experiences, job performance evaluations, and career outcomes. *Academy of Management Journal, 33,* 64–86; Powell, G. N., & Graves, L. M. (2003). *Women and men in management* (3rd ed.). Thousand Oaks, CA: Sage.

16. Kraiger, K., & Ford, J. K. (1985). A meta-analysis of ratee race effects in performance ratings. *Journal of Applied Psychology, 70,* 56–65; McKay, P. F., & McDaniel, M. A. (2006). A reexamination of black-white mean differences in work performance: More data, more moderators. *Journal of Applied Psychology, 91,* 538–554; Roth, P. L., Huffcutt, A. I., & Bobko, P. (2003). Ethnic group differences in measures of job performance: A new meta-analysis. *Journal of Applied Psychology, 88,* 694–706.

17. Greenhaus et al. (1990); Pulakos, E. D., White, L. A., Oppler, S. H., & Borman, W. C. (1989). Examination of race and sex effects on performance ratings. *Journal of Applied Psychology, 74,* 770–780.

18. McKay & McDaniel (2006); Roth, Huffcutt, and Bobko (2003) reported smaller job performance differences between Hispanics and whites than between blacks and whites.

19. Kraiger & Ford (1985).

20. Greenhaus, J. H., & Parasuraman, S. (1993). Job performance attributions and career advancement prospects: An examination of gender and race effects. *Organizational Behavior and Human Decision Processes, 55,* 273–297.

21. Heilman, M. E., & Guzzo, R. A. (1978). The perceived cause of work success as a mediator of sex discrimination in organizations. *Organizational Behavior and Human Performance, 21,* 346–357.

22. Ilgen, D. R., & Youtz, M. A. (1986). Factors affecting the evaluation and development of minorities in organizations. In K. Rowland & G. Ferris (Eds.), *Research in personnel and human resource management: A research annual* (pp. 307–337). Greenwich, CT: JAI; Kanter, R. M. (1989). Differential access to opportunity and power. In A. Alvarez (Ed.), *Discrimination in organizations* (pp. 52–68). San Francisco: Jossey-Bass.

23. Greenhaus et al. (1990); Lyness, K. S., & Thompson, D. E. (1997). Above the glass ceiling? A comparison of matched samples of female and male executives. *Journal of Applied Psychology, 82,* 359–375.

24. Kanter (1989); Martin (1991).

25. Greenhaus et al. (1990).

26. Fernandez, J. P. (1988). Human resources and the extraordinary problems minorities face. In M. London & E. M. Mone (Eds.), *Career growth and human resource strategies* (pp. 227–239). New York: Quorum Books; Greenhaus et al. (1990); Ibarra, H. (1995). Race, opportunity, and diversity of social circles in managerial networks. *Academy of Management Journal, 38,* 673–703; Kanter (1989).

27. Blake-Beard, S. D., Murrell, A., & Thomas, D. (2007). Unfinished business: The impact of race on understanding mentoring relationships. In B. R. Ragins & K. E. Kram (Eds.), *The handbook of mentoring at work: Theory, research, and practice* (pp. 223–247). Thousand Oaks, CA: Sage; McKeen, C., & Bujaki, M. (2007). Gender and mentoring. In Ragins & Kram, pp. 197–222.

28. Allen, T. D. (2006). Mentoring. In Greenhaus & Callanan, pp. 486–493; Dreher, G. F., & Cox, T. H. (1996). Race, gender, and opportunity: A study of compensation attainment and the establishment of

mentoring relationships. *Journal of Applied Psychology, 81,* 297–308; Ragins, B. R. (1997). Diversified mentoring relationships in organizations: A power perspective. *Academy of Management Review, 22,* 482–521.

29. Allen (2006).

30. Blake-Beard et al. (2007).

31. Jenkins, M. (2005, March). Why you need a mentor: Mentors are the most important resource for success on the job. Finding them can be a task: Positioning yourself to be selected as a mentee is another. Here's how to accomplish both. *Black Enterprise,* pp. 1–5.

32. Ibid.

33. Allen (2006); Ragins (1997); Ragins, B. R., & McFarlin, D. B. (1990). Perceptions of mentor roles in cross-gender mentor relationships. *Journal of Vocational Behavior, 37,* 321–339.

34. McKeen & Bujaki (2007).

35. Kanter, R. M. (1977). *Men and women of the corporation.* New York: Basic Books; Yoder, J. D. (2006). Tokenism. In Greenhaus & Callanan, pp. 810–811.

36. Ilgen & Youtz (1986); Kanter (1977).

37. Ilgen & Youtz (1986).

38. Yoder, J. D. (2006).

39. Block, C. J. (2006). Stereotyping of workers. In Greenhaus & Callanan, pp. 766–767.

40. Ashburn-Nardo, L., Morris, K. A., & Goodwin, S. A. (2008). The confronting prejudiced responses (CPR) model: Applying CPR in organizations. *Academy of Management Learning & Education, 7,* 332–342; Lyness (2006).

41. Jones, E. (1986). Black managers: The dream deferred. *Harvard Business* Review, *64*(3), 84–93.

42. Fernandez (1991). *Managing a diverse workforce.* Lexington, MA: Lexington Books.

43. Eddleston, K. A., Veiga, J. F., & Powell, G. N. (2006). Explaining sex differences in managerial career satisfier preferences: The role of gender self-schema. *Journal of Applied Psychology, 91,* 437–445.

44. Gutek (2006).

45. Green, S. G., & Mitchell, T. R. (1979). Attributional processes of leaders in leader-member interactions. *Organizational Behavior and Human Performance, 23,* 429–458; for research on the impact of ethnic differences on a supervisor's liking of a subordinate, see Tsui, A. S., & O'Reilly, C. A., III. (1989). Beyond simple demographic effects: The importance of relational demography in superior-subordinate dyads. *Academy of Management Journal, 32,* 402–423.

46. Korman, A. K. (1988). *The outsiders: Jews and corporate America.* Lexington, MA: Lexington Books.

47. Ilgen & Youtz (1986).

48. Joplin, J. R. W., & Daus, C. S. (1997). Challenges of leading a diverse workforce. *Academy of Management Executive, 11*(3), 32–47; Robinson and Dechant (1997).

49. Rosener, J. B. (1990, November–December). Ways women lead. *Harvard Business Review,* pp. 119–125.

50. Grant, J. (1988, Winter). Women as managers: What they can offer to organizations. *Organizational Dynamics,* pp. 56–63.

51. Cox & Blake (1991).

52. Carter, S. L. (1991). *Reflections of an affirmative action baby.* New York: Basic Books; quote is on p. 32.

53. Horwitz, S. K., & Horwitz, I. B. (2007). The effects of team diversity on team outcomes: A meta-analytic review of team demography. *Journal of Management, 33,* 987–1015.

54. Thomas (1991); quote is on pp. 171–172.

55. Blake-Beard, S. (2006). Multicultural organization. In Greenhaus & Callanan, pp. 518–519; quote is on p. 518.

56. Cox, T. H. (1991). The multicultural organization. *Academy of Management Executive, 5*(2), 34–47; also see Cox, T. H. (1993). *Cultural diversity in organizations: Theory, research & practice.* San Francisco: Berrett-Koehler.

57. Thomas (1991).

58. Cox (1991).

59. Ibid.; quote is on p. 46.

60. Linnehan, F. (2006). Affirmative action. In Greenhaus & Callanan, pp. 6–10; Thomas (2006); Thomas, R. R., Jr. (1990, March–April). From affirmative action to affirming diversity. *Harvard Business Review,* pp. 107–117; Thomas (1991).

61. Linnehan (2006); quote is on p. 6.

62. Thomas (1990); quote is on p. 107.

63. Thomas (1991).

64. Konrad, A. M., & Linnehan, F. (1999). Affirmative action: History, effects and attitudes. In G. N. Powell (Ed.), *Handbook of gender in organizations* (pp. 429–452). Thousand Oaks, CA: Sage; Linnehan (2006).

65. Thomas (1991); quote is on p. 24.

66. Ibid.

67. Ibid; quote is on p. 167.

68. Ibid; quote is on p. 26.

69. Gatewood, R. D., Field, H. S., & Barrick, M. (2007). *Human resource selection* (6th ed.). Mason, OH: Southwestern Thomson.

70. Cox & Blake (1991); Thomas (1991).

71. Thomas (2006); quote is on p. 242.

72. Hanson, B., & Walker, B. (1988). *Valuing differences at Digital Equipment Corporation.* Paper Presented at the Careers Division Pre-Conference Workshop at the Annual Meeting of the Academy of Management, Anaheim, CA; Kulik, C. T., & Roberson, L. (2008). Common goals and golden opportunities: Evaluations of diversity education in academic and organizational settings. *Academy of Management Learning & Education, 7,* 309–331.

73. The discussion of Sodexo's diversity learning program is based on material presented in Anand, R., & Winters, M. (2008). A retrospective view of corporate diversity training from 1964 to the present. *Academy of Management Learning & Education, 7,* 356–372.

74. Thomas (1991); quote is on p. 174.

75. Nelton, S. (1988, July). Meet your new work force. *Nation's Business,* pp. 14–21.

76. Fisher, C. D., Schoenfeldt, L. F., & Shaw, J. B. (1990). *Human resource management.* Boston: Houghton Mifflin; quote is on p. 134.

77. Bose-Sperry, L. (2006). Sexual harassment. In Greenhaus & Callanan, pp. 734–738; Fitzgerald, L. F., Drasgow, F., Hulin, C. L., Gelfand, M. J., & Magley, V. J. (1997). Antecedents and consequences of sexual harassment in organizations: A test of an integrated model. *Journal of Applied Psychology, 82,* 578–589.

78. Thomas (1991); quote is on p. 10.

79. Thomas (2006); Martin (1991).

80. Cox & Blake (1991); quote is on pp. 52–53.

81. Faircloth, A. (1998, August 3). Guess who's coming to Denny's? *Fortune,* pp. 108–110.

82. Avery, D. R. (2006).

83. Thomas (1991); quote is on p. 180.

84. Fernandez (1991); Morrison, A. M., White, R. P., & Van Velsor, E. (1987). *Breaking the glass ceiling: Can women reach the top of America's largest corporations?* Reading, MA: Addison-Wesley.

ENDNOTES FOR CHAPTER 12

1. U.S. Census Bureau. (2008). *Statistical abstract of the United States,* Table 738, Firm Births and Deaths by Employment Size of Enterprise: 1990 to 2004. Available at http://www.census.gov

2. U.S. Census Bureau. (2008). *Statistical abstract of the United States,* Table 735, Establishments, Employees, and Payroll by Employment-Size Class: 1990 to 2004. Available at http://www.census.gov

3. Anonymous. (2007). Entrepreneurs in the U.S. economy. *Monthly Labor Review, 130*(12), 38; Burch, J. G. (1986, September–October). Profiling the entrepreneur. *Business Horizons,* pp. 13–16; Salwen, K. G. (1998, March 30). Editors note. *Wall Street Journal,* p. R4; Sexton, D. L., & Smilor, R. W. (1997). (Eds.). *Entrepreneurship 2000.* Chicago: Upstart Publishing; Swanbrow, D. (2006). *Number of U.S. entrepreneurs reaches eight-year high.* Retrieved June 13, 2008, from http://www.umich.edu/news/index.html?Releases/2006/Jan06/r011906c; U.S. Bureau of the Census. (1997). *Statistical abstracts of the United States: 1997* (117th ed.). Washington, DC: Government Printing Office.

4. Anonymous. (2007). *A (little) bit of government can go a long way.* Retrieved June 13, 2008, from http://www.forbes.com/entrepreneurs/2007/11/05/small-business-government-ent-law-cx_kw_1105whartonregulation.html; Freear, J., Sohl, J. E., & Wetzel, W. E. (1997). The informal venture capital market: Milestones passed and the road ahead. In D. L. Sexton & R. W. Smilor (Eds.), *Entrepreneurship 2000* (pp. 47–69). Chicago: Upstart Publishing; Hubbard, J. (2007). Small business, big picture. *RMA Journal, 90*(1), 32–33.

5. Mill, J. S. (1848). *Principles of political economy with some applications to social philosophy.* London: John W. Parker.

6. Schumpeter, J. A. (1934). *The theory of economic development.* Cambridge, MA: Harvard University Press.

7. Cunningham, J. B., & Lischerson, J. (1991). Defining entrepreneurship. *Journal of Small Business Management, 29*(1), 45–61.

8. Cunningham & Lischerson (1991); DeCarolis, D. M., & Litzky, B. E. (2006). Entrepreneurship. In J. H. Greenhaus & G. A. Callanan (Eds.), *Encyclopedia of career development* (pp. 284–288). Thousand Oaks, CA: Sage; Gunderson, G. (1990). Thinking about entrepreneurs: Models, assumptions, and evidence. In C. A. Kent (Ed.), *Entrepreneurship education: Current developments, future directions* (pp. 41–52). New York: Quorum; Hisrich, R. D., & Brush, C. G. (1985). *The woman entrepreneur: Characteristics and prescriptions for success.* Lexington, MA: Lexington Books; Kirzner, I. (1997). Entrepreneurial discovery and the competitive market process: An Austrian approach. *Journal of Economic Literature, 35,* 60–85; Shane, S., & Venkataraman, S. (2000). The promise of entrepreneurship as a field of research. *Academy of Management Review, 25,* 217–226.

9. Shane & Venkataraman (2000); Singh, R. P. (2001); A comment on developing the field of entrepreneurship through the study of opportunity recognition and exploitation. *Academy of Management Review, 26,* 10–14.

10. Knaup, A. E. (2005, May). Survival and longevity in the business employment dynamics data. *Monthly Labor Review,* pp. 50–56.

11. Donkin, R. (2004, November 25). New entrepreneurs can carve their place: With social hierarchies in the news, it is a good time to consider how life can be made easier for young people who want to start up their own business. *Financial Times,* p. 9; Labich, K. (1990, December 17). Breaking away to go on your own. *Fortune,* pp. 40–56.

12. Kuratko, D. F., Hornsby, J. S., & Naffziger, D. W. (1997). An examination of owner's goals in sustaining entrepreneurship. *Journal of Small Business Management, 35*(1), 24–33; Luke, B., Verreynne, M. L., & Kearins, K. (2007). Measuring the benefits of entrepreneurship at different levels of analysis. *Journal of Management and Organization, 13,* 312–330; Rauch, A., & Frese, M. (2007). Let's put the person back into entrepreneurship research: A meta-analysis on the relationship between business owners'

personality traits, business creation, and success. *European Journal of Work and Organizational Psychology, 16,* 353–385; DeCarolis & Litzky (2006).

13. Hall, D. T., & Richter, J. (1990). Career gridlock: Baby boomers hit the wall. *Academy of Management Executive, 4,* 7–22.

14. Ibid.

15. Capowski, G. S. (1992). Be your own boss? Millions of women get down to business. *Management Review, 81*(3), 24–31.

16. Collins, O. F., & Moore, D. G. (1964). *The enterprising man.* East Lansing: Michigan State University Press.

17. Capowski (1992); Davidsson, P. (2006). *Researching entrepreneurship.* Boston: Springer; Cassar, G. (2007). Money, money, money? A longitudinal investigation of entrepreneur career reasons, growth preferences and achieved growth. *Entrepreneurship and Regional Development, 19*(1), 89; Douglas, E. J., & Shepherd, D. A. (2002). Self-employment as a career choice: Attitudes, entrepreneurial intentions, and utility maximization. *Entrepreneurship Theory and Practice, 26*(3), 81–90; Frese, M., Brantjes, A., & Hoorn, R. (2002). Psychological success factors of small scale businesses in Namibia: The roles of strategy process, entrepreneurial orientation and the environment. *Journal of Developmental Entrepreneurship, 7,* 259–282; Kuratko, D. F., Hornsby, J. S., & Naffziger, D. W. (1997). An examination of owner's goals in sustaining entrepreneurship. *Journal of Small Business Management, 35*(1), 24–33; Rauch & Frese (2007).

18. Cassar (2007); Choo, S., & Wong, M. (2006). Entrepreneurial intention: Triggers and barriers to new venture creations in Singapore. *Singapore Management Review, 28*(2), 47–64; Frese et al. (2002); Koellinger, P., Minniti, M., & Schade, C. (2007). "I think I can, I think I can": Overconfidence and entrepreneurial behavior. *Journal of Economic Psychology, 28*(4), 502–518; Levie, J. (2007). Immigration, in-migration, ethnicity and entrepreneurship in the United Kingdom. *Small Business Economics, 28*(2–3), 143–157; Noora, A., Tuunanen, M., & Alon, I. (2005). The international business environments of franchising in Russia. *Academy of Marketing Science Review, 5,* 1–18; Schwartz, D., & Malach-Pines, A. (2007). High technology entrepreneurs versus small business owners in Israel. *Journal of Entrepreneurship, 16*(1), 1–9.

19. McClelland, D. C. (1967). *The achieving society.* New York: Free Press.

20. Apospori, E., Papalexandris, N., & Galanaki, E. (2005). Entrepreneurial and professional CEOs: Differences in motive and responsibility profile. *Leadership & Organization Development Journal, 26*(1/2), 141–162; Babb, E. M., & Babb, S. V. (1992). Psychological traits of rural entrepreneurs. *Journal of Socio-Economics, 21*(4), 353–362; Buttner, E. H., & Moore, D. P. (1997). Women's organizational exodus to entrepreneurship: Self-reported motivations and correlates with success. *Journal of Small Business Management, 35*(1), 34–46; Johnson, B. R. (1990, Spring). Toward a multidimensional model of entrepreneurship: The case of achievement motivation and the entrepreneur. *Entrepreneurship Theory and Practice,* pp. 39–54; Shaver, K. G. (1995). The entrepreneurial personality myth. *Business and Economic Review, 41*(3), 20–23; Shaver, K. G., & Scott, L. R. (1991). Person, process, choice: The psychology of new venture creation. *Entrepreneurship Theory and Practice, 16*(2), 23–36; Stewart, W. H., Jr., Watson, W. E., Carland, J. C., & Carland, J. W. (1999). A proclivity for entrepreneurship: A comparison of entrepreneurs, small business owners, and corporate managers. *Journal of Business Venturing, 14*(2), 189–214; Yonca, G., & Nuray, A. (2006). Entrepreneurial characteristics amongst university students: Some insights for entrepreneurship education and training in Turkey. *Education & Training, 48*(1), 25–38.

21. Bowen, D. D., & Hisrich, R. D. (1986). The female entrepreneur: A career development perspective. *Academy of Management Review, 11,* 393–407; Chen, C. C., Greene, P. G., & Crick, A. (1998). Does entrepreneurial self-efficacy distinguish entrepreneurs from managers? *Journal of Business Venturing, 13*(4), 295–316; Nair, K. R. G., & Pandey, A. (2006). Characteristics of entrepreneurs: An empirical analysis. *Journal of Entrepreneurship, 15*(1), 47–61.

22. Cunningham, B., Gerrard, P., Chiang, F. P., Lim, K. Y., & Linn, C. S. (1995). Do undergraduates have what it takes to be entrepreneurs and managers of small businesses in Singapore? *Journal of Asian Business, 11*(4), 35–50; Ganesan, R., Kaur, D., Maheshwari, R. C., & Sujata, S. (2003). Demographic correlates of locus of control and perceived ladder of success: A study of women entrepreneurs. *International Journal of Entrepreneurship, 7,* 1–16; Yonca & Nuray (2006).

23. Davidsson (2006).

24. Donkin (2004); Pitt, L. F., & Kannemeyer, R. (2000). The role of adaptation in microenterprise development: A marketing perspective. *Journal of Developmental Entrepreneurship, 5,* 137–155; Vella, N. (2001). *Entrepreneurial attributes in Malta.* Unpublished doctoral dissertation, Maastricht School of Management, The Netherlands; Wincent, J., & Westerberg, M. (2005). Personal traits of CEOS, inter-firm networking and entrepreneurship in their firms: Investigating strategic SME network participants. *Journal of Developmental Entrepreneurship, 10,* 271–284.

25. Cunningham et al. (1995); Douglas & Shepherd (2002); Frese et al. (2002); Kreiser, P. M., Marino, L. D., & Weaver, K. M. (2002). Assessing the psychometric properties of the entrepreneurial orientation scale: A multi-country analysis. *Entrepreneurship Theory and Practice, 26*(4), 71–94; Kropp, F., Lindsay, N. J., & Shoham, A. (2008). Entrepreneurial orientation and international entrepreneurial business venture startup. *International Journal of Entrepreneurial Behavior & Research, 14,* 102–117; Stewart et al. (1999); Yonca & Nuray (2006).

26. Low, M. B., & MacMillan, I. C. (1988). Entrepreneurship: Past research and future challenges. *Journal of Management, 14,* 139–161; Ray, D. M. (1994). The role of risk-taking in Singapore. *Journal of Business Venturing, 9,* 157–177.

27. Busenitz, L. W. (1999). Entrepreneurial risk and strategic decision making: It's a matter of perspective. *Journal of Applied Behavioral Science, 35,* 325–340.

28. DeCarolis & Litzky (2006).

29. Brockhaus, R. H., & Horwitz, P. S. (1986). The psychology of the entrepreneur. In D. L. Sexton & R. W. Smilor (Eds.), *The art and science of entrepreneurship* (pp. 25–48). Cambridge, MA: Ballinger; Koellinger et al. (2007); Rauch & Frese (2007).

30. Schein, E. H. (1985). *Career anchors: Discovering your real values.* San Diego, CA: University Associates.

31. Ibid; quote is on p. 30.

32. Rauch & Frese (2007).

33. Ganesan et al. (2003); Kolvereid, L. (1996). Prediction of employment status choice intentions. *Entrepreneurship Theory and Practice, 21*(1), 47–57; Nair & Pandey (2006); Shapero, A., & Sokol, L. (1982). The social dimensions of entrepreneurship. In C. A. Kent, D. L. Sexton, & K. H. Vesper (Eds.), *Encyclopedia of entrepreneurship* (pp. 72–90). Englewood Cliffs, NJ: Prentice Hall.

34. Hisrich, R. D., & Brush, C. (1986). Characteristics of the minority entrepreneur. *Journal of Small Business Management, 24*(4), 1–8; Malach-Pines, A., Dvir, D., & Sadeh, A. (2004). The making of Israeli high-technology entrepreneurs: An exploratory study. *Journal of Entrepreneurship, 13*(1), 29–53.

35. Robinson, P. B., Ahmed, Z. U., Dana, L. P., Gennady, R. L., & Smirnova, V. (2001). Towards entrepreneurship and innovation in Russia. *International Journal of Entrepreneurship and Innovation Management, 1,* 230–240; Robinson, P. B., Stimpson, D. V., Huefner, J. C., & Hunt, H. K. (1991). An attitude approach to the prediction of entrepreneurship. *Entrepreneurship Theory and Practice, 15*(4), 13–32.

36. Cooper, A. C., & Dunkelberg, W. C. (1987). Entrepreneurial research: Old questions, new answers, and methodological issues. *American Journal of Small Business, 11,* 1–20; Kolvereid (1996); Mazzarol, T., Volery, T., Doss, N., & Thein, V. (1999). Factors influencing small business start-ups: A comparison with previous research. *International Journal of Entrepreneurial Behaviour & Research, 5*(2), 48–59; Murray, S. (2006, January 26). Gearing up for a new battle of the bulge. An unprecedented demographic phenomenon presents global challenges and opportunities. *Financial Times,* p. 1.

37. Hisrich & Brush (1986).

38. Low & MacMillan (1988).

39. Cunningham et al. (1995); Frese et al. (2002); Low & MacMillan (1988); Nair & Pandey (2006); Rauch & Frese (2007); Yonca & Atsan. (2006).

40. Schein (1985).

41. Beaudoin, T. (1988, September). Pushed out of the nest and flying. *Management Review,* p. 10; Page, H. (1996, July). Executive decision. *Entrepreneur,* pp. 149–153; Stanworth, C., & Stanworth, J. (1997). Reluctant entrepreneurs and their clients—The case of self-employed freelance workers in the British book publishing industry. *International Small Business Journal, 16*(1), 58–73.

42. Shapero & Sokol (1982).

43. Brockhaus & Horwitz (1986); Hyytinen, A., & Ilmakunnas, P. (2007). Entrepreneurial aspirations: Another form of job search? *Small Business Economics, 29*(1–2), 63–80.

44. Manzella, J. (2008). Globalization benefits American workers. *World Trade, 21*(1), 8; Santomero, A. M. (2004). Preparing for the 21st century economy. *Executive Speeches, 19*(1), 24–30.

45. Anonymous. (2005, October 25). Innovative furniture is child's play for P'kolino. *PR Newswire,* p. 1; Bounds, G. (2007, July 31). Enterprise: Almond business expands its identity to kick-start growth; revenue shoots up thanks to move to popular peanuts. *Wall Street Journal,* p. B10; Selz, M. (1991, November 22). Follow your heart. *Wall Street Journal,* p. R6; Tibken, S. (2008, June 16). Beyond fair trade: The Web has given artists an easier way to pursue their passions—and make money from them. *Wall Street Journal,* p. R9; Trotter, C. (2007, March 27). CA Boom 4: The west coast independent design show showcases cutting-edge green products and homes; exhibitors offer the latest in green materials, technologies and manufacturing. *PR Newswire,* p. 1; Whitford, D. (2006). Her sister is gone. Can their business . . . ride on? *Fortune Small Business, 16*(9), 82.

46. Baughn, C. C., Cao, J. S. R., Le, L. T. M., Lim, V. A., & Neupert, K. E. (2006). Normative, social and cognitive predictors of entrepreneurial interest in China, Vietnam and the Philippines. *Journal of Developmental Entrepreneurship, 11*(1), 57–77; Chay, Y. W. (1993). Social support, individual differences and well-being: A study of small business entrepreneurs and employees. *Journal of Occupational and Organizational Psychology, 66,* 285–303; Rodriguez, L. T. (2000). *The wind beneath their wings: The moderating effects of social support on the entrepreneur and entrepreneurial performance outcomes.* Unpublished doctoral dissertation, University of Nebraska–Lincoln; Summers, D. F. (1998). *An empirical investigation of personal and situational factors that relate to the formation of entrepreneurial intentions.* Unpublished doctoral dissertation, University of North Texas; Williams, O. (2007). *Examining Africultural values as mediators on the relationship between institutional racism and the survival of African-American entrepreneurship.* Unpublished doctoral dissertation, Howard University, Washington, DC.

47. Van Auken, H., Fry, F. L., & Stephens, P. (2006). The influence of role models on entrepreneurial intentions. *Journal of Developmental Entrepreneurship, 11,* 157–167.

48. Jones, M. (2002). *Empowered by choices of entrepreneurship: An intervention for female African American high school students through the My Entrepreneurial Journey (MEJ) program.* Unpublished doctoral dissertation, Alliant International University, San Francisco; Munk, N., & Oliver, S. (1996). Women of the valley. *Forbes, 158*(15), 102–108; Scherer, R. F., Adams, J. S., Carley, S. S., & Wiebe, F. A. (1989). Role model performance effects on development of entrepreneurial career preference. *Entrepreneurship Theory and Practice, 13*(3), 53–71.

49. Johnson, R. (1999, February 16). Family businesses fret about taxes and estate planning—Having finally "made it," entrepreneurs try to figure out how to keep it. *Wall Street Journal,* p. B2; Tralka, D. W. (2003). Business succession: Keeping ownership in the family. *Agency Sales, 33*(6), 24–26.

50. Upton, B., & Heck, R. K. Z. (1997). The family business dimension of entrepreneurship. In D. L. Sexton & R. W. Smilor (Eds.), *Entrepreneurship 2000* (pp. 193–214). Chicago: Upstart Publishing.

51. *The Forbes 400: #239 Margaret Magerko,* retrieved June 22, 2008, from http://www.forbes.com/lists/2007/54/richlist07_Margaret-Magerko_AE2I.html; *The Forbes 400: #17 Abigail Johnson,* retrieved

June 22, 2008, from http://www.forbes.com/lists/2007/54/richlist07_Abigail-Johnson_WTEB.html; *The 100 most powerful women: #85 Christie Hefner,* retrieved June 22, 2008, from http://www .forbes.com/lists/2007/11/biz-07women_Christie-Hefner_QFJI.html

52. Minerd, J. (1999). A "gray wave" of entrepreneurs. *Futurist, 33*(6), 10.

53. Andrews, E. S. (1992). Expanding opportunities for older workers. *Journal of Labor Research, 13*(1), 55–66; Singh, G., & DeNoble, A. (2003). Early retirees as the next generation of entrepreneurs. *Entrepreneurship Theory and Practice, 27*(3), 207–226.

54. Visit Web sites: *U.S. Small Business Administration, Small business planner,* retrieved June 22, 2008, from http://www.sba.gov/smallbusinessplanner/plan/index.html; and *SCORE: Counselors to America's small business,* retrieved June 22, 2008, from http://www.score.org/

55. *Venture Associates: Venture capital clubs or groups,* retrieved June 22, 2008, from http://www.venturea.com/clubs2.htm

56. Connecticut Venture Group, retrieved June 22, 2008, from http://cvg.org/about_cvg.asp

57. Savannah Area Chamber, retrieved June 22, 2008, from http://www.savannahchamber.com/ about.php

58. Kuratko, D. F. (2005). The emergence of entrepreneurship education: Development, trends, and challenges. *Entrepreneurship Theory and Practice, 29,* 577–597.

59. Ewing Marion Kauffman Foundation, retrieved July 8, 2008, from http://www.kauffman .org/foundation.cfm

60. Babson College, retrieved June 22, 2008, from http://www3.babson.edu/Newsroom/ factsandfigures.cfm; *U.S. News & World Report,* retrieved July 8, 2008, from http://grad -schools.usnews.rankingsandreviews.com/grad/mba/search/specialities+progam_entrepreneurship

61. Lord, M., & Westfall, R. G. (1996, March 10). *Running their own show: With corporate jobs no longer offering security, entrepreneurship has become hot, hot, hot.* Retrieved July 8, 2008, from http://www.usnews.com/usnews/edu/articles/960318/archive_010017_2.htm

62. Kuratko (2005); Solomon, G. T., Duffy, S., & Tarabishy, A. (2002). The state of entrepreneurship education in the United States: A nationwide survey and analysis. *International Journal of Entrepreneurship Education, 1*(1), 65–86.

63. Global Consortium of Entrepreneurship Centers (GCEC), retrieved July 8, 2008, from http://www.nationalconsortium.org/index.cfm

64. *Key facts about women-owned businesses.* Retrieved July 8, 2008, from Center for Women's Business Research Web site: http://www.nfwbo.org/facts/index.php

65. Ahl, H. (2003). *The scientific reproduction of gender inequality: A discourse analysis of research articles on women's entrepreneurship.* Paper presented at Gender and Power in the New Europe, the 5th European Feminist Research Conference, Jonkoping University, Sweden; Dolinsky, A. (1993). The effects of education on business ownership: A longitudinal study of women's entrepreneurship. *Entrepreneurship Theory and Practice, 18*(1), 43–53; Kroll, L. (1998, May 18). Entrepreneurial moms. *Forbes,* pp. 84–92; Olson, S. F., & Currie, H. M. (1992). Female entrepreneurs in a male-dominated industry: Personal value systems and business strategies. *Journal of Small Business Management, 30*(1), 49–57; Sarri, K., & Trihopoulou, A. (2005). Female entrepreneurs' personal characteristics and motivation: A review of the Greek situation. *Women in Management Review, 20*(1/2), 24–36; Schoenberger, C. R. (1998, July 2). Understanding the spirit of entrepreneurship. *Boston Globe,* p. D1; Sexton, D. L., & Bowman-Upton, N. (1990). Female and male entrepreneurs: Psychological characteristics and their role in gender-related discrimination. *Journal of Business Venturing, 5,* 29–36; Tan, J. (2008). Breaking the "bamboo curtain" and the "glass ceiling": The experience of women entrepreneurs in high-tech industries in an emerging market. *Journal of Business Ethics, 80,* 547–564; Zapalska, A. (1997). A profile of woman entrepreneurs and enterprises in Poland. *Journal of Small Business Management, 35*(4), 76–82.

66. Smith, J. (2008, March 25). Men and women entrepreneurs are driven by different motivations. *McClatchy–Tribune Business News.*

67. Hughes, A. (2002). More work, less pay. *Black Enterprise, 33*(5), 32; Morrison, A. M., White, R. P., & Van Velsor, E. (1992). *Breaking the glass ceiling: Can women reach the top of America's largest corporations?* Reading, MA: Addison-Wesley.

68. Flowers, L. (2001). *Women, faith and work: How ten successful professionals blend belief and business.* Nashville, TN: World Publishers; Kephart, P., & Schumacher, L. (2005). Has the "glass ceiling" cracked? An exploration of women entrepreneurship. *Journal of Leadership & Organizational Studies, 12*(1), 2–15; Mincer, J. (2002). Area mirrors national picture of low number of women CEOs. *Kansas City Star,* p. E32; Moreno, L., & Murphy, M. (1999, March 22). Generational warfare. *Forbes,* pp. 62–66; Smith (2008); Walker, E. A., & Webster, B. J. (2007). Gender, age and self-employment: Some things change, some stay the same. *Women in Management Review, 22,* 122–135.

69. Main, J. (1990, February 12). A golden age for entrepreneurs. *Fortune,* pp. 120–125; quote is on p. 121.

70. Fisher, A. (2004). Why women rule. *Fortune Small Business,* (14), p. 47.

71. Smith (2008).

72. Kephart & Schumacher (2005); Walker & Webster (2007).

73. Kroll (1998).

74. Shiffman, K. (2006). Big is beautiful. *Profit, 25*(5), 40–43; Stoner, C. R., Hartman, R. I., & Arora, R. (1990, January). Work–home role conflict in female owners of small businesses: An exploratory study. *Journal of Small Business Management,* pp. 30–38.

75. Cooper, A. C., & Artz, K. W. (1995). Determinants of satisfaction for entrepreneurs. *Journal of Business Venturing, 10,* 439–457; Smith (2008); Zhao, H., Seibert, S. E., & Hills, G. E. (2005). The mediating role of self-efficacy in the development of entrepreneurial intentions. *Journal of Applied Psychology, 90,* 1–14.

76. *Self-employed women: 1976–2003.* Retrieved July 8, 2008, from the Bureau of Labor Statistics Web site: http://www.bls.gov/opub/ted/2004/apr/wk4/art04.htm

77. *Survey of business owners (SBO).* Retrieved July 8, 2008, from the U.S. Census Bureau Web site: http://www.census.gov/econ/sbo

78. Smith (2008).

79. Bowen & Hisrich (1986); Coleman, S. (2000). Access to capital and terms of credit: A comparison of men- and women-owned small businesses. *Journal of Small Business Management, 38*(3), 37–52; Fabowale, L., Orser, B., & Riding, A. (1995). Gender, structural factors, and credit terms between Canadian small businesses and financial institutions. *Entrepreneurship Theory and Practice, 19*(4), 41–65; Fay, M., & Williams, L. (1993). Gender bias and the availability of business loans. *Journal of Business Venturing, 8,* 363–376.

80. Cuba, R., Decenzo, D., & Anish, A. (1983). Management practices of successful female business owners. *American Journal of Small Business, 8,* 40–46; Daniel, T. A. (2004). The exodus of women from the corporate workplace to self-owned businesses. *Employment Relations Today, 30*(4), 55–61.

81. Buttner, E. H., & Moore, D. P. (1997). Women's organizational exodus to entrepreneurship: Self-reported motivations and correlates with success. *Journal of Small Business Management, 35*(1), 34–46.

82. Buttner & Moore (1997); Robinson, S. (2001). An examination of entrepreneurial motives and their influence on the way rural women small business owners manage their employees. *Journal of Developmental Entrepreneurship, 6,* 151–167.

83. U.S. Census Bureau. (2006). *2002 survey of business owners.* Retrieved July 8, 2008, from the U.S. Census Bureau Web site: http://www.census.gov/econ/sbo

84. U.S. Census Bureau. (2006). *2002 survey of business owners;* U.S. Census Bureau. (2001). *1997 economic census, survey of minority-owned business enterprises;* U.S. Census Bureau. (1996). *1992 economic census, survey of minority-owned business enterprises.* All retrieved July 8, 2008, from http://www.census.gov/econ/sbo

85. *Survey of business owners.* (2009). Retrieved July 8, 2008, from http://www.census.gov/econ/sbo

86. Rhodes, C., & Butler, J. S. (2004). Understanding self-perceptions of business performance: An examination of black American entrepreneurs. *Journal of Developmental Entrepreneurship, 9*(1), 55–71.

87. Dadzie, K. Q., & Cho, Y. (1989, July). Determinants of minority business formation and survival: An empirical assessment. *Journal of Small Business Management,* pp. 56–61; Smith-Hunter, A. E., & Boyd, R. L. (2004). Applying theories of entrepreneurship to a comparative analysis of white and minority women business owners. *Women in Management Review, 19*(1/2), 18–28.

88. Dadzie & Cho (1989); Dickson, R. D. (1992, January–February). The business of equal opportunity. *Harvard Business Review,* pp. 46–53; Edmondson, V. C. (1999). The elite theory of entrepreneurship challenged: It's a new day and a new niche. *Journal of Career Development, 26*(1), 37–49; Hisrich & Brush (1986); Smith-Hunter & Boyd (2004).

89. Schein, E. H. (2006). Career anchors. In Greenhaus & Callanan, pp. 63–69.

90. Hyatt, J. (1992, February). Should you start a business? *INC.,* pp. 48–58.

91. *Joseph Segel.* Retrieved July 10, 2008, from http://en.wikipedia.org/wiki/Joseph_Segel

92. The description of the entrepreneur John Paul Jones DeJoria was taken from several sources, including Palmeri, C. (1991, March 4). Often down but never out. *Forbes,* p. 138; also from the company Web site: http://www.paulmitchell.com and from http://www.wikipedia.org/wiki/John Paul_DeJoria

93. Naughton, T. J. (1987, Fall). Quality of working life and the self-employed manager. *American Journal of Small Business,* pp. 33–40; Prottas, D. (2008). Do the self-employed value autonomy more than employees: Research across four samples. *Career Development International, 13*(1), 33–45.

ENDNOTES FOR CHAPTER 13

1. Bartlett, C. A., & Ghoshal, S. (2002, Winter). Building competitive advantage through people. *MIT Sloan Management Review,* pp. 34–41; Becker, B. E., Huselid, M. A., & Ulrich, D. (2001). *The HR scorecard: Linking people, strategy and performance.* Boston: Harvard, Business School Press; Powell, T. C. (1992). Organizational alignment as competitive advantage. *Strategic Management Journal, 13,* 119–134.

2. Colarelli, S. M., Hemingway, M., & Monnot, M. (2006). Strategic human resource management (SHRM). In J. H. Greenhaus & G. A. Callanan (Eds.), *Encyclopedia of career development* (pp. 767–771). Thousand Oaks, CA: Sage; Bartlett & Ghoshal (2002); Becker et al. (2001).

3. Wang, D. S., & Shyu, C. L. (2008). Will the strategic fit between business and HRM strategy influence HRM effectiveness and organizational performance? *International Journal of Manpower, 29,* 92–110.

4. Arthur, J. B. (1994). Effects of human resource systems on manufacturing performance and turnover. *Academy of Management Journal, 37,* 670–687; Green, K. W., Wu, C., Whitten, D., & Medlin, B. (2006). The impact of strategic human resource management on firm performance and HR professionals' work attitude and work performance. *International Journal of Human Resource Management, 17,* 559–570; Huselid, M. A. (1995). The impact of human resource practices on turnover, productivity, and corporate financial performance. *Academy of Management Journal, 38,* 635–672; Paré, G., & Tremblay, M. (2007). The influence of high-involvement human resources practices, procedural justice, organizational commitment, and citizenship behaviors on information technology professionals' turnover intentions. *Group & Organization Management, 32,* 326–353; Sun, L. Y., Aryee, S., & Law, K. S. (2007). High performance human resource practices, citizenship behavior, and organizational performance: A relational perspective. *Academy of Management Journal, 50,* 558–577; Valle, R., Martin, F., Romero, P. M., & Dolan, S. L. (2000). Business strategy, work processes and human resource training: Are they congruent? *Journal of Organizational Behavior, 21,* 283–297; Wang & Shyu, (2008).

5. Appelbaum, S. H., Ayre, H., & Shapiro, B. T. (2002). Career management in information technology: A case study. *Career Development International, 7,* 142–158; Baruch, Y. (2003). Career systems in transition: A normative model for organizational career practices. *Personnel Review, 32,* 231–251; Baruch, Y. (2004). Transforming careers: From linear to multidirectional career paths: Organizational and individual perspectives. *Career Development International, 9,* 58–73; Baruch, Y., & Peiperl, M. (2000). Career management practices: An empirical survey and implications. *Human Resource Management, 39,* 347–366; Egan, T. M., Upton, M. G., & Lynham, S. A. (2006). Career development: Load-bearing wall or window dressing? Exploring definitions, theories, and prospects for HRD-related theory building. *Human Resource Development Review, 5,* 442–477; Gutteridge, T. G., & Leibowitz, Z. B. (1993). A new look at organizational career development. *Human Resource Planning, 16,* 71–84; McDonald, K. S., & Hite, L. M. (2005). Reviving the relevance of career development in human resource development. *Human Resource Development Review, 4,* 418–439; Morgan, R. (2006). Making the most of performance management systems. *Compensation and Benefits Review, 38,* 22–27.

6. Christenson, R. (2006). *Roadmap to strategic HR: Turning a great idea into a business reality.* New York: AMACOM.

7. Becker et al. (2001); Christenson (2006).

8. Ulrich, D. (1997). *Human resource champions.* Boston: Harvard Business School Press.

9. Christenson (2006); quote is on p. 53.

10. London, M. (1991). Career development and business strategy. In J. W. Jones, B. D. Steffy, & D. W. Bray (Eds.), *Applying psychology in business* (pp. 430–437). New York: Lexington Books; quote is on p. 433.

11. Christenson (2006).

12. Dunn, J. (2006). Strategic human resources and strategic organization development: An alliance for the future? *Organization Development Journal, 24,* 69–76; McCowan, R. A., Bowen, U., Huselid, M. A., & Becker, B. E. (1999). Strategic human resource management at Herman Miller. *Human Resource Management, 38,* 303–308.

13. Capelli, P. (2008, March). Talent management for the twenty-first century. *Harvard Business Review,* pp. 74–81; Ulrich, D., & Lake, D. (1990). *Organizational capability.* New York: Wiley.

14. Capelli (2008).

15. Ulrich & Lake (1990).

16. Ibid.

17. Nicholson, N. (1996). Career systems in crisis: Change and opportunity in the information age. *Academy of Management Executive, 10,* 40–51.

18. Christenson (2006).

19. Holt, D. J. (2006). Redeployment. In Greenhaus & Callanan, pp. 679–681.

20. Retrieved August 1, 2008, from http://solutions.3m.com/wps/portal/3M/en_US/global/sustainability/our-people/learning-career-growth/

21. McDougall, P. (2006). IBMers blue, big time. *InformationWeek, 1110,* 17; Wong, N. C. (2006, September 6). Thousands already cut from HP adjust to losing HP way of life. *Knight Ridder-Tribune Business News,* p. 1.

22. Wanous, J. P. (2006). Realistic recruitment. In Greenhaus & Callanan, pp. 672–675.

23. Anonymous. (1998, May). Case study: At the vanguard of successful recruiting. *HR Focus,* p. 9.

24. Wheatley, M. (1996, June). The talent spotters. *Management Today,* pp. 62–66.

25. Terpstra, D. E. (1996). The search for effective methods. *HR Focus, 73,* 16–19; Wiley, C. (1992). Recruitment research revisited: Effective recruiting methods according to employment outcomes. *Journal of Applied Business Research, 8,* 74–79.

26. Kupperschmidt, B. R. (2001). UAPs: To have and to hold. *Nursing Management, 32,* 33–34; Thorsteinson, T. J., Palmer, E. M., Wulff, C., & Anderson, A. (2004). Too good to be true? Using realism to enhance applicant attraction. *Journal of Business and Psychology, 19,* 125–137.

27. Information on internships at Aetna (http://www.aetna.com/working/students/index.html), Allstate (http://www.allstate.com/careers/internships.aspx), Boeing (http://www.boeing.com/employment/collegecareers/index.html), Kodak (http://www.kodak.com/US/en/corp/careers/students/newindex), Hewlett-Packard (http://h10055.www1.hp.com/jobsathp/content/informations/students graduates.asp), and Procter & Gamble (http://www.pg.com/jobs/jobs_us/recruitblue/internships .shtml).

28. *Undergraduate admissions,* retrieved August 4, 2008, from http://www.drexel.edu/em/undergrad/coop/coop-options.aspx; *Guide to cooperative education,* retrieved August 4, 2008, from http://www.drexel.edu/provost/scdc/coop/index.html

29. Christenson (2006).

30. Kaeter, A. (2000). Virtual cap and gown. *Training, 37,* 114–122.

31. Ibid; quote on p. 119.

32. Ibid.

33. Anonymous. (2002). Motorola adapts training to modern business demands. *Human Resource Management International Digest, 10,* 21–23.

34. Meister, J. (1998). Extending the short shelf life of knowledge. *Training and Development, 52,* 52–53; Anonymous (2002); Ellis, K. (2002). Corporate U's: High value or hot air? *Training, 39,* 60–64; Vitiello, J. (2001). New roles for corporate universities. *Computerworld, 35,* 42.

35. Fender, C. M. (2006). On-the-job training. In Greenhaus & Callanan, pp. 571–572.

36. Bernthal, P., & Wellins, R. (2006). Trends in leader development and succession. *Human Resource Planning, 29,* 31–41.

37. Anonymous. (1996, October). Where it's an inside job. *Management Today,* p. 13; Messmer, M. (2003). Building an effective mentoring program. *Strategic Finance, 84,* 17.

38. Anonymous. *The career development program.* (2009). Air Products and Chemicals, Inc. Retrieved June 19, 2009, from http://www.airproducts.com/Careers/NorthAmerica/UniversityRecruiting/Welcome .htm; Brockington, J. (Personal communication with the Director of University Relations, Air Products and Chemicals, Inc., January 25, 1999).

39. Derr, C. B. (2006). Succession planning. In Greenhaus & Callanan, pp. 785–789.

40. McCall, M. W., Jr. (1998). *High flyers: Developing the next generation of leaders.* Boston: Harvard Business School Press; Zenger, J. H., & Folkman, J. (2002). *The extraordinary leader: Turning good managers into great leaders.* New York: McGraw-Hill.

41. Zenger & Folkman (2002).

42. Derr (2006).

43. Ibid.

44. *Training & leadership development programs for college applicants.* (2009). Retrieved June 19, 2009, from http://www.lockheedmartinjobs.com/college_leadershipdev.asp

45. Groysberg, B., Nanda, A., & Nohria, N. (2004). The risky business of hiring stars. *Harvard Business Review, 82,* 92–100.

46. Briscoe, J. R., & Derr, C. B. (2003, August). *The roundabout model: A flexible approach to managing leadership development.* Paper presented at the Academy of Management meeting, Seattle; Heise, S. (1994). Disney approach to managing. *Executive Excellence, 11,* 18–20.

47. Heise (1994); Martinez, M. N. (1992). Disney training works magic. *HR Magazine, 37,* 53–57.

48. Find information about careers at ARAMARK from their Web site: http://www.aramark.com

49. Tracey, J. B., & Charpentier, A. (2004). Professionalizing the human resources function: The case of ARAMARK. *Cornell Hotel and Restaurant Administration Quarterly, 45,* 388–397.

50. Bird, A. (1994). Careers as repositories of knowledge: A new perspective on boundaryless careers. *Journal of Organizational Behavior, 15,* 325–344; Mirvis, P. H., & Hall, D. T. (1994). Psychological success and the boundaryless career. *Journal of Organizational Behavior, 15,* 365–380.

51. Harris, B. R., Huselid, M. A., & Becker, B. E. (1999). Strategic human resource management at Praxair. *Human Resource Management, 38,* 315–322.

52. Information about Praxair can be found online at http://www.praxair.com/

53. Kets de Vries, M. F. (2005). Leadership group coaching in action: The Zen of creating high performance teams. *Academy of Management Executive, 19,* 61–76; quote is on p. 62.

54. Ibid; quote is on p. 61.

55. Feldman, D. C., & Lankau, M. J. (2005). Executive coaching: A review and agenda for future research. *Journal of Management, 31,* 829–848.

56. Ellinger, A. D., Ellinger, A. E., & Keller, S. B. (2003). Supervisory coaching behavior, employee satisfaction, and warehouse employee performance: A dyadic perspective in the distribution industry. *Human Resource Development Quarterly, 14,* 435–458.

57. Boyatzis, R. E., Smith, M. L., & Blaize, N. (2006). Developing sustainable leaders through coaching and compassion. *Academy of Management Learning & Education, 5,* 8–24.

58. Christenson (2006).

59. Ibid.

60. Prochaska, S. (2006). Three-hundred-sixty-degree (360°) evaluation. In Greenhaus & Callanan, pp. 807–572.

61. Edwards, M. R., & Ewen, A. J. (1996). 360-degree feedback: The powerful new model for employee assessment & performance improvement. New York: AMACOM; quote is on p. 4.

62. Atwater, L. E., Brett, J. F., & Charles, A. C. (2007). Multisource feedback: Lessons learned and implications for practice. *Human Resource Management, 46,* 285–307; Gebelein, S. (1996). Employee development: Multi-rater feedback goes strategic. *HR Focus, 73,* 1–5; Newbold, C. (2008). 360-degree appraisals are now a classic: Good preparation and execution are the keys to success. *Human Resource Management International Digest, 16,* 38–40.

63. Atwater, L. E., & Brett, J. F. (2006). 360-degree feedback to leaders: Does it relate to changes in employee attitudes? *Group & Organization Management, 31,* 578–600; Atwater et al. (2007).

64. LaRock, S. (2001). Key components, topics of successful preretirement counseling program. *Employee Benefit Plan Review, 56,* 30–31.

65. Ibid.

66. Ibid.

67. Ibid.

68. Wiley, J. L. (1993). Pre-retirement education: Benefits outweigh liability. *HR Focus, 70,* 11.

69. Lengnick-Hall, M. L. (2006). Human resource information systems (HRIS). In Greenhaus & Callanan, pp. 362–366.

70. Beckers, A. M., & Bsat, M. Z. (2002). A DSS classification model for research in human resource information systems. *Information Systems Management, 19,* 41–50.

71. Ngai, E. W. T., & Wat, F. K. T. (2006). Human resource information systems: A review and empirical analysis. *Personnel Review, 35,* 297–314.

72. Hussain, Z., Wallace, J., & Cornelius, N. E. (2007). The use and impact of human resource information systems on human resource management professionals. *Information & Management, 44,* 74.

73. Broderick, R. F., & Boudreau, J. W. (1992). Human resource management, information technology and the competitive edge. *Academy of Management Executive, 6,* 7–17; Sadri, J., & Chatterjee, V. (2003). Building organizational character through HRIS. *International Journal of Human Resources Development and Management, 3,* 84–98.

74. Christenson (2006).

75. Hunt, J. M., & Weintraub, J. R. (2007). *The coaching organization: A strategy for developing leaders.* Thousand Oaks, CA: Sage; quote is on p. 3.

76. Ibid; quote is on p. 15.

77. Anonymous. (2007). BT Wholesale pilots online coaching and mentoring: Individual productivity improvements of up to 15 percent seem feasible. *Human Resource Management International Digest, 15,* 20–22; Rowold, J. (2008). Multiple effects of human resource development interventions. *Journal of European Industrial Training, 32,* 32–44.

78. Coffey, C., & Tombari, N. (2005). The bottom-line for work/life leadership: Linking diversity and organizational culture. *Ivey Business Journal Online,* 1; Maiden, R. P., Attridge, M., & Herlihy, P. A. (2005). *The integration of employee assistance, work/life, and wellness Services.* New York: Haworth Press.

79. Ibid.

80. Beutell, N. J., & Wittig-Berman, U. (2008). Work-family conflict and work-family synergy for generation X, baby boomers, and matures: Generational differences, predictors, and satisfaction outcomes. *Journal of Managerial Psychology, 23,* 507–523.

81. Perri, D. (2006). Morale. In Greenhaus & Callanan, pp. 510–511.

82. Ibid.

83. Christenson (2006).

ENDNOTES FOR CHAPTER 14

1. Greenhaus, J. H., Callanan, G. A., & DiRenzo, M. (2008). A boundaryless perspective on careers. In J. Barling & C. L. Cooper (Eds.), *The Sage handbook of organizational behavior* (Vol. 1, pp. 277–299). Thousand Oaks, CA: Sage.

2. Tams, S., & Arthur, M. B. (2006). Boundaryless career. In J. H. Greenhaus & G. A. Callanan (Eds.), *Encyclopedia of career development* (pp. 44–49). Thousand Oaks, CA: Sage.

3. Bierema, L. L. (2006). Lifelong learning. In Greenhaus & Callanan, pp. 473–475.

Name Index

Subject Index

About the Authors

Jeffrey H. Greenhaus, Professor and William A. Mackie Chair in the Department of Management at Drexel University's LeBow College of Business, received his PhD degree in Industrial/Organizational Psychology from New York University. Jeff's research, which focuses on career dynamics and work–family relationships, has been published in many of the field's leading journals. In addition, Jeff is coauthor (with Stew Friedman) of *Work and Family—Allies or Enemies? What Happens When Business Professionals Confront Life Choices*, is coeditor (with Saroj Parasuraman) of *Integrating Work and Family: Challenges and Choices for a Changing World,* and is coeditor (with Gerry Callanan) of the *Encyclopedia of Career Development*. A member of the Academy of Management, Jeff is a Fellow of the Society for Industrial and Organizational Psychology and the Association for Psychological Science.

Gerard A. Callanan is a Professor of Management in the School of Business at West Chester University. He received his PhD in Organizational Behavior from Drexel University. Prior to his appointment at West Chester, he was a vice president with the Federal Reserve Bank of Philadelphia. During his 22 years at the Federal Reserve, Gerry held a number of senior posts. He is a member of the Academy of Management and the American Psychological Association and his research on a variety of management topics has appeared in a number of scholarly publications. Gerry is coeditor (with Jeff Greenhaus) of the *Encyclopedia of Career Development*, published in 2006.

Veronica M. Godshalk is a Professor of Management and Chair of the Business Administration Department at the University of South Carolina, Beaufort. Having received her PhD degree in organizational behavior from Drexel University, Ronnie has focused her research on career management and mentoring issues. She has published articles in the *Journal of Vocational Behavior, Journal of Organizational Behavior, Group and Organizational Management,* and *Leadership Quarterly*. Ronnie is an active member of professional associations, such as the Academy of Management, the Eastern Academy of Management, and the Society for Industrial and Organizational Psychology. She had worked in the computer industry in sales and sales management prior to entering academia, and has been a consultant for several Fortune 500 companies.